KU-517-345

THE LIBRARY
UNIVERSITY OF
WINCHESTER

KING ALFRED'S COLLEGE
WINCHESTER

To be returned on or before the day marked below:—

-4 DEC 1997

PLEASE ENTER ON ISSUE SLIP:

AUTHOR WALSH

TITLE Fourteenth-century scholar and primate

ACCESSION No. 2671

KA 0005341 4

A FOURTEENTH-CENTURY SCHOLAR AND PRIMATE

CAMBRIDGE, Corpus Christi College MS 180, fol. 1r (ante 1381). Text of *De Pauperie Salvatoris* made for Adam Easton OSB. FitzRalph is depicted as an archbishop, while representatives of the four mendicant orders are plagued by devils.

A FOURTEENTH-CENTURY SCHOLAR AND PRIMATE
RICHARD FITZRALPH IN OXFORD, AVIGNON AND ARMAGH

by
KATHERINE WALSH

CLARENDON PRESS · OXFORD
1981

Oxford University Press, Walton Street, Oxford OX2 6DP
London Glasgow New York Toronto
Delhi Bombay Calcutta Madras Karachi
Kuala Lumpur Singapore Hong Kong Tokyo
Nairobi Dar es Salaam Cape Town
Melbourne Wellington
and associate companies in
Beirut Berlin Ibadan Mexico City

© Katherine Walsh 1981

Published in the United States by
Oxford University Press, New York

All rights reserved. No part of this publication may be reproduced, stored in a retrieval system, or transmitted, in any form or by any means, electronic, mechanical, photocopying, recording, or otherwise, without the prior permission of Oxford University Press

British Library Cataloguing in Publication Data

Walsh, Katherine
A fourteenth-century scholar and primate.
1. Fitzralph, Richard
2. Christian biography
I. Title
270.5'092'4

ISBN 0-19-822637-3

KING ALFRED'S COLLEGE
WINCHESTER.
270'5
WAL
2671

Typeset by Anne Joshua Associates, Oxford
Printed in Great Britain
at the University Press, Oxford
by Eric Buckley
Printer to the University

VIRO DOCTISSIMO
AUBREY GWYNN S.J.
OMNIUM QUI IN HIBERNIA
RERUM MEDIAEVALIUM STUDIA PROFITENTUR
PRINCIPI
HOC OPUS
D.D.D.
AUCTRIX

Preface

Richard FitzRalph was a prolific writer on a range of issues which were crucial to late medieval European society. His sermons, academic treatises, and polemical works were recognized almost half a century ago by Fr. Aubrey Gwynn as a fundamental source for their author's long and varied career, for his pivotal role between the strife-torn world of the Anglo-Irish border and the intellectual and ecclesiastico-political milieu of Oxford and Avignon. These writings also ensured him a place in the wider intellectual-cultural history of the period: his part in the Greek and Armenian debates attracted attention in centres as diverse as Cracow and Cesena, while his acknowledged influence on Wyclif and Hus and consequently on the ecclesiological turmoil in central Europe guaranteed the survival of his works in an extraordinarily large number of manuscripts in circles close to the universities of Prague and Vienna, as well as in the monastic and cathedral centres of the Germania Sacra. FitzRalph is primarily remembered as the impetuous 'Armachanus', who pursued a vendetta against the mendicant friars and in doing so developed the – subsequently notorious – doctrine of dominion by grace. It is a partial aim of the present study to correct this perspective and to allow a more complex personality to emerge. Hence we meet the 'iron chancellor' who filled Oxford jail to bursting point with recalcitrant students, the lazy letter-writer in Avignon pursuing private intellectual interests and nearly driving his canons in Lichfield to despair, the advocate of missionary activity and reconciliation with the eastern Christians, and the zealous reforming prelate who built his pastorate on the example of Becket, the martyred archbishop of Canterbury. FitzRalph experienced a problem not unknown to many who exchange the relative freedom of academic speculation for the episcopal mitre: the theologian and biblical scholar could afford the luxury of high ideals concerning an unstructured, apostolic church, but the prelate-administrator was confronted with the sheer impracticability of those ideals. Also in Ireland he was faced with a range of moral issues, from the perennial problem of the high level of violence in his ecclesiastical province to natural methods of birth control and clerical celibacy. Although on the one hand he defended the rights of the Gaelic population and on the other denounced the 'immorality' of their clergy (the social and legal explanation for whose practices he would scarcely have understood), he clearly had little direct pastoral experience of the Gaelic elements among his flock. Hence the legend that he was the first to translate the Bible into Irish, doubtless created by exponents of 'sola scriptura' and with Lollard overtones, must be dismissed as a pious fiction.

Despite the considerable body of archival material which is used, the core of this study is based on FitzRalph's own writings, whose internal contradictions and occasional confusion, as in the dialogue *De Pauperie Salvatoris*, can be seen as a barometer of his own developing reactions to new situations. As individual writings frequently have a significance for more than one set of problems, the combination of a chronological with a thematic approach has made some repetition unavoidable. Most of FitzRalph's writings are available only in manuscript form or in unsatisfactory early printings, hence research for this book involved much travelling. In the course of these travels I have incurred many obligations, and it is a pleasure to acknowledge them here. Above all the generosity of the Alexander von Humboldt-Stiftung, which elected me to a research fellowship for the period 1976–78, made possible the pursuit of the scattered manuscript material. Prof. Dr. Horst Fuhrmann, President of the Monumenta Germaniae Historica in Munich, and Prof. Dr. Reinhard Elze, Director of the German Historical Institute in Rome, provided optimal facilities for a wandering scholar. Miss Beryl Smalley, Dr. Jeremy I. Catto and Dozent Dr. Alexander Patschovsky gave constructive and critical advice at all stages of preparation and each undertook the considerable burden of reading the penultimate draft in its entirety. I owe a special debt of gratitude to Don Alfons M. Stickler, SDB, and Msgr. José Ruysschaert, Prefect and Vice-Prefect of the Biblioteca Apostolica Vaticana, and to Msgr. Dr. Hermann Hoberg, Vice-Prefect of the Archivio Segreto Vaticano, while Prof. Agostino Paravicini Bagliani of the Biblioteca Apostolica Vaticana provided valuable codicological information. Sir Richard Southern, P. Dr. Marc Dykmans S.J., Prof. Dr. Isnard W. Frank O.P., Prof. Dr. Paul Händel, the late Dr. Richard Hunt, Prof. Dr. Achim Masser, Mr. Charles Morgenstern, Prof. Dr. Hans Martin Schaller, and Prof. Dr. Paul Uiblein answered queries on various topics. The Master and Fellows of Corpus Christi College Cambridge gave permission for the manuscript in their care from the collection of Archbishop Matthew Parker to be used for the frontispiece. To all I am most grateful. However my greatest debt is to the dedicatee, Fr. Aubrey Gwynn, without whose initiative and constant encouragement this study of FitzRalph would scarcely have been written.

Innsbruck, January 1981

Contents

Abbreviations

AA	*Analecta Augustiniana* (Città del Vaticano, 1905 ff.)
Acta Ioannis XIII	*Acta Ioannis XXII (1317-1334)*, ed. Aloysius L. Tautù (Pontificia Commissio ad Redigendum Codicem Iuris Canonici Orientalis, Fontes, Series III, vol. vii, Tom. ii, Rome, 1952)
Acta Benedicti XII	*Acta Benedicti XII (1334-1342)*, ed. Tautù, ibid., vol. viii (Rome, 1958)
AFH	*Archivum Franciscanum Historicum* (Quaracchi, 1908 ff.)
AFP	*Archivum Fratrum Praedicatorum* (Rome, 1931 ff.)
AHC	*Annuarium Historiae Conciliorum* (Paderborn, 1969 ff.)
AHDLMA	*Archives d'histoire doctrinale et littéraire du moyen âge* (Paris, 1926 ff.)
AHP	*Archivum Historiae Pontificiae* (Rome, 1963 ff.)
Archbishop Alen's Register	Charles McNeill (ed.), *A Calender of Archbishop Alen's Register, c.1172-1534* (Royal Society of Antiquaries of Ireland, Dublin, 1950)
Arch. Hib.	*Archivium Hibernicum* (Dublin, 1912 ff.)
ASOC	*Analecta Sacri Ordinis Cisterciensis* (Rome, 1945 ff.)
ASV	Archivio Segreto Vaticano
Ausgehendes Mittelalter	Anneliese Maier, *Ausgehendes Mittelalter. Gesammelte Aufsätze zur Geistesgeschichte des 14. Jahrhunderts*, 3 vols. (Storia e Letteratura 97, 105, 138, Rome, 1964-77). First printings of each article are cited in the bibliography
B	Oxford, Bodleian Library, MS Bodl. 144
BAV	Biblioteca Apostolica Vaticana
BF	*Bullarium Franciscanum* (i-iv, Rome, 1759-68; v-vii, Rome, 1898-1904; n.s. Quaracchi, 1929 ff.)
BL	British Library (formerly British Museum)
Boyle, *Vatican Archives*	Leonard E. Boyle, *A Survey of the Vatican Archives, and of its Medieval Holdings* (Toronto, 1972)
BRUC	Alfred B. Emden (ed.), *A Biographical Register of the University of Cambridge to A.D. 1500* (Cambridge, 1963)
BRUO	Alfred B. Emden (ed.), *A Biographical Register of the University of Oxford to A.D. 1500*, 3 vols. (Oxford, 1957-9)

Cal. Reg. Fleming	Henry J. Lawlor (ed.), 'A Calendar of the Register of Archbishop Fleming', *PRIA* 30 C (1912), 94–190
Cal. Reg. Sweteman	Henry J. Lawlor (ed.), 'A Calendar of the Register of Archbishop Sweteman', *PRIA* 29 C (1911), 213–310
CCR	Calendar of Close Rolls
Chart. Univ. Paris.	Heinrich Denifle and Émile Chatelain (eds.), *Chartularium Universitatis Parisiensis*, 4 vols. (Paris 1891–9)
CLM	Codex Latinus Monacensis (= MS collection, Bayerische Staatsbibliothek, München)
Clyn, *Annals of Ireland*	*Annals of Ireland by Friar John Clyn*, ed. R. Butler (Irish Archaeological Society, Dublin, 1849)
Colledge, *Richard Ledred*	Edmund Colledge, *The Latin Poems of Richard Ledred, OFM Bishop of Ossory, 1317–1360 (Toronto, 1974)*
Courtenay, *Adam Wodeham*	William J. Courtenay, *Adam Wodeham. An Introduction to his Life and Writings* (Studies in Medieval and Reformation Thought, vol. xxi, Leiden, 1978)
CPL	*Calendar of Entries in the Papal Registers relating to Great Britain and Ireland. Papal Letters* (London, 1893 ff.)
CPL Petitions I	*Calendar of Entries in the Papal Registers relating to Great Britain and Ireland. Petitions to the Pope* (London, 1896)
CPR	Calendar of Patent Rolls
CVP	Codex Vindobonensis Palatinus (MS collection, Österreichische Nationalbibliothek, Wien)
DHGE	*Dictionnaire d'histoire et de géographie ecclésiastiques* (Paris, 1912 ff.)
Dowdall Deeds	Charles McNeill and Annette J. Otway-Ruthven (eds.) *Dowdall Deeds* (Irish Manuscripts Commission, Dublin, 1960)
DNB	*Dictionary of National Biography* (London, 1917 ff.)
DPS	*De Pauperie Salvatoris*, FitzRalph's dialogue in seven books (completed 1356)
DTC	*Dictionnaire de théologie catholique* (Paris, 1930 ff.)
Dulaurier, *Docs. arméniens*	*Recueil des historiens des Croisades. Documents arméniens*, ed. Édouard Dulaurier, 2 vols. (Paris, 1869–1906)
EETS	Early English Texts Society (London, 1864 ff.)
EHR	*English Historical Review* (London, 1886 ff.)
Eubel, *Hierarchia Catholica*	Conradus Eubel *et al.* (eds.), *Hierarchia Catholica medii et recentioris aevi* (Münster–Padua, 1913 ff.)
Friedberg	*Corpus Iuris Canonici*, ed. E. L. Richter and E. Friedberg, 2 vols. (Leipzig, 1879–81)
FS	*Franciscan Studies* (1941 ff.)

Goldast, *Monarchia*	Melchior Goldast von Haiminsfeld, *Monarchia sancti Romani imperii*, 3 vols. (Frankfurt, 1610–14)
Grandisson's Register	F. C. Hingeston-Randolph (ed.), *The Register of John de Grandisson, Bishop of Exeter 1327–1369*, 3 vols. (London–Exeter, 1894–9)
Gwynn, *English Austin Friars*	Aubrey Gwynn, *The English Austin Friars in the Time of Wyclif* (Oxford, 1940)
Gwynn, 'Sermon Diary'	Idem, 'The Sermon Diary of Richard FitzRalph, Archbishop of Armagh', *PRIA* 44 C (1937), 1–57
Gwynn, *Studies*	Idem, 'Richard FitzRalph, Archbishop of Armagh', *Studies* 22 (1933), 389-405, 591-607; 23 (1934), 395–411; 'The Black Death in Ireland', 24 (1935), 25–42; 'Archbishop FitzRalph and George of Hungary', 24 (1935), 558-72; 'Richard FitzRalph, Archbishop of Armagh', 25 (1936), 81–96; 'Archbishop FitzRalph and the Friars', 26 (1937), 50–67
Hammerich, *FitzRalph and the Mendicants*	Louis L. Hammerich, 'The Beginning of the Strife between Richard FitzRalph and the Mendicants, with an edition of his autobiographical prayer and his Proposition "Unusquisque" ', *Det Kgl. Danske Videnskabernes Selskab. Historisk-filologiske Meddelelser*, 26, 3 (Copenhagen, 1938)
*HBC*²	Frederick M. Powicke and Edmund B. Fryde (eds.), *Handbook of British Chronology*, 2nd edn. (London, 1961)
Hoberg, *Einnahmen*	Hermann Hoberg, *Die Einnahmen der apostolischen Kammer unter Innocenz VI., I. Die Einnahmen-Register des päpstlichen Thesaurars* (Vatikanische Quellen zur Geschichte der päpstlichen Hof- und Finanzverwaltung, vol. vii, Paderborn, 1955)
Hoberg, *Servitienquittungen*	Idem, *Die Einnahmen der apostolischen Kammer unter Innocenz VI., II. Die Servitienquittungen des päpstlichen Kamerars* (ibid., vol. viii, Paderborn, 1972)
IHS	*Irish Historical Studies* (Dublin, 1938 ff.)
ITQ	*Irish Theological Quarterly* (Dublin, 1906–22, 1951 ff.)
J	Oxford, St. John's College, MS 65
JEH	*Journal of Ecclesiastical History* (London, 1950 ff.)
JRSAI	*Journal of the Royal Society of Antiquaries of Ireland* (Dublin, 1849 ff.)
JTS	*Journal of Theological Studies* (London, 1899 ff.)
Kaeppeli, *Script O.P.*	Thomas Kaeppeli, *Scriptores Ordinis Praedicatorum Medii Aevi* (Rome, 1970 ff.)
Kleine Schriften	Joseph Koch, *Kleine Schriften*, 2 vols. (Storia e Letteratura 127–8, Rome, 1973). First printings of each article are cited in the bibliography

L	BL, MS Lansdowne 393
Leff, *FitzRalph Commentator*	Gordon Leff, *Richard FitzRalph, Commentator on the Sentences. A Study in Theological Orthodoxy* (Manchester, 1963)
*LTK*²	*Lexikon für Theologie und Kirche*, 2nd edn. (Freiburg i. Br., 1957 ff.)
Medieval Religious Houses. England and Wales	David Knowles and R. Neville Hadcock, *Medieval Religious Houses. England and Wales* (London, 1953)
Medieval Religious Houses. Ireland	Aubrey Gwynn and R. Neville Hadcock, *Medieval Religious Houses. Ireland* (London, 1970)
Mohler, *Einnahmen*	Ludwig Mohler (ed.), *Die Einnahmen der apostolischen Kammer unter Klemens VI.* (Vatikanische Quellen zur Geschichte der päpstlichen Hof- und Finanzverwaltung, vol. v, Paderborn, 1931)
MOPHist.	*Monumenta Ordinis Fratrum Praedicatorum Historica* (Louvain-Rome, 1896 ff.)
MPG	*Patrologia Graeca*, ed. J. P. Migne (Paris, 1857 ff.)
MPL	*Patrologia Latina*, ed. J. P. Migne (Paris, 1878 ff.)
MS	*Mediaeval Studies* (Toronto, 1939 ff.)
Obl. et Sol.	*Obligationes et Solutiones*, in ASV, Fondo camerale
OCP	*Orientalia Christiana Periodica* (Rome, 1935 ff.)
OHS	Oxford Historical Society
Owst, *Literature*²	Gerald R. Owst, *Literature and Pulpit in Medieval England*, 2nd edn. (Oxford, 1961)
Owst, *Preaching*	Gerald R. Owst, *Preaching in Medieval England* (Cambridge, 1926)
P	Paris, Bibliothèque nationale, Lat. 15853
PBA	*Proccedings of the British Academy* (London 1904 ff.)
Perini, *Bibl. Aug.*	David Perini, *Bibliographia Augustiniana*, 4 vols. (Florence, 1929)
Proc. Am. Phil. Soc.	*Proceedings of the American Philosophical Society* (Philadelphia, 1840 ff.).
Proc. ICHC	*Proceedings of the Irish Catholic Historical Committee* (Dublin, 1955 ff.)
PRIA	*Proceedings of the Royal Irish Academy* (Dublin, 1840 ff.)
Rashdall's Universities	*The Universities of Europe in the Middle Ages by the late Hastings Rashdall*, Frederick M. Powicke and Alfred B. Emden (eds.), 3 vols. (Oxford, 1936)
Raynaldus, *Ann. Eccl.*	Odericus Raynaldus, *Annales Ecclesiastici*, 38 vols. (Lucca, 1738-59)
RB	*Revue Benédictine* (Lille, 1884 ff.)
Reg. Burgh. Lincoln	Register of Henry Burghersh, Bishop of Lincoln 1320-40 (Lincoln Cathedral Archives)

Reg. John Swayne	David A. Chart, *Register of John Swayne, Archbishop of Armagh and Primate of Ireland* (Belfast, 1935)
Reg. Lat.	*Registra Lateranensia*, ASV, Dataria apostolica (1389 ff.)
Reg. Northburgh	Register of Roger Northburgh, Bishop of Coventry and Lichfield (1322–58) (Lichfield Cathedral Archives)
Reg. Suppl.	*Registra Supplicationum*, ASV, Dataria apostolica (1342 ff.)
Reg. Vat.	*Registra Vaticana*, ASV (1073 ff.)
RHE	*Revue d'histoire ecclésiastique* (Louvain, 1900 ff.)
RS	Rolls Series (London, 1858–96)
Rymer's *Foedera*	Thomas Rymer (ed.), *Foedera, Conventiones et Litterae*, 6 vols. (London, 1816–69)
S	*Summa Domini Richardi Radulphi Archiepiscopi Armachani . . . in Questionibus Armenorum* (i.e. *Summa de Questionibus Armenorum*), ed. Johannis Sudoris (Paris, 1511)
Salter, *Snappe's Formulary*	Herbert E. Salter (ed.), *Snappe's Formulary and other Records* (OHS, 1923)
SB München	*Sitzungsberichte der Bayerischen Akademie der Wissenschaften zu München, historisch-philosophische Klasse* (Munich, 1871 ff.)
SB Wien	*Sitzungsberichte der (since 1947: Österreichischen) Akademie der Wissenschaften, philosophisch-historische Klasse* (Vienna, 1831 ff.)
Schäfer *Ausgaben . . .* Johann XXII	Karl E. Schäfer, *Die Ausgaben der apostolischen Kammer unter Johann XXII., nebst den Jahresbilanzen von 1316–1375* (Vatikanische Quellen zur Geschichte der päpstlichen Hof- und Finanzverwaltung, vol. ii, Paderborn, 1912)
Schäfer, *Ausgaben . . . Benedikt XII, Klemens VI, Innocenz VI*	Idem, *Die Ausgaben der apostolischen Kammer unter Benedikt XII., Klemens VI. und Innocenz VI.* (ibid., vol. iii, Paderborn, 1914)
Smalley, *English Friars*	Beryl Smalley, *English Friars and Antiquity in the Early Fourteenth Century* (Oxford, 1960)
Statuta Antiqua	M. Stickland Gibson, *Statuta Antiqua Universitatis Oxoniensis* (Oxford, 1931)
Studies	*Studies – an Irish Quarterly Review* (Dublin, 1911 ff.)
Summa	*Summa de Questionibus Armenorum*
Tr. Am. Phil. Soc.	*Transactions of the American Philosophical Society* (Philadelphia, 1769 ff.)

TRHS	*Transactions of the Royal Historical Society* (London, 1871 ff.)
VCH	*Victoria History of the Counties of England*
Walsh, 'FitzRalph and the Friars'	Katherine Walsh, 'Archbishop FitzRalph and the Friars at the Papal Court in Avignon, 1357–60', *Traditio* 31 (1975), 223–45
Walsh, 'Hardeby'	Idem, 'The "De Vita Evangelica" of Geoffrey Hardeby, OESA (*C*.1320–*c*. 1385). A study in the mendicant controversies of the fourteenth century', *AA* 33 (1970), 151–261; 34 (1971), 5–83, and separate (Rome, 1972)
WS	Wyclif Society (London, 1884 ff.)
ZBLG	*Zeitschrift für Bayerische Landesgeschichte* (Munich, 1928 ff.)
ZKG	*Zeitschrift für Kirchengeschichte* (Gotha–Stuttgart, 1876 ff.)
ZKT	*Zeitschrift für Katholische Theologie* (Innsbruck, 1877 ff.)

I Oxford

i. Anglo-Irish background, youth, and early education

COMMENCING with the period which he spent as a student of theology at Oxford University, the career of Richard FitzRalph is documented with a wealth and precision of detail remarkable for a man of his epoch. However, the details of his background, parentage, and birth have remained more obscure. FitzRalph himself, despite his voluminous writings on a wide range of topics which permit us to draw a well-rounded picture of his personality and temperament, gives few precise details of an autobiographical nature. One such detail is nevertheless, in view of the doubtful state of the evidence from other sources and of the claims made in older English historiography,[1] a most important clue as to his place of birth. During a sermon preached in the Franciscan convent at Avignon on the feast of St. Francis, 4 October 1349, he told the audience of his family's close links with their order, informing them that the only religious community in his native town was a Franciscan one and that at any given time at least one if not more of his relatives were friars in that community.[2] That FitzRalph was a native of the archdiocese of Armagh, whose archbishop he was to become, is made plain by the earliest reference to him in the papal registers when for the first time he received a benefice by papal provision

[1] John Prince, *Damnonii Orientales Illustres: or The Worthies of Devon* (Exeter, 1701), pp. 294–8, claimed FitzRalph as a native of Devon, a member of the FitzRalph family of Norral near Widecombe, in spite of those who 'tell us, that he was an Irishman, and born in the Town of Dundalk in that Kingdom' (p. 294). The claim was based on the fact that FitzRalph sought episcopal consecration in Exeter Cathedral, and of the subsequent presence of a family of the same name in Devon. Prince attributed the latter's coat-of-arms, Barule of 6 Arg. and Azure 3 Buckles Gul., to the archbishop on the basis of this alleged identification. Although Reginald L. Poole corrected the picture (*DNB* vii. 194), this error was repeated by Workman, *John Wyclif*, i, 126.

[2] B, fol. 194^{v}; J, fol. 142rb. A further indication in the diary that FitzRalph was a native of Dundalk is provided by a passage in a sermon preached in that city on 24 April 1348. It was the first sermon preached by him upon his return as archbishop, and he stated that he was addressing it to those 'de sanguine meo', B, fol. 42^{v}; J, fol. 34^{va-b}.

on 27 September 1331,[3] and Fr. Gwynn used gleanings from a range of calendared record material to work out that he was of Anglo-Norman burgess stock from the north-east corner of the Pale.[4] This detail concerning the Franciscans confirms that the town in question cannot have been Drogheda, which contained communities of all four mendicant orders within or near its walls, but must have been Dundalk, the only other reasonable possibility in the archdiocese which also lay within the confines of the Anglo-Irish lordship.[5] The probability that Dundalk was his birthplace is further strengthened by the testimony of the annalist who recorded FitzRalph's death at the papal curia – the various sources differ as to the exact day of his death, whether 10, 14, or 16 November 1360 – and added 'cujus ossa per venerabilem patrem Stephanum, Episcopum Midie, in Hibernie dilata sunt ad recondendum in ecclesia Sancti Nicolai de Dondalk, unde fuit oriundus'.[6] Despite the annalist's further laconic comment, 'sed dubium est aliquibus si sunt ossa illius vel alterius', the tradition is recordable within a generation of his death that the tomb in his native city was the scene of 'many great miracles' and that he was venerated locally as St. Richard of Dundalk.[7] Consequent upon this swiftly established cult, a papal commission was appointed during the pontificiate of Urban VI (1378–89) to examine the case for his canonization, while under the succeeding pope, Boniface IX (1389–1404), these investigations had made sufficient progress for FitzRalph's canonization to have been seriously under consideration.[8]

The actual date of FitzRalph's birth cannot be established

[3] ASV, *Reg. Vat.* 101, fol. 225^{r}, in which he is described as a cleric of the archdiocese of Armagh who has previously held no benefice.

[4] *Dowdall Deeds, ad indicem,* for the families of Rauf (or Rowe) and Dowdall, who were prominent in the Dundalk area in the fourteenth century.

[5] *Medieval Religious Houses. Ireland,* pp. 224, 247–9, 288, 298.

[6] There is a consensus among older authorities for 16 November; see Prince, p. 298, who may have taken his information from Sir James Ware, *De Praesulibus Hiberniae Commentarius* (Dublin, 1665), p. 21. For the account of the transfer of the remains to Ireland see J. T. Gilbert (ed.), *Chartularies of St. Mary's Abbey, Dublin: with the Register of its House at Dunbrody, and Annals of Ireland,* 2 vols. (RS, London, 1884), i. 393. This transfer cannot have taken place before 19 February 1369 when Stephen Vale (Wall) was translated from Limerick, nor after his death 10 November 1379, *HBC*², 320.

[7] This local veneration is summed up in the lines of English verse copied into the manuscript of the *Martyrologium Dungallense:* 'Manny a mile have I gone | and manny did I walk | but neuer sawe a hollier man | than Richard of Dundalk', in Brussels, Bibl. nat. MS 506, fol. 115^{r}.

[8] ASV, Indice 320, fol. 42^{r} (11 November 1389), and *Reg. Lat.* 69, fols. 181^{v}–183^{r} (28 January 1399), record the successive stages of this investigation.

precisely, and one can only infer by working backwards from the known milestones of his academic career that he must have been born around 1300 or slightly earlier. Since he came to Oxford as a secular student of arts and did not, as was usually the case with members of religious orders who had undergone a philosophical training in their own schools, seek 'graces' or dispensations from the normal progression of studies through the arts faculty, we can for purposes of computation assume that FitzRalph followed the then accepted procedures. The first piece of concrete information about his Oxford career establishes him on 25 July 1325 as a master of arts and fellow of Balliol Hall. On that date the chancellor of the university, Henry Gower, formally ratified a ruling made by two external masters concerning the college statutes of Balliol.[9] By statute Balliol was then reserved for students in the arts faculty, and under the terms of this ruling those members of the college who were students in the higher faculties, including theology, were required to leave. Four members of the college were thus affected and obliged to resign their fellowships: Richard Campsall and Walter Horkestaw, both doctors of theology, and Richard Radford and Richard 'filius Radulphi', both masters of arts.[10] The sources give no indication of the length of FitzRalph's residence at Balliol, nor how he came to be there. In the traditional division of students between northerners and southerners for academic purposes the Welsh and Irish came to be grouped together with the southerners, while Balliol Hall was something of a stronghold for the northern elements.[11] Nor can it be established definitely whether FitzRalph was subsequently admitted to a fellowship elsewhere. It has been suggested that he became a fellow of the Hall which later became University College, but Merton is also, in view of its strong associations with theology in the university and of FitzRalph's own links with Mertonian circles, a distinct possibility.[12] The enforced resignation of his

[9] Herbert E. Salter (ed.), *The Oxford Deeds of Balliol College* (OHS 1913), p. 285.

[10] See respectively *BRUO* I, 344–5 (supplemented by James A. Weisheipl, 'Repertorium Mertonense', *MS* 31 (1969), 208–9); *BRUO* II, 963; ibid., III, 1541–2; II, 692–3.

[11] Alfred B. Emden, 'Northerners and Southerners in the Organization of the University to 1509', *Oxford Studies presented to Daniel Callus* (OHS 1964), p. 2.

[12] Gwynn, *Studies,* 22 (1933), p. 400, suggested University College, but he was unaware of the extent of FitzRalph's Merton connections. On the Mertonians see Weisheipl, 'Repertorium Mertonense', 177–244, and his detailed examination of their works and surviving manuscripts in 'Early Fourteenth-Century Physics of the Merton "school" ' (MS D.Phil., d. 1776, Oxford, 1956).

Balliol fellowship may have compelled him to seek other sources of financial support and on 26 April 1326 he was collated by Edward II to the church of Athboy in the diocese of Meath.[13] However, although this church was located within the confines of the Anglo-Irish lordship where the king's writ ran, there is no definite evidence that FitzRalph ever actually got possession of the church or its revenues, and the argument used by Grandisson in his later attempts to secure papal patronage for his protégé to the effect that FitzRalph held no benefice already would suggest that the Irish collation did not take effect.

The registers of Bishop John Grandisson of Exeter, a powerful patron who subsequently smoothed the path of FitzRalph's rise to prominence at Avignon, contain several entries which throw light on the young Anglo-Irishman's progress towards the doctorate in theology. Grandisson had studied in Paris from 1313 to 1317 under the Cistercian master, Jacques Fournier, who became pope as Benedict XII on 16 December 1334, and appears also to have spent a period of study in Oxford, probably before his departure for Paris.[14] He was provided to the see of Exeter by John XXII on 12 August 1327, was consecrated in Avignon, and enthroned on 22 August 1328 in Exeter. The register for his first year as bishop contains a letter in which Grandisson addressed FitzRalph as 'magister Ricardus', but not yet as 'bachalarius', while in a further letter a year later he is mentioned as 'in Sacra Pagina Egregius bachalarius',[15] and finally in the summer of 1331 we can date with certainty his inception as doctor of theology.[16] In view of the statutory requirements for candidates in theology proceeding to the doctorate at Oxford in the thirteenth and fourteenth centuries, a procedure which required nine years to complete, FitzRalph must have begun his studies in theology no later than 1322, i.e. three years before he resigned his fellowship at Balliol.[17] It is conceivable that he carried out the mandatory two years' teaching as regent master in

[13] CPR 1324–27, 258, but there is no evidence that he ever got possession of the church or its revenues.

[14] *BRUO* II, 800–1, but the dating of Grandisson's sojourn at Oxford remains a problem.

[15] *Grandisson's Register*, i. 173, 233.

[16] 24 May 1331 Grandisson addressed FitzRalph as bachelor of theology, ibid., ii. 616, whereas by 27 September of the same year the papal letter conferring upon him a benefice in the diocese of Exeter addressed him as doctor. The entry in *Grandisson's Register*, i. 106–7, recording the bishop's petition to John XXII for this benefice has been incorrectly dated in the printed register to *c.*1328–9.

[17] *Statuta Antiqua*, pp. 48–51.

arts concurrently with the initial stages of his theological studies and may have been teaching Balliol students in arts until his resignation. However, he was obliged to have completed his own arts courses and incepted as master of arts before embarking on the study of theology, hence by 1322 he must have followed courses in the seven liberal arts and the three philosophies: natural philosophy, moral philosophy, and metaphysics, and participated in the necessary disputations, all of which normally required about seven years.[18] This chronology would place his arrival at Oxford no later than *c.*1314–15, and it could have been several years earlier. The initial stages of university training in arts then corresponded to what in modern terms might roughly be described as 'grammar school education' and students came correspondingly younger to university, usually aged about fourteen or fifteen; thus we can arrive at a hypothetical date of birth for FitzRalph around 1300, possibly slightly before, but definitely not later.

The next question to be considered concerns the conditions of Anglo-Irish urban society at the beginning of the fourteenth century, which provided the background to FitzRalph's formative years. His native archdiocese of Armagh can be regarded as a microcosm of the tensions and racial divisions then endemic in Irish society as a whole. Within a generation of the 'invasion' of Ireland by the Cambro-Normans under the leadership of the Earl of Clare (Strongbow) this area had felt the effect of the Norman presence,[19] and almost half of its territory had been permanently occupied by the new settlers. Town life had developed largely along English lines in the eastern coastal parts of the diocese (modern County Louth), especially in Drogheda and Dundalk.[20] By the early fourteenth century both the secular and ecclesiastical administration had been forced to recognize that the diocese was irrevocably divided into two almost evenly balanced parts. The northern half still clung to the old order, the ancient kingly family of the O'Neill ruled and gave judgement according to Gaelic law; Gaelic speech and customs

[18] For the curriculum and regulations governing it see Weisheipl, 'The Curriculum of the Faculty of Arts at Oxford in the Early Fourteenth Century', *MS* 26 (1964), 143–85; idem, 'Developments in the Arts Curriculum at Oxford in the Early Fourteenth Century', *MS* 28 (1966), 151–75.

[19] See Annette J. Otway-Ruthven, *A History of Medieval Ireland* (London, 1968), pp. 70–101.

[20] There is no comprehensive treatment in English of the rise and growth of towns in medieval Ireland, but see Gearoid MacNiocaill, *Na Búirgéisí,* 2 vols. (Dublin, 1964); J. J. Webb, *Municipal Government in Ireland* (Dublin, 1918).

prevailed, even the clergy were regarded as a race apart and referred to in official diocesan records as 'clerus inter Hibernos'.[21] In the southern half of the diocese, dominated by the towns of Drogheda and Dundalk and lying close to the Pale and the nerve-centres of government of the English lordship, the rule of law was that of the justiciar's court, and the clergy here were designated 'clerus inter Anglos'. This cleavage was given what amounted to official recognition with regard to ecclesiastical administration in that the northern part of the archdiocese, together with the primatial city of Armagh, was ruled by a native-born dean who resided in Armagh with some of the Gaelic Irish canons of the chapter. Visitation in those dioceses within the metropolitan jurisdiction which lay 'inter Hibernos' – in this case the vast majority – was entrusted to native commissaries, or even in some cases to the bishop of the diocese in question. The primate resided at one or other of his two manors of Termonfechin and Dromiskin in County Louth, was assisted in the government of the 'English' half of his diocese by an Anglo-Irish archdeacon, used the parish church of St. Peter in Drogheda as his pro-cathedral, and only rarely ventured to his cathedral city of Armagh.[22]

Furthermore there were ominous signs, becoming increasingly evident, that the rule of law in the Anglo-Irish lordship was breaking down, that racial tensions on the borders of the Pale were becoming so acute that government officials were either unable or unwilling to discharge their duties.[23] Above all, the parliamentary legislation of 1297, 1310, and 1320 illustrated how serious the problem had become by the early fourteenth century, while the Scottish invasion led by Edward Bruce, 1315-18, which came to be recognized by the English government, Anglo-Irish settlers, and native Irish alike, as an unmitigated disaster, highlighted these tensions even though it did not

[21] For relations between the Gaelic lordship in Ulster and the archbishops of Armagh see Katharine Simms, 'Gaelic Lordships in Ulster in the Later Middle Ages' (unpublished Ph.D. thesis, University of Dublin, 1976); idem, 'The Archbishops of Armagh and the O'Neills 1347-1471', *IHS* 19 (1974), 38-55; Michael Glancy, 'The Primates and the Church Lands of Armagh', *Seanchas Árdhmacha,* 5 (1970), 370-96.

[22] See Aubrey Gwynn, *The Medieval Province of Armagh 1470-1545* (Dundalk, 1946), pp. 73-7. Although attention here is primarily focused on the last hundred years before the Reformation, the situation was basically the same in the fourteenth century.

[23] James F. Lydon, *Ireland in the Later Middle Ages* (Dublin, 1973), p. 48. For a reinterpretation of the 'Gaelicization' of the Anglo-Irish see Robin Frame, 'Power and Society in the Lordship of Ireland, 1272-1377', *Past and Present*, 76 (1977), 3-33.

actually cause them.[24] It certainly underlined the increasing weakness of the central government of the lordship and its failure to implement the most crucial objective in its policy, i.e. to 'keep the peace'.[25] This tension between the two nations was evident in every sphere, in the industrial and trading life of the towns as in ecclesiastical organization and religious communities. The guilds, which by the fourteenth century were an accepted feature of trades and crafts in all urban communities throughout western Europe, practised in Ireland their own particular form of 'closed shop', usually by excluding the native Irish from membership, a practice which was to be strongly condemned by FitzRalph when he returned to Ireland as archbishop of Armagh.[26] Such condemnation might seem surprising, coming as it did from a member of the Anglo-Irish burgess section of the population, but FitzRalph was indisputably a conscientious and pastorally-minded prelate, whose sermons provide ample testimony to his constant efforts to promote justice, fair dealing, and peace among his divided flock.

One of the areas of tension in later medieval Ireland which is most amply documented and which has a definite relevance for the formation of FitzRalph's personal attitudes as well as for the problems which he had to face during the penultimate stages of his career is that of Irish ecclesiastical life. Here the problem was made more acute by the dominant role played by the regular clergy, and strife between the two nations in communities of monks, canons, and friars was a constant feature of religious life. Not only did episcopal authority, diocesan life, and the quality of pastoral care in the parishes suffer from these political and racial tensions which had developed in the course of the thirteenth century and were to divide Irish society irretrievably for the remainder of the medieval period,[27] but they also affected communities of religious, most intensely Cistercians and Franciscans. The orders of mendicant friars were to be the special target of FitzRalph's criticisms during the last years of his life, when he had been forced to cope with their activities in the pastoral context, and it will be a contention of this study that his volte-face from cordial relations with the friar-scholars

[24] Lydon, 'The Bruce Invasion of Ireland', *Historical Studies*, 4 (1963), 111–25; Otway-Ruthven, *Medieval Ireland*, pp. 224–51.

[25] Lydon, *Ireland in the Later Middle Ages*, p. 50.

[26] FitzRalph preached in Drogheda on this subject, 28 June 1355.

[27] Vividly described in John A. Watt, *The Church and the Two Nations in Medieval Ireland* (Cambridge, 1970), esp. pp. 173–83, 189–91.

whom he knew at Oxford and Avignon to total opposition to the mendicant way of life can be most satisfactorily explained in terms of this confrontation, made more acute in the highly-charged Anglo-Irish situation. The concentration of anti-mendicant criticism among Anglo-Irish churchmen in the late Middle Ages was striking, and if FitzRalph received little more than lukewarm support from his brother bishops throughout western Christendom, this may at least partly be explained by a failure – even on the part of English prelates – to appreciate the dimensions of his problem.

The mendicant orders had come to Ireland from England and had settled initially in the Anglo-Irish towns. Even though all four orders soon drew substantial support from the native race as well, there was little evidence of tension among Dominican, Carmelite, and Augustinian friars. But by the later thirteenth century the Franciscans were coming to be regarded by the Dublin government as a potentially subversive element, 'a political risk', and it was being advocated that they, like the Cistercians, should be subjected to careful screening with a view to securing control of the houses in the marcher districts in the hands of sound, hand-picked English religious, a policy for the implementation of which Edward II finally secured the support of John XXII.[28] By 1307 the Cistercian abbey of Mellifont, which contained a large proportion of native Irish monks, was in a state of chaos, strife over the choice of the next abbot had reached such proportions that private armies were being employed to back the claims of the rival contenders, and at this point the situation was brought to the attention of the justiciar. It is scarcely a coincidence that the next parliament, which sat at Kilkenny three years later, passed legislation which illustrated the thinking of the colonial authorities about native Irish religious, and subsequent events in the course of the Bruce invasion only served to reinforce these impressions in the minds of English ecclesiastical and royal servants.[29] A statute was promulgated forbidding the profession or reception of any native Irish religious, whether monk, canon, or friar, in communities among the colonists. Though the statute was soon recognized as inappropriate and hastily revoked, the very fact of its promulgation revealed the extent of estrangement between

[28] Ibid., pp. 181–2.
[29] Ibid., pp. 176, 183.

the two nations, even among members of supranational religious corporations.[30]

Although *gravamina* from all over Christendom were heard by Pope Clement V at the Council of Vienne, including the complaints of the *ecclesia Hibernica,* concerning oppression of the Church by secular powers, this was mainly a question of a Church/State clash and the problem of the two nations was not specifically brought to light. That this was so is not surprising when one considers that the *gravamina* were prepared and presented by Archbishops John Lech of Dublin and Walter Jorz of Armagh, the latter being subsequently accused by Domhnall O'Neill, in the Remonstrance presented to the papal legates in England on behalf of the native Irish, of responsibility for the partisan legislation of 1310.[31] This Remonstrance, which can be dated to the spring of 1318, was a somewhat belated justification for the rejection of English lordship in Ireland and support for Edward Bruce, and it listed among the *gravamina* of the Gaelic Irish in ecclesiastical and civil law the complaint that it was not regarded as a crime for an Englishman to deprive an Irishman of his property or even to take his life.[32] It further alluded to an episode which took place shortly after Bruce had landed in northern Ireland in May 1315. In the presence of Bruce a disputation had taken place concerning the rights and wrongs of the Anglo-Irish situation, and a Franciscan, who has been tentatively identified as Simon Mercer of the Drogheda convent,[33] took part. When the argument became heated Friar Simon maintained that it was not a sin to kill an Irishman, and if he had done so himself he would not hesitate to say Mass the following morning. In retaliation for such sentiments, Irish

[30] For the text of the statute passed at Kilkenny see *Statutes and Ordinances and Acts of the Parliament of Ireland, King John to Henry V,* ed. H. F. Berry (Dublin, 1907), pp. 270–7.

[31] For the Latin text see John Fordun, *Scotichronicon,* ed. T. Hearne, 5 vols. (Oxford, 1722), iii. 908–26, and Eng. trans. in Edmund Curtis and Robert B. McDowell, *Irish Historical Documents 1172–1922* (London, 1943), pp. 38–42. For Walter Jorz's difficulties as archbishop of Armagh see *BRUO* II, 1023–4.

[32] 'For not only their laymen and secular clergy but also some of their regular clergy dogmatically assert the heresy that it is no more a sin to kill an Irishman than a dog or other animal', Curtis–McDowell, p. 43. The effect of such teaching, and the operation of the *lex marchie* in justification of the murder of Irishmen and plunder of their property, was roundly condemned by FitzRalph in his sermons forty years later.

[33] The Remonstrance referred to him as 'frater Simon', and a Simon Mercer is recorded as a member of the Drogheda convent in 1317, when he visited England on a mission to Edward II, E. B. FitzMaurice and A. G. Little, *Materials for the History of the Franciscan Province of Ireland, A.D. 1230–1450* (Manchester, 1920), p. 101.

forces who took and sacked the town of Dundalk later that summer burned the Franciscan friary to the ground and massacred the entire community of twenty-two friars.[34] If FitzRalph's statement concerning his family connections with the convent is taken literally, then it is virtually certain that at least one of his relatives perished as a result. There is a certain tragic irony in the situation that nearly forty years later he would have to accuse the Franciscans of Gaelic origin within his archdiocese of abusing the confessional to excuse similar partisan crimes when committed against those of his own race.[35]

Yet a further indication of the divisions within the Irish Franciscan province is provided by the counter-accusation of the following year. Armed with letters dated 20 August 1316 from Edward II, the provincial in Ireland, Thomas Godman and an English Franciscan, Geoffrey of Aylsham, who was the royal candidate for the vacant see of Cashel,[36] went to Avignon to seek the intervention of their minister-general, Michael of Cesena, against those Irish friars who were working up support for Edward Bruce and thereby fomenting rebellion against the rightful lordship of the English Crown in Ireland.[37] At the same time Edward II was proving reasonably successful in his attempts to persuade John XXII of the urgent need for politically reliable episcopal appointments at such a time of crisis for royal power in Ireland.[38]

During these turbulent years of FitzRalph's youth the lack of any university or *studium generale* in the country made it imperative for an Irishman, whether secular or religious, in pursuit of higher studies and of the career opportunities open to university graduates to go elsewhere, and from the thirteenth century onwards the most usual place for Irish students of both Gaelic and Anglo-Norman backgrounds to choose was

[34] Ibid., p. 93; *Medieval Religious Houses. Ireland,* p. 249.

[35] FitzRalph's statement rings true, especially as a member of the Rauf family, Joannes Radulphi, was Franciscan prior-provincial until the chapter at Kilkenny in May 1332, FitzMaurice–Little, pp. 135, 209.

[36] This disputed election is discussed in John A. Watt, 'Negotiations between Edward II and John XXII concerning Ireland', *IHS* 10 (1956), 2–3. For evidence of the king's intervention see FitzMaurice–Little, pp. 97–8.

[37] On 20 August 1316 the Franciscan minister-general issued letters from Avignon, ordering his friars in Ireland not to make common cause with the Scots, nor to foment rebellion, FitzMaurice–Little, pp. 98–9.

[38] Edward II recommended to John XXII, 25 March 1317 that for the duration of the political unrest no Irishman be appointed to a bishopric in Ireland without royal approval, Rymer's *Foedera,* ii. 318–19. Watt, 'Negotiations', 1–16, shows the extent to which John XXII complied with this request.

Oxford,[39] though the great wave of university expansion on the Continent during the later fourteenth and fifteenth centuries took Irish students further afield. The problems caused by the lack of facilities for higher studies in Ireland were set out in considerable detail in a petition addressed to Pope Clement V when Archbishop John Lech of Dublin attended the Council of Vienne in 1311-12, and as a result that pontiff issued a bull on 13 July 1312 authorizing the establishment of a university in Dublin with all the privileges usually accorded by the papacy to a *studium generale.*[40] The new university was to be located in St. Patrick's Cathedral, whose chapter was the largest and richest in Ireland, the only one comparable with those of English cathedrals.[41] The next step was taken by Lech's successor in the see of Dublin, Alexander de Bicknor, who appears to have brought the university *de facto* into being in 1320, and on 10 February 1321 he issued the *Ordinatio pro Universitate Dublinensi,* thereby giving statutory implementation to the papal decree.[42] The Avignonese popes, including John XXII (1316-34) who had more extensive contacts with Ireland than any other medieval pope,[43] were outstanding patrons of universities and the reasons for the failure of the Dublin enterprise lay not in the lack of papal patronage but in conditions nearer home. Fr. Gwynn has argued that the entire scheme for a university in Dublin was the work of Alexander de Bicknor, that as the king's treasurer in Ireland and the unanimous choice of the chapters both of St. Patrick's and Holy Trinity to succeed as archbishop

[39] *BRUO, passim,* provides numerous examples of Gaelic Irish students in Oxford during the 13th and 14th centuries, many of whom subsequently became bishops in Irish sees, e.g. in the early 14th century, Maurice MacCarwell, Cashel, 1303-16 (*BRUO* III, 2193); David MacMahon, Killaloe, 1299-1317 (III, 2194); Alan Ahern, Ardfert, 1331-47 (III, 2203).

[40] ASV, *Reg. Vat.* 59, fol. 196^{v}, inaccurately printed in W. H. Monck Mason, *History and Antiquities of the Collegiate and Cathedral Church of St. Patrick, near Dublin* (Dublin, 1820), Appendix, pp. ix-x. See also Heinrich Denifle, *Die Entstehung der Universitäten des Mittelalters* (Berlin, 1885), pp. 639-43; Aubrey Gwynn, 'The Medieval University of St. Patrick's, Dublin', *Studies*, 27 (1938), 199-212, 437-54; most recently, Fergal McGrath, *Education in Ancient and Medieval Ireland* (Dublin, 1979), pp. 216-20.

[41] See Geoffrey J. Hand, 'The Medieval Chapter of St. Patrick's Cathedral, Dublin', *Repertorium Novum,* 3 (1964), 229-48. Only the first part: 'The early period (*c.*1219-*c.*1279)' was published.

[42] Also printed in Monck Mason, Appendix, pp. x-xi, and Eng. trans., ibid., pp. 100-1 n. For Bicknor see *BRUO* I, 186-7; *HBC*², 336; on Bicknor's election, Geoffrey J. Hand, 'The Rivalry of the Cathedral Chapters in Medieval Dublin', *JRSAI* 92 (1962), 205.

[43] Gwynn, 'The Medieval University', 207-8.

of Dublin in 1310-11 (though Clement V provided another royal servant instead), he had been the master-mind behind the original petition presented by Archbishop Lech to the pope.[43] When Bicknor finally returned to Dublin as archbishop in 1318 he set about implementing the plan. William Rodyard, dean of St. Patrick's since 1310, was named as the first chancellor of the new university, and at the same time appointed to the professorship of canon law.[44] However, Bicknor's own subsequent financial troubles, disgrace, and excommunication in the years between 1322 and his death on 14 July 1349 ruined whatever slender hope there might otherwise have been for the survival of an infant university based on St. Patrick's in Dublin.

The statement drawn from Lech's petition to Clement V, 'quod licet nonnulli doctores seu baccalarii saltim in theologica facultate, aliique in grammatica sive artibus magistri legentes, in terra Ibernia habeantur, . . . scolarium universitas vel studium generale propter quod pauci reperiuntur in terra ipsa viri decori scientia litterarum'[45] invites some consideration of the educational opportunities and facilities available in early fourteenth-century Ireland. Where, for example, could FitzRalph have received an elementary education in preparation for his studies at Oxford? In his remarks to the Franciscans at Avignon in 1349 he did not explicitly say so, but it is possible that he received his early education at their convent in Dundalk. Although we know from Bicknor's *Ordinatio* that both the Franciscans and Dominicans had schools of theology in Dublin, whose position alongside the new university was to be safeguarded and from which it was clearly envisaged the university would be supplied with teachers of theology, probably in analogy to university procedures elsewhere,[46] it is doubtful whether the prescriptive legislation of the mendicant orders concerning the establishment of provincial and conventual schools of theology

[44] Monck Mason, p. 101. Rodyard is described as doctor of canon law, but it is not known where he obtained this degree. Of the remaining 'doctors of divinity' appointed professors of theology – William Hardite OP, Henry Cogry OFM, and Edward Kermerdyn OP – only the latter has a recorded university career, *BRUO* II, 1040. Rodyard was still dean of St. Patrick's and vicar-general of the archdiocese of Dublin during Bicknor's absence on 2 July 1328, but then disappeared from the records, *Archbishop Alen's Register*, pp. 199-200, though according to Monck Mason, pp. 118-22, he remained dean until after 1335.

[45] Ibid., p. 100.

[46] Ibid., pp. 100-1. They were to provide the regent masters, who could elect the chancellor, and two proctors, who were also to be regent. The *lector* on the Bible, who was to lecture at St. Patrick's, was apparently also to be recruited from the mendicant communities.

and philosophy were fulfilled in every case in Ireland. However, it is to be expected that the Franciscans in a busy trading town such as Dundalk would have had the facilities for imparting a rudimentary or elementary education, and for the relative of a member of the community doubtless a little Latin grammar could have been provided.[47]

If we turn from the general background of Irish society during FitzRalph's youth to the more particular situation of his home town of Dundalk, we are in a more fortunate position with regard to sources than is the case for most Anglo-Irish towns of this period. Before the end of the twelfth century the town had become the most important urban centre in the lordship granted in 1185 by Prince John as *dominus Hibernie* to his seneschal Bertram de Verdon. The original borough of Dundalk was founded before Bertram's death in 1192 and by the middle of the thirteenth century it was sharing in the general prosperity of the Anglo-Irish towns on the eastern seaboard.[48] Despite Fitz-Ralph's subsequent disclaimer before the Franciscans in Avignon that his family was of lowly birth – 'licet de humili loco nati'[49] – and presumably had therefore a particular affinity with the followers of St. Francis, the evidence indicates otherwise. The family of Rauf, to which Richard FitzRalph ('Fyrauf, *filius Radulphi*') belonged, was a burgess family of reasonable prominence by the first half of the fourteenth century. It was connected with the more distinguished family of Douedale (Dowdall), whose surviving collection of 'Deeds' – an unbroken series of records from the thirteenth to the seventeenth centuries – contains valuable information about the personal history of FitzRalph's family in Dundalk. In the Balliol deed of 1325 FitzRalph had already changed his name from plain 'Rauf' to the more aristocratic sounding *filius Radulphi.* Consequently it does not become conclusively established until the 1340s that he is to be identified with the Dundalk family of Rauf which suddenly sprang to prominence in the early 1320s, appearing frequently both in the Dowdall Deeds and the Calendars of

[47] For Franciscan legislation concerning the appointment of teachers see John Moorman, *A History of the Franciscan Order* (Oxford, 1968), pp. 365–8, with guide to sources.

[48] *Dowdall Deeds,* pp. x–xi. In the years after FitzRalph's death the area around Dundalk was hard pressed by the Gaelic Irish, especially the O'Neill. In June 1369 owners of the De Verdon lands petitioned for a reduction of scutage because large parts of the manors of Dundalk and Loughsewdy were in enemy hands, Otway-Ruthven, *Medieval Ireland,* p. 301 n. 54.

[49] B, fol. 194^{v}; J, fol. 142rb.

Patent and Close Rolls.[50] The name of John Rauf occurred regularly as witness to various grants from 1322 onwards, and there are other indications that he was a man of substance: on 23 April 1330 he received exemption for life from Edward III from being put on assizes, juries, or recognizances, and from service as mayor, sheriff, coroner, or other officer of the Crown against his will, while on 30 June of the same year he admitted to a debt of 30*s.* which he owed to a cleric named Thomas Bannburgh. In default of payment the sum was to be levied from John's goods and lands.[51] From a further deed concerning family lands dating from the year 1345 we learn that this John Rauf had both a son and a grandson of the same name,[52] of whom the son may possibly be identical with that John Rauf who acted as attorney for local families during the 1330s and in the same capacity for FitzRalph after the latter had become archbishop of Armagh but was still detained in England on business.[53] Yet another of the same name is to be found, as Johannes Radulphi, who held office as Franciscan provincial minister until the chapter held at Kilkenny in May 1332. Yet the first conclusive piece of evidence linking FitzRalph with this family complex is to be found in a petition which he laid before Clement VI on 8 May 1344, when he sought and obtained a benefice in Ireland for each of his three nephews, Richard and Edmund 'Radulphi' and John Brisbon, all clerics of the archdiocese of Armagh and all at that date apparently studying at Oxford.[54]

From this accumulation of evidence it is clear that the Rauf family had emerged as persons of some substance in the first half of the fourteenth century, were able to send some of their sons to avail themselves of the benefits of a university education in Oxford, and, through the career of Richard FitzRalph, open for them the channels to ecclesiastical preferment. Apart from his namesake, the younger Richard Radulphi, none of these clerical members of the archbishop's family left any further record of their existence,[55] but the lay members continued to

[50] John Rauf first appears as witness in several grants 1322–3, *Dowdall Deeds,* pp. 31–5, for six such occasions, 16 April 1322–10 June 1323.

[51] CPR 1327–30, 514, 529, 531; CCR 1330–33, 142.

[52] 20 July 1345, *Dowdall Deeds,* pp. 67–8.

[53] CPR 1345–48, 272, 356; CCR 1346–49, 477; CPR 1348–50, 118.

[54] ASV, *Reg. Suppl.* 6, fol. 343^{v}; *CPL Petitions* I, 53.

[55] 10 September 1360, shortly before his death, FitzRalph secured a canonry and prebend in Ferns for his relative Walter Dowdall, *Reg. Suppl.* 33, fol. 252^{v}, *CPL Petitions* I, 359. Another member of the Dowdall family, George, became archbishop of Armagh during the Marian restoration, 1553–8, *HBC*^{2}, 383.

figure, if less prominently than before, in the life of the area, a factor which doubtless contributed to the cult of 'St. Richard of Dundalk' and the drive for his canonization in the decades immediately after his death.

Although his change of name was clearly accepted for purposes of college records and by his patron, Bishop Grandisson of Exeter,[56] the change did not go completely unnoticed and this information was passed on to the next generation of irreverent but perspicacious students. While FitzRalph was chancellor of Oxford University in 1332–4 he was, as we shall see, faced with a major university crisis generally known as the Stamford Schism, and in this context he was the subject of a set of satirical verses composed by one of the students who had seceded to Stamford and who alluded quite unequivocally to the recent improvement in the chancellor's social status.[57] If indeed FitzRalph made the change in the belief that such an elegant Latinization would help rather than hinder his career in the academic hierarchy, he certainly succeeded in his purpose and opened even wider horizons for the future.

ii. Oxford at the time of FitzRalph

Oxford during the first half of the fourteenth century, when FitzRalph spent some twenty of the formative years of his life there, interrupted as far as we know only by his visit to Paris in the academic year 1329–30,[1] was intellectually one of the most exciting and stimulating places in Europe. This was a particularly brilliant period for the university, one in which it could rival the schools of Paris in distinction and originality. It was not merely the chauvinism of a proud English prelate and servant of the Crown which led Richard de Aungerville (de Bury), bishop of Durham and the most learned book-collector and patron of scholars in fourteenth-century England, to boast in his *Philobiblon* that 'admirable Minerva . . . has passed by Paris, and has now happily come to Britain', and to reflect that the whole academic world was then fascinated by English subtleties and

[56] They may not have regarded the Latinization as a change of status. In academic debates at Oxford he was frequently referred to as 'Firauf', or 'Phyrauf', see Courtenay, *Adam Wodeham*, pp. 79 ff.

[57] Ed. in Herbert E. Salter, 'The Stamford Schism', *EHR* 37 (1922), 249–53.

[1] As tutor to Grandisson's nephew, John Northwode, *Grandisson's Register*, i. 233. For Northwode, *BRUO* II, 1371–2.

calculations.[2] He considered Paris as solidly conservative, even a little sleepy by comparison, and was immensely proud of the way in which his Alma Mater was forging ahead and making new discoveries in the various fields of scholarship. Both William of Ockham's innovations in the realm of logic and the developments in natural science, especially physics and mathematics, emanating from the Mertonian school[3] had contributed much to this new situation, and both of these influences in their different ways underlined the fact that the great scholastic syntheses of the previous century were breaking down. Similar tendencies were still further illustrated by renewed emphasis among the friars, in Oxford and elsewhere, on biblical rather than systematic theology, and the mendicant doctors working in English universities during these years produced much biblical commentary of quality and distinction.[4] This was the period which Etienne Gilson had in mind when he made the oft-quoted remark that the marriage between theology and philosophy was being dissolved and that each party was making claims on the other.[5] If one may be forgiven for pushing his metaphor a step further, it may reasonably be argued that, whereas this marriage had originally been solemnized in Paris, Oxford was more active in providing grounds for initiating divorce proceedings.

FitzRalph's autobiographical prayer, for which there is substantial evidence that he composed it at Avignon during his case against the friars and that it should therefore be dated to within a year or two of his death in 1360, is something of an 'apologia pro vita sua', and it provides valuable insights into the author's view of his own intellectual development. It has survived in a large number of manuscripts because it was invariably copied as an appended chapter to the last book of the *Summa de Questionibus Armenorum.* It pertains more properly to the later phases of the archbishop's career and will be considered in the appropriate context. However, one passage in the prayer is relevant to the progress of FitzRalph's earlier studies at Oxford

[2] *Philobiblon,* ed. and trans., E. C. Thomas (London, 1888), cap. 9, pp. 212–13. For Bury, *BRUO* I, 323–6; Wieland Schmidt, 'Richard de Bury – ein anti-höfischer Höfling', *Philobiblon,* 19 (1975), 156–88. On the dispute whether *Philobiblon* was composed by Bury himself, or was largely the work of his protégé Robert Holcot, see Smalley, *English Friars,* pp. 67–8.

[3] Gordon Leff, *William of Ockham. The Metamorphosis of Scholastic Discourse* (Manchester, 1975); Weisheipl, *Early Fourteenth-Century Physics.*

[4] These are studied in Smalley, *English Friars.*

[5] Etienne Gilson, *La Philosophie au moyen âge. Des origines patristiques à la fin du XIVe siècle* (Paris, 1952^{2}), p. 605.

and the influences to which he was exposed there: he related how in those days 'putabam enim antea per Aristotelica dogmata et argumentationes quasdam profundas', whereas he now looked back on this scholastic period as one in which he was croaking like a frog or a toad in the swamp: 'quomodo cum ranis et bufonis in paludibus crocitabam'.[6] We shall have to consider subsequently the reasons, both practical and intellectual, for FitzRalph's 'conversion' from a scholastic method of theological proof to a stronger reliance on the Bible, a change which became strikingly clear in the sermons and treatises belonging to the Avignon and Irish periods of his life.

There is no reason to doubt the veracity of FitzRalph's statement that he had formerly been influenced by 'Aristotelica dogmata'. Not merely does the only surviving work from his years at Oxford, his *Commentary on the Sentences*, provide ample evidence in support of this claim, but the central position of the corpus of Aristotle's works in the teaching of logic and natural science in the arts faculty made it almost inevitable that this should have been the case. The two disciplines which dominated the arts faculty at Oxford during the first half of the fourteenth century were logic and natural philosophy or science. In the former case, which occupied almost half of the arts curriculum in practice, all the books of the old and new logic of Aristotle had to be heard at least once and in the case of the *Prior Analytics, Topics,* and *Sophistici Elenchi* a second reading was obligatory before the student was admitted to determinations.[7] Equally in the case of natural philosophy, teaching was founded in the *libri naturales* of Aristotle, with the greatest emphasis being placed on his *Physics* as the philosophical foundation of all academic speculation.[8] Although FitzRalph does not appear to have joined in with the young masters of arts, many of them Mertonians, who revelled in the academic exercises of the logic schools and left numerous treatises 'de sophismatibus' and 'de obligatoriis',[9] determinations in logic were a statutory part of his arts course.

Logic was primarily an instrument to further inquiry into other areas, notably natural science and theology, and it was in these areas that the new logic which emerged in the Oxford

[6] Edited Hammerich, *FitzRalph and the Mendicants,* pp. 18-22, at p. 20. The MSS upon which this edition was based are frequently defective.

[7] Weisheipl, 'Curriculum', 174; *Statuta Antiqua,* pp. 26, 1-6.

[8] Weisheipl, 'Curriculum', esp. 173-5.

[9] e.g. Richard Kilwington, *BRUO* II, 1050-1; William Sutton, *BRUO* III, 1826.

schools, especially in the lectures of William of Ockham in the years following 1317[10] was to make the most profound impact, above all in the 1330s and 1340s. However, an investigation into the intellectual foundations of FitzRalph's *Commentary on the Sentences* will reveal the crucial role which the *libri naturales*, and especially the *Physics* and *De anima*, played in the formation of his thought. *De anima* was of particular importance in the medieval study of human psychology, especially as it also involved confrontation with the Averroist interpretation of Aristotle. However, whereas it is true to argue that such problems received more attention on the Continent, as the Paris condemnations of 1270 and 1277 reveal, than in Oxford, there are some indications of a Latin Averroism in Oxford which, largely through the influence of Walter Burley, was also to leave its mark on FitzRalph.[11] Oxford discussions of psychological problems and especially of Averroist teaching on the intellect tended to take place within the context of commentaries on the Sentences and therefore within the faculty of theology, whereas problems in physics such as quantity and matter, motion, and the intension and remission of forms, were more usually discussed in the course of lecturing in arts, though they might also come up for discussion in commentaries on the Sentences.[12]

To a large extent Oxford masters were concerned with specific problems raised in Aristotle's *Physics*, including those of the continuum and the nature of the infinite which were also attracting the attention of their Paris contemporaries.[13] This interplay of logic and physics owed much to the nominalism of

[10] The chronology of Ockham's writings has long been the subject of controversy, and a definitive solution is particularly difficult because many of his works were composed simultaneously over a number of years. It is generally accepted that he was lecturing on the Sentences in Oxford by 1317, *BRUO* II, 1384–7, and despite considerable advances in the study of individual works and their internal relationship since Emden wrote, the general chronological picture has changed little. See Léon Baudry, *Guillaume d'Occam: sa vie, ses œuvres, ses idées sociales et politiques* (Paris, 1949), supplemented by Leff (as n. 3) and Arthur S. McGrade, *The Political Thought of William of Ockham* (Cambridge, 1974).

[11] Burley's Averroism has been much disputed. See Anneliese Maier, 'Ein unbeachteter "Averroist" des 14. Jahrhundert: Walter Burley', *Ausgehendes Mittelalter*, i. 101–21, and opposing her, M. Jean Kitchel, 'Walter Burley's Doctrine of the Soul: another view', *MS* 39 (1977), 387–401.

[12] Maier, *Die Vorläufer Galileis im 14. Jahrhundert. Studien zur Naturphilosophie* (Rome, 1966²); idem, 'Diskussionen über das aktuell Unendliche in der ersten Hälfte des 14. Jahrhunderts', *Ausgehendes Mittelalter*, i. 41–85; idem, 'Das Problem der Evidenz in der Philosophie des 14. Jahrhunderts', ibid., ii. 367–418.

[13] Maier, 'Diskussionen über das aktuell Unendliche', 62 ff., drew attention to these parallel developments.

Ockham, but was really developed into a valuable scientific contribution by Thomas Bradwardine and the other Mertonians who tried to study physical problems in terms of mathematical principles. In doing so, they developed a method of arguing which has been termed 'letter-calculus' and which became widely used also in theology, especially in commentaries on the Sentences.[14] Although few commentaries on Aristotle's *Physics* have survived from early fourteenth-century Oxford, apart from the major contributions of Ockham and Burley, such commentaries must have been common currency among the regent masters in arts. Cases in point were FitzRalph and his slightly younger contemporary, Richard Kilwington, who as regent master at Oriel took issue with him on the questions of infinity and eternity, but neither of their commentaries or lectures on the topic survive.

Having established that FitzRalph was at least for a time under the influence of 'Aristotelica dogmata', one must consider the problem: what or who were the sources of his understanding of Aristotle? Who were his teachers and guides? The most influential commentator on Aristotle in Oxford during the early fourteenth century was unquestionably Walter Burley, who has been the subject of a substantial amount of recent research.[15] Born *c.*1274–5, he was already a master of arts and fellow of Merton by 1301.[16] As that college had been founded with the intention (apart from the education of the founder's relatives) of enabling bachelors of arts to become masters, after which they might remain beyond their statutory three years as regent masters in arts or proceed to study theology,[17] it is possible

[14] Originally suggested by Aristotle in his *Physics,* its application by the Mertonian 'Calculators', including Bradwardine, is discussed in Weisheipl, *Early Fourteenth-Century Physics,* pp. 174–274. See also John E. Murdoch, 'Mathesis in Philosophiam Scholasticam Introducta: The rise and development of the application of mathematics in fourteenth-century philosophy and theology', *Arts libéraux et philosophie au moyen âge* (Paris, 1969), 215–54.

[15] *BRUO* I, 312–14; Stephen F. Brown, 'Walter Burleigh's Treatise "De suppositionibus" and its influence on William of Ockham', *FS* 32 (1972), 15–64; idem, 'Walter Burley's "Quaestiones in librum Perihermeneias" ', *FS* 34 (1974), 200–95; Agustin Una Juárez, 'Aristóteles y Averroes en el siglo XIV. Las Autoridades "Mayores" para Walter Burley', *Antonianum,* 52 (1977), 326–58, 680–94; M. Jean Kitchel, 'The "De Potentiis Animae" of Walter Burley', *MS* 33 (1971), 85–113; M. L. Roure, 'Insolubilia Walteri Burlei', *AHDLMA* 37 (1970), 262–84; Herman Shapiro, 'A Note on Walter Burley's Exaggerated Realism', *FS* 20 (1960), 205–14; idem, 'More on the "Exaggeration" of Burley's Realism', *Manuscripta,* 6 (1962), 94–8.

[16] *BRUO* I, 312.

[17] *Rashdall's Universities,* iii. 192. Merton graduates in arts were obliged to spend

that he had already begun his theological studies while at the same time continuing to teach in the arts faculty. He moved to Paris *c.*1310 and is recorded as still at the Sorbonne, now regent master in theology in 1324.[18] While he continued to write political and philosophical commentaries almost until the end of his life, his subsequent career was primarily that of a 'court cleric'. He was special envoy on a number of occasions from Edward III to the French court and to Avignon, chaplain to Edward's queen, Philippa of Hainault, and subsequently appointed tutor to their son, the Black Prince, as soon as young Edward was of an age to 'learne his booke'.[19] At court, in Avignon, and above all in the circle of intellectuals who gathered at the London residence of Bishop Richard de Bury, and which included secular and mendicant scholars alike[20] – the Dominican Robert Holcot, several Mertonians including Walter Burley and Thomas Bradwardine, Richard Kilwington the future dean of St. Paul's and FitzRalph's principal ally in the anti-mendicant campaign, as well as civil servants and lawyers – FitzRalph would have had ample opportunity to meet Burley in person. But here we are more concerned with the influence exercised at Oxford by Burley's Aristotelian commentaries while their author was absent in Paris. Burley began to comment on Aristotle no later than 1301 and continued at least until 1337, if not later. By the then prevailing standards he taught for a remarkably long time in the arts faculty and was in the habit of revising at frequent intervals his various commentaries, for example he commented on the *Perihermeneias* four times. Burley dealt with both the *libri naturales* and Aristotle's logical treatises, and the quality of his work earned him the title 'doctor planus et perspicuus'. Even though his long absence in Paris *c.*1310–24 makes it improbable that FitzRalph heard him lecture in person while he was a student in the arts faculty, the influence of Burley's commentaries on the teaching of that faculty in these years should not be underestimated. Oxford scholars were kept well informed about new developments in Paris and elsewhere on the Conti-

three years as regents in that faculty instead of two, as required in the rest of the university, *Merton College Injunctions of Archbishop Kilwardby 1276*, ed. H. W. Garrod (Oxford, 1929), p. 15.

18 Pierre Feret, *La Faculté de théologie de Paris*, iii (Paris, 1896), p. 243.

19 Rymer's *Foedera*, iv. 269, 422; Raphael Holinshed, *Chronicles*, iii (London, 1586), 414, 464.

20 Described by William de Chambre, *Continuatio Historie Dunelmensis*, printed in Henry Wharton, *Anglia Sacra*, i (London, 1691), 766.

nent, largely through the mobility of the friars, and the speed with which Burley began to take issue with Ockham's new logic indicates that the reverse was also true.[21]

Hence it may be suggested that in Burley we have one of the principal sources for that Aristotelianism tinged with Averroism which is reflected in FitzRalph's *Commentary on the Sentences* and which, above all in relation to problems concerning the will and intellect, was criticized by some of FitzRalph's contemporaries in Oxford and Paris.[22] Recent work on the chronology of the Ockham–Burley debate is significant for any consideration of the thorny problem of FitzRalph's attitude to the new logic and its implications for theology. The first part of Burley's *De puritate artis logicae tractatus longior* was devoted to an explicit attack on Ockham's teaching concerning simple supposition and the reality of universals, and has been dated after the completion of Ockham's own *Summa logicae* in mid-1324.[23] Recent research has tended to confirm the impression that Ockham had left Oxford before the end of 1320 and that the bulk of his non-political writings were composed in the London Greyfriars between his departure from Oxford and his delation to Avignon on heresy charges in 1324. Among these writings was the revised version of his *lectura* on the Sentences, which aroused the opposition of Burley, and the latter's *Tractatus de Universalibus Realibus* contained the first indications of that opposition which would govern the subsequent debate. Before this work Burley had a long list of Aristotelian commentaries and treatises to his credit, all of which were found by Weisheipl to be free from any reaction to Ockham's new logic, and for which we thus have a *terminus ad quem* of about 1323.[24] Although Burley was working in Paris when he published his first reactions to the new teaching, he adopted the practice which became common among its Oxford critics: he rejected Ockham's teaching, but without mentioning him by name. Perhaps due to

[21] That Ockham's views were already being attacked in Paris *c.*1319–20 has been demonstrated by Maier, 'Zu einigen Problemen der Ockhamforschung', *Ausgehendes Mittelalter,* i. 175–208.

[22] Above all by Adam Wodeham in Oxford and Gregory of Rimini in Paris, respectively a Franciscan and an Augustinian friar, but there is no indication at this stage of anti-mendicant antagonism.

[23] The *terminus ad quem* for Ockham's *Summa Logicae* is now held to be prior to his departure for Avignon in mid-1324; see modern edition by Philotheus Boehner (St. Bonaventure, N.Y., 1957–62). Leff, *William of Ockham,* p. xvii, follows the older view that Ockham wrote it in Avignon, i.e. between 1324 and 1328.

[24] *BRUO* I, 312–13.

a spirit of collegiality, even though the colleague was no longer physically among them, the tendency was to take issue with the doctrines but not to conduct polemic against the man. FitzRalph, as we shall see, followed this practice, but the former chancellor of the University, John Lutterell, who denounced Ockham in Avignon as a propagator of heresy, did not.[25] However, these developments belong to the period after FitzRalph had completed his arts courses and was already a student of theology, though possibly still regent in arts. Before the reaction to Ockham gathered momentum we can presume a substantial body of 'conservative' Aristotelian commentaries were circulating in Oxford, reflecting the attitudes which were basic to most of the teaching in the arts faculty and which would have been readily absorbed by all but the most original minds, a situation which might help to explain FitzRalph's oft-cited indifference to the exciting new teaching when he himself began to lecture on the Sentences in 1328.[26]

Nevertheless, the problem of FitzRalph's attitude to Ockham remains a complex one. When he came to deal with topics in his *Commentary on the Sentences,* where he had at least to take cognizance of Ockham's views, his own opinions were expressed only in the most cautious and guarded of terms. He was clearly aware of Ockham's teaching and of those implications for theology which the events of 1324–8 had brought to the forefront of the debate, hence his lack of involvement in these controversies cannot be explained by lack of opportunity. In purely intellectual terms, and considering only the interplay of influences and opportunities, a satisfactory explanation for FitzRalph's attitude is difficult to find, and one is tempted to think also in terms of the young scholar's own personality, his ambitions, his profound respect for authority, and desire to remain on the side of orthodoxy. Ockham first emerged in Oxford records *c.*1317 when he was admitted a bachelor in the faculty of theology, apparently having begun his theological studies around 1307–8 and previously studied philosophy at a Franciscan *studium*, whether in London, Oxford, or elsewhere

[25] For Lutterell, *BRUO* II, 1181–2, and Fritz Hoffmann, *Die Schriften des Oxforder Kanzlers Iohannes Lutterell* (Leipzig, 1959). For his opposition to Ockham see Josef Koch, 'Neue Aktenstücke zu dem gegen Wilhelm Ockham in Avignon geführten Prozess', *Kleine Schriften,* ii. 275–363.

[26] e.g. Leff, *FitzRalph Commentator,* pp. 4–18, argued for FitzRalph's complete indifference to contemporary theological debates.

is not clear.[27] He spent considerably longer than the statutory minimum period commenting on the Sentences, and even in the first version of his *lectura*, which have been tentatively dated 1317-19, they presented a challenge to older and more conservative theologians. The revised version of his lecture manuscript, dated around 1321-3, showed a bolder development of his new logic and a rejection of the modes of thought of his predecessors.[28] By now the main features were clear which were to mark him out as the chief spokesman of the 'moderni' or 'nominalist' school that was soon to make such a decisive impact on the *studia* in France and the German lands as well as in England. But not even the brilliance and influence of the Franciscan school at Oxford in the early fourteenth century, where Scotist tradition of opposition to strict Thomism and of commenting on both Aristotle and St. Augustine was being continued by Ockham's slightly older contemporary and confrère at Oxford, Robert Cowton,[29] could protect Ockham from the watchdogs of orthodoxy once the implications of his logic and of his theory of knowledge in the sphere of theology became apparent. In view of the fact that there were usually several 'formed bachelors' at the Oxford Greyfriars awaiting their turn for the single chair allotted to the Franciscans, it is tempting to consider the possibility that Ockham was regarded by his superiors as a slight embarrassment and made to wait his turn in the years after 1320. Hence his inception was delayed and his ultimate failure to incept may be linked with the summons to Avignon in 1324 to answer charges arising out of his teaching.[30]

By 1324 John Lutterell was active at the curia in his attempts to secure the condemnation of Ockham's entire teaching as 'doctrina pestifera'. Lutterell's career has certain parallels with that of FitzRalph, and there is consequently some justification for looking at the issues here more closely. Lutterell had been elected chancellor in October 1317 in place of Henry Harclay,

[27] *BRUO* II, 1384-5.

[28] See combined evidence of Auguste Pelzer, 'Les 51 articles de Guillaume Occam censurés en Avignon, en 1326', *RHE* 18 (1922), 240-70, and Koch (as n. 25), for the revised version of the Sentences as the subject of Lutterell's denunciation of Ockham for heresy.

[29] *BRUO* I, 507; Little, *Grey Friars at Oxford*, p. 222. See also Michael Schmaus, 'Zur Diskussion über das Problem der Univozität im Umkreis des Johannes Duns Scotus', *SB München, phil. hist. Klasse*, 4 (Munich, 1957); Barnabus Heschich, *De immaculata conceptione beatae M. V. secundum Thomas de Sutton OP et Robertum de Cowton OFM* (Rome, 1958).

[30] Baudry, pp. 80-5.

who had died at Avignon on 25 July 1317 while representing the university in the perennial dispute with the Dominicans.[31] Lutterell, who seems to have had a capacity for incurring hostility from many quarters, notably among the monks of Durham then studying in Oxford,[32] took up the university's case. Attempts were made to terminate his chancellorship and Edward II, who had always been a generous patron of the friars, at first refused permission for Lutterell to leave the kingdom and pursue the matter at the papal court on the grounds that 'if disputes be divulged in parts beyond the seas, to wit in universities and other public places, scandals and other dangers may arise, not only to the said master John and the masters and scholars, but also to the realm and its inhabitants.'[33] Not until the summer of 1323 did the king, after due inquiry into the causes of the dispute, sanction his departure for the curia, probably because Lutterell had presented himself personally before the king and explained the matters at issue. He was so successful in the statement of his case that the king ordered letters of recommendation for him to be so formulated 'that the pope may perceive the king's affection for his clerk and may show him grace and favour'.[34] Armed with royal protection for two years,[35]. Lutterell set out for Avignon in August 1323. Neither royal nor university sources specify the precise nature of the dispute between him and the masters and scholars of the university, and it is tempting to see in it evidence that Lutterell had become alarmed at the heretical character of Ockham's teaching. Beginning with Tanner,[36] historians have argued that Lutterell resigned his position as chancellor in order to carry his denunciation of Ockham to the papal curia. But apart from the difficulties created for this interpretation by modern research into the chronology and dating of the various redactions of Ockham's

[31] *BRUO* II, 874–5. See also Carol Balić, 'Henricus de Harclay et Ioannes Duns Scotus', *Mélanges offerts à Etienne Gilson* (Toronto–Paris, 1959), pp. 93–121.

[32] As chancellor he and his household took up residence in rooms belonging to Durham College (*Rashdall's Universities,* iii, 186–8), normally reserved for monk-students from Durham. The attempt of prior Gilbert de Elwyk (*BRUO* I, 637) to terminate this expensive tenancy was unsuccessful, and the prior had to capitulate on the grounds that Lutterell 'vero universitatis caput est, et oculus Archiepiscopi', *Collectanea,* III (OHS 1896), 74–6. This is the only indication that Lutterell owed his powerful position in the university to the protection of Archbishop Walter Reynolds of Canterbury.

[33] CCR 1318–23, 675.

[34] Cal. Chancery Warrants, 1244–1326, 533.

[35] CPR 1321–24, 329, 336.

[36] Thomas Tanner, *Bibliotheca Britannico-Hibernica* (London, 1748), p. 489.

work, there are other issues to be considered. Firstly there are allusions to attempts to terminate his office as chancellor, and a glance at the list of confirmations of chancellors published in *Snappe's Formulary* shows that he held the office for five years, much longer than any of his near-contemporaries.[37] In December 1322, two months after his tenure of office was finally terminated, the university passed a statute which was to govern the election of the chancellor for the next century and a half, and which limited tenure to two years.[38] Consequently it is more probable that the original dispute which Lutterell wished to take to the curia concerned his clinging to office despite opposition from within the university, and that subsequently the question of a possible condemnation of Ockham came to the fore.

Lutterell may have gone to Avignon with other plans in mind also: a copy of an undated letter addressed to him as chancellor by a friend then residing at the papal curia, who has been tentatively identified as Stephen de Kettlebergh,[39] urged him to abandon the academic life for a career in Avignon.[40] The chancellor was informed that the pope, who had previously reserved his choicest favours for lawyers, was now beginning to turn his attention to theologians, and especially to those highly qualified in the Scriptures: 'dominus noster summus pontifex magnam et specialem affeccionem quam pre hiis temporibus pretextu sapiencie civilis erga iuristas conceperat, modo de novo ad theologos, et maxime ad magistros in sacra pagina transtulit integre et perfecte'.[41] Although the term 'magistri in sacra pagina' was applied indiscriminately to doctors of theology regardless of any special talents in the field of biblical studies, Lutterell's informant may have recognized the trend in curial circles to emphasize the study of the Bible as against the more speculative theology of the scholastics.[42] In any case, he warned that a

[37] Salter, *Snappe's Formulary*, pp. 70–1, 325, respectively for his confirmation by the bishop of Lincoln and the list of early 14th-century chancellors.

[38] Idem, *The Mediaeval Archives of the University of Oxford*, i (OHS 1917), 105–6, 286; *Statuta Antiqua*, p. 118.

[39] *BRUO* II, 1043. Kettlebergh also enjoyed the favour of Grandisson of Exeter, and subsequently received the canonry and prebend of Crediton in Devon, which FitzRalph had vacated by 1343, *Grandisson's Register*, iii. 1349. He was in Avignon *c.*1319–20, and in 1343–44.

[40] Printed in *Snappe's Formulary*, pp. 303–4.

[41] Ibid., p. 303.

[42] On John XXII's promotion of biblical studies – 'he reproved, directed, encouraged and rewarded', see Smalley, *English Friars*, pp. 31–2. His letter of reproof to the masters of arts and theology in Paris, 8 May 1317, who engaged in frivolous speculation instead of serious study of the Bible and theology is printed in *Chart. Univ. Paris*, ii. 200–1.

master who was skilled in theology and made for himself a name need never leave the papal court. Dignities and prebends, bishoprics, and even archbishoprics were to be had for those who sought them: Lutterell should come in search of such rewards. His adviser continued with the assurance that if he should come and give two public disputations, carefully studied and prepared, on suitable theological subjects in the presence of curial theologians, he would do more for his reputation and advancement than in all his years in the schools.[43] Cynical advice perhaps, but the writer was practical and the available evidence shows that his remarks held more than a grain of truth. John XXII was a lawyer by talent and training, but he was becoming increasingly more interested in theology, and the careers of those who sat on papal theological commissions in the 1320s and 1330s were in some cases spectacular, in most, comfortable. Lutterell's participation in the proceedings against Ockham and subsequently in the debates about the beatific vision, in which he supported the – theologically dubious – views propounded by the pope, did not go unrewarded.[44]

Whatever the motives for his original decision to set out for Avignon, he was from 1324 onwards demonstrably engaged in building up a case against Ockham. He was given a copy of Ockham's lectures on the Sentences by John XXII and requested to examine it from the standpoint of strict orthodoxy. He picked out fifty-six propositions and denounced them as 'contra veram et sanam doctrinam', supporting his charges with a detailed exposition of the theological errors in the text as submitted to him. As Koch noted in his important article on Lutterell's contribution to the case, the purpose of the latter's list of errors and his treatise against them was to lay bare the roots of Ockham's philosophical thinking and to point out the dangers for theology which might result from it – and in the light of subsequent developments in later medieval thought Lutterell's warnings sound almost like prophecy.[45] The weight of evidence lies in favour of the view, held by both Pelzer and Koch, that Lutterell was the person originally responsible for bringing a formal accusation of heresy against Ockham and delating him to the curia, an action on the part of a former chancellor which must have caused embarrassment among supporters

[43] *Snappe's Formulary*, p. 304.
[44] For Lutterell's benefices see *BRUO* II, 1182.
[45] Koch, *Kleine Schriften*, ii. 297.

of speculative research in Oxford. During this period all the original work seems to have been done by the bachelors, particularly in their lectures on the Sentences and in their disputations among themselves. Relatively few masters were productive and original authors in their mature years, and such charges of heresy levelled against those who were developing their most exciting ideas within the relatively confined atmosphere of the schools can scarcely have been regarded as a stimulant to creative research.

The course of events which followed Ockham's summons to Avignon is well known and needs only brief comment. Clearly aware of the dangers facing him, Ockham produced what he claimed was the sole authentic text of the lectures on the Sentences as he had given them in Oxford. The commission, which had already examined the copies of these lectures hitherto available in Avignon, had condemned a series of propositions as erroneous, but had carefully refrained from stating that they were heretical. When they compared this new text and notes submitted by Ockham with the text already examined, they were unanimously of the opinion that the second text had been recently altered – erasures and additional marginalia altered the general character of the text wherever suspect opinions were being asserted or defended.[46] Thereupon the commission revised its earlier judgement and issued another report which was signed by all six commissioners, though the Dominican bishop of Meaux, Durandus de Saint-Pourçain, who was to play a prominent part in the beatific vision controversy on the anti-papal side, recorded his dissent on a minor question.[47] The presence of Durandus, a Dominican who had experienced considerable difficulty with his own superiors for failing to follow the 'orthodox Thomist' line within the order of Preachers, is an indication of the extent to which the papacy was careful to avoid the impression of a hostile board of censors. The period of the Avignonese papacy saw considerable developments in the concept of authoritative teaching and of the *magisterium* of the papacy, with, as a result, greater emphasis on theological commissions under general papal direction but with extensive discretionary powers.[48] Under the Avignonese popes these commissions were

[46] Pelzer, pp. 246 ff.

[47] See Kaeppeli, *Script. O.P.*, i. 339–50, with extensive bibliography.

[48] See remarks on the expansion of this magisterial dimension in Walter Ullmann, 'Boniface VIII and his Contemporary Scholarship' *JTS* n.s. 27 (1976), 87. While the future Benedict XII sat on the commission which examined Ockham, Pierre Roger (Clement VI) sat on that of Waleys, Smalley, *English Friars*, p. 78.

distinguished by the breadth of talent and variety of opinions represented, and not even John XXII, when his cherished theory of the beatific vision came under attack, was afraid to listen to a wide range of opinion, regardless of whether it supported him or not. In the case of Ockham the pope continued to seek expert opinion for several years after the commissioners had presented their report. It was not simply a question, as the traditional picture of John XXII's relations with the Franciscan order might suggest, of yet another 'nail in their coffin'. The fact that heresy proceedings initiated against Ockham were never brought to a conclusion, neither judgement nor sentence were passed,[49] probably illustrates – as FitzRalph would also discover to his own disadvantage – that the Franciscans never lacked friends in high places, and most especially at the papal curia.

After Ockham, Thomas Bradwardine was unquestionably the most influential mind in Oxford during the first half of the fourteenth century. An almost direct contemporary of FitzRalph and subsequently a member of the same circle around Richard de Bury, he was born *c.*1280 and was a fellow of Balliol 1321–3. In that year he was elected to a fellowship in Merton and by 1326 had completed the three-year regency in arts which was a statutory requirement of that college.[50] He followed the Oxford tradition established by Grosseteste, combining science and theology.[51] Originally a mathematician with a keen interest in logic, he is claimed to have 'led the way in the renewed application of mathematics to scientific problems'.[52] He appears to have undergone a 'conversion' from natural philosophy to theology and, like FitzRalph, he is chiefly remembered by historians of fourteenth-century thought for work completed outside the strictly scholastic environment, in Bradwardine's case *De causa Dei contra Pelagium et de virtute causarum ad suos Mertonenses*, completed by 1344.[53] Having commented on the

[49] The later stages of these proceedings, up to Ockham's flight, 26 May 1328, are obscure, but it is known that Cardinal Jacques Fournier presented his opinion in a document since lost, Koch, as no. 25, 297.

[50] *BRUO* I, 244–6.

[51] See *Robert Grosseteste, Scholar and Bishop*, ed. Daniel A. Callus (Oxford, (1955), esp. the editor's 'Robert Grosseteste as Scholar', pp. 1–69; A. C. Crombie, 'Grosseteste's Position in the History of Science', pp. 98–120.

[52] *BRUO* I, 245–6.

[53] Ed. Henry Saville (London, 1618), and studied in Gordon Leff, *Bradwardine and the Pelagians* (Cambridge, 1957). Bradwardine's thought is more comprehensively studied in Heiko A. Oberman, *Archbishop Thomas Bradwardine, a fourteenth-century Augustinian. A study of his theology in its historical context* (Utrecht, 1958²).

Sentences and fulfilled the other statutory obligations as bachelor of theology at Merton, he left Oxford as a 'formed bachelor' in 1335 to join the household of Bishop Richard de Bury, incepting as doctor at a later, but unknown date.[54] Although he vacated his fellowship in 1335, the year after FitzRalph's departure from Oxford, the closing words of *De causa Dei* indicate that he remained closely bound to that college which was then the most distinguished intellectual centre of the university. It has been argued that Bradwardine was preaching and teaching the doctrine of predestination which is so characteristic of *De causa Dei* for many years, both in Oxford and later in London, before completing his comprehensive and devastating assault on Pelagianism.[55] In a famous passage he complained that while a student he had heard nothing but Pelagian doctrine, a complaint which revealed his long-standing interest in problems of grace, free will, and God's foreknowledge even in the earliest stages of his academic career. As a student of philosophy he recalled that he had been led astray by Pelagian errors: 'ego autem stultùs a scientia Dei et vanus, quando philosophicis litteris intendebam, errore contrario seducebar, quandoque enim audivi theologos tractare materiam, et pars Pelagii michi verior videbatur'.[56] The preface to his completed work was written as chancellor of St. Paul's in London, a benefice to which he was collated on 19 September 1337 and which he surrendered on becoming archbishop of Canterbury shortly before his death as a victim of the plague on 26 August 1349,[57] but it is clear that the substance of *De causa Dei* had been worked out in the form of lectures while he was still among the Mertonians, and these were probably the friends who put pressure upon him to cast his lectures in final written form.[58]

Modern studies of Bradwardine's treatise have been for the most part inclined to emphasize that he was a 'determinist' who, in his insistence on the primacy of God's universal causality, denied the true freedom of human choice. It has been argued that *De causa Dei* rests on the fundamental assumption that

[54] *BRUO* I, 245. William de Chambre included him in Bury's circle, ed. cit., 766.

[55] Leff, *Bradwardine and the Pelagians*, pp. 265–6.

[56] Ed. cit., i. 308.

[57] *BRUO* I, 245; though elected upon the death of John de Stratford a year earlier, the papal provision did not take effect until 19 June 1349, and he was consecrated in Avignon a month later, *HBC*², 211.

[58] Reference to pressure by friends and colleagues to publish one's findings was common; see the similar claim made by Geoffrey Hardeby OESA concerning the publication of his *Liber de Vita Evangelica* against the friars' critics, Walsh, 'Hardeby', *AA* 33, 192–3.

man has no natural autonomy, that direct control of the world and its deeds lies with God, and that as such Bradwardine's work is an extreme statement of a theology based entirely on faith as opposed to the scepticism of many of his contemporaries. Consequently he was regarded as being – to a far greater degree than FitzRalph, and even more so than Gregory of Rimini – the staunch defender of authority against scepticism, the man who provided the answer of faith and dogma to those who upheld the power of human reason and the freedom of the will. Even when it is attempted to mitigate this 'determinist' view by placing Bradwardine's work firmly in the context of early fourteenth-century theological debate, no more satisfactory alternative answer presents itself to the problem of the identity of the 'Pelagians' with whom Bradwardine took issue, other than the followers of Ockham and members of the Mertonian circle such as Thomas Buckingham, who attempted to find a middle way between Pelagianism and a Stoicism which denied all power to the human will.[59] FitzRalph also discussed the issue in his *lectura* on the Sentences and attempted, although cautiously, to find a 'middle way'. He did not pursue the matter as far as Buckingham, his contemporary and possible friend – a fellow of Merton 1324-40 and chancellor of Exeter from 25 March 1346, who may well have been a further link between FitzRalph and that diocese when the archbishop-elect of Armagh sought consecration at the hands of Grandisson.[60]

Bradwardine's theological work on predestination reveals also a considerable preoccupation with the Latin classics, and it has been suggested that he – like Walter Burley, whose writings include the somewhat unlikely treatise *De vita et moribus philosophorum*, a collection of biographies of the leading sages of the ancient world, together with excerpts from their works – cultivated his 'classicizing' interests in Bury's household.[61] It is worth questioning whether, and to what extent, FitzRalph was receptive to similar influences. In any case these, like Ockham's new logic, were unfolding and developing before his eyes at Oxford during the years 1315-35.

For the origins of this 'classicizing' movement among biblical scholars we have to turn to the Dominican *studium* in Oxford.

[59] Leff, *Bradwardine and the Pelagians,* pp. 165-254. He identified the Pelagians attacked by Bradwardine as Ockham, Aureole, Holcot, Buckingham and Wodeham.

[60] For Buckingham see *BRUO* I, 298-99.

[61] Smalley, *English Friars,* pp. 73-4.

Here relations with the university had been stormier than in the case of the Franciscans, originally because of the opposition of older masters to the new forms of Aristotelian-Thomist teaching. Subsequently these problems crystallized into more formal, constitutional issues. FitzRalph must have arrived at Oxford as a young student while the Dominicans were still engaged in their struggle with the university. The issue was twofold: on the one hand the Dominicans were seeking recognition in Oxford for the privileges granted to them by custom in Paris, above all that of exemption for their students from the obligation of inception in arts and of regency in that faculty before being admitted to the study of theology, while on the other hand they wished the order of study in Oxford to conform to that of Paris. In Oxford, unlike Paris, a bachelor lectured on the Sentences before, not after he had spent two years lecturing on the Bible, a situation which had obvious implications for the theological formation of the candidates.[62] The compromise reached after papal and royal intervention was expressed in the *Compositio* of November 1313 and confirmed by royal letters patent on 7 April 1314,[63] seems to have brought an uneasy peace, though there are indications that the issues involved were still the subject of litigation at the papal curia as late as the chancellorship of John Lutterell (1317-22), and there is definite evidence that his predecessor Henry Harclay had sought out the new pope after the long vacancy from 1314 to 1316 with this, among other university problems, in mind.[64]

One can only speculate whether Dominican fears of provoking further ill-feeling in the university, together with the fate of Ockham (a scion of the much more favoured Franciscan *studium* at Oxford), might explain the undoubted fact that the two most prominent Dominican theologians of the next generation, Nicholas Trevet and Robert Holcot, contemporaries of Bradwardine and FitzRalph, began to break away from the militant Thomism of their predecesssors and sought to establish contact with a more literary and humanist tradition, which they expressed, not in terms of speculative theology, but of biblical commentary with a clear pastoral purpose.[65] Beryl Smalley has demonstrated that, after a decline in the quality of biblical

[62] *Statuta Antiqua,* p. 50, ll. 16-19.

[63] *Collectanea,* II (OHS 1890), 237, 241-4, 251-2. For the course of the struggle see Bede Jarrett, *The English Dominicans* (London, 1921), pp. 76-81.

[64] *BRUO* II, 875.

[65] Smalley, *English Friars,* pp. 29 ff.

commentary from *c.*1280 until the second decade of the fourteenth century, there was a spectacular upsurge again *c.*1320–50, and biblical studies flourished in response both to papal pressure, encouragement and reward from above, and prodding from below.[66] This prodding from below was also indirectly a result of papal educational policy. A new type of student was reading theology: alongside the friar-students and secular clerks there were now older men, rectors of parishes who had obtained licences permitting them to absent themselves from their churches for a number of years in order to pursue a recognized course in theology. But they rarely obtained permission to absent themselves for long enough to graduate through the arts to a degree in theology, and consequently they could only choose the courses most helpful for their subsequent duties in the confessional and pulpit. In addition monk-students were now being sent by their superiors with the expressed aim of teaching them to preach, and for both of these groups of students the most basic element in their course would have been the lectures on Scripture.

The vast bulk of this scriptural teaching in the faculty of theology appears to have been done by the friars, whose work in this area often extended far beyond the statutory requirements of the *bachalarius biblicus.* They produced the great biblical commentaries of the period, while the secular doctors scarcely competed in this field and left remarkably little exegetical writing until the days of Wyclif, although the renewed emphasis among systematic theologians on the Scriptures as the source of all truth and the foundation of theology may be linked with the teaching of the friars.[67] The virtual monopoly of biblical scholarship in mendicant hands had the twofold result of stimulating the friars to even greater efforts in their own lecturing on the Bible and further of ensuring that the pastoral care of lay communities not directly served by friars might be served by those trained in preaching and pastoral theology by members of the mendicant orders.[68] The situation can only have added to the jealousy and resentment of the friars which was already

[66] Ibid., p. 31.

[67] See Gustav A. Benrath, *Wyclifs Bibelkommentar* (Berlin, 1966).

[68] William A. Pantin, *The English Church in the Fourteenth Century* (Cambridge, 1955), p. 119 drew attention to the pastoral influence of mendicant teachers in their *studia particularia*, such as London, Norwich, York, or Northampton, which were attended by members of the secular clergy, while the documentary evidence for the planned university in Dublin suggests that a similar situation operated there.

rampant among monks and seculars and which FitzRalph would further feed in the course of his own campaign against the virtual pastoral monopoly enjoyed by the mendicants. As a student of theology in the 1320s FitzRalph must have acquired direct experience of the situation. While he was hearing lectures on the Bible in the early stages of his theological studies *c.* 1322–5, both Nicholas Trevet and Thomas Waleys may still have been at the Oxford Blackfriars,[69] and when he came to lecture on a book of the Bible himself as part of the requirements for the *magisterium*, his direct contemporaries were Robert Holcot, who incepted as doctor of theology in or soon after 1332, and John Ridevall, the only Oxford Franciscan among the classicizing friars before John Lathbury in the 1350s, who incepted in 1331.[70] Trevet, 'a true polymath',[71] was regent in Oxford from 1303 to 1307, when he participated in various theological disputations and published a series of *quodlibeta.* Following a period of study in Paris from 1307 to 1314, he returned for another term of regency in Oxford and was to be found as *lector* at the London Blackfriars in September 1324. By 1307 his work as a biblical commentator was sufficiently recognized that the Dominican chapter-general formally approved his commentaries on Genesis and Exodus and issued a mandate to the entire order that he was to be assisted in the completion of a commentary on the whole Pentateuch. This however seems never to have been written, although he published a commentary on the entire Psalter between 1317 and 1320.[72] He commented also on texts of late antiquity, including Augustine's *De civitate Dei*, Boethius' *De consolatione Philosophiae*, pseudo-Boethius' *De disciplina scholarium* and on classical and pseudo-classical texts without making any sharp distinction between Christian and pagan texts. The commissions which he received from John XXII and from the dean of the Sacred College, the Dominican cardinal Niccolò da Prato (*c.* 1315–18)[73] for commentaries on the

[69] For Trevet see *BRUO* III, 1902–3, and Waleys, ibid., 1961–2.

[70] For Holcot, *BRUO* II, 946–7; Ridevall, ibid., III, 1576; Lathbury, ibid., II, 1104–5.

[71] 'being theologian, biblicist, hebraist, historian and classicist', Smalley, *English Friars*, p. 58. Also Ruth J. Dean, 'Nicholas Trevet, Historian', *Medieval Learning and Literature,* ed. J. J. G. Alexander and M. T. Gibson (Oxford, 1976), pp. 328–52.

[72] Smalley, *The Study of the Bible in the Middle Ages* (Oxford, 1952²), pp. 346–55.

[73] Ruth J. Dean, 'The earliest known Commentary on Livy', *Mediaevalia et Humanistica*, 3 (1945), 86–98; idem, 'Cultural Relations in the middle ages: Nicholas Trevet and Nicholas of Prato', *Studies in Philology*, 45 (1948), 541–64.

younger Seneca's Tragedies and on Livy's *Ab Urbe condita* demonstrate that there was now a market for guides to the classics for the uninitiated, and that biblical commenting was regarded as a useful training for this kind of work also. Even the *Declamationes* of the elder Seneca, on which Trevet had commented before 1315, could be put to practical uses by a busy preacher – they provided exciting material for *exempla* with which to adorn a sermon, illustrate a scriptural point, and help to retain the interest of the audience.[74]

Clearly with some misgivings Beryl Smalley relegated Trevet to the 'forerunners' of her classicizing group of English friar-doctors because his successors surpassed him as commentators on *De civitate Dei*, and above all because the classicizing biblical commentary, the most characteristic production of the group, was their invention not his.[75] Thomas Waleys, whose subsequent career was to involve unpleasant notoriety and a sojourn in papal and inquisitorial prisons on charges of heresy while FitzRalph was in Avignon – even if they did not meet, Waleys must have been a household name for FitzRalph during the beatific vision controversy – must be placed, in the light of the revised chronology of his academic career, as regent master in Oxford during the early 1320s before his departure to lecture at the Dominican *studium* in Bologna. He left a set of *Moralitates* on a number of books of the Old Testament, from Exodus to Ruth inclusive, in the form of lecture notes, and it has been argued convincingly that a set of lecture notes covering so many books of the Bible could hardly have been compressed into one tenure of a university chair, hence it can be established that he had begun his cycle of lectures at Oxford and then continued it at Bologna. This conclusion would make it probable that FitzRalph heard him give some of these lectures during his Oxford regency, though in their less sophisticated, pre-Italian form, before he had developed a taste for ancient history and had acquired access to a wider range of the classics as source material for his *exempla*.[76] Next in chronological order came the Franciscan John Ridevall, who incepted in the same year as FitzRalph (1331) and whose *lectura in Apocalypsim*, given presumably during his regency at Greyfriars from 1331 to 1332, was founded

[74] Smalley, *English Friars*, p. 64. [75] Ibid., p. 65.

[76] He cannot have been regent in Oxford before *c.*1321 and, having resigned his chair to make way for younger confrères, was assigned to the Dominican *studium* at Bologna in or before 1326, Smalley, *English Friars*, pp. 75–6, 79–80.

on the work of Trevet and Waleys. Ridevall introduced a new dimension into this type of biblical commentary, the element of the fantastic which further stimulated Robert Holcot when he came to comment on the Scriptures during his own regency from 1332 to 1334.[77] Although Holcot's commentary on the Sentences was frequently copied and even printed in the early sixteenth century, his reputation throughout Europe rested less on his nominalism or 'Ockhamism' and much more on his biblical commentaries – on Ecclesiastes, the Twelve Prophets, and above all, on Wisdom, which made its author famous almost overnight and was largely responsible for the popular circulation of his other writings.[78] As well as bringing together 'the traditional teaching of Scripture and a type of pre-humanist study deriving from Richard of Bury and his circle',[79] he developed a special technique of illustrating his moral position by means of 'pictures' of his own devising and *exempla* drawn from classical sources.[80]

These circumstances should be borne in mind when we come to consider the scriptural approach of FitzRalph in his later theological work, the *Summa de Questionibus Armenorum*, and above all his approach to pastoral literature and use of the Bible in his sermons. He too during his preaching career had to vary the diet for different types of audiences, but the kind of public he faced as dean of Lichfield, in London, and in Anglo-Irish trading towns such as Drogheda and Dundalk, cannot have differed much from the public described by Beryl Smalley as forming the lay background to the development of scholarship in later medieval England. However, as will emerge from this study, FitzRalph did not share the flights of fancy which coloured the work of some of the friar-commentators, but adhered more strictly to the literal sense of the text. He did occasionally use stories as illustration, but he did not have their classical background. His sermons and dialogues displayed an impressive knowledge of the Bible and suggest a sound exegetical training,[81] and this at least he may have gained from the friars who were

[77] Ibid., pp. 109–32.

[78] Maier, 'Diskussionen über das aktuell Unendliche', *Ausgehendes Mittelalter*, i. 81–2, argued that Holcot's commentary on the Sentences was overestimated.

[79] Smalley, *English Friars*, p. 141. The following remarks are drawn from her study of Holcot's manner of commenting, pp. 137 ff.

[80] Ibid., pp. 9–27.

[81] His *Questio Biblica*, known to Wodeham and his contemporaries, has not survived in any identifiable form, Courtenay, *Adam Wodeham*, pp. 78–81.

preaching and teaching in Oxford during his student years, with the further possible advantage of exposure to the foremost biblicist of the day, Nicholas of Lyra, who was at the height of his influence in Paris *c.*1330, when FitzRalph spent a brief period of study there. In his later work FitzRalph was to anticipate Wyclif on a number of points, although his emphasis on the central position of Scripture as the main source of authority never went as far as a doctrine of *sola scriptura.* On biblical problems, as in the *Commentary on the Sentences*, he was prepared to settle for a middle way, showing due respect for authority and convention.

iii. Commentator on the Sentences

The only surviving work which testifies to FitzRalph's intellectual development during his years as a student and teacher of philosophy and theology at Oxford, apart from a group of *determinationes* which must be dated to his period as regent master in the faculty of theology 1331–2, is his *lectura* or *Commentary on the Sentences of Peter Lombard*, and the aural exposition of these was a statutory requirement for all candidates for degrees in theology.[1] Unlike his later, unquestionably more original works which reflect his direct experiences and which by virtue of the circumstances of their composition are less abstract in character, this commentary shows signs of having originated as an academic exercise in which standard authorities are cited with respect by an aspiring candidate for the doctorate in theology. Of all his writings, apart from some occasional sermons which were copied individually or in small groups, the commentary had the most limited manuscript circulation of all FitzRalph's works, and the text survives in an unsatisfactory state which may have been occasioned by a partial revision undertaken while he was acting as *magister regens* and when several bachelors disputing under his supervision – notably the Franciscan Adam Wodeham – challenged some of his views. Certain sections of the work attracted the attention of the late Anneliese Maier, who employed FitzRalph's views on creation, infinity, and eternity to illustrate her studies on the diversity of scholastic thinking on problems of natural philosophy, especially in the first half of the fourteenth century.[2] Subsequently J. A. Robson

[1] *Statuta Antiqua,* p. 50; *Rashdall's Universities*, iii. 159.

[2] Maier, *Die Vorläufer Galileis, ad indicem;* idem, 'Diskussionen über das aktuell Unendliche', esp. 75–85.

submitted it to a brief, but perceptive analysis in the course of his study of Wyclif's early philosophy and of the influences at work on the latter while he was a student and teacher in the arts faculty at Oxford.[3] The entire text was studied in greater detail by Gordon Leff,[4] and most recently William J. Courtenay threw fresh light on the text in the course of his important biographical and codicological study of FitzRalph's slightly younger contemporary, Adam Wodeham.[5] However, given the complex nature of the manuscript problems posed by the text and the fact that the planned edition is still only in the early stages of preparation,[6] definitive judgements about the text itself are not possible. Leff's study, which grew out of his work on the conservative tradition in the schools, the conflicts between 'antiqui' and 'moderni', and especially out of his books on Thomas Bradwardine and Gregory of Rimini,[7] is very much in the nature of a commentary on FitzRalph's commentary and displays its author's philosophical rather than historical leanings. Hence it devotes little attention to the historical context, which is crucial to the present inquiry. Courtenay, on the other hand, is primarily concerned to employ information which can be gleaned from FitzRalph's *curriculum vitae* and from his *lectura* in order to establish Wodeham's own chronology, but – as will be argued below – mistaken dating of FitzRalph's academic career on his part has distorted his entire argument.[8]

FitzRalph's commentary attracted interest among his immediate contemporaries and successors in Oxford and Paris and, especially in Oxford, it was received with some enthusiasm and minutely discussed by mendicant and secular scholars working out their own commentaries on the Sentences.[9] However the manuscript tradition, which provides further evidence of

[3] John A. Robson, *Wyclif and the Oxford Schools* (Cambridge, 1966²), pp. 70-96.

[4] Leff, *FitzRalph Commentator.* [5] Courtenay, *Adam Wodeham.*

[6] By Prof. James McEvoy, Department of Scholastic Philosophy, The Queen's University, Belfast.

[7] *Bradwardine and the Pelagians* (Cambridge, 1957); *Gregory of Rimini* (Manchester, 1961); idem, 'The Changing Patterns of Thought in the earlier fourteenth century', *Bull. J. Rylands Library*, 43 (1961), 354–72.

[8] On the assumption that FitzRalph was already doctor of theology when Grandisson wrote to him, 24 May 1331, *Grandisson's Register*, ii. 616, Courtenay placed his reading of the Sentences in the academic year 1326-7, *Adam Wodeham*, pp. 75-6. For a more detailed critique of this dating see Walsh, 'The later medieval Schoolman in Theory and Practice', *Innsbrucker Historische Studien*, 2 (1979), 171-6.

[9] Apart from Wodeham, it was vigorously debated by Robert Holcot, the Mertonian Nigel of Wavere, and the Franciscan bachelor Reppes. For the identification of the latter see Courtenay, pp. 84–5.

Franciscan interest, is weaker in England than in either France or Italy. There are four main surviving manuscripts, two each of French and Italian provenance,[10] in addition to three less complete versions, two of which are to be found in English collections and are of English provenance,[11] and four further fragments of Continental origin.[12] As will emerge from this study, the *lectura* was used and quoted in England primarily in those circles which had direct contact with Oxford while FitzRalph was actually lecturing there, whereas Paris was the centre of a slightly later Continental dissemination, and knowledge of it had reached the Sorbonne no later than the early 1340s.[13] Hence the commentary was in circulation at a relatively early stage in FitzRalph's ecclesiastical career. All of the most important manuscripts date from the fourteenth century and all of these, except one dated 1389,[14] refer to him as 'Magister Ricardus (H)ybernicus', or even 'Phyraph', if they identify the author at all. By contrast his subsequent writings, the sermons, the *Summa de Questionibus Armenorum, De Pauperie Salvatoris*, and the anti-mendicant polemical literature, circulated exclusively under the title of his archiepiscopal see, 'Armachanus'. Consequently such interest as his *Commentary on the Sentences* generated, which in any case is most clearly identified during the two decades after its composition, did not derive from his subsequent fame or notoriety

[10] Respectively Paris, Bibl. nat., Lat. 15853 (= P); Florence, Bibl. naz., A. VI. 611, and A. III. 508; BAV, Vat. Lat. 11517.

[11] MS Worcester Cathedral Q 71, and Oxford, Oriel College MS 15, are of English provenance, and Troyes, Bibl. mun. MS 505 is French. For a recent note on the contents of the latter see William J. Courtenay, 'The Sentences-Commentary of Stukle: a new source for Oxford theology in the fourteenth century', *Traditio*, 34 (1978), 435–8.

[12] BAV, Ottobon. Lat. 179 and 869, and Pisa, Seminario arcivescovile MS 159 contain individual *questiones*; CVP 5076 contains part of a *questio* on the clear vision of God, and it is doubtful if this was part of the *Commentary on the Sentences.* It may have been occasioned by the debates in the schools when John XXII's unorthodox views became known *c.*1332–3. These fragments, with the exception of CVP 5076, which he did not consult and whose importance he denied, and of the Pisa fragment, of which he was not aware, are discussed in Leff, *FitzRalph Commentator*, pp. 176–93. A further series of *questiones* are attributed to FitzRalph in Cambridge, MS Peterhouse 223, fols. 71^r–178^r. These are not part of his *lectura*, nor of any other identifiable work by him, and his authorship is uncertain.

[13] By 1342 both Wodeham and FitzRalph were known to Gregory of Rimini in Paris, see William J. Courtenay, 'Ockhamism among the Augustinians: the case of Adam Wodeham', *Scientia Augustiniana. Festschrift Adolar Zumkeller* (Würzburg, 1975), 269; Leff, *Gregory of Rimini*, pp. 3–4. See also *BRUO* III, xxviii, for the creation, by Luke Wadding and others, of a figmentary Franciscan theologian, 'Adam Hibernicus', through the conflation of marginalia in Gregory's commentary referring to Adam (Wodeham) and Hibernicus (FitzRalph).

[14] MS Oriel 15, fol. 1^{ra-va}, 'Sermo in opus armachani'.

in other areas.[15] None of the extant manuscripts appear to have been based on an *ordinatio* text, completely revised by its author and published as his definitive text, and it is possible that FitzRalph never completed the revision upon which he was working as regent master. The wide variations in the extant manuscripts, even in the selection of *questiones* which they contain, together with occasional confusion and conflicting arguments, are consistent with the possibility that FitzRalph's original *lectura* was revised in places in the light of his magisterial teaching and disputations, but that the scribe may have retained in the revision passages which were part of the original lectures. Despite these wide variations in the manuscripts, it does however seem clear that all of them contain some version of the corrected lectures, and that none of them represent a version of the original *lectura* which FitzRalph delivered as a *bachalarius sententiarius*. Further, it is clear that the surviving manuscripts do not all depend upon a common source, a factor which suggests that some at least must be based upon *reportationes* of opinions which he can only have expounded as regent master,[16] when such an exposition might more properly be described as *Questiones ordinarie* or *Questiones magistrales super Sententias*.[17]

The most important surviving text is that contained in Paris, Lat. 15853, formerly the property of Jean de Gorre whose presence as regent master in the faculty of arts and on two separate occasions rector of the University of Paris is documented.[18] Upon his death in 1360, the same year as FitzRalph, he bequeathed the manuscript to the Sorbonne,[19] and its numerous informative marginalia indicate that the text was closely studied, either by its original owner or by near-contemporaries.[20]

[15] A rare exception, clearly deriving from a text which circulated before FitzRalph's elevation to the see of Armagh, is CLM 16058, containing his sermon on the Immaculate Conception preached at Avignon, 8 December 1342, and entitled 'Sermo Richardi radulphi anglici doctoris in Theologia et decani Lithefeldensis', fol. 172r.

[16] For the debates under FitzRalph's regency see Courtenay, *Adam Wodeham*, pp. 53–112.

[17] For a discussion of these see Palémon Glorieux, 'Sentences', *DTC* xiv. 1877, and for their application in the Oxford context of the 1320s and 1330s, see Courtenay, *Adam Wodeham*, pp. 51–2.

[18] *Chart. Univ. Paris.*, ii. 444, 467, 489, 559, 635.

[19] 'Iste liber est pauperum magistrorum de sorbona ex legato magistri johannis gorre', P, fol. 191va. A 15th-century hand subsequently attributed the text to 'Thomas Hibernicus', P, fol. 192r. All quotations are from this MS unless otherwise stated.

[20] Leff, *FitzRalph Commentator*, p. 179, suggested that these marginalia might have been written by FitzRalph himself. But this hand is not the same as that of the marginalia in CVP 1430, for which there is also reason to suppose it might be Fitz-

Leff suggested that whereas this manuscript clearly cannot be considered an *ordinatio* text, it may have provided the original for the other texts of French and Italian provenance,[21] and this suggestion is supported by the fact that the transmission of the commentary from Paris to Italy is documented in the case of a manuscript which originated in the Franciscan *studium* at Paris and was subsequently taken to their convent at Santa Croce in Florence.[22] Against this view must be placed the consideration that the second Florentine manuscript, also from Santa Croce and apparently copied there, contains the magisterial *determinationes* which are not to be found in any other manuscript, and which the scribe was able to identify as being the work of 'ybernici sive phyraph'.[23]

The collective testimony of all the manuscripts and fragments of the commentary demonstrates that when FitzRalph lectured on the Sentences he followed the pattern which had become firmly established,[24] especially in Oxford where the candidate was required to spend a shorter period of preparation between the 'Admissio ad lecturam libri Sententiarum' and inception as doctor of theology than was the case in Paris.[25] No comprehensive treatment of the questions posed by the Lombard was attempted, and FitzRalph concentrated almost exclusively on those topics usually discussed in the first two books of the Sentences, after which the commentary tailed off to a virtually complete neglect of the sacraments in the course of Book IV, which is represented almost 'pro forma' by a single question on the Eucharist.[26] However, he did manage to extend the range of his discussion of a number of questions, above all in Book I, which takes up more than two-thirds of the entire commentary, to touch upon most of the major issues then occupying the attention of his contemporaries in the schools. In terms of the

Ralph's. At this stage of research into the MS tradition of his work his hand has not been identified, and the annotator of P may have been one of the bachelors at the Sorbonne who debated FitzRalph's views in the 1340s.

[21] Leff, *FitzRalph Commentator,* p. 181.

[22] Florence, Bibl. naz., MS A. VI. 611.

[23] Florence, Bibl. naz., MS A. III. 508, fols. 109vb–129vb. Furthermore Vat. Lat. 11517 does not derive from either of the Florentine MSS. The work of an Italian scribe, it may have been made in Avignon from a text in circulation there during FitzRalph's lifetime. See José Ruysschaert, *Codices Vaticani Latini 11414–11709,* (Città del Vaticano, 1959), pp. 209–10.

[24] Glorieux, 'Sentences', 1861–3, for the 14th-century regulations in Paris.

[25] See *Rashdall's Universities*, i. 476–8, iii. 159.

[26] P, fols. 187ra–191va.

formal construction of his commentary, FitzRalph also followed the pattern which by the 1320s had become traditional, and did not adopt the new 'conclusiones' system which was being developed during the years 1315-25, and which by *c.*1340 – especially in Paris – had become a major structural feature of commentaries on the Sentences, and of some philosophical commentaries in the arts faculty as well.[27] Such 'conclusiones' were intended to be tested rather than accepted uncritically, and they were not regarded as an unambiguous representation of their author's thought. They were more in the nature of propositions deriving from individual questions or groups of questions. The method was relatively rare in Oxford, though it was used occasionally by Ockham, by his confrère Walter Chatton, and by the Carmelite John Baconthorpe, but not by either FitzRalph or his 'Ockhamist' contemporaries among the friars, Adam Wodeham and Robert Holcot. Like them FitzRalph invariably reached his solutions by means of a statement of his own opinion, followed by replies to the principal arguments. Leff used this criterion of FitzRalph's normal procedure in order to argue that several questions in the Worcester and Oriel manuscripts, on future contingents and the 'ymago Dei' respectively, not to be found in all the main manuscripts and adopting the 'conclusiones' method of argument, must be regarded as spurious additions.[28]

Leff's second and 'decisive reason' for rejecting the authenticity of the question on future contingents is because the author referred to his already having treated of these problems, 'quas alias in lectura mea tractavi'.[29] However, the evidence provided by Adam Wodeham's *lectura* to the effect that FitzRalph as regent master revised his commentary, and the indications in the manuscripts that the scribe working on the corrected version may have included parts of the original versions as well as the corrected passages without eliminating the resulting discrepancies[30] might solve this particular difficulty. In such circumstances experimentation with a new, alternative method of

[27] William J. Courtenay, 'John of Mirecourt and Gregory of Rimini on whether God can undo the past', *Recherches de théologie ancienne et médiévale*, 39 (1972), 243-44.

[28] *FitzRalph Commentator*, pp. 180, 187.

[29] P, fol. 99ra. The *questio* concerned was 'Utrum creatura rationalis possit prescire in verbo aliquid futurum contingens', fol. 98va.

[30] For evidence that the surviving form of the commentary in all MSS is really the *Opus correctum* see Courtenay, *Adam Wodeham*, esp. pp. 77-8.

constructing arguments – already known in Oxford – is a possibility which in FitzRalph's case, and in the present state of the manuscript study of his text, cannot be rejected out of hand. This new method was used extensively by the Augustinians in Paris, Thomas of Strassburg and Gregory of Rimini, with whose thinking FitzRalph shared much in other, less formal and structural respects, although these were to criticize him on a number of crucial issues.[31] Nevertheless, if the division of fourteenth-century thinkers into those who adopted a logico-critical approach largely dependent on Ockham, and those whose historico-critical methods owed much to the school of Augustinian theologians, were to be applied to FitzRalph, he would have to be accorded a place among the latter.[32]

Towards the end of his life he was to reflect on his period in the schools, in which his thinking was governed – but not exclusively as we shall see – by 'Aristotelica dogmata', and which he professed subsequently to have rejected.[33] Nevertheless, his statement must be treated with some caution, as the attitude reflected in the autobiographical prayer is subtly different from that of an almost contemporary letter written from Avignon during the hearing of his case against the friars. Writing to Giovanni Marignola, bishop of Bisignano, while the latter was in Prague at the court of Charles IV and was apparently being summoned by his fellow-Franciscans to join in their defence against the 'Armachanus', FitzRalph boasted of his public disputations in Oxford some thirty years earlier when he denounced the systems of Ockham and Burley,[34] a statement which might be deemed to apply to the rival systems of logic developed by these two in interplay with one another during FitzRalph's student days. However, the central points which emerge from Leff's examination of FitzRalph's only surviving purely scholastic offering, in which we would expect to find some reflection of

[31] For Parisian use of this method see Courtenay, 'John of Mirecourt and Gregory of Rimini', 243.

[32] Courtenay, 'Ockhamism among the Augustinians', 267; idem, *Adam Wodeham*, pp. 40–2, who shows that although Wodeham tended towards the logical approach, he cited a wider range of patristic literature than FitzRalph.

[33] Hammerich, ed. cit., p. 20, ll. 74–5.

[34] Ed. in Gelasius Dobner, *Monumenta Hist. Boemia*, ii (Prague, 1768), 73–4. See also Girolamo Golubovich, *Bibliotheca bio-bibliografica della terra santa e dell'oriente francescano*, iv (Quaracchi, 1923), 269–70. For Giovanni see Anna-Dorothee v. den Brincken, 'Die universalhistorischen Vorstellungen des Johann von Marignola OFM. Der einzige mittelalterliche Weltchronist mit Fernostkenntnis', *Archiv für Kulturgeschichte*, 49 (1967), 297–339.

these conflicts, are their author's remoteness from contemporary issues, his safe, non-combative, conventional orthodoxy. FitzRalph 'was unable to grasp the full range of implications and to devise solutions to meet them', he evinced 'little . . . participation in, or perhaps more correctly permeation by, contemporary thinking'.[35] If this estimate of FitzRalph's performance in the scholastic arena is accepted, the archbishop's statement late in life must be dismissed as defensive boasting, wishful thinking coloured perhaps by the militant situation in which he found himself at the time of writing this letter, perhaps subconsciously projecting backwards in time the subsequent developments in his own thinking which in the meantime would certainly have led him to reject in public the systems propounded by both Ockham and Burley. Yet the statement appears to have a ring of truth, especially when considered in the light of the available knowledge of his independence of thought and action in other spheres, and of the response evoked by the commentary among younger bachelors lecturing and disputing at Oxford while he was still present and active as regent master and as chancellor.[36] Hence the remark need not be dismissed as groundless, and further examination of the controversy is justified in order to discover more about its author's attitude to and place in developments in Oxford thought of the 1320s and 1330s.

The first problem to be clarified concerns the dating of FitzRalph's commentary and the consequent chronology of his subsequent academic career. On the basis of the internal evidence of Adam Wodeham's lectures on the Sentences, Courtenay could establish both that the Franciscan had heard FitzRalph dispute while the latter was a bachelor and the former a student of theology, and further that FitzRalph was a regent master who took an active part in the debates between Wodeham and his 'socii' when these were lecturing on the Sentences.[37] Courtenay started from the irrefutable evidence that the Dominican William Crathorn began to lecture on the Sentences in the autumn of 1330,[38] an argument which is amply reinforced by Crathorn's reference at the beginning of his own *lectura* to an eclipse of the

[35] *FitzRalph Commentator*, p. 12.

[36] Courtenay, *Adam Wodeham*, pp. 75–112.

[37] FitzRalph seems to have been an exception to the increasing tendency among regent masters after the 13th century to confine themselves solely to a general direction of students and to participation in the public functions of the university, see Glorieux, *Répertoire des maîtres en théologie de Paris au XIIIe siècle*, i. 23.

[38] For Crathorn see *BRUO* I, 550–1, and Courtenay, *Adam Wodeham*, pp. 76, 96–9.

sun as having taken place 'isto anno', and which can be dated precisely to 16 July 1330.[39] From this *terminus a quo* Courtenay set out to establish the identity of the 'socii' with whom Wodeham debated, and in doing so he based his entire case for the dating on a questionable hypothesis which seemed to imply that FitzRalph was being referred to as doctor of theology as early as the autumn and winter of 1330–1.[40] In the light of this Courtenay established FitzRalph's inception as doctor at some point before the autumn of 1330, his lectures on the Sentences as having taken place in the academic year 1326–7, and further maintained that by the time he was elected chancellor in May 1332, he had already completed his term of regency.[41] Although it may have been possible to construct such a chronology on the basis of internal manuscript evidence alone, it is sharply at variance with other types of evidence. The entries in Grandisson's episcopal register are remarkably precise in the use of academic titles and they provide a clear guide to FitzRalph's progress towards the doctorate in theology. In Grandisson's first letter to FitzRalph, to be dated after the bishop's visit to Oxford on 17 May 1328 *en route* from Avignon to Exeter, as it was written from his diocese, he addressed FitzRalph as 'magister (i.e. artium) Ricardus', but not yet as 'bachalarius', whereas in a further letter of 4 October 1329 the title 'in Sacra Pagina egregius Bachalarius' indicates that the reading of the Sentences had been completed in the meantime.[42] Further, on 24 May 1331 the bishop wrote of FitzRalph as 'bachalarius sacre theologie', whereas the benefice which he received from John XXII in response to Grandisson's petition of 27 September 1331 was issued to him as 'in sacra pagina doctori',[43] which appears to indicate that inception lay in between, i.e. in the summer of 1331. Yet another factor in favour of this dating is to be found

[39] See Heinrich Schepers, 'Holcot contra dicta Crathorn', *Philosophisches Jahrbuch*, 77 (1970), 325–6, 340.

[40] The argument for FitzRalph's regency as having already begun in 1330 depends upon Crathorn's reference to him as 'iste doctor', and on the assumption that the written version of Crathorn's commentary was not even subjected to a perfunctory revision at the end of his aural exposition on the Sentences, Courtenay, *Adam Wodeham*, p. 76. This would be of minor significance but for the fact that FitzRalph's alleged regency in 1330–1 is made the foundation for a number of important conclusions, especially concerning the chronology of Wodeham's career and the identification and dating of the 'socii' who read the Sentences with him.

[41] Ibid., p. 76.

[42] *Grandisson's Register*, i. 173, 233. For Grandisson's presence in Oxford on 17 May 1328, ibid., i. 342.

[43] Ibid., ii. 616; *Reg. Vat.* 101, fol. 255^{r}.

in the register of the bishop of Lincoln who, in confirming FitzRalph in office as chancellor on 30 May 1332, described him not merely as professor of theology at Oxford, but 'inter vos actualiter nunc regenti'.[44] Hence the evidence clearly points to FitzRalph reading the Sentences in 1328, either in the academic year 1327–8 or (less likely in view of his absence in Paris during 1329–30 and his inception as doctor the following year) 1328–9,[45] but not as early as 1326–7, while the year of regency in which he disputed with the bachelors Adam Wodeham, William Skelton, Reppes, and the otherwise unknown Benedictine 'socius' must have been 1331–2.[46]

These debates indicate that, whereas the bachelors accepted some and rejected other aspects of FitzRalph's thought, they did not regard it as irrelevant. Leff's view of the commentary had to some extent been anticipated by Fr. Gwynn, whose views were based on a cursory examination of the limited number of manuscripts known to him more than forty years ago, when Ockham-research was at a much less advanced stage than it is now. With scarcely-veiled surprise and reluctance he argued that FitzRalph had worked out his lectures on the Sentences in apparent oblivion of developments all around him in the faculties of arts and theology. As an explanation for this lapse on FitzRalph's part, Gwynn made a suggestion which was scarcely flattering to the intellectual prowess of the young *bachalarius sententiarius*, namely that by the time Ockham had come to lecture on the Sentences and formulate publicly his new logic and theories of knowledge — lectures which in the light of investigations at Avignon from 1324 onwards must have been given no later than 1321–3 and which are now known to have been

[44] Printed in *Snappe's Formulary*, p. 76.

[45] Even the most extensive version of his *lectura*, in P and Vat. Lat. 11517, points to his having spent only one year lecturing on the Sentences and not two, as in the case of Wodeham's Oxford lectures.

[46] This dating affects Courtenay's chronology of Wodeham's three series of lectures on the Sentences, at London, Norwich, and Oxford, *Adam Wodeham*, pp. 30–76. But this dating is consistent with the information provided in Vat. Lat. 1110, fol. 135v: 'Et sic finitur quartus liber fratris ade Wodeham doctoris in theologia, qui legit Oxon. anno domini M° CCCXXXIJ'. This colophon indicates that Wodeham was reading the Sentences in 1332, but not that he had completed all four books (whose length suggests a two-year reading) by that date. It was clearly written after Wodeham's inception as doctor, and the 'explicit' of the *Tabula* which follows raises the possibility that it was written after Wodeham's death (1358): 'explicit tabula super quartum librum fratris ade Woddam magistri in theologia, de ordine fratrum minorum, et est anglicus nacione vel fuit' (fol. 141r). The problems of dating presented by this manuscript are discussed in Courtenay, *Adam Wodeham*, pp. 14–15, 23–5.

germinating in earlier versions from *c*.1317 – FitzRalph's thought had already been sufficiently formed as to allow no room for the reception of the novelties being expounded by Ockham and no opportunity to take issue with them. The influence most directly responsible for forming FitzRalph's approach to metaphysical problems while he was a student in the arts faculty and whose views he would both have expounded as a regent master in that faculty and used as a philosophical basis for his approach to theological questions was, according to Gwynn's reasoning, none other than the man whose system, FitzRalph declared towards the end of his life, he had worked to refute, i.e. Walter Burley.[47] This reasoning may be based on an over-literal interpretation of FitzRalph's claim, also made *c*.1358–9 in the autobiographical prayer, that he had rejected 'Aristotelica dogmata' in favour of Scriptural truth, a claim which must be examined more critically in the context of his more mature theological work, especially the *Summa de Questionibus Armenorum*.[48] Apart from all other considerations, it seems improbable that a student of FitzRalph's undoubted intellectual curiosity, combined albeit with a respect for authority, would have adopted such a 'blinkered' attitude and simply accepted on a lifelong basis the philosophical guidelines received from Burley's commentaries on Aristotle, even if these were circulating as teaching manuals in the arts faculty during FitzRalph's student years. His own teaching activity in the faculty of theology provides evidence of his willingness to revise his opinions in response to intellectual challenge, and his subsequent public career provides numerous examples of his ability to change his mind in accordance with changed circumstances. Whether this feature ought to be considered a mark of flexibility or a talent for opportunism is in this context irrelevant. What is significant is the clearly documented capacity for development in the thinking which lay behind his public actions, and which would contrast oddly with such an interpretation of his alleged neglect of the new teaching.

[47] In his letter to Giovanni Marignola, above, n. 34. Gwynn's arguments were worked out in unpublished notes, but his conclusions on the 'Aristotelian Averroism' of Burley coincide largely with the published views of Anneliese Maier. Her interpretation of the sense in which Burley's 'Averroism' was to be understood is also largely valid for FitzRalph, *Ausgehendes Mittelalter*, i. 102–3.

[48] Robson, *Wyclif and the Oxford Schools*, pp. 90–5, viewed this claim sceptically, but most of the examples he chose to show continuity rather than change between the Sentences and the Armenian questions were taken from precisely those books of the *Summa* which refuted recent scholastic developments, and not those which debated the Armenian issues.

Furthermore, we are faced with the problem of identifying the foundations of FitzRalph's metaphysical teaching as it is revealed in his lectures on the Sentences, the seven magisterial *determinationes*, and in his own and others' references to works by him which are no longer extant, but which clearly belong among his Oxford lectures and disputations. These include a commentary on Aristotle's *Physics*, to which he frequently referred in his *Commentary on the Sentences* and which probably represented the substance of a course of mandatory lectures given during his regency in the arts faculty.[49] A *questio biblica*, composed during his regency in theology, 1331-2 and surviving in no identifiable manuscript, is known to us only through the references to it contained in Wodeham's lectures on the Sentences.[50] Lecturing on the Bible was one of the ordinary duties of the regents in theology, although by the early fourteenth century only the mendicant masters took this obligation seriously and most, if not all, biblical instruction was in their hands.[51] This *questio* may represent some attempt on FitzRalph's part to meet this statutory requirement, though Wodeham's references to it indicate that it discussed more general philosophical and theological problems as well, and may have been used by its author as a vehicle to answer his critics among the disputing bachelors. It must have been composed after the (partial) revision of FitzRalph's *lectura* on the Sentences, as it contained a further radical revision of his views on future contingents.[52] That this revision took place in response to criticism by Wodeham in the course of their disputations might be suggested by the fact that the Franciscan knew FitzRalph's treatment both in the *lectura* and in the *questio biblica*, that he opposed the former and favoured the latter treatment of the topic. Hence it might be regarded as one of several examples of mutual influence and

[49] Weisheipl, 'The Curriculum', 173-5. On FitzRalph's lost commentary, and that of his opponent in the schools, Richard Kilwington, see Maier, 'Verschollene Aristoteles-kommentare des 14. Jahrhunderts', *Ausgehendes Mittelalter*, i. 237-64. From Wodeham's lectures on the Sentences she deduced that there had been controversy over problems of infinity and eternity between FitzRalph and Kilwington while the latter was still regent in arts, 'Diskussionen über das aktuell Unendliche', ibid., i. 74-8. FitzRalph's own subsequent references to his commentary on the *Physics* were mainly confined to two questions in Book II of his *lectura*: 'Utrum includit contradiccionem deum produxisse mundum ex nihilo', and 'Utrum motus et tempus distinguantur realiter a subiectis suis et inter se', P, fols. 139ra-142va.

[50] Wodeham cited it ten times in his own *lectura*, Paris, Univ. MS 193, fols. 192vb-198rb, Courtenay, *Adam Wodeham*, p. 79.

[51] Smalley, *English Friars*, pp. 29-30.

[52] Courtenay, *Adam Wodeham*, pp. 77-9.

borrowing which is characteristic, not only of these two, but of numerous scholars of their day. There is of course no sure method of determining whether FitzRalph had actually revised this section of his bachelor lectures, or whether the views on future contingents criticized by Wodeham were those of the original version. Equally difficult to determine is whether all of the changes which FitzRalph made in his *lectura* were a response to criticism during debates under his regency, or whether contact with Paris theologians two years earlier had helped to refine and alter his opinions.

Unfortunately it is not possible from Wodeham's references to the *questio biblica* to work out what other topics FitzRalph might have considered in it, nor to decide what approach to biblical exegesis it might have revealed during his scholastic period – information which in the light of his subsequent self-confessed 'conversion' to the Scriptures would be particularly valuable. The only other work alluded to by a contemporary is a gloss or commentary on Augustine's *De Trinitate*, which might be a separate work, or may be a reference to his revision of the questions 'de imagine Dei', which relied extensively on *De Trinitate* and might loosely have been described as a commentary on it.[53]

On the basis of the assumption mentioned above, that the guiding spirit for FitzRalph was Burley, one would expect to find the former's work also displaying an Aristotelianism tinged with some Averroist leanings,[54] but lacking (if one follows Leff's judgement) the ability to make finer distinctions. At least one contemporary believed he could identify Averroist tendencies in FitzRalph, above all in his readiness to accept the Arab philosopher as an authority on problems connected with the intellect.[55] Above all, the commentary reveals a mind more sensitive to current controversy than has previously been conceded.

[53] The former is more likely in view of Wodeham's remark, 'et haec est etiam via Firauf in Lectura et similiter in glosulis super 5 Trinitate c.19', Paris, Univ. MS 193, fol. 119vb, and in view of FitzRalph's own frequent references to Augustine's *De Trinitate* in his vernacular and Latin sermons.

[54] Above all acceptance of the central Averroist tenet of the unity of the intellect, Maier, *Die Vorläufer Galileis*, p. 174.

[55] Vat. Lat. 4353, fol. 38^{r}, contains in Kilwington's commentary on the Sentences a reference to an 'argumentum fundatum super Averroym, qui mihi est nullius auctoritatis', which is apparently directed against an opinion of FitzRalph, Maier, as n. 54, p. 174 n. Leff, *FitzRalph Commentator*, pp. 151–8, argued that FitzRalph's approach to the mind and its faculties was of an 'essentially Augustinian nature', but he did not deny the influence of Aristotle and Averroes.

FitzRalph occasionally admitted to having been temporarily influenced by contemporary opinions which he had heard being expounded but which, subsequently and on the basis of better information, he decided to reject, an admission on his part whose significance is further enhanced in the light of Courtenay's discoveries concerning the cut-and-thrust debates which took place under his regency.

In his own *lectura* the treatment of many questions is not particularly searching: in these he contented himself with a perfunctory statement of arguments for and against, followed by the acceptance of a conventional solution. Although the statutory requirement, in Oxford as in Paris, implied a reading of all four books of the Lombard, it had by the early fourteenth century become common for commentators on the Sentences to 'specialize', and to focus their attention on a small group of problems in which they had a special interest. This was especially true of secular bachelors such as FitzRalph who were limited to a one-year reading of the Sentences. They did not have the additional opportunity enjoyed by a number of mendicant theologians, including Adam Wodeham, who could lecture on the Sentences in one of the *studia* of their order as well as in the *studium generale* and thereby complete a much more comprehensive commentary. Of special interest among Oxford theologians of this generation were questions concerning the relationship between nature and grace, particularly as this concerned man's free will, God's omnipotence, and future contingents, interests which they shared with Paris and which were gradually becoming the common content of later medieval scholasticism. FitzRalph did not stray far from this favoured group, and his main themes are creation, psychological problems of the mind and its faculties, God's omnipotence and foreknowledge, future contingents, and – almost as a leitmotiv for the entire commentary – the question of free will.[56]

This latter topic, together with the related issues of grace and merit, was one of the most enthusiastically debated at Oxford and was to call forth the wrath of Thomas Bradwardine directed against all latter-day Pelagians, and it was a subject on which the disputing bachelors of FitzRalph's day were also divided.

[56] Leff, *FitzRalph Commentator*, pp. 90–109, discussed FitzRalph's views of the will in relation to the intellect, showing that his assertion of the primacy of the will was so extreme that he was at times in danger of adopting the semi-Pelagian position criticized by Bradwardine; see Leff, *Bradwardine and the Pelagians*, esp. pp. 127 ff.

Courtenay has indicated that closer study of these commentaries, with a view to discovering the several attitudes to this group of problems which they contain, might result in some surprises. We find, for example, FitzRalph strongly maintaining the unlimited capacity of the soul for grace and beatitude through its own powers and receiving somewhat wavering support from the Dominican 'Ockhamist' Robert Holcot, but not from the Franciscan 'socius' Wodeham, who is inclined to condemn this position as Pelagian.[57] Such evidence suggests that not merely is the view of Wodeham as the 'archetypal semi-Pelagian' which some recent historians have taken over from Gregory of Rimini, in need of drastic revision, but also that which takes Wyclif at his face value and postulates a triumvirate consisting of FitzRalph, Bradwardine, and Wyclif.[58] It also indicates that FitzRalph's younger contemporaries did not restrict themselves to taking up his, in theological terms, less contentious views on motion, time, and infinity,[59] that these debates gave him yet another opportunity to hold out with some tenacity for his cherished position on free will, and they may have helped to provoke Bradwardine's reactions, whose initial expression was to be found in his own Oxford lectures from the early 1330s onwards.[60]

However, we can in the final analysis identify the mind behind the *lectura* as basically orthodox and eager to resolve problems in a compromise between the extremes of 'antiqui' and 'moderni'. Hence FitzRalph's commentary is primarily of interest as a witness for his age, the work of a man who was familiar with, but unable to make an outstandingly original contribution to, the intellectual problems which were then exercising some of the finest minds of the age, a factor which did not escape some of his younger contemporaries. They generally treated him with respect, but not infrequently dismissed his arguments as inadequate. A particularly striking example of this is to be found in the attitude of Wodeham, who challenged FitzRalph more

[57] Courtenay, *Adam Wodeham*, p. 106.

[58] Workman, *John Wyclif*, i. pp. 121–32, linked them thus. He also discussed Wyclif's attempts to steer a middle course between FitzRalph and Bradwardine on the question of predestination, ibid., p. 125.

[59] Maier showed that these were the topics upon which FitzRalph was most frequently quoted by near-contemporaries, especially Wodeham and Holcot. But she assumed that, because Wodeham quoted FitzRalph so often, he therefore copied him on these issues, 'Diskussionen über das aktuell Unendliche', *Ausgehendes Mittelalter*, i. 79; *Die Vorläufer Galileis*, p. 302.

[60] Leff, *Bradwardine and the Pelagians*, pp. 265–6, discusses genesis and dating of *De causa Dei*.

than any other living author, despite the latter's seniority in the hierarchical rank of the schools, and who flouted convention by criticizing him by name. Nevertheless, he clearly respected FitzRalph and sheltered behind the weight of the regent's obvious influence within the university on occasions when he agreed with him, referring to him as 'doctor certe non minus imputatus in hac universitate'.[61]

Leff's judgement of this commentary is basically a negative one. He sees the work as characterized only by its conventional orthodoxy and by a 'traditional' Augustinianism derived primarily from Henry of Ghent, conceived in pre-Scotist terms, and therefore outside of and irrelevant to the main currents of his time.[62] But this judgement can only be accepted with substantial qualifications, and it must be conceded that FitzRalph concentrated on topics which lay at the heart of scholastic controversy during these years. Far from being anachronistic, the range of subjects he treated is strikingly similar to the themes preoccupying both his own near-contemporaries among English theologians and also the most influential commentator in Paris a decade later, Gregory of Rimini, although the latter would reject many of the views expressed both by FitzRalph and by his mendicant disputants in Oxford.[63] Even Leff occasionally felt obliged to qualify his judgements, above all with regard to FitzRalph's exclusive debt to the Augustinians and his apparent imperviousness to contemporary Oxford currents, but it is primarily due to the work of Anneliese Maier that we are able to place FitzRalph more precisely in the context of these currents.[64] She has done much to establish that, far from being a complete outsider whose discussions seem 'unreal' and 'superficial' because he was not involved in the controversies which these currents provoked, on the contrary, his reactions to Ockham, to Bradwardine's pupil and friend Richard Kilwington,[65]

[61] Vat. Lat. 1110, fol. 21^{v}. [62] *FitzRalph Commentator*, p. 18.

[63] Especially Wodeham, Kilwington, and Bradwardine, despite FitzRalph's differences with each of these on various counts, see Leff, *Gregory of Rimini*, pp. 101-3, 163-84. Gregory of Rimini opposed FitzRalph's views on infinity several times in his own commentary on the Sentences, Book I (ed. Venice, 1522), *dist.* 42-44, *q.*4; Bk II, *dist.* 1, *q.* 3, *dist.* 2, *q.* 2 a.1, *dist.* 3, *q.* 1 a.1, in *Gregorii Arimensis OESA Lectura super Primum et Secundum Sententiarum*, ed. Damasus Trapp *et al.*, Tomus IV super Secundum (*Dist.* 1-5), (Spätmittelalter und Reformation, Texte und Untersuchungen, vol. 9, Berlin-New York, 1979), 102, 297-307, 345-51.

[64] e.g. *Die Vorläufer Galileis, passim*, and the articles collected in *Ausgehendes Mittelalter*, i.

[65] For his dispute with Kilwington on infinity and motion see above, n. 49, and Maier, *Die Vorläufer Galileis*, pp. 209-15; Francesco Bottin, 'Un testo fondamentale

and his affinity with some of the Mertonians locate him firmly within these currents and help to explain why – in the company of Ockham, Bradwardine, and Wodeham – he became one of the four most frequently cited English theologians of the fourteenth century.[66]

Maier's work further renders unnecessary the several explanations put forward by Leff in different sections of his book for the alleged lack of involvement on FitzRalph's part. One explanation is a charitable one, that FitzRalph was still under the age of thirty when he composed his commentary, and that therefore the work of a man of immature years should not be compared with the contributions of the great schoolmen. Further, it was written before the full impact of Ockhamism became clear,[67] and before the period *c.* 1340 when theology became truly controversial. On the other hand he offered the explanation that FitzRalph simply regarded these lectures as the formal completion of his academic training, the necessary precondition for a non-academic career in public life, for which he already had a patron to facilitate entry and advancement.[68] In such circumstances a cautious, traditional approach, suitably deferential to the acknowledged authorities, might be politically wise, especially if FitzRalph was able to recognize his own limitations as a speculative thinker. The first explanation ignores the undoubted fact that so much of the original work in the universities of the period was done by bachelors in their lectures, 'responsiones', and disputations among themselves and with the regent masters. These bachelors were, if secular clerks, on average the same age as FitzRalph when they came to lecture on the Sentences, though members of religious orders might be correspondingly older. The second explanation seems dubious in the light of our knowledge of FitzRalph's activities as regent master, especially his constant revision of his views in response to criticism in the course of debates, all of which point to a deeper

nell'ambito della "nuova fisica" di Oxford', *Antiqui und Moderni. Traditionsbewusstsein und Fortschrittsbewusstsein im späten Mittelalter* (Berlin–New York, 1974), 201–205.

[66] Courtenay, *Adam Wodeham*, p. 158, stressed that Wodeham, unlike FitzRalph and Bradwardine, was quoted as an authority on a wide range of topics, whereas the other two were quoted almost exclusively on divine volition and future contingents. As applied to FitzRalph, this remark must be understood as referring only to those works which originated in an Oxford academic context before 1332–3.

[67] *FitzRalph Commentator*, p. 13.

[68] Ibid., p. 174.

interest in and commitment to the work of the schools than simple careerism.

Furthermore, the evidence of some of the wide range of scholastic texts used by Maier in her studies of the natural philosophy of the fourteenth-century schoolmen suggests that the remark of Bishop Grandisson in 1329, made when recommending his protégé on the occasion of FitzRalph's visit to Paris, that he 'inter omnes studentes et legentes Universitatis Oxoniensis eminenter dinoscitur intelligens et subtilis', was not mere rhetoric and flattery.[69] In Maier's work most of the Oxford figures are relegated to a subsidiary role behind their Parisian contemporaries, and her view of the relative importance of the two schools in this generation needs revision in the light of Weisheipl's work on the Mertonians. Yet despite this unconscious bias on her part, FitzRalph's place in the history of these developments and debates is brought to light. Above all, his alleged Averroism and his affinity with some, though significantly not with all of his contemporaries among the Mertonians, emerge more clearly – in this respect one of the major dividing issues was sympathy for Ockham even after he had caused consternation and embarrassment among his devotees by his flight from Avignon to the 'schismatic' court of Ludwig of Bavaria on 26 May 1328.[70] Her work also reveals a clearer total view of FitzRalph's cosmology, which owed much to Augustine, to Averroes, and to Grosseteste as well as to Henry of Ghent, and is combined with an aversion to some emerging implications of the 'moderni' – in short that FitzRalph combined a moderate Augustinianism with a moderate realism, and represented what Gilson characterized as 'augustinisme averroisant'.[71]

In his own chosen areas FitzRalph displayed close acquaintance with the writings of St. Augustine, though notably with little else in the standard corpus of patristic literature cited by the schoolmen, and his series of questions 'De imagine Dei in anima humana' borrows extensively from Augustine's *De Trinitate.*[72] However, he attempted for the most part to achieve a *via media* between an extreme Augustinianism such as that of

[69] *Grandisson's Register*, i. 233.

[70] See Karl Bosl, 'Die "geistliche Hofakademie" Ludwigs des Bayern', *Der Mönch im Wappen* (Munich, 1961), pp. 97-129.

[71] *La Philosophie du moyen âge*, p. 687.

[72] Sent. I, *q.* 5, *art.* 1-6, P, fols. 24vb-35vb. It is possible that he subsequently expanded this *questio* into the work which Wodeham knew as 'Firauf . . . super 5 Trinitate', above, n. 53.

Bradwardine and the new teaching of Ockham. His lack of sympathy with the latter is most clearly demonstrated in a *questio* 'Utrum motus et tempus distinguatur realiter a subiectis suis et inter se',[73] where he rejected the opinions of 'quidam valens' which he had heard being expounded orally some time earlier. Maier argued with some conviction that this reference was intended to imply Ockham,[74] and it is reasonable to assume that FitzRalph had heard the view expressed in the course of a lecture or disputation at Oxford. He admitted that he had initially been impressed by the arguments of this unnamed scholar when they were being expounded, but now on maturer reflection he felt obliged to reject them. It is tempting to speculate on the reasons for this change of mind. If his remark is intended to refer to Ockham, FitzRalph must have heard the Franciscan airing his views in Oxford prior to his summons to Avignon. Especially after the condemnation of fifty-one propositions derived from Ockham's commentary on the Sentences in 1326 and in the knowledge that John XXII was still collecting opinions about Ockham's orthodoxy several years later – even if FitzRalph was writing 'before the full impact of Ockhamism had become clear'[75] – he might have been encouraged to revise his views on Ockham and refer to him only obliquely and anonymously when composing his own lectures. The condemned articles were not directly linked with the views on motion at issue here, but it is at least possible that this was one of the sections of the original *lectura* which were not revised during the period of FitzRalph's regency, and it was not customary for bachelors to attack by name the opinions of those who were their seniors in the hierarchy of the schools, even if, as in the case of Ockham, these were under suspicion of heresy.[76] Nevertheless, we are left with the interesting possibility that FitzRalph, during the early stages of his theological studies, when Ockham was lecturing as *bachalarius sententiarius* and working out the ideas which caused so much excitement in the university and disapproval at

[73] P, fol. 142va, 'et aer lucidus esset lumen, sicut ego quendam valentem audivi dicentem' (Sent. II, *q.* 1, *art.* 2).

[74] *An der Grenze von Scholastik und Naturwissenschaft* (Rome, 1952^2), p. 16. The term 'valens' was regularly used of a contemporary whose opinion was deemed to carry weight, whether one agreed with it or not. Wodeham used it with reference to FitzRalph, Vat. Lat. 955, fol. 8^r.

[75] Leff, *FitzRalph Commentator*, p. 13.

[76] Burley accepted this convention when he criticized Ockham and never named him, but Courtenay's evidence shows that the rules were far from rigid, *Adam Wodeham*, pp. 77–81, 116–17.

the curia, was originally impressed by the arguments of the *venerabilis inceptor*, but that by the time he had come to lecture on the Sentences himself the tide had turned and the climate for such speculations in the course of academic exercises in the faculty of theology was less favourable. In the past Oxford had often been deemed to enjoy greater freedom than Paris in the expression of daring opinions in the course of academic debate, partly because the bishop of Lincoln as the ordinary ecclesiastical authority was far removed from the schools. However, the example of Lutterell, as chancellor, making the content of academic debate the basis for heresy proceedings against an individual, changed this climate.

On the problem of motion, as elsewhere when dealing with physical problems such as the theory of velocity, which FitzRalph, like most of his contemporaries, took over from Aristotle's *Physics,*[77] FitzRalph belonged in the Mertonian rather than the Ockhamist line of interpretation.[78] Yet he did not see eye to eye with the Mertonians on all matters, and we learn from Wodeham's commentary that there had been some controversy between FitzRalph and Bradwardine's pupil, Richard Kilwington, in which each took up diametrically opposed positions on the subject of infinity and eternity. The disputed issues were worked out by both contestants in the course of their commentaries on the *Physics*, neither of which survive, but from their respective remarks on the subject in their lectures on the Sentences it has been possible to gain a rough idea of the issues involved.[79] FitzRalph's case is stated in the course of a *questio* 'Utrum includit contradictionem Deum produxisse mundum ab eterno', in which he cited Aquinas, Scotus, and Henry of Ghent in support of his approach to the problem of infinity, but in his conclusion he followed the line of the Aristotelian Averroists, perhaps even directly Walter Burley.[80] When Kilwington discussed a similar topic in the course of his own *lectura* on the

[77] Maier, *Zwischen Philosophie und Mechanik* (Rome, 1958), p. 150 and n.

[78] Ibid., pp. 133-4, 138.

[79] 'Diskussionen über das aktuell Unendliche', 75-8. Only a fragment of Kilwington's commentary on the Sentences has survived, a few questions in Vat. Lat. 4353, fols. 34^{v}-50^{r}. Kilwington, like Burley, spent a long period of regency in arts, and for the MSS of his other Aristotelian commentaries see *BRUO* II, 1051. When he began to lecture on the Sentences he followed FitzRalph on a number of topics, but differed on others, including infinity and the latter's Averroist sympathies, see Maier, *Die Vorläufer Galileis,* pp. 174, 209-15, 302-3.

[80] P, fols. 139ra-142va, esp. fol. 142rb. See Leff, *FitzRalph Commentator,* pp. 112-16.

Sentences, he rejected an 'argumentum fundatum super Averroym, qui mihi est nullius auctoritatis', he almost certainly had FitzRalph in mind.[81] It is characteristic of FitzRalph's *lectura*, in which he cited numerous authorities (many passages of his text contain no recognizable argument, but consist simply of a series of authorities set out one after another), that he cited Averroes as an authoritative source to be listened to with some respect.[82]

Here in this controversy with Kilwington, a Mertonian who, like Walter Burley, had a long and active career in the arts faculty, was an experienced commentator on philosophical texts, and must be regarded as a more reliable authority than FitzRalph on natural philosophy and the new cosmology, we may have the key to the somewhat obscure allusions in the satirical poem directed at FitzRalph during his chancellorship by one of the secessionists in the Stamford Schism.[83] The latter may have been satirizing something which we can only dimly sense, because the crucial texts of the controversy do not survive: the object of his ridicule may have been a more traditional approach to the physical universe and to the mathematical possibilities of scientific inquiry, which must have seemed unsophisticated when compared with the ideas being generated by some of his contemporaries, with which the satirist must have been familiar. Few Mertonian contributions to the discussion of the philosophical aspects of the problem of motion survive, as all of them treated it in their lost commentaries on the *Physics*, commentaries which must have been series of lectures delivered in the arts faculty and which had a wider aural than written circulation among their immediate contemporaries. FitzRalph's treatment in the single question in his lectures on the Sentences, in which he referred back to his earlier work on the *Physics*, was exceedingly cautious. He limited himself to an exposition of the various authorities, especially on the question of time, weighed up their various pros and cons, while the only really decisive statement of opinion in the *questio* is the rejection of 'Ockhamist' teaching mentioned already.[84] None the less the decision to treat the topic at all, and the interest in Aristotelian physics reflected in the fact of his having commented on them and

[81] Maier, as n. 55. She maintained that FitzRalph's Averroist tendencies were 'well-known' among contemporary thinkers.

[82] P, fols. 32^{ra-b}, 47ra, 48vb, 65vb.

[83] Ed. Salter, in *EHR* 37, 249-51.

[84] Above, nn. 72-3.

provoked some debate about them, combine to link him with the Mertonians of his generation, even though the *Physics* was by statute a crucial text in the teaching of the arts faculty.[85] A further indication that FitzRalph's interest in problems of mathematics and physics may have been more lively and more informed than either modern historical research or the satirizing students in Stamford were prepared to allow, is contained in a note of possession in a manuscript of Euclid's *Geometry*, originally in the possession of Jacques Pantaléon, patriarch of Jerusalem and later Pope Urban IV (1261-4), which contains in a fourteenth-century hand the note 'Iste liber fuit domini armachani'.[86] As the manuscript subsequently passed into the hands of the Cistercians at Aulne-sur-Sambre (Hainault, Belgium), the archbishop of Armagh in question presumably acquired or at least consulted it in Avignon. Among fourteenth-century archbishops of Armagh who both had scholarly interests and are known to have visited the papal curia, FitzRalph and Stephen Segrave stand out, though the latter spent an extremely brief period there and no intellectual activity in Avignon is documented in his case, and FitzRalph is the more realistic possibility.[87] Even if FitzRalph were the possessor of this manuscript, which cannot be determined with certainty, his treatment of scientific problems lacked the assurance and originality of the 'armchair physicists' around Thomas Bradwardine, and he may himself have realized his inadequacy in the field of natural philosophy. That he regarded this as being the case in matters of logic and metaphysics is indicated by a passage in his *questio* on the Eucharist: he alluded briefly to the opinions of an unnamed 'modernus', which might have been either Ockham or one of his followers, but then dismissed these controversies as belonging to the school of philosophy rather than theology.[88]

In other respects FitzRalph stood far apart from, if not

[85] *Statuta Antiqua*, pp. xcvi, 26, 390; Weisheipl, 'The Curriculum', 174.

[86] Formerly Phillipps MS 4633, now Columbia University (N.Y.), MS Plimpton 156, fol. 165^{v}. For references to this MS I am grateful to Dr Agostino Paravicini Bagliani, of the Biblioteca Apostolica Vaticana. For further references see his article 'Un matematico nella corte pontificia del secolo XIII: Campano da Novara (+ 1296)', *Rivista di storia della Chiesa in Italia*, 27 (1973), 114 n. 80.

[87] Other possibilities are members of the Jorz family, of whom Thomas, a Dominican and confessor to Edward II, became cardinal of S. Sabina on 15 December 1305, while his brothers Walter and Roland, also Dominicans, became successively archbishops of Armagh, had difficulty in establishing residence there, and returned to England as auxiliary bishops, *BRUO* II, 1023-4, but they are improbable candidates.

[88] P, fol. 192rb.

actually opposed to Bradwardine, especially over the related questions of predestination and free will. Bradwardine, initially in his Oxford lectures and subsequently in *De causa Dei*, attacked what he called the 'Pelagiani moderni', by which he meant those whose doctrine of sin and grace attached too little weight to the sovereign action of God's love, and whose scepticism, originating in Ockham's theory of knowledge, could have disastrous consequences for theology.[89] FitzRalph attempted in his treatment of the intellect and will to steer a middle course between the determinism of the Averroists, whom he was prepared to follow on some issues but not on all, and what might be described as the 'scepticism' of some of his contemporaries. However, the attitude of FitzRalph to the soul's capacity for beatitude, to which Wodeham took exception,[90] might have had a similar effect on Bradwardine. FitzRalph formulated the theory of cognition, upon which his treatment of the mind and will depended, by drawing from Averroes and Henry of Ghent as well as directly from Augustine, and in opposition to many of the 'moderni' he insisted on separating the faculties of the mind, intellect, and will, thereby distinguishing cognition from volition.[91] The whole problem turned on whether the will is controlled by man's knowledge, and at the root of the discussion lay the conflict between a Pelagian and a Stoic interpretation. It would however be a total misrepresentation of the situation to imply that only polarized positions were represented in scholastic thinking on the problem. On the contrary, extreme positions were the less frequent, and most of those who devoted their attention to the question attempted, like FitzRalph, to find a median solution, accepting some elements from each side of the argument.

Wyclif subsequently paid tribute to both Bradwardine and FitzRalph as the two Oxford teachers upon whom he relied most,[92] but on this issue he followed the former and not the latter. Wyclif's realist predestinarianism contrasted sharply with FitzRalph's efforts to 'reconcile' free will with a moderate acceptance of divine predestination, and this factor may help to explain why Wyclif quoted from *De Pauperie Salvatoris* on dominion and from the *Summa de Questionibus Armenorum* on a wider range of theological issues, but never from the *lectura*

[89] Leff, *Bradwardine and the Pelagians*, pp. 15, 127–35, 186–254.
[90] Courtenay, *Adam Wodeham*, p. 106.
[91] Robson, *Wyclif and the Oxford Schools*, pp. 78–82.
[92] Ibid., pp. 31, 70; Workman, *John Wyclif*, i, pp. 123–31.

on the Sentences.[93] Although he could not have used any of the extant manuscripts, it is improbable that a text of FitzRalph's *lectura* was not available to him. MS Oriel 15, which was made for a Benedictine of Glastonbury in 1389 and was still in Canterbury College in 1524,[94] must have been copied from a partly revised text circulating in Oxford after FitzRalph's regency.[95] But FitzRalph's strong emphasis on the primacy of the will made his text useless as a source of authority for Wyclif when he was working out his own positions. Despite FitzRalph's lack of sympathy with the trends of the 'moderni' on many issues, it cannot be categorically stated at the present state of research into the Oxford debates of the early 1330s, that his doctrine was free from all traces of the tendencies which Bradwardine was to describe as 'Pelagian' or 'semi-Pelagian'. While he did not deny the reality of predestination, but merely sought to interpret it with less rigour, he nevertheless went to considerable lengths to safeguard the freedom of the will, and the fluid and uncertain state of the debate during his regency may be indicated by the state of his own arguments, in which he sometimes qualified his own previous statements almost to the point of contradiction. This tendency, which marred his entire *lectura* on the Sentences and which originated largely in the author's habit of picking and choosing among a variety of authorities in his quest for a middle way, was criticized by Wodeham as 'hedging'.

FitzRalph's eclecticism and its consequences were particularly evident when he came to apply his philosophical conclusions

[93] Wyclif lifted large sections of *De Dominio Divino* from *DPS* almost literally, in *De Civili Dominio* he quoted extensively from the same work, and he further took a substantial number of citations concerning the divine will, the functions of the clergy, and of ecclesiastical authority from the *Summa*. More surprisingly perhaps, the *Summa* is also cited extensively in one section of Wyclif's *Summa de Ente: lib. ii, tractatus tertius, de voluntate Dei*, where both FitzRalph and Bradwardine are discussed exhaustively and often critically, see Michael Dziewicki, ed. (WS, London, 1909), pp. 134–6, 162, 182, 184–5.

[94] Montague R. James, *The Ancient Libraries of Canterbury and Dover* (Cambridge, 1903), p. 167.

[95] A miscellaneous compendium of Oxford theologians, its crude standard of workmanship suggests a student's notebook. Leff, *FitzRalph Commentator*, p. 186, had doubts about this MS, arguing that it cannot be accepted as 'the authentic work of FitzRalph'. It diverges more than any other extant MS from the corpus of questions which must have formed the bulk of FitzRalph's *lectura*, and it is the only one to include the text of the principial sermon, which he preached as 'bachalarius sententiarius' in the church of St. Mary the Virgin, fol. 1^{ra-va}. For the statutory requirements regarding the 'principium' see *Statuta Antiqua*, pp. xcvii, 39; Glorieux, 'Sentences', 1862–3.

about intellect and will to theological problems – to the role of the will in perceiving the 'clear vision' of God and the relative importance of intellect and will in attaining eternal life. Throughout his commentary he is frequently to be found in opposition to the teaching of Scotus, slightly less often does he take issue with Aquinas, but here he tried to steer a middle course between Scotus's view of the will as a power superior to the intellect, which appealed to FitzRalph personally, and the opposite position held by Aquinas, which he appears to have regarded as the more authoritative. Here especially Wodeham took him to task for trying to have things both ways.[96] Although the Franciscan had touched on this question in what appears to have been his principial lecture at the beginning of his Oxford commentary, citing FitzRalph's views on the soul's capacity for beatitude,[97] he returned to the topic again in his principial debate with his 'socii' at the beginning of the second book on the Sentences.[98] In view of the extreme length of Wodeham's commentary on Book I of the Lombard, he cannot have reached the second book before the spring of the academic year in which he began his biennial reading of the Sentences at Oxford. If we accept that Wodeham's first year and FitzRalph's regency are to be dated 1331–2, then it is possible to conjecture that by the time the 'socii' came to the principial debate at the beginning of Book II the question of the beatific vision had acquired a new importance in the light of the sermons of John XXII. The pope had begun to expound his views on the vision of God enjoyed by the souls of the just immediately after death, in a series of sermons, of which the first was delivered on 1 November 1331. The others followed on 15 December 1331, 5 January and 3 February 1332, and in view of the speed with which the news of their potentially heretical contents travelled around Europe it is not improbable that it had reached the disputing bachelors in Oxford before the end of the academic year. In FitzRalph's own statements on the subject in the course of his revised *lectura*, the clear vision enjoyed by the souls of the blessed is taken for granted, without any implication of doubt that these might not enjoy such a vision of the divinity until after the General Judgement. However, the criticism of Wodeham at the beginning of his *lectura*, before he realized that FitzRalph had altered his opinion, may have a deeper significance which escapes

[96] Robson, *Wyclif and the Oxford Schools*, p. 78.
[97] Courtenay, *Adam Wodeham*, p. 77.
[98] Ibid., pp. 90–1.

us as we have no record of the original version of the latter's *lectura* on this topic.[99] Nevertheless, it is probable that the detailed questions on problems of the clear vision as related to intellect and will in these lectures attracted sufficient attention for his opinion on the pope's problem to be sought in theological circles at the curia, especially as by the time he arrived at Avignon FitzRalph had just completed a term of office as chancellor and his views were being debated in the schools by known sympathizers of Ockham.

FitzRalph's doctrinal position in these confused years cannot have appeared as totally and irrelevantly conservative as Leff's assessment would suggest. Despite FitzRalph's oft-repeated aversion to the opinions of the 'moderni' on some topics, his *lectura* caused a vigorous reaction among the younger 'Ockhamist' friars, favourable on some issues and critical on others, but in any case quoting him and publicizing his views to a remarkable degree. The main question on which he was taken up and cited over the next two decades was infinity, where his arguments were adopted by a number of authors who incorporated them, modified and criticized in varying degrees, into their own lectures on the Sentences.[100] However, nobody discussed FitzRalph's views so frequently or so vigorously as Adam Wodeham, who cited him in either the margin or text of over forty of his seventy questions.[101] Although Wodeham treated him with respect,[102] he was also extremely outspoken in his criticism of his academic superior. Wodeham opposed FitzRalph's views more often than the reverse, but was always respectful and frequently acknowledged the quality of the arguments even though he was not prepared to agree with the conclusions and, as has recently been demonstrated, it would be misleading to convey the impression that Wodeham was a committed opponent of FitzRalph. On the contrary, the fact that Wodeham had access to the revised version of the regent master's lectures on the Sentences and could quote extensive passages from it verbatim while it was still in the stages of preparation does not indicate strained relations.[103]

[99] Ibid., pp. 77-81.
[100] Maier, 'Diskussionen über das aktuell Unendliche', 78-9.
[101] Courtenay, *Adam Wodeham*, p. 75.
[102] Vat. Lat. 1110, fol. 21^{V}; Courtenay, *Adam Wodeham*, p. 80 n.
[103] Ibid., p. 78. The intellectual relationship between these two illustrates once more Maier's point that the question of infinity demonstrated in a particularly acute manner the diversity of late scholastic thinking, *Die Vorläufer Galileis*, p. 215.

There are several indications of give and take on the part both of the regent master and the Franciscan bachelor, with each prepared to learn from and revise their own opinions in the light of the other's work. At the beginning of Wodeham's Oxford commentary he cited an opinion of FitzRalph on the soul's capacity for beatitude which he must have derived from the original lectures delivered by FitzRalph as *bachalarius sententiarius* which Wodeham, as a theological student, appears to have attended. In the course of his aural exposition Wodeham became aware that FitzRalph had in the meantime changed his opinion on the matter and was able in the next session to quote the revised version.[104] The episode conveys a lively picture of teaching and debating in the schools: FitzRalph as regent master was obviously present and objected that he no longer held the view being attributed to him, and promptly provided the text of his revised opinions for the information of a bachelor under his regency. Again on the subject of future contingents, there appears to have been a continuing debate between the two, which resulted in FitzRalph changing his views for the first time in the revision of his *lectura* and yet again in his *questio biblica*, the latter very probably in the light of Wodeham's criticism.[105] However, it was not all one-way traffic, and Wodeham can also be demonstrated as having changed his opinions in the light of those of FitzRalph, especially on infinity. The question in Book III of Wodeham's *lectura*, in which he followed FitzRalph verbatim on the issue, involved a total rejection of his own arguments as expressed in Book I.[106]

Almost simultaneously, but not quite as literally, Wodeham's confrère Robert Halifax followed FitzRalph's arguments on cosmology while lecturing on the Sentences at Cambridge.[107] Also lecturing at roughly the same time, and probably the Dominican 'socius' with whom Wodeham disputed under FitzRalph's regency, was Robert Holcot. He has always been regarded as an enthusaistic follower of Ockham and in his commentary he devoted considerable attention to the problem of free will. However, his position in the conflicts revolving around such problems in Oxford and Paris during these years is still disputed. Whereas

[104] Vat. Lat. 955, fol. 10r. [105] Courtenay, *Adam Wodeham*, p. 79.

[106] Maier, *Die Vorläufer Galileis*, p. 176. This change of opinion appears to have escaped Courtenay's notice.

[107] Maier, as n. 106; idem, 'Diskussionen über das aktuell Unendliche', 79–81. For Halifax see *BRUC*, 280.

Oberman was convinced he was to be regarded as one of the 'Pelagians' opposed by Bradwardine, Maier could find no clearly established position or line of thought at all in his commentary, seeing it as a colourful mosaic of diverse opinions, some of them irreconcilable.[108] Although she considered his work completely unoriginal and overrated,[109] she recognized him as belonging to the same group as FitzRalph, Wodeham, and Halifax, all of whose views would come in for searching criticism at the hands of Gregory of Rimini. The latter recognized FitzRalph as the source for the common view of infinity held by this group and gave his arguments almost verbatim in refutation of it.[110] FitzRalph continued to be quoted frequently in the schools of Paris throughout the rest of the fourteenth century, especially by the Augustinian friar Johannes Hiltalingen of Basel, but also by Ceffons, Mirecourt, and D'Ailly, though they tended to use his *lectura* only for a restricted group of problems, revolving around infinity, future contingents, and divine volition,[111] but none of these cited him as often as did Gregory of Rimini.

Gregory is an example *par excellence* of the eclecticism common to all schools of thought of the period. While this is not the place to attempt a review of his theology, it may be pointed out that whereas he rejected FitzRalph on infinity, he shared his view on the primacy of the will over the intellect and on other related topics. At the same time, while differing sharply from Bradwardine on sin, Gregory shared much of his rigorous Augustinian interpretation of grace and predestination, which on the other hand FitzRalph could not accept.[112] Thus in the first half of the fourteenth century we are faced in theology as in philosophy with a situation in which, not merely had the marriage between the two disciplines broken down, but the overlapping and borrowing across conventional lines of division

[108] 'Diskussionen über das aktuell Unendliche', 81–2, but her opinion that Holcot knew FitzRalph only through Wodeham is, in the light of Courtenay's work on the debates under FitzRalph's regency, highly improbable.

[109] Holcot's commentary had a wide MS circulation and was printed at Lyon in 1518, see *BRUO* II, 946, and Leff, *Bradwardine and the Pelagians*, pp. 216–27. But Maier failed to consider Holcot's reputation as a biblical commentator, whose commentary on the book of Wisdom made him 'famous overnight' (Smalley, *English Friars*, p. 141), and the circulation of his non-biblical work owed much to this reputation.

[110] Maier, 'Diskussionen über das aktuell Unendliche', 82–3.

[111] Courtenay, *Adam Wodeham*, pp. 116–59.

[112] Above, n. 63; Damasus Trapp, 'Augustinian Theology of the Fourteenth Century', *Augustiniana*, 6 (1956), esp. 182–213.

and schools of thought had become so complex as to make such rigid divisions and designations meaningless.[113] The later scholastics displayed such a wide variety of opinions, shadings, reservations, and doubts on almost every topic which they touched, that an 'orthodox' line was becoming impossible to establish. This confusion was neatly summed up by a remark of FitzRalph at the end of his own question on infinity, 'Nolo ulterius implicare me hoc sophismate quia est chaos infinitum.'[114] In the circumstances it is not difficult to sympathize with his attempts to find a safe middle road, and with those who tried to follow in his footsteps.

iv. Chancellor of Oxford University

All the available evidence indicates that during the later stages of his academic career at Oxford, FitzRalph owed much to the patronage of a man subsequently described as 'the wealthiest lord bishop that Exeter had hitherto possessed'.[1] John Grandisson, who ruled his diocese with a deep sense of commitment from 1328 until his death on 16 July 1369,[2] was the scion of an aristocratic family which owned estates in Burgundy as well as Herefordshire, and he was already described as a student of civil law on 13 February 1306 when he received at his father's request a papal dispensation to hold several benefices despite his uncanonical age of fourteen.[3] On 7 July 1312 he received additional benefices, including the archdeaconry of Nottingham, together with a dispensation to visit the latter by deputy for the next three years.[4] These benefices were presumably intended as a financial provision for his studies, and by May 1313 he was

[113] Maier, *Die Vorläufer Galileis*, p. 215.

[114] P, fol. 142va.

[1] George Oliver, *Lives of the Bishops of Exeter and a History of the Cathedral* (Exeter, 1861), p. 80. On the death of his brother Peter, Lord Grandisson, in 1358 – preceded by other members of the family – the bishop succeeded to the peerage, thereby augmenting his already substantial resources.

[2] Oliver, p. 82, gave 15 July as date of death, but Hingeston-Randolph argued for 16, on the evidence for the obsequies in *Grandisson's Register*, iii. lxvii. *BRUO* II, 801 followed the latter dating.

[3] *CPL* 1305-42, 5. He received permission to hold benefices to the value of 300 marks, including canonries in Wells and York, and on the same day his brother Thomas, also under the canonical age, was permitted to hold a canonry in Lincoln. The boys' tutor in civil law was also permitted to receive an additional benefice, ibid., 5.

[4] Ibid., 101. Five years later on the death of his brother Thomas, John was permitted to add the vacant canonry and prebend to his existing accumulation of benefices, ibid., 161.

included in a list of scholars at the University of Paris, where he studied theology under the Cistercian master and future Pope Benedict XII, Jacques Fournier, who incepted as doctor of theology no later than the academic year 1313–14.[5] From royal letters issued to Grandisson in December 1316 we know that he intended to pursue his studies in Paris for at least one more year, but there is no indication that he ever graduated either as bachelor or doctor of theology.[6] He gained the patronage of John XXII, to whom he presented a book he had written, possibly his *Life of Becket.* He was appointed a papal chaplain,[7] and on 13 November 1326 he received a papal indult for two years to have the archdeaconry of Nottingham visited by deputy.[8] Some authorities have argued that he received this dispensation in order to continue his studies and that he was at Oxford in 1326–7, thus encountering FitzRalph,[9] but the record of his activities in these years excludes the possibility of a period of study. On 27 October 1326 John XXII appointed him, together with the archbishop of Vienne and the bishop of Orange, as his nuncios to negotiate a peace settlement between Edward II and the French king Charles IV on the one hand, and to resolve the dispute between Queen Isabella and the English

[5] *Chart. Univ. Paris.*, ii. 162. On the date of the Fournier's inception as master of theology see Robert E. Lerner, 'A note on the University Career of Jacques Fournier, O. Cist., later Pope Benedict XII', *ASOC* 30 (1974), 66–9, which corrects the view that Fournier had been a Paris master by 1310 and had participated in the heresy trial of Marguerite Porete, and dates his inception to 1313–14. Bernhard Schimmelpfennig, 'Zisterzienserideal und Kirchenreform. Benedikt XII. (1334–42) als Reformpapst', *Zisterzienser-Studien*, iii (Berlin, 1977), 14, followed the older dating and maintained that Fournier became abbot of Fontfroide in 1311 shortly after inception in Paris. But the dating of Grandisson's studies in Paris, combined with the evidence of his letter to the newly elected Benedict XII 'whom he had heard as a doctor in Paris' (*Grandisson's Register*, i. 110) supports Lerner's argument that Fournier was regent in Paris after 1313–14.

[6] CPR 1313–17, 569, 573. There are an extremely large number of extant papal letters to Grandisson, but they never mention an academic title. He is not included in Glorieux, *Repertoire des maîtres en théologie de Paris au XIIIe siècle*, though it contains some names up to *c.*1320. Nor in idem, *La Faculté des arts et ses maîtres au XIIIe siècle* (Paris, 1971).

[7] He was already a papal chaplain, 7 August 1322, *CPL* 1305–42, 224. An earlier letter, incompletely dated but apparently written in August 1317, thanked Grandisson for a gift which the pope described as a compendium of edifying material, ibid., 417. Oliver, p. 85, stated that Grandisson presented a copy of his Life of Becket to Benedict XII in 1342. The work survives in manuscript in MS Bodl. 493, which belonged to Cardinal Reginald Pole, though there is no longer any trace of the copy which Grandisson donated to Exeter Cathedral Library.

[8] *CPL* 1305–42, 254. But the original letter makes no reference to Grandisson's petition as being for purposes of study, *Reg. Vat.* 82, fol. 61^r.

[9] Including Emden, *BRUO* II, 800.

factions on the other,[10] while on 3 November 1326 he received a safe-conduct from Edward II to come to England as the papal representative.[11] The registers of John XXII indicate that he continued to work in this capacity until his appointment by papal provision to the see of Exeter on 12 August 1327.[12] He was in England for most of this period, but as a papal diplomat and not as a student in Oxford. Tempting as this explanation for his connection with FitzRalph might be, it is ultimately unsatisfactory.

However, the tone of Grandisson's correspondence suggests some existing contact with the Anglo-Irish scholar before 1328–9, and we have Grandisson's own testimony that he had been a student at Oxford with William of Exeter, a royal clerk and for many years physician to Queen Philippa.[13] But William's academic career is of little help in dating Grandisson's sojourn at Oxford as William spent an unusually long time there, was master of arts by 1319, and at various stages over the next fifteen years graduated as doctor of both medicine and theology.[14] Nevertheless, it is possible that Grandisson had encountered FitzRalph there at an earlier stage of his scholastic career and that they had remained in contact. The earliest reference to FitzRalph in Grandisson's register suggests that the former was more assiduous in pursuing the contact after Grandisson's elevation to the see of Exeter, and it is possible that they met when the newly consecrated bishop was in Oxford on 17 May 1328 on his way to Exeter.[15] This reference is a curious letter, clearly written in 1328 though undated in the register. In it Grandisson referred to an earlier letter, no longer preserved, in which he had told FitzRalph not to come to Exeter because of 'certis ex causis que nostrum animum tunc movebant: earum, tamen, veritate lacius sciscitata visceraliter consolamur'.[16] Grandisson further

[10] *CPL* 1305–42, 481; *Grandisson's Register*, iii. 315–21.

[11] CPR 1324–27, 340. He was occupied on the same papal mission until the late summer of 1327, ibid., 480–4.

[12] Ibid., 482–3.

[13] *Grandisson's Register*, i. 360, where he acknowledges a debt of six marks, owed to William since they had been students together at Oxford.

[14] *BRUO* I, 659–60.

[15] Grandisson spent much of the spring of 1328 in the Oxford area. He did homage for the temporalities at York 9 March, attended parliament at Northampton, and visited his father's manor near Gloucester before setting out for Devon, where he arrived 9 June. He was in Oxford on 17 May, where he issued a licence permitting a priest of his diocese to continue his studies, *Grandisson's Register*, i. 342.

[16] Ibid., i. 173. His return to favour is further documented by Grandisson's attempts to supply him with the loan of theological books, including on 5 December (1329) a copy of the sermons of St. Augustine, ibid., i. 240.

implied that he had heard unfavourable reports about FitzRalph, had these investigated, and discovered them to be without foundation. Hence if FitzRalph was interested in being raised to orders, Grandisson had no further objections and FitzRalph should visit him in Exeter to discuss the matter further. There is no record of the date or place of FitzRalph's ordination to the priesthood, a fact which is surprising if Grandisson was the ordaining prelate. The bishop of Exeter was a model for his contemporaries, not only because of the way in which he built his cathedral, endowed its library, or provided for the poor,[17] but in the administration of his diocese. His registers are a remarkable series, displaying meticulous attention to the everyday details of diocesan life. However, in view of FitzRalph's lifelong admiration for Grandisson and, as archbishop-elect of Armagh nearly twenty years later, his choice of Grandisson as consecrating prelate and Exeter Cathedral, the nave of which had in the meantime been completed,[18] as the place of consecration, together with his conscious attempt to model his own administration on that which he had learned in Exeter, it does not seem improbable that he was ordained to the priesthood by the patron whom he had been fortunate enough to meet as a student, before he presented himself to the regent masters of the university as *bachalarius sententiarius*.

Whatever initial reservations Grandisson may have entertained about FitzRalph were clearly dispelled soon, and he sent FitzRalph as *curator* of his nephew John de Northwode, who was to continue his studies in Paris. Grandisson's letter of 4 October, which the editor of his registers dated 1329, was addressed to an unnamed ecclesiastic, who must have been of some distinction and influence in the academic world.[19] In it the bishop thanked the recipient for the honours and favours he had received personally and commended to his protection Grandisson's young

[17] Oliver, pp. 80 ff., and evidence of *Grandisson's Register*.

[18] On Grandisson's building activity see John M. Dalton, *The Collegiate Church of Ottery St Mary* (Cambridge, 1917); H. F. Fulford Williams, 'The Vestments of Bishop Grandisson now in the Azores', *Report and Transactions of the Devonshire Association*, 94 (1962), 613-22. Grandisson built most of the nave of Exeter Cathedral and began work on the west front which was finished by his successor in 1392. His part included the small chapel at the south side of the great door where he is buried, while his special reverence for Becket is illustrated in the boss depicting the martyrdom, in the nave, F. Rose-Troup, *Bishop Grandisson, Student and Booklover* (Plymouth, 1929), p. 16. He also collected ivories depicting the Becket legend, Tancred Borenius, *St Thomas in Art* (London, 1932), pp. 124-5.

[19] *Grandisson's Register*, i. 233.

nephew, a student of the University of Paris. The bishop requested that the same favours be extended to Northwode's tutor and mentor, FitzRalph, 'virum utique preclare sciencie et conversacionis honeste', of whom he further declared: 'Magister in Artibus et in Sacra Pagina egregius Bacularius inter omnes studentes et legentes Universitatis Oxoniensis eminenter dinoscitur intelligens et subtilis, prout apud vos et scolasticos vestros experiencia declarabit'.[20] The editor suggested as recipient of this letter the Cistercian cardinal, Jacques Fournier, a suggestion which would help to explain the preferment which FitzRalph received during the next pontificate. However, the tenor of the letter suggests that it was directed to a master still regent in Paris who might offer more practical guidance than could be expected from a curial cardinal and theological adviser to John XXII far away in Avignon.[21] In any case the letter makes plain that FitzRalph could avail himself of a range of contacts which an influential – though not particularly learned – alumnus of the schools of Paris might wish to place at the disposal of his relative. Northwode was still in the elementary stages of his studies and would presumably have heard lectures in the faculty of arts,[22] but what of the bachelor of theology accompanying him? Despite Oxford's claims to greater originality in some areas, Paris was still the fountain-head of theological authority, and FitzRalph never failed to grasp an opportunity when it came his way. We know that he formally registered in Paris and that he paid fees for himself and Northwode – a fragment of the Bursar's rolls from these years records that payment was

[20] Compare these remarks with John Leland, *Commentarii de Scriptoribus Britannicis*, p. 372, who recorded that FitzRalph was 'not only a finished dialectician and philosopher, but also had such a happy skill in theology that the whole University crowded to his lectures like bees to their hives'. Leland gave no source, but he may have seen a description of FitzRalph similar to that by Grandisson.

[21] Ed. cit., i. 233 n. The form of address would permit this interpretation: 'Reverende Dominacioni vestre de innumeris et immeritis beneficiis et honoribus nobis exhibitis, corditer regraciamur . . . Reverende Pater et Domine karissime . . .' But it could equally apply to Pierre Roger (the future Clement VI), whose career as student and master at Paris dated back to *c.*1307, and he could easily have known Grandisson. In 1329 Roger exchanged the bishopric of Arras for the archbishopric of Sens, and was already an influential figure in Paris, at court and in the university. See John E. Wrigley, 'Clement VI before his pontificate: the early life of Pierre Roger, 1290/91–1342', *The Catholic Historical Review*, 56 (1970), 433–73, though some of his dating was criticized in Maier, *Ausgehendes Mittelalter*, iii. 554 n.

[22] *BRUO* II, 1371–2 for Northwode's career. He was MA by 1334, master of theology at an unknown date, and chancellor of the university in 1345. His uncle maintained him in appropriate style, securing him additional benefices to cover his Oxford expenses, *Grandisson's Register*, i. 192–3.

made by 'Richardus filius Rodolphi cum discipulo suo,[23] but we do not know what lectures he attended. Unlike his charge, he presumably heard lectures in theology and may have heard the Franciscan Nicholas of Lyra, whose biblical commentaries were then attracting considerable attention in Paris.[24] But we have all too little information about this visit to Paris or the impressions which FitzRalph might have gained from the experience. Its duration cannot have been longer than one academic year, and upon his return to Oxford we find Grandisson's patronage opening up further horizons for the young scholar from Dundalk.

FitzRalph's earliest benefices, as known to us from both papal sources and from Grandisson's register, point to the same source of patronage as that which made possible the visit to Paris. On 24 May 1331 Grandisson, addressing him as 'clerico nostro familiari', granted him an annual pension of 100*s.* until it should be possible to secure for him a benefice for life in Exeter.[25] Was FitzRalph planning to settle permanently in the diocese, or was such a benefice simply intended as an income to finance a university career, which he may have considered adopting until the events of 1333-4 led him along other paths? He did not have to wait long for better things: on 1 September 1331 he received a benefice in the diocese and by 27 September he had become a canon and prebendary of Exeter Cathedral by papal provision.[26] From Grandisson's petition, of which there is an undated copy in the register,[27] we learn that the bishop sought the permission of John XXII to increase the number of canons in Exeter which, he alleged, was very small by comparison with other English cathedrals, and more canons were needed to cope with the cure of souls and the defence of the rights of his church. He then sought canonries for his nephew Northwode

[23] *Chart. Univ. Paris.*, ii. 670.

[24] Other possibilities whom FitzRalph might have heard in Paris were Jean Buridan, Nicholas d'Autrecourt, and the English Carmelite, John Baconthorpe, whom older accounts frequently mentioned as FitzRalph's teacher. However the chronology of Baconthorpe's academic career makes a direct teacher-pupil relationship improbable, though FitzRalph may have occasionally heard the Carmelite lecture. For Baconthorpe see *BRUO* I, 88-9; *BRUC* 669-70; Beryl Smalley, 'John Baconthorpe's Postill on Matthew', *Mediaeval and Renaissance Studies*, 4 (1958), 91-145; Walter Ullmann, 'John Baconthorpe as a Canonist', *Church and Government in the Middle Ages* (Cambridge, 1976), 223-46.

[25] *Grandisson's Register*, i. 616.

[26] Ibid., iii. 1286; *Reg. Vat.* 101, fol. 224^{r-v}; *CPL* 1305-42, 355. On 1 September FitzRalph was collated to the precentorship of the Collegiate Church at Crediton, but exchanged it on 3 October for a prebend in the same church.

[27] *Grandisson's Register*, i. 106-7.

and for FitzRalph who, although he is a doctor of theology, Grandisson is ashamed to have to report has not yet received a benefice.[28] FitzRalph's inception as doctor of theology can be dated to this summer of 1331, as in the letter of 24 May he was still addressed as a bachelor, but with the implication that he was being rewarded for his theological prowess and that his inception was imminent. The benefices which he received the following September were all granted to him as doctor of theology, and it is probable that Grandisson deliberately waited until FitzRalph had incepted before presenting his petition to the pope, in order to lend weight to his arguments for more canonries in his cathedral.

Thus when Grandisson went to Avignon in October 1331 and remained there for about three months, FitzRalph was almost a member of his episcopal household. But it is unlikely that FitzRalph accompanied him to the curia, as he was lecturing in Oxford as regent master during the academic year 1331–2. When he was elected chancellor of the university and confirmed in office by Bishop Burghersh of Lincoln on 30 May 1332, the bishop described him as professor of theology 'inter vos actualiter nunc regenti'.[29] We have already seen that the revised version of his *lectura* on the Sentences was a major element in his teaching activity as regent master. It is possible that he also engaged in some scriptural teaching, on the basis of which he composed his *Questio Biblica*, though the testimony of Robert Holcot, which is confirmed by the manuscript tradition,[30] would not suggest that scriptural teaching formed a major part of FitzRalph's work as regent.

His election as chancellor within a year of inception may be taken as an indication that he was held in some esteem by his peers. If this was the case, it was probably for qualities of soundness and orthodoxy, a commitment to university teaching, and a willingness to undertake administrative responsibilities, rather

[28] Ibid., 107. Dalton, *The Collegiate Church*, p. 118, incorrectly dated the collation of FitzRalph and Northwode to canonries in Exeter as 29 March 1334. However, Grandisson's successful petition to John XXII to augment the number of canonries in his cathedral met with opposition from officials of the court of Canterbury, and the bishop was forced to seek a renewal of the papal mandate providing for his two protégés. This latter document was confused by Dalton with the original provision, *Grandisson's Register*, i. 719–21.

[29] Printed in *Snappe's Formulary*, pp. 75–6.

[30] The remark in his inaugural lecture at Oxford *c.*1334 that the friars had to carry the main burden of scriptural teaching as it was neglected by others, is quoted in Smalley, *English Friars*, p. 31 n.

than because he was regarded as having made a distinctly original contribution to the intellectual life of the university. Then as now, original spirits in an academic community were rarely to be found in high administrative positions, and we may take the election as chancellor in 1335 of the powerfully-connected Robert de Stratford[31] while still a student of theology as an indication that qualifications other than seniority in the academic hierarchy were regarded as necessary for the position – especially in the difficult circumstances following the secession of masters and students from Oxford to Stamford (Lincs.) known as the Stamford Schism. Confusion among earlier historians concerning FitzRalph's tenure of the chancellorship was finally clarified by Salter's publication in 1924 of the list of confirmations of the chancellors by the bishop of Lincoln as the ordinary of the diocese in which the university was located.

The early stages of FitzRalph's two-year term of office seem to have been relatively uneventful. The long struggle between the university and the absentee archdeacon of Oxford, Cardinal Gailard Lamotte (or 'de Mota'), whereby the attempts of the cardinal's proctors to extend his authority in the archdeaconry brought him into conflict with the privileged position of the university and consequently with the chancellor, dragged on intermittently from 1325 until 1345.[32] The cardinal had initiated legal proceedings against the university in Avignon, and on two separate occasions proctors were sent to the curia to represent the university in the case. The first of these occasions, in which Simon Bredon[33] was sent as proctor, fell within Fitz-Ralph's period as chancellor, and in a letter to Bishop John de Stratford of Winchester, which must be dated before the latter's translation to Canterbury on 26 November 1333,[34] the chancellor expressed distress over the expense of a long lawsuit at the curia and referred also to the 'varias et graves vexaciones

[31] Confirmed 9 May 1335; see *Snappe's Formulary*, pp. 76–7, where he is described as a scholar in theology. He subsequently held office as keeper of the Great Seal, Chancellor of the Exchequer, and Chancellor of England, *BRUO* III, 1799–1800. His predecessor, Hugh Willoughby, who succeeded FitzRalph in office and was unsuccessful in his dealings with the Stamford secessionists, did not remain for the statutory two-year period.

[32] Charles R. L. Fletcher, 'The University and Cardinal Gailard de Mota (1325–1345)', *Collectanea*, i. 16–26.

[33] *BRUO* I, 257–8. He may have been a member of both delegations, in 1333 and again during the chancellorship of Stratford, as he is named in a letter from the university to the chancellor concerning the case, Fletcher, pp. 20–1.

[34] *HBC*², 211.

burgensium Oxonie'.[35] Already by the spring of 1333 the first signs of the impending crisis were emerging, and FitzRalph was to have the doubtful distinction of presiding over one of the most serious episodes in the history of the medieval university. The Stamford Schism occurred when a group of masters and students broke away from the main body of the university and established their headquarters at Stamford, where the Dominicans had an important convent and the Carmelites a thriving *studium particulare* for students of their own order.[36] This type of secession was nothing new in university life: there had been several during the thirteenth century, the most famous and permanent being that from Oxford to Cambridge in 1206. Others of less permanence had taken place to Northampton and Salisbury, while the Cambridge students also migrated to Northampton in 1260, to be followed three years later by a number of Oxford students who moved there during the upheavals of the baronial revolt.[37] Contemporary sources and above all, royal intervention in favour of the two by now permanently established universities, illustrate the insecurity of both Oxford and Cambridge in face of possible rival *studia*. This uneasiness and the memory of earlier secessions seem to have been the major factors in forming the attitude of the university authorities to the events of these years.

The causes of the Stamford Schism have never been satisfactorily explained. Rashdall put forward the suggestion that it had resulted from a dispute between masters and students,[38] but without specifying whether this might have been over disciplinary or intellectual questions. However, in view of the fact that as early as March 1329 there was an attempt in some episcopal circles to organize an assembly to raise funds to help the university in its struggles against the townspeople of Oxford,[39] there are stronger grounds for accepting the explanation of the Schism which became current in Oxford itself. This was that there was tension between northern and southern students, that the townspeople and especially the servants and

[35] Fletcher, p. 19.

[36] *VCH Lincoln*, ii. 226–9; *Medieval Religious Houses. England and Wales*, pp. 187, 199. On 4 June 1333 Edward III confirmed private benefactions made to the Carmelites there, and at that stage there were no signs of trouble, CPR 1330–34, 456.

[37] *Rashdall's Universities*, iii. 276, 86–88.

[38] Ibid., iii. 89, though he also conceded that it might have been caused by the Northerners, 'worsted in their battles with the Southerners'.

[39] Reg. Northburgh, ii. fol. 102^r, the bishop of Worcester appealed in March 1329 for an assembly to raise funds for this purpose.

'familiares' of the university body became involved on the side of the southern elements. Consequently a state of hostility developed between these elements in the town and a group of masters and students, presumably northerners, who felt that their lives and property were at risk. None of the extant documents make clear the issues involved and, as we shall see, the problem consisted of a mixture of various elements, including the poverty of some masters who appear to have been the victims of discrimination in the distribution of fellowships and benefices.[40] As a result a body of northern students left the university and settled in Stamford, about one hundred miles to the north-east. But it was not a secession of students only, and these were accompanied, or at least soon followed by a group of masters, who directed their studies and disputations at the rebel *studium*. The role of Merton College in the episode requires some examination. Anthony à Wood in his *Annals of the University* gave detailed consideration to the various explanations for the schism which had been put forward up to the end of the eighteenth century, and he cited as the main reason the refusal of the Fellows of Merton to admit northern scholars, as these were the alleged cause of friction between the college and the university. He further pointed out that the monks of Durham had had reason to complain about Merton in this respect,[41] and the involvement of the Durham Benedictines is by no means improbable as they owned the priory of St. Leonard's in Stamford and could send their students there.[42] Apart from Wood's account, other sources emphasized a strong link between the Stamford schismatics and Merton[43] and after the schism had been finally brought to an end its ringleader was identified by Robert de Stratford, then chancellor of the university, as one William de Barneby, a regent master and fellow of Merton.[44]

Wood had stated that the schism began in May 1334 and that further secessions took place in June and July of the same

[40] A common feature of medieval university life; see the letter of John XXII, 1 March 1317, urging all prelates as far as possible to collate benefices in their gift to masters and doctors of the University of Paris, who were often deserving cases, *Chart. Univ. Paris.*, ii. 198.

[41] See *The History and Antiquities of the University of Oxford*, i (Oxford, 1792), at 426.

[42] *Medieval Religious Houses. England and Wales*, p. 78.

[43] Especially Francis Peck, *Academia Tertia Anglia, or the Antiquarian Annals of Stamford*, xi (1727), 19, with list of the principal secessionists.

[44] Printed in *Collectanea*, i. 15–16. For Barneby, who had been a proctor in the university's case against the Dominicans in Avignon, 1317, *BRUO* I, 112.

year,[45] a dating which would have placed the entire episode outside FitzRalph's chancellorship. However, the early eighteenth-century historian of Stamford and its schools, Francis Peck, who had access to a remarkable range of sources, conjectured that the secession had probably taken place at the beginning of Michaelmas term 1333.[46] A Latin poem or satire discovered and published by Salter shows that this conjecture was correct.[47] The verses are somewhat obscure, but there can be no doubt that they came from the pen of one of the secessionists at Stamford. They must be dated no later than the spring of 1334, since they are addressed to FitzRalph as chancellor, an office which he ceased to hold on 14 May 1334 in accordance with the statutory ruling of December 1332,[48] and they were certainly written before the king's attitude to the *studium* had become known. Royal opposition to the school at Stamford was clearly expressed in an order to the sheriff of Lincoln on 2 August 1334 to go in person to Stamford and disperse the school set up there by masters and students of Oxford University 'colore quarundam dissensionum'.[49] Academic life there was obviously in full swing: not only were the secessionists studying, but the king had been informed that 'actus scholasticos exercere praesumant', and he therefore ordered the sheriff to send the secessionists back to Oxford and to proclaim throughout his bailiwick that only the two existing universities were to be recognized for purposes of study and academic acts.

The tenor of the order suggests that the school at Stamford had been in existence for some time, probably for the entire academic year 1333-4, and this would tally with the boast of the writer of the satirical verses against FitzRalph that the schism had already lasted for more than half a year. The verses throw a good deal of light on the action of the chancellor during these stormy months. The powers of the chancellor were extensive, especially as the ordinary of the diocese, whose official the chancellor theoretically was,[50] resided far away in Lincoln and

[45] As n. 41, p. 425.

[46] Peck, xi, 9, argued that a series of secessions took place between November 1333 and July 1334.

[47] *EHR* 37 (1922), 249-51, ed. from BL, MS Royal 12. D. XI, which also contained a formulary of letters written to and from the university 1330-9, which are printed in *Collectanea*, i. but incorrectly dated.

[48] *Snappe's Formulary*, p. 326.

[49] Rymer's *Foedera*, II. ii. 891. The same letter was sent to the mayor and bailiffs of Oxford.

[50] For the chancellor's powers see Herbert E. Salter (ed.), *Registrum Cancellarii Oxoniensis*, i (OHS 1932), xiii-xxvi.

was frequently a royal servant in addition to his other obligations.[51] FitzRalph was thus responsible for the good order of both town and university and he apparently felt obliged to take action as soon as the first signs of trouble emerged among the student body. The earliest documents concerning the masters' and students' grievances do not reflect any issues of northern-southern rivalry, but they do point to an atmosphere of violence in the community and to a belief that only royal intervention could solve the problem adequately. Before taking any more drastic steps these masters and students appealed to Edward III for help, and only when this petition failed to have the desired effect did they depart for Stamford. From their place of refuge they appealed to the king once more, explaining the reasons for their action. They claimed that on account of the presence in Oxford of people from various places (a veiled allusion to the separateness of the northerners?), many robberies and acts of violence were being committed, with which neither the civic authorities nor the chancellor were in a position to deal. Many masters and scholars dared not remain to study there, they feared loss of property and even death, and as a result they had removed themselves to Stamford and other centres, from which they sought royal protection.[52]

Even allowing for some exaggeration to justify their own actions, the situation they described amounted to the implication that university authority had broken down, that the surroundings were no longer conducive to study, and that neither FitzRalph, who by custom would have been classified as a southerner, nor the proctors, one of whom was by statute a northerner,[53] were in a position to offer the necessary protection of authority. The charge, if justified, was a serious one. In this petition nothing was said about a permanent settlement in Stamford, but in a further petition, known to Peck and printed in his *Annals of Stamford*, the king was informed that the secessionists had left Oxford 'a estudier et profiter plus en quiete & en pees quils ne soleient faire'.[54] According to this petition they had been at Stamford for some time and were

[51] For Burghersh as holder of office under the Crown see *BRUO* III, 2157-8, where he is included because of his association with the university, though it is doubtful if he ever studied or taught there.

[52] Their petition to this effect, dating from January or February 1334, is printed in *Collectanea*, iii. 133.

[53] Emden, 'Northerners and Southerners', 2; *Statuta Antiqua*, pp. lxxiv, 148.

[54] Peck, xi, 16.

now seeking royal approval for their school, and permission to remain there permanently. It would appear that at this point the anonymous satirical verses were composed by one of the secessionists.

The core of the satire lies in the constant allusion to a wager involving a man's head, and its editor quoted a suggestion made privately to him by A. G. Little that FitzRalph as chancellor had been misguided enough to wager his head in public against the continuance of the schism beyond six months.[55] This period had now passed and the author of the verses taunted the chancellor with the unhappy fate which must await him. If Little's suggestion is correct and this indeed was the case, the verses must be dated to the spring of 1334 and it is possible that FitzRalph had used words to this effect at the autumn meeting of Congregation, around 15 October, when the schism was still only a few weeks old, and when the principal officer of the university would naturally have tried to minimize the extent of the crisis. His embarrassment and discomfiture when it assumed greater dimensions must have been considerable, even without such taunts issued from the relative security of Stamford which lay beyond his jurisdiction and where respect for his person must have been at a low ebb.

In the opening verses of the satire FitzRalph's newly-acquired name 'Fy-Rauf' came in for unfavourable comment, together with an oblique reference to his lack of wealth upon which to base such social pretensions: he was taunted with the folly of wagering his head rather than his personal property, but from all that we know of his background and career by that date, he could have had little opportunity to accumulate any property beyond a few books and the income from a – by contemporary standards – modest accumulation of benefices since becoming doctor of theology.[56] The writer went on to boast that the new *studium* at Stamford (Vada Saxosa), far from being suppressed within six months, would get legal sanction from the king, but that this would not help FitzRalph who was in grave danger of losing his head for his folly. The next allusion is obscure, and

[55] *EHR* 37, 251.

[56] In addition to the canonry and prebend 'de la Crosse' which he held in Exeter, FitzRalph acquired, 3 April 1334, the prebend of Westbroke in the Collegiate Church of Bosham, *Grandisson's Register*, iii. 1300. On his resignation of 'de la Crosse', Thomas Pateshull was collated to it, 14 March 1335, ibid., iii. 1311. He may by then also have had provision to a canonry and prebend in Armagh Cathedral, mentioned in the bull of appointment as dean of Lichfield in 1335, *Reg. Vat.* 120, fol. 55^{r}.

FitzRalph is apparently represented as claiming knowledge of the future through observation of the course of the stars.[57] Was this perhaps intended to imply a possible argument used by the chancellor in support of his belief that the schism would last no longer than six months? Or a reference to something he had mentioned in a lecture, possibly on the topic of future contingents? One would like to know more about any possible knowledge of astronomy on FitzRalph's part and his connections with the Mertonian circle of natural scientists, as these remarks of the satirist, taken out of their original context, are not easy to interpret. Are they to be regarded as a student's imperfectly understood and inaccurately reported version of a chance remark made during a lecture, or was the misrepresentation deliberate on the satirist's part? It may have been intended as a slightly malicious allusion to a defect in FitzRalph's intellectual make-up which has already been noted, and which would not have escaped the sharp-witted students under his care, i.e. his inability to subject the physical universe to any searching analysis. The verses concluded with a triumphant affirmation that Oxford would be denuded of students, while Stamford would become a peaceful refuge for the fruitful pursuit of scholarship – a claim which is borne out by the correspondence of both Crown and university. While each opposed the *studium*, they had to concede that academic life was flourishing there.

One feature of the satire stands out, and that is its remarkable freedom from any traces of racial rancour or resentment. If the writer was a northerner, as might seem probable from the known circumstances of the schism, he did not admit to any sentiments of provincialism. Nor did he, as might have been tempting in the circumstances, taunt the chancellor with his non-English background. Irish students were a constant feature of Oxford life, and both Gaelic and Anglo-Irish were often known to be troublesome. Furthermore, sufficient details of the contemporary political scene on the other side of the Irish Sea must have penetrated to Oxford for it to be known that, whereas the Anglo-Irish town-dwellers might differentiate themselves clearly from the native Irish, they were regarded with almost equal suspicion in English government circles, even in the aftermath of the Bruce invasion when FitzRalph's native area of Dundalk had distinguished itself in loyalty to Edward II. The possible explanation that FitzRalph had during his Oxford years

[57] Ed. cit., 251.

so 'acclimatized' himself that his Irish background passed unnoticed, or that his friendship with Bishop Grandisson led to the assumption that he came from Devon, is in the circumstances unsatisfactory. FitzRalph was unequivocally known during his academic career as 'Hybernicus' and his *Commentary on the Sentences* circulated exclusively under this title, although the entire corpus of his later works circulated under the name of 'Armachanus'. Hence his Irish origins were well documented in Oxford, and it may be regarded as a mark of the good sense of late medieval university students that whereas their quarrels often savoured of 'campanilismo' or provincialism, they did not necessarily resort to academic sectarianism, even when fighting their case against superiors of a different cultural tradition.

The Stamford Schism continued during the whole of 1334 and was not finally brought to an end until Edward III, having ordered an inquiry into the issues under dispute, commissioned William de Trussel to suppress the school on 28 March 1335.[58] A small number of contemporary documents helps to piece the story together during the eighteen months which the schism lasted. In the meeting of Congregation of 14 December 1333 a statute was passed enforcing the payment of lecture fees by students of logic and physics, while a second obliged all masters of arts except those of royal or noble birth to collect their fees, because if those who did not need their salaries did not collect money for lecturing, poor masters who were obliged to teach for money, would have no students.[59] On the same day two further statutes were passed which bear even more directly on the chancellor's problems. One provided for the expulsion of any student who might in future make an assault on the person of the chancellor, while the other ordered that the chancellor should be obliged to resign his office if he was absent from the university for more than one month during term-time unless his absence was made necessary by university business.[60] This legislation seems to suggest that FitzRalph's person was exposed to physical danger during these months, and he may have considered seeking a safer place of refuge until the troubles had died down. However, nothing that we know of FitzRalph's character and methods would lead one to accuse him of cowardice –

[58] Rymer's *Foedera*, II. ii. 903–4.

[59] Edited in Henry Anstey, *Munimenta Academica* (RS 1868), i. 128–9; *Statuta Antiqua*, p. 131.

[60] Anstey, p. 127; *Statuta Antiqua*, p. 133.

rather did he have a talent for impetuous, even foolhardy action, and later disputes were to show his tenacity, as in the case against the friars, against impossible odds. Another possible explanation for this preventive legislation may be that he was considering taking the case to the papal curia, whereas the university was safeguarding its right in principle to decide in Congregation whether this course of action should be taken and when. Nor is there any indication that FitzRalph was prematurely removed from office as a result of these incidents. He remained in office for the statutory period and it would appear that when he resigned on 14 May 1334 in accordance with the statutory procedures he continued to play a part in the final settlement of the dispute.

Although Edward III on 2 August 1334 ordered the sheriff of Lincoln to disperse the scholars assembled at Stamford, and at the same time sent similar instructions to the major and bailiffs of the city of Oxford, the situation remained unchanged. The king's instructions also contained a clause requiring all those who had complaints to make concerning acts of violence within the city of Oxford to appear before the king's justices who had been specially deputed to investigate these charges. On 2 September an order was issued requiring the new chancellor and his proctors to appear before the king at Westminster, and a similar order went out to the mayor of Oxford to present himself together with four suitable representatives of the townspeople. These orders seem to suggest that the root of the matter lay in some sort of conflict between the town and the university – a frequent-enough occurrence – or at least the situation was thus interpreted by the king's advisers.[61] On 21 September, and presumably as a result of these discussions with urban and university representatives, Edward III appointed a special commission to investigate the matter. Three bishops were nominated as the royal commissioners, of whom the most prominent was the king's chancellor and recently installed bishop of Durham, Richard de Bury.[62] With him were appointed the bishop of Norwich, William Ayermine, and the long-lived Roger Northburgh of Coventry and Lichfield, whose dean FitzRalph was soon to become and in this capacity to gain valuable experience as a litigant at the papal court. Each of the three bishops were given full powers to act alone in the matter, and Bury, with whom FitzRalph was to have considerable contact over the next

[61] Rymer's *Foedera*, II. ii. 891–2.

[62] For Bury's career see *BRUO* I, 323–6.

few months, appears to have been the only one to intervene personally. He visited Oxford during October 1334 with instructions to obtain evidence from the chancellor, proctors, masters, and students of the university and to take all necessary precautions to restore order and peace in both the urban and academic communities. The mandate given to the commissioners, upon which Bury acted, also implied that the core of the dispute was to be found in dissension between 'town' and 'gown', as in the document of 20 September setting up the commission, Edward III stated that he was doing so in reply to a petition from the chancellor of the university, in which it was stated that in Oxford 'a diu est, estitit et existit inter scolares ejusdem universitatis & eorum familiares et servientes, graves dissensiones et discordiae subortae fuerant'.[63] As this must have been based directly on the petition of Hugh de Willoughby, who had succeeded FitzRalph as chancellor the previous May,[64] it can be taken as a fairly accurate representation of the situation.

One of the main problems for the university administration in the course of these troubles seems to have been the inability (or unwillingness?) of the civic authorities to bring offenders to justice, and when the former petitioned the king concerning the matter they requested that the right of arresting and detaining disturbers of the peace be temporarily transferred from the mayor and bailiffs of the city to the sheriff. The reason given is significant: the mayor and bailiffs had been found unwilling to make arrests on the denunciation of the chancellor for fear of ill-feeling in the town – 'pour peur de leur comune'.[65] But when the sheriff received these powers from the king, he too found himself unable to handle the situation. Consequently there was another petition to the king, this time from William de Spersholt, sheriff of Oxford and warden of Oxford Castle, complaining that the county gaol in the castle was full. In spite of that the chancellor, every day and without a warrant, issued orders to his beadles to arrest and deliver to the sheriff southern and northern clerks who had been committed to the chancellor's court for acts of violence and whom the chancellor wished to have imprisoned in the castle.[66] But the sheriff protested, maintaining that his gaol was full to bursting point, that real security had become impossible, and dangerous criminals could escape. Therefore he requested a royal order that no clerk

[63] Rymer's *Foedera*, II. ii. 892.

[64] For his career see *BRUO* III, 2051.

[65] *Collectanea*, iii. n° 83, 134.

[66] Ibid., n° 84, 134.

be sent to his gaol unless he be a notorious criminal who had been tried and judged in the king's courts. His petition appears to have met with little success, but it does illustrate the difficulty in such a situation of maintaining in a small community such as Oxford the separate jurisdictions of the king's courts and that of the university chancellor.[67]

The schism appears thus to have arisen because of the dual problem of relations between the town and the university on the one hand and the clash between northern and southern elements on the other, and a group of petitions dating from early in 1335 indicate that the case had not yet been resolved. These petitions, from the chancellor Hugh de Willoughby and the masters of the university to Queen Philippa, to Bishop Burghersh of Lincoln, and to the king, demonstrate that the schism was regarded as part of a wider set of *gravamina* of the university, including the case of the Cardinal de Mota and the problem of benefices for impoverished masters. The letter to Queen Philippa is dated 'le Jour de Seint Valentin', which is unquestionably to be dated to 14 February 1335, since it requested her to commend her 'petite Universite de Oxenford' to the newly-elected pope Benedict XII.[68] The university also lamented its poverty, reminded her of her generosity in the past, and requested her to write to Cardinal de Mota to plead for a settlement granting the university its rights. At about the same time the chancellor and masters wrote to the bishop of Lincoln, informing him of their decision to send 'certos nostros nuncios' to the new pope to seek favours which might assist the university in its difficulties. Here again the poverty of the university was stressed, presumably with the intention of implying its inability to pay for lengthy litigation at the curia. The bishop was asked to seek support from the king to the pope and to anybody else who might help, and especially to intervene with Cardinal de Mota. He was also requested to use his influence with the king to bring the Stamford Schism to an end, and in this context the university authorities described the secessionists as 'filii degeneres, quos dicta Universitats de pulvere produxit in viros et honoribus quamplurimis decoravit'.[69] Evidently the secessionists could count some distinguished scholars among their ranks, which

[67] On the competence of the various jurisdictions see *Rashdall's Universities*, iii. 81 ff.

[68] Text in *Collectanea*, i. 8–9, but mistakenly dated 14 February 1334.

[69] Ibid., 9–10.

probably helps to explain their ability to survive for so long in defiance of university and royal authority. The third petition from the university was addressed directly to the king, who was requested to write to Cardinal de Mota, and also to the pope on behalf of poor masters – the papacy should not hand out English benefices indiscriminately, but should use them to finance impoverished teaching masters in Oxford.[70] This petition concluded with a plea to the king to put an end to the rival studium at Stamford:

reliquum siquidem malum quod per omnem modum nocivum et pestiferum arbitramur, novum scilicet concursum scolarium ad oppidum Stanfordie pretextu scolastice discipline, quod fortassis quia tam in dispendium studii nostri quam in tocius Regni discordiarum seminarium generale redundare presumitur per potenciam Regiam obsecramus et petimus extirpare, ut quod improvida temeritate fuerat incohatum, per providenciam Regiam ad malorum futurorum cautelas cicius finiatur.[71]

At last the king took decisive action by sending William de Trussel in March 1335 with a mandate to conduct a full inquiry into the situation.[72] Trussel's orders were almost a literal repetition of those issued to the sheriff of Lincoln in August 1334. The latter had plainly failed to take effective measures against the secessionists, but Trussel was more peremptory. He went to Stamford accompanied by the sheriff and ejected the students. But as soon as he had left the town they were reinstalled, encouraged by the citizens of Stamford who did not wish to lose their new-found source of income.[73] Edward III was no longer willing to tolerate such insubordination and Trussel was ordered to return to Stamford. On 25 July 1335 the property of all scholars there was confiscated for the king's use, while a list of the principal offenders was prepared and dispatched to the king. In all the list contained thirty-eight names: seventeen masters, one bachelor, fourteen students, and six parish priests.[74] First on the list was William de Barneby, who was evidently considered the master-mind behind the schism. A regent master of some seniority at Merton, he had in 1317 represented the university in Avignon as a proctor in the case against the Dominicans. As a penalty for his activities in Stamford he was deprived of his degree in Oxford, and two years later it was rumoured that he wished to incept in Cambridge, whereupon the chancellor, Robert de Stratford, wrote to the authorities in the sister

[70] Ibid., 10–11. [71] Ibid. [72] Rymer's *Foedera*, II. ii. 903–4.
[73] Peck, xi, 18–19. [74] Listed ibid., 19.

university, warning them against this 'incentor precipuus periculosi dissidii pridem in Universitate suscitati'. According to Stratford, Barneby had been principally responsible for the Stamford affair, and Cambridge should treat him as a convicted perjurer (the subject of alleged perjury is not more precisely defined) and close its doors against this rebel.[75] One can only speculate on the reasons for such harsh treatment and on Barneby's motives. Was he moved to protest against his college's exclusive attitude towards northern trouble-makers?

Meanwhile the king paid a visit to Stamford, staying briefly at the Dominican convent and ensuring that his orders were effectively carried out.[76] One might query whether the decisive action finally taken by Edward III in the spring and summer of 1335 was not connected with the announced intention of the university to send representatives to consult with Benedict XII on the matter.[77] That FitzRalph is to be counted among these 'nuncii', if not the sole spokesman for the university who actually went to the curia at this point, seems probable. In the final analysis the Stamford Schism, far from clouding his term of office as chancellor, appears to have added to his standing. Soon after he laid down the office he was collated on 10 July 1334 to the chancellorship of Lincoln on the recommendation of Bishop Burghersh, thereby suggesting that the diocesan ordinary responsible for the university had no reservations about FitzRalph's handling of the situation, but opposition from the dean and chapter of Lincoln prevented his formal inauguration and he never succeeded in making good his claim to the office.

At the same time he is recorded in the well-known passage by William de Chambre as being one of the distinguished Oxford scholars who frequented the London household of the chancellor of England and king's treasurer, Richard de Bury. FitzRalph's contact with the powerful bishop of Durham may have originated at an earlier stage, but the circumstances of the Stamford Schism certainly provided him with closer access to yet another powerful English ecclesiastic with contacts at the papal curia. Nor did FitzRalph lack royal favour in the following decades, despite a clash over a Lichfield benefice for one of the

[75] *Collectanea*, i. 15-16. [76] *VCH Lincoln*, ii. 227.

[77] Also in the summer of 1335, on 6 June the king issued instructions to the chancellor that Oxford students be neither permitted to wear arms within the city precincts nor keep them in their lodgings, a more drastic prohibition than the compromise solution of 1313, *Collectanea*, i. 14.

king's clerks, and although Edward III was to utter some sharp words about the archbishop of Armagh in the 1350s and attempt to curb his activities, this was due more to the ties of patronage and friendship which bound both Edward and his queen to the mendicant orders than to any long royal memory of troubles involving FitzRalph twenty years earlier. Most important, the schism provided at least one reason for FitzRalph's first visit to Avignon, where curial contacts and papal patronage were to have a decisive effect on his subsequent career.

II Avignon

i. The beatific vision controversy

When FitzRalph arrived at Avignon during the later months of 1334 the city on the Rhone was not yet the cultural crossroads of western Christendom which it would become during the pontificate of Clement VI (1342–52), when the papal building programme and intensive cultivation of the visual and literary arts lent it a distinction unique in mid-fourteenth-century Europe. However, the city was already something more than a temporary administrative centre for the papacy, its bureaucratic structure, and its courts of law.[1] Petrarch had arrived there in 1326 and was in the service of Cardinal Giovanni Colonna when Richard de Bury, in Avignon as ambassador of Edward III, made contact with him in the summer of 1333.[2] Although Petrarch recorded the meeting in his *Epistolae ad Familiares,*[3] there is no indication that it had any serious implications for the beginnings of English humanism – the mendicant doctors around Bury in London continued to use the classics for their own purposes without any indication of awareness of Petrarch's new approach to classical scholarship.[4] Despite the advice given to John Lutterell about the promising openings for theologians at the curia, the main functions of the papal court were necessarily legal and administrative, and both in the creation of cardinals and in the selection of their 'familiares', who were also invested with curial offices, the strong preponderance of lawyers is clearly in evidence.[5]

[1] Guillemain, *La Cour pontificale*; for descriptions of living conditions in the city under John XXII see letters of Aragonese ambassadors to Jaume II, Finke, *Acta Aragonensia*, ii. 224–7, 396–7.

[2] See N. Denholm-Young, 'Richard de Bury (1287–1345)', *TRHS* 4th ser. 20 (1937), 135–68.

[3] Ed. Vittorio Rossi (1933), iii. 1. Although Petrarch complained that his questions often met with total silence, because Bury either could not or would not answer him, he nevertheless described Bury as 'vir ardentis ingenii nec litterarum inscius abditarum rerum ab adolescentia supra fidem curiosus', ed. cit., 106.

[4] Smalley, *English Friars*, pp. 5–8, 280–307, on the difference between English 'classicism' and Italian 'humanism' in the 14th century.

[5] Guillaume Mollat, 'Contribution à l'histoire du Sacré Collège de Clément V à Eugène IV', *RHE* 46 (1951), 32–3; and for a representative case, Norman P. Zacour, 'Talleyrand: the Cardinal of Périgord (1301–64)', *Tr.Am.Phil.Soc.* n.s. 50, pt. 7 (1960), 1–83.

Despite the cosmopolitan atmosphere at the curia where most countries were permanently represented, few Englishmen tended to remain there for any length of time, though a small number of English lawyers and theologians are recorded as having spent longer periods there.[6]

Even the University of Avignon, in existence since 1303, was heavily weighted in the direction of legal studies, while the study of theology remained the preserve of the *studium* attached to the curia which, before the period of papal residence in Avignon, itinerated with the papal household. This *studium* was intended as an organ for the transmission of orthodox dogma under immediate papal jurisdiction and was considerably strengthened – paradoxically – during the celebrated controversies in which the orthodoxy of the pope himself was at issue. Above all during the pontificate of John XXII (1316–34), a lawyer by training and inclination who developed an interest in speculative theology during the later years of his life, the study of theology and ancillary disciplines at the curia acquired an added impetus, partly in response to the dispute about the beatific vision and partly with a view to preparing missionaries through the study of eastern languages and theology.[7] John's interest has often been dismissed by historians as the dabblings of an old man, trained in the law but not in theology, in areas beyond his competence – a view not supported by recent research, which reveals the extent to which he took pains to inform himself in theological problems by private study.[8] Also during this pontificate, and primarily in the course of debate about Franciscan poverty,

[6] Guillemain, *La Cour pontificale*, p. 612. FitzRalph was the only exception he recognized, though an equally long-standing resident in Avignon was the Carmelite procurator-general and later archbishop of Cashel, Ralph Kelly. For English lawyers in Avignon in the 1340s see Michael J. Haren, 'A Study of the "Memoriale Presbyterorum", a fourteenth-century confessional manual for parish priests', 2 vols. (MS D.Phil. d. 6097–8, Oxford, 1975), i. 30–1.

[7] *Acta Ioannis XXII (1317–34), passim*, for his constant preoccupation with the Christian East. For the application of legislation promoting such studies see Roberto Weiss, 'England and the decree of the Council of Vienne on the teaching of Greek, Arabic, Hebrew and Syriac'; idem, 'The study of Greek in England in the fourteenth century', *Medieval and Humanist Greek*, respectively pp. 68–79, 80–107. To the examples cited there, 71 ff. for the provision of teachers of Hebrew in England, especially at Oxford, should be added the contribution of Wells Cathedral chapter, Hist. MSS Comm. IX. report, p. 208. Before his elevation to the see of Exeter, Grandisson was a canon of Wells, and his interest in Hebrew is documented in the possession of a Hebrew Pentateuch (now Westminster Abbey, MS 1) and a Hebrew–French vocabulary with Latin glosses (now Bodl., MS Hebr. 1466).

[8] Maier, 'Annotazioni autografe di Giovanni XXII in codici vaticani', *Ausgehendes Mittelalter*, ii. 81–96.

the view that the pope possessed a key of knowledge ('clavis scientie') was being used to develop the idea of papal infallibility, not by the canonist theorists of papal sovereignty, but rather by their largely Franciscan opponents.[9] Contrary to older research, it has been recently demonstrated that John XXII did not claim for himself the key of knowledge which would give him the power to decide in matters of doctrine and make pronouncements which were intrinsically irrevocable; that he understood clearly that he, as pope, was bound by the articles of faith as set out in Scripture, and that his canonistic theory of papal sovereignty left no room for a theology of papal infallibility.[10] These contentions are further reinforced by the pope's willingness to seek as many opinions as possible on the orthodoxy or otherwise of his own interpretation of the vision of God enjoyed by the blessed before the Last Judgement.

By the time of FitzRalph's first sojourn at the curia from 1334 to 1336, the number of lawyers, administrative and legal clerks, proctors, and visitors pursuing in person their claims to benefices or engaging in other forms of litigation, was substantially augmented by theologians whose views were being sought by the pope in this, his most recent and most serious theological dilemma. The controversy about the nature of the beatific vision enjoyed by the just immediately after death and before the Last Judgement, in which FitzRalph also became involved, was a burning issue not only at the curia but also in the universities, not least because of the possible implications of a heretical pope.[11] The controversy surrounding Franciscan interpretations of the poverty of Christ and the implications of their views for the visible structure of the hierarchical Church had resulted in a series of papal condemnations. These undermined not merely the extreme doctrine of poverty held by the Spiritual Franciscans and Fraticelli, but also that of the main body of the order, the Conventuals, which had been approved by Nicholas III in *Exiit qui seminat* in August 1279 and which, the Franciscans claimed, had been accepted as valid dogma by the universal

[9] Malcolm D. Lambert, 'The Franciscan Crisis under John XXII', *FS* 32 (1972), 123–43, argued that the pope's attitude to the order was less indefensible than Manselli and E. Pásztor had been prepared to allow; see also Brian Tierney, *Origins of Papal Infallibility 1150–1350* (Leiden, 1972), pp. 172 ff. for a more positive view of John XXII's actions.

[10] Ibid., pp. 189–94.

[11] Ockham, writing his *Tractatus contra Ioannem* from Munich, was aware of these implications, ed. H. S. Offler, *Opera Politica*, iii (Manchester, 1956), 49, 65, 67, 140, 152, and Tierney, pp. 214–34.

Church.[12] The discussions leading to these condemnations had represented John XXII's first public venture into the realms of theological debate, and here he had stressed his juridical sovereignty rather than the papal capacity for dogmatic definitions, and consequently found essentially legal solutions which did not fully meet the theological aspects of the problem.[13] On that occasion, in sharp contrast to the subsequent discussions about the beatific vision, he had on his side the bulk of learned opinion, not only that of secular theologians and members of the older endowed monastic orders who had always viewed the mendicant way of life with scepticism, but also that of many friar-doctors from other mendicant orders.[14]

In many respects John XXII was theologically unadventurous, and his characteristic remark in a letter of 18 January 1331 that it was more fitting to imitate the purity of the Blessed Virgin than to engage in speculation about it,[15] was a calculated side-swipe at those debating the theology of the Immaculate Conception. He himself usually took the precaution of putting doubtful propositions before a commission of theologians before making an official pronouncement.[16] But he was also a frequent and a good preacher, if occasionally imprudent in his choice of words. On solemn feasts it was his custom to preach before a curial audience, when he would expound upon and attempt to solve disputed theological problems. The theologians among his audience appear to have become accustomed to the often paradoxical remarks which he threw out in the course of these sermons and tended to lend them a deaf ear – until protest from outside, and from a particularly challenging quarter, forced them to take issue in this case, even though the pope's view was not intended as an official pronouncement.[17] The 'rebel' Franciscans, including the former minister-general, Michael of

[12] Discussed in Lambert, and Tierney, pp. 173–82. [13] Tierney, p. 190.

[14] For Augustinian participation in the dispute see Fulgence A. Mathes, 'The Poverty Movement and the Augustinian Hermits', *AA* 31 (1968), 136–47; the Dominican general Hervaeus Natalis opposed the Franciscan concept of poverty, Kaeppeli, *Script. O.P.* ii. 242, as did the former Carmelite general Guido Terrena, see Bartomeu M. Xiberta, *Guiu Terrena, carmelita de Perpignà* (Barcelona, 1932); Thomas Turley, 'Guido Terreni and the Decretum', *Bulletin of Medieval Canon Law*, n.s. 8 (1978), 29–34.

[15] Cited in Guillemain, *La Cour pontificale*, p. 131.

[16] The function of such commissions in providing expert advice on doubtful propositions is illustrated in Koch, 'Der Kardinal Jacques Fournier (Benedikt XII.) als Gutachter in theologischen Prozessen', *Kleine Schriften*, ii. 367–86.

[17] Marc Dykmans, *Les Sermons de Jean XXII sur la vision béatifique* (Rome, 1973). p. 12 '. . . les théologiens de curie savaient fermer l'oreille.'

Cesena, the canonist Bonagratia of Bergamo, and William of Ockham, who had taken refuge in Munich at the court of Ludwig the Bavarian, had already been arguing that the pope who revoked a decree of his predecessor and condemned what they considered to be not merely a fundamental principle of their order but a dogma of the Church, was a heretic and had forfeited all claims to obedience.[18] They now seized on the latest papal exposition as further proof of their claim.

In the sermons preached on the feast of All Saints, 1 November and 15 December 1331, 5 January and 2 February 1332, and 25 March 1332/3,[19] John XXII developed a doctrine of the beatific vision which was widely denounced as erroneous and unorthodox. While he accepted that there were two Judgements, a particular and a general, he argued that after the first the blessed saw only the humanity of Christ and not the vision of the Deity face to face. He argued that the souls of the blessed were still in an imperfect state until the resurrection of the body and Last Judgement, hence they could only enjoy in their imperfect state a peace and happiness caused by the contemplation of the humanity of Christ. For this view he adduced both a philosophical and a theological reason, the first that the soul as an imperfect being cannot claim a perfect reward, the second that the Last Judgement, according to Scripture (Apoc. xx. 4-6), seems to mark a change in the fate of the blessed, opening up for them the true kingdom of heaven.[20] In the first sermon John based his view on the authority of Bernard of Clairvaux, who had expressed similar sentiments in the course of his sermons, and the pope was careful to state that his and Bernard's interpretation was an opinion.[21] Clearly the first sermon caused unfavourable comment, and in the subsequent sermons the pope was concerned to present an array of scriptural and patristic authorities, especially that of St. Augustine, in support of his view. But he continued to insist that the question was open, and if he was mistaken he wished the subject to be clarified on the basis of Scripture and the teaching of the Church.[22] Despite his caution his views were transmitted to Munich as further proof

[18] Ibid., pp. 165-97, for a chronology of the controversy and the contributions to it.

[19] Edited ibid., pp. 85-161. [20] Ibid., pp. 93-4. [21] Ibid., p. 99.

[22] Ibid., p. 152; J. E. Weakland, 'Pope John XXII and the Beatific Vision controversy', *Annuale Medievale,* 19 (1968), 76-84; Joseph N. Tylenda, 'Calvin and the Avignon sermons of John XXII', *ITQ* 41 (1974), 37-52. The latter shows how Calvin totally misunderstood John XXII's opinions.

of his heresy, while at the same time they became the subject of debate in the schools, and the issue became a controversy of major proportions.

It has been the subject of a remarkable amount of recent research, principally from the pens of the late Anneliese Maier, whose work concentrated on the largely Dominican-inspired opposition which the pope's views engendered in curial and theological circles, and of Fr. Marc Dykmans, who has been mainly concerned with the views actually expressed by John XXII in his sermons, with the minority who supported him, and with the origins and subsequent fate of the disputed doctrine.[23] In spite of the impressive amount of manuscript literature which each has discovered, analysed, and to some extent edited, their various contributions have been something of a running debate, and consequently their findings have not yet been synthesized in convenient form. Hence it is necessary to survey briefly here the development of the issue, in order to explain the involvement of FitzRalph and the subsequent preferment which he received at the hands of John XXII's immediate successors, both of whom participated actively in the dispute.

The concern aroused by the papal deviation from accepted teaching, which even if it was not defined dogma was nevertheless the traditional common understanding, was not limited to those actually present, and soon the matter was being debated, not only in Munich, but also at the court of Robert d'Anjou in Naples, where once more the king felt himself compelled to commit to paper his dissatisfaction with the papal teaching,[24] and in Paris, whose theologians were, according to the French king, Philip VI, the proper judges of orthodoxy in doctrinal matters: these ought not to be left in the hands of curial lawyers.[25] The main problem caused by the pope's view, according to current opinion, was that it involved accepting the theory that the humanity and divinity of Christ were divisible, i.e. the Nestorian heresy, and that one could have the vision of the humanity without that of the deity. Hence the question of the

[23] Maier's more important contributions are printed in *Ausgehendes Mittelalter*, iii. 319–590. See also Dykmans, *Pour et contre Jean XXII en 1333. Deux traités avignonnais sur la vision béatifique* (Città del Vaticano, 1975), at p. 11, a list of his contributions to the controversy.

[24] Idem, *Robert d'Anjou: la vision bienheureuse. Traité envoyé au pape Jean XXII* (Rome, 1970).

[25] Maier, 'Die Pariser Disputation des Geraldus Odonis über die Visio Beatifica Dei', *Ausgehendes Mittelalter*, iii. 326.

indivisibility of the two natures of Christ, which became a significant issue in the debates with the Armenians,[26] had already become a subject of controversy in the early 1330s. Despite the pope's protests that it was possible to have vision of the humanity without in any way jeopardizing or questioning the dual-nature doctrine, members of the Dominican order were quick to point out the heterodox origins of the views being propounded. Initially Giovanni Regina da Napoli stressed that the erroneous doctrine was held by the Greek churches, a point subsequently repeated by the English Dominican Thomas Waleys in the famous sermon preached in the church of his order at Avignon on 3 January 1333 which landed him in the Inquisitor's prison.[27] The Dominican bishop of Meaux, Durandus de Saint-Pourçain, no longer resident at the curia but summoned back by John XXII in order to express his opinion, stated in effect that the doctrine being propounded by the pope was the same as that taught by the Cathars and persecuted by John's predecessors over a century earlier.[28]

Much of the support which John XXII attracted came from those members of the Franciscan order who had remained loyal to him in spite of the dissensions over the doctrine of evangelical poverty and even in spite of the cloud which hung over their most talented and original theologian, William of Ockham, now in Munich. Adherents of John's view included the new minister-general of the Franciscans, Guiral Ot, whose *disputatio* before the assembled Paris theologians in the autumn of 1333 was far from being a piece of slavish flattery of the pope, but was a

[26] For FitzRalph's contribution during the later debates see *Summa*, esp. Bk. I: S, fols. 2ra-6vb; Vat. Lat. 1033, fols. 1^{r}-7^{r}; Vat. Lat. 1035, fols. 1rb-8ra.

[27] On the former see Kaeppeli, 'Note sugli scrittori domenicani di nome Giovanni di Napoli', *AFP* 10 (1940), 48-76; idem, *Script. O.P.*, ii. 495-8; Maier, 'Zur Textüberlieferung einiger Gutachten des Johannes de Napoli', *Ausgehendes Mittelalter*, iii. 481-504. On Waleys, Kaeppeli, *Le Procès contre Thomas Waleys O.P. Études et documents* (Rome, 1936). The sermon is edited, pp. 93-108. Towards the end of February 1333 John XXII wrote to the French king arguing that Waleys was not imprisoned for his views on the beatific vision, but for other errors, Dykmans, *Les Sermons de Jean XXII*, pp. 173-4. Idem, 'À Propos de Jean XXII et de Benoît XII. La libération de Thomas Waleys', *AHP* 7 (1969), 127, argued that the decision to release Waleys in the summer of 1334 was the beginning of the pope's retraction of his own view.

[28] Idem, 'De Jean XXII au concile de Florence ou les avatars d'une hérésie gréco-latine', *RHE* 68 (1973), 30-9. For Durandus see Koch, *Durandus de S. Porciano* (Münster, 1927); idem, 'Die Magister-Jahre des Durandus de S. Porciano O.P. und der Konflikt mit seinem Orden', *Kleine Schriften*, ii. 7-118. The text of his opinion is in Vat. Lat. 4006, fols. 307^{r}-312^{r}. His views were consistent with 13th-century anti-Greek polemic among Dominicans, Antoine Dondaine, ' "Contra Grecos". Premiers écrits polémiques des dominicains d'Orient', *AFP* 21 (1951), 320-446.

discriminating analysis of the entire problem. In the face of opposition from the theologians who had been summoned for the occasion by Philip VI, Ot's views underwent some development and refinement, and he ended by arguing basically for three different kinds of vision, allowing the souls of the blessed immediately after death a vision of God which was less perfect than the 'visio eterna' which they would enjoy only after the Last Judgement.[29] This view, with some variation of emphasis and degree, gained the private support of the two men who succeeded John XXII in the papacy, Jacques Fournier and Pierre Roger, the latter also a former professor of theology at the Sorbonne and now as archbishop of Rouen and French ambassador to the papal curia, a frequent visitor to Avignon while the controversy was raging.[30] This middle course, in the version expounded by Fournier and others, allowed the possibility of a 'duplex visio', of which that vision enjoyed after the Last Judgement was the more perfect and complete. But it did not imply that the previous vision was not a vision of God, but rather a diminished capacity of the soul to perceive and appreciate God's divinity. When Fournier as Benedict XII published *Benedictus Deus* (29 January 1336) this version was not condemned but simply ignored and was allowed to remain as tacitly accepted within the boundaries of orthodoxy.[31] FitzRalph publicly declared his opposition to the pope's opinion in terms which seem not to permit such a compromise solution, but as the revision of his Oxford *lectura* also involved some reconsideration on his part of the soul's capacity for beatitude, it is possible that at this stage he may have shared to some extent the view represented by Fournier. The latter's private views differed, however, in important respects from the interpretation which was published early in his pontificate, after consultation with a commission of theologians which included FitzRalph.[32] This formulation in *Benedictus Deus* made no concessions to the Greek and Armenian interpretations, and it had a profound

[29] Maier, 'Die Pariser Disputation des Geraldus Odonis', *Ausgehendes Mittelalter*, iii. 327-33.

[30] Dykmans, 'La libération de Thomas Waleys', 127-8, for the sermon preached by Pierre Roger in the Dominican convent in Paris before the university orators, passionately opposing the papal view. Idem, *Les Sermons de Jean XXII*, pp. 167 ff., for Roger's numerous interventions in the case.

[31] For Benedict's contributions as a cardinal see Maier, 'Zwei Prooemien Benedikts XII.', *Ausgehendes Mittelalter*, iii. 447-89.

[32] For the members, *Chart. Univ. Paris.*, ii. 454.

effect on East–West relations and on the fate of the reunion negotiations over the subsequent decade.[33]

Two English Franciscans at the curia joined in the debate but, unlike most of the Dominicans, they supported the papal case, and they led Dykmans to posit a pro-papal Franciscan front in opposition to the group of Dominicans studied by Anneliese Maier.[34] William of Alnwick had had a long career of anti-papal activity, both in support of Philip the Fair against Boniface VIII and in defence of Franciscan poverty against John XXII, when his trenchant criticism of papal policy compelled him to avail himself of the protection of Robert of Naples. He had meanwhile been reconciled with the pope and was rewarded in 1329 with the bishopric of Giovinazzo in southern Italy.[35] Also on the papal side was his younger confrère, Walter of Chatton, who had been a regent master in Oxford slightly before FitzRalph and had departed for Avignon no later than the spring of 1333. He took part in a number of consultations about the beatific vision under John XXII and Benedict XII, displaying in the process great animosity towards the Dominican critic of the papal view, Thomas Waleys.[36] John Lutterell was still in residence in Avignon as a papal theological adviser, having presumably followed the advice given to him over a decade earlier, and he also wrote in support of the papal view in the summer of 1333. He appears to have helped to formulate the pope's arguments during the later stages of the controversy. However, Lutterell took the content of his own arguments from the archbishop of Naples, Cardinal Annibale de Ceccano, who together with his chaplain Gaspert de Laval, a Cluniac monk from La Charité-sur-Loire, Francesco C(h)ristiani, and the Cistercian abbot of Casamari, wrote and preached diligently in favour of the pope.[37] Ceccano

[33] Dykmans, 'De Jean XXII au concile de Florence', 47.

[34] Idem, 'Le Dernier sermon de Guillaume d'Alnwick', *AFH* 63 (1970), 259–79; 'Les Frères Mineurs d'Avignon au début de 1333 et le sermon de Gautier de Chatton sur la vision béatifique', *AHDLMA* 38 (1971), 232–53.

[35] Idem, 'Le Dernier sermon', 259; *BRUO* I, 27. His sermon survives only as a fragment, ed. in Dykmans, art. cit., 269–79.

[36] For Chatton, *BRUO* I, 395–6; Courtenay, *Adam Wodeham*, pp. 66–74; Dykmans, as n. 34.

[37] Dykmans, 'Le Cardinal Annibal de Ceccano et la vision béatifique', *Gregorianum*, 50 (1969), 343–82; 'Le Cardinal Annibal de Ceccano (vers 1284–1350), étude biographique', *Bulletin de l'institut historique belge*, 43 (1973), 145–344; for the text of Ceccano's defence of John XXII, idem, *Pour et contre Jean XXII*, pp. 59–166. Ceccano held a number of English benefices, *CPL* 1305–42, 379, 384–5. Lutterell's contribution, the *Epistola de visione beatifica*, is edited in Hoffmann, *Die Schriften des Oxforder Kanzlers*, pp. 103–119.

was one of the first of the theologians at the curia to compromise himself by coming out openly in support of the papal view, for which he was in the short term amply repaid with a number of important benefices *in commenda* and the cardinal bishopric of Tusculum-Frascati, although in the testament composed shortly before his death in 1350, he had to retract a number of questionable views on the Church, the Trinity, evangelical poverty, and the beatific vision.[38]

A Franciscan, tentatively identified as Walter Chatton,[39] preached in Avignon on 13 December 1332 in favour of the papal view, and in response to this sermon Waleys came out in opposition, accusing the pope's supporters of being mere flatterers, as did his Oxford confrère Robert Holcot in lectures on the Sapiential books 1333-4.[40] Waleys was taken into the custody of the Inquisition on papal orders. Although John XXII insisted that Waleys was being investigated for other reasons, he ordered a commission of theologians to investigate Waleys's sermon, together with opinions on the beatific vision problem by Durandus de S. Pourçain and by Cardinal Fournier, which the pope had requested but which turned out to be in opposition to the papal view. The commission, chaired by Cardinal Annibale, picked out a few theses of both Durandus and Waleys dealing with minor matters not directly relevant to the beatific vision, and with qualifications described these as erroneous but not heretical. But a decision in favour of the papal view could not be achieved,[41] whereupon John XXII wrote around Europe ordering the topic to be examined in formal disputations and seeking opinions. Concerning the Paris disputations the evidence is substantial, but the situation in the English universities is less clear. There are several indications that the question was discussed there, but no precise details. Ceccano referred in his treatise, to a 'magister . . . qui determinavit in Anglia',[42] and Maier argued that this referred to FitzRalph, that he had discussed the matter in an Oxford disputation, that the pope – who was well informed about events and opinions in Oxford – heard about it and asked him for a written version, and that

[38] Dykmans, 'Étude biographique', 281-2; 'Annibal de Ceccano et la vision béatifique', 343.

[39] Ibid., 346.

[40] Smalley, *English Friars*, p. 141.

[41] Maier, 'Zu einigen Disputationen aus dem Visio-Streit', *Ausgehendes Mittelalter*, iii. 416-17.

[42] Ed. cit., p. 149.

FitzRalph *sent* this to Avignon in 1332 or early 1333.[43] Against this Dykmans argued that FitzRalph came to Avignon after May 1334 and before the death of John XXII on 4 December 1334, and participated in the discussions in person, having previously in England maintained in a university disputation the imperfection of the beatific vision before the Last Judgement.[44] We know further that an English Franciscan, Richard de Chassam, sought permission to go to England on business and that he held a university disputation there, but its topic is unknown.[45] On 5 September 1334 John XXII issued letters to the Cistercian abbot of Combe, John Brid, whom he had appointed bishop of Cloyne the previous year in spite of the expressed wish of Edward III that the see be united with Cork.[46] Brid was a member of papal theological commissions and his letters were addressed to the faculty of theology in Cambridge concerning a confidential matter which was to be explained verbally. The possibility that the pope wished to secure the faculty's approval for his views, or at least to hear the opinion of the Cambridge theologians, who in this period were less frequently represented at Avignon than those from Oxford, deserves consideration, but further information is unfortunately not available.

At the same time the pope requested every theologian who came to the curia on business to give his opinion and refused them permission to leave until his request had been complied with, as in the case of Thomas Poucyn, abbot-elect of St. Augustine's Canterbury, a doctor of theology and possessor of a rich library of scholastic works, who came to get confirmation of his office.[47] He duly got it on 3 June 1334, but was not permitted to leave Avignon until he had expressed himself on the burning

[43] Maier, 'Schriften, Daten und Personen aus dem Visio-Streit unter Johann XXII', *Ausgehendes Mittelalter*, iii. 559–61.

[44] 'Annibal Ceccano et la vision béatifique', 372. In 'La libération de Thomas Waleys', 127, he had argued that FitzRalph and a Benedictine abbot (Thomas Poucyn?, below, n. 47) had presented written opinions to the pope, a view based on the discovery of an anonymous text which he was then inclined to attribute to FitzRalph, but whose authorship he has since rejected (private communication of Fr. Dykmans).

[45] For his mission to England 'pro negotiis et libris missus est', *Chart. Univ. Paris.*, ii. 454n., and Dykmans, 'Annibal Ceccano et la vision béatifique', 371. John XXII may have sent him to seek written opinions.

[46] Dykmans, art. cit., pp. 371–2. The former abbot of Combe (in the diocese of Lichfield) had been consecrated in Avignon by Ceccano before 11 August 1333, *CPL* 1305–42, 384.

[47] *BRUO* III, 1508, probably the Benedictine abbot who wrote on the topic in summer 1334 in Avignon. For the assistance he gave to Waleys, lecturing and writing in his defence and procuring books for him from the papal library see Pantin, *The English Church in the fourteenth century*, p. 121.

topic. This he finally did, and with some reluctance stated his opposition to the papal view, and also expressed his solidarity with the position of Thomas Waleys.[48] FitzRalph appears to have found himself in a similar situation when he arrived at the curia and came in contact with John XXII. Whatever the original motives for the visit – whether in order to present the case of his university and justify his handling of the difficult situation which had arisen during his term of office as chancellor, or to attempt to surmount the opposition from the dean and chapter of Lincoln which was preventing him from taking possession of the chancellorship of that diocese in spite of the recommendations of Bishop Burghersh, or a combination of several motives – it is clear from his own statement that he had arrived in Avignon while John XXII was still alive, whereupon the pope had requested him to set down in writing his own views on the beatific vision. He duly did so and delivered into the pope's own hands an opinion that the souls of the just enter into their full reward as soon as they have made complete satisfaction and not only after the Last Judgement.[49] Unfortunately no such statement or treatise has survived from the pen of FitzRalph and we can only seek to reconstruct his views and his position in the controversy from other writings and sermons in which he touched upon the matter.

During his original course of lectures on the Sentences, delivered in Oxford before the topic had become a matter of general concern, there had been no particular reason for FitzRalph to have made it a subject for detailed discussion, and even in the revised version contained in the extant manuscripts the specific issue raised by the pope had not yet become a burning question in the schools. However, because of FitzRalph's strong concentration on the mind and its faculties, he had been obliged to consider whether knowledge was controlled by the will. In this context he argued that the blessed in heaven, who have seen God clearly, may be absolutely necessitated to will what He reveals, but that this was not the case with mortals who have not yet seen God in His perfection.[50] From these remarks it may be concluded that FitzRalph assumed without further argument that the blessed whose will he was trying to reconcile with the 'clear vision' were already enjoying that vision immediately after death. But we cannot deduce from the *Commentary*

[48] *Chart. Univ. Paris.*, ii. 436–7 n.

[49] B, fol. 158^{v}; J, fol. 117vb.

[50] P, fols. 24ra, 25rb.

on the Sentences more than an informed interest in problems related to that raised by John XXII, because in it FitzRalph's interest lay elsewhere and his discussion of the primacy of the will involved some inconsistencies in his statements about the 'clear vision'.[51] But whereas the commentary contained no direct statement of the position which FitzRalph would adopt when faced with the pope's request, its revised version and the debates of Wodeham and his 'socii' under FitzRalph's regency pointed in the direction of that position.[52]

The clearest statement of his views in relation to the interpretation propounded by John XXII is contained in a sermon which he preached six months after the death of that pope but while the issue was still *sub iudice.* Preaching before a predominantly English audience in the Dominican church at Avignon on 7 July 1335, the feast of the translation of the relics of St. Thomas of Canterbury, which was something of a national holiday commemorated annually by the English community at the curia, FitzRalph delivered a panegyric on St. Thomas, taking as his text: 'Transtulit illum dominus' (Ad Hebr. xi. 5).[53] However, he digressed slightly from his main theme in order to consider the burning topic of the day, i.e. the nature of the 'visio deitatis' at that moment being enjoyed by the saint whose feast they were celebrating.[54] By the date of FitzRalph's sermon the new pope had retreated to his summer palace at Pont-de-Sorgues where, in addition to his work on broader plans for the reform of the Church, curia, and religious orders,[55] he spent most of the summer and autumn studying the voluminous body of literature which the controversy had engendered: the sermons of John XXII and Waleys, his own contributions written as a cardinal, and the judgements on these which had been requested both by himself and by his predecessor from a representative selection of eminent theologians present at the curia over the previous three years. We can only surmise that FitzRalph's verdict was among these.

On 7 July 1335 FitzRalph stressed that he would present a

[51] Robson, *Wyclif and the Oxford Schools*, pp. 76-9.

[52] Courtenay, *Adam Wodeham*, pp. 77, 106, on the soul's capacity for beatitude.

[53] B, fols. 155^{v}-161^{r}; J, fols. 115vb-119rb.

[54] B, fol. 158^{r}; J, fol. 117vb.

[55] On papal reform programme, Schimmelpfennig, 'Benedikt XII als Reformpapst', 11-43; Clémens Schmitt, *Un Pape réformateur et un défenseur de l'unité de l'Eglise. Benoît XII et l'ordre des frères mineurs* (Quaracchi, 1959); Jean-Berthold Mann, *Le Pape Benoît et les cisterciens* (Paris, 1949).

similar argument to that which he had already delivered to the late pope: 'Dico sicut aliter dixi, et de precepto domini Johannis scripsi, et in manus eiusdem tradidi, quod hec merces redditur immediate post plenam purgacionem anime separate: intelligo post plenam satisfaccionem pro suis peccatis.'[56] He then proceeded to argue that the justice of God would not permit Him to deprive the blessed of their reward as soon as they had been purified in purgatory, and disposed of the objection that before the resurrection and Last Judgement even a soul that had been saved was still, because of original sin, 'misera et ita non vere beata'.[57] Hence his argument for a total vision of God on the part of the blessed before the Last Judgement placed him very definitely among the – largely Dominican – opposition to John XXII, and here FitzRalph showed no concession to the intermediate view privately held by Benedict XII. It is unlikely that he shared this view, even privately, because at that stage he still advocated strongly the intercession of the saints as an important element in popular spirituality, an element which would have lost much of its significance if the view were accepted that not even the saints enjoyed the full 'visio deitatis' before the Last Judgement. Here too he circumvented somewhat uneasily a problem which was the corollary of his stated opinion, and which had been raised by John XXII in the sermon of 5 January 1332: whether the souls of the damned also received their final punishment immediately after death. John XXII had maintained that this was not the case until after the Last Judgement, and that in the meantime they remained in a condition of semi-darkness from which they were able to move about the world as demons tempting the living,[58] whereas the implication of FitzRalph's remarks is to the contrary: '. . . Deus summe bonus et summe iustus non est iustior aut promptior ad puniendum quam ad premiandum.' However, he dealt with the matter at length in Book XI of the *Summa de Questionibus Armenorum*, and there is strong evidence that the question preoccupied him on yet another occasion and that he made it the subject of one of the short *questiones disputate* contained in CVP 5076: 'Queritur utrum dampnati in inferno ante iudicium videntes gloriam beatorum post iudicium omni luce privati penitus

[56] B, fol. 158^{v}; J, fol. 117vb. In the light of FitzRalph's explicit remark, Maier's argument (above, n. 43) that it is not to be taken literally and that FitzRalph had sent his views to the pope through a third party as early as 1332 is not convincing.

[57] B, fol. 159^{r}; J, fol. 118ra.

[58] *Les Sermons de Jean XXII*, p. 145.

excecentur.'[59] This is the second of four extremely brief questions which had been assumed by both Leff and Gwynn (neither of whom had seen the manuscript personally) to have formed collectively a single question and to be a fragment of the *lectura* on the Sentences.[60] Their conclusions had been based on the title of the first question contained in the printed catalogue: 'Queritur utrum creatura rationalis clare videns deum necessaria diligat ipsum', which commences at the top of folio 65ra. However, closer examination of the manuscript raises a further problem, as at the bottom of folio 64vb the rubric is given: 'Sermo Reverendissimi doctoris domini Richardi Archiepiscopi armachani primatis ybernie', followed immediately by a new gathering and a new hand. The text that follows is definitely not a sermon in the conventional sense, which FitzRalph, like most medieval preachers, always opened with a scriptural quotation upon which the sermon was then based. The work has rather the form of *questiones ordinarie* in the manner of magisterial disputations in the schools, and could have originated during a period of regency in the faculty of theology.[61] Although the external evidence for the attribution of these questions to FitzRalph is far from conclusive, the internal evidence of the text itself strongly indicates his authorship. The work is preserved in a unique copy and has no literal parallel with any of his identified writings; the problems posed and the arguments adduced are sufficiently similar in content and treatment to his discussions elsewhere, especially in the *Summa de Questionibus Armenorum*, to justify tentatively assigning it to him in default of evidence to the contrary.

The questions, which are incomplete, the fourth one breaking off at folio 69ra and thus implying an incomplete exemplar, are based directly on *distinctiones* drawn from the Sentences of Peter Lombard; they are not a direct contribution to the beatific vision controversy and they take no notice of its central problem. They clearly originated in an academic environment, but it is impossible to state categorically that they did so independently of renewed interest in these topics as a result of the papal sermons of 1331–2. The title of the first question reflects the pseudo-Augustinian *Liber de diligendo Deo*, and here as

[59] CVP 5076, fol. 66ra. [60] Leff, *FitzRalph Commentator*, p. 176.

[61] Courtenay, *Adam Wodeham*, pp. 78–9. For other *determinationes* attributed to FitzRalph see Leff, pp. 191–2. These are in Florence, Bibl. Naz. A. III. 508, fols. 109vb–129vb.

elsewhere the author's arguments demonstrate FitzRalph's respect for what he believed to be the teaching of the bishop of Hippo.[62] Although Gwynn suggested that FitzRalph's patristic knowledge left much to be desired, and it is true that his knowledge of the Fathers cannot be compared with his mastery of Scripture, nevertheless he did follow the Scotist–Augustinian tradition in Oxford sufficiently to have become familiar with the writings of Augustine and, to a lesser extent, of Jerome. Beyond these, however, his patristic knowledge, like his acquaintance with the Jewish and Islamic traditions, was perfunctory.[63]

Whereas the *lectura* on the Sentences provides some guidelines to FitzRalph's thinking with regard to the beatific vision, the *Summa de Questionibus Armenorum*, which originated in the discussions at the curia during the years 1338-44, is much more illuminating on the subject. The *Summa*, its genesis, composition, dating, and content will be examined in greater detail below, but in this context it must be considered briefly in the light of the most recent theological controversy which also had implications for eastern Christendom. FitzRalph clearly recognized that this issue, together with the related questions of the humanity and divinity of Christ, the intercession of the saints, and the doctrine of purgatory, were crucial to the reunion attempts then in progress, and in Books XI–XIV he and his discussion partner returned to these issues frequently and under various guises, providing an exhaustive treatment of the possible opinions. Although the dialogue form allowed FitzRalph to express views, on these and on other topics, which he did not personally hold, it nevertheless emerges clearly that FitzRalph continued to hold the opinion which we have already encountered in the sermon preached in the Dominican church on 7 July 1335.

The genesis of the pope's unconventional views on the beatific vision has remained something of a problem despite the research of both Maier and Dykmans, both of whom tried to identify a possible line of development in the thinking of John XXII by examining his letters and the marginalia in his own hand on a large number of manuscripts known to have been in his possession during his pontificate, but without success. It is,

[62] The apocryphal *Liber de diligendo Deo*, a pot-pourri of writings of Hugh of St. Victor, St. Bernard, and St. Anselm, printed *MPL* 40, 847–68.

[63] Norman Daniel, *Islam and the West. The Making of an Image* (Edinburgh, 1960), pp. 50–3. Grandisson's apparent familiarity with current Hebrew scholarship was not reflected in FitzRalph's work.

however, clear that the pope's views on the subject changed radically during the period 1317-31. The bull of canonization of the Franciscan archbishop of Toulouse, Louis d'Anjou, on 7 April 1317 shows clearly that the pope then envisaged the saint as already enjoying the perfect vision of God face to face, i.e. that he still held fast to the traditional interpretation of the beatific vision. Four years later in the course of his correspondence with representatives of the Armenian Church and again in 1326, when writing to the Patriarch of Jerusalem, John XXII touched generally on the question of the saints in heaven with the implication that they were already enjoying their eternal reward, but did not make any specific statement about the precise nature of the vision they were enjoying.[64] Hence it was not until the autumn of 1331 that he was seen to have changed his mind on the subject, and the records do not show at what point or under what circumstances he might have been led to do so. In default of other possible solutions a tentative hypothesis may be suggested here. A striking feature of the pontificate of John XXII, fostered no doubt by the length of the pontificate and the increasing stability of the papal curia at Avignon, was the increased interest in Armenian and Greek theology, linked with attempts to achieve a better understanding of the problems of the Eastern Churches. Although the Inquisition, under the control of the Dominicans, was given extensive powers to deal with 'heretics' in this area, its methods were not the only ones employed. Two teachers of Armenian were appointed at Avignon in 1322-3 and financed out of papal funds, and subsequently the pope wrote to the bishop of Paris on 25 July 1326, urging him to investigate whether the decree of the Council of Vienne with regard to the erection of chairs of Greek, Hebrew, Aramaic, and Chaldaic had been carried out.[65] The pope wanted to know how many teachers were giving instruction in these languages, what their source of income was, and how many students were attending such courses. Meanwhile the Venetian crusading propagandist, Marino Sanudo Torsello, had altered his previously hostile attitude towards Byzantium and was now urging the

[64] *Reg. Vat.* 63, fols. 372^{v}-374^{r}; Raynaldus, *Ann. Eccl.* (1321), 151-2; (1326), 330-1; also Weakland, art. cit., 76-7. Lambert, *Franciscan Poverty*, p. 204, suggested that John XXII developed his view of the beatific vision in opposition to the doctrines of Petrus Ioannis Olivi, but did not elaborate on this theory.

[65] Guillemain, *La Cour pontificale*, p. 383. For the two teachers sent by the king of Armenia, Schäfer, *Ausgaben . . . Benedikt XII . . .*, 573; *Chart. Univ. Paris.*, ii. 293-4.

elderly emperor Andronikos II to work towards union between the Eastern and Western churches. As a result of this influence the emperor changed his attitude of disengagement from the West and sent envoys to discuss possibilities with the pope.[66] By 1326 John XXII was displaying an unusually tolerant attitude towards the Greek Church, especially in Crete,[67] and by the time he came to deliver the series of controversial sermons on the beatific vision the lines of communication on the interrelated questions of reunion and crusade between Constantinople and Avignon were less tenuous than they had been at any time since the abortive attempt to reach an understanding at the Second Council of Lyons in 1274.[68] For the reunion negotiations which took place at Avignon under the next pontiff, Benedict XII, and for all subsequent attempts up to and including the Council of Ferrara-Florence, the doctrine of the beatific vision, together with the related problems of purgatory and the intercession of the saints, were to be of crucial importance, and we know from FitzRalph's own testimony in his *Summa de Questionibus Armenorum* that his discussion of the different Latin and Greek interpretations of the beatific vision was undertaken at the express wish of Barlaam of Calabria. Perhaps the pope's remarks during the winter of 1331-2 were intended for eastern ears and his undogmatic, somewhat hypothetical, formulation of an opinion which to Latin ears sounded distinctly suspect, was intended as a gesture in the general direction of Byzantium and Armenia – a hint that certain matters might still be open to discussion in the light of biblical and patristic authority?

The subsequent debate on the topic also supports this suggestion at least in one limited respect, in that it revealed just how varied were the opinions on the subject held by a wide range of theologians of considerable stature. Even among those who supported the pope there was not an absolute concensus: whereas they accepted his general premiss, they frequently

[66] Angeliki Laiou, 'Marino Sanudo Torsello, Byzantium and the Turks', *Speculum*, 45 (1970), 381-2.

[67] John Gill, 'Pope Urban V (1362-70) and the Greeks of Crete', *OCP* 39 (1973), 461-8, esp. 465-6. But at the same time John XXII entrusted to the Dominicans the operation of the Inquisition in the Latin possessions in Greece, Wilhelm de Vries, 'Die Päpste in Avignon und der christliche Osten', ibid., 30 (1964), 92. John XXII's bull to this effect, issued 25 July 1318, is printed in *Acta Ioannis XXII*, pp. 30-3.

[68] Donald Nicol, 'Byzantine requests for an oecumenical council in the fourteenth century', *Byzantium: its Ecclesiastical History and Relations with the Western World* (London, 1972), 69-85.

expressed reservations and modifications, developing their own views with a number of subtle distinctions, while the situation in the anti-papal camp was no different. After the initial cry of protest, they also began to develop subtle distinctions on the subject. Hence it emerged that the pope had touched on an issue concerning which there had been a generally accepted but tacit understanding, although the subject had not previously been examined according to the criteria of theological orthodoxy. When they were actually faced with the necessity of making decisions about it, the foremost theologians of the day found themselves without clear-cut answers. However, when John XXII composed on 3 December 1334, the day before his death, a testament in which he retracted his errors – though with an important saving clause[69] – he arrived at a position privately held by his most influential opponents, namely that of a more perfect vision after the resurrection of the body and, in a later passage, expressed a view which almost anticipated that contained in the bull *Benedictus Deus.*[70]

During the conclave which followed John XXII's death neither this doctrinal issue nor the projected crusade which the pope had been trying to organize with the assistance of the French king were the primary considerations. The deliberations were dominated by the fear of the French party led by Talleyrand, the cardinal of Périgord, who – according to the well-informed but not always reliable Florentine chronicler, Giovanni Villani – played a decisive role in the election of the next four popes,[71] that a pontiff might be elected who would transfer the papacy back to Rome. Although contemporary reports suggest that Fournier was elected almost by accident when neither of the opposing parties could secure a majority for their candidate, the speed with which the Cistercian cardinal held two consistories in which he outlined his plans for reform in Church and curia suggests that he was not totally unprepared for the honour which fell upon him. From a recent study of Benedict XII as reforming pope emerged the plausible suggestion that the cardinals who elected him knew Jacques Fournier primarily as a theologian and as an active opponent of heretics, and that precisely for this reason they elected him in succession to John

[69] *Chart. Univ. Paris.*, ii. 440–1. The saving clause was 'anime purgate . . . vident Deum . . . facie ad faciem clare *in quantum status et conditio compatitur anime separate*' (my italics).

[70] Printed in *Enchiridion Symbolorum*, pp. 296–7.

[71] Quoted in Zacour, 'Cardinal of Périgord', 20.

XXII, whose theological errors threatened to compromise the papacy as an institution as well as the person of the pope.[72] This 'accidental' election inaugurated a pontificate which not only saw the beginnings of the building programme that was to confer upon the residence of the papal curia at Avignon an air of stability and permanence, but was also characterized to an unprecedented degree by austerity and reforming zeal. Papal activity in the area of reform extended beyond the immediate confines of the college of cardinals, curial administration, and the distribution of benefices, to include also the religious orders – his own confrères the Cistercians, also the Benedictines and Canons Regular, and the four mendicant orders, although the Dominican opposition to papally imposed reform measures was to result in a running battle between the order and the pope for the whole of this pontificate. Many of these debates concerning reform of the religious, and especially the mendicant orders took place during the years which FitzRalph spent at the curia, a factor which must be borne in mind when considering the genesis of his own opposition to the role of the friars in the pastoral sphere and their place in the ecclesiastical structure. It must be considered to what degree, if any, FitzRalph subsequently took over the reforming attitudes of the Cistercian pope, which, however, were not, despite Benedict's re-issue of the decretal *Super Cathedram*, characterized by animosity towards the mendicant orders *per se*.[73] In the short term the election of the Cistercian meant, whether the cardinals in conclave intended this or not, that one of their number most directly involved in the beatific vision controversy was now in a position to bring about a solution to the problem, and Benedict set himself to study all the documentation which the debate had produced during the first months of his pontificate.

On 4 October 1335 Benedict XII issued instructions to his chamberlain, Arnaud Isarn, to make payments to sixteen masters of theology who during the two months from 4 July to 4 September had worked with him at Pont-de-Sorgues on the problem

[72] Schimmelpfennig, 'Benedikt XII als Reformpapst', 15.

[73] Schimmelpfennig's argument, p. 29, that the mere fact of Benedict's re-issue of *Super Cathedram* indicated that he was not well disposed towards the friars, needs some modification. *Super Cathedram* was the only instrument available to 14th-century popes to regulate relations between the friars and the secular clergy, and it was re-issued regularly by successive popes, including Innocent VI on the eve of FitzRalph's case against the friars in Avignon.

of the beatific vision.[74] Although the papal instruction gave only the Christian names in many cases, the editors of the *Chartularium Universitatis Parisiensis* identified all of the group at least tentatively, and its composition is remarkable for the fact that whereas it contains – as might be expected – a strong preponderance of theologians drawn from the mendicant orders, of these at least five are Franciscans, five Friars Hermits of St. Augustine, and only one each from the ranks of the Dominicans and Carmelites.[75] Benedict XII clearly did not intend a heavily weighted jury which would absolve the Dominican Thomas Waleys at the expense of the deceased pope, and while the Carmelites had been linked with the Franciscans in sympathy with the papal view, the Augustinians had, as in the case of the poverty controversy a decade earlier, been closer to the Dominican position.[76] Of the two secular masters on the list, the 'Walter' has been identified as Walter Burley, of whom we know that during these years he travelled constantly in the service of Edward III and Queen Philippa, and his presence at the curia and participation in a theological commission is not improbable.[77] That the 'Richard' on the list should be identified as FitzRalph is much more probable than the Franciscan Richard de Chassam suggested by the editors,[78] in view both of FitzRalph's known preoccupation with the problem at this time and also in consideration of the patronage which he began to enjoy immediately after the accession of Benedict XII.

The deliberations at Pont-de-Sorgues during this summer of 1335 resulted in the formulation of a doctrine of the beatific vision which the new pope promulgated on 29 January 1336, and which declared:

quod secundum communem Dei ordinationem animae Sanctorum omnium, qui de hoc mundo . . . decesserunt, . . . mox post mortem suam et purgationem prefatam in illis, qui purgatione huiusmodi indegebant, etiam ante resumptionem suorum corporum et iudicium generale post ascencionem Salvatoris Domini nostri Iesu Christi in coelum, fuerunt, sunt et erunt in

[74] Maier, 'Schriften, Daten und Personen', *Ausgehendes Mittelalter*, iii. 581–2.

[75] *Chart. Univ. Paris.*, ii. 453–4, and discussion of their identification Maier, art. cit., 569 n.

[76] Smalley, 'John Baconthorpe's Postill on St Matthew', 138. This Carmelite, writing in or soon after 1336, insisted that John XXII only expressed a private opinion and never deviated from the faith. He clearly thought Waleys deserved his fate for his imprudence. The studies of Maier and Dykmans indicate that the Augustinian friars were not prominent in the controversy.

[77] *BRUO* I, 313.

[78] As n. 75.

coelo . . . viderunt et vident divinam essentiam visione intuitiva et eciam faciali, nulla mediante creatura in ratione obiecti visi se habente, sed divina essentia immediate se nude, clare et aperte eis ostendente . . .[79]

It made clear that the view adopted by John XXII was totally false, though without naming him or identifying him as the author of the condemned teaching. Equally the doctrinal statement in the bull made no explicit concession to the view which was widely expressed by many who had opposed the papal opinion, including Benedict himself and Pierre Roger, that the vision enjoyed immediately after death was less perfect than that which would be enjoyed after the Last Judgement. Hence despite the presence at Pont-de-Sorgues of a substantial representation of sympathizers with the pope's opinion, the bull effectively stated that this view was not compatible with orthodox teaching. For the Franciscan rebels in Munich, Benedict XII did not go far enough in the condemnation of his predecessor and simply provided them with the opportunity of declaring him also a heretic. The formula in the bull coincided, however, to a remarkable degree with the view expressed by FitzRalph on 7 July 1335 when the commission had only begun to work, and it was only to be expected that his subsequent comments on the subject during the Armenian debates would stress his adherence to the officially sanctioned view. In *Benedictus Deus* the new pope also dealt with the related question which had preoccupied FitzRalph, and came out strongly in favour of the opinion expressed more tentatively by FitzRalph, namely that those who died in the state of mortal sin 'mox post mortem suam ad inferna descendunt ubi poenis infernalibus crucientur . . .'[80] This new formulation had the merit of clarity, it restored order and stability to the theological scene at the curia after four years of heated debate, but it did not make easier the task of those working for reunion with the Eastern Churches over the next decade.

For FitzRalph, however, recognition and reward came swiftly and on 17 December 1335 Benedict XII provided him to the deanery of Lichfield Cathedral.[81] Although the papal letter mentioned the provision to the chancellorship of Lincoln, it must have been clear by now that in spite of the expectative which FitzRalph had procured from John XXII before the latter's death, the opposition of dean and chapter in Lincoln

[79] Ed. cit., p. 297. [80] Ibid. [81] *CPL* 1305–42, 524.

to his appointment was insurmountable and a suitable alternative benefice had to be found. The purpose of this appointment was not to provide him with a source of income upon which he could continue to live and work at the curia as theologian and preacher, as it carried with it the duty of residence, and it was part of Benedict's reform plan to enforce such residence.

ii. Dean of Lichfield

The combined efforts of Bishop Burghersh of Lincoln and Benedict XII to provide the former chancellor of Oxford University with a suitable benefice were not without their difficulties. On 10 July 1334 Burghersh had collated FitzRalph to the chancellorship of Lincoln, vacant since the departure of Anthony Bek.[1] In the letter of collation issued from the bishop's castle at Newark-on-Trent, Bek was named as the previous chancellor. But there was considerable friction between the bishop, chancellor, and the dean and chapter of the diocese, understandable in view of the fact that Bek had been elected bishop by the chapter and received the royal assent only to have his election quashed by a papal provision in favour of Burghersh, and an unusually long time was allowed to elapse between the collation of FitzRalph and the communication of this appointment to the dean and chapter on 23 March 1335. Bek had been appointed dean in 1329, and there were two subsequent collations to the chancellorship, Roger Mundham on 26 November 1330 and John de Combe on 23 October 1331,[2] but neither of these was mentioned in the collation of FitzRalph, nor is there any further record of the collation of a successor to FitzRalph before the death of Burghersh on 4 December 1340.[3] However, the Act and Chapter Book of Lincoln has a number of entries for the years 1329-37, which indicate that the dean (and in his absence at the papal curia the sub-dean) and chapter were adopting an independent stance with regard to the establishment of grammar schools on the grounds that the chancellorship was vacant. At some point which cannot be determined precisely, Bek, who as a master of theology had been one of the Oxford proctors in Avignon when the university's case against the Dominicans was being heard in 1314 and was provided to

[1] No record of this expectative has survived in the papal registers, and we know of the collation only from the registers of Bishop Burghersh, Reg. Burgh. Linc., iv. fol. 411^{r}. For Bek see *BRUO* I, 152-3.

[2] Reg. Burgh. Linc., iv, fols. 402^{v}-405^{v}.

[3] *BRUO* III, 2157-8.

the chancellorship of Lincoln in 1316,[4] either resigned the chancellorship on becoming dean, or else continued to maintain both dignities in violation of the papal mandate.[5] After 1330 he was continually absent from Lincoln, and while in Avignon he appears to have taken little part in capitular business. It is possible that the independent-minded canons of the chapter refused to accept either FitzRalph or any of the previous episcopal collations to the chancellorship, and that the office was quietly allowed to languish during the remaining years of Burghersh's episcopate.[6]

In any case FitzRalph had to seek another benefice. Grandisson was experiencing difficulties with the proctors of the see of Canterbury concerning the creation of the additional canonries in Exeter for his nephew Northwode and his Anglo-Irish protégé,[7] and the revenues from the canonry in Armagh, to which he had in the meantime been provided, cannot have been substantial.[8] By now he had to some extent distinguished himself by his stance on the 'orthodox' side of the beatific vision controversy and Benedict XII, possibly prodded by the continued influence of Grandisson and Burghersh,[9] was willing to provide for him. On 17 December 1335 FitzRalph was appointed to the deanery of Lichfield, another English benefice which had been the subject of friction for some years past.[10] The deanery had been

[4] *CPL* 1305–42, 167.

[5] The evidence of the papal registers is not clear on this. On 30 July 1318 John XXII addressed him as chancellor of Lincoln, ordering him to resign this office as incompatible with the canonry and prebend in Lincoln Cathedral to which he had also been collated, *CPL* 1305–42, 178. Yet as late as 1 July 1331 John XXII still addressed him as chancellor of Lincoln, ibid., 322.

[6] 31 May 1334, when Bek was already a papal chaplain and in Avignon, he was addressed as dean of Lincoln. Presumably the chancellorship was vacant and Burghersh intended it for FitzRalph, ibid., 408.

[7] *Grandisson's Register*, i. 719–21.

[8] *Reg. Vat.* 120, fol. 55^{r-v}, but this only stated that FitzRalph had been provided to a canonry and prebend in Armagh, as well as benefices in Exeter and the chancellorship of Lincoln. We know that the Lincoln provision did not take effect, while in Exeter *Grandisson's Register* shows that FitzRalph held at least two prebends, that of Westbroke in the collegiate church of Bosham (collated 3 April 1334, ibid., iii. 1300), and that of 'de la Crosse', which he had acquired earlier and vacated no later than 14 March 1335, ibid., iii. 1311. There is some negative, but inconclusive evidence that he had given up his prebend in Bosham by 3 October 1336, ibid., iii. 1314.

[9] Gwynn, *Studies*, 22 (1933), 594, suggested that the influence of Bradwardine might also have been behind FitzRalph's promotion because Bradwardine, already a canon of Lincoln and therefore likely to have been involved in the dispute over the collation to the chancellorship, was one of those who received a concurrent mandate announcing FitzRalph's provision to Lichfield, *Reg. Vat.* 120, fol. 55^{v}.

[10] Ibid., fol. 55^{r-v}, *CPL* 1305–42, 524.

held from December 1320 until his appointment on 16 March 1324 as archbishop of Armagh by the former chancellor of Cambridge University, Stephen Segrave. As soon as Segrave had been consecrated in Avignon on 29 April 1324, John XXII exercised his right of provision and on 1 May nominated Roger de Convenis, despite the right which the canons had acquired in 1222 of electing their own dean.[11] Oblivious of the papal decision the chapter had elected William de Arimine, whose election was then quashed in favour of the papal nominee, a Gascon and therefore particularly resented by the chapter, and the capitular nominee was soon provided by the pope to the see of Norwich.[12] But the matter did not end there: Convenis sought and received a dispensation for non-residence for three years in order to study civil law, and on 21 August 1328 he exchanged the deanery with John Gasci, later bishop of Marseilles, for a canonry of Lerida, whereupon on Gasci's death on 13 October 1335 the canons attempted unsuccessfully to recover their right of election.[13] Two months later they had to accept another papal provision, in circumstances which did not make FitzRalph's initial dealings with the chapter particularly easy. However, in FitzRalph's case one of the most compelling arguments against papal providees, that of non-residence, did not seem to be a problem. In compliance with Benedict XII's decree of 10 January 1335, ordering all those at the curia who held benefices with cure of souls to leave Avignon and return to their posts, FitzRalph duly set out for England.

On 12 April 1336 he was received by the bishop of Coventry and Lichfield, Roger Northburgh, a royal servant who was none the less a diligent bishop and whose registers over a long episcopate from 1322 to 1358 indicate a smoothly-functioning diocesan organization and searching visitation of monastic houses.[14] The meeting took place at the bishop's residence at Brewood Manor. With Adbaston, Brewood was one of the two prebends

[11] *Reg. Vat.* 77, fol. 342^{r}, *CPL* 1305–42, 240. On the statutory position of dean see Hester T. Jenkins, 'Lichfield Cathedral in the fourteenth century' (MS B.litt. d. 538–9, Oxford, 1956), i, 46–9.

[12] *Reg. Vat.* 113, fol. 72^{v}, *CPL* 1305–42, 472.

[13] *Reg. Vat.* 80, fols. 362^{r}, 372^{r}; *Reg. Vat.* 87, fol. 368^{r}; *Reg. Vat.* 89, fol. 14^{r}; *Reg. Vat.* 102, fol. 43^{r}, *CPL* 1305–42, 249, 279, 281, 357.

[14] Northburgh held several offices under Edward II, as keeper of the Wardrobe, keeper of the Privy Seal, and treasurer of the Exchequer, and had a long episcopate in Lichfield, 1322–69. See Rymer's *Foedera*, II. 433 for Edward II's attempts to have him made a cardinal in 1320. For his career, *BRUC* 427. His unpublished register is in Lichfield Cathedral.

normally held by the dean of Lichfield, and on the following day FitzRalph was instituted to the deanery, and on 21 April was installed in the cathedral.[15] Non-residence was a regular feature of fourteenth-century deans of Lichfield – in the period 1320 to 1390 they are recorded as having spent no more than ten years there in all. FitzRalph's extremely active interest in the affairs of the diocese over the next sixteen months gave no hint that he also would fit into the pattern of absentee deans for most of his tenure of office, spending some seven of the next ten years before his elevation to the see of Armagh engaged in litigation at the papal court, and certainly for no more than part of that time directly serving the interests of the cathedral chapter of Lichfield.[16]

Immediately after his installation it became clear that a new broom had arrived to disturb the somewhat haphazard manner in which the canons had conducted their affairs during the years in which there had been no resident dean. FitzRalph was obviously filled with good intentions, intended to be an active dean and to supervise every detail of the management of cathedral and chapter. To what extent this business-like approach to capitular affairs was due to the various influences to which he had recently been subjected – Bishop Bury's household in London and at Auckland Castle, the increasingly reform-conscious papal court under Benedict XII, or his brief stay with his bishop at Brewood Manor before installation in Lichfield Cathedral – can only be a matter for speculation. Yet it was only to be expected that a man of FitzRalph's calibre and temperament, if he chose to be resident and conscientious, would make his presence felt in a chapter which had recently experienced the advantages and disadvantages of an absentee, pluralist foreigner as their dean. This phase of FitzRalph's career was to be a significant one, not least because it provided him with his first experience of diocesan life, of the day-to-day administration, and of the intricate balance between episcopal authority and the aspirations of the capitular clergy, experience which

[15] Much of the following is drawn from the Chapter Acts Book of Lichfield Cathedral, which was removed from the cathedral *c.*1347, later acquired by Elias Ashmole, and bequeathed with the rest of his collection to the Bodleian Library, now MS Ashmole 794. However, it contains no reference to the dean's installation, but see Reg. Northburgh, ii. fol. 159^{v}. Alan de Assheborn's continuator mistakenly gave 1337 as the year of installation, *Anglia Sacra*, i. 443.

[16] MS Ashmole 794, fols. 55^{r}–58^{v}, provides ample evidence of his involvement in the affairs of cathedral and chapter during his first months in Lichfield.

would be of considerable advantage to him when he came to deal with the see of Armagh and its clergy in the later years of his life. Not merely the teaching and example of his friend and mentor, Grandisson, but also his own practical training-ground in Lichfield left their mark on a prelate whose sermons and diocesan legislation yield considerable insight into the problems of the mid-fourteenth-century archdiocese of Armagh and their author's attempts to deal with them.

But if FitzRalph learned something from his years in Lichfield, he also brought with him a valuable asset when he arrived, namely first-hand knowledge of curial proceedings and legal formalities which would subsequently assist him in the course of litigation, both on his own behalf and on behalf of his chapter, during his next visit to Avignon. The entries in the Chapter Acts Book[17] for these years indicate not only the new dean's minute attention to the details of capitular and cathedral business, but also a change of tone in the proceedings – more business-like but also more litigious, more concerned with effective legal safeguards. The dean was relentless in pursuit of his objectives, at least one of which was to be significant for his future relations with the chapter, i.e. a high standard of observance of their obligations and duties on the part of the cathedral clergy subject to his authority.[18]

The changed circumstances were already made clear at a special meeting of the chapter summoned two days after FitzRalph's installation, at which he presided and at which a new and intricate system of proxies was evolved for the various lawsuits in which the chapter was engaged – at the papal court, in the provincial court of the archbishop of Canterbury, and ordinary local cases in the bishop's court. In the first category a distinction was now to be made between the proctor who presented appeals and the one who appeared in consistory – a distinction which accorded with curial practice as FitzRalph would recently have learned – although in procedure both commissions were still to be held by Robert de Thresk. With regard to the court of Canterbury, new regulations were drawn up ensuring the tighter supervision on the part of dean and chapter of their proctor in litigation before the metropolitan's legal

[17] The evidence it provides for FitzRalph's work as dean was surveyed briefly in a lecture delivered by a subsequent dean of Lichfield, Henry E. Savage, *Richard FitzRalph, sometime dean* (Lichfield, 1928).

[18] MS Ashmole 794, fols. 44^{v}, 57^{r}.

officers.[19] Initially FitzRalph's relations with the canons appear to have been good, and his innovations were accepted as being in their own best interests. On 26 June 1336 they nominated him to investigate the financial position of the parish church of Cannock, which had been exempted from the archdeacon's jurisdiction and placed under the direct authority of the dean and chapter, in whose gift the living was.[20] Three months later relations were still harmonious, when an order was passed unanimously by the dean and canons to the effect that if the dean or any other member of the chapter was involved in litigation on behalf of the chapter in any suit against the bishop, and as a result subjected to molestation of his person or his goods, or any other violation of his rights, he was to be defended at the expense of the dean and chapter.[21] Clearly the dean was taking precautions against all eventualities: possibly the litigation which was to take him back to Avignon was already pending, and he was making advance preparations. In any case the same provision was re-enacted in February 1340 while FitzRalph was absent at the curia.[22] The entries in the Acts Book indicate that the dean was mainly concerned with the advancement of the authority which he considered appropriate to his office and frequently went beyond the prerogatives accorded to him by right and custom. These entries also indicate that, whereas he was interested in power and influence, he was less concerned with his own material interests. Only one episode is recorded in which such interests were at stake, and even this was a minor issue. On 21 March 1337 he obtained the approval of the chapter for some structural changes in his two prebends of Adbaston and Brewood. In the case of the former he was permitted to demolish several houses in order to use the materials for improvements at Brewood – was he deliberately establishing his personal headquarters close to the bishop's manor? The chapter granted permission without further comment or explanation, other than the understandable proviso that the agricultural life of Adbaston be protected and the farm buildings there remain intact.[23]

[19] Savage, op. cit., pp. 10–11.

[20] MS Ashmole 794, fol. 57r.

[21] Ibid., fol. 55v.

[22] Ibid., fol. 75v.

[23] Ibid., fol. 57r. Since the mid-13th century there had been trouble between the dean and chapter on the one hand and the Augustinian canons at Ronton (Staffs.) on the other over Adbaston farms, and this controversy was still smouldering under Dean John Derby, Henry E. Savage, *The Great Register of Lichfield* (Lichfield, 1923), pp. 15–16.

The principal duty of the dean was the care of the cathedral, in its physical aspects as well as in the ordering of the liturgy and supervision of the cathedral clergy. In the case of Lichfield the first years of FitzRalph's tenure of office coincided with a crucial phase in the rebuilding of the cathedral. The Norman church built by Bishop Roger Clinton during the first half of the twelfth century was gradually replaced in successive building phases between 1195 and 1340 by a structure which, apart from the Victorian restorations, is basically that which still exists today.[24] The Early English choir, whose preservation was to present considerable structural problems to the local builders in FitzRalph's period, had been completed during the first of these building phases, *c.*1195–1208. Then followed the chapter house (completed 1249), the rebuilding of the nave in Decorated style (completed 1285), and the imposing west front, which was finally completed *c.*1320. This latter phase of the building had been carried out under the direction of Bishop Walter Langton (1296–1321), who had also commenced a new building programme at the east end.[25] Although work on the Lady Chapel was only in its early stages when Langton died, he left a substantial amount of money in his will for its completion. Despite the fact that the money was requisitioned in July 1322 by Edward II as a contribution to his campaign against the Scots, and that the dean and chapter did not finally secure repayment of the entire sum for more than fifty years (and then without interest), the building programme continued remarkably quickly over the next two decades. In the absence of a dean in residence between the departure of Stephen Segrave and the arrival of FitzRalph, the work of the chapter in this respect was doubtless furthered by the energetic Bishop Roger Northburgh, and by the time FitzRalph arrived the Lady Chapel had been completed and work had begun on the presbytery, which was to extend the new portion in Decorated style until it joined up with the Old English choir near the centre of the cathedral. Here the local masons encountered formidable technical problems, partly because when building the Lady Chapel they had made use of a natural bed of sandstone as its foundation and this resulted in a slight bend to the north in the wall of the

[24] The best account of the 14th-century cathedral and building operations is Jenkins, op. cit.

[25] See also Henry E. Savage, *The Fourteenth Century Builders* (Lichfield, 1916); John E. W. Wallis, *Lichfield Cathedral* (London, 1975), pp. 10–14.

cathedral. They tried to counteract this as they built from east to west, one bay after another, and the careful observer may still notice that the piers on either side of the altar rails are not quite opposite one another. When, however, the builders reached the final bay of the presbytery and had to join up the new portion to the three bays of the Old English choir which were for various reasons to be preserved, the problem became more acute. Now they realized that the new Decorated presbytery was narrower than the older choir, and FitzRalph in agreement with the other members of the chapter decided to call in an outside expert. Their choice fell upon William Ramsey, master builder to Edward III and then in charge of work on the royal castles south of the Trent, and sought his 'sanum consilium' on the best way to complete the work. On 23 May 1337 a contract was agreed upon by the dean and chapter, whereby Master William was to receive payment of twenty shillings for each visit to Lichfield as his consultation fee, with an additional 6*s.* 8*d.* for the travelling expenses of himself and his attendants from London to Lichfield and back.[26] Ramsey found a harmonious solution to the chapter's problem, and the work was brought to completion in accordance with his plans in 1340, while FitzRalph was still absent in Avignon.

Indications of his close supervision of the cathedral personnel are provided by the cases of the former chorister Robert 'of the Peak', who was nominated as one of the vicars in the cathedral by a local lay patron, Sir John de Marisco, and who was accepted in office on condition that he be ordained to Holy Orders within one year and in the intervening time subject himself to examination by the dean, and also of John le Valeys, whose neglect of his chantry duties had been reported to FitzRalph. However, in this case the dean's attempt to intervene and impose a penalty failed, and he was compelled to allow the matter to subside quietly.[27] Yet another episode indicates action on the dean's part which was clearly considered unprecedented in Lichfield. In any case it was sufficiently rare for the chapter clerk, John de Pulton, who was responsible for keeping the record of capitular acts, to report the proceedings in some detail, although he normally omitted any record of the installation of prebendaries, or at most mentioned them briefly. However, in the case of

[26] MS Ashmole 794, fol. 37^{v}. For Ramsey see John Harvey, *English Medieval Architects* (London, 1954), pp. 215–18.

[27] MS Ashmole 794, fols. 56^{v}, 57^{v}.

Robert Kirklington, who was installed as prebendary of Bobenhull on 2 May 1337, the story is told in some detail, not once but twice.[28] For reasons which are not made clear, FitzRalph chose to make this an issue in principle and insisted that the prebend in question was a priest's stall, that the incumbent was obliged to celebrate Mass in the cathedral every day, and that he would bind this incumbent under oath to fulfil the obligation – a course of action which was both high-handed and in such circumstances unusual, and which inevitably aroused resentment. His action may have been intended as a warning to negligent prebendaries, and he may have been guided, as Dugdale suggested,[29] by his own pledge upon installation that he would ensure that all those subject to his authority would perform in full their duties in the cathedral, but ignored in his impetuous zeal the rest of his own promise, that he would exercise humility and patience in his dealings with his subordinates. In this matter FitzRalph clearly did not succeed in carrying the canons with him; they supported the new prebendary (who appears to have been a local man), and here we have the first sign of a rift between the dean and the members of his chapter, though there is no indication in the record that this episode had anything to do with his decision to return to Avignon.

On the contrary, the ostensible purpose of the dean's mission to Avignon must have been capitular business, most probably one or more of the burning issues which the chapter had seen fit to bring before the papal courts. One of these was the long-standing dispute between the two rival cathedral chapters of Coventry and Lichfield, the one Benedictine and the other a chapter of secular canons, which until FitzRalph's arrival in Lichfield had been in the hands of the Lichfield chapter's proctor at the curia, Robert de Thresk. Under FitzRalph's personal management the issue was to be at least temporarily resolved with certain concessions in favour of Lichfield, but the final settlement simply reaffirmed the old arrangement whereby each chapter would have the right to elect the next bishop alternately in the case of vacancy,[30] a right which soon ceased to have any practical value as episcopal appointments became exclusively a papal and Crown prerogative. A second possible bone of contention was the question of visitation of the cathedral chapter.

[28] Ibid., fols. 53^{v}, 57^{v}.

[29] Dugdale, *Monasticon Anglicanum*, iii. 255. Ibid., 248 ff. for the statutes concerning the dean's duties.

[30] *VCH Stafford*, iii. 8–14.

Northburgh was a diligent 'visitor' of the religious houses in his diocese and subjected them often to searching supervision. He also countered the claims of the archbishop of Canterbury to 'visit' the Lichfield Cathedral chapter by advancing his own right to conduct such a visitation, and both claims aroused bitter opposition on the part of the canons.[31] Unless some such issue were involved, it would be difficult to explain the financial arrangements made at the chapter meeting of 21–22 August 1337, which was summoned in response to FitzRalph's announcement of his intended visit to Avignon.[32] He received from the chapter letters of commendation to the pope and the sum of £100 sterling, an unusually large payment in such circumstances, even allowing for the fact that part of it was intended as remuneration due to the chapter's proctor, Robert de Thresk.[33]

Even if not already *sub iudice*, the matter of relations between the dean and chapter was already considered by the canons as a possible area of litigation, and they clearly recognized that FitzRalph might be tempted to use his sojourn in Avignon to press the question of his own jurisdiction as dean. Hence they took the precaution of securing from him a pledge that he would not procure any fresh bulls to the detriment of the chapter with regard to the disputed points concerning his jurisdiction, points which are not precisely described in the account in the Acts Book, but which, it can be surmised, were related to the dean's authoritarian approach to the choice, examination, and supervision of the cathedral prebendaries.[34] In return the chapter promised not to undertake during his absence any course of action which would infringe upon the dean's rights as generally understood, and it appears that the canons respected this promise, even though they could scarcely have foreseen that the absence being legislated for would last for seven years.

The problem of the hospitality which by custom and statute the dean was expected to extend to members of the cathedral chapter arose frequently during FitzRalph's tenure of office in Lichfield, and even became the subject of representations by

[31] Edwards, *English Secular Cathedrals*, pp. 131–3.

[32] MS Ashmole 794, fol. 72^{v}.

[33] In August 1333 when William Skelton, canon of Lichfield, was sent by the chapter to Avignon he received an allowance of £11 per year, £5 travelling expenses, and the promise of £40 on his return, ibid., fol. 47^{v}. Skelton was still a canon of Lichfield 4 March 1342, *CPL* 1305–42, 557.

[34] MS Ashmole 794, fol. 58^{v}.

him to Clement VI towards the end of his sojourn in Avignon.[35] During his first year as dean the question had already arisen, when FitzRalph met the vicars in the chapter house on 25 January 1337 and secured from them an agreement that they had no claims as of right to be entertained by him on the anniversaries of bishops and deans, as the capitular statutes only required him to extend hospitality to the vicars on St. Chad's day, i.e. the patron saint of the cathedral, and on the feast of the Assumption. Any further hospitality towards his vicars was a matter of his own good will and not a question of obligation.[36] A similar problem arose during FitzRalph's absence in the case of the further statutory obligation towards the canons of the cathedral chapter on certain major feast days – Christmas, Purification, Trinity, and Assumption. In this case the two proctors appointed by FitzRalph to represent him in England while he was at Avignon, Nicholas de Lasci and John Pryne, appeared before the canons in the chapter house on 19 December 1337 and declared their readiness to meet the absent dean's obligations on these four feasts, together with all other duties recognized by custom or by statute.[37] This offer was, however, declined by the canons in terms which obscure rather than clarify the reasons for FitzRalph's prolonged absence. They did so on the grounds that they would not do anything derogatory to the archbishop or the court of Canterbury, or contrary to the rights of the cathedral or the position of the dean.[38] It is difficult to see how all these various interests might be affected by the acceptance of an invitation to which the canons were entitled by statute. The reference to the archbishop of Canterbury and his court indicates that the litigation which FitzRalph had taken to the curia was a case which had either previously been heard in Canterbury and was now being taken on appeal to Avignon, or else that it concerned a matter deemed to be within the competence of the metropolitan. FitzRalph was therefore bypassing the jurisdiction of the archbishop of Canterbury, then the powerful John de Stratford, confidant of Edward III and several times chancellor of England.[39] The latter possibility is consistent with the explanation for FitzRalph's excommunication offered by Jenkins. She argued that Stratford was more strict

[35] *Reg. Vat.* 159, fol. 362^r, *CPL* 1342–62, 117. For the increasing number of Lichfield canons in residence and the rising cost of hospitality see Edwards, *English Secular Cathedrals*, pp. 64–5.

[36] Dugdale, *Monasticon Anglicanum*, iii. 250.

[37] Ibid., 256.

[38] MS Ashmole 794, fol. 59^v.

[39] *BRUO* III, 1796–8.

than his predecessors in the exercise of his right to have the wills of all deceased canons in English dioceses proved in the court of Canterbury. In Lichfield matters came to a head in May 1337 following the death of a member of the chapter, Master Philip de Turville, whose will was proved before the chapter in Lichfield. As he was wealthy and also held a rectory in Kent, the matter came to the archbishop's notice, who thereupon challenged the dean's usurpation of metropolitan rights.[40] In the light of this evidence the claim made by the royal clerk, William Kildesby, that FitzRalph had been excommunicated by the archbishop in the course of litigation seems plausible and this might account for the increasingly cautious attitude of the cathedral chapter. The canons continued to adopt this attitude throughout 1338, when they rejected the subsequent invitations issued by FitzRalph's proctors with the explanation that they did not wish to burden the dean during his absence.[41] After this the Acts Book is silent on the matter, and one would be left with the impression that the canons avoided making any claims involving a financial burden on the absent dean were it not for a letter issued by Clement VI on 16 May 1344 in response to a petition of FitzRalph to the effect that he was being harassed on this score during his absence. The papal attitude was cautious, and Clement ordered the bishop and chapter to investigate the statutory obligations of the dean which had been laid down under the previous bishop, Walter Langton (1296-1321),[42] and if these were found to be unreasonably onerous upon the dean and his financial position (and the pope implied he did not think they were) they should be mitigated. The Acts Book records no further action on the matter, and it can only be presumed that FitzRalph was covering himself for all eventualities preparatory to his return to Lichfield later in 1344.

More important matters disturbed relations between the dean and his canons during his absence, above all his constant requests for further financial support and, in the later years, his apparently inexplicable continued residence at Avignon long after he had completed to the apparent satisfaction of the Lichfield canons the task for which they sent him there. Through his proctors in England, whom he appointed or re-confirmed every two years, FitzRalph drew on the chapter for his expenses and the substantial sums which he received for the years 1337-40

[40] Jenkins, i. 44-5. MS Ashmole 794, fol. 72^v^.
[41] Ibid., fols. 59^v^, 63^v^. [42] *HBC*², 234.

are recorded in the Acts Book.[43] Unfortunately the entries for the years 1341-3 are very sparse and the records for the period 1343-55 are lost entirely, leaving us with no evidence either of the chapter's reactions to FitzRalph's activities in his last years in Avignon – when we know he was engaged in other matters – or of his administration of his deanery upon his return. However, he continued to appoint proctors to represent him in England: on 28 September 1340 he nominated as his attorneys for the next two years John Pek of Brewood, clerk, and Thomas de la Hurne of Milton, layman, while on 16 July 1342 he nominated, also for two years, Godfrey Fremond and John de Skelton.[44]

Business transactions between Lichfield and Avignon were cumbersome and time-consuming, and FitzRalph was not the best of correspondents. Unless the chapter was prepared to incur the added expenditure of a special messenger, the delay between forwarding documents to FitzRalph for approval and signature and having them returned for them to act upon was considerable, and clearly the authority delegated to his attorneys in England was limited. By the spring of 1340 the chapter was clearly becoming impatient, and in a letter dated 10 March some of the reasons for their dissatisfaction become clear.[45] The canons stated that their former proctor at the curia, Robert de Thresk, whom the dean had replaced personally, had written to one of the canons pointing out that he still held documents belonging to the chapter and that he intended to retain them until he was paid for services over the past two years. But the canons had sent FitzRalph out to Avignon equipped with funds to pay the proctor for the year ending at Michaelmas 1337 and they had not employed him since. Without actually insinuating that FitzRalph had misappropriated their funds and not made the authorized payments three years earlier, the canons politely inquired into the nature of the services for which Thresk was claiming payment and of the documents which he claimed to hold. They also sought from FitzRalph a reply to letters written on their behalf by the dean's proctors in England, which FitzRalph had apparently chosen to ignore. Most significantly of all the canons requested that the dean have sent to them the bull proclaiming the decision handed down in their favour by the curial court in their case against the Benedictine prior and

43 MS Ashmole 794, fols. 68^{v}, 69^{r}, 69^{v}.

44 CPR 1340-43, 34, 488.

45 MS Ashmole 794, fol. 77^{r}.

monks of Coventry, or at least a copy of it. This indicates that the case between the Coventry and Lichfield chapters had been decided in favour of Lichfield during the winter of 1339-40, and that from the viewpoint of the chapter the principal reason for FitzRalph's absence in Avignon had been resolved satisfactorily. They make no reference to any further litigation in which the dean might be engaged on their behalf, and the inference is that the infringement of their rights through episcopal visitation of the chapter was not, or at least no longer, an issue in Avignon.[46] Such an interpretation leaves unanswered the question as to why FitzRalph in a sermon preached before Clement VI on 6 December 1349 stated that he had spent seven years engaged in litigation at the curia, and that he had to battle his way through fifteen appeals before finally winning his case.[47]

However, a further explanation for FitzRalph's prolonged absence and for the apparent anomalies and obscurities in the Acts Book lies in an entry in the Close Rolls dated from Westminster 28 May 1346, but referring to legal proceedings which had begun by 28 September 1337.[48] The case originated in a dispute between the dean and chapter of Lichfield on the one hand and William Kildesby, one of the most powerful clerks in the royal household, who in 1338 became keeper of the Privy Seal. Kildesby claimed that he had been lawfully collated to the living of Cannock, a parish which was in the gift of the dean and chapter of Lichfield and which, it may be recalled, had been the subject of financial investigations during the years 1332-6. During the same period attempts had been made to secure into royal hands the gift of Cannock, which lay close to the king's free chapel of Penkridge, but the first attempts to collate a royal nominee had failed due to the successful resistance of dean and chapter.[49]

[46] The controversy flared up again towards the end of Northburgh's episcopate 1357-9, and frequently during the 14th century the dean and chapter went to the unusual trouble and expense of seeking advice from other secular chapters. They also appealed to the pope against attempts both by the bishop of Lichfield and the archbishop of Canterbury to visit the chapter, Edwards, *English Secular Cathedrals*, p. 132. By 1397 Richard Scrope was visiting the cathedral with the consent of the chapter. For Scrope, later archbishop of York and possessor of a manuscript of FitzRalph's *Summa de Questionibus Armenorum* and sermon diary (now MS New College 90), see *BRUO* III, 1659-60, *BRUC* 513-14.

[47] B, fol. 202^{v}; J, fol. 147va.

[48] CCR 1343-46, 577-8.

[49] The royal free chapel of Penkridge (Staffs.), diocese of Coventry and Lichfield, was a collegiate foundation established by King John and given by him to the archbishops of Dublin, who were therefore *decani nati*, see *Archbishop Alen's Register*, pp. 307-12; Jeffrey H. Denton, *English Royal Free Chapels 1100-1300. A constitutional study* (Manchester, 1970), *ad indicem*.

With the collation of Kildesby in the summer of 1337 and the continued resistance of dean and chapter, the matter came to a head and the case was heard in the king's court on Monday 'three weeks before Michaelmas', i.e. 7 September 1337. On that date William Kildesby came before the king's court and claimed that the dean's suit in the name of the chapter ought not to be heard since he was under sentence of major excommunication by authority of the archbishop of Canterbury. Kildesby brought letters which were deemed as proving his point and FitzRalph's case was accordingly dismissed – by no means the last time this argument was used against him in order to discredit a lawsuit initiated by him.[50] A further indication of the methods to which Kildesby was prepared to resort is provided by a letter of Benedict XII to Edward III on 7 July 1341.[51] The pope protested that the papal messenger sent to England with letters to the bishop of Lichfield and to Kildesby's brother Robert concerning the disputed benefice was seized by the brothers Kildesby and imprisoned on a false charge of homicide in order to prevent him from executing the mandate issued by the curial auditor charged with the investigation of the case. At this point it is a reasonable inference that FitzRalph was keeping the pope well informed about the injustices being perpetrated by the opposition in order to keep the collation of benefices in royal hands, and apparently with the king's tacit consent.

Although these entries in the papal registers and Close Rolls go part of the way to explain some of the events revealed by the Acts Book and discussed above, they do not answer the most basic question as to why FitzRalph was under sentence of excommunication in the late summer of 1337. Clearly this sentence of excommunication was the principal personal reason for FitzRalph's decision to set out for the curia, even though the record of the chapter meeting of 21-22 August does not indicate whether the sentence had already been handed down or whether it was still only threatened, nor does it throw any further light on the possible reasons for the excommunication. However, the most probable explanation, and one which would explain both the cautious attitude of the chapter and their willingness to finance him during his protracted absence at Avignon is that FitzRalph had chosen to bypass the court of Canterbury and

[50] CCR 1343-46, 577-8. The friars subsequently used a similar argument.
[51] *CPL* 1305-42, 590-1.

take the dispute with the monks of Coventry, and possibly also the questions of probate of wills and episcopal visitations of the chapter to the curial courts – a move which, given English royal attitudes to appeals to Rome, was unlikely to endear him either to Edward III or to an archbishop of Canterbury who by 1337 had already served two periods of office as chancellor of England.[52] Even if the chapter did not necessarily approve of FitzRalph's methods of capitular administration and had reservations about the way in which he conducted their legal affairs, he had done so while representing their best interests and they probably felt obliged to lend their support. On the other hand their cautious attitude over the question of hospitality in 1337-8[53] and their decision to indemnify themselves against possible action arising out of correspondence on their behalf between the dean's proctors in England and FitzRalph in Avignon from 1339 to 1340[54] are consistent with the possibility that their dean was still regarded as under sentence of excommunication in the ecclesiastical province of Canterbury. This hypothesis would also help to explain why, after the Coventry-Lichfield dispute had ended in favour of the dean and his chapter, FitzRalph continued in residence at the curia and also the very personal note in the sermon of 6 December 1349 in which he paid tribute to the integrity of papal judges who had heard his case and after seven years of litigation and fifteen appeals had vindicated him against an opponent who was considerably more powerful than he ('contra adversarium multum me potenciorem'), a remark which would very aptly apply to the archbishop of Canterbury.[55]

By 1341 Stratford had disengaged himself to a considerable degree from affairs of the realm and was able to devote himself more exclusively to metropolitan duties, so it is not improbable that his proctors at the curia were given instructions to pursue the case against FitzRalph with renewed vigour, and that the proceedings therefore dragged into the next pontificate.[56] Stratford's change of interests was reflected in the statutes which he had issued after the provincial council held in London in 1342. His legislation was characterized by concern for the

[52] McKisack, *The Fourteenth Century*, pp. 152 ff. He was chancellor 1330-4, 1335-7, and briefly 1340.

[53] MS Ashmole 794, fols. 59^{v}, 63^{v}.

[54] Ibid., fol. 70^{v}.

[55] B, fol. 202^{v}; J, fol. 147va.

[56] For Stratford's quarrels with Edward III and withdrawal from office see McKisack, pp. 169-79.

parochial structure and for the defence of property at parochial level against encroachments by religious orders and other elements, a concern which FitzRalph would at a later stage of his career represent to an extreme degree,[57] although in the early 1340s the two men represented opposing interests. Even then, however, a fundamental difference in the attitude of both is clearly distinguishable. Stratford was concerned to keep the legal business of the *ecclesia Anglicana* within the confines of the kingdom of England, and thereby conformed to the known wishes of Edward III, whereas FitzRalph from the beginning of his ecclesiastical career adopted a policy which he would maintain to the end of his life – when in doubt or difficulty appeal to the papal curia. This 'Rome-running' was a general feature of the Irish Church, where the situation caused by the 'two nations' increased the number of appeals to the papal curia, and it is possible that FitzRalph adopted a similar stance in analogy to prevailing circumstances in Ireland.

However, FitzRalph's second visit to the curia was not solely devoted to litigation and, apart from his increasing interest in the relations between the Roman Church and the Greek and Armenian 'schismatics', and participation in negotiations with representatives of these eastern Churches which shall be considered below, at least two other areas of activity on his part are identifiable which had a major impact on his future career. First and foremost in his work as a preacher, which will also be the subject of a separate discussion. To a lesser extent, and an aspect which might easily escape notice, is his development of particular areas of 'expertise' within the wider scope of curial business and, especially in the last year of Benedict XII's pontificate and the first years of that of Clement VI he is increasingly to be found dealing with the problem of apostate religious who are to be reconciled with their orders, and with the provision of suitable candidates for benefices within the Anglo-Irish lordship in general, and in the archdiocese of Armagh in particular. In the former case, his years as a litigant in Avignon coincided with the period in which Benedict XII was engaged in promoting the reform of the religious orders – monks, canons, and friars alike – sometimes as in the Dominican case in the

[57] Brenda Bolton, 'The Council of London of 1342', *Councils and Assemblies* (Cambridge, 1971), 147-60. His constitutions were those of a lawyer not a theologian, but the situation they reflected was such that it is not difficult to anticipate support for FitzRalph's subsequent stand from members of the English hierarchy. What is surprising is the eventual weakness of that support.

face of most bitter opposition from the order concerned, who denied the necessity of papally imposed reform.[58] A side-effect of this reforming activity was a drive, especially noticeable in the registers of Benedict XII, to reconcile apostate members of the regular clergy with their religious superiors and convents, and particularly in the case of members of the older monastic orders – significantly not any friars – we find FitzRalph during the period 1341-3 frequently receiving a papal mandate to execute the reconciliation of this or that particular English religious with his convent.[59]

During the same period his role as an 'Irish expert' at the curia can be seen developing. A number of benefices, mainly in the Anglo-Irish lordship or at least in dioceses where in the mid-fourteenth century a residue of 'English' influence was still to be expected, were the subject of papal provisions in the early 1340s and an increasing proportion of them were issued with a concurrent mandate to FitzRalph, thereby suggesting that while the dean of Lichfield was in residence at the curia, he may have personally helped to further the petition of the ultimate providee from his native land.[60] A small minority of such benefices in which his name figures was intended for candidates of Gaelic Irish stock and these were usually located within the archdiocese of Armagh, in which at some unknown point in the early 1330s FitzRalph had been provided to a canonry.[61] We have no evidence whether, in compliance with the terms of Benedict XII's bull providing him to the deanery of Lichfield, FitzRalph had actually resigned all his other benefices. It is at least possible that in the case of his canonry in Exeter together with the prebend of Crediton he did not resign immediately, as these were the subject of a petition by the dean of Lincoln, William of Norwich, for his nephew on 20 February 1343 in terms which suggested that the resignation had occurred relatively recently and that Grandisson had collated another to these benefices,

[58] For his sermons to the Dominicans and attitude to their reform problems, Walsh, 'An Irish Preacher at Avignon', 401-15.

[59] e.g. *Reg. Vat.* 129, fols. 120^{v}, 192^{r-v}; *Reg. Vat.* 162, fol. 147^{v}; *CPL* 1305-42, 550, 552; 1342-62, 139.

[60] Some of these also concerned members of Oxford University, as the case of Adam Pothow, *Reg. Vat.* 129, fols. 307^{v}-308^{r}; *CPL* 1305-42, 555. For the latter as proctor for the university see *BRUO* III, 1505.

[61] But including Hugh O'Kelly, provided to a canonry in St. Patrick's Cathedral, Dublin, 30 September 1343, *CPL* 1342-62, 100.

or was about to do so.[62] In the case of FitzRalph's canonry in Armagh there is no evidence that he ever resigned it, and it is probable in view of the minimal revenues which he could have drawn from such a benefice that the obligation to resign was not enforced either by Benedict XII or by Clement VI and that FitzRalph remained an absentee canon of Armagh until his election as archbishop by the cathedral chapter in June 1346.

This view is further reinforced by the fact that he was in contact, while still at Avignon, with the diocese of Armagh and its Gaelic Irish archbishop, David O'Hiraghty, when the latter was obviously willing to employ Anglo-Irish or English agents for his transactions at the curia. Closer study of relations between Armagh and the curia during this episcopate leads to the more general reflection that Gaelic Irish prelates in the fourteenth century may regularly have used 'English' agents in their dealings with Avignon, where the latter were numerous, well versed in curial procedures, and apparently influential, at a time before the expansion of the observant movement among the mendicant orders in fifteenth-century Ireland was to provide a constant stream of Irish friars on the path to Rome as the agent of their orders and of their bishops.[63] In any case the papal registers testify to the fact that Archbishop O'Hiraghty used Roger Sampford as his agent, sending him at least six times to the curia on diocesan business and finally requesting Clement VI to provide him with a suitable benefice. On 20 September 1343 the pope issued letters to the abbot of Mellifont and the deans of Lichfield and Armagh, making these executors of the mandate to provide Sampford with the church of Tamlachan in the gift of the archbishop.[64] On the same day a further letter was issued to Sampford himself, together with the usual executive letters to the abbot of Mellifont and the deans of Lichfield and Lincoln,[65] providing him in further compliance with the petition of Archbishop O'Hiraghty to a canonry in Armagh with expectation of a prebend, notwithstanding the church of Tamlachan to which he had already been provided, i.e. with tacit

[62] *Reg. Vat.* 153, fol. 84^{r-v}, with more detailed information about the circumstances than *CPL* 1342-62, 78.

[63] The evidence of *CPL* for the 15th century supports this view, and for Roman leanings of the observant friars see Francis X. Martin, 'The Irish Augustinian reform movement in the fifteenth century', *Medieval Studies presented to Aubrey Gwynn S.J.* (Dublin, 1961), 230-64.

[64] *Reg. Vat.* 157, fol. 249^{v}; *CPL* 1342-62, 96; *CPL Petitions* I, 116.

[65] *Reg. Vat.* 158, fols. 110^{v}-111^{r}; *CPL* 1342-62, 100.

papal approval for the retention of both benefices, doubtless in view of their low income – benefices in Gaelic Ireland and in border areas were frequently so poor that provision to them was expedited gratis without payment of the usual taxes.[66] It is reasonable therefore, in view of FitzRalph's connection with these provisions and of Sampford's frequent presence in Avignon, to assume that the two men were in contact at the curia. FitzRalph's own employment of Sampford as his personal representative in Avignon after his election to the see of Armagh, to petition the pope for his *pallium*, lends further weight to the argument that they had been in contact at the curia during the early 1340s.

Further significant indications of the dean of Lichfield's continued association with the Church in Ireland during his prolonged absence are contained in a series of petitions which received a favourable response from Clement VI on 8 May 1344. Here FitzRalph secured for each of three nephews provision to an important benefice in Ireland: Edmund Radulphi (Rauf) was to get a canonry in Ossory, John Brisbon a canonry in St. Patrick's in Dublin, while the dean's namesake, Richard Radulphi, was to receive a benefice in the diocese of Meath.[67] All three were then students at Oxford, and the examination of their suitability for the benefices concerned was to be undertaken either by the chancellor of Oxford University or by the chancellor of Lichfield.[68] Richard Radulphi was the only one of the three described as holding a degree: he was already a bachelor of arts, would subsequently become master of arts and a student of theology, and was to act as FitzRalph's personal agent in Avignon during the 1350s when the archbishop was occupied in Ireland.[69] These provisions are an indication of more personal concerns which helped to prolong FitzRalph's residence at the curia. His concern for the education and advancement of his nephews, the two members of the Rauf family and one of the Brisbon – a Dundalk family related by marriage to the Rauf[70] – had already

[66] Walsh, 'Ireland, the Papal Curia and the Schism: a border case', Genèse et débuts du Grand Schisme d'Occident. Avignon, 25–28 settembre, 1978 (Colloques Internationaux du Centre National de la recherche scientifique, 586, Paris, 1980), 561–74, at 563.

[67] *Reg. Vat.* 158, fols. 189^{v}, 231^{v}–232^{r}, 372^{v}; *CPL* 1342–62, 107; *CPL Petitions* I, 53.

[68] The university chancellor was then William de Bergeveney, who held office 1341–3 and 1343–5, *BRUO* I, 173–4.

[69] For Richard FitzRalph jr. see *BRUO* II, 694.

[70] *Dowdall Deeds, passim.*

secured for the three young Anglo-Irishmen the opportunity to study at Oxford. The next step up the ladder towards a successful ecclesiastical career involved the provision of each of them to a suitable benefice, something which FitzRalph could achieve through personal influence and intervention at the curia, and once this had been achieved we find him making preparations for his return to Lichfield.[71] One is tempted to speculate whether FitzRalph may not have had other motives in mind when arranging the strategic distribution of his relatives in several important cathedral chapters. The placing of Edmund Radulphi and John Brisbon respectively in Ossory and Dublin may have been intended to strengthen FitzRalph's ties with the ecclesiastical life of the Anglo-Irish lordship, and it certainly placed a relative in each of two cathedral chapters where the diocesan ordinaries were engaged in bitter strife and where, at least in the case of Dublin the death or eventual deposition of an elderly and discredited prelate might have been regarded as an opportunity for personal advancement.

Nevertheless, FitzRalph appears to have served his chapter to their satisfaction during his stay in Avignon. He was unable to halt the strong infiltration of Italian providees in the diocese, especially in the archdeaconries in the 1330s, and while he himself was in Avignon the precentorship of the cathedral of Lichfield was conferred, on 15 July 1343, on none other than Cardinal Annibale de Ceccano, the staunch supporter of John XXII's position in the beatific vision controversy.[72] However, he negotiated a successful interim solution to the conflict with the chapter of Coventry and during his term of office as dean the claims of the bishop to visit the chapter were successfully resisted without allowing a crisis situation to develop as had happened in 1322-4 under Stephen Segrave and was to occur

[71] Only one more sermon is recorded in Avignon before FitzRalph's departure, on 7 July 1344, B, fols. 187^{r}–193^{r}; J, fols. 137ra–141rb, and he was in Lichfield before 25 November 1345.

[72] *Reg. Vat.* 157, fol. 137^{r}; *CPL* 1342-62, 95. Ceccano held several English benefices, including the archdeaconries of Nottingham and Buckingham, and the treasurership of York, ibid., *ad indicem*. FitzRalph was not the only link between Lichfield and the curia in the early 1340s. On 10 March 1345 after FitzRalph's return to Lichfield, Clement VI wrote to Bishop Northburgh, thanking him for letters sent through the bishop's nephew Laurence (described as bachelor of canon law), and also for the gift of a valuable cope, *Reg. Vat.* 138, fol. 224^{r}; *CPL* 1342-62, 15. Clement VI assured Northburgh that he would look with favour on him and his church, which may have been simply a polite formula, or may have indicated that the bishop was taking independent action to preserve his own rights against the chapter, whose agent was FitzRalph.

again in 1357–9.[73] In the case of Lichfield the powerful position of the dean enabled the chapter to resist episcopal visitation very much longer than other cathedral chapters with similar statutes, and the dean and chapter were for the remainder of the fourteenth century to expend considerable resources in time and money in their attempts to cope with the problem before finally submitting to episcopal visitation under Bishop Richard Scrope in 1397.[74]

While in Lichfield, before his departure for Avignon, and during the two years which elapsed between his return and his election to the see of Armagh, FitzRalph proved himself a diligent administrator and pastor. Whereas the evidence for the first period in Lichfield tells us more about his relations with the chapter, his attempts to restore a high standard of observance of their duties on the part of the cathedral clergy, his general concern for discipline and good order in his cathedral and for his own personal authority as dean, and his interest in the building programme then being undertaken, the evidence for the later period is revealing in a different direction. It shows us for the first time FitzRalph as an active and practically-minded pastor, concerned with preaching and with the inculcation of basic truths and standards in his flock. The sermons preached in his cathedral and in numerous churches throughout the diocese in the period 1345–7 are cast in a very different mould from those preached before curial audiences during the previous seven years. The latter testify to the fact that, regardless of the differences which might have existed between the dean of Lichfield and the archbishop of Canterbury, these were not regarded as a hindrance in the circles close to the pope and did not prevent his continued rise in the estimation of both Benedict XII and Clement VI. They also provide, together with the sermon of 7 July 1335, the earliest examples of FitzRalph's developing talent as a preacher and, understandably, here he concentrated his attention on general theological problems and the reform of ecclesiastical abuses, whereas the Lichfield sermons provided him with his first opportunity to preach in a

[73] See Jenkins, i, 40 ff., and *VCH Stafford*, iii. 155 ff. The Acts Book contains no entries pertaining to FitzRalph's activities as dean after his return from Avignon, and the records are lost for the years 1343–55, Savage, *Richard FitzRalph*, pp. 19–20. MS Lichfield Cathedral 89 contains correspondence concerning the cathedral for the years 1340–52, but FitzRalph does not figure in it.

[74] See B. S. Benedikz, *A Catalogue of the Cathedral Library Manuscripts* (rev. version, Birmingham, 1978).

pastoral context. Hence the period which FitzRalph spent as dean of Lichfield was formative in a number of ways which were to be significant for his future work in Armagh. He received his first taste of diocesan administration and pastoral activity under a bishop whose own concern for good organization and high standards among the secular and regular clergy under his jurisdiction might well have provided a model for future guidance, and whose scholarly interests were at least sufficient to ensure that Lichfield under his care acquired the nucleus of a respectable cathedral library. This office provided FitzRalph with the opportunity for a lengthy stay in Avignon, where he acquired experience of curial legal procedures, emerged as a preacher of stature, and participated in those debates between eastern and western Christians which resulted in the *Summa de Questionibus Armenorum.*

iii. Armenian debates and the Summa de Questionibus Armenorum

The *Summa de Questionibus Armenorum*, a dialogue in nineteen books, has a strong claim to be considered FitzRalph's most important and influential contribution to medieval theological literature. In many respects it is the most revealing work for a study of his thought, personal intellectual development, attitudes to Scripture and speculative theology, cultural contacts, and place in the history of medieval thought, in spite of the fact that it did not have the immediate impact among his contemporaries of either his theory of dominion or his campaign against the mendicant friars. Apart from the *Defensio Curatorum*, the polemical statement of his case against the pastoral privileges of the friars, it had of all his writings the widest manuscript circulation in the fourteenth and fifteenth centuries. It was also printed by Je(h)an Petit, bookseller to the University of Paris, under a licence issued by Louis XII on 12 March 1511, and the preparation of the edition was carried out by Johannis Sudoris, who also added a text of the four principal anti-mendicant sermons preached by FitzRalph in London at St. Paul's Cross during the winter of 1356-7.[1] These sermons, which had an

[1] Magister Johannis Sudoris identified himself in the 'incipit' of the printed text: 'Incipit summa domini ricardi radulphi archiepiscopi armachani totius hybernie primatis de erroribus armenorum correcta e emendata a johanne sudoris caletibestensi diocesis rothomagensis sacre militie doctore meritissimo gimnasii regalis navarre quadam bursario theologo', ed. Paris, 1511, fol. 1ra. On the title page he described the work correctly as *Summa . . . in Questionibus Armenorum*, and FitzRalph origi-

extensive manuscript circulation independently of the rest of the sermon diary, were printed on fifteen folios at the end of the volume, but their pagination was confused by the printer.[2] In spite of the fact that some of the better manuscripts of the *Summa* emanated from Sorbonne circles and are still in Paris, where they were presumably available to the university bookseller, the text both of the *Summa* and of the sermons is a particularly bad specimen of early printing. Frequently it is possible to glean no more from the printed page than the general sense of the original text, and recourse to one of the better manuscripts is essential. The manuscript tradition of the *Summa* is exceptionally good, as the work circulated widely, above all from two centres: Avignon, where the papal library possessed copies from an early date, one of which must have been that presented by FitzRalph to Clement VI for his inspection and approval,[3] and Paris, from where the text was transmitted to university centres as far distant as Leipzig and Cracow.[4] For purposes of this study two Vatican manuscripts have been used throughout, Vat. Lat. 1033, which was written in Perugia in 1393 for Boniface IX, and Vat. Lat. 1035, written in Paris in the later fourteenth century and purchased there by a student of theology, the Dominican (later cardinal) Juan de Torquemada.[5]

nally called his work *questions*, avoiding the implication that the opinions held by the Armenians which they discussed in Avignon had already been condemned as erroneous.

[2] The foliation is as follows: 163–167, 161–162, 161–163, 174–177, but in spite of this the text follows consecutively in the order in which these leaves were bound.

[3] This dedication copy can no longer be traced, and it was possibly in that section of the papal library which became dispersed as a result of the travels of Benedict XIII, see Maier, 'Die "Bibliotheca Minor" Benedikts XIII (Petrus de Luna)', *Ausgehendes Mittelalter,* iii. 1–53. In the catalogue of this library, nos. 90 and 127 were copies of FitzRalph's *Summa*, but these must have been made later than Clement's copy, see Maier, 'Der literarische Nachlass des Petrus Rogerii (Clemens VI.) in der Borghesiana', *Ausgehendes Mittelalter*, ii, 255–315. No work by FitzRalph appeared in the catalogue made for Urban V in 1369, but by 1375 a copy of the *Summa* was in the catalogue made for Gregory XI, see Franz Ehrle, *Historia Bibliothecae Romanorum Pontificum*, i (Rome, 1890), 274 ff., 588.

[4] Cracow, Bibl. Jagelliónska, MS 1599 (DD. VI. 1) was copied in Paris in 1375 and is the earliest dated text still extant. It has a note indicating that the Polish clergy used the *Summa* against the errors of the Ruthenian Christians: 'Iste liber est datus per mag. Laurencium de Ratibor, professorem, pro libraria magistrorum, in quo continetur Armachanus Anglicus de questionibus Armenorum seu Ruthenorum', fol. 1^{r}. During the reign of Casimir the Great (1333–70) the Armenian presence in Poland increased substantially and in 1367 they were permitted to establish an archbishopric at Lemberg, see J. Krajcar, 'The Ruthenian Patriarchate', *OCP* 30 (1964), 65–84.

[5] For a description of Vat. Lat. 1033–1036, four copies of the *Summa*, see Pelzer, *Cod. Vat. Lat.* II. i, 541–4.

The manuscript circulation, above all in the humanist circles linked with the Council of Ferrara–Florence and the revival of negotiations for reunion of the eastern and western Churches, need not detain us here, and the primary considerations are the place of the text in FitzRalph's *œuvre* and intellectual development, the contents and context of the work, and the information which it provides for FitzRalph's interests and contacts during his longest period of residence at the curia.

The date of composition has been the subject of controversy, above all because earlier scholars, including R. L. Poole,[6] based their conclusions on the preface of the work in which FitzRalph, as archbishop of Armagh and primate of Ireland, dedicated his dialogue to the two Armenian prelates with whom he had discussed the topics concerned: 'Reverendis in Christo patribus Nersi archiepiscopo Managartensi ac fratri Iohanni electo Clatensi Maioris Armenie Ricardus Radulfi archiepiscopus Armacanus Hybernie primas.'[7] As FitzRalph could not describe himself thus until after his consecration on 8 July 1347, the preface must have been composed after that date. The *terminus ad quem* for the completion of the work is set by a further passage in the preface, in which the author submitted his work to the judgement of Pope Clement VI: 'et ipsum opus, cuius titulum volui esse de questionibus armenorum, quod in 19 particulas sive libros distinxi, singulis libris materiam fidei et ipsius capitula premittendo approbacioni et reprobacioni nostri patris Clementis sexti universalis ecclesie summi pontificis, in toto et in parte commicti'.[8] As Clement VI died on 6 December 1352, these passages might seem to point to a date of composition in the years 1347–52. Based on the fact that FitzRalph was in Avignon from the summer of 1349 until early in 1351, Poole had concluded that the archbishop of Armagh debated with the Armenian prelates in Avignon during the course of this visit and then composed the dialogue for their guidance in matters of faith. This impression might be further strengthened by the consideration that when FitzRalph returned to Avignon in 1349 the question of reunion with the Greeks had been revived. Two embassies were sent from Constantinople by the emperor John

[6] *DNB* vii. 195.

[7] S, fol. 1ra; Vat. Lat. 1033, fol. 1^{r}; Vat. Lat. 1035, fol. 1ra.

[8] Ibid. There are a number of minor variations in the MSS, but reference will only be made to them when they fundamentally alter the meaning of the text. All MSS agree on the title which FitzRalph intended for his work '. . . de questionibus armenorum'.

Cantacuzenus, the first consisting of Greeks accompanied by the emperor's Latin servant Franciscus, the second two years later and consisting of two western bishops, presumably friars.[9] Hence it would not be unreasonable to conclude that reunion negotiations were inaugurated with Armenian as well as Greek representatives during these years and, as will become clear, recent research on pro-union elements within the Armenian Church tends to support rather than reject such a possibility. This is, however, a probable explanation – not for the original composition of FitzRalph's dialogue – but for his feeling compelled to complete it and seek a public imprimatur for his views by submitting it to the reigning pope, who was then adopting a more conciliatory attitude towards the eastern Christians.[10]

The dating of the text to 1349–51 was questioned by Fr. Gwynn in a brief paper published some forty years ago,[11] and shortly afterwards the debate was taken a stage further by the critical textual studies of L. L. Hammerich, which centred on the autobiographical prayer included in most manuscripts and in the Paris edition as Chapter 35 of the final book of the dialogue.[12] Poole had raised doubts about the authenticity of this prayer, arguing on the basis of its difference in style from the rest of the dialogue that it might be a spurious addition,[13] but the prayer, which was edited by Hammerich,[14] contains allusions to various episodes in the archbishop's life and is one of the most personal and illuminating documents which we have from his pen.[15] In it he gave thanks to the Incarnate Word for special graces granted to him during his active life, including

[9] Raymond-Joseph Loenertz, 'Ambassadeurs grecs auprès du pape Clément VI (1348)', *Byzantina et Franco-Graeca*, ed. Peter Schreiner, i (Rome, 1970), 285–302; Günther Weiss, *Joannes Kantakuzenos – Aristokrat, Staatsmann, Kaiser und Mönch – in der Gesellschaftsentwicklung von Byzanz im 14. Jahrhundert* (Wiesbaden, 1969), did not refer to this embassy, but pointed out that the emperor held discussions about reunion after 1 September 1347 and again through envoys with Innocent VI in 1353, while Clement frequently put out 'feelers' among prominent Greeks, ibid., pp. 61–3. On 14th-century reunion negotiations see Wilhelm de Vries, *Rom und die Patriarchate des Ostens* (Munich, 1963), pp. 52–64.

[10] Jules Gay, *Le Pape Clément VI et les affaires d'orient (1342–1352)* (Paris, 1904).

[11] *Studies*, 22 (1933), 598–606, where Gwynn located the genesis of the *Summa* precisely in the events at Avignon during the late 1330s and early 1340s.

[12] With the exception of Vat. Lat. 1034.

[13] *DNB* vii. 195.

[14] In *FitzRalph and the Mendicants*, pp. 18–22. He based his edition on a group of Paris MSS, but for several passages Vat. Lat. 1033 gives better readings. Citations below are generally taken from Hammerich's edition, but dubious passages are corrected from the Vatican MS.

[15] See Hammerich's notes and commentary on the prayer, pp. 22–5.

three cases of pursuit by his enemies – persecutors and royal officers – when he nevertheless managed to escape to safety: once while travelling and accompanied only by a young monk and a novice, which might have occurred *en route* to or from Avignon,[16] and a second time when he and some of his servants were captured by robbers but suffered no harm other than the loss of his purse.[17] But even this loss, he felt, had been made good on several occasions in the hour of need: 'cum amplius me urgebat necessitas diversis temporibus per partes eam fecisti restitui'.[18] This episode, in which he travelled with money and servants, might easily have taken place in Ireland after he had become archbishop, where conditions on the fringe of the Anglo-Irish lordship and in the Gaelic parts of his ecclesiastical province were positively conducive to such occurrences, and where FitzRalph's own denunciations of the violence of life reveal overtones of personal experience. A further possible occasion for this fracas involving the archbishop and his household might have been his attempt in 1348 to have his primatial rights established within the confines of the see of Dublin.

Finally there had been an occasion when FitzRalph was fleeing from the king's officers who held a writ for his arrest: however, he managed to evade them and reached his destination, which was clearly Avignon:

> Via eras michi recta cum ergo a facie ministrorum regalium fugiens latitarem qui litteras quas brevia nominant plurimas in portibus diversis regni nostri acceperant ut me caperent et tenerent: quoniam tu preveniendo ipsorum insidias nunc me interius premonebas ut fugerem, me nunc exterius dirigebas quo pergerem, tandem via breviori apud homines declinata multo celerius per te viam rectissimam me perduxeras quo tendebam.[19]

Hammerich argued that this episode involving pursuit by royal officials took place in 1337 when FitzRalph, as dean of Lichfield, made his way to Avignon in defiance both of Edward III and of the archbishop of Canterbury, who in the course of litigation had excommunicated him.[20] In support of this view one might adduce the passage in which FitzRalph gave thanks for the joys which were granted to him amidst the sorrows of a long exile, referring to his lengthy lawsuit at Avignon: 'Eras michi in curia veritas lucida in tantum quod patefacta iusticia questionum mearum et adversancium michi calumpniis denudatis apud palacii apostolici auditores graciam in oculis cunctorum

[16] Ed. cit., p. 18, ll. 11-21. [17] Ibid., pp. 18-19, ll. 22-30.
[18] Ibid., ll. 27-9. [19] Ibid., p. 19, ll. 31-8. [20] Ibid., pp. 24-5.

invenirem'.[21] His final triumph came after seven long years of servitude: 'Tu, Veritas valida, triumphasti, et post servitutem inibi vj annorum vij° anno, ut lex tua preceperat, me liberum a loco illi servitutis abire iussisti.'[22] Here he was definitely referring to the period 1337-44, and it is certain that the prayer, together with the completion of the *Summa*, belongs after this period at the curia when FitzRalph claimed to have rejected scholasticism for the more immediate truth of the Scripture. But how soon after?

Hammerich argued for dating the concluding prayer almost immediately after FitzRalph's return to Lichfield and before the prologue in which he submitted the work to Clement VI on his next visit to the curia. Hammerich did so on the grounds that the prayer contained no explicit references either to FitzRalph's work in Ireland, or the bitter struggle against the mendicants which dominated the last years of his life, or to the Black Death which was a much greater danger than either robbers or royal officers.[23] In doing so he opposed Gwynn's suggestion that the prayer was a much later addition to the *Summa* and was composed in Avignon during the last visit from 1357 to 1360,[24] and that the episode involving flight from officers of the Crown had taken place during the spring or early summer of 1357, after the archbishop had stirred up a hornets' nest during his series of anti-mendicant sermons preached at St. Paul's, whereby he had aroused not merely the hostility of the friars but also the displeasure of Edward III whose patronage the mendicant orders enjoyed and who had a further interest in preventing the dispute being taken on appeal to the papal court.[25] Hence on 1 April 1357 the king issued a mandate expressly forbidding the archbishop of Armagh to leave the kingdom without royal licence, while a few days later mayors and bailiffs in all ports on the south-eastern coast were ordered to be specially watchful lest anybody attempt to leave the country without royal permission.[26] The parallel with the situation described by FitzRalph in his prayer is striking, and this seems a more persuasive argument for the later date than a further

[21] Ibid., p. 20, ll. 57-60. FitzRalph's encounters with curial lawyers made a deep and not always favourable impression on him, and he returned to the problem of curial lawyers and litigation on several occasions during his Avignon sermons.

[22] Ed. cit., p. 20, ll. 66-8. [23] Ibid., p. 25. [24] *Studies*, 22, 606-7.

[25] Gwynn, *English Austin Friars*, pp. 83-9.

[26] Rymer's *Foedera*, III. i. 352, 353. Clearly the king's officers were attempting to enforce the recently enacted (1353) Statute of Praemunire.

criterion adduced by Gwynn on the basis of manuscript evidence. In support of his conjecture that the prayer was a later addition to the dialogue, and therefore that its different style presented no serious objection to its authenticity, he pointed to the fact that it was missing from one of the earliest extant manuscripts, Vat. Lat. 1034, dating from 1380. In this manuscript the explicit states that the text is complete, which might seem excellent contemporary evidence for the existence of a manuscript tradition in which the autobiographical prayer had not yet been added to the original (complete) text, but for the fact that the table of contents at the beginning of Book XIX in this manuscript includes the title of Chapter 35, with the subject-matter of the prayer.[27] Hence whatever the reasons for the scribe's omission of the text of the prayer, the premiss on which this hypothesis is based cannot be correct. However, the evidence of FitzRalph's escape to Avignon in 1357, despite the royal writs intended to detain him, seem to be the most important criterion for dating the prayer, even though there was a previous case of royal involvement, and possible royal displeasure over his actions as dean of Lichfield in 1337. But there is no official record of a royal attempt to restrain him in England on the first occasion, and the Acts Book of Lichfield reflects the canons' unease over the dean's clash with the archbishop of Canterbury yet gives no hint of a serious breach with the Crown.[28]

Several episodes during the 1340s, including the sermons preached by FitzRalph on official occasions connected with the English victory in the war with France and the mission to Avignon to plead for an extension of the Jubilee indulgence without the obligation of personal pilgrimage, to the subjects of Edward III, indicate that FitzRalph still enjoyed the confidence of the English king to an extent which was incompatible with the sentiments expressed in the prayer, and that the king's delay in restoring to him the temporalities of the see of Armagh was not caused by hostility or suspicion. On the other hand Fitz-Ralph's actions in 1357 caused a more fundamental breach

[27] Vat. Lat. 1034, fol. 96va. The short Ch. 34 ends with the same 'explicit' as in Vat. Lat. 1033, and then follows: 'Explicit liber totus Summe etc. inceptus Anno dominij M^{o} ccc^{o} lxxx^{o} mensis Ianuarij die viij^{o}. finitus autem mensis aprilis die vi^{o} eiusdem Anni per manus presbiterj Gorij de Cora qui ad instantiam dominj fratris A(ugustini) de urbe Callensis Episcopi sui Amici preintimj sola dilectione Scripsit quibus in presenti gratia et in futuro gloria Amen' (fol. 96va). Augustinus de Urbe OESA was bishop of Cagli 1378–95; see Eubel, *Hierarchia Catholica*, i^{2}. 158; *Reg. Aven.* 204, fol. 160^{r-v}.

[28] MS Ashmole 794, fol. 59^{v}.

between the archbishop and the Crown, and his description – even allowing for a highly-coloured emotional outburst – conforms more precisely with the official record of royal reactions on this occasion. Even English chroniclers writing in the later fourteenth century indicated that because of his actions towards the end of his life, FitzRalph found himself out of royal favour.[29] Hence it is more probable that the experience depicted so vividly in the prayer had occurred shortly before its composition, that FitzRalph composed it during the last years of his life, and that he anticipated that the faith in the guidance of Scripture and the tenacity which had brought success in the past would prove equally effective in his case against the friars upon which he was presently engaged.

However, to argue for a late date in the case of the autobiographical prayer with which FitzRalph concluded his *Summa*, is not to suggest that the entire work was a later composition, nor even that it belonged to the period 1349-51 suggested by Poole. The archbishop adopted this style of formal prayer on at least one other occasion, at the end of the seventh (which was originally intended to be the final) book of the dialogue *De Pauperie Salvatoris*, a work which was also composed in the 1350s.[30] It was the next major work composed by FitzRalph after the completion of the *Summa* and its opening chapter contains a statement which rather emphatically refutes the possibility that he could have been working on the Armenian questions during his third visit to the curia from 1349 to 1351. In the *De Pauperie Salvatoris* FitzRalph tried to apply his developing theories of lordship and jurisdiction to the pastoral and theological problems posed by the mendicant orders, his concern for which had already emerged by the summer of 1350 when on 5 July he preached on the question at a public consistory in the presence of Clement VI.[31] *De Pauperie Salvatoris* is, like the *Summa*, in dialogue form and the same two speakers, Ricardus and his disciple Iohannes, reappear. The latter pressed his teacher to enter upon a new discussion with him and instruct him on the

[29] Thomas Walsingham, *Historia Anglicana 1272–1422*, ed. H. T. Riley, i (London, 1863), 285; John of Reading, *Chronica*, ed. James Tait (Manchester, 1914), p. 131.

[30] Only the first four books of *DPS* were printed by Reginald L. Poole, as an appendix to his edition of Wyclif, *De Dominio Divino* (WS, London, 1890), pp. 273–476. All quotations from Books IV–VII in this study are taken from the earliest datable text, CVP 1430, and for Book VIII from Paris, Bibl. nat., Lat. 3222. For a description of these manuscripts see Appendix, p. .

[31] Ed. Hammerich, *FitzRalph and the Mendicants*, pp. 53–73.

vexed questions of property, dominion, and religious poverty. Among other reasons he urged the fact that his master was at the moment unusually free from other work: 'Unde, quia iam cerno te preter solitum a studio ociosum, in Ihesu nomine te require . . .'[32] We know that FitzRalph came to Avignon both as envoy of Edward III and to secure concessions on behalf of his archdiocese, and whereas his plea on behalf of Edward III concerning the Jubilee indulgence had met with only partial success, he continued to work in Avignon from 1349 to 1351 both for the various privileges which the ecclesiastical peculiarities of the northern dioceses of the province of Armagh required and also to solve the question of the disputed primacy which had caused so much trouble under the former archbishop of Dublin, Alexander de Bicknor (†14 July 1349). By now FitzRalph had also been confronted with the difficulties in the pastoral sphere caused by the activities of the friars and had emerged in support of the secular clergy on this issue. If we added to this list of activities a long series of discussions with the Armenian representatives, and the composition of an elaborate and far-ranging theological dialogue in nineteen books, then the phrase used by Iohannes, 'preter solitum a studio ociosum' would seem singularly inappropriate. Furthermore, as we know that FitzRalph presided over a commission established by Clement VI to discuss the mendicant issue and that he had completed five, if not six, of the seven books of *De Pauperie Salvatoris* before his departure from Avignon in the spring or early summer of 1351,[33] and in view of his varied interests and commitments it would have been virtually a physical impossibility for him to have been working on the *Summa* at the same time.

The most convincing evidence for the dating of FitzRalph's work on the Armenian questions is to be found in the history of the controversies surrounding the Armenian Church, its alleged heresies, and the possibility of reunion with the western Church which developed during the pontificate of Benedict XII and continued into that of Clement VI. Both of the Armenian prelates to whom FitzRalph addressed himself in the prologue of the *Summa* figured prominently in these developments. Nerses Balientz was a native of Greater Armenia, the classical

[32] *DPS*, Bk. I, Ch. 1, ed. cit., p. 277.

[33] For the commission established under Clement VI and consisting of FitzRalph and two other theologians, *DPS*, prologue, ed. cit., p. 273.

Cilicia, who had become bishop of Ourmiah in Lesser Armenia. Here he came under the influence of a group of Dominican missionary friars, whose presence in Armenia had helped to form a 'Latinizing' party within the Armenian Church with the ultimate objective of bringing about reunion with Rome. Nerses became an active member of the *Fratres Unitores*, the United Brethren of St. Gregory the Illuminator, who had been founded under Dominican influence and became a focal point for these Latinizing Armenians,[34] working under the guidance of Dominican missionary bishops and ultimately adopting most of the constitutions of the Order of Preachers.[35] Meanwhile Nerses' Latinizing contacts and tendencies led him to doubt the validity of his own Armenian baptism, ordination to the priesthood, and episcopal consecration, while his recently acquired knowledge of Latin doctrines and practices led him to accuse the orthodox Armenians of heresy. As a result he was excommunicated by the Catholicos of Sis, Jacob II of Tarsus, who had consecrated him bishop and whose powers Nerses had therefore called into question. The Catholicos secured his imprisonment by the Armenian king Leo IV for a brief period, and upon his release refused to allow him to resume his priestly functions.[36] Thereupon Nerses set out for Avignon, where he soon won sympathy and papal favour as the innocent victim of an Armenian Church which was ill disposed towards the Church of Rome and towards the advocates of reunion. On 9 October 1338 Benedict XII confirmed him as archbishop of Manazgard in Greater Armenia on the frontiers of the Christian kingdom, to which it would appear from the papal account Nerses had been unanimously

[34] For the 'Fratres Unitores' see Loenertz, *La Societé des frères pérégrinants*, pp. 142 ff.; Gregorio Petrowicz, 'I Fratres Unitores nella Chiesa Armena', *Euntes Docente*, 22 (*Festschrift Cardinal Agaganian*, 1969), 309–47; M. A. van den Oudenrijn, *Das Offizium des hl. Dominicus des Bekenners im Brevier der "Fratres Unitores" von Ostarmenien* (Rome, 1935), pp. 1-3. The best over-all view of the situation in Armenia in this period is still Henri-François Tournebize, *Histoire politique et religieuse de l'Arménie depuis les origins des Arméniens jusqu'à la mort de leur dernier roi (l'an 1393)* (Paris, 1900); idem, 'Arménie', *DHGE* iv. 290–391. For papal relations with the orient, see Jean Richard, *La Papauté et les missions d'orient au moyen âge (XIII*^e^*–XV*^e^ *siècles)* (Collection de l'École française de Rome, 33, Rome, 1977), esp. pp. 121–225. There is no modern critical study of Nerses and the 'Latinizing' Armenian prelates who shared his views. Petrowicz's study is a mine of information not easily available elsewhere, but it tends towards an 'apologia' for Armenian traditions. Nevertheless, I profited greatly from a discussion with Fr. Petrowicz, Pontificio Collegio Armeno, Rome, which helped to clarify some of the issues considered here.

[35] Petrowicz, 318. He regarded Nerses as a 'disciple' of John of Kerna, the Armenian leader of this monastic movement, ibid., 337.

[36] Schmitt, *Benoît XII et l'ordre des frères mineurs*, p. 325.

elected by the clergy and people of the diocese. The pope also complied with the Armenian's request by conferring upon him the *pallium* and having him consecrated in accordance with the Roman rite by the vice-chancellor, Cardinal Pierre Després, but – significantly – Benedict was careful to stipulate that this consecration was only conditional in case he might not have been previously consecrated.[37] At this stage Benedict XII was clearly not prepared to deny the validity of the powers of Armenian bishops.

The elevation of Nerses to the see of Manazgard was later the subject of considerable friction between his followers and the Armenian hierarchy. The papal document had made it clear that there had been some sort of election prior to the papal provision, and that the pope was merely giving apostolic sanction to a popularly expressed wish. But this was indignantly denied by the Armenian clergy assembled at the Council of Sis in 1343, who maintained that no such election had taken place, that Nerses was an intruder who had falsely claimed the archbishopric, whereupon the patriarch had been obliged to expel him from the country as an instigator of dissension within the Armenian Church, and that furthermore Nerses had shown himself abroad as an intriguer and hostile to the rights and traditions of that Church.[38] However, in view of Nerses' known sympathy for the Latinizing and pro-union party in Armenia before his departure for the west, it is reasonable to conjecture that he may have been elected to the see of Manazgard by such Latinizing elements and that this election may have been represented to Benedict XII as a unanimous choice. But the Latinizing party was in a minority, the much larger party favoured an independent Armenian Church with its own rites and religious tradition, and when the Council of Sis met, the assembled Armenian prelates had received more than enough evidence of the way in which the Latinizing Nerses had discredited those traditions at the papal court.

Nerses' movements in the period immediately after his papal confirmation are difficult to work out precisely. Four months later he received a further papal letter, permitting him to visit Jerusalem with five companions and to choose a confessor if in danger of death,[39] privileges which would suggest that he

[37] J.-M. Vidal, *Benoît XII. Lettres communes*, ii (Paris, 1904), 4-5 n. 5284.
[38] *Acta Benedicti XII*, p. 213.
[39] Vidal, *Lettres communes*, 180 n. 7059; 196 n. 7291. It has been argued that

planned a journey back to Armenia to take possession of his see. However, it is unlikely that he ever undertook this journey, as on 8 January 1340 he received a pension from the Apostolic Camera, and the terms of this grant make clear that he had already received a number of other payments since his arrival at the curia. Over the next two years when, as we shall see, the beliefs and practices of the Armenian Church were under considerable scrutiny at the curia, the payment of this pension was frequently confirmed, and by 7 August 1342 he was described as a teacher of Armenian at the curia, a task for which he also received additional payments.[40] He was one of the principal architects of the list of 117 errors attributed to the Armenian Church and drawn up following a series of investigations conducted by Benedict XII.[41] These had been sent by the pope to the king, Leo V of Armenia, and to the patriarch on 1 August 1341, and they provoked the angry response of the Armenian prelates assembled at the Council of Sis two years later together with the accusation that Nerses had been responsible for circulating at the papal curia such distorted and slanderous misrepresentations of Armenian doctrine.[42] At this stage Nerses

Nerses was still in Armenia when this letter was issued to him and that the journey in question was *towards* Avignon, Delaurier, *Docs. arméniens*, i, 702. But the tenor of Benedict's bull of 9 October 1338 suggests that, whereas at that date Nerses was still in Armenia and might receive conditional re-consecration if he could find a suitable prelate in Armenia, he had come to the curia in person to receive the *pallium*. Schmitt, p. 325, argued on the assumption that Nerses was already at the curia by the autumn of 1338.

[40] Nerses had clearly been in receipt of payments under terms which expired 7 January 1340, and on 8 January new arrangements were made, to be valid until 20 December 1340, Schäfer, *Ausgaben . . . Benedikt XII . . .* , p. 112. On 18 February 1341 and 8 January 1342 he received further payments, ibid., pp. 138, 157, but only on 7 August 1342 was he actually described as 'in curia legenti', ibid., p. 198. This was not the first papal attempt to provide for the teaching of Armenian in Avignon, in order to facilitate missionary activity and theological discussion. John XXII ordered payment for two Armenians sent to Avignon in 1322 by the king of Armenia, who were teaching the language at the curia, Schäfer, *Ausgaben . . . Johannes XXII*, pp. 564, 566, 573. In 1342 there may have been a special need for language teachers at the curia in view of the negotiations with representatives of the Greek and Armenian Churches, and on the same day the pope ordered a larger provision for the teaching of Greek, below, n. 88.

[41] Edited in *Acta Benedicti XII*, pp. 119–55.

[42] The Armenians' reply is printed ibid., pp. 160–229. The assembled Armenian prelates directed their attack on Nerses in reply to error 75, in which the papal document had alleged that a certain Armenian doctor had come to Avignon and attacked the practice of elevating the Host during the Mass, maintaining that the Eucharist was to be celebrated in private and not be seen by the people, ed. cit., p. 144. The Armenians replied that this error was held by Nerses, the council fathers had investigated its origins, but Nerses' claim that the Armenian Catholicos Jacob held this view was

disappeared from the papal records for a while, and it is not clear whether he stayed on in Avignon or returned to Armenia soon after these discussions had taken place. In any case he was in Armenia in 1353 when Innocent VI appointed him as official interpreter to a group of papal theologians who had gone there in the hope of negotiating a lasting union. Papal policy had changed considerably in the meantime, and although recent research has done much to modify the picture of Benedict XII as hostile to the eastern Churches and intolerant of any concession to their local cultural traditions[43] nevertheless Clement VI adopted a more conciliant attitude to the native spokesmen of the eastern Churches, including that of Armenia. The reply of the Council of Sis that the 117 errors were a malicious misrepresentation of their beliefs and practices arrived in Avignon no later than 1345 and the following year Clement VI sent out two special nuncios to negotiate with the Armenian leaders. The instructions given to the papal representatives on this occasion indicate that papal policy had become more lenient towards Armenian traditions during the previous five years, but the question of reunion was once more lost from sight in the troubles which beset the kingdom of Armenia over the next few years, while in Avignon as throughout western Christendom, the Black Death proved to be a rude interruption of large-scale diplomatic plans.[44] By the time equilibrium was restored and the next papal delegation could be sent, Clement VI was already

false and slanderous, ibid., p. 213. *c.* 1341 the Armenian Catholicos had sent a profession of faith, with a brief description of the sacraments as celebrated in the Armenian rite, to the pope. It is printed in *Acta Benedicti XII,* pp. 156-9, but the discussion of the Eucharist makes no specific reference to the elevation of the Host, ibid., p. 157.

[43] See Schmitt, *Benoît XII et l'ordre des frères mineurs*, pp. 318-78, for East-West relations during this pontificate. The subsequent fate of Nerses is unclear: he may be identical with Nerses, abbot of the monastery of St. George in Lesser Armenia who, with another monk James, was permitted to remain in England for one year under royal protection as his native land was overrun by Saracens, 7 February 1364, *CPR* 1361-4, 459.

[44] For internal difficulties in Armenia see Charles Kohler, 'Lettres pontificales concernant l'histoire de la Petite Arménie au XIVe siècle', *Florilegium Melchior de Vogüé* (Paris, 1909), 308-23. In a letter of 8 September 1344 Clement VI referred to reports he had received concerning repeated Saracen molestation of Armenia, ibid., 320, and it can be assumed that his informant was either Nerses or John of Kerna, the second dedicatee of the *Summa.* From this correspondence it is clear that Armenia was sharply divided on the question of reunion with Rome or the maintenance of an independent religious tradition, and that the vast majority favoured the latter solution and had little sympathy with the Latinizing movement promoted by Nerses and others.

dead but his successor, the vacillating and indecisive Innocent VI, did, however, continue to negotiate. In such circumstances there was probably no man more competent than Nerses to act as interpreter between the Latin theologians and the Armenian prelates, but his influence must have been regarded with great suspicion in Armenia on account of his openly Latinizing tendencies and lack of sympathy for local traditions. At some stage during his life, probably initially in the Dominican circles close to the *Fratres Unitores* and subsequently while living and working in Avignon, he acquired a sufficiently good grasp of the Latin language to be able to translate into Armenian the Latin chronicle of the Dominican Martin of Poland. To his translation he appended additional material concerning the history of Armenia and its kings up to *c.*1335,[45] and his work is still regarded as an important, if not totally objective, witness to local Armenian traditions in the fourteenth century.

When Nerses, already discredited in Armenia, set out for Avignon *c.*1338 he was accompanied by another advocate of the Latinizing policy of the *Fratres Unitores*, Simon Beg, bishop of Erzeroum, and at Avignon they met other members of the Brethren who had left Armenia in 1336 as a result of the hostile measures of Leo IV.[46] These included John Kernatzi (of Kerna), identifiable as the second dedicatee of FitzRalph's preface to the *Summa de Questionibus Armenorum* and at least as prominent, if not more so, in the deliberations of the early 1340s which occasioned FitzRalph's work. John of Kerna was an orthodox monk who *c.*1328 came under the influence of the Bolognese Dominican, Bartolomeo da Poggio. The latter had been created the first Latin bishop of Maraghà by John XXII[47] and founded a congregation of *Fratres Peregrinantes* for mendicant friars who were voluntarily engaged in missionary work in the East. John of Kerna had been sent by his Armenian superiors to Maraghà in order to learn more about these Dominican missionaries, and he spent two years there learning Latin

[45] Delaurier, *Docs. arméniens*, i. 608 n.; Anna-Dorothee v. den Brincken, *Die "Nationes Christianorum Orientalium" im Verständnis der lateinischen Historiographie* (Cologne–Vienna, 1973).

[46] Petrowicz, 329. For Simon Beg, a Latinizer who also sought episcopal reconsecration, see *DHGE* xv, 833.

[47] Petrowicz, 316; Leonertz, *La Societé des frères pérégrinants*, pp. 142–4, 162. For Bartolomeo see Kaeppeli, *Script. O.P.* i. 154–5. None of his writings have survived, apart from six sermons on the sacrament of penance, but he apparently engaged in a disputation with John of Kerna on the dual nature of Christ, a topic which was to be central to FitzRalph's discussions with the Armenians, Kaeppeli, 155.

and scholastic theology and at the same time teaching the Dominicans Armenian. Having returned with Bartolomeo to Kerna in 1330, they invited a number of Armenian doctors and abbots to come and discuss the doctrine and rite of the Armenian Church and the possibility of reunion with Rome. A substantial number of Armenian abbots adopted union for themselves and their convents, including Kerna. In order to promote the union among their people, they further organized themselves under the direction of the Dominican Bartolomeo into the *Congregatio Unitorum*, or *Ordo Fratrum Unitorum S. Gregorii Illuminatoris*, adopting the rule of St. Augustine and most of the Dominican constitutions and receiving the approval of John XXII in 1331.[48] Kerna, under the rule of John who was the real founder of the *Fratres Unitores* and their first superior, became the centre of the Latinizing movement in Armenia; in order to achieve union at all levels of Armenian society the Brethren established Latin schools and colleges, and by 1334 had provided for the Armenian translation of some of the most fundamental works of scholastic – and especially Dominican – theology.[49] However, they were occasionally more zealous than prudent, especially John of Kerna who, like Nerses, doubted the validity of the Armenian sacraments and re-baptized the laity and re-ordained the clergy. Their attempts to replace the Armenian rite, which they saw as conducive to theological error, with the Latin rite translated into the Armenian language tended to increase the hostility of the defenders of Armenian tradition, including the king, Leo IV, and a wave of persecution dispersed the *Fratres* throughout the East and from the Crimea up into Poland.[50]

Having encountered such difficulties for his programme in the East, John of Kerna came to Avignon in order to gain first-hand experience of western religious life, and Loenertz dated his stay at Avignon to *c.*1337-44, which coincided exactly with FitzRalph's most lengthy period in residence there.[51] After that John seems to have returned to Armenia, where his death is recorded as having taken place in 1348, a date which raises a problem concerning the dating of FitzRalph's dedication. Fitz-Ralph described him as elect of 'Clatensis', and no such episcopal

[48] Petrowicz, 317-18. Bartolomeo also translated the rule of St. Augustine (as observed by the Dominicans) into Armenian, Kaeppeli, 155.

[49] Petrowicz, 319. [50] Ibid., 321-5.

[51] *La Societé des frères pérégrinants*, pp. 142-6.

see can be identified. However, in view of the number of sees created in the East during these years, especially in Armenia and Persia, many of which never had any practical effect, it is at least possible that the monastic centre at Kerna, which was also the centre of the Latinizing movement, may have been elevated to an episcopal see and the movement's guiding spirit nominated its first bishop. Even if the report of his death in 1348 is correct, it would have taken time for the news to reach Avignon and it is not impossible that FitzRalph wrote the dedicatory letter to his former negotiating partners and presented the work to Clement VI without being aware of the death of one of them.[52]

The papal-Armenian correspondence during the pontificate of John XXII reflected the danger of the Islamic threat to the little country, the decimation of the nobility in constant warfare, and repeated appeals to the West for help.[53] Appeals continued to be made to Benedict XII, but by now the mounting criticism of the Armenian Church vocally expressed by the Latinizers who had come to Avignon, perturbed him, and he set up an inquiry into the charges of doctrinal errors, bizarre practices, and superstitions attributed to the Armenian Church. Information was collected from Armenians summoned to Avignon for this purpose, from others who had come voluntarily, and from Latins who had direct personal experience of conditions in Armenia – presumably friar-missionaries – in a series of hearings which cannot have begun before the autumn of 1339, as they took place under the presidency of Cardinal Bernard d'Alby. He was created cardinal on 18 December 1338 and entered the curia on 2 August 1339.[54] The witnesses included both those who could neither speak nor understand Latin as well as those who knew both languages, while a number of Armenian books, theological and liturgical, were examined for errors with the aid of interpreters and papal notaries in order to avoid misrepresentation.[55] It would be reasonable to assume, and Armenian sources confirm that this was so in the

[52] Loenertz, ibid., did not indicate that John was a bishop, but in the light of other evidence for the Armenian debates at the curia in this period he is the only possibility for this identification.

[53] See documents printed in Kohler, art. cit. and *Acta Ioannis XXII, passim,* though the latter contains more letters dealing with matters of ecclesiastical organization and discipline, urging closer conformity with Roman practices. See also Schmitt, *Benoît XII et l'ordre des frères mineurs*, pp. 321–3.

[54] Eubel, *Hierarchia Catholica*, i². 17.

[55] *Acta Benedicti XII*, p. 120.

case of Nerses, that such Latinizing Armenians as Nerses and John of Kerna, who had come to Avignon freely and independent of any inquiry, also gave evidence. *Fratres Unitores* and Dominicans also apparently submitted evidence, and the findings of the commission were expressed in the 117 articles which were regarded at Avignon as being elements in the *fides Armenorum*, and which were formulated by those competent in both languages, a phrase which suggests Latinizing Armenians and mendicant missionaries, as such facility in both languages was to be found principally among the *Fratres Unitores*, who had learned Latin under the influence of Dominican missionaries, while western students of Armenian were usually friars.[56] Of the 117 'errors' the first three dealt with the procession of the Holy Spirit (*filioque*) and the Armenian rejection of the teaching of the Council of Chalcedon on the subject; the central part of the document, articles 25 to 103, dealt with problems of Christology and the sacraments in no particularly logical order, while articles 4 to 19 and 104 to 106 concerned questions relating to the beatific vision, judgement, and purgatory, 20 to 21 with the dual nature of Christ, and 22 to 24 with the punishment of souls in hell – all of those topics which had preoccupied theologians at the curia, including Benedict XII and FitzRalph, during the beatific vision controversy earlier in the decade.[57] This concentration of topics helps to explain why FitzRalph, who had no direct experience of Armenia or anywhere else in the East to qualify him as a witness in the inquiry, was nevertheless engaged in discussions with the Armenian representatives. Furthermore, the extreme detail of his consideration of this group of related problems in the *Summa*, especially in Books XI to XIV,[58] tends to support this suggestion that he was consulted as an 'expert' on the Latin interpretation of these doctrines.

We may presume that FitzRalph's associates in negotiations with the Armenians at the curia included friars with missionary

[56] Ibid., p. 120.

[57] e.g. in article 8 the papal document claimed that the Armenians conceded to the souls of the just – even after the Last Judgement – not a vision of the 'essentiam Dei', but merely of the 'claritatem Dei, quae ab eius essentia manat', *Acta Benedicti* XII, p. 123. The Armenians denied this, using arguments from Scripture to prove the reverse, ibid., pp. 168–9. The question of the dual nature of Christ, which had already been under discussion in Armenia (see n. 47), and on which the papal view of the Armenian position was stated in articles 20–1 (ibid., p. 127), was discussed by the Council of Sis, ibid., pp. 176–81.

[58] S, fols. 82va–118vb; Vat. Lat. 1033, fols. 83^{r}–123^{r}; Vat. Lat. 1035, fols. 114vb–166vb.

experience, who would normally have been associated with the Latinizing party in Armenia. They were dealing with those Armenians whose very presence and willingness to debate matters involving doctrinal differences and possible reunion illustrated their own Latinizing tendencies. From the preface to the *Summa* it is clear that FitzRalph shared, or at least came to adopt, similar views. He was a conscious and open Latinizer and whereas he was careful to describe his work as a discussion of Armenian 'questions' rather than as 'errors', he introduced his remarks by stating that he had been informed that certain heresies had arisen in Armenia owing to an absence of sound knowledge of the Scriptures, information which he had clearly received from Nerses and John of Kerna:

Ex relacione vestre sancte devotionis accepi ob defectum exercicii in sacris scripturis antiquas quasdam hereses a sanctis patribus reprobatas et nonnullas contra sacram scripturam novellas asserciones erroneas in vestris partibus pullulasse: propter quas per doctores latinos ex sacris litteris convincendas, eo quod earum patroni auctoritatem Romane ecclesie non admittunt, estimantes eius auctoritatem ex sacris litteris probari non posse, ad Romanam curiam zelus domus dei et Christi caritas vos adduxit.[59]

These words indicate that FitzRalph was speaking to men who were seeking guidance from Latin theologians: 'per doctores Latinos ex sacris litteris convincendas', words which accurately describe the attitude of the Latinizing party in Armenia and their representatives in Avignon, with whom FitzRalph had ample opportunity for contact since their arrival in 1337-8.

Unlike the Armenian Franciscan, Daniel of Täbriz, who arrived in Avignon early in 1341, accompanied by a knight, Thoros Mikaelentz, and bearing letters from Leo V pleading for assistance against the Muslim invaders, FitzRalph composed his dialogue without any specific reference to the list of 117 errors. Friar Daniel on the other hand, an Armenian convert who then became a Franciscan, taught theology at Sis, and was a staunch defender of Armenian orthodoxy and traditions, was requested by Benedict XII to express his views on the 117 errors. Daniel's reply, the *Responsio ad errores impositos Hermenis*, anticipated that of the Council of Sis in that it combined an indignant refutation of the articles as a misrepresentation of Armenian doctrine with a bitter denunciation of Nerses as the instigator of such treachery against the Armenian Church and people.[60]

[59] S, fol. 1ra; Vat. Lat. 1033, fol. 1^{r}; Vat. Lat. 1035, fol. 1ra.

[60] Golubovich, *Biblioteca bio-bibliographica della Terra Santa*, iv. 333-41; Schmitt, *Benoît XII et l'ordre des frères mineurs*, pp. 321-8.

Nevertheless, it is clear from the plan of the *Summa de Questionibus Armenorum* that FitzRalph was not prepared to take the 117 errors, with which he must have been familiar, at their face value. If he had chosen to base his dialogue on the list, the entire plan of his work would have been different. The papal list was highly controversial in tone and deliberately placed greatest emphasis on those doctrines in which the differences between the Roman and Armenian traditions were most marked; in other words it was intended to involve the defenders of Armenian tradition in difficulties. FitzRalph, however, adopted a different scheme, and he followed the natural order of the main articles of the Christian faith, proving the divinity and humanity of Christ, the dual procession of the Holy Spirit, the primacy of Rome, and the authenticity of the Roman sacramental tradition, judgement and reward, free will and predestination, and the unique position of the Catholic faith against Muslims and Jews. The order of his treatise is thus determined by the relative importance of the points under discussion, beginning with the divinity of Christ, then going on to deal with the question of the Holy Spirit, the Church of Christ, the sacraments, heaven, hell, and purgatory, scripture and ceremonial. Although the individual sections are often repetitive and lacking a logical line of argument, the external structure upon which FitzRalph built up his work was more systematic than that of the 117 errors, and very much more fair to the Armenian (and as we shall see, also to the Greek) point of view. He strove to present a reasonable discussion of the main points of disagreement, and his approach to these problems is entirely from the angle of a theologian who wished to prove the truth of the Catholic faith from Scripture with no more than a slight appeal to tradition. There is indeed a curious absence of all patristic and liturgical arguments in the dialogue, also lacking is all reference to the earlier Councils of Constantinople and Ephesus which the Armenians would have accepted as authoritative. Nor is there any reference to the detailed reply which the Armenian prelates composed at the Council of Sis and sent back to Avignon in or before 1345 and which contained, not merely a rejection of some of the doctrines imputed to them in the list of 117 errors but also a detailed statement of Armenian beliefs and practices in a number of the disputed areas.

Although FitzRalph gave the title *Summa de Questionibus Armenorum* to the entire nineteen books of his dialogue, many of them have only a loose connection with the main issues. The first ten books deal almost exclusively with the Armenian doctrines, whereas Books XI–XIV consider errors more generally attributable to the Eastern Churches including the Greeks. After Book XIV a caesura is clearly to be seen, and the final five books indicate, especially in the case of Books XV–XVII where problems of grace, free will, and predestination are discussed, that they may well have been added after the wave of condemnations in Paris during the mid-1340s and included in the over-all defence of the Christian faith before FitzRalph wrote the final dedication.[61] In his dialogue FitzRalph began with the most important issue which divided the Armenians from the West and from the other eastern Churches, that of the two natures of Christ. Since the Council of Chalcedon, when the Armenians separated themselves from the Greeks, this doctrine had been a stumbling-block for them. They confused the teaching of that council with Nestorianism or rejection of the hypostatic union, largely because of misunderstandings in the relevant texts, and in their insistence on the single nature of Christ they had become tainted with the Monophysite heresy.[62] FitzRalph took as his guideline the literal interpretation of Scripture, both Old and New Testament, as the one source of authority which would be accepted without question by all parties to the discussion, though the implication is that the Latinizing prelates whom FitzRalph was addressing would be amenable to other arguments but could not use them in dealing with their fellow Armenians, and then dealt with the points at issue systematically, beginning with the Nestorian heresy. He devoted Book I to proofs from the New Testament that Christ was God, and in Books II–IV produced an impressive display of knowledge of the Old Testament, above all from the Prophets and the Psalms, to prove that Christ was indeed the promised Messiah.[63] Book V refuted the heresies of Arius, Apollinarius, and the Manichaeans and proved the humanity of Christ, as well as his divinity and Messianic character,[64] and once more the proofs are virtually an exercise

[61] S, fols. 118vb–144rb; Vat. Lat. 1033, fols. 123^{r}–149^{r}; Vat. Lat. 1035, fols. 167ra–202va. The condemnation, following an examination of the work of Nicholas d'Autrecourt in Avignon before 19 May 1346, is printed in *Chart. Univ. Paris.*, ii. 576–86, and is discussed in Leff, *Gregory of Rimini*, pp. 14–17. Leff also argued that Bks. XV–XVII of FitzRalph's *Summa* followed these events, *FitzRalph Commentator*, p. 2.

[62] *DHGE* iv. 303.

[63] S, fols. 2ra–31rb; Vat. Lat. 1033, fols. 1^{r}–32^{v}; Vat. Lat. 1035, fols. 1rb–45va.

[64] S, fols. 32ra–38vb; Vat. Lat. 1033, fols. 32^{v}–39^{v}; Vat. Lat. 1035, fols. 45va–55va.

in *sola scriptura*. In Book VI the procession of the Holy Spirit was discussed and FitzRalph expounded the views of the Greeks and the Armenians who, under late Byzantine influence, had also deleted *filioque* from the Creed.[65] Book VII argued the primacy of the see of Rome as head of the Church, again with exclusively scriptural arguments, without any legal or historical considerations.[66] Book VIII, one of the longest in the dialogue, is devoted to the Armenian teaching on baptism, its sacramental character and its proper form, criticizing the Armenian view (which FitzRalph had presumably learned from Nerses) that total immersion was the only valid form of baptism, and that it and confirmation were almost inseparable.[67] Book IX continued the discussion of Armenian sacramental theology, considering some of their practices regarding the Eucharist, confirmation, and extreme unction, while Book X dealt with the sacramental character of Holy Orders, with the nature and limits of ecclesiastical jurisdiction, with the power of the priest to forgive sin, with simony, and the problem of ordination and acquisition of ecclesiastical office by hereditary right.[68] Hence even in these first ten books FitzRalph included discussion of several issues which were common to other eastern Churches. A case in point was Book VI, where his discussion of the *filioque* issue was extended to include also the doctrinal views which he attributed to the Greeks and the information he had acquired from a Greek source in Avignon.

Books XI to XIV were mainly devoted to topics which equally concerned all the eastern Churches and which impinged on western Christendom directly in the 1330s. As the view put forward by John XXII concerning the beatific vision had been recognized both by the pope's Dominican opponents and by the advocates of union to be the traditional Greek interpretation, there was a close link between the Greek and Armenian discussions taking place in Avignon *c.*1338-44 and the controversy which had caused so much excitement at the curia and in the universities several years earlier. Curiously enough the implications

[65] S, fols. 39ra–44rb; Vat. Lat. 1033, fols. 39^{v}–45^{r}; Vat. Lat. 1035, fols. 55vb–63va.

[66] S, fols. 45ra–52vb; Vat. Lat. 1033, fols. 45^{r}–53^{v}; Vat. Lat. 1035, fols. 63va–73ra.

[67] S, fols. 53rb–65rb; Vat. Lat. 1033, fols. 53^{v}–67^{r}; Vat. Lat. 1035, fols. 73ra–92ra.

[68] S, fols. 66ra–82ra; Vat. Lat. 1033, fols. 67^{r}–82^{v}; Vat. Lat. 1035, fols. 82ra–114vb.

of the Greek origins of the pope's view were not subjected to a serious critical-historical discussion by FitzRalph or by the authors of the extant treatises pertaining to the controversy. We have already encountered FitzRalph's brief references to his own position among the opponents of the papal view, although the work in which he communicated this opposition to the pope does not survive in any identifiable form. However, these four books provide an exhaustive discussion of the topic and all related issues and are the most comprehensive statement of his views. But one must be careful to avoid reading them backwards in an attempt to reconstruct his original contribution in 1334. Now he was writing after the publication of the papal judgement and expressing himself for the benefit of the Armenian prelates, and whereas Iohannes might raise contentious issues and even opinions with which both Benedict XII and Clement VI, and possibly FitzRalph, might have privately sympathized, Ricardus now taught his pupil in accordance with what had become the orthodox norm.[69]

The subject-matter of the first half of Book XI followed naturally out of the previous discussion of ecclesiastical jurisdiction, lordship, and priestly powers. FitzRalph considered the powers of the simple priest to administer absolution, and also the punishment of the impious before the Last Judgement, a topic which he had considered briefly on other occasions. His emphasis here on the full sacramental power of the simple priest, equal to that of any prelate as regards absolution from all kinds of sin, and with no suggestion of an exalted notion of episcopal powers to absolve, is of more than passing interest in the light of his own subsequent attitude as archbishop to encroachments upon his jurisdiction by the Franciscans, especially in the area of confession and absolution from grave or 'reserved' sin.[70] In Book XI, Chapter 16, a new theme was introduced when Iohannes asked FitzRalph to give his opinion on the Armenian doctrine that there is no punishment for the impious

[69] Bk. XII, Ch. 1: S, fol. 91^{rb-va}; Vat. Lat. 1033, fol. 93^{r-v}; Vat. Lat. 1035, fol. 128^{ra-b}. Again in Bk. XIV, Ch. 29 FitzRalph rejected the possibility of a 'duplex visio', which was suggested by Iohannes in terms reminiscent of the discussions in the early 1330s, and which had been neither condemned nor approved in *Benedictus Deus*, S, fol. 118va; Vat. Lat. 1033, fol. 123^{r}; Vat. Lat. 1035, fol. 166vb.

[70] Bk. XI, Chs. 1–7 discussed in detail the powers of the 'simplex sacerdos', but here FitzRalph was arguing the question of the priest's sacramental powers as a theological issue, without considering the practical application of the canon law in specific areas of jurisdiction, S, fols. 82va–85va; Vat. Lat. 1033, fols. 83^{r}–86^{r}; Vat. Lat. 1035, fols. 115rb–119vb.

before the Last Judgement. FitzRalph replied with an elaborate defence of the traditional view that such punishment was accorded immediately after death and before the resurrection and final judgement,[71] a view which the Armenian prelates to the Council of Sis claimed that they also shared.[72] Books XII–XIV were devoted to an exhaustive discussion of the Greek denial of purgatory and the problem of the beatific vision. In the latter case FitzRalph introduced his emphatic defence of the orthodox version as contained in *Benedictus Deus* with Christ's words to the good thief on the Cross (Luc. xxiii. 43).[73] Even when Iohannes specifically questioned him about the 'duplex modus visionis', which was clearly intended as a literary technique to provide Ricardus with the opportunity to discuss one of the possible solutions raised in the course of the earlier debates, FitzRalph was reluctant to concede any restrictions on the quality of the 'visio nuda et clara divine essencie' enjoyed by the souls of the blessed immediately after death.[74] This contribution to the beatific vision debate differs in one striking respect from the bulk of contributions in the 1330s in that, whereas these had depended in varying degrees on an intermingling of authorities – the Bible, the Fathers, conciliar decrees, Bernard of Clairvaux, Peter Lombard, and Aquinas – here the only authority considered is the Bible.

However, another source of information is cited, specifically as regards FitzRalph's knowledge of the Greek doctrine of purgatory originally formulated by Athanasius – a doctrine which was still an acute source of controversy at the Councils of Basel and Ferrara-Florence in the reunion negotiations with the Greeks.[75] Here FitzRalph cited as authority for his knowledge of Greek teaching the Calabrian abbot, Barlaam of Seminaria, who was clearly his guide to Greek theology in the same manner as Nerses and John of Kerna supplied him with information concerning Armenian opinions.[76] Barlaam first appeared in Book

[71] S, fol. 88^{r-v}; Vat. Lat. 1033, fols. 89^{v}-90^{r}; Vat. Lat. 1035, fols. 123rb-124ra.

[72] Article 7, *Acta Benedicti XII*, p. 122.

[73] '. . . a christo dictum latroni hodie mecum eris in paradiso', S, fol. 91rb; Vat. Lat. 1033, fol. 93^{r}; Vat. Lat. 1035, fol. 128rb.

[74] Above, n. 69. The entire topic is discussed at length in Bk. XIV, S, fols. 109vb–118vb; Vat. Lat. 1033, fols. 113^{v}-123^{r}; Vat. Lat. 1035, fols. 134vb-166vb.

[75] Dykmans, 'De Jean XXII au concile de Florence', 29–66.

[76] The best recent discussion of Barlaam's place in Byzantine thought is contained in Gerhard Podskalsky, *Theologie und Philosophie in Byzanz. Der Streit um die theologische Methodik in der spätbyzantinischen Geistesgeschichte* (Munich, 1977), pp. 126–42. For his political and intellectual activity see Martin Jugie, *DHGE* vi,

VI, Chapter 1 of the *Summa*, when Iohannes requested Ricardus to expound Greek teaching on the procession of the Holy Spirit: 'Vellem ut michi ex sacra scriptura et ex hiis que Greci et Armeni nobiscum confitentur plena et clara deduccione ostenderes sicut illi doctori Greco Barlaham spopondisti quod Spiritus Sanctus ita est et ita procedit sive spiratur a Patre.'[77] Barlaam is here introduced as a well-known personality ('illi doctori Greco'), with whom FitzRalph must already have had personal contact. Again in Book VI, Chapter 12, Iohannes stated a number of objections to the orthodox doctrine and invited Ricardus to answer these objections. These have been attributed to Barlaam: 'quod nos ponimus quaternitatem personarum, et etiam trinitatem et dualitatem personarum restringimus'.[78] FitzRalph replied to these objections in the following chapter, treating them with some contempt: 'multos enim audivi et scripsi difficiliores obiectus de incarnacionis misterio et de eucharistie sacramento'.[79] Finally at the beginning of Book XIII FitzRalph stated the Greek doctrine of purgatory, citing Barlaam as his authority and with considerable respect: 'ut ex relatu venerabilis viri abbatis et doctoris Greci Barlaham, cuius intuitu sextum librum huius libri conscripsisti, tibi innotuit quod quidam Athanasius Grecus omnino negat purgatorium',[80] a passage which once again makes it clear that there was a certain amount of communication between the two men and that they exchanged ideas on topics of current interest.

FitzRalph's adviser concerning Greek theology was described

817-34; idem, 'Barlaam est-il né Catholique?', *Échos d'Orient*, 39 (1940), 100-23; Nicol, 'Byzantine Requests for an Oecumenical Council', *Byzantium* . . . , 69-85; idem, 'The Byzantine Church and Hellenistic Learning in the fourteenth century', ibid., 23-57; Mario Scaduto, *Il monachismo basiliano nella Sicilia medioevale* (Rome, 1947), pp. 323-5; Guiseppi Schirò, 'I rapporti di Barlaam Calabro con le due Chiese di Roma e di Bisanzio', *Arch. stor. per la Calabria e la Lucania*, 1 (1931), 325-57; 2 (1932), 71-89, 426-37; 5 (1935), 59-77; 6 (1936), 80-99, 302-25; 8 (1938), 47-71; Kenneth M. Setton, 'The Byzantine Background to the Italian Renaissance', *Proc. Am. Phil. Soc.*, 100 (1956), 1-76, esp. 40-5. A negative, even hostile approach to Barlaam is reflected in the works of John Meyendorff, 'Un mauvais théologien de l'unité au XIVe siècle: Barlaam le calabrais', *1054-1954, L'Eglise et les églises. Études et travaux offerts à Dom Lambert Beauduin*, ii (Chevetoque, 1955), 47-64; idem, *Introduction à l'étude de Grégoire Palamas* (Paris, 1959), trans. as *A Study of Gregory Palamas* (London, 1964), but with a reduced critical apparatus.

77 S, fol. 39ra; Vat. Lat. 1033, fol. 39^{v}; Vat. Lat. 1035, fols. 55vb-56ra.

78 S, fol. 43^{va-b}; Vat. Lat. 1033, fol. 44^{v}; Vat. Lat. 1035, fol. 62^{va-b}.

79 S, fol. 43vb; Vat. Lat. 1033, fol. 44^{v}; Vat. Lat. 1035, fol. 63ra.

80 Bk. XIII, Ch. 1, S, fol. 102ra; Vat. Lat. 1033, fol. 105^{r}; Vat. Lat. 1035, fol. 143rb.

by the contemporary Greek historian, Nikephoros Gregoras, as 'the man who came over from Italy wearing the habit of a Greek monk. He was versed in the dogmatic wisdom of the Latins and had sampled the outside (i.e. secular) wisdom of the Hellenes'.[81] This somewhat partisan assessment illustrates the tensions within the Greek Church and also the opinion, current in both eastern and western circles, that Barlaam had a capacity for changing his commitment as circumstances dictated. He was a colourful and controversial figure who played an important role in East–West relations during the 1330s and 1340s. Mathematician and astronomer, philosopher and theologian, he has been described as 'one of the most versatile minds of his age',[82] but regrettably he has never been the subject of a major critical study, though he figures marginally in numerous studies on fourteenth-century Byzantine religious and intellectual history. From these it emerges that modern Byzantinists have succeeded little better than his contemporaries in establishing a consensus of opinion about him. Some details of his career are still obscure, though the main outline can be established. Born in Seminaria in Calabria *c.*1298, he entered a Greek monastery in southern Italy and was, according to Meyendorff, 'Greek by language and sentiment, but western educated and imbued with the spirit of the Italian Renaissance'.[83] In 1328 he left Italy for Constantinople, 'leaving his native land for love of true piety', according to Gregorios Palamas with whom he was later to engage in bitter dispute, to study Aristotle in the original, or 'eager to instruct the Greeks in the beautiful simplicities of scholastic theology'.[84] Upon his arrival in the imperial capital he was appointed to teach Aristotle there, and by 1331 he was both professor at the imperial university and abbot of the Basilian monastery of St. Salvator. He believed that knowledge of Greek philosophy was essential for theologians and that the

[81] Nikephoros Gregoras, *Historia* XI. 10, ed. L. Schopen–I. Bekker (Bonn, 1829–55), i. 555, and discussed in Nicol, 'Byzantine Church and Hellenistic Learning', 47–8. In *Historia* XIX, 1 (ed. cit., ii, 919), he maintained that the emperor John Cantacuzenos patronized Barlaam in order to learn from him, and further reported that Barlaam suffered defeat and humiliation in a disputation at Constantinople in 1331, a story which Weiss, *Joannes Kantakuzenos*, p. 103, is inclined to doubt.

[82] Steven Runciman, *The Last Byzantine Renaissance* (Cambridge, 1970), p. 68. In his own *Historia* Cantacuzenos described Barlaam as a man of 'sharp intelligence, perspicacious, and a master at imparting his ideas, learned in Euclid, Aristotle and Plato, and therefore of widespread fame', cited in Setton, art. cit., 41.

[83] *Gregory Palamas*, p. 42.

[84] Meyendorff, 'Un mauvais théologien de l'unité', 48; Nicol, 'Byzantine Church and Hellenistic Learning', 47.

truths of theology were within the reach of secular or outside learning, a rationalist approach which was soon to cause friction. However, he was extremely successful, both as a theologian and secular scholar, was patronized by John Cantacuzenos, and consulted on a wide range of topics, though he never established good relations with his colleagues the Byzantine humanists.

When John XXII sent two Dominican bishops, Francesco da Camerino and Richard of England, to Constantinople in 1333-4 to discuss the possibility of reunion, Andronikos III commissioned Barlaam to engage in public disputations with them on the *filioque* issue, and Barlaam's conviction that Aristotelian methods of proof could be applied to such a theological problem was violently attacked by Gregorios Palamas, the chief exponent of Byzantine mystical theology and monastic spirituality.[85] He also incurred thereby the hostility of the leading figures in Byzantine monasticism, and because of this he was rebuffed by the patriarch, although he still retained great prestige in imperial circles where his reputation for orthodoxy was not yet seriously challenged. He continued to work for reunion and presented to the synod in Constantinople a plan to this effect which was cautiously received.[86] Meanwhile Benedict XII had renewed hopes that union might be achieved through the empress Anna of Savoy, and Barlaam was sent as imperial ambassador to Robert the Wise in Naples, to the French king, and to Avignon, but without any mandate from the Greek Church. The main reason why Andronikos III sent Barlaam to the West was to seek help against the Turks, but in an address to Benedict XII and the assembled cardinals soon after his arrival at the curia, the imperial ambassador tried to persuade the pope to reduce tension between Greeks and Latins (which he argued was a much

[85] Podskalsky, pp. 126 ff.; Ursula Bosch, *Andronikos III Palaiologos* (Amsterdam, 1965), p. 139. The two Dominicans returned from the Crimea to Avignon via Constantinople in 1333, and in 1334 they returned to the imperial court, charged by John XXII with investigating the possibilities of reunion. Nikephoros Gregoras, who knew nothing about Latin theology, attempted to persuade the emperor and patriarch not to negotiate, and his own refusal paved the way for the choice of Barlaam as negotiator with the Dominicans. Podskalsky described Barlaam's performance as one of the most important achievements in Byzantine theology (p. 127). See also *Nikephoros Gregoras, Rhomäische Geschichte: Historia Rhomäike*, German trans. by Jan Louis van Dieten, i (Stuttgart, 1973), pp. 13–14; Meyendorff, *Byzantine Hesychasm: historical, theological and social problems* (London, 1974); Lowell M. Clucas, 'Eschatological Theory in Byzantine Hesychasm: a parallel to Joachim da Fiore?', *Byzantinische Zeitschrift*, 70 (1977), 324–46.

[86] *Gregory Palamas*, p. 47.

greater obstacle to union than any doctrinal differences) and to reopen discussion of disputed issues, if possible within the framework of an ecumenical council.[87] The pope ordered the payment of Barlaam's expenses through the Apostolic Camera on 30 August 1339, but refused to accept the suggestion of a conciliar solution to the problem.[88] The main flaw in Barlaam's plan, as western observers viewed it, was that he tended to ignore or minimize the doctrinal differences between the two traditions, while his philosophical position led him into a theological relativism which appealed to curial theologians at Avignon no more than it had done to Gregorios and his monks. Barlaam regarded *filioque* and unleavened bread as the two main questions to be considered, and seemed to ignore the fundamental problems of the primacy of Rome and the infallibility of the Church.[89] Meyendorff argued that it was not until Barlaam came to Avignon and met with opposition to his views that he really came to appreciate that the matter was one of ecclesiology and required the Greeks to return to obedience to the Roman Church as a precondition of unity.[90]

In the East Barlaam's views on union also met with opposition on the ecclesiological front. Gregorios Palamas now criticized Barlaam not only on the *filioque* issue but also on his understanding of the relations of God with man as revealed in the New Testament. When Barlaam returned to Constantinople in 1340, or very early in 1341, further controversy flared up between the Calabrian abbot and those mystical Byzantine monks who looked to Palamas as their leader and whose methods of prayer Barlaam denounced as heretical. The beginnings of this Palamite controversy have been interpreted as the confrontation of humanistic nominalism with the theology of grace of Byzantine monasticism, and at a council held on 10 June 1341 Barlaam's denunciation of the monks was condemned. Five days later his main support in Constantinople,

[87] For Anna of Savoy, who patronized the Franciscans in Constantinople, as negotiator of reunion, see Schmitt, *Benoît XII et l'ordre des frères mineurs*, p. 318. Barlaam's address to the pope and cardinals is printed in Raynaldus, *Ann. Eccl.* (1339), ed. cit., vi. 167–72, and *MPG* 151, 1331–2, and summarized in Nicol, 'Byzantine requests', 77–80.

[88] Schäfer, *Ausgaben . . . Benedikt XII*, p. 91 for payment of 50 fl. to Barlaam.

[89] Meyendorff, 'Un mauvais théologien de l'unité', 49.

[90] Ibid., 50; idem, *Gregory Palamas*, p. 47, where he argued that Barlaam's plan for union was based on the dogmatic relativism which had been criticized in Constantinople when he used it against the hesychasts, and in Avignon his method found as little favour as among the Greek monks.

Andronikos III, died, and Barlaam soon left for the West once more.[91] By 23 August 1341 he was in Avignon where he, together with his *socius* Giorgios of Saloniki and two *familiares* were to receive a regular pension from the papal Camera. By 10 January 1342 the two *familiares* had disappeared from the papal pay-roll, but Barlaam and Giorgios were still in receipt of bounty, and by 7 August 1342 Barlaam was receiving a regular salary for teaching Greek.[92] A scholar of some distinction, his was obviously regarded as a more highly-priced talent and he received 50 per cent more than Nerses was paid in an entry of the same day for teaching Armenian. Clement VI was supporting them but also making use of them, and one can conjecture that the purpose of such teaching was partly missionary and partly to facilitate dialogue with eastern envoys at Avignon. How long Barlaam continued to teach Greek at Avignon or whom – apart from his most famous pupil – he actually taught, is not clear, as he soon made his doctrinal submission to Rome and on 2 October 1342 received the bishopric of Gerace in southern Italy which was invariably reserved for Greek-speaking clients of the curia during the fourteenth century.[93] This preferment Barlaam received partly through the good offices of Petrarch, who described in the *Epistolae ad Familiares* how he and the abbot used to meet daily for purposes of studying Greek, and that Barlaam's textbook for his illustrious pupil was a manuscript of some of Plato's dialogues.[94] In spite of his submission Barlaam continued to hold views on the Roman primacy and on the four marks which distinguished the true from the schismatic Church, which were not totally in accord with Roman teaching, while at the same time he was anathematized in Byzantium. In terms of eastern theology the Barlaam episode represented the defeat of western scholasticism and of the – largely Thomist – rational approach to dogma, and the triumph of orthodoxy which drew on a long tradition of eastern patristic theology, mysticism, and monastic ascetism, most of whose exponents were vehemently opposed to union with the

[91] Idem, 'Un mauvais théologien de l'unité', 61–2; *Gregory Palamas*, pp. 54–5.

[92] Schäfer, *Ausgaben . . . Benedikt XII*, pp. 138, 157, 198.

[93] Eubel, *Hierarchia Catholica*, i^2. 263. Barlaam had already renewed his contacts with southern Italy early in 1339, when he visited the court of Robert of Naples as Byzantine envoy, and may have presented Greek manuscripts to the king, Weiss, 'The Translators from the Greek at the Angevin Court of Naples', *Medieval and Humanist Greek*, pp. 118–19.

[94] Idem, 'Petrarca e il mondo greco', ibid., pp. 173–7, 181–2.

West.[95] Because of his change of heart, moving from staunch defence of Byzantine theological tradition to extreme criticism at the papal curia in the 1340s, Barlaam was mistrusted by his contemporaries. Nevertheless, Meyendorff's contention that Barlaam set out on the path towards union with Rome without doctrinal conviction because rationalist philosophy prevented him from having any, and that other sympathizers with the union in the East were 'seduced by the apparently Greek flavour of the Thomist synthesis'[96] can only be accepted with grave reservations.

Barlaam was therefore in Avignon in 1339–40 as imperial ambassador, and in a private capacity as a teacher of Greek from the latter part of 1341, though he seems to have resided in his bishopric for at least some part of the period 1342–7, returned once more to Avignon in 1347, and died in Gerace before 13 July 1348, when another Byzantine monk Simone Atumano, who had also come to Avignon as a Greek scholar, was provided to the see by Clement VI.[97] FitzRalph could have made contact with him in Avignon on either or both of his first visits, in 1339–40 and 1341–2, and it is not surprising that when the Anglo-Irish theologian was collecting information from the Armenians Nerses and John of Kerna, he should at the same time seek to broaden the picture by consulting a known Greek authority in Avignon. Hence on Greek matters, as in the case of his Armenian information, FitzRalph was dependent on a source who was known for his Latinizing tendencies and who might not be relied upon to be totally fair to the Greek doctrines being expounded. Whereas one might have expected that Barlaam who, unlike the two Armenians, left a substantial *œuvre*, would himself provide a useful corrective to the representation of his thinking offered by FitzRalph in the *Summa*, this is unfortunately not the case. The problem of the chronology of his literary activity has not been clarified, and this is further complicated by the fact that Barlaam wrote on the same

[95] Constantine N. Tsirpanlis, 'The career and political views of Marc Eugenicus', *Byzantion*, 44 (1974), 460–1. On Barlaam's dubious theological views after his formal 'conversion' see Meyendorff, 'Un mauvais théologien de l'unité', 62.

[96] *Gregory Palamas*, pp. 27, 239.

[97] Giovanni Mercati, *Se la versione dall'ebraico del codice Veneto Greco VII sia di Simone Atumano arcivescovo di Tebe* (Città del Vaticano, 1916), pp. 26–7, 31. Jugie, *Echos d'Orient*, 39, 124–5, argued that Barlaam lived until 1350, but the evidence for his view is unsatisfactory. For Simone Atumano's Greek scholarship see Weiss, 'The Greek culture of South Italy in the later middle ages', *Medieval and Humanist Greek*, pp. 41–2.

controversies more than once, defending the Greeks against the Latins and subsequently the Latins against the Greeks, making it extremely difficult to establish his personal convictions until the chronological and textual problems of his writings have been properly studied.[98]

FitzRalph's allusions to Barlaam suggest that their discussions took place before the latter's submission to Rome, when Barlaam had come to Avignon as a distinguished Greek theologian representing Byzantium, personally favouring union, well-known at the curia, and on friendly terms with residents there. In both of the passages of the *Summa* in which Barlaam's views are considered, FitzRalph broadened the discussion from strictly Armenian topics to include views held also by the Greeks. It would be consistent with both the structure of the work and with our knowledge of the relative chronologies of the Armenian debates and Barlaam's presence at Avignon to assume that FitzRalph, having become involved in the Armenian discussions, availed himself of the opportunity to acquire comparative information concerning the Greek positions which were being referred to constantly in the deliberations which resulted in the composition of the 117 errors. Subsequently when FitzRalph put his *Summa* together, he incorporated the arguments which he had gathered from his conversations with Barlaam, using the dialogue form to solve the problem of digressions, and thus employing all that he had been able to learn during these years about the Greek and Armenian Churches, in addition to stray pieces of information about Jews, Saracens, and Tartars which were to be picked up by any resident at Avignon during a period when envoys from the East were a regular feature.[99]

FitzRalph's knowledge of Judaism, apart from that which could be gleaned from a minute study of the Old Testament, also depended on one particular source which he encountered at Avignon, a convert Jewish scholar whom he never identified by name. In Book II, Chapter 11, of the *Summa* he cited a long series of Messianic texts from the Old Testament, among them the verse of the vulgate text: 'Ego occidam et ego vivere faciam: percutiam et ego sanabo' (Deut. xxxii. 39), and indicated his awareness of the philological and textual difficulties caused by

[98] On Barlaam's *œuvre* see Giannantonio Mandalari, *Fra Barlaamo Calabrese maestro del Petrarca* (Rome, 1888), pp. 69–97, 119–20.

[99] On this kind of information see Schmitt, *Benoît XII et l'ordre des frères mineurs*, pp. 318–28, 362–78.

this passage. Were the verbs to be understood as active or passive, and what had they been in the Hebrew text? In support of his own interpretation he quoted the authority of a converted Jewish doctor ('maximus doctor Hebreorum factus Christianus'), probably a member of the substantial Jewish community in Avignon.[100] FitzRalph then recalled a curious story which he had learned from this source, concerning a copy of the Pentateuch preserved in the Dominican convent in Bologna, and allegedly written by Ezra (Esdras), the Hebrew lawgiver and reformer in the fourth century BC, in his own hand. Some Jewish doctors, who had consulted the manuscript, used it to deny the Messianic character of Christ, and were challenged by FitzRalph's source, who had also used the manuscript. Although this convert Jewish scholar cannot be identified, the story of the allegedly authentic text of Ezra in Dominican possession in Bologna continued to circulate, and the text was examined by a number of late seventeenth- and eighteenth-century scholars before it suffered mutilation and elimination of the disputed passages in the Napoleonic era.[101] However, FitzRalph's account, and the discussions provoked by the text both in the fourteenth century and later, throw some light on early scientific study of the textual history of the Bible by western scholars. The Dominicans had obviously allowed themselves to be persuaded of the antiquity of their text (now generally held to be a thirteenth-, or at the earliest a twelfth-century product), and showed it to all distinguished visitors. FitzRalph's acquaintance must have seen it there before this meeting at Avignon, a meeting which can be given a precise *terminus ad quem*. Although FitzRalph mentioned this text only once in the *Summa*, he told exactly the same story in almost the same words while preaching before Benedict XII in the vice-chancellor's chapel on 16 December 1341. The text for the third Sunday in Advent was 'Gaudete in domino semper' (Ad Phil. iv. 4), but in the

[100] S, fol. 9vb; Vat. Lat. 1033, fol. 11^{r}; Vat. Lat. 1035, fol. 13ra.

[101] Interest in this MS was aroused when the Maurist Benedictine Bernard de Montfaucon recorded in his *Diarium Italicum* (Paris, 1702) having visited the Dominican convent in Bologna in 1698, where he examined the text (op. cit., pp. 399–400). Although subsequent examinations by 18th-century biblical scholars established it as no earlier than the 13th century, Napoleon included it in the list of treasures which were to be transported to the Louvre in 1796. Finally returned to Bologna in 1815, it was severely mutilated and the inscriptions which had led FitzRalph's Jewish source to argue for its antiquity, and whose genuineness was rejected by 18th-century scholars, were now missing. See Leonello Modana, *Catalogo dei codici ebraici . . . di Bologna* (Florence, 1889), p. 323.

course of the sermon the preacher had occasion to cite the crucial text 'percutiam . . .', whereupon he told his audience the story of the Bolognese manuscript, though without specifying the source of his information.[102] In view of the ambiguous position of the large Jewish community in Avignon he may have decided that in the papal presence discretion was the better part of valour,[103] but the exact parallel of this sermon with the passage in the *Summa* is a clear indication of FitzRalph's non-litigious activities during these years.

Another important aspect of FitzRalph's thinking whose genesis is illuminated by a study of his work on the Armenian questions is that of lordship and dominion. The theory of just lordship founded on grace was to become the leitmotiv of his later work and the doctrine of lordship which he then evolved became the basis of his attack on the jurisdictions, privileges, and poverty of the mendicant orders. He developed this doctrine largely during the period after 1350, when he began to make a detailed study of mendicant poverty, its underlying principles, and their justification in Scripture and canon law, and in the *Summa* it is evident that these doctrines have not yet been worked out, nor was there yet any evidence of anti-mendicant feeling on his part. Indeed the reverse might be regarded as true, and in the series of sermons preached to the mendicant communities at Avignon between 1335 and 1349, his sympathy and admiration for their work occasionally finds expression. One such occasion also occurred in the *Summa*, where he considered the missionary work of the friars in pagan lands and discussed the problem of pastoral jurisdiction in lands so remote from the ordinary governmental framework of the Church – a foretaste of his own subsequent preoccupation with the problem of the friars' relationship with that framework? Ricardus allowed

[102] B, fol. 233^{v}; J, fol. 167va.

[103] On the Jewish community in Avignon see Guillemain, *La Cour pontificale*, pp. 642 ff. FitzRalph's first contacts with Jewish scholarship were probably these Avignon encounters. Although there is some evidence for a vigorous intellectual life of Oxford Jews in the 12th and 13th centuries (even though their primary function was as moneylenders to impecunious students from whom they often took books as pledges), their expulsion in 1290 meant that no opportunities for Hebrew scholarship survived in 14th-century Oxford. On expulsion they took their books with them and none of the Bodleian's Hebrew books is known to have reached Oxford before the 16th century, Cecil Roth, *The Jews of Medieval Oxford* (OHS 1951), pp. 121–32. But Roth's claim that after 1290 there is no record that any person of Jewish birth set foot in Oxford for the next three centuries (p. 168) may need modification in the light of attempts to comply with the legislation of the Council of Vienne by having convert Jews teach Hebrew in Oxford.

Iohannes to raise the problem of the source of the friars' authority to preach, hear confessions, and administer the sacrament of penance: 'Quid dices de viris multis devotis qui ad Tartaros et ad Saracenos accedunt ut eos convertant, et hoc est sine superioris cuiuscunque licencia?'[104] Ricardus replied that the friars got their jurisdiction from Christ's general mandate to go teach all nations, and provided that they were not defying some positive prohibition they were free to do so. The nature of their work was so excellent ('eximie caritatis'), that they could claim their jurisdiction directly from the Gospel precept.[105] Similar sentiments are contained in a sermon which FitzRalph preached to the Franciscans at Avignon on the feast of St. Catherine of Alexandria, on 25 November 1338. Here he considered the psychology of infidels who accepted the Christian faith without full understanding of its doctrines and of some Christians who – so he had been told by an allegedly well-informed witness – had lost their faith through contact with Saracens.[106] Again it is scarcely coincidental that this sermon was preached while a Mongolian delegation was present at the curia. It had arrived in May 1338, bringing letters from the Khan Togan-Temour, who was interested in exchanging ambassadors with the pope, and from Christian residents at his court who had been without a chaplain for the past eight years and feared that without spiritual guidance they would lose their faith.[107] On their departure in December 1338 they were accompanied by a papal delegation which included the Franciscan Giovanni Marignola da Firenze, with whom FitzRalph was to engage in acrimonious correspondence over the mendicant issue some twenty years later,[108] but their presence at the curia, followed by other Saracen and Tartar delegations over the next two years helped to broaden the range of FitzRalph's knowledge of conditions in the Christian and non-Christian East. This sermon of 25 November 1338 displayed already a minute interest in the problems of missionary countries and he occasionally cited examples which indicated that he had been in contact with returned missionaries, possibly Franciscans: in a brief discussion of miracles, and of the gift of driving devils out of those possessed, he reported the information that the latter

[104] Bk. X, Ch. 7, S, fol. 76ra; Vat. Lat. 1033, fol. 76^{v}; Vat. Lat. 1035, fol. 106va.
[105] S, fol. 76rb; Vat. Lat. 1033, fols. 76^{v}–77^{r}; Vat. Lat. 1035, fol. 106^{va-b}.
[106] B, fol. 181^{v}; J, fol. 133va.
[107] Schmitt, *Benoît XII et l'ordre des frères mineurs*, p. 365.
[108] Ibid., pp. 368–71.

occurred more frequently in eastern countries. In reply to those who might be inclined to doubt such statements, his advice was simple and direct: 'Vade igitur illuc et poteris esse securus.'[109] In view of the fact that he was preaching to friars who regarded their missionary work in the Orient as one of the glories of their order, and precisely at a time when a delegation consisting mainly of Franciscans was being sent from Avignon to China – a detail of which both FitzRalph and his audience must have been well aware – one wonders whether the preacher was not deliberately encouraging recruits for the missions? The sermon certainly indicated both the widening of FitzRalph's cultural horizons and growing interest in the East, as well as illustrating an attitude towards the friars which was diametrically opposed to his later and much-publicized one.

He returned to the problem of miracles on several occasions in the course of this *Summa*, alluding to it briefly in his argument from apologetics for the two natures of Christ and discussing it in greater detail in Book XIX, Chapter 25,[110] where he distinguished four categories of possible miracles: those worked by God or angels without human participation; those in which God or angels used human participation; those worked by God or angels in response to a direct intervention of saints or angels, but not of God; those worked as a result of direct divine intervention. FitzRalph was prepared to accept only the fourth and final category as satisfying the criteria for a genuine miracle, and he reflected contemporary Oxford opinion – including both Bradwardine and the Augustinian Geoffrey Hardeby – in being prepared to accept only a circumstantial attitude to miracles. A miracle was identifiable only in accordance with individual circumstances.[111]

The question of lordship as distinct from jurisdiction was the subject of discussion in Book X, Chapter 3, and here FitzRalph's views were more tentative than in the later anti-mendicant writings and sermons. Ricardus had been asked by his pupil to

[109] B, fol. 186^{v}; J, fols. 136va–137ra.

[110] S, fol. 158^{v}; Vat. Lat. 1033, fol. 165^{r-v}; Vat. Lat. 1035, fol. 221^{ra-va}.

[111] See Albert Lang, *Die Entfaltung des apologetischen Problems in der Scholastik des Mittelalters* (Freiburg, 1962), pp. 125, 150–1, 199–200. He pointed out that whereas the question of miracles had previously been a metaphysical one, by the early 14th century it had become largely a problem of cognition – whether it was possible for man to recognize a miracle as such. While the Carmelite John Baconthorpe attempted to employ the prophecies to prove God's exclusive power to transmit miraculous signs, FitzRalph's division into four categories convincingly illustrated this shift from the metaphysical to the cognitive, ibid., p. 125.

explain the problem and he began his reply with a word of warning: 'In questione quam tangis de iuribus regnorum, scilicet quo iure expedit ut reges sibi succedant magistri philosophi disseciunt.'[112] Scripture, he explained, did not necessarily provide a definite ruling concerning the conditions necessary for lawful rule in temporal affairs as it did in the case of bishops and deacons, and it seems that at this stage in the development of his thinking he had not yet begun to study either the canonists or the political publicists on the subject, where for example Aquinas would concede the deposition of a tyrannical king while John XXII held fast – in theory if not in practice – to the view that even evil kings ruled by divine right.[113] Hence Ricardus expressed a personal opinion with extreme caution: a kingdom founded on violence was no true kingdom, but if the people gave their free consent, temporal power received divine approbation.[114] Then Iohannes sought further clarification of the position and Ricardus argued that God could not approve the rule of an infidel, who might therefore be king but had no just lordship or dominion. Just lordship was founded on justice, and could not exist where such justice was absent. These opinions naturally led to a consideration of the ruler's authority when he was known to be in a state of sin, and once more Fitz-Ralph was cautious by comparison with his later work. Hesitantly he put forward an opinion which had not yet become a fundamental element in his theology, but which would figure frequently in the anti-mendicant treatises:

> Unde quantum michi videtur nullus existens in peccato mortali habet aliarum creaturarum verum dominium apud Deum, sed tyrannus aut fur sive raptor merito est vocandus quamvis nomen regis aut principis aut domini propter possessionem seu propter successionem hereditariam aut propter approbacionem populi sibi subiecti aut propter aliam legem humanam retineat: nec verum habet dominium donec vere peniteat et penitencie gracia eum in statum Deo acceptum instituat.[115]

He then drew the necessary conclusions in two brief sentences and dismissed the topic as of lesser significance: it is doubtful if he was yet aware of the deeper implications of the theory or the manner in which it might be employed.

[112] Bk. X, Ch. 3, S, fol. 75ra; Vat. Lat. 1033, fol. 75^{v}; Vat. Lat. 1035, fol. 105ra.

[113] For a brief and clear discussion of this problem see Jean Dunbabin, 'Aristotle in the Schools', *Trends in Medieval Political Thought*, ed. Beryl Smalley (Oxford, 1965), pp. 65–85.

[114] S, fol. 75rb; Vat. Lat. 1033, fols. 75^{v}–76^{r}; Vat. Lat. 1035, fol. 105rb.

[115] Bk. X, Ch. 4, S, fol. 75va; Vat. Lat. 1033, fol. 76^{r}; Vat. Lat. 1035, fol. 105^{va-b}.

Among those present at Avignon in 1337-44 it has been possible to identify several personalities from whom FitzRalph received information which was incorporated into the *Summa*. Is this also possible in the case of his first tentative formulation of a doctrine which was to have profound implications for the friars in general and for Oxford intellectual life in particular? Consideration of the genesis of this doctrine belongs more properly to the context of *De Pauperie Salvatoris*, but a general remark is necessary. It has been shown that the basic elements of FitzRalph's doctrine were already to be found in the *De Ecclesiastica Potestate* of Aegidius Romanus. But the Augustinian school of theology, which venerated Aegidius as the Aquinas of their order and elevated him to the position of official doctor to be studied by all students of theology within the Augustinian order,[116] was not prepared to follow him on this particular issue – with the significant exception of Guglielmo Amidani of Cremona. He had employed Aegidius' doctrine to defend the 'potestas directa in temporalia' of the papacy against the authors of the *Defensor Pacis* and supporters of Ludwig the Bavarian,[117] and as Augustinian prior-general from 1326 to 1342 he was regularly in residence in Avignon while FitzRalph was collecting the information for his *Summa*. Directly or indirectly he provided the original impetus for FitzRalph's subsequent development of the doctrine of dominion by grace.

Most scholars who consulted the *Summa* have pointed to a perceptible caesura in its construction after the first fourteen books, and Hammerich, whose argument for an early date of composition of the first section is supported by the evidence adduced above for FitzRalph's contacts at the curia *c.*1338-42, suggested that this break coincided with FitzRalph's return to Lichfield in the winter of 1344-5 before becoming archbishop of Armagh.[118] The evidence of the sermon diary shows that in this period he worked and preached in the immediate vicinity of Oxford and might reasonably have availed himself of the opportunity to renew his academic contacts and supplement

[116] For the Augustinian origins of FitzRalph's theory of dominion see Gwynn, *English Austin Friars*, pp. 35-73; for Augustinian legislation about the role of Aegidius in the teaching of the order see Adolar Zumkeller, 'Die Augustinerschule des Mittelalters: Vertreter und philosophisch-theologische Lehre', *AA* 27 (1964), 169-71.

[117] See also Ugo Mariani, *Chiesa e Stato nei teologi agostiniani del secolo XIV* (Rome, 1957), pp. 103-11, 213-14; Perini, *Bibl. Aug.* i. 28-32.

[118] Hammerich, pp. 13-16.

the Lichfield library with whatever books he needed from Oxford. In one respect, however, this caesura is more apparent than real, as Book XV began with Iohannes reminding Ricardus that up to now he had argued exclusively from the literal sense of Scripture, and that he had promised to consider proofs for the authority of Scripture, a topic which FitzRalph then discussed extensively in the early chapters of Book XV, thereby providing a methodological support for his own earlier arguments, before moving on to problems which he had discussed in his *Commentary on the Sentences*, i.e. God's omniscience, future contingents, and free will.[119] This section is at variance with what had gone before, and in Books XV–XVII where his opponents are also schoolmen, he returned to the scholastic method of proof employed in the *lectura* on the Sentences, borrowing substantially from his own earlier work. Undoubtedly these final five books deal with subjects which bear no direct relationship with the controversies between the Latins and the eastern Churches, Greek or Armenian, although the fiction of a dialogue about the Armenian controversy was maintained. It would appear that FitzRalph decided to round off his work by making it a compendium of his views on all 'enemies' of orthodox western Christianity, including the 'moderni' of the western schools as well as Muslims and Jews. In Books XVIII–XIX, dealing with the latter two communities, he returned to the leitmotiv of the earlier part of the *Summa*, reliance on Scripture as the one authority which could usefully be adduced when dealing with all 'enemies' of orthodox Christianity.

In Books XV–XVII, when he turned to the topics of free will and predestination, his adversaries became a very different group from those whom he had been discussing previously. He was now concerned with what he regarded as a new heresy being propagated by certain elements in the schools. In this context he appealed to the good sense of all thinkers, pagan and Christian alike, against the folly of the new generation: 'soli vos moderni iuvenes estis docti',[120] and he expressed his abhorrence of their new teaching in language more violent than

[119] Bk. XV, Chs. 1–7, S, fols. 119rb–122rb; Vat. Lat. 1033, fols. 123^{r}–126^{v}; Vat. Lat. 1035, fols. 167ra–171vb.

[120] Bk. XV, Ch. 2, S, fol. 120ra; Vat. Lat. 1033, fol. 124^{v}; Vat. Lat. 1035, fol. 158va. In the immediately preceding passage he had been discussing modern methods, arguing that difficulties could not be solved by means of exercises in logic and sophistry, but only through Scripture combined with the writings of the great commentators on Scripture and on the Sentences.

anything else we find in his writings before the mendicant controversies, when the debate would assume a tone of unparalleled bitterness. At no stage did he identify his opponents in this section, and it has been suggested that he wrote it in reply to the extreme Augustinian predestinarianism of Bradwardine's *De Causa Dei*. If, as seems probable, FitzRalph was working out this section during his last years in Lichfield, he must have been familiar with the work of Bradwardine, not merely in the early version which had been expounded in a series of lectures at Oxford during the early 1330s, but with the finished work which was circulating no later than 1344, and whose contents were well known both in England and in Paris. However, a consideration of FitzRalph's choice of words in the light of Bradwardine's career makes it seem impossible that he was the target of attack. The phrase 'moderni iuvenes' is scarcely applicable to a man of considerable maturity and stature, at least as old as FitzRalph himself, if not older. Bradwardine's death as a victim of the plague on 26 August 1349 shortly after his consecration as archbishop of Canterbury had occurred soon after FitzRalph set out for Avignon on his mission for Edward III, when he must have had the completed, or near-completed dialogue with him for presentation to Clement VI. It is improbable that he would have written with such bitterness about a man who had died so recently and enjoyed a reputation for learning and sanctity.

The 'moderni iuvenes', if these were Oxford men, are more likely to have been the younger disciples of Bradwardine who – perhaps in direct confrontation with the 'Pelagians' among the followers of Ockham whom Bradwardine had in mind – may have taken the doctrines of the 'doctor profundus' farther than their propagator had ever intended. Unfortunately there is a large gap in our knowledge of Oxford intellectual life during the years immediately before and after the Black Death. After the hectic – and productive – turmoil of the 1320s and early 1330s, when Ockham, Wodeham, FitzRalph, Bradwardine, and the Mertonians, together with the mendicant biblical scholars, provided a broad spectrum of serious and occasionally exciting scholarship, there is something of a no-man's land until the age of Wyclif. This was a period in which the influence of Ockham and of Bradwardine must have dominated teaching and disputing in the schools, but individual exponents remain shadowy figures lurking in the pages of Emden, awaiting evaluation of their thought and its assimilation in the contemporary picture.[121] These may have included some of the 'iuvenes' whom FitzRalph had in mind, and whose doctrine he disliked and rejected as 'dyabolicam sapienciam', while Paris provides at least one even more likely candidate. Here the Cistercian bachelor of theology, Jean de Mirecourt, had pushed Bradwardine's teaching to its logical and most extreme conclusions, but without any of Bradwardine's qualifying clauses, in the years following the circulation of the English doctor's views in Paris, and a list of his errors and those of others teaching and disputing in the schools on the Seine was condemned by forty-three Parisian masters of theology in 1347.[122] If FitzRalph had Mirecourt and his Parisian pupils and colleagues in mind concerning free will and predestination, and possibly Nicholas d'Autrecourt in the section on 'modern' theories of knowledge,[123] he must either have been following the course of debates in the University of Paris more minutely than would have been usual for a schoolman no longer regent or else he completed this section after the condemnations of 1347 had highlighted developments there, most likely working on it after his return to Avignon in 1349.[124]

However much FitzRalph and Bradwardine might have differed on their approach to predestination, the future archbishops of Armagh and Canterbury shared certain interests in common, including 'orientalia'. A Merton manuscript which can be traced to Bradwardine's possession at the time when he was engaged on the composition of *De Causa Dei*, contains a text of Hayton's *Flos Historiarum Terre Orientis* bound together with an early Latin version of Marco Polo's narrative of his travels, and Bradwardine quoted these two texts more than once in the long prologue to *De Causa Dei.*[125] Apparently both scholars, who belonged to the same group of Oxford theologians, were attracted to the literature arising from contemporary expansion of European interest in the East, and not simply the Near East. Whereas Bradwardine was interested in Marco Polo's travels in

[121] See Robson on trends in Oxford speculation 1350–70, in *Wyclif and the Oxford Schools*, pp. 97–112; Stephen L. Forte, 'A Study of some Oxford Schoolmen of the middle of the fourteenth century' (MS B.Litt., c. 10–11, Oxford, 1949).

[122] Printed in *Chart. Univ. Paris.*, ii. 610–14.

[123] As n. 120.

[124] See Leff, *FitzRalph Commentator*, p. 2, for a similar dating.

[125] MS Merton H. 3. 12 (now MS 340), Frederick M. Powicke, *The Medieval Books of Merton College* (Oxford, 1931), pp. 127–8. See also Wolfgang Giese, 'Asienkunde für den kreuzfahrenden Westen. Die "Flos historiarum terre orientis" des Hayto von Gorhigos (O. Praem.) aus dem Jahre 1307', *Secundum Regulam Vivere. Festschrift für P. Norbert Backmund O.Praem.* (Windberg, 1978), 245–64.

the far Orient, FitzRalph's horizons were by no means limited to Armenia and the Greek empire and more than once his speculations concerned the missionary activities of the friars in Tartary, his awareness possibly having been aroused by the Tartar envoys and returned missionaries in Avignon. For example, he allowed his disciple Iohannes to argue that Daniel's prophecy cannot yet have been fulfilled since so large a portion of the world was still inhabited by pagan peoples: 'ita ut pauce regiones nunc inhabitentur per Christianos et plurime per paganos tartaros, sarracenos et alios infideles',[126] while his discussion of the problem created by his friar-contemporaries who went to work among the infidel without any more precise claim to jurisdiction than the evangelical precept reflected a similar concern. Finally there is a striking passage in Book XVIII which shows FitzRalph as fully alive to the practical problems caused by controversy with those who do not accept the authority of the Old and New Testament as the inspired word of God. In a long objection Iohannes urged the weakness of using scriptural argument from the New Testament against the Jews, or from either the Old or the New Law against the Tartars, Saracens, or other infidel peoples, whereupon FitzRalph set about the task of proving the intrinsic superiority of the Christian message. Whereas his arguments are not particularly original or otherwise noteworthy, the discussion indicates that FitzRalph was deeply concerned with the missionary problems of the Avignonese papacy.[127]

Yet another point of contact between the *Summa de Questionibus Armenorum* and the evidence of contemporary Oxford reading, above all the wide interests of the Mertonians, is reflected in FitzRalph's interest in the Koran. More than half of Book XVIII is devoted to an elaborate comparison of Muslim teaching as revealed in the Koran and that of Christ as made known through the Gospels.[128] The single source of FitzRalph's knowledge of Islam was the translation and paraphrase of the Koran made by Robert of Ketton at the behest of Peter the Venerable which was part of the compilation of Islamic lore

[126] Bk. III, Ch. 3, S, fol. 14va; Vat. Lat. 1033, fol. 16^{r}; Vat. Lat. 1035, fol. 20rb.

[127] Bk. XVIII, Chs. 8-9, respectively Iohannes's objection and FitzRalph's reply, S, fol. 147^{rb-vb}; Vat. Lat. 1033, fol. 152^{r-v}; Vat. Lat. 1035, fol. 206^{ra-vb}.

[128] For FitzRalph's knowledge of the Koran see Daniel, *Islam and the West*, pp. 23-5, 33, 50-3, 76-7, 276, 326.

known as the 'Cluniac corpus',[129] but FitzRalph studied his single text minutely, and like many others who considered the problem he set out to 'prove' that the Koran guaranteed the authenticity of the Bible. This is one of the weakest sections of his work, and his arguments are thorough to the point of tedium but quite unoriginal, except for the fact that he appears to have taken the scriptural defence against Islam further than other medieval authors, further than the Spaniards faced with the practical problem of the *reconquista*, and further than the earlier Cluniacs from whom FitzRalph took over his Islamic lore.[130] However, he had no desire for originality and had no personal contact with the doctrines of Islam; hence he had no way of checking up on his source and repeated some bizarre notions which the Muslims were alleged to have of Christ, in several cases quoting passages from the Koran which had been so distorted in translation that they seemed almost pure invention.[131] His discussions on the subject lack the range and depth of a man like Nicholas Cusanus a century later who had to work from the same translation of the Koran, but who considered a broader range of authorities as well.[132]

Whereas FitzRalph's developing interest in the East is most clearly documented at Avignon, there were possibilities for such interests while he was still at Oxford, where both the Mertonians and the classicizing biblical scholars were widening the accepted dimensions of academic scholarship.[133] At Oxford FitzRalph would also have had access to books on the subject, including his single Islamic source, Robert of Ketton's translation of the Koran, which was contained in a Merton manuscript (MS

[129] See Giles Constable, *The Letters of Peter the Venerable* (Cambridge, Mass., 1967), i. 294–5; ii. 275–84; James Kritzeck, *Peter the Venerable and Islam* (Princeton, 1964); Marie-Thérèse d'Alverny, 'Deux traductions latines du Coran au moyen âge', *AHDLMA* 16 (1947–8), 69–131. It is possible that FitzRalph, in the choice of title for his dialogue, had the *Summa totius haeresis Saracenorum* of Peter the Venerable in mind, printed in *Bibliotheca Cluniacensis*, ed. Martin Marrier-André Duchesne (Paris, 1613), cols. 1109–15.

[130] Daniel, p. 51.

[131] Ibid., p. 173. FitzRalph discussed the question in Bk. XVIII, Ch. 13 (Ch. 12 in S, where Chs. 1-2 were run together), S, fol. 148^{va-b}; Vat. Lat. 1033, fol. 153^{v}; Vat. Lat. 1035, fols. 207vb–208rb.

[132] Daniel, p. 276. For the *Cribratio Alkoran* (1461) of Nicholas Cusanus see Georges C. Anawati, 'Nicolas de Cues et le problème de l'Islam', *Niccolò Cusano agli inizi del mondo moderno* (Florence, 1970), pp. 141–73, esp. 160–70 for plan and summary of the contents of Cusanus' text. There is no modern edition: it was printed in *Opera Omnia* (Basel, 1565), and translated into German by Gustav Hölscher-Paul Naumann, *Sichtung des Alkoran* (Hamburg, 1948).

[133] There is no study of the state of Islamic studies, or knowledge of Islamic doctrine in 14th-century Oxford, but see Roth, as n. 103.

H. 3. 13). Merton acquired the text as part of a legacy from one of Bradwardine's contemporaries John Raynham, fellow of Merton and possessor of a vast library.[134] It also contained a translation of the *Chronica mendosa et ridiculosa Saracenorum* by Robert of Ketton, and Hermann of Carinthia's *Doctrina Mahumet.*[135] It is even possible that FitzRalph actually used this manuscript, if he worked on the later part of the *Summa* at Oxford after his return to Lichfield, as the translation of the Koran it contained is incomplete, breaking off at Azoara LXXVII, and none of FitzRalph's references pertain to later sections of the Koran.[136] Similarly the Merton library provided material for study of other problems beyond the normal range of the Christian Church, including the perennial controversy with the Jews which had taken on a new lease of life in France, Italy, and Spain since the Council of Vienne. A new wave of controversial treatises appeared, and some of them were represented in the Merton library, having emanated from circles around Thomas Bradwardine. FitzRalph's interest in the Jewish controversy is plain from every section of the *Summa*, probably fostered through his contact with the converted Jewish scholar in Avignon, and this interest is related to his attitude to biblical scholarship, which is among the most important problems arising from a study of his *Summa.*

In its formal aspects the *Summa* differed from the dialogue which followed it, *De Pauperie Salvatoris*, and especially with regard to the nature of proof used in the argument. In the preface to the later work FitzRalph outlined his argument from authority as follows:

> Et ne propter librorum tuorum carenciam te excuses, ecce tradendi modum hunc tibi prescribo ut si ea que michi querenti affirmari conaberis sacris scripturis diffinicionibus, seu assercionibus summorum pontificum seu sacrosancte Romane ecclesie, aut racionibus vivis communias respondendo, nullius testimonio doctoris adiecto, michi satisfieri reputabo.[137]

This outline implied the usual four arguments: from Scripture, from the declarations of popes and church councils, from theological authority which in this case had to be omitted due to the lack of books, and the argument from reason. The third argument

[134] Powicke, p. 129. For Raynham, a fellow of Merton by 1335, doctor of theology, and later rector of Holingborne (Kent) see *BRUO* III, 1570–1.

[135] See Powicke, p. 129.

[136] FitzRalph referred to Azoara 76 in Bk. XVIII, Ch. 15, S, fol. 149rb (as Ch. 14); Vat. Lat. 1033, fol. 155^{r}; Vat. Lat. 1035, fol. 209^{ra-b}.

[137] Put into the mouth of Iohannes, ed. cit., p. 277.

may have been a literary device to excuse any gaps caused by the fact that the dialogue was completed in Ireland, where he is unlikely to have had access to a wide range of books, and he needed to justify himself before his old university and the curial theologians. On the other hand at the beginning of the *Summa* he had made it clear that the arguments against the errors he was combating would be derived almost exclusively from Scripture, owing to the lack of agreement between the two parties concerning the authority of the Roman see and of the accepted Latin theologians.[138] Hence the introductory words of Iohannes: 'Quia ex litterali sensu scripture sacre intendis in hoc opere tractare Armenorum propositas questionis, ostende michi primo quis sensus scripture sacre dici debeat litteralis',[139] served as an invitation to Ricardus to provide a curious and instructive dissertation on the problems to be faced by an interpreter of the Bible who was not prepared to evade obvious difficulties by an appeal in true medieval style to the 'sensus tropicus' or 'allegoricus'. As a student in Oxford FitzRalph must have been exposed to the techniques of the friar-doctors lecturing on the Bible in the 1320s, who employed an ingenious variety of approaches in their commentaries.[140] However, the view he expressed here was straightforward 'Thomist' doctrine on the literal sense. Sweeping aside all objections to the definition of the 'sensus litteralis', FitzRalph maintained that the main clue to the interpretation of the Scriptures was to know the mind of the author: 'non refert quis sensus proprie dici debeat litteralis alicuius scripture, dum tamen scias mentem auctoris', and then stated the guiding principle of his *Summa*, namely that the literal interpretation of scriptural passages would be determined by the obvious meaning of the author.[141] Clearly this method evaded a number of awkward objections and assumed as a working rule a 'common-sense' interpretation of the Bible, and

[138] But he ignored other possible authorities who should have been equally acceptable (below, n. 142). His approach to Scripture has been the subject of a stimulating paper which, despite some historical inaccuracies, throws valuable light on his place in 14th-century biblical scholarship, Alistair J. Minnis, ' "Authorial intention" and "literal sense" in the exegetical theories of Richard FitzRalph and John Wyclif: an essay in the medieval history of biblical hermeneutics', *PRIA* 75 C (1975), 1–30. Minnis is primarily concerned to show that the link from Nicholas of Lyra to the Lollard Bible passed through FitzRalph. For him the presumed author of the Lollard Bible, John Purvey, 'reads Lyra with FitzRalph in mind', art. cit., 30.

[139] Bk. I, Ch. 1, S, fol. 2ra; Vat. Lat. 1033, fols. 1^{v}–2^{r}; Vat. Lat. 1035, fol. 2ra.

[140] Bk. I, Ch. 5, S, fol. 3^{rb-va}; Vat. Lat. 1033, fols. 3^{v}–4^{r}; Vat. Lat. 1035, fols. 3vb–4vb. See Smalley, *English Friars, passim*; idem, *The Study of the Bible*.

[141] Bk. I, Ch. 1, S, fol. 2^{ra-b}; Vat. Lat. 1033, fol. 2^{r}; Vat. Lat. 1035, fol. 2^{rb-va}.

FitzRalph could disregard exact theological or exegetical criteria. In a work such as the *Summa* it was easier to proceed in this manner, and the approach is consistent with the characteristics of its author which have already been observed in the *lectura* on the Sentences. Throughout his long life FitzRalph was involved in many controversies and invariably aimed at a quick decision in accordance with practical considerations. In the *lectura*, where a rigorous approach to philosophical and theological problems was required, and where his own peculiar combination of talents was not displayed to advantage, he was conspicuously less successful than in his later more subjective work. The careful examination of all possible arguments and objections, reflective consideration of a range of interpretations of other biblical scholars, were methods which present a sharp contrast to the subjective and emotional approach often to be found in FitzRalph. His approach was essentially practical rather than speculative, a characteristic which was also to determine his relations with the friars in the last decade of his life.

For most of the *Summa* he was true to the programme outlined in the first chapter. Each of the main errors attributed to the Armenian and Greek Churches by the theologians he had consulted were countered with arguments derived almost entirely from the Bible, but with little exegetical analysis of the texts cited. Many chapters, especially in the earlier books, consist of little more than a string of scriptural quotations, which his impressive knowledge of the Bible enabled him to produce in support of western positions. On the other hand it would be misleading to assume that he set out to establish the Bible as the sole rule of faith, to be interpreted personally and without regard for authority. On the contrary he was careful to stress that this approach was determined by the circumstances: he was arguing against those who did not accept the authority of the Roman Church or its theologians, and the only common ground for such discussion was the Bible. But subconsciously, and unintentionally, he contributed another milestone in the direction of *sola scriptura*, especially because of the subjective manner in which he chose to interpret the literal sense, and also because of his almost total neglect of arguments from early Christian tradition which the Greeks and Armenians would have recognized.

The argument from Scripture could easily have been supplemented by the authority of the Greek Fathers and the councils of the early Church, but FitzRalph's knowledge in this area was so deficient as to represent a major defect in his *Summa*. He was not a patristic scholar, his knowledge of the Fathers being limited to a reasonable familiarity with Augustine and a lesser acquaintance with St. Gregory, Origen, and John Chrysostomos – sparse by comparison with his contemporary Bradwardine.[142] He did, however, present an unusually detailed discussion of the doctrines of the pseudo-Dionysius in Books XIII–XIV when discussing the beatific vision, purgatory, and eternal reward. It is possible that he may have developed this knowledge through his discussions with Barlaam, but in any case there were a number of Latin translations of the pseudo-Dionysius to hand.[143] Occasionally he attempted to argue from tradition, as in his refutation of the Jewish position on the Messiah, where he confined himself to the Old Testament, but 'multa de ipso et per ipsum ac suos gesta recepi que in nostro evangelio et in scripturis apostolicis et aliorum innumerabilis fide dignorum historicorum litteris referuntur . . . aut talis scriptura debet ab hominibus approbari aut nulli historico adhibenda est fides quod est nimium absurdum'.[144] Again in the section on the beatific vision he pointed out: 'in isto articulo etiamsi ex scriptura expresse probari non posset . . . adherendum esset fidelibus historicis viris sanctis qui passiones sanctorum scripserunt et referunt ostensiones angelicas'.[145] He was himself aware of the limitations of his chosen method of argument: 'non enim est dubium quin anime alique aliquod premium habeant in presenti nec ipsi qui hoc querunt in hoc dubitant, sed querunt de vera beatitudine animarum quam vellent si fieri potest ex scriptura sacra aut ex racione habere probatam auctoritatem aliam non curantes'.[146] In Books XV–XVII, where he was opposing the

142 Oberman, *Bradwardine*, esp. pp. 23–4; idem, *Werden und Wertung der Reformation. Vom Wegestreit zum Glaubenskampf* (Tübingen, 1977), pp. 83–90. Esp. in Books XV–XVII, where his main topic was not the Armenians, FitzRalph cited a range of sources other than the Bible and Augustine – Boethius, Origen, Chrysostomos, Aristotle, and Averroes, S, fols. 119vb, 126va, 131vb, 140vb, 144^{va-b}; Vat. Lat. 1033, fols. 124^{r}, 130^{v}, 134^{v}, 145^{r}, 148^{r-v}; Vat. Lat. 1035, fols. 167va–168ra, 177^{ra-b}, 183ra, 196^{ra-b}, 201rb.

143 Esp. Bk. XIII, Ch. 11 (against the Greeks), and Bk. XIV, Chs. 9–29 (against Greeks and Armenians), S, fols. 105^{rb-vb}, 112rb–118vb; Vat. Lat. 1033, fols. 108^{v}–109^{r}, 116^{r}–123^{r}; Vat. Lat. 1035, fols. 148^{ra-b}, 157vb–166vb.

144 Bk. III, Ch. 21, S, fol. 19rb; Vat. Lat. 1033, fol. 21^{r}; Vat. Lat. 1035, fol. 27^{va-b}.

145 Bk. XII, Ch. 26, S, fol. 100va; Vat. Lat. 1033, fol. 103^{v}; Vat. Lat. 1035, fols. 141va–142ra.

146 Bk. XII, Ch. 1, S, fol. 91rb; Vat. Lat. 1033, fol. 93^{r}; Vat. Lat. 1035, fol. 128ra.

younger generation of western schoolmen and where the exclusively biblical argument was superfluous, he returned to the normal scholastic method of proof and authorities, but in Books XVIII–XIX he altered his line of argument again and appealed to Saracens and Jews with arguments from reason and the testimony of natural history. Here, however, we find passages of circular argument, where he tried to prove the authority of the Old Testament from the witness of the New, and vice versa.[147]

Despite the defects in his methods of argument, FitzRalph displayed an impressive knowledge of the Bible. It has been suggested that he developed a special interest in Scripture as a student of theology in Oxford, and the phrase used by Grandisson – 'in sacra pagina egregius bachalarius/doctor' – was used to illustrate this contention. But the phrase was part of a conventional academic title and form of address and need have no further significance. There is no sermon evidence for FitzRalph's years as a student and master in Oxford, and he became prominent as a preacher only after his arrival in Avignon. Only one sermon survives from the first visit in 1334–5, that preached in the Dominican church on the feast of the translation of St. Thomas of Canterbury, and from this single example it is not possible to make generalizations about the preacher's biblical talent, especially in view of the sermon's preoccupation with the then current beatific vision controversy and with the Becket legends which were intended to entertain as well as enlighten the audience. But the sermons from 1338 onwards displayed that intense preoccupation with the Bible as the source of all Christian authority which also characterized the *Summa*. It was to be found both in his popular devotional homilies preached in Lichfield from 1345 to 1346 and in the formal sermons at the curia, which were occasionally used as a parade of theological learning. At Oxford he must have encountered, among the Franciscans and Dominicans who were his teachers and colleagues, biblical scholarship of a high order. Furthermore, his sojourn in Paris in 1329–30 must have exposed him to the work of Nicholas of Lyra, probably the most influential biblical commentator of his day, especially on the Old Testament. We can

[147] Bk. XVIII, Ch. 6, S, fols. 146vb–147ra; Vat. Lat. 1033, fols. 151^{v}–152^{r}; Vat. Lat. 1035, fol. 205^{va-b}. See also Daniel, pp. 50–3, and Joseph R. Zenner, 'Armachanus über Widersprüche und Irrthümer in der hl. Schrift und in den approbierten kirchlichen Übersetzungen. Ein Beitrag zur Geschichte der Hermeneutik', *ZKT* 15 (1891), 348–61.

only surmise that FitzRalph was influenced by either or both of these sources – he was certainly exposed to them, and by the time he emerged as a preacher in Avignon and as a writer on the Armenian questions the effect of these or similar influences was in evidence.

In this development he was in tune with official papal policy, which was in favour of a more attentive study of Scripture. The decrees of the Council of Vienne had been intended to foster a revival of biblical studies, by providing the necessary machinery for linguistic studies – Hebrew, Greek, Aramaic, and Syriac – which were the necessary precondition, although the effect of these decrees was sporadic. We know that a tax was being levied in the diocese of Lincoln in the years up to 1325 to pay for teachers of these languages in Oxford, but the state of Greek studies there had not improved by the early 1330s, though there is some evidence for increased knowledge of Hebrew.[148] During the pontificates of John XXII and Benedict XII various attempts were made at Avignon to promote the study of oriental languages, but for missionary rather than biblical reasons. However, Clement VI, to whom FitzRalph submitted the *Summa* for approval, was deeply concerned about the promotion of biblical studies. On 20 May 1346, writing to the University of Paris after the sceptical propositions of Nicholas d'Autrecourt had been discussed and condemned at the curia, and when the progress of nominalist ideas derived from Ockham was causing concern among the older and more conservative generation of scholars in Paris, Clement urged a return to the sounder traditions of Aristotle in philosophy, and to the study of the Bible and orthodox tradition in theology. Writing to the masters and students of Paris, Clement stated: 'Plerique quoque theologi, quod deflendum est amarius, de textu Biblie, originalibus et dictis sanctorum ac doctorum expositionibus . . . non curantes, philosophicis questionibus et aliis curiosis disputationibus et suspectis opinionibus doctrinisque peregrinis et variis se involvunt.'[149] He commanded them to return to the sources of revealed truth 'ex quibus vera illa acquiritur theologia, cui non attribuendum est quicquid ab hominibus scire potest'. FitzRalph's approach in the *Summa* differed from the programme

[148] Text in *Chart. Univ. Paris.*, ii. 154–5. See Weiss, 'England and the teaching of Greek', 76–9; idem, 'The study of Greek in England', 96–106.

[149] *Chart. Univ. Paris.*, ii. 588. See also the similar edict of John XXII, 8 May 1317, ibid., 200–1.

outlined by the pope in the former's neglect of the 'originalia et dicta sanctorum', but in this case he could defend the predominance of the scriptural argument in the light of the special nature of the work and the audience for whom it was intended. At another point he was also out of step with the papal dictum, in his denunciation of the 'Aristotelica dogmata' in the autobiographical prayer, a factor which lends further credence to the view that this prayer at the end of the *Summa* was not part of the original text which FitzRalph presented to Clement VI for inspection and approval. Whether this is to be interpreted as careerism or conviction, the parallel between the papal injunction and the sentiments expressed in the *Summa* is striking, and it is at least probable that FitzRalph was a genuine supporter of the papal endeavour to bring theological studies back to first principles.

Compared with the earlier *lectura* on the Sentences, the *Summa* is – with the understandable exception of the section dealing with the errors of western schoolmen – notably free from the dialectics otherwise characteristic of the works of the medieval scholastics, and FitzRalph recognized this change in his own work, attributing it to a special divine grace. The extent of this change, and the possibility that he may have exaggerated it, have been the subject of some discussion,[150] but the evidence of the *Summa* and of the sermon diary indicates that there was a substantial change in outlook and in the tone of his writings. When FitzRalph looked back on his intellectual career in the prayer which, it is suggested, should be dated after 1357, he saw as the turning-point in his development the years spent in litigation at the curia, when he was exposed to the contacts and influences which led to the composition of the *Summa*: 'Nec illis sex annis michi solida veritas abfuisti, sed in tuis sanctis scripturis que de Te veritate incarnata a Te atque propter Te erant tuis populis promulgate, me veluti in quodam radioso speculo illuxisti, qui annis meis prioribus in philosophorum nugis me quasi ita in quadam tenebrosa caligine latitasti.'[151] Alluding to his earlier work as a teacher of philosophy and theology at Oxford, he further emphasized the change which he felt had come about in the striking metaphor of the toad in the swamp based on Ovid,[152] and connected this new knowledge

[150] See Robson, *Wyclif and the Oxford Schools*, pp. 71–2, 89–90, for criticism of Gwynn's view of this change.

[151] Ed. Hammerich, p. 20, ll. 69–74.

[152] See Ovid, *Metamorphoses*, vi. 376.

of the Scriptures with controversies in which he opposed Jews, Saracens, Greeks, and Armenians. The language in which he denounced his opponents here was very different from the courteous treatment which both Barlaam and the two Armenian prelates received at his hands in the *Summa* and its prologue. In the prayer he asserted that he had come to the conclusion that truth was to be found only in Scripture, despite 'garrencium philosophorum, pertinacium Iudeorum, simigentilium Grecorum, carnalium Sarracenorum, atque indoctorum Armenorum tumultum, qui fraudulenter et callide decorticabant tuam scripturam'.[153] This phrase scarcely suggests open and unprejudiced discussion with those non-adherents of the Roman Church whom he had encountered at Avignon, and this basic lack of sympathy with the representatives of the Greek and Armenian Churches implicit in his statement, may have been directed against those of less 'Latinizing' tendencies who also presented their case at the curia. On the other hand both of the Armenians must have appeared – by the standards of an Oxford doctor of theology – to possess a defective acquaintance with the kind of knowledge which impressed western observers at the curia. Even Barlaam's undoubted talents, and especially his secular interests in mathematics and astronomy as well as in ancient Greek literature, are less likely to have impressed FitzRalph.[154]

The capacity for insulting polemic displayed in this passage is a characteristic which became more prominent towards the end of his life. He displayed it in the letter to the Franciscan bishop of Bisignano, and especially in his outbursts against the friars. In itself the tone of this passage is therefore an argument in favour of the late dating of the prayer. In it FitzRalph also linked these controversies with representatives of other religious and cultural traditions with the protracted litigation which was the chief trial for his own experiences in Avignon – for which he was amply rewarded. He regarded his years at the curia as a season of bounty during which his mind was illuminated and his eyes opened to the truth of Scripture in a manner which had not been possible at Oxford. Now he claimed to realize at last

[153] Ed. cit., pp. 20–1, ll. 81–5.

[154] There is no evidence for contact between FitzRalph and Petrarch in Avignon, nor that the former attempted to learn Greek, despite his interest in the eastern churches, Weiss, 'The study of Greek in England', 97–8 n. But the note in MS Plimpton 156 at least raises a question against his alleged lack of all scientific interests.

the folly of those who neglected this truth and could rejoice at the end of his court case in the possibility of being able to devote himself more completely to the prayerful study of the Bible, presumably on his return to Lichfield.[155]

Allowances must be made for the changed perspective of an old man's reminiscences in interpreting the testimony of this prayer, and apart from any spectacular 'conversion' the circumstances of his later career would in any case have dictated a less scholastic, more biblical approach to theology – the successful pastor and preacher does not hold his flock by means of scholastic proofs, but through his use of the Scriptures. Yet this personal confession does illuminate a fundamental principle of the *Summa*. Here the argument was almost exclusively scriptural, not merely because he was dealing with men who did not recognize proofs that depended on the authority of the Roman Church, but also because of his conviction that the errors of the Armenians derived from their imperfect knowledge of the Bible. The lack of argument from early Christian tradition and from a comparative study of the Christian liturgies has already been noted and this, the chief defect in FitzRalph's case – must in the first instance be attributed to his own ignorance of Greek and Armenian literature. But there was also a more positive factor underlying this defect, i.e. FitzRalph's conviction that a careful study of the Bible was in itself sufficient to prove the truth of Roman doctrines, and that the Scriptures must be interpreted in a literal sense if his adversaries were to be convinced (and convicted) of their errors.

Although his knowledge of the Bible was already impressive in the earliest recorded sermons, the later development of his talent as a preacher does support the testimony that a change had come over his intellectual interests during the seven years at Avignon. This change was probably due to a combination of circumstances: contact with new surroundings and intellectual currents at the papal curia; his own developing interest in the missionary problems of the Avignonese papacy and in the politically-charged attempts to secure reunion of the eastern Churches with Rome as soon as possible in the face of the Islamic threat; the papal drive for a return to the supernatural sources of revealed truth, the 'fontes revelationis' which Clement VI commended to the Paris masters and students as contrasted

[155] For the sermon preached on 7 July 1344 before his departure from the curia, B, fols. 187^{r}–193^{r}; J, fols. 137ra–141rb.

with the more sceptical attitudes which had been common at Oxford and Paris since the days of Scotus, Durandus de Saint Pourçain, and Ockham, and with which FitzRalph was already familiar. Such a climate and combination of circumstances provided both the setting and the opportunity for FitzRalph to reflect on his own intellectual position and engage in what he regarded as a new search for truth, spurred on by the need to sustain his own morale in the face of adversity in the law courts.

It is striking that FitzRalph's interest in biblical studies was accompanied by a marked distaste even for the traditional Aristotelianism of the schools, and his condemnation was an open rejection of much of his own activity as a schoolman. In this respect he was out of harmony with the directions given to the University of Paris by Clement VI, when the pope ordered masters and students not merely back to the text of the Bible and to the 'originalia et dicta sanctorum', but also to the acknowledged masters of scholastic philosophy, and above all to Aristotle, to whom the pope gave pride of place but whom, he claimed, the Paris philosophers were neglecting. Here FitzRalph went farther than the pope in his reaction against the eccentricities of contemporary philosophy, a reaction which coincided with the defiant challenge to Aristotelian authority which was issued in Paris, debated, and then severely censured at Avignon during these very years.

This issue had begun to assume significant dimensions when on 21 November 1341 Benedict XII had summoned one of the most distinguished masters of the arts faculty in Paris, Nicholas d'Autrecourt, to answer before papal judges for the orthodoxy of his teaching. The resulting inquiry is well known from the *Discussio et reprobatio errorum magistri Nicolai de Ultricuria*, which was published shortly before Clement's letter of 20 May 1346 to the university. This represented the result of some four years of discussion of his teaching at the curia, most of which had taken place while FitzRalph was still there.[156] The nature and significance of the various opinions attributed to Nicholas d'Autrecourt, and which he finally abjured on 25 November 1347, are still the subject of debate, but it is clear that his views marked a definite reaction against the authority of Aristotle and a tendency to criticize the value of arguments and proofs previously accepted as self-evident, and that he presented them with

[156] *Chart. Univ. Paris.*, ii. 576–87.

an audacity of phrasing that aroused the more conservative Paris doctors to indignant protest. In essence d'Autrecourt was arguing for a common-sense approach to philosophy, as is indicated by the condemned proposition in which he was accused of teaching that absolute certitude could not be attained 'per apparentia naturalia', but that some degree of certainty could be attained if only men would pay attention to realities rather than to the study of Aristotle and Averroes. No wonder that Clement VI was alarmed that such teaching could undermine the established authorities of scholastic philosophy which were the foundation of the university curriculum in theology. Nicholas was further accused, among other tenets, of having criticized those who abandon the 'res morales et curam boni communis' for the sake of the logic of these two philosophers – a folly which so amazed Nicholas that he likened himself to a friend of truth who blew his trumpet to waken men from their slumbers but that these, far from showing gratitude for his good deed, were indignant and fell upon him as their deadly enemy. Not even the papal judges were prepared to take this seriously as a challenge to orthodox thought and, whereas they condemned other doctrines as false, erroneous, or heretical, they described this merely as presumptuous. The episode has a general interest as an indication of the increasing scepticism of fourteenth-century university teaching, but it also has a particular significance for FitzRalph's change of attitude. The episode coincided exactly with the reaction of a man who had previously been a staunch defender of the university system, its prerogatives, and teaching programme. FitzRalph's reaction from Aristotle in favour of the Bible, and the Paris master's reaction from the predominance of Aristotle to a half-humorous, half-earnest appeal for a philosophy of common sense 'per apparentia naturalia' and his willingness to divert 'ad res morales et curam boni communis' the time and energy which many scholars were spending on the barren dialectics of scholastic logic seem to have occurred simultaneously. In other respects these two were poles apart, and this coincidence indicates that the reaction away from Aristotle was not confined to sceptical minds. Here, as in other respects, FitzRalph anticipated Wyclif and future developments in English theological thinking. It was not a mere accident that he should have spent much of the later years of his life defending a thesis of lordship and jurisdiction which was based on a dubious interpretation of Augustinian doctrine and which was radically opposed to the principles of Aristotelianism. However, in the short term his conversion to the study of the Bible was to have a profound effect on his approach to the 'res morales et curam boni communis' both as a preacher and prelate.

III The Preacher and his Sermon Diary

FitzRalph's activity as a preacher is almost unique in one important respect, in the detailed sermon diary which he kept, and the care and precision with which he revised and polished his formal Latin sermons, possibly with the intention of publishing them in collected form towards the end of his life, though he failed to complete the task. He never put the Latin sermons in chronological order, hence they are copied in all the extant manuscripts of the diary in an order which makes neither thematic nor chronological sense, but more or less as the collector of his papers found them after his death in Avignon. The diary, in two of the main manuscripts entitled 'Sermones domini Ricardi dei gracia Archiepiscopi Ardmachani Hybernie primatis habiti Avinione et aliis locis quampluribus de diversis sanctis et temporibus prout inferius intitulantur',[1] provides an unusually complete and balanced picture of his work, as court theologian and plaintiff in Avignon, as pastor and administrator in Lichfield, and as prelate in the ecclesiastical province of Armagh, over a period of almost twenty-five years. Although the entire collection of ninety-two items, which survive in four complete manuscripts and numerous fragments ranging from substantial partial collections to copies of individual sermons, has been loosely termed the 'sermon diary', this title properly belongs only to the first part of the collection, which consists mainly of Latin summaries of, or excerpts from sermons preached almost exclusively in the vernacular in England and Ireland. But the collection also contains the full text of his formal Latin sermons and *Proposiciones* preached in Avignon and the anti-mendicant sermons delivered in London. With remarkably few exceptions the rubric contains precise details of the date and venue of each sermon, thus providing a reasonably detailed *itinerarium* for FitzRalph's pastoral activities in Lichfield and Armagh as well

[1] J, fol. 1^{r}. This rubric is missing from B, while L has instead of the original medieval rubric a *Tabula Sermonum* written in a 17th-century hand which occasionally provides more information concerning individual sermons than the rubric in J. For this *Tabula* and its scribe Paulus Veridicus (= Paul Harries, a bitterly anti-mendicant English priest active in Dublin *c.*1630) see Appendix, p.

a clear indication of the circles in Avignon where he was welcomed as a preacher.[2]

Although it is necessary to deal with the formal aspects of the diary and attempt a systematic evaluation of its contents and of its author's place in the fourteenth-century preaching tradition, the most valuable aspect of the sermons for the biographer of FitzRalph is their intensely personal quality. They are forthright, committed, and often passionate to a degree which was impossible in the context of formal theological treatises, and they illuminate his personality, interests, and prejudices, his changing and developing views, his opportunism, his moods, hopes, and fears. Furthermore, they reveal a concern for Church reform at all levels, from the curia through prelates and parish curates to the laity, long before he became embroiled in controversy with the friars. This concern was expressed in *ad hoc* terms, applied to specific situations, especially in Ireland where his sermons present a striking contrast to the conventional (and expected) denunciations of clerical vices in synodal and visitation sermons. In his academic, more reflective treatises, even when dealing with controversial subjects as in the *Summa de Questionibus Armenorum* and *De Pauperie Salvatoris*, he had recourse to dialogue form which had the advantage of permitting him to ventilate extreme opinions without actually committing himself to them. But in the pulpit he did not mince his words, though he did tend to exercise discrimination in marrying theme and mood to audience, especially in Avignon where interests of self-preservation dictated a degree of prudence, at least in the early stages. He could and did express himself in elegant Latin, expounding complex theological themes in formally constructed discourses in accordance with the contemporary 'artes predicandi'. He was also capable of unleashing his wrath over contemporary abuses and injustices with forthright if not brutal clarity, even when his criticism was directed against curial courts and lawyers, prelates, and higher clergy. In this respect his tone became distinctly more moderate on being elevated to the episcopal dignity himself, when he learned to restrict much of this criticism to the privacy of provincial synods. Nevertheless, his occasional outbursts in Avignon about

[2] Only two of the 95 items are totally devoid of clues to date and place of preaching; in five further cases the feast but not the year is given, and a tentative dating can be attempted. For the remainder the rubric in B supplies the necessary information, occasionally supplemented by L and MS Tanner IV. These rubrics are missing in J, whose *Themata sermonum*, fols. 202vb–203vb, has much less information.

place-hunters and pluralists, immoral prelates and double-dealing lawyers can be matched in England and Ireland with attacks on those who incite to and condone violence and dishonesty, fraudulent treatment of women and of the Gaelic Irish in matters of testamentary dispositions and inheritance laws, tithe-evasion and business malpractice, immorality, and neglect of their duties by the clergy. His strongly expressed views on racial tensions, in the case of England and France as well as in Anglo-Ireland, on the status of women, pastoral care, personal piety, honesty, and fair dealing, further enhance the value of the diary as a contemporary document, important and revealing on a wide range of social, political, and ecclesiastical issues. In the sermon diary lies the key to the most problematic aspect of FitzRalph's career, why the curial theologian and friend of the mendicant communities in Avignon, concerned with their oriental and missionary undertakings, in tune with their scholarly interests and willing to imitate their preaching techniques and their practice of writing out in Latin sermons originally delivered in the vernacular,[3] should suddenly change direction and pursue what amounted to a vendetta against his former friends. This development can be traced in the diary and his changed attitude, based on his view that the friars were abusing the confessional against what he felt to be the interests of rectitude and justice, is in keeping with many of the sentiments which he uttered from the pulpit.

The evidence of the diary shows that he had become conscious of his role as preacher – 'predicator devotus' was his own description of himself upon his return from Avignon to Lichfield in 1344 – and had begun to develop his talent in this direction during his early years at the curia. Formal sermons in the presence of the pope in his private chapel, before cardinals and higher curial dignitaries in the vice-chancellor's chapel and in the *audientia causarum*, were a regular feature of life in Avignon. These sermons were usually devoted to the exposition of strictly theological subjects, though with an eye to seasonal topics in the liturgical year, and they were both the means of providing the pope and his advisers with a range of informed theological opinion and an opportunity for theologians visiting the curia to display their talents and perhaps secure for them-

[3] Owst, *Preaching*, p. 227, maintained that this practice was a mark of the friars' exclusiveness and vastly superior intellectual attainments, reflecting a desire to keep the fruits of their labours among their equals.

selves some preferment. The nature of the sermon diary and above all the probability that its several parts were put together in the present form after FitzRalph's death by a friend in Avignon – for which the most likely candidate is the dean of St. Paul's, Richard Kilwington – from the archbishop's personal papers and with a view to having them circulated in England, makes it impossible to discern whether the sermon of 7 July 1335 was the only one delivered on this first visit to the curia.[4] FitzRalph appears to have begun to keep a sermon diary, or notes for his further use after each sermon he preached, soon after his return to Lichfield in the autumn of 1344. This return can be dated with some accuracy, as the last sermon preached in Avignon was on the feast of the translation of St. Thomas of Canterbury on 7 July 1344, and the first recorded sermon in Lichfield was on 28 November of the same year.[5] From internal evidence it seems that he wrote up the diary personally for the period 1344–57, and included in it the predominantly vernacular sermons preached in England and Ireland, but not those preached during his third visit to Avignon, 1349–51.[6] These sermons are copied, with only minor variations in the chronological order, in the main manuscripts, beginning with the short notes on sermons preached in Lichfield during Advent 1344 and ending with the famous series of anti-mendicant sermons preached in London during the winter and spring of 1356–7. These last four sermons were delivered in the vernacular, but were subsequently revised, expanded, and polished in Latin for wider circulation and belong properly to the literature of the anti-mendicant campaign. Of the remainder, some sermons were copied out at length if not in full, while others were simply noted as having been preached at a given time and place, with the scriptural text upon which each was based and a few short notes on their contents. That FitzRalph was personally responsible for its compilation is indicated by a number of small factors within the diary itself: the author of the notes frequently spoke in the first person singular, referred from one sermon back to

[4] B, fols. 155^{v}–161^{r}; J, fols. 115vb–119rb, and Walsh, 'An Irish Preacher at Avignon', 409–11.

[5] The rubric does not always indicate which Becket feast is intended, the martyrdom (29 December) or the translation of the relics, but the preacher's introductory remarks usually provide a clue. For this sermon, B, fols. 187^{r}–193^{r}; J, fols. 137ra–141vb, and for the Lichfield sermon in his cathedral, B, fol. 2^{v}; J, fol. 2^{rb-va}.

[6] For the list of sermons, in the order of the three principal MSS, see Gwynn, 'Sermon Diary', 48–57. MS New College 90 also has a complete collection, but see Gwynn, ibid., 8–9.

another, and occasionally when several sermons dealt with similar topics, he noted in the later case that he was repeating the contents of the earlier sermon. Again in several sermons in which he cited well-known tales and legends, or the life of a saint (veneration of the saints was a frequent theme of both his popular and his formal sermons, though he had some harsh things to say about the abuse of popular devotional aids such as Marian shrines at Walsingham and elsewhere),[7] the compiler of the notes merely gave a brief indication of the matter, as though realizing that if he wished to refer back to it he could rely on memory.[8] A further feature of the notes, which shows conclusively that they could only have been compiled by the preacher in person, is his discussion of an Advent sermon preached in the vernacular in Lichfield Cathedral. He referred to a particular point arising out of the subject-matter of the sermon, with the comment that he had not actually dealt with this point in the sermon itself as the laity were present. Clearly he had already learned to distinguish between the kind of criticism which might be expressed in front of the laity and the norms of preaching 'ad cleros'.[9]

Unlike the texts of the Avignon sermons, which FitzRalph obviously revised himself, the notes in the diary for these vernacular sermons seem not to have been intended for publication. Informal in character, with frequent cross-references and reminders for personal use, the diary was intended as a working instrument for a busy preacher, who constantly reiterated his view of the pulpit as a means of instruction in the most basic elements of the Christian faith. Hence a closer examination of the sermons contained in this first part of the collection, in the diary proper, reveals more about FitzRalph as an active pastor, engaged in the daily problems of ministering to his flock, strongly concerned with the role of the preacher (be he dean or bishop) as a teacher, engaged in the practical application rather than in theoretical reflections about the duties of prelates and

[7] In a sermon preached at Deddington near Oxford, 1 November 1356, B, fols. 91^{r}–92^{v}; J, fols. 74ra–75ra. Wyclif quoted this sermon at length, invoking the authority of 'Armachanus' against superstition and idolatrous worship of the saints, see Benrath, *Wyclifs Bibelkommentar*, pp. 34–5.

[8] e.g. the fragments of sermons on St. Catherine preached annually on the appropriate feast-day in Lichfield, where he could rely on the elaborate sermon of 25 November 1338 to the Franciscans in Avignon, B, fols. 1^{v}–2^{v}, 2^{v}–3^{r}, 179^{v}–187^{r}; J, fols. 1vb–2rb, 2^{va-vb}, 131va–137ra.

[9] e.g. in his last sermon in Lichfield, 3 December 1346, B, fol. 39^{r}; J, fol. 31^{v}. See Owst, *Preaching*, p. 251.

of parish priests charged with the cure of souls. Exceptions to this general rule are the Maundy sermon on the Eucharist preached to the Lichfield Cathedral clergy in 1345 and two sermons preached in Ireland, respectively in 1352 and 1354/5, to the bishops and clergy of his ecclesiastical province.[10] However, by and large a distinction can be made between the sermons contained in this part of the collection and the Avignon sermons as between the formal, Latin, and theologically-orientated contributions to sermon literature – some of which are closely linked with the development of ideas expressed in the discussion of the Armenian problems – and those which translate into practice FitzRalph's ideal of preaching as primarily a practical exposition of the teaching of the Church related to the major feasts of the ecclesiastical calendar.[11] In this respect the latter type has a special value as a set of pastoral sermons illustrating the labours of a zealous prelate in the pulpit, but understandably they did not have a wider circulation than the late fourteenth- early fifteenth-century English context to which they applied, whereas the Avignon sermons, with their polished Latin style, and in several cases the appeal of high theological content and pungently expressed criticism of ecclesiastical abuse, circulated individually and in small groups even on the Continent. In view of the very extensive recent discoveries of manuscripts of individual sermons, of theological as well as anti-mendicant interest, in German and Austrian libraries, the view that 'there is very little evidence that FitzRalph's sermons were much read outside England . . . with the single exception of . . . Defensorium Curatorum',[12] requires considerable modification. This statement still applies to Italy, where little interest was expressed in the anti-mendicant campaign and only FitzRalph's *Summa de Questionibus Armenorum* circulated freely, and to a lesser extent in France, where the *Summa*, the *Commentary on the Sentences*, and some of the anti-mendicant sermons were read, but not to central Europe and most definitely not to the libraries of the great monastic centres within the *Reichskirche*.[13]

[10] For the Maundy sermon, to which he frequently returned in later discussions of the Eucharist, B, fols. 4^{r}–7^{v}; J, fols. 2vb–5vb. Only the *Tabula Sermonum* in L gives the date and place of this sermon.

[11] Especially in Lichfield, e.g. while preaching in the chapel of St. Nicholas in Lichfield on 22 May 1346, he explained the custom of Rogation Days, B, fols. 33^{v}–34^{r}; J, fol. 27ra. For sermons and processions connected with Rogation Days see Owst, *Preaching*, pp. 200–2, 243.

[12] Sermon Diary, 2.

[13] e.g. the MSS cited below, nn. 51 and 70.

i. Avignon

The most important and substantial section of the manuscript-collections is that of the Avignon sermons, although representing merely twenty-four out of ninety-two items. However, these are without exception given in full and were clearly preserved by their author in a form intended for private circulation and possibly for publication. Of this group four items are not sermons in the strict sense and will be considered according to their subject-matter: the formal *Proposicio* preached on behalf of Edward III in August 1349, requesting the extension of the Jubilee indulgence to the population of his territories without the obligation of making pilgrimage to Rome in person, because of the devastation and travel difficulties caused by the Black Death. Two further items are the anti-mendicant *Proposiciones* of 1350 and 1357, while the fourth is FitzRalph's public response to his opponents' objections to the *Proposicio* of 1357.[14] The remaining sermons are significant not only for the range of topics discussed, but also for the venues in which they were delivered: four in the Franciscan church, two to the Dominicans, and one to the Carmelites in Avignon; five each in the papal chapel and in that of the vice-chancellor, and three in the *Audientia Causarum*, or *Apostolica Audientia*. As might be expected the majority of these, fourteen in all, were preached during FitzRalph's longest sojourn at the curia from 1337 to 1344, whereas only one can be located in his first visit, three apart from the *Proposiciones* of 1349 and 1350 during the third visit from 1349 to 1351, and only two – one each in the papal and vice-chancellor's chapel – during the final visit of 1357–60, when his animosity towards the friars and the court case *sub iudice* had deprived him of a preaching forum to which he previously had access. Curiously enough, in view of his later allegiances, no sermon is recorded to any monastic community, neither Benedictine, Cistercian, nor Augustinian canons regular. Nor apparently were any held in the convent of the Augustinian friars in Avignon, despite his probable connection with the prior-general who was the source of his theory of dominion and grace.

Four of these Avignon sermons were preached on feasts of St. Thomas of Canterbury, the acknowledged patron of the

[14] B, fols. 246^{v}–279^{r}; J, fols. 177vb–202va. The first of these *Proposiciones* survives only in copies of the sermon diary, including less complete versions such as Bibl. Casanatensis MS 948 (fols. 87^{r}–93^{v}), in contrast to the wider circulation of the anti-mendicant texts.

English nation at home and abroad and regarded with special veneration by English representatives at the papal curia, who celebrated both his feasts – that of the martyrdom on 29 December and that of the translation of the relics to their new shrine in Canterbury on 7 July. On each occasion it was customary to invite a distinguished visitor from England to preach a suitable panegyric,[15] and such an occasion provided FitzRalph with his first known opportunity to preach before an Avignon audience, on 7 July 1335 in the Dominican church. As a representative of Oxford University at the curia and a member of the papal commission on the beatific vision, FitzRalph's milieu, which he clearly enjoyed, was still that of academic theology, where many of the most respected theologians with whom he was in contact over the next decade were friars. This invitation to preach before the Dominicans may have been extended by Dominicans who like himself were involved in the debates on the beatific vision, who knew him to be a supporter of their own champion Thomas Waleys, and at that stage the development of FitzRalph's thinking about the friars over the next two decades could not have been foreseen.

For his first Avignon sermon on Becket, he took as his text the passage: 'Transtulit illum dominus' (Hebr. xi. 5) and expounded on the various possible interpretations of 'translatio'. He enumerated the reasons for veneration of the martyr, explaining the justification for the saint's relics being transferred to a more worthy shrine, which then became the most popular place of pilgrimage in England until its destruction by royal command in 1538, as the cult of St. Thomas the Martyr fell victim to the Henrician Reformation.[16] In this early sermon, it is striking that FitzRalph accepted wholeheartedly, almost naïvely, the veneration of the saints without any qualification or warnings about possible abuses caused by ignorance, superstition, or excessive zeal, which characterized some of his later

[15] For the English 'nation' in Avignon see Guillemain, *La Cour pontificale*, pp. 612–14. Better documented is the 'Hospice of St. Thomas the Martyr', established on the initiative of English merchants and travellers soon after the Jubilee year 1350, see 'The English Hospice in Rome', *The Venerabile*, Sexcentenary Issue, 21 (Rome, 1962).

[16] B, fols. 155^{v}–156^{v}; J. fols. 115vb–116rb. The shrine was the most popular place of pilgrimage in later medieval England until its destruction following the royal edict against saints and their cult, September 1538. On pilgrimages to Canterbury see J. J. Jusserand, *English Wayfaring Life in the Middle Ages* (London, 1950^{4}), pp. 197–204. For the cult of St. Thomas and its hagiography see Borenius, *St Thomas in Art*; Brita Puschel, *Thomas à Becket in der Literatur* (Bochum, 1963).

utterances as archbishop. By then he had become a seasoned campaigner in the pastoral field and had learned by experience some of the more common pitfalls. However, the use which Wyclif was to make of FitzRalph's particularly outspoken criticism of the Marian shrines of Walsingham, Lincoln, and Newark, should not lead automatically to the assumption that FitzRalph was a forerunner of the Lollards or a crypto-Protestant in his attitude to the veneration of images or shrines.[17] As we shall see, he must be given a large share of the credit for an elaborate publicity campaign for the shrine of St. Patrick, popularly known as St. Patrick's Purgatory, on an island in Lough Derg in a remote corner of his ecclesiastical province, which through the exploits of George of Hungary acquired some international notoriety during FitzRalph's episcopate.[18] In this first Becket sermon FitzRalph showed himself to be in tune with the trend among medieval preachers of illustrating the moral with a slightly exotic tale, and the achievements of Becket in life and in death are highlighted by an account of his alleged parentage: the once-cherished legend of how the mother of the saint, a Saracen princess named Mathilde, had encountered the Anglo-Norman merchant from London, Gilbert, in the Holy Land and had followed him to London, knowing only two words of English – 'Gilbert' and 'London'. On arrival she was jeered by the crowd for her ignorance, but was recognized by Gilbert's servant. Following her baptism which in deference to her royal rank was attended by three bishops, she was married to Gilbert Becket and Thomas was born of the marriage[19] – a charming and fanciful tale which was common currency among medieval hagiographers and was colourful enough to entertain as well as edify the mendicant audience at Avignon. The version told by FitzRalph bore close resemblance to the early fourteenth-century pictorial representation in 'Queen Mary's Psalter' which contains the most detailed surviving artistic rendering of events from Becket's life.[20] FitzRalph may have owed his interest and

[17] Above, n. 7. But for the veneration in which FitzRalph was held in Lollard circles see Anne Hudson, 'A neglected Wycliffite text', *JEH* 29 (1978), 263–5, and the 15th-century vernacular treatise formerly attributed to Wyclif, in MS Roy. 17. A. xxvi, fol. 12^{r}: 'As expouneth Seynt Rich. Armachan . . .'

[18] At the curia also he publicized the cult of St. Patrick, citing in a sermon before Clement VI, 14 February 1350 an example concerning the angel who appeared to St. Patrick in Wales, showing him the true field of his labours, B, fol. 211^{v}; J, fol. 153ra.

[19] B, fol. 157^{r-v}; J, fol. 117ra.

[20] It acquired its popular title because it subsequently passed into the possession of Mary Tudor, George Warner, *Queen Mary's Psalter. Miniatures and drawings by an*

knowledge of the Becket legend to his patron Grandisson of Exeter, who composed a life of St. Thomas of Canterbury, probably the book which he presented to John XXII at Avignon. Then followed a digression, in which FitzRalph alluded to the beatific vision controversy and his own contribution to it, which he had presented to Pope John XXII in person and whose dramatic purpose in the context of this sermon was to illustrate the perfect nature of the beatific vision then being enjoyed by the saint whose feast they were commemorating.[21] In this passage FitzRalph made his own position in the controversy clear: the deliberations which the commission of theologians undertook under the direction of Benedict XII during the summer of 1335 had barely begun when FitzRalph preached this sermon, but he used the opportunity thus presented to express his solidarity with the opinion expressed by the Dominican Thomas Waleys, which subsequently became the basis of the bull *Benedictus Deus*.

The remainder of the sermon was devoted to a discussion of the self-imposed austerities practised by the saint, and the preacher exhorted his hearers to take Becket as their model and practise mortification in their daily lives, following the saint's example when faced with temptation in matters of the spirit and the flesh.[22] Although FitzRalph did try to use the subject as a vehicle for edification and relate it to specific features of the friars' religious life, this was a fairly impersonal sermon by a visiting preacher on a topic of little more than passing interest to a Dominican community, and his other three surviving sermons on the same topic emphasize the fact that this was a national feast-day to be commemorated each year at some venue in Avignon. In this respect it differed both from FitzRalph's second sermon to the Dominicans six years later and from the several sermons of edification and exhortation on various aspects of the religious life, observance, duty, and morality which he was to preach, above all during his second visit to the curia and especially before Franciscan audiences. It

English artist of the 14th century, reproduced from Royal MS 2 B VII (London, 1912), Plates 282–94. The origin of the legend that Becket was the grandson of a Saracen emir is uncertain, but it was common currency by the later 13th century, and the version quoted by FitzRalph is similar to that of the 15th-century English poet, Robert of Gloucester, in *The Life and Martyrdom of Thomas Becket Archbishop of Canterbury*, ed. W. H. Black (Percy Society, xix, London, 1845).

[21] B, fol. 158^{r-v}; J, fol. 117vb.

[22] B, fols. 160^{v}–161^{r}; J, fol. 119^{ra-b}.

is, however, the only surviving testimony to his public activity during his first visit to Avignon and, together with his involvement in the beatific vision debates, may have helped him towards the substantial prize of an important English benefice. This early sermon differed from the later ones, when he had gained considerably in confidence and stature as a preacher who did not hesitate to voice his criticism of princes and prelates, lay and religious, and to draw moral lessons from his criticism. It also differed from his own later sermons on Becket during the period 1340–4, which he tended to make the vehicle for expression of his concept of the ideal prelate, a topic which had clearly begun to preoccupy him. The sermons of the early 1340s illustrate his developing ideas on the subject[23] – possibly in anticipation of the possibility that his favoured position under both Benedict XII and Clement VI might lead him to a bishopric. Such a possibility cannot have appeared remote, especially as suitably qualified candidates for Irish bishoprics within the Anglo-Norman sphere of influence, who were both potentially acceptable to the English Crown and enjoyed the necessary curial patronage, were not numerous. In any case the image of himself which he projected at the curia, both in sermons within the papal court and in the churches of the friars which were frequented by cardinals and other dignitaries on major feasts, was one likely to make an impression on the circles close to Benedict XII. It was that of a man committed to pastoral care and the encouragement of popular devotion, to high standards of observance on the part of the regular clergy, critical of abuse but sympathetic to their *modus vivendi*, and capable of sensitive discrimination between rule, observance, and objective of the various orders. He also displayed a commitment to securing high standards of conduct on the part of the secular clergy, opposing place-hunting, nepotism, immorality, and the absenteeism of prelates, this latter a surprising feature when one considers his own record on the subject, both as dean of Lichfield and archbishop of Armagh: exactly two-thirds of the period between his installation in Lichfield in April 1336 and his departure around Christmas 1346 was spent abroad, while of his fourteen years as archbishop of Armagh he spent a little over six years in Ireland.

[23] Esp. the Becket sermon of 29 December 1340, and the sermons preached in the Franciscan church on the feast of St. Martin, 11 November 1338, and the undated one for the feast of St. Anthony (17 January), B, fols. 236^{r}–241^{r}, 175^{r}–179^{v}, 141^{r}–145^{v}; J, fols. 169va–173rb, 128rb–131va, 105rb–108vb.

However, as we shall see in later sermons preached in Avignon when he was in the same position as an absentee prelate, he was sufficiently sensitive on the subject to feel obliged to justify himself in public, arguing that his own presence at the curia was necessary for the welfare of his flock and outweighed the disadvantages of his prolonged absence from his archdiocese.[24]

For his next sermon on Becket, preached in the *Audientia Causarum* in 1340, almost certainly on 29 December in view of the extent to which it was devoted to the question of Becket's martyrdom, he chose the theme of the good shepherd: 'Bonus pastor animam suam ponit pro ovibus suis' (Ioh. x. 11) and discussed at considerable length the model prelate and his duties.[25] His audience appears to have included a number of English prelates who had come to Avignon on business, and the preacher exhorted them to self-examination, returning yet again to the problem of whether their business at the curia was sufficiently pressing to warrant neglect of their flocks while they were in Avignon.[26] Here Becket was praised above all as a pastor – it was not necessary for every prelate to be a doctor of theology, and there were many worthy men with a particular talent for teaching the truths of the faith to their people even though they had only simple intelligence. But they applied this with diligence and faith to the Scriptures and were, according to FitzRalph, often more worthy of their office than doctors learned in theology.[27] Here the emphasis is different from the sermon of 25 February 1338, in which he had denounced the acquisition of benefices and ecclesiastical offices through simony and nepotism to the detriment of candidates with high academic qualifications who were unable to achieve promotion.[28] But the flexible preacher took his arguments as he required them, and here he needed to illustrate his case by praising Becket's strong sense of pastoral commitment despite his lack of theological expertise – a defect which Becket sought to remedy by having

[24] Preaching before Clement VI on 6 December 1349, B, fol. 204^{r}; J, fols. 147vb–148va.

[25] B, fols. 236^{r}–241^{r}; J, fols. 169va–173rb. Only MS Tanner IV, a 14th-century collection of six Avignon sermons by FitzRalph, fol. 418^{r}, gives the year as 1340. Gwynn, 'Sermon Diary', 57, therefore suggested 7 July 1340, but the extensive discussion of the martyrdom makes 29 December more probable.

[26] B, fol. 237^{v}; J, fol. 170^{rb-va}.

[27] B, fol. 237^{r}; J, fol. 170ra.

[28] Here he contrasted the easy path of promotion for the 'filios proprios' of prelates, though he was careful to add the qualification 'spirituales, intelligo, non carnales', with the difficulties often facing scholars of proved reputation, B, fol. 149^{v}; J, fol. 111vb.

Scripture read and expounded to him at table and by consulting the best available theologians.[29] This emphasis on the bishop as pastor and teacher is consistent with FitzRalph's exhortation to his own bishops in synod at Drogheda in 1352 when he put before them a clear statement of their obligations, as subjects of higher ecclesiastical authority, as rulers of their own flocks, and, above all, as teachers. Another feature of contemporary prelates which was regularly criticized by late medieval preachers, including FitzRalph, their greed as expressed in the drive for accumulation of benefices, was also reflected in this sermon, where the preacher explicitly held up Becket as a model for all prelates with a mercenary streak.[30]

The third Becket sermon, dating from 1341, continued the same theme of the martyred archbishop of Canterbury as a model prelate, the preacher and teacher of his flock. Here FitzRalph discussed the problem of courage and fear, distinguishing between fear of man ('timor servilis') and fear of God ('timor filialis'), attributing the latter but not the former to his hero, before launching a remarkably outspoken attack on the prevailing vices of the age, not least at the papal court. Here he gave vent to his anger and frustration on the general topic of endless and indiscriminate litigation, a topic which must have touched personally many of his audience in the *Audientia Causarum*, and then returned to his other favourite targets, nepotism and simony.[31] This sermon is that of a man of established reputation – he had already achieved some success in his litigation – and could afford to speak out boldly concerning the practices which were not merely prevalent in the daily life of the curia but, as the administration grew in complexity, had become a necessary part of that administration. The final Becket sermon, preached on 7 July 1344 shortly before FitzRalph's departure, on the text: 'Contempnit timorem nec cedit gladio' (Iob. xxxix. 22) is much more conciliant and devotional in tone, as befitted the occasion.[32] In it the preacher expressed relief that his seven-year ordeal in the curial courts had come to an end and, with a certain note of self-irony, likened both Becket and himself to the ass or mule who was tenacious and stubborn, patient, and willing to carry loads – presumably qualities he found necessary

[29] B, fol. 237^{r}; J, fol. 170ra.
[30] B, fol. 237^{v}; J, fol. 170^{va-b}.
[31] B, fols. 138^{r}–140^{v}; J, fols. 102vb–105ra.
[32] B, fols. 187^{r}–193^{r}; J, fols. 137ra–141rb.

in order to survive lengthy litigation.[33] By now he must have become a familiar figure to curial audiences, and he bade them farewell with a further story about Becket, whose hair shirt had become torn and was miraculously mended by the Blessed Virgin in return for Becket's piety and devotion: the preacher extended the story to include a personal application, likening his own soul to a rag which had been torn by the years of worry, anxiety, and distractions of the papal court ('huius palacii' – he was preaching once more in the *Audientia Causarum*), and praying that the Virgin might do another mending job and permit him to return once more to his proper duties as a devout preacher.[34]

Even in this farewell sermon FitzRalph could not refrain from emphasizing Becket's lack of a mercenary streak, citing the example of Becket's action in resigning his archbishopric to Alexander III for fear of committing 'symonia mentalis', and feeling himself unworthy of the office because his election had taken place at the behest of the king – a passage which may be interpreted as an elaborate hint at the position of FitzRalph's legal adversary, the royal servant, Archbishop Stratford of Canterbury.[35] This significance is heightened by the consideration that there appear to have been no 'Becket' sermons dating from FitzRalph's later visits to the curia as archbishop of Armagh and during the primacy in Canterbury of Simon Islip (1349-66) with whom he had no quarrel. Hence on the basis of the available evidence it may tentatively be suggested that the Becket sermons of 1340, 1341, and 1344 – all of which were preached in the *Audientia Causarum* – had a subtle purpose. These sermons emphasized Becket the model pastor, not the litigant, and may have been chosen with FitzRalph's own case against the then reigning archbishop of Canterbury in mind, hoping that the implicit contrast would not escape an audience in one of the principal centres for the dispensation of papal justice. Nevertheless, despite a possible ulterior motive in the choice and treatment of subject in these sermons, it is clear that FitzRalph had a deep personal admiration for Becket, and that he did in his own pastoral and primatial activities, and especially in his militant and tenacious defence of what he believed to be the rights of his Church, model himself – consciously or unconsciously – on the martyred archbishop of Canterbury.

The question of lawyers and litigation preoccupied FitzRalph

[33] B, fol. 192^{v}; J, fol. 141ra.

[34] B, fol. 187^{r}; J, fol. 127^{ra-b}.

[35] B, fol. 192^{r}; J, fol. 140vb.

in a particularly acute manner during the seven years of his second sojourn at Avignon, and this preoccupation is reflected in several sermons of the period, especially two early ones, both of them preached in November 1338 in the Franciscan convent at the curia. Clearly FitzRalph, after one year in Avignon pursuing the case which, as we have seen, concerned both his own personal interests and those of the cathedral chapter of Lichfield, had suffered his baptism of fire and discovered, as many a litigant before and since, that the curial advocates could be an obstacle as well as an avenue to the dispensation of papal justice. In the first of these two sermons, celebrating the feast of St. Martin of Tours on 11 November 1338,[36] FitzRalph raised a number of issues to which he would return in more detail later: the model prelate, for whom the saint should be an ideal because he combined his work with a spirit of prayer and chastity; the model religious who should be characterized by the observance of poverty and chastity; the duty of almsgiving in life and not simply the adoption of a selfish attitude by enjoying one's goods in life and making testamentary bequests after death; the oppression of subjects by secular rulers.[37] He set St. Martin before his audience as an example of a soldier for Christianity and went on to lament that modern soldiers did not live according to the Gospel precepts (did he have the horrors of the Bruce invasion in his own native area in mind?), before turning to the main target of his attacks, the 'soldiers' in the Church whom he identified as the lawyers, the 'advocati, promotores, and procuratores' fighting for their stipends. Some, though he is careful to stipulate not all, he accused of taking on and promoting causes, regardless of whether they were just or not, and of charging the same high fee for all of them – he seems oblivious of the irony that with such a remark he was himself pre-empting the judicial procedure. Others he accused of taking double, or even treble salaries for their services, and of resorting to fraudulent methods in order to secure the success of their clients.[38]

A fortnight later on the feast of St. Catherine of Alexandria he preached once more before a Franciscan audience. While this sermon was primarily a formal and lengthy panegyric of the

[36] B, fols. 175^{r}–179^{v}; J, fols. 128rb–131va.

[37] B, fol. 176^{v}; J, fol. 129^{ra-b}. This was his first reference to the duty of almsgiving in life, and he returned to it in Avignon on 8 December 1342 (to the Carmelites), 4 October 1349 (to the Franciscans), on numerous occasions in Ireland, and in ever more extreme terms again in Avignon, 1 November 1358 and 6 January 1359.

[38] B, fols. 175^{v}–176^{r}; J, fol. 129ra.

saint, for whom he shared the veneration which was widespread in fourteenth-century Europe and on whom he was to preach again on several occasions in Lichfield, with an excursus on missionary activity among the Saracens and Tartars – a subject not without particular relevance to a Franciscan audience – FitzRalph found an opportunity to return once more to the controversial topic of curial lawyers. Here, however, the approach was more general and was formulated as a plea for the study of theology, and especially of the Scriptures, as the most important of all sciences. FitzRalph criticized bitterly those who devoted themselves to the profane sciences to the exclusion of even the most rudimentary knowledge of the Bible. This sermon is the first indication of his interest in the study of Scripture and the development of his arguments for scriptural authority as the 'scientia fidei', and it may coincide chronologically with the awakening of interest in textual interpretation which was reflected in the opening chapters of the *Summa de Questionibus Armenorum*. Various categories of offenders came under attack: those 'negligentes et tepidos qui gerunt curam animarum, et raro aut numquam instruant aut informant in fide', and also those 'qui habent in cavernis magnam copiam librorum legum aut medicine, et non est inter omnes una parva biblia quam possent in fine diei respicere . . .'; furthermore, the presumptuous, who knew a few scriptural quotations contained in the *Decretum* and assumed that they had thereby mastered the 'scientia scripturarum', while remaining ignorant of the greater portion of the Bible, and the 'mere historians' ('nudos historicos') who avoided the difficult questions of interpretation and contented themselves with the literal-historical sense, ignoring the remaining three traditional senses according to which medieval exegetes interpreted the Bible.[39] The intensity of the preacher's feelings on the subject might suggest that he had already in the later months of 1338 come in contact with such problems and possibly that the early debates with the Armenian and Greek representatives had begun to arouse his concern, especially if such debates were in his opinion being dominated by curial officials who were primarily canonists and not theologians. His attempt to counter the objection that if everybody studied theology and nobody was learned in the law – an objection

[39] B, fol. 183^{r-v}; J, fol. 134rb. He returned again to the problem of the Hebrew text on 16 December 1341, and to the relationship of Scripture to apologetics on 29 March 1342.

which might reasonably be raised in Avignon – no experts could be found to judge genuine cases of litigation among members of the Christian Church, was not particularly successful, amounting to no more than a further denunciation of excessive legal activity and a lamentation that no people was as litigious as the Christian. Much of this litigation was in his opinion unnecessary, and he chose the opportunity to display his incipient interest in and knowledge of Jewish society by arguing in favour of the jurisprudence of the Old Law as reflected in the Old Testament which, he claimed, gave the Jewish regime a tranquillity unknown to contemporary Christian society.[40] Although he denied wishing to appear contemptuous of other faculties, especially that of law, he made no secret of his own preference for theology and of his belief that this should be of primary importance to his Franciscan audience.

At no stage was his animosity towards lawyers more clearly expressed than in these two sermons of November 1338, and from them it might be deduced that at that stage his case was not faring very well and that he had little reason to expect justice at the hands of curial advocates. He may also have used sermons to mendicant audiences as a forum to make statements which he could hardly make in the curia, and the Franciscans would hardly have been expected to be unduly sympathetic towards the horde of legal functionaries who inhabited the courts at Avignon. It is significant that FitzRalph's tone was substantially different when he had occasion to return to a similar theme during a sermon preached on 6 December 1349 in the papal palace in the presence of Clement VI.[41] On this latter occasion his criticism of the malpractices of curial lawyers was no more than a mild inference in a general discussion of the station and duties of various groups and professions when he was dealing with the questions of bribery and fraud,[42] and this criticism was overshadowed by a *laudatio* of papal justice as it had been dispensed to him at the end of his seven-year ordeal. His tribute to the integrity of the judges who had heard his case was patently genuine, and it can only be concluded that FitzRalph was behaving in the subjective, passionate manner which is so consistent with his other actions. Paradoxically, the very inconsistency of his statements over a period of eleven years is

[40] B, fol. 183^{r}; J, fol. 134ra.

[41] B, fols. 199^{v}–205^{r}; J, fol. 145va–149ra.

[42] B, fols. 202^{r}–204^{r}; J, fols. 147rb–148vb, contain a lengthy discussion of standards of legal practice and the grounds upon which the duty of restitution were based.

consistent with what we know of his experiences in this period and of his own personality and character, while on the purely human level what could be more natural than to criticize the system when it appeared to be working against the cause one believed to be just and to praise it when it produced one's desired objective?

It might be suggested that this discrepancy of mood and attitude was due to the fact that the later sermon was preached in the papal presence and that a more deferential attitude to papal judicial procedures was therefore prudent. But there are indications that FitzRalph, even when in a more vulnerable position than he was as archbishop of Armagh in 1349, was not always prepared to adopt a prudent and deferential attitude in his appearances before the pope, most strikingly so in the case of an Ash Wednesday sermon preached in the presence of Benedict XII.[43] Although the sermon is undated in the main manuscripts of the complete collection, the date is given in Munich CLM 23474, a fourteenth-century miscellany containing this single example of FitzRalph's preaching and clearly deriving from an early text which circulated before the preacher's elevation to the see of Armagh.[44] Hence in default of external evidence to the contrary, and as this dating is consistent with the internal evidence of the sermon itself, the date of Ash Wednesday, i.e. 25 February 1338, may be tentatively accepted, a dating which would make it the earliest recorded sermon in Avignon apart from the Becket sermon of 1335 and the first which FitzRalph preached in the papal curia itself. If FitzRalph were selected to preach before the pope in his private chapel within a short time of his return to the curia, it may be because his work on the beatific vision issue three years earlier was still remembered and held in esteem. He certainly used the occasion to preach a sermon which ranged over a wide selection of topics, both theological and reforming. The major portion of the sermon is theological, and it contains a particularly interesting passage in which the preacher sought to explain the nature of God's foreknowledge by an illustration which he had used in the *lectura* on the Sentences, comparing God's intellect with a mirror, capable of representing all transitory natures without any physical change in itself. He continued his argument with a phrase which foreshadowed his later rejection of the scholastic method:

[43] B, fols. 145^{v}–150^{r}; J, fols. 108vb–112ra.

[44] CLM 23474, fol. 6^{r}. The provenance of this manuscript is unknown.

'Quando exercitabar in sophismatibus, solebam sic arguere', but here he was not concerned with scholastic arguments and simply referred his audience back to the text of the Lombard himself.[45] A further section of the sermon was devoted to moral problems, and here he based his arguments on the treatise of Innocent III *De condicionis humane miseria*,[46] before turning to the theme of ashes in order to expound on the dangers of high ecclesiastical life. This section is extremely outspoken in its criticism of a range of abuses, in particular the rapacity of prelates who neglect their flocks in order to accumulate still more benefices and wealth. Throughout the sermon the preacher combined a devotional and rhetorical approach which was very direct and in parts moving, and his apparently genuine and passionate concern for the well-being of the Christian community cannot have failed to impress his audience. He was doubtless aware that sentiments such as these were guaranteed to meet with the approval of the austere and reform-conscious Cistercian pope, who was well known for his reluctance to help his relatives to positions of wealth and influence. FitzRalph may therefore have been deliberately playing to the gallery with expressions of moral outrage such as: 'Sunt multi in ecclesia dei presidentes rapaciter congregantes, gulose sive tenaciter reservantes, et suos pullos scilicet spirituales filios contempnentes. Suntne prelati plurimi rapaciter congregantes . . . ?'[47] He developed also the theme which was to be a favourite one for the rest of his life, the duty of giving alms from one's goods in life rather than waiting to make donations 'ad pios usus post mortem', recalling the Sermon on the Mount (Luc. vi. 20 ff.; Matt. v. 3 ff.) and observing that 'predecessores vestri solent esse quasi nichil habentes et omnia possidentes, . . . set iam a contrario plures sunt quasi omnia habentes et nichil possidentes'. The final diatribe against those who acquire fat benefices through nepotism rather than their own merits, to the disadvantage of 'doctores in theologia, doctores in decretis, et alii probi viri . . . in mendicitate miserrima finiant suos dies',[48]

[45] B, fol. 147^{r-v}; J, fol. 110^{ra-b}, '. . . Super isto eos remitto ad di.XL. primi libri sententiarum, et ad exemplum predictum de speculo.'

[46] B, fols. 146^{v}, 148^{r}, 150^{r}; J, fols. 109va, 110vb, 112ra. See *Lotharii Cardinalis (Innocentii III) de miseria humane conditionis*, ed. Michele Maccarrone (Lucca, 1955).

[47] B, fol. 149^{r}; J, fol. 111rb. One of the rare exceptions was Benedict's nephew, the Cistercian Guillaume Court, who became a cardinal and subsequently presided over the hearing of FitzRalph's case against the friars. See also Schimmelpfennig, 'Benedikt XII. (1334–42) als Reformpapst', 16 ff.

[48] B, fol. 149^{v}; J, fol. 111va.

may owe its particularly bitter note to the fact that FitzRalph himself, although highly qualified in theology, had to wait a long time for a benefice, and then only managed through the patronage of Grandisson, when the bishop of Exeter was providing for the future of his own youthful and unqualified nephew, who received at the same time a much more lucrative collection of benefices than the regent master of theology.[49] He may have also had in mind the complaints of Oxford masters who were unable to support themselves on their teaching fees and whose unbeneficed plight had been a source of concern during the troubles in the university around the time of the Stamford Schism. For whatever reason, the topic continued to preoccupy FitzRalph, long after he had reached the peak of his own career and could not complain of unfavourable treatment of his own person. He returned to it in the theologically important sermon on the Immaculate Conception preached to the Carmelites at Avignon on 8 December 1342, in his last sermon to the Franciscans on 4 October 1349, and during a formal discourse on sin and temptation preached before Clement VI in Lent (14 February 1350).

Although there are several undated sermons among the Avignon collection which may belong to the years 1339-40, none can be definitely assigned to this period. The lacuna may be due to the defective state of the collection as it has survived, or it may have had a more positive cause. Was FitzRalph's case going badly and had he temporarily fallen out of papal favour or, more probably, was he becoming involved in the Armenian negotiations to the exclusion of other activities? The next datable sermon is the second Becket one, dating most probably from 29 December 1340, which contained the pointed exhortation that prelates who had come to Avignon on legal business should return to their flocks. Here he used an argument which would also become a familiar theme in the later sermons – responsibility for one's own conscience and the duty of regular and rigorous self-examination, in this case in order to determine whether the reason for being at the curia was genuinely in the

[49] The special claims of graduates to benefices featured regularly in university petitions to late 14th-century popes, e.g. the roll of the English nation in Paris and that of the masters of Oxford (which included Mag. John Wyclif), both 1362 and calendared in *CPL Petitions* I, 389-92. See also Ernest F. Jacob, 'Petitions for benefices from English universities during the Great Schism', *TRHS* 4th ser. 27 (1945), 41-59.

interests of one's flock or purely selfish.[50] Practical in tone, it suggests that the preacher was reasonably sure of his ground, and the invitation to preach in the *Audientia Causarum* may be an indication that at this stage his case was progressing favourably. By now the discussions with the Armenian representatives leading to the formulation of the 117 *errores* must have been nearing completion, and the possibility cannot be excluded that FitzRalph's work in this area enhanced his status in the curia, and consequently his chances against the archbishop of Canterbury.

One of the essential preconditions of the conscientious prelate, apart from blameless personal morality and attainment of office through merit not nepotism, was – in the ideal picture gradually built up by FitzRalph in the sermons of the late 1330s and early 1340s – that of residence in his diocese and personal attention to the duties of his office, including preaching and teaching as well as administration, but not the pursuit of secondary objectives at the papal curia. Hence it must have been a source of personal embarrassment when, as archbishop, his own prolonged visits to the city on the Rhone became the subject of criticism. We know that in the case of his visit in 1349-51, which had the twofold objective of presenting Edward III's indulgence plea and his own personal problem of the exercise of his primatial jurisdiction, and especially his right to have his cross carried before him even within the precincts of the archdiocese of Dublin, this visit became so protracted that even the English king – for motives other than genuine pastoral concern – felt obliged to remind him of his duties and order his return to Ireland. Clement VI had, as archbishop of Rouen and ambassador of the French king, been a regular visitor to, and preacher in, Avignon. Then, and subsequently as cardinal, he moved in circles to which FitzRalph also had access, and the tone of FitzRalph's sermons preached before him in the papal chapel indicate a certain familiarity between the two men. Furthermore, both were prominent preachers, whose sermons bore sufficient stylistic similarities and circulated together among their contemporaries as those of a particular Avignon circle, to warrant consideration of the possibility of mutual influence or exchange of ideas about the technique and content of their sermons.[51] In chrono-

[50] B, fol. 237^{v}; J, fol. 170va. He had also stressed this on 6 December 1338, and would do so again in the sermons on St. Anthony the Hermit and St. Francis to the Franciscans in Avignon.

[51] Their sermons appear together in Brussels, Bibl. royale MS 2582 (new); St. Paul im Lavanttal (OSB) MS 23; Klosterneuburg MS 204; Innsbruck, Universitäts-

logical terms it would seem probable that when FitzRalph came to Avignon he learned from his older and more distinguished contemporary, and a passage in his sermon of 4 October 1349 strengthens this impression. Here he discussed the qualities of the ideal sermon and the pitfalls facing the unskilled preacher, remarking 'accepi a pluribus quod sermonum prolixitas dominos hic sepe accediat, sermonum difficilitas eorum animos sepe perturbat, sermonum curiositas eos aut alios (*sic*) nunquam edificat, sed loquentem ostentat.'[52]

Clement cannot have failed to remember the earlier outbursts of the dean of Lichfield against absentee prelates living in Avignon on inadequate pretexts. Hence in the sermon of 6 December 1349,[53] when FitzRalph discussed the duties of various offices including prelates and parish priests, he raised the delicate problem of dispensation for purposes of a visit to the curia. While he criticized the parish clergy for running to Avignon at every possible opportunity, he naturally felt obliged to justify his own presence there instead of in his diocese. He built up an elaborate, but not wholly convincing argument to the effect that one can get a dispensation, but that might not be enough; one must question whether the motives for it are justified, whether the purpose of the visit is a selfish and therefore a sinful one, or whether it is meritorious, and he warned that a dispensation for the wrong reasons could be dangerous for the personal salvation of those 'qui curam animarum habentes gratis morantur in curia'.[54] But whereas here, as on so many other occasions, FitzRalph stressed the importance of personal decisions in conscience, he carefully avoided specifying the actual reasons for his own prolonged stay at the curia or submitting their merit to the judgement of his audience. As yet the mendicant question had not become acute, the sermon preached two months earlier to the Franciscans had not indicated any radical

bibliothek MS 234 (formerly in the Cistercian abbey, Stams). See Philibert Schmitz, 'Les Sermons et discours de Clément VI, OSB', *RB* 41 (1929), 15–34; Diana Wood, 'Maximus sermocinator verbi Dei: the sermon literature of pope Clement VI', *The Materials, Sources and Methods of Ecclesiastical History* (Studies in Church History, 11, Oxford, 1975), 163–72. Hammerich, *FitzRalph and the Mendicants*, p. 31, also noted the connection, though in unflattering terms, describing some of FitzRalph's sermons as 'very longwinded panegyrics of the same kind as several of the sermons preached by the later Clement VI'.

[52] B, fol. 193^{r}; J, fol. 141rb. Compare this criticism with the criteria for a successful sermon adduced by Clement VI and discussed in Wood, 164–5.

[53] B, fols. 199^{v}–205^{r}; J, fols. 145va–149ra.

[54] B, fol. 204^{r-v}; J, fol. 148vb.

change of front, although FitzRalph had already in several of his sermons given indications that certain aspects of the pastoral scene which involved also the role of the religious did not meet with his approval, and around this time he must have begun to work out the anti-mendicant arguments which found their first concrete expression in the *Proposicio* preached seven months later on 5 July 1350 in the presence of Clement VI. Hence the most convincing reasons for FitzRalph's continued presence at Avignon in the winter of 1349–50 were connected with his archdiocese, with the need to secure mass dispensations for ordinations and intermarriages in spite of the peculiarities caused by the clash between Gaelic and canon law in parts of his ecclesiastical province,[55] and above all, the need to secure a judicial decision in favour of Armagh on the primacy question in the favourable circumstances caused by the interregnum in Dublin between the death of the discredited archbishop Alexander de Bicknor (+ 14 July 1349) and the consecration of his successor John of St. Paul, on 14 February the following year. As we shall see when we come to consider his role as archbishop of Armagh, FitzRalph was successful with regard to securing papal approval for all internal arrangements within his metropolitan jurisdiction, including the necessary dispensations, but the problem of the primacy was to prove more complex and was not solved, even temporarily, until the next pontificate.

Hammerich's brief study of the sermon diary was undertaken with the specific objective of trying to solve a problem alluded to above, namely the precise identification of the origins of FitzRalph's anti-mendicant attitudes up to the moment of preaching the *Proposicio* of 5 July 1350, and as a result his study is in one important respect misleading. Despite his brief general characterization of the sermon diary as a whole,[56] he was primarily concerned to pick out the passages which discussed property and poverty, confession, absolution, and restitution, and also testamentary bequests, which might be deemed as laying the foundation for the mendicant crisis, and therefore he tended to ignore the far greater bulk of sermons which dealt with theological and hagiographic themes, as well as those of general moral exhortation which were part of the stock-in-trade of the late medieval preacher. It would of course be equally misleading to suggest that the dominant factor in these sermons was the criticism of abuses in the curia or throughout Christendom. The majority of

[55] *CPL Petitions* I, 206–7.

[56] *FitzRalph and the Mendicants*, pp. 25–42.

sermons preached in the early years in Avignon were principally concerned with theological subjects and with the preacher's concept of the ideal pastor. One of his earliest sermons in curial circles, and the first of a number preached in the chapel of the vice-chancellor,[57] was preached on the second Sunday of Advent, 6 December 1338.[58] A very strict and formal sermon, which gives the impression that the preacher is, theologically speaking, on his 'best behaviour', a possibility which would be consistent with the view that he was in difficulties with his law-suit and consequently gave vent to his frustration in the sermons to the Franciscans a month earlier, FitzRalph is here at his most careful and orthodox. He discussed the standard theological problems arising out of both the Last Judgement and the resurrection of the body, both issues which had been brought back into the limelight by the beatific vision debates, but the sermon contained little personal comment. Instead all the best authorities are cited – the Fathers, including Origen, Chrysostom, and Hilary, as well as Augustine – and of medieval authorities, Anselm and the Lombard. Most of the patristic quotations could have been found in the pages of the Lombard, but not all of them. Hence this sermon is one of the few examples of a greater degree of familiarity with patristic literature in FitzRalph's entire *œuvre*, and it at least raises a question mark against the view that his patristic knowledge, with the single exception of St. Augustine, was minimal whereas his knowledge of the Bible was indisputable.

This is an unusually long, rhetorical, and subtle sermon, divided into a formal schema which was unusual in FitzRalph's sermons, though it might be argued that its tripartite construction in twenty-seven paragraphs, all in groups of three, had been carried to such extremes that comprehension suffered. Even by Avignon standards, this sermon was exceptional, but it seems to have been a constant feature of FitzRalph's sermons in the vice-chancellor's chapel that they should be among his more formal and impersonal ones, three of them being for Advent, the remaining two respectively for Good Friday 1342 and All Saints 1358 (though this latter would have been in the papal chapel

[57] The other sermons preached there included one for the first Sunday of Advent, undated in all MSS; 16 December 1341, also an Advent sermon; a Good Friday sermon dated only in MS Tanner IV to 1342 (29 March 1342); 1 November 1358, B, fols. 212^{v}-217^{r}, 231^{r}-236^{r}, 150^{r}-155^{v}, 127^{r}-134^{v}; J, fols. 153vb-156vb, 165vb-169va, 112ra-115vb, 90va-100vb.

[58] B, fols. 217^{r}-222^{v}; J, fols. 156vb-160va.

but for the illness of Innocent VI).[59] In that of 16 December 1341, the third Sunday of Advent, he took as his text: 'Gaudete in Deo semper' (Ad Phil. iv. 4) and returned once more to the discussion of the Last Judgement, thereby indicating that it had not ceased to be a topic for discussion but had probably received a new lease of life in the course of the Armenian debates at the curia.[60] Here the preacher built his sermon very closely on the text, expounding on the various causes of spiritual joy and avoiding all moral applications of the theological problem. The third such sermon, undated in all manuscript collections except for the rubric of the first Sunday of Advent and devoted to the doctrine of the Incarnation,[61] is again formal and impersonal in style. It is, however, unusual for its devotional, almost mystical tone which is largely modelled on Bernard of Clairvaux, with occasional appeals to the authority of Anselm of Canterbury.[62] It was recognized as one of FitzRalph's most successful exercises in devotional preaching by the compiler of the *Omne bonum*, a monk and probably a Cistercian (in which case the treatment of Bernard of Clairvaux must have had a particular appeal) working in the London area around 1360, an enemy of the mendicant friars and admirer of the preaching capacity of the recently deceased archbishop of Armagh.[63]

On the other hand, the Good Friday sermon of 29 March 1342, preached in the vice-chancellor's chapel shortly before the death of Benedict XII and essentially theological in tone and content, adopted a different approach.[64] Dealing with the Redemption as a problem of apologetics, FitzRalph examined in detail the various doctrinal errors frequently propagated – those of the Jews, the Manichees, and of the Philosophers – and illustrated once more his development away from scholastic philosophy as a guide to theological problems. The sermon also indicates his increasing interest in comparative religious problems

[59] B, fol. 127^r^, includes the rubric: 'Sermo eiusdem Ricardi in capella domini Vicecancellarii in festo omnium sanctorum propter infirmitatem domini pape qui in sua capella factus esse debebat.' This suggests that FitzRalph included the explanation in his own copy of the sermon, and it was taken over by the unknown compilator of the collection – if Kilwington, he may have attended the sermon.

[60] B, fols. 231^{r}–236^{r}; J, fols. 165vb–169va.

[61] B, fols. 212^{v}–217^{r}; J, fols. 153vb–56vb.

[62] Esp. *Cur Deus homo.* For the most recent edition see: *Anselme de Cantorbéry, Pourquoi Dieu s'est fait homme*, ed. with French trans., René Roques (Sources chrétiennes. Séries des textes monastiques d'occident, xi, Paris, 1963).

[63] BL, MS Royal 6. E. vii, fol. 234^{r}.

[64] B, fols. 150^{r}–155^{v}; J, fols. 112ra–115vb.

as expressed in the *Summa de Questionibus Armenorum*, which must at this point have been in the course of preparation.

Although FitzRalph's approach to theological method can be seen changing in the course of these sermons, some of the topics which had preoccupied him as a schoolman at Oxford continued to do so, not least that of predestination. The passage in the Ash Wednesday sermon of 1338 in which he returned to it indicated that he was still unable to reconcile that personal commitment to the primacy of the will which was so strongly expressed in his *Commentary on the Sentences* with the anti-Pelagian teaching then being propounded by his friend Bradwardine. The latter was moving back and forth, to Italy and Avignon and still in contact with theological circles in Paris and Oxford, while intermittently completing his work on the treatise *De Causa Dei* against those in both universities whom he regarded as pushing the doctrine of free will to Pelagian limits. These controversies cannot have been unknown to some of FitzRalph's audience in Avignon, and he introduced the topic by reminding his hearers that God had chosen them for their high estate and then expounding on God's foreknowledge in terms of the mirror image mentioned earlier: 'Sic cogitent deum esse speculum sine macula quod de sui natura representet non tantum existencia set eciam omnia futura et omnia possibilia.'[65] However, the tone is uncertain, and FitzRalph had either not yet clarified the matter for himself sufficiently to make a clear statement of his views or else he regarded the topic as so delicate that he preferred, especially before such an audience, to expound arguments rather than proffer an opinion. On a later occasion, when he might reasonably have been expected to climb down from the fence, in a Lenten sermon preached in the chapel of Clement VI on 14 February 1350 on the topic of sin and temptation, he avoided the question of free will altogether.[66] Here the tone of his discussion of the fall of Adam and Eve, their sin, and prospects of redemption, is almost Puritan-predestinarian, but again a pronouncement on the doctrinal issue is carefully avoided. The preoccupation of late medieval preachers with the Devil, above all discussion of the equality of the Devil's powers with those of angels, is here illustrated in an *exemplum* dealing with Ireland and St. Patrick, the patron saint of the see of Armagh whose cult was to be substantially furthered during the next

[65] B, fol. 147^{r-v}; J, fol. 110^{ra-b}.

[66] B, fols. 205^{r}–212^{v}; J, fols. 149ra–153va.

pontificate.[67] In the same way as the Devil was able to show Christ the whole world, including Ethiopia, India, Arabia, so could the angel who appeared to Patrick working in Wales show him the various regions of the world including Ireland, indicating to him where God intended him to work,[68] an illustration which is one of FitzRalph's very few references in his Avignon sermons to his Irish background and its local particularities.

One controversial topic upon which he was prepared to commit himself in public was the much disputed issue of the Immaculate Conception which in the fourteenth century sharply divided the religious, especially the mendicant orders, with the Dominicans generally opposed to the doctrine, while the Carmelites and a large element of the Franciscans supported it.[69] The devotional and rhetorical sermon which FitzRalph preached on the subject to the Carmelites in Avignon on 8 December 1342 had the widest independent manuscript circulation of any individual sermon by him which did *not* pertain to the mendicant controversy, and is indicative of the interest which the issue aroused at the level of parochial instruction as well as in the strictly theological sphere.[70] Its text was known to, and often quoted by, the Paris master and canon of Regensburg, Konrad von Megenberg. As proctor of the English nation in Paris he was a frequent visitor to the curia from 1337 to 1341, while he represented the city of Regensburg in Avignon on later occasions. On four separate occasions he preached on the feast of the Immaculate Conception in Avignon, and it is possible that he may have heard FitzRalph on the topic as well.[71] For a

[67] For the discussion of reprobation and punishment for sin, and on the sin of Adam and Eve, B, fols. 206^{r}–207^{r}; J, fol. 150^{ra-vb}.

[68] B, fol. 211^{v}; J, fol. 153ra. For preoccupation with the Devil in later medieval preaching see Owst, *Preaching*, pp. 175–7, 335–44.

[69] Bartomeu M. Xiberta, 'De elementis doctrinalibus in controversia de immaculata B. V. Mariae conceptione', *Carmelus*, 1 (1954), 199–235; Francisco da Leire Guimaraens, 'La Doctrine des théologiens sur l'Immaculée Conception de 1250 à 1350', *Études Franciscaines*, n.s. 3 (1952), 181–203; 4 (1953), 23–51, 167–87; Ignatius Brady, 'The Development of the Doctrine of the Immaculate Conception in the fourteenth century after Aureoli', *FS* 15 (1955), 175–202; E. M. Buytaert, 'The Immaculate Conception in the writings of Ockham', *FS* 10 (1950), 149–63; G. E. Mohan, 'The "Quaestio de Relatione" attributed to Ockham', *FS* 11 (1951), 273–303; Zumkeller, 'Die Augustinerschule des Mittelalters', 191–2, and bibliographical notes.

[70] Contained in MS Klosterneuburg 789; CLM 16058 (formerly in the collegiate church of St. Nicholas in Passau); Salzburg, Erzabtei Sankt Peter, MS b. X. 18; Hamburg, Staatsbibl., MS St. Petri-Kirche 30 b.

[71] In his *Commentarius de laudibus B. V. Marie*, composed after FitzRalph's death, Konrad frequently cited approvingly the views of 'reverende memorie domini

different reason the sermon attracted attention among later fourteenth-century Carmelites: in it FitzRalph upheld the traditional account of the ancient origins of the Carmelite order, of Elias and Elijah living as hermits on Mount Carmel near Nazareth and of a continuous community presence there until the time of Christ when they were converted to the teaching of the apostles, thereby claiming to be the oldest Christian monastic community in existence.[72] Here FitzRalph was exclusively concerned with the antiquity of the order and its special veneration, implied in the order's full title, for the Blessed Virgin, and neither the function and duties of its members, in the pastoral sphere or elsewhere, nor the question of mendicancy arose in the discussion, but the sermon reflects the same friendship and sympathy which characterized all his links with the friars before 1350. When he turned to the actual doctrine in question, his interpretation was favourable and he admitted having changed his mind since his discussion in the *lectura* on the Sentences. At that stage his attitude had been negative, when in the course of a discussion of the creation of the soul and original sin he had contented himself with the enumeration of ten principal arguments against the doctrine and avoided committing himself to acceptance of it.[73] The Avignon sermon indicates not merely that he had changed his mind during the intervening years, at least eleven since he had revised the *lectura* on the Sentences, but also that the basis of his argument had altered, and once more we find an example of FitzRalph appealing to faith and scripture rather than to rational and scholastic proof, with a final appeal to the 'mens devota fidelium'. Yet even at this stage he was cautious and, aware that the doctrine was far from universally accepted and that it was opposed by a number of distinguished Dominican theologians whom he would otherwise have reason to respect, he insisted that his view was a private one and commended it to the judgement of the cardinals, prelates, and doctors present in his audience.[74]

Although his views on the subject had undergone a substantial change since his Oxford days, it is not improbable that he

mei Richardi quondam Armacani archiepiscopi, cuius anima requiescat coram vultu virgineo in deliciis paradisiacis', CLM 14190, fol. 29ra, and quoted in: *Konrad von Megenberg, Werke: Ökonomik* (Buch I), ed. Sabine Krüger (MGH, Staatsschriften des späteren Mittelalters, iii, Stuttgart, 1973), IV-XV.

[72] Ed. cit., 166, and for Carmelite interest in this sermon, ibid., 163.

[73] P, fols. 178^{v}–179^{r}; ed. cit., 170.

[74] Ibid., 168.

would already have encountered there the favourable view of the doctrine which by the beginning of the fourteenth century had become current through the work of William of Ware, François de Mayronne, and, above all, Duns Scotus, though in his sermon he cited none of these recent views on the subject, preferring older 'authorities', especially Scripture, St. Augustine, Innocent III, and, above all, Anselm of Canterbury. The latter he seems to have respected enormously, but many of the passages he cited as the work of Anselm are in fact drawn from Eadmer.[75] In this sermon he presented – when compared with many of his other sermons – an unusually wide range of authorities, on one occasion even citing Horace, *De arte poetica*, though he appears to have known the work only through quotation in Innocent III's *De miseria conditionis humane*, but nevertheless indicating that he had gone to unusual pains to prepare this particular sermon.[76] Above all, however, his argument was firmly rooted in the scriptural evidence and in this respect the sermon conformed to the usual pattern of being primarily an exposition of biblical texts, reflecting his increasing preoccupation with the Bible during the years of the Armenian debates.

One of the most constant features of these Avignon sermons, especially during the years 1337-44, was his preoccupation with the pursuit of perfection, the religious life, sin, and the duties of restitution and of almsgiving, topics which would eventually, and inevitably, lead him to consider the role of those who by the mid-fourteenth century had the spiritual care and pastoral leadership of a vast body of the laity, whereby the latter sought guidance in the confessional on precisely these moral problems. On the question of poverty he adopted the traditional approach to the Sermon on the Mount and stressed that the poor were the beloved of Christ, and therefore that voluntary renunciation of one's property for the benefit of the poor was meritorious. Again he engaged in the sermon on St. Martin in an exhaustive proof that good works *ex voto* – by which he meant a life of poverty and chastity such as that adopted by religious – was more meritorious than good works performed without such a vow. However, despite frequent references to the meritorious

[75] FitzRalph knew Anselm's *De conceptione virginis gloriosae*, but occasionally cited Eadmer instead, ed. cit., 168, 169, 178.

[76] Innocent's treatise is cited 5 times, ed. cit., 164, 174 (twice), 176, 177, *De miseria conditionis humane*, ed. Maccarrone, pp. 7, 16 (twice), 43, 44. The passage from Horace is on p. 16, while a quotation from Juvenal was also taken from the same source, p. 44.

nature of voluntary renunciation of property, he never explicitly gave his approval to the corollary of that poverty – corporate and individual – practised by the friars, especially by the Franciscans, namely mendicancy 'after the manner of Christ and the apostles'.[77] He frequently returned to the theme of almsgiving, in the sermons to the Franciscans on 11 November 1338 and 4 October 1349, and to the Carmelites on 8 December 1342, but always with the implication that such alms were intended for the involuntary poor, for whom a life of poverty and mendicancy was a matter of necessity not of choice,[78] and always stressing the greater merit of giving to the poor during one's own lifetime rather than by means of a testamentary disposition which only had validity after death. This sermon on St. Francis of 4 October 1349 contained one of the few pieces of autobiographical information which FitzRalph let slip over a long preaching career: he told his audience that from childhood he had been closely connected with the Franciscan order, the Franciscans being the only religious community in his native city of Dundalk and that several members of his family had been members of it. However, the main body of the sermon, friendly in tone but devoted to the question of poverty and its corollary, the duty of almsgiving, may be interpreted as a first veiled hint of the way in which FitzRalph's thoughts were moving. His attitude to poverty and its devotees is not as yet hostile, but the problems presented by its profession as a chosen way of life have aroused his attention, possibly even his suspicions, sufficiently for him to commence a deeper study of it. The Franciscans at Avignon may have been startled at the bitterness of FitzRalph's hostility when it was finally aroused, but attentive listeners may already have noticed more than exhortation in a positive vein when they gathered to commemorate their founder's feast-day in 1349.

FitzRalph returned to the question of almsgiving again in the course of two sermons during his last visit to the curia when the case against the friars was *sub iudice* and when the topic had a rather more acute significance. On the feast of All Saints, 1 November 1358, when he must have been one of the most controversial figures in Avignon, he was invited to preach in the vice-chancellor's chapel. Innocent VI was originally to have

[77] B, fol. 176^{v}; J, fol. 129^{rb-va}.

[78] Treated in the Carmelite sermon, ed. cit., 174–5, and in the later sermon to the Franciscans, B, fols. 193^{v}–194^{r}; J, fols. 141vb–142vb.

attended the sermon but was prevented through illness, a factor which seems to have disappointed the preacher, who had evidently hoped to use the occasion to restore himself in papal favour, despite his attacks on the friars.[79] In it he returned in the course of a homily on love of God and of one's neighbour to the problem of almsgiving, reviewing the reasons why both are to be loved and how, and clearly indicating his view that one's neighbour could only be helped by alms given in life. At this stage in his career his preoccupation with the issue might have been interpreted as arising out of his animosity towards the friars, who gained a considerable part of their alms in the form of legacies and bequests from those to whom they had ministered in life and who were perhaps even buried in their churches, a situation which lay at the root of the secular clergy's grievances against the friars and was fundamental to the case which FitzRalph was then pursuing. The friars could afford to wait until the benefactor died, but the involuntary poor – and many parish curates were genuinely poor – could not.[80]

But FitzRalph's statement of his views on almsgiving in this sermon further inflamed the situation at the curia, it aroused fierce criticism on the part of his mendicant opponents, and the preacher eagerly sought another opportunity to clarify himself on the subject. He was invited to preach in the papal chapel on the feast of the Epiphany, 6 January 1359, and this time Innocent VI did attend. This sermon was made the occasion for FitzRalph's most elaborate exposition of his views and also the most severe: he cited the example of the generosity of the Magi, unlike the greedy who thought to store up 'insurance' for their salvation by making promises during their lifetime, but still enjoying all their property until death.[81] He argued that a man who failed to give alms in life and continued to enjoy all his property, but who attempted to remedy the situation by generous benefactions and legacies after death, could not be absolved from his sin of avarice and was equally doomed to eternal punishment – a doctrine which would scarcely have commended itself to the friars who consoled their penitents and encouraged them to make precisely this type of donation to

[79] Walsh, 'FitzRalph and the Friars', 223–45.
[80] B, fol. 133^{r-v}; J, fol. 100^{ra-vb}.
[81] B, fols. 241^{r}–246^{v}; J, fols. 173va–177vb. This sermon also had an independent circulation, MS Klosterneuburg 204; Mainz, Stadtbibl. MS 217.

pious foundations.[82] Whether it appealed to the pope can only be a matter for speculation, but the speed with which the entire controversy was allowed to die down at the curia once Fitz-Ralph had died would suggest that Innocent VI was not particularly sympathetic. However, it would be misleading to suggest that FitzRalph had only developed this line of argument about testamentary bequests in and after 1349, and with specific reference to the friars. Already in a Pentecost sermon preached in Lichfield Cathedral on 15 May 1345 he had included a dogmatic section on the *filioque* as befitted the occasion, and also some moral exhortations, emphasizing the need to strive for total purification from sin in this life, '. . . nec per distribuccionem illorum bonorum post mortem iuvantur in purgatorio, cum non vadant in purgatorium, sed in profundum infernum'.[83] Although he made other allusions in the same vein, notably in the sermons of 9 April 1346 (Palm Sunday) at Burton in Staffordshire and of 11 April 1347 in London, the latter which he also repeated a year later upon his arrival in Dundalk,[84] none had been as severe as that of Pentecost 1345. His constant warnings against such testaments appear not to have been specifically directed at the friars but once more they indicated the direction in which his thoughts were moving.

Another topic upon which he adopted, as a moral theologian, an extremely severe stance was the duty of restitution, to which he would return constantly in his pastoral sermons in England and Ireland but upon which he also aired his views in Avignon. He did so both in the sermon before Clement VI of 6 December 1349 and in that to the Franciscans two months earlier. He was to have considerable trouble with their confrères in Ireland in the early 1350s and, whereas this last sermon to the Franciscans showed no external signs of friction, the possibility cannot be excluded that already during his first year of direct contact with his archdiocese in 1348–9 he had perceived the difficulties which could arise in a divided community if confessors were prepared to confuse morality with politics. If confessors were to adopt the attitude that theft from an Anglo-Norman neighbour or the withholding of lawful tithes due to an Anglo-Norman

[82] B, fol. 243^{r-v}; J, fol. 175va. He then repeated, more elaborately, the statement of 1 November: 'Avarus . . . defraudat animam suam bonis eternis, et eciam quia ex diviciis superfluis taliter congregatis et usque ad mortem continue reservatis fructus non capiet', B, fol. 133^{r}; J, fol. 100rb.

[83] B, fol. 16^{r}; J, fol. 12va.

[84] B, fols. 29^{r-v}, 39^{v}–40^{r}, 42^{v}; J, fols. 23^{ra-b}, 32^{rb-va}, 34^{va-b}.

parish priest was justifiable resistance to the conquerors when practised by members of the Gaelic race, and the Franciscans were regarded as prone to adopting this attitude, then the archbishop might reasonably doubt the efficacy of their ministry in terms of pastoral theology. Consequently his elaborate examination of questions of justice and fraud, and the grounds upon which the duty of restitution was based, might be interpreted as a hint of the struggle to come. Even if FitzRalph had not had much time in his first year to sort out the rights and wrongs of the situation, the position of the Franciscans in his ecclesiastical province, whose Gaelic members had a large and influential convent with a small school of theology on the very doorstep of his primatial cathedral, while he as an Anglo-Irish prelate could only visit that cathedral under conditions of extreme danger to his person as well as his authority, cannot have appeared other than provocative,[85] with consequent effects on his attitude to the friars in general.

FitzRalph's Avignon sermons equally indicate concern for the affairs and well-being of the Dominican order and the pursuit of perfection in accordance with the model of St. Dominic, whose life and work he expounded in a sermon preached to the general chapter of the Dominican order held at Avignon on 27 May 1341.[86] This, the 113th general chapter of the order and held in the papal curia at the express command of Benedict XII, was a tense occasion, as papal attempts to impose reforming measures had met with the most effective resistance from the Dominicans and resulted in a violent clash between Hugues de Vaucemain, master-general of the order from 1333 to 1341, and the Cistercian pope whose pontificate coincided approximately with Hugues's generalate. Having succeeded in imposing reforming measures on his fellow Cistercians, though even here not without some difficulty,[87] and on the Benedictines and Augustinian canons, as well as on the Franciscans,[88] the pope met with

[85] For the importance of the Armagh convent see FitzMaurice-Little, op. cit., p. 30; Gwynn, *Medieval Province of Armagh*, pp. 109–10; *Medieval Religious Houses. Ireland*, p. 242.

[86] B, fols. 161^{r}–168^{v}; J, fols. 119rb–124ra. The date in the principal MSS, 4 August 1341, cannot be correct as the chapter was no longer in session by that date. For the circumstances of this chapter see Daniel A. Mortier, *Histoire des maîtres généraux de l'ordre des frères precheurs*, iii (Paris, 1907), 87–167. The *Acta* of the chapter were edited by Benedictus M. Reichert, *MOPHist.* iv (Rome, 1899), 269–79.

[87] See Mahn, *Benoît et les cisterciens,* esp. pp. 31–49.

[88] Schmitt, *Benoît et l'ordre des frères mineurs.* There is no comparable study for the other mendicant orders during this reforming period, but see Guillaume Mollat, *Les Papes d'Avignon* (Paris, 1964^{10}), pp. 77–83.

strong opposition from the Dominicans, who particularly disliked his measures concerning the reception of apostates, the corporate poverty of the order and its privilege of mendicancy. Benedict had retaliated by depriving the order of its legislative powers, with the result that no constitutions were promulgated at the general chapters of Clermont (1339), Milan (1340), or Avignon (1341), where the chapter originally summoned to Carcassonne was compelled to meet under papal supervision, and by the death of Benedict XII on 25 April 1342 when the running battle between the order and the pope finally came to an end, most of the leading dignitaries of the order were in the papal prison for refusing to accept the reforming edicts.[89]

Surprisingly the *Acta* of the general chapters of these years make no reference to the difficulties then being debated within the order, and FitzRalph was equally reticent in his address to the assembled friars at the chapter of 1341. It was in any case normal procedure to extend to a distinguished preacher an invitation to preach before the assembled capitular fathers, and it may have been intended as a conciliatory gesture on the order's part that their choice for the Avignon chapter was a man of blameless theological orthodoxy towards whom the pope was known to be favourably disposed. FitzRalph's choice of topic was also a tactful one, and he concentrated attention principally on the life and virtues of the order's founder St. Dominic, though even this might have been intended as a subtle reminder to the pope that he had, at the beginning of his pontificate and before his campaign for the reform of the religious orders had got under way, paid special tribute to the Dominicans' founder in terms which had led the order to believe that they were not really in need of papal reform measures.[90] This was the sermon of a sympathetic and well-informed friend of the order, not of a man whose criticism of the mendicant way of life would subsequently call into question the very foundations upon which the orders of friars were built. When dealing with the saint's life and work FitzRalph described with obvious approval how St. Dominic sold his property, distributing the proceeds among the poor, and also the charity and humility which made him reject the opportunity of promotion to a bishopric.[91] Once more FitzRalph exalted the idea of voluntary poverty and almsgiving, but avoided

[89] Mortier, p. 162.
[90] Mahn, p. 11, though he exaggerates Benedict's affection for the Dominicans.
[91] B, fol. 165^{v}; J, fol. 122rb.

all discussion of the practice of mendicancy, a silence which might be interpreted as deference to the delicate situation existing between the order and the pope. The sermon did contain one digression devoted to one of the topics which, as we have seen, constantly preoccupied him during this second visit to Avignon – incompetent, indolent, and unworthy 'viri ecclesiastici'. Here he allowed himself a provocative allusion to the old pun of the Dominicans being the *domini canes*, when he referred to these negligent ecclesiastics as 'canes muti non valentes, aut ut verius proferam, non scientes', in an extension of his constant complaint that ecclesiastical offices were given through simony and nepotism to those who were unworthy, ill educated, and generally unsuitable. Then he applied this to the listening friars by exhorting them to remain in the station appropriate to their vocation and not to seek higher ecclesiastical offices and honours, by which he presumably meant that their humility should prevent them from becoming bishops, as it could not be argued that they were less worthy in respect of educational standards for episcopal office than the then pertaining norms.[92]

Much of the sermon was devoted to eloquent praise of St. Dominic's missionary work among the heretics of Toulouse and Carcassonne, though repeated references to the latter town may have had more immediate associations for the capitular fathers than the conversion of the Cathars and the papal Crusade, and may have been interpreted as a veiled reminder that their chapter had been translated from there to Avignon on papal orders. All was, however, not flattery and FitzRalph reminded his audience of the duty imposed on those entrusted with the goods of the Church not to misuse them, and issued a general exhortation to conform to the norms and ideals of religious community life.[93] The capitular fathers were warned about the danger to true humility, towards which every religious should strive, by the struggle for higher status and offices – all friars should be equal in dignity. Here therefore FitzRalph displayed, not hostility to the friars' status, aspirations, activities, and financial arrangements *per se*, but a keen awareness of their problems and a positive commitment, a warm and apparently well-intentioned concern for the health of their religious life.

[92] B, fol. 167^{r}; J, fol. 123rb. There is no comparable study to that of Thomson, *Friars in the Cathedral. The first Franciscan bishops*, for Dominican attitudes to friars becoming bishops.

[93] B, fols. 166^{r}–167^{v}; J, fols. 122va–123vb.

The capitular fathers could have had little reason to be dissatisfied with their choice of preacher.

FitzRalph's emphasis on their founder's missionary activity was guaranteed to appeal to the assembled friars at a time of highly developed missionary activity under the aegis of the Avignon papacy, especially in Persia, Armenia, and along the shores of the Black Sea. Both Franciscans and Dominicans had been responsible for a renewal of contacts between the Roman and eastern Churches, and the Dominicans made an added contribution in the case of the Latinizing Christians in Armenia through the *Fratres Unitores.* Already in the sermon to the Franciscans on the feast of St. Catherine, 25 November 1338, FitzRalph had shown some of that interest in missionary activity which was subsequently to find its most complete expression in the *Summa de Questionibus Armenorum.* Here he had dealt with the problem of converts who had accepted the Christian faith on the basis of inadequate instruction and cultural preparation, and subsequently – he had been reliably informed – were seduced by the Saracens away from belief in Christ.[94] This information, which he presumably received from returned friar-missionaries, led him to a discussion of the psychology of the infidel who freely accepted truth which he could not understand or vice versa remained an infidel because of an incapacity for belief,[95] and whether the latter actually sinned by his unbelief. He finally came to the conclusion that such infidels, while not sinning actually, were through their lack of baptism excluded from the vision of God and true beatitude, a view which was in accord with the orthodox conclusions emerging from the beatific vision debates earlier in the decade. From the tone of FitzRalph's sermon, especially the familiar way in which he explained how the missionary ought to argue with those whom he wished to convert, it is clear that the preacher was consciously addressing potential missionaries, while the occasional examples cited 'on good authority', including one about the frequency with which missionaries among Saracens and Tartars expelled demons,[96] sound like authentic tales from the mission field and suggest that he had been discussing these problems with men who had returned from missionary territory, many of whom were regular visitors to Avignon.

From these Avignon sermons it is possible to draw some

[94] B, fol. 181^{v}; J, fol. 133ra.

[95] B, fols. 181^{v}–182^{r}; J, fol. 133$^{ra–va}$.

[96] B, fol. 186^{v}; J, fol. 136vb.

general conclusions about FitzRalph's personality, his development as a preacher, and preaching technique, the widening range of interests and influences to which he was exposed, the subtle shift in theological interests away from scholastic argumentation towards a strongly biblical approach. They further permit us to monitor the developing preoccupations and opinions which were subsequently reflected in the completed version of the *Summa de Questionibus Armenorum*, and the faint beginnings of the views on dominion and on the role of the friars which were to be of decisive importance for the later stages of his career. We have seen him on some occasions careful and cautious, as before curial audiences with whom he was not familiar, on others more audacious, as in the sympathetic presence of Benedict XII when that pontiff was trying to send absentee benefice-holders back to their duties and to reform the religious orders, and here FitzRalph could launch a tirade of polemic against the greed of pluralists and the nepotism and worldliness of prelates. At one time he might appear as the formal doctor of theology, expounding a theoretical problem, or wrestling with questions of free will and predestination which concerned him personally. At other times he was to be seen as the impassioned, moralizing reformer, exhorting in a not unfriendly manner the mendicant communities at the curia to a stricter religious observance and selfless charity, or expounding the lives of the saints as examples of the model prelate and pastor, or again criticizing the laity for breaches of justice and charity by neglecting their duties of restitution and almsgiving. On the one hand his own very genuine personal piety and sense of commitment is apparent, his devotion to the Blessed Virgin (although the doctrine of the Immaculate Conception caused him problems) and to the saints, while on the other hand his bitter criticism of the curial lawyers in private when he was in difficulties and his *laudatio* of their fairness in public when he was winning show him as a man of ordinary human weakness, capable of blatant prejudice and subjectivity.

His second and most lengthy stay at the curia occasioned a number of sermons which reflected his widening contacts, with missionaries and biblicists, orientalists and Hebraists, and thus provided a commentary on the genesis of his major theological work. Strangely, however, neither Barlaam, his main authority on Greek topics, nor the two Armenians, Nerses and John of Kerna, were cited by him in any forum, though they must have been familiar figures to Avignon audiences. The reason for this may have been the need for discretion, reluctance to make these topics a matter for public debate as long as the discussions were in progress and there was a possibility of success. If this were the case, and FitzRalph left for England in the autumn of 1344 before the negative reaction from the Council of Sis had penetrated to the West, the entire topic of the negotiations could have passed without comment in the sermons which he preached before his departure, whereas by the time of his return when there was no longer a need for reticence he was in any case presenting the *Summa* to the pope and therefore making public his views on these eastern questions. Above all, the sermons of this formative period of the second sojourn were characterized by their versatility of theme, mood, and treatment. They ranged from formal tripartite sermons in the best structural traditions of the *Artes Praedicandi*, through the more direct exposition of the gospel of the day – a category which suggests that he was familiar with the sentiments expressed in the *De modo componendi Sermones* of his Dominican contemporary, Thomas Waleys[97] – to the informal haranguing interspersed with lively stories delivered to the Franciscans. These latter give the impression that his contacts were closer to the Franciscans than to the other mendicant orders, a factor which must have added to the subsequent bitterness when FitzRalph's case, though technically directed against all four orders of friars, singled out the Franciscans as the special target for his animosity. The topics ranged from complex theological to simple devotional, from the virtues of the saints to a tirade of abuse, and according to topic and circumstances he chose the form of his sermons, thereby making it difficult to fit his preaching technique into any of the patterns available for contemporary composers of sermons. Sometimes he yielded to the temptation to preach sermons which, even by the standards of later medieval preaching, can only be described as long-winded panegyrics. He had learned much from the type of university sermons which an Oxford chancellor almost a century later, William Gascoigne, was inclined to attribute to the coming of the friars – sermons whose formality and logical distinctions appealed to learned and fashionable audiences such as those at Avignon, who may have overlooked the

[97] For Waleys's contribution to this genre see Thomas M. Charland, *Les Artes praedicandi. Contribution à l'histoire de la rhétorique du moyen âge* (Paris–Ottawa, 1938).

sermon's content in their enthusiasm for the form.[98] FitzRalph was aware of this tendency and consciously tried on occasion to avoid it, and in the sermon to the Franciscans of 4 October 1349 he remarked: 'accepi a pluribus quod sermonum prolixitas dominos hic sepe accediat, sermonum difficilitas eorum animos sepe perturbat, sermonum curiositas eos aut alios nunquam edificat, set loquentem ostentat'.[99] Hammerich, on the basis of his own argument that the mendicant controversy had already begun when this sermon was preached, maintained that FitzRalph was making a last attempt to secure the favour of his audience on this occasion.[100]

In formal terms these sermons vary considerably. A considerable proportion, especially the Avignon sermons, show a clear debt to the standard forms of contemporary *Artes Praedicandi*, with a clearly defined theme, subdivision, citation of authorities, and 'anti-theme', whereas the less complex homilies in Lichfield and Ireland owed more to the simple exposition of the gospels praised by Waleys. But for all their diversity of theme, style, and form, FitzRalph's sermons have certain features in common, above all, a fluent and easy Latin style, a wide range of expression, a capacity to marry mood and style to the appropriate occasion, and an exceptional familiarity with the books of the Bible. He also showed a certain sensitivity to the susceptibilities of his audiences, and used the occasions where he was apparently among friends to give vent to his more outrageous – and outraged – feelings of frustration, even if he lacked the earthy sense of humour so common among mendicant sermons of the period. One cannot avoid the impression that he used sermons preached before the friars, especially the Franciscans, to make public feelings which he could not permit himself to express in the papal or vice-chancellor's presence. However, in view of the indications that these Avignon sermons were polished and revised by their author late in life, it is difficult to establish a line of development, and an argument that the later sermons displayed more erudition, greater familiarity with the Bible or the Fathers, a further shift away from the scholastic method, would be tendentious. A clear distinction can, however, be made between the Becket sermon of 1335, when the preacher was a newcomer to Avignon audiences and both topic and

[98] Owst, *Preaching*, p. 312. For Gascoigne see *BRUO* II, 745–8.
[99] B, fol. 193^{r}; J, fol. 141rb.
[100] Hammerich, *FitzRalph and the Mendicants*, p. 41.

treatment were general, informal, and impersonal, and the later sermons beginning with the passionate denunciation of abuses in the benefice-hunting system, of Ash Wednesday 1338. This was the sermon of a man in familiar surroundings, where his utterances could reflect his experiences, interests, hopes, grievances, and disappointments. In the second visit he developed a fine talent for matching theme and treatment to his audiences and cannot have failed to make a favourable impression. He displayed an undeniable capacity for using his preaching talents to his own advantage, thereby furthering his ecclesiastical career. If he decided to 'play the system' and follow the advice which had been given many years earlier to his predecessor in office as chancellor in Oxford, his success must be acknowledged.

ii. Lichfield

When FitzRalph returned from Avignon in the autumn of 1344 to resume his duties as dean, having successfully pursued the chapter's case – even if he also spent, from the canons' point of view, an excessively long time pursuing his own interests at the curia – he had greatly increased both his stature as an expert in ecclesiastical litigation and his reputation as a preacher. There is no evidence of much preaching activity on his part in the diocese of Lichfield during his first year there, 1336–7, nor that he had kept a sermon diary then, though presumably he observed his statutory obligations,[1] since no complaints to the contrary were indicated in the Act and Chapter Book. However, on his return at the end of seven years of litigation he was, as he had told his last audience in Avignon, eager to take up the work of a devout preacher,[2] and the decision to keep a diary coincided with his return. The text of this diary, as it survives in the main manuscripts, is defective both at the beginning and in several places throughout. The first two sermon-notes are given without any title, place, or date and are written together on one folio. Internal evidence shows that the first of these was an Ash Wednesday sermon, and a reference in it to St. Patrick's Purgatory – which was to acquire fame as a result of the pilgrimage of the Hungarian 'Ritter Georg' in 1353 – suggests that it was preached in Ireland, while a reference to the controversy with the mendicant

[1] As dean he was obliged to preach on certain major feasts, Dugdale, *Monasticon Anglicanum*, iii. 248 ff.

[2] '. . . et ego ad officium meum, scilicet devoti predicatoris restituar', B, fol. 187^{r}; J, fol. 137ra.

friar-confessors further confirms the impression that it should be dated after 1350. It is followed by a second fragment, which breaks off in mid-sentence at the end of the first folio,[3] and which seems to have been the opening of a sermon preached to some prelates assembled in a synod or provincial council. It also suggests a date after FitzRalph's return to his archdiocese in the summer of 1351.[4] As the remainder of the diary is in roughly chronological order, beginning with the feast of St. Catherine, 25 November 1344, and concluding with the last of the anti-mendicant sermons preached in London at St. Paul's Cross on 12 March 1357,[5] Gwynn suggested that this first folio had become misplaced, and that it had originally belonged to the central part of the diary, i.e. among the sermons of the years 1351–55, which are also in several cases misplaced.[6]

However, neither form nor content of the sermons immediately following upon these two fragments is consistent with the possibility that one of them could have been the first sermon preached by the dean upon his return from Avignon. As regards content, one would have expected him to make some reference in the first sermon in his cathedral to his recent homecoming, or to the mission satisfactorily completed. Instead this sermon is a devotional panegyric on the life of St. Catherine of Alexandria, his special veneration for whom had already been expressed in one of his early sermons in Avignon. With regard to its form, the sermon-note began: 'Sermo eiusdem in vulgari in ecclesia lichfeldensi', a somewhat unlikely rubric for the first sermon. Though FitzRalph's name was given in full in the title of the sermon diary in two of the three main manuscripts,[7] he might still be expected to have repeated his name at the beginning of the first sermon, as he had the habit of writing his name, with the addition of a new title, whenever he was promoted to a

[3] B, fol. 1^{r-v}, sermon no. 3 begins fol. 2^{r}; J, fol. 1^{ra-vb}, with sermon no. 3 beginning on the same folio. L presents a similar picture, with the two fragments on fol. 11^{r-v}, and no. 3 beginning on fol. 11^{v}. Hence there is no reason to assume that B originally had the continuation of the second fragment.

[4] In view of the existence of synodal sermons for 1352 and 1355, this fragment may pertain to 1353–4, or 1356. His return to Ireland must have been before 8 September 1351 and, apart from a brief visit to England in 1353, he was in Ireland until June 1356, B, fols. 51^{v}, 81^{r}; J, fols. 42va, 66va.

[5] B, fols. 2^{r}–127^{r}; J, fols. 1vb–100vb. The first three sermons are not strictly chronological, but in the following order: (3) St. Catherine's Day, 25 November 1345; (4) first Sunday in Advent, 28 November 1344; (5) St. Catherine's Day undated, probably 1344, making this the first recorded sermon after the dean's return to Lichfield.

[6] Gwynn, 'Sermon Diary', 19–22.

[7] J, fol. 1^{r}; L, fol. 11^{r}.

higher office, or on particularly solemn occasions. For example in the sermon preached in Lichfield Cathedral on the first Sunday of Advent three days later, 28 November 1344, an occasion upon which it was the dean's statutory obligation to preach, the title is given: 'In prima dominica adventus sermo ad populum . . . per Ricardum decanum'.[8] Again on becoming archbishop-elect of Armagh, the first sermon-note after his election pertaining to a sermon preached in London at a procession of thanksgiving in September 1346 after the English victory at Creçy, FitzRalph was careful to note in his diary his change of status: 'Sermo Ricardi electi Ardmachani in processione Londoniensi facta pro rege et fiebat in vulgari'.[9] Yet again upon his return to his archdiocese in 1351 after a prolonged absence in Avignon, he included his full title of archbishop of Armagh and primate of Ireland in one form or another in the first two sermons preached upon his return, on 8 September at Coleraine and on 4 December in Dromiskin, a small town south of Dundalk which was also the location of one of his two archiepiscopal manors.[10] Here of course the emphasis on his title as primate of Ireland had a deeper significance, but the repetition of these formal titles at various intervals in the course of the diary suggest that it was unlikely for FitzRalph to have begun his collection with the phrase 'sermo eiusdem', and it is probable that at least one if not more sermons preached in Lichfield upon the dean's return must have originally inaugurated the diary in the autumn of 1344, and that these folios had detached themselves from the text which became the common exemplar for the extant complete manuscripts.

These reflections raise the further question of the original form in which FitzRalph maintained the diary before it was copied for wider circulation. The present state of the manuscript evidence suggests that, whereas smaller collections or even individual sermons – exclusively however, those preached in Avignon – circulated in a form which clearly indicated that they had been copied before FitzRalph became archbishop of Armagh, the copies of the complete collection in its present form were probably not made for wider circulation until after

[8] B, fol. 2^{v}; J, fol. 2rb. Gwynn, 'Sermon Diary', 19, drew attention to this habit.

[9] B, fol. 36^{v}; J, fol. 29vb.

[10] In the Coleraine sermon he described himself as 'Ricardi primatis Hibernie', and in Dromiskin gave his full title 'Ricardi Archiepiscopi Ardmachani primatis Hibernie', B, fols. 51^{v}, 53^{v}; J, fols. 42va, 44ra.

his death. When FitzRalph as dean of Lichfield began to keep his diary in 1344, it is improbable that he acquired a large volume in which to write down a complete collection over the following years. Much more likely, especially in view of the 'lacunae', is the suggestion that he worked with 'quaderni' of eight, ten, or at most twelve leaves, taking a new one as each was filled. These 'quaderni' might have been preserved loose, or might have been stitched together, but it is unlikely that they would have resulted in the sort of carefully-produced book that was sold on the commercial market.[11] This might also explain the repetition of his title every time his status changed, or he entered upon a new phase of duties in Lichfield or Armagh, when it is likely that he could have commenced a new 'quadernus' on each of these occasions. A further complicating factor in the genesis of the diary is the indication that it does not consist of the day-to-day entries made immediately after he had preached each sermon. The fact that he noted in several cases that individual sermons had been entered by himself in the wrong order, indicates that he often copied entries in later from sermon-notes which he had made at the time of preaching, and the most probable explanation is that in the course of his preaching tours, often away from home both in Lichfield and Armagh, he used a mixture of both methods according as circumstances dictated.

In all there are twenty-five sermons recorded in the diary as having been preached between FitzRalph's return to Lichfield and the restoration to him of the temporalities of the see of Armagh by order of Edward III on 15 April 1347.[12] The vast majority of these were simple homilies preached 'in vulgari ad populum', to the people of the diocese either in the cathedral or in the neighbouring prebends, parishes, hospitals, and cemeteries within his jurisdiction. By comparison with the formal Latin sermons preached at Avignon, these are very much more simple and direct in their appeal. They were rarely copied out in full in the diary, and the Latin notes made by the preacher vary considerably: sometimes the text seems almost complete, while in other cases a few short lines indicate the contents of the sermon, together with details of place and date of preaching. Between these extremes are others which contain

[11] Gwynn, 'Sermon Diary', 20.

[12] CPR 1345–48, 272; CCR 1346–49, 477. The sermons are in B, fols. 2^{r}–42^{v}; J, fols. 1vb–34va.

a summary, or the opening paragraphs, or even a portion of the argument – all probably information which the preacher wanted to keep for future reference. These sermons, together with the even larger number of twenty-nine recorded as having been preached in Ireland during the years 1348-9 and 1351-6, are for the most part noted in the diary as having been preached in the vernacular. The areas in Ireland in which he preached also had English as their vernacular, and there is no indication that he made any serious attempt to deal directly with the people of Gaelic Ireland in the northern dioceses of his province. The only Latin sermons recorded in this part of the collection are a Maundy Thursday sermon preached to the cathedral clergy in Lichfield and two before provincial synods within his own metropolitan jurisdiction.[13] The only sermon in the vernacular to a clerical audience was that preached in the Carmelite church in Drogheda on the feast of the Annunciation, 25 March 1349, which may have been an indication of the low level of learning among the Irish Carmelites in the aftermath of the Black Death,[14] or alternatively because the sermon was a public occasion on which the laity was welcome, and for whom in this stern and severe sermon the preacher had a particular word of warning.[15]

A rare exception among the Lichfield sermons to the simple and popular vernacular homily was that preached in Latin to the cathedral clergy in the recently completed choir at Lichfield on Maundy Thursday 24 March 1345. Here FitzRalph, taking as his text the words of consecration: 'Hoc est enim corpus meum . . .' (Luc. xxii. 19), expounded at length his views on Eucharistic theology, and these views were impeccably orthodox. In this respect at least Wyclif could not have claimed 'sanctus Ricardus episcopus Armachanus'[16] as an authoritative support for the teaching on the Eucharist which he developed during the later years of his life. Clearly FitzRalph regarded this sermon as the definitive statement of his own opinions, and he

[13] The Maundy sermon (B, fols. 4^{r}–7^{v}; J, fols. 2vb–5vb) is undated in the main MSS and this rubric is given only in the *Tabula Sermonum* in L.

[14] For the effect of the Black Death on mendicant communities, as reflected in the reduction of recruitment requirements see Francis X. Martin and Alberic de Meijer, 'Irish Material in the Augustinian Archives Rome, 1354-1624', *Arch. Hib.* 19 (1956), 64.

[15] According to the rubric the sermon was preached *in vulgari*, but the text was preserved in Latin. See edition by Benedict Zimmermann, *Anal. Ord. Carm. Discalc.* 3 (1931), 179-89.

[16] Wyclif's description in *De Blasphemia* (1381), ed. Michael H. Dwiewicki (WS, London, 1893), p. 232.

frequently referred back to it whenever a matter concerning the doctrine of the Eucharist came up for discussion in later sermons. However, the vast majority of the Lichfield sermons follow a definite pattern which FitzRalph had evolved for instructing popular audiences, taking his subject usually from the epistle or gospel of the day according to the Sarum rite, or else from the life of the saint being commemorated, though the latter case occurred here much less frequently than in Avignon. Apart from a sermon in honour of St. Catherine for each of his years in Lichfield, and on each occasion preached in the cathedral, there is only one panegyric on a saint. This is a sermon preached on the feast of St. Mark the Evangelist, in the chapel of the hospital of St. John the Baptist, an early thirteenth-century foundation for poor men under the rule of a master and with a public cemetery attached, which was the venue of two sermons to open-air audiences during 1345-6, and which are preserved almost complete in the diary.[17] By far the more frequent type of sermon in Lichfield were those 'de tempore', above all for Lent and Advent, and for the feast-days associated with Passiontide, Easter, the Ascension, Pentecost, or the feasts of the Blessed Virgin. It would appear that in this purely pastoral capacity FitzRalph was much more concerned to instruct his audiences concerning the major events in the ecclesiastical year and the doctrines associated with these, than with inculcating a particular veneration of the saints. It may be that he was already becoming aware of the abuses to which such veneration, if not properly informed and guided, might lead, an awareness which was clearly visible in the sermon preached on All Saints' Day 1356 at Deddington near Oxford.[18] This sermon was subsequently lifted out of context by Wyclif, to show that such an impeccable authority as FitzRalph had strong reservations about the veneration of the saints, pilgrimages to Marian shrines, and similar cults. In any case, these sermons usually took the form of a reading of the gospel text in Latin and then in English, a careful explanation of the text sentence by sentence, followed by a homily on the subject-matter of the text. As far as can be judged from the Latin summaries in the diary, these homilies must have been fairly simple and free from

[17] B, fols. 7^{v}–9^{r}, 9^{r}–13^{v}, 34^{r}–36^{v}; J, fols. 5vb–7ra, 7ra–10vb, 27rb–29va. For this hospital see *Medieval Religious Houses. England and Wales*, p. 284; *VCH Stafford*, iii. 279–89.

[18] B, fols. 91^{r}–92^{v}; J, fols. 74ra–75ra.

theological complications, concerned with instruction and exhortation to a better way of living rather than with doctrinal debate. Occasionally he devoted his attention to explaining details of the liturgical calendar, as for example in the sermon preached in the church of St. Nicholas in Lichfield, when he explained in elaborate detail the various customs associated with processions held on Rogation Days.[19]

The general pattern shows that he was an active dean: although he must have spent a considerable amount of time in routine administration and in the supervision of the rebuilding of the cathedral, he preached regularly both in his cathedral and in nearby churches. He also paid occasional visits to outlying parts of his deanery, preaching on several occasions at Brewood and Cannock in Staffordshire.[20] That he should spend time in Brewood and feel obliged to preach there at least once a year is not surprising. Of the two prebends attached to his office by statutory right, Brewood and Adbaston, the former was clearly his favourite. The approval which he sought and secured from the chapter in March 1337 for his plan to demolish several houses in Adbaston in order to make improvements at Brewood suggest that he had a residence in the latter, conveniently situated close to the episcopal manor favoured by Bishop Northburgh. Only rarely did the dean move farther afield during the period of slightly over two years in office between his return from Avignon and his departure early in 1347, probably via Oxford,[21] to London to do homage to Edward III for the temporalities of Armagh before moving to Exeter for his episcopal consecration.

One such occasion is indicated by an important but undated

[19] B, fols. 33^{v}-34^{r}; J, fol. 27ra. It is only a tiny fragment, a reminder of the theme of the sermon.

[20] At Brewood on 9 October 1345 and 26 March 1346, in Cannock on 21 May 1346, and in Burton (Staffs.) on Palm Sunday, 9 April 1346, B, fols. 22^{v}-24^{r}, 27^{r-v}, 32^{v}-33^{v}, 27^{v}-30^{r} respectively; J, fols. 17va-18vb, 21^{rb-vb}, 26ra-27rb, 22ra-23vb.

[21] He preached at Burford, about 19 miles west of Oxford on the feast of the Epiphany, B, fol. 42^{r-v}; J, fol. 34^{ra-va}. No year is given in the diary, but its position suggests 1347. An argument against this dating is the rubric, which describes the preacher as dean of Lichfield, not as 'electus Ardmachani'. The sermon may, however, have been preserved on a loose sheet and without rubric, and it was included erroneously by the unknown 'editor'. Hammerich, p. 27, suggested Epiphany 1348, in which case FitzRalph was already archbishop and the rubric equally incorrect. His argument was based on an alleged similarity between this sermon and the fragment at the beginning of the diary which criticized mendicant confessors, and he further argued that this undated fragment belonged to FitzRalph's first year in Ireland as archbishop and was therefore evidence for his thesis that the struggle with the friars had begun *before* his departure for the curia in the early summer of 1350.

sermon whose rubric and place in the diary suggests that it must have been preached during the late summer or early autumn of 1346. The rubric describes it as 'Sermo Ricardi electi Ardmachani in processione Londoniensi facta pro rege et fiebat in vulgari',[22] thereby indicating that it was preached after FitzRalph's appointment by papal provision to the see of Armagh on 31 July of that year had been made known in England. Furthermore, internal evidence, especially references to the recent English victories in France, suggests a date around late September or early October, when news of the battles of Creçy (26 August) and Poitiers (19 September) would have reached the English capital.[23] The diary contains only a brief outline of the content of this sermon, doubtless because the preacher incorporated in it material from earlier sermons and from one in particular. This was not the first occasion upon which he had preached at a public procession on behalf of English political interests and ambitions in France. An earlier sermon, also undated, but on account of its position in the diary between sermons of May and August 1345 respectively and because of the text upon which it was based ('Orate pro invicem ut salvemini', Jacob. v. 16), which the preacher explicitly stated was the gospel of that week, is most likely to have been preached on or around the fifth Sunday after Trinity, i.e. 26 June 1345.[24]

This sermon must be considered in the light of the intensive preparations for war which occupied the attentions of Edward III's court during this summer. FitzRalph exhorted the participants at the procession how they should pray, and which objectives should be made the theme of their petitions, reminding them that they had a special duty to pray for their king, that he might live justly and sincerely, lest the nation should fall victim of the sins of its sovereign. He asked them to pray that Edward III would be guided by sane and wise counsellors, and that he should achieve a just and happy outcome in the forthcoming military campaigns.[25] On the other hand the preacher tried not to allow either himself or his audience to be carried

[22] B, fol. 36^{v}; J, fol. 29vb.

[23] B, fols. 36^{v}–37^{v}; J, fols. 29vb–30va. For these campaigns in France when the king was accompanied by Bradwardine, see McKisack, *The Fourteenth Century*, pp. 133–40. The sermon allegedly preached by Bradwardine before Edward III and his army when the news of the victory against the Scots at Neville's Cross (17 October 1346) has been edited by Heiko A. Oberman and James A. Weisheipl, 'The *Sermo Epicinius* ascribed to Thomas Bradwardine (1346)', *AHDLMA* 33 (1958), 259–329.

[24] B, fols. 17^{r}–20^{r}; J, fols. 13rb–15va, one of the few sermons in J in which the rubric is given in full.

[25] B, fol. 19^{r}; J, fol. 14vb.

away from their Christian obligations by misguided patriotism, and he warned them not to pray for bloodshed and loss of life on the part of the enemy. To do so would be to violate the gospel precept of loving one's neighbour as oneself and therefore to damage the cause of their own sovereign.[26] At the same time he was emphatic in his insistence that the law of nature required both that all subjects prayed for their king as protector and defender of his people, and that they supported the work of their armed forces. FitzRalph's difficulty in establishing adequate criteria for a theory of the just war,[27] in reconciling the patriotic sentiments appropriate to an Anglo-Irish subject of Edward III with his own calling as priest and preacher, became even more patent when he moved on to consider problems of pacifism and the defensive war. He had to counter the objections of those who argued that whereas a war for the defence of the realm was justified, this did not apply in the case of an invasion of France across the Channel, and his reply was one which would have certainly commended itself to the king. It was perhaps thus intended. But his argument that the superior hereditary right of Edward III to the throne of France, according to the judgement of English succession law, meant that *de iure* and *de facto* one man was king of both France and England, that the two kingdoms were therefore to be considered as two members of one unit, the indivisible realm of the English king, is to modern ears utterly tendentious.[28] It is noteworthy, however, that FitzRalph based Edward's claims exclusively on hereditary right, without any explicit application of the theory of dominion and grace, which he was subsequently to employ in a startling manner.

At this stage FitzRalph had been back in England for less than one year, and did not yet have any reason to assume that he was destined for higher office in Ireland. In view of his difficulties with the English Crown and its servants, especially with the archbishop of Canterbury and with the keeper of the Privy Seal, William Kildesby, over the disputed prebend of Cannock,

[26] B, fol. 19^{r-v}; J, fol. 14vb. Gwynn, *Studies*, 23 (1934), 404–5, suggested that the first of these sermons concerning the war was also preached in 1346, but in 'Sermon Diary', 49, he revised this to the summer of 1345. In view of its position in the diary, and the fact that none of the immediately preceding or following items are displaced, the latter is more probable.

[27] For a recent discussion of this problem, Frederick H. Russell, *The Just War in the Middle Ages* (Cambridge, 1975).

[28] B, fol. 19^{v}; J, fol. 15rb.

the dean of Lichfield may have felt the need to give strong and public expression of his support for the aspirations of Edward III. He returned once more to the same theme, the obligation to pray that the king might make the best use of talents and resources, in the second of these sermons, preached as archbishop-elect of Armagh after the spectacular and to some extent unexpected English victories in France in August–September 1346.[29] In the earlier sermon an attentive observer might have interpreted FitzRalph's remarks about the need for wise counsellors as an implied criticism, as a warning to the zealous proponents of the war, who included prominent ecclesiastics, not to overreach the available resources, not to engage in over-ambitious campaigns which would harm rather than improve the English position. But in the later sermon he too joined in the general euphoria with which the news from France was greeted, and he argued that the victories were God-given signs of the justification of earthly claims. He used examples of excessive royal pride from the Old Testament in order to explain the downfall of Philip VI and his allies, and here one can identify faint hints of what was to come – the notion that conspicuous success was a proof of divine favour, and its corollary that the successful exercise of lordship was dependent upon its holder being in the state of grace.[30]

Such processional sermons were a regular feature of the ecclesiastical calendar, especially in connection with Rogation Days, when the theme of prayer was particularly appropriate. FitzRalph's last recorded sermon, before he set out for Devon and episcopal consecration at the hands of his old friend and benefactor, John Grandisson of Exeter, was preached in London at a procession in the church of Corpus Christi on the Thursday following Low Sunday, 11 April 1347, after he had done homage to Edward III but before he had received back the temporalities of the see of Armagh.[31] Once more the central issue was prayer, and the archbishop-elect presented to his audience an exposition and commentary, phrase by phrase, on the Lord's Prayer. He had clearly taken great pains to work out his views for this sermon, and the form in which it survives in the diary is more complete than comparable homilies delivered during this period. Consequently he was able to use it for future reference, and he

[29] He prefaced his remarks '. . . secundum fuit narrata historia nostri triumphi in francia', B, fol. 37^{r}; J, fol. 30ra.

[30] B, fol. 37^{r-v}; J, fol. 30^{rb-va}.

[31] B, fols. 39^{v}–42^{r}; J, fols. 32rb–34ra.

repeated it on at least one subsequent occasion in circumstances when he may have had little opportunity to prepare a new sermon.[32]

Although the evidence of Bishop Grandisson's register makes plain that FitzRalph, after his episcopal consecration, spent some months in Devon performing the functions of an auxiliary bishop[33] and presumably availing himself of the opportunity of an 'apprenticeship' under one of the most successful diocesan administrators of the fourteenth-century English Church in order to prepare himself for his tasks in Ireland, no sermons are recorded in the diary for this period. The bishop of Exeter's register specifically mentioned that FitzRalph travelled around Devon consecrating churches, confirming children, and blessing sacred vessels, functions which might reasonably have been combined with a sermon preached by the visiting prelate. We have already considered the form in which FitzRalph may have maintained his diary, 'quaderni' of a small number of folios rather than a large cumbersome volume. In these circumstances it is probable that the sermons belonging to his period in Devon, one of which in accordance with his usual custom of including every change of status or additional office would have announced him in the rubric as 'archiepiscopus' (and no longer 'electus') of Armagh, were copied in a separate 'quadernus' which never found their way into the surviving diary.[34] This impression is further strengthened by the state of the diary for the period between FitzRalph's departure from Lichfield in the winter of 1346-7 and arrival in Ireland more than a year later. The last recorded Lichfield sermon of 3 December 1346 is followed immdiately by the London procession sermon of 11 April 1347, the Epiphany sermon at Burford – also apparently belonging to the year 1347 but nevertheless out of the correct order – and the first surviving sermon which the new archbishop preached upon his arrival in Ireland, that delivered at Dundalk on 24 April 1348, and whose tone suggests that it actually was the first sermon delivered by FitzRalph on Irish soil since his return. Here he repeated his earlier sermon on the Lord's Prayer, and the entry contained in the diary is a typical example of the kind of brief note he occasionally included for his own information.

[32] In his first recorded sermon in Ireland as archbishop he repeated it in Dundalk 24 April 1348.

[33] *Grandisson's Register*, ii. 1022, and the commission is printed, ii. 1024.

[34] Such a solution would correspond with Gwynn's theory concerning the composition of the diary, 'Sermon Diary', 20.

He remarked that he had mentioned to his audience three reasons for taking this particular topic as the theme of his sermon before them, though only one of these reasons is further explained – that he was following Christ's example, who had taught this prayer as the first of all prayers to his own people the Jews. In like manner FitzRalph had returned among his own people 'eos de sanguine meo', by which he clearly meant the citizens of Dundalk among whom he had numerous family connections, and to whom he wished to impart the same message.

iii. Ireland

FitzRalph's last years in Lichfield represented in purely numerical terms his most active period of preaching, at least as far as the evidence of the sermon diary can be trusted. In the space of slightly over two years from the end of November 1344 until the feast of Epiphany 1347 he noted twenty-five sermons in the diary, an average of almost one per month. However there is reason to assume that the portions of the diary compiled in Lichfield represented a more complete record of his preaching activity than did any of the subsequent sections. Here FitzRalph had been employed in a round of duties which involved some travelling, but within a restricted area. He had in the deanery at Lichfield a more stable base, with the corresponding facilities for keeping his records in order, than was possible later in Ireland. For the Lichfield period there are no obvious gaps in the diary, and no reason to assume that any sermon which the preacher might have chosen to record has since been lost. The situation with regard to the Irish sermons is very different. Although FitzRalph spent the better part of six years in Ireland as archbishop, there are only thirty-one recorded sermons, of which one contains no identification of date or place of preaching but which on internal grounds must be identified as an Ash Wednesday sermon to an Irish audience,[1] while a further fragment must have been part of a homily preached to the clergy and possibly some of the suffragan bishops at a provincial council.[2] The surviving Irish sermons belong to the central core which is properly termed the sermon diary,[3] but their primary

[1] The reference to a knight who 'solus post Patricii tempus eius purgatorium pro dei amore intravit' is unlikely to have been understood without further comment except by an Irish audience, B, fol. 1^{r}; J, fol. 1^{ra-b}.

[2] B, fol. 1^{v}; J, fol. 1^{va-b}.

[3] B, fols. 42^{v}–81^{r}; J, fols. 34va–66vb. The single exception in this section is the London sermon preached at St. Mary's Newchurch, 25 March 1357, which was misplaced and included at fols. 56^{v}–58^{r}, and 46va–48ra.

significance is not restricted to the evidence which they provide for FitzRalph's development as a preacher. Their real importance in this context lies in the extent to which they contribute to our knowledge of his work as archbishop, ecclesiastical politician, and mediator in Armagh, as pastor, reformer, and diocesan administrator, as commentator on the conditions of Irish life as he observed them, and of the measures which he tried to adopt in order to improve these conditions. This importance is heightened by the absence of both his episcopal register and of the text of the statutes of the provincial synods over which he presided and whose legislation he attempted to implement during his visitations and preaching tours. These sermons are therefore among the most revealing documents of his episcopate. Consequently they will be subjected to a more detailed examination in the appropriate context, and here no more will be attempted than a few general remarks about their characteristics and place in the collection as a whole.

According to the evidence of the diary, FitzRalph's preaching activity in Ireland fell into three definite, but numerically unequal, parts and there is reason to assume that one or more 'quaderni' of Irish sermons is wholly or partly missing. The first period coincides with his first visit to Ireland after his consecration, when in the spring of 1348 he preached a series of five sermons in quick succession in the area around Drogheda and Dundalk, in what was clearly an attempt to make contact with his flock as soon as possible, and in which he made extensive use of material already recorded in his diary from London and Lichfield sermons. The outbreak of the plague, which arrived in the towns on the eastern coast in August 1348, was responsible for a cessation of preaching activity until the following spring. Hence the only other sermon recorded in the diary as having been preached before the archbishop's departure for London and then Avignon in the early summer of 1349 was that on the Immaculate Conception delivered in the Carmelite church in Drogheda on 25 March 1349, but it does seem probable that he also preached in Dublin later in that spring when he ventured to the capital in an attempt to enforce his primatial claims against the archbishop of Dublin. The second group of sermons was preached in 1351–2, after his return from Avignon and in the circumstances surrounding the first provincial synod which he opened at Drogheda on 7 February 1352. Then followed a long gap which appears to have been caused at least in part by his decision to place the city of Drogheda under interdict with the consequent cessation of public liturgical functions. Other contributory factors to this silence were FitzRalph's visit to the king's court at Westminster in the late spring or summer of 1353 followed by a bout of illness, from which he appears to have been only gradually recovering when the Hungarian knight George Grissaphan arrived on pilgrimage to St. Patrick's Purgatory during the winter of 1353-4. The final phase of FitzRalph's preaching activity in Ireland dated from 1354 until his departure for England in June 1356 never to return, of which the most intensive period was that of February to June 1355. During these months, following his second synod held at Drogheda, he went on visitation both in the diocese of Meath and in the English part of his own diocese. In addition to the sermon with which he opened the synod of 5 February, he preached nine sermons over the next four and a half months, in which he attempted to promote the practical application and enforcement of the synodal legislation enacted at Drogheda.[4]

Apart from the synodal sermons delivered in Latin and the 1349 sermon preached in the Carmelite church in Drogheda, these Irish sermons are mainly preserved as brief Latin notes referring to vernacular sermons characterized by moral exhortation and pastoral zeal. Probably because of the topic discussed, the Immaculate Conception, and the fact that this sermon to the Carmelites had a higher theological content than was customary in most of FitzRalph's homilies to an Irish audience, he regarded it as worth preserving. Hence it is the only example of these sermons in Ireland in which the text is given in a virtually complete form, apparently a Latin text of the sermon which he actually delivered, and subsequently polished for inclusion in his sermon collection. However, the end of the text is defective in all of the extant manuscripts,[5] a factor which lends support to the view that at least one and probably more folios of the original 'quadernus' of the archbishop's notes went astray, and the missing portion may well have contained the text of a sermon preached in Dublin later in the same spring.

The preaching tour with which FitzRalph commenced his

[4] The synodal sermons were edited by Gwynn, *Arch. Hib.* 14 (1949), 53–65; the sermons of the subsequent tour are in B, fols. 65^{r}–70^{r}, 71^{r}–72^{r}; J, fols. 54rb–58va, 59^{ra-vb}.

[5] He had been discussing sin and damnation and the argument tailed off with 'saltem quod homo non nisi per hominem sui generis et nature redimi omnino non debuit, hoc modo ostenditur . . .', B, fol. 49^{r}; J, fol. 40va.

official career as archbishop of Armagh brought him into contact with an area with which he must in any case have been familiar from childhood, and which was to remain the core of his activities for the remainder of his working life in Ireland. The opening sermon on the Lord's Prayer to the people of Dundalk on 24 April 1348 was followed in quick succession by four more: on Sunday 27 April in Louth, two days later at Ardee, the following Sunday (4 May) at Drogheda, and a week later at Mansfieldstown.[6] The text of the second of these sermons, the account in St. John's Gospel of Christ's first appearance to the apostles after the resurrection (Ioh. xx. 19),[7] was justified by the ecclesiastical calendar, but it may also have been intended to imply a subtle parallel. In these sermons FitzRalph made clear to his new flock that he had come to them imbued with a sense of purpose, and a programme of moral reform was high on his list of priorities. He made no attempt to cajole them or win popularity by flattery, and the tenor of these sermons would have been more appropriate to a Lenten preacher exhorting to repentance than a new archbishop introducing himself in the course of the Easter celebrations. His topics ranged from denunciations of immorality and lust (in these he cited examples of the peccadilloes of Oxford youths in terms which both reflected his experience of the problems of undergraduate life and his preference for calling a spade by its proper name),[8] of avarice and lack of charity, through an explanation of the reasons why God is obliged to punish sinners, to exhortations on the love of God and of one's neighbour, the need for baptism in order to achieve salvation, problems of merit and beatitude. The sermon preached at Drogheda, on the text 'Qui crediderit et baptizatus fuerit salvus erit' (Marc. xvi. 16), anticipated in several respects FitzRalph's thinking about the necessity for baptism as a precondition for the righteous exercise of dominion which would find expression in *De Pauperie Salvatoris*, but for the main body of the text he simply referred back to a sermon which he had preached as dean of Lichfield in the cemetery of the hospital of St. John the Baptist on 4 May 1345, for which the diary

[6] B, fols. 42^{v}–45^{v}; J, fols. 34vb–37rb.

[7] Only a brief fragment survives, B, fols. 42^{v}–43^{r}; J, fols. 34vb–35rb.

[8] In the Louth sermon he used an 'exemplum de scolari oxoniensi pulcherrimo iuvene qui a suo confessore requisitus cur numquam de peccato luxurie voluit confiteri respondit quod cum cogitabat ingenuitatem anime sue nunquam poterat sibi in consensum venire quod eius generositatem carnis infime turpitudinibus macularet . . .', B, fol. 42^{v}; J, fol. 34vb.

contained extremely detailed notes.[9] Similarly in the second of these five sermons, preached at Louth, he referred for the main body of his argument back to the Pentecost sermon in Lichfield Cathedral in 1345.[10] Hence these five sermons confirm the impression that FitzRalph had but recently arrived in Ireland, and as yet had not found time to work out a new series of sermons appropriate to the conditions he found there. Consequently he drew heavily on that existing stock which was recorded in detail in his diary – in the first case repeating a previous sermon absolutely verbatim, in two of the others adapting Lichfield sermons, while in the two remaining sermons he rearranged material which he had used in Avignon in other contexts. These sermons provide therefore a practical illustration of the purpose of the diary, a useful tool for the assistance of a busy preacher.

Of the twenty-nine sermons preached in Ireland for which the diary gives particulars of date and place, a singularly high proportion – ten in all – are recorded as having been preached in Drogheda, the city which FitzRalph made the administrative centre for the English half of his diocese, using the parish church of St. Peter as his 'pro-cathedral'.[11] Of the remainder, four were preached in his native Dundalk, three in Ardee, two in his nephew's rectory at Trim in the neighbouring diocese of Meath, and one each in Louth, Mansfieldstown, Dromiskin, Termonfechin (all in the Armagh diocese), Coleraine (Down and Connor), Greenoge, Screen, Athboy, and Kells (Meath). Hence apart from the single visit to the isolated group of English colonists in the remote coastal town of Coleraine far to the north, virtually cut off from the main centres of English influence and soon after FitzRalph's death to fall into Gaelic Irish hands, he never moved outside the English half of his diocese centred on Drogheda and Dundalk and the diocese of Meath which was strongly under the influence of the Dublin government.

Because of the additional details which the diary contains concerning place and date of preaching, FitzRalph's sermons provide for at least part of his episcopate a rough itinerary of

[9] B, fol. 44^{v}; J, fol. 36va.

[10] '. . . sicut in sermone illo in die penthecostes: Paraclitus spiritus sanctus.' In a further passage he referred for his arguments on the forgiveness of sin to the sermon on the 'Pater noster' delivered in London and Dundalk, B, fol. 43^{r}; J, fol. 35ra.

[11] Respectively 1348, 1349, 1351, 1352 (two including a synodal sermon), 1355 (four including a synodal sermon), and 1356. He preached in Drogheda at least once in each year he spent in Ireland, with the exception of 1353–4, when the city may have been under interdict.

his movements. Further, because of his frequently repeated and impassioned denunciations of local abuses we gain a vivid impression of some of the more pressing problems which he had to face during his years in Ireland. Consequently this section of the diary helps to supplement the deficiencies in our sources of information caused by the loss of his episcopal register. In view of his known zeal for the good order of his diocese and the long years of apprenticeship provided by his close contacts with men such as Grandisson of Exeter and Northburgh of Coventry and Lichfield, who were in this respect exemplary among their fourteenth-century English colleagues, it is scarcely conceivable that FitzRalph did not keep such a register. An indication that he did so is provided by the evidence of subsequent volumes of the Armagh episcopal registers, both in the form of individual fragments dating from his pontificate and bound into later volumes and in the form of cross-references from later registers back to decrees promulgated or decisions reached by the 'Lord Archbishop Richard'.[12] Hence the existence in the later fourteenth and fifteenth centuries of a body of record material emanating from his own episcopate can be assumed, and it was clearly available to his successors in the diocese. However, it is more probable that the actual register itself travelled with him on his final journey to Oxford, London, and then Avignon in 1356-7. He set out with the intention of conducting business connected with the welfare of his diocese, and both in London and at the curia during the last years of his life he engaged in a considerable amount of routine diocesan business, in addition to his case against the mendicant orders. In such circumstances, and in view of the rather haphazard form in which the sermon diary (apart from the formal Avignon sermons and several others which he had clearly prepared himself for publication and circulation) survived and returned to England, it is easy to understand how the episcopal register, especially if it consisted mainly of unbound sheets, might have become scattered to the four winds. Whoever collected the sermons in the form in which they have survived, possibly Richard Kilwington and in any case a supporter of the archbishop's anti-mendicant cause, was more concerned with the preservation of material connected with the latter than with the minutiae of daily life in a remote Irish diocese. Such a register, however, whose existence may be

[12] In the registers of Milo Sweteman (1361-80) and John Swayne (1418-39) and in the statutes of Nicholas Fleming (1404-16) now bound into Swayne's register.

presumed with reasonable certainty, would have been a mine of information concerning the attempts of a curially-orientated and reforming prelate, especially in the years 1351-6 when he tried to be resident and conscientious, and the difficulties which he encountered. In the absence of such a register, the diary assumes a particular significance – though its limitations as a record source will emerge in the following discussion of Fitz-Ralph at work as archbishop of Armagh.

IV Archbishop of Armagh

i. The Irish Church and the primatial question

The death on 16 May 1346 of Archbishop David O'Hiraghty of Armagh highlighted two important problems in Irish ecclesiastical and political life. The first, and most immediate, was whether the death of this archbishop of Gaelic stock – the first since Nicholas MacMaol Iosa (1270–1303) – would mean that the see reverted to a prelate of English birth or background, firmly rooted in the English sphere of influence.[1] The second, and related issue, concerned the location of the primacy in the Irish Church, whether in Dublin and therefore closely identified with the government of the English lordship, or in Armagh where the divisions and tensions between the two 'nations' in medieval Ireland were strongly in evidence.[2] MacMaol Iosa had been able to hold a balance between these two nations in his divided archdiocese and ecclesiastical province, preventing excessive interference by Crown officials in the affairs of the Irish Church. However, his three immediate successors, the Dominicans Walter Jorz (1307 until his resignation in 1311), and Roland Jorz (1311–22), and Stephen Segrave who had been one of Fitz-Ralph's predecessors as dean of Lichfield,[3] had all been of English birth, largely absentee, and all had ended their lives in England. O'Hiraghty had been dean of Armagh under Segrave, in accordance with an arrangement which continued under Fitz-Ralph that an English, or Anglo-Irish archbishop resided at one or other of his two manors of Dromiskin and Termonfechin, respectively close to the towns of Dundalk and Drogheda and within the sphere of influence of the Anglo-Norman lordship. His half of the diocese was administered by the archdeacon, while the northern half including the primatial city of Armagh remained under the control of a native Irish dean.[4] However, upon the death of Segrave on 27 October 1333 neither John

[1] For the archbishops since Nicholas MacMaol Iosa see *HBC*², 308.

[2] Watt, *The Church and the Two Nations*, pp. 173–215.

[3] Respectively *BRUO* II, 1023–4, 1023; *BRUC* 516–17.

[4] Gwynn, *Medieval Province of Armagh*, pp. 73–5. The English 'half' consisted of the deaneries of Drogheda, Dundalk, and Ardee, *Cal. Reg. Sweteman*, 289.

XXII nor Edward III made any hasty move to fill the see and it remained vacant until July of the following year, when O'Hiraghty was unanimously elected by the chapter of Armagh and almost simultaneously on 4 July provided to the see by John XXII. At this point O'Hiraghty was already at the curia, and it is possible that he had been aware of the chapter's wishes before the election took place and had come to Avignon to secure papal approval for his candidature before John XXII might decide on a royal candidate who would carry out the wishes of Edward III regarding the Irish Church.[5] The new archbishop was consecrated with all haste on 26 July by the cardinal bishop of Porto and instructed by the pope to set out for his archdiocese as soon as possible.[6] During his twelve years in office he was, like most of his English predecessors during the fourteenth century, hampered by the financial difficulties of the see. He was constantly in debt and was unable to pay even the relatively mild curial taxes imposed on his impoverished diocese,[7] while the problem seems in his case to have been made particularly acute by the financial exactions of royal officials in those parts of the diocese which lay within the Anglo-Irish Pale and which included the thriving commercial towns of Drogheda and Dundalk – the most prosperous parts of his territory, which might otherwise have been able to help him out of his difficulties.

In view of the fact that O'Hiraghty's presence at the curia is documented for the summer of 1334 and his date of departure for Ireland is unknown, one is led to speculate whether he might not have been in contact with FitzRalph there. The latter had already aspirations to a canonry in the Cathedral of Armagh

[5] Watt, pp. 192–7; idem, 'Negotiations between Edward II and John XXII', 120.

[6] John XXII confirmed the election on 4 July and by 26 July he had been consecrated, *Reg. Vat.* 106, fols. 454^{v}, 457^{r}; *CPL* 1305–42, 403.

[7] O'Hiraghty's financial difficulties are well documented. On 18 May 1343 the papal nuncio in England was authorized to collect a large debt from him, computed on the basis of the *ad limina* payments which had not been paid for the previous 14 terms. By analogy with the archbishop of Canterbury, who was obliged to make an *ad limina* visit every 3 years, this meant that no archbishop of Armagh had either visited the curia or paid the necessary taxes in the event of non-appearance for 42 years. The tax to be collected amounted to 50 marks for each of the outstanding 14 terms, at the exchange rate of 1 mark = 5 florins, thus amounting to 700 marks or 3,500 florins, *Reg. Vat.* 137, fol. 2^{r}; *CPL* 1342–62, 1. O'Hiraghty protested inability to pay, and on 3 August 1344 the papal registers show that he had been subjected to further penalties for non-payment, that he had managed to produce securities for the whole of the outstanding debt, whereupon the nuncio was ordered to relax the penalties, *Reg. Vat.* 138, fol. 58^{v}, *CPL* 10. O'Hiraghty also left other debts, which continued to play a part in FitzRalph's relations with the papal Camera.

and may even have been technically a member of the chapter which elected O'Hiraghty, though presumably an absentee member at the time of the election in view of his presence in the household of Richard de Bury before his departure for Avignon. Although no record of such a provision survives in the papal registers, FitzRalph had at some date between 1331 and 1335 been provided to a canonry and prebend in Armagh, which Benedict XII ordered him to resign upon becoming dean of Lichfield. Regardless of whether FitzRalph complied with this papal order or not, he continued to remain in close contact with his native diocese while in England and Avignon. The evidence that O'Hiraghty pursued higher studies in Oxford is flimsy,[8] and his apparent lack of theological qualifications might have meant that John XXII had no further interest in retaining him at the curia during the beatific vision debates, but sent him off to his diocese with all possible speed. Hence a meeting of the new archbishop and the former chancellor of Oxford University during the late summer or autumn of 1334 was possible, but cannot be assumed.

During the twelve years of his episcopate O'Hiraghty tried to improve the administration of his ecclesiastical province, maintaining a regular representative at the papal curia in the person of the 'English' cleric, Roger Sampford, who travelled to Avignon at least six and possibly eight times on his behalf, sometimes carrying money to pay off part of the Armagh debts, on other occasions presenting the archbishop's petitions. On O'Hiraghty's behalf Sampford began the process, continued by FitzRalph when the latter represented the interests of the diocese at the curia in person in 1349-51, of securing the necessary multiple dispensations to enable the sons of the Gaelic Irish to conform to the requirements of the canon law and be ordained, and to ensure the gradual provision of suitably qualified public notaries for an ecclesiastical province which, according to the petition presented and duly granted for the provision of four notaries on 23 November 1343, scarcely had a single one for its entire eleven dioceses.[9] At home the archbishop anticipated

[8] Emden included him among the possible alumni of Oxford, *BRUO* III, 2204.

[9] *Reg. Suppl.* 5, fol. 72^{r}; *CPL Petitions* I, 30. On 29 January 1344 he received a further dispensation for Isaac O'Culan, who figured frequently in the papal registers. The son of a deacon and one of the few Gaelic Irish canon lawyers in the diocese, O'Culan received dispensations permitting him to be ordained, and to hold benefices including a canonry and prebend in Armagh Cathedral, *Reg. Suppl.* 4, fol. 166^{r}; *Reg. Suppl.* 6, fol. 163^{v}; *CPL Petitions* I, 40, 72.

FitzRalph also in his attempts to conduct regular visitations in his province. A fragmentary record of one such visitation in the diocese of Meath has survived by a happy accident: although his episcopal register, like that of FitzRalph, has failed to survive, individual items including this one were bound into later registers, especially that of Milo Sweteman, FitzRalph's immediate successor (1362-80).[10] A further difficulty which O'Hiraghty shared with his successor, was caused by the attempts of the archbishop of Dublin, Alexander de Bicknor (1317-49) – the first for over a hundred years to do so – to enforce his claim to the title 'primas Hibernie', traditionally accorded to the successors to the see of St. Patrick in Armagh.[11] Bicknor's predecessors, especially John Lech (1311-13), had resisted Armagh's claims to the primacy in so far as these involved their assertion within the precincts of the Dublin metropolitan jurisdiction, as is illustrated by the incident which took place in Dublin in 1313. Archbishop Roland Jorz of Armagh, having been summoned to attend Parliament, landed in Howth and proceeded towards the city with his primatial cross carried before him in order to take up residence in the Cistercian abbey of St. Mary's, whereupon he was intercepted by the servants of the archbishop of Dublin before the convent of Augustinian nuns of Grace Dieu to the north of Dublin and after a violent clash had to retire in defeat.[12] Successive archbishops of Armagh then sought dispensation from the obligation of attending Parliament in Dublin in order to avoid a repetition of such scenes, and O'Hiraghty especially showed little inclination to press his claims within the area of the Anglo-Irish Pale. There is no evidence that he pursued his claims with anything like the determination that FitzRalph was to display, nor indeed is there any indication that in this case the claims of an otherwise discredited Archbishop Bicknor were taken seriously either by the papacy or the English Crown.

We have already seen evidence for the suggestion that while FitzRalph was still in Avignon as dean of Lichfield, he was already in contact with the proctor of the archbishop of Armagh, and that he continued at least for the first year after his appointment by Clement VI to employ the services of

[10] *Cal. Reg. Sweteman*, 219.

[11] For the earlier phases of the conflict see Watt, pp. 108-16, and for the titles accorded respectively to the archbishops of Armagh and Dublin during the 12th and 13th centuries, Maurice P. Sheehy, *Pontificia Hibernica,* 2 vols. (Dublin, 1962-5), *passim.*

[12] Reported in Annals of St. Mary's (1313), *Chart. St Mary's Abbey*, ii. 342.

Sampford who, as a canon of Armagh, was a member of the chapter which in turn elected FitzRalph, unanimously as it would seem.[13] When the new archbishop-elect petitioned for and duly received the *pallium*, from the terms of the bull of Clement VI of 28 August 1347 it emerges that Sampford was representing FitzRalph in Avignon on this matter.[14] At that date Sampford was once more, or still at the curia and presumably it was intended that he would continue to act for FitzRalph as he had done for his Gaelic Irish predecessor. Such a situation did not, however, materialize, and after this mission concerning the *pallium* Sampford disappears from the records: he may have died, perhaps also a victim of the plague, or alternatively FitzRalph's own personal and lengthy visits to the curia, followed in the early and mid-1350s by those of his nephew and namesake who took over the duties of his uncle's proctor in Avignon, may have rendered superfluous the services of another representative of the archbishop of Armagh.

A further indication of FitzRalph's continued close association with the Church in Ireland in general, and with his native archdiocese and ecclesiastical province in particular, was provided by the benefices which he secured for his three nephews, all at the time students at Oxford University, on 8 May 1344. However, it will emerge that his influence within Irish ecclesiastical circles while he was still dean of Lichfield was not sufficient to secure undisputed possession of these benefices for the three young men. Upon his accession to the see of Armagh he had to intervene personally before Edward III in order to secure royal directives to English Crown officials in Ireland, dated respectively 4 July and 3 August 1348,[15] guaranteeing that the

[13] Sampford's own search for benefices met with obstacles: at the request of O'Hiraghty Clement VI provided him 21 August 1343 with the church of Tamlachan in the diocese of Armagh and a canonry in Armagh Cathedral with expectation of a prebend, *Reg. Vat.* 157, fol. 249^{v}, *Reg. Vat.* 158, fols. 100^{v}–111^{r}; *CPL* 1342–62, 96, 100; *Reg. Suppl.* 4, fol. 166^{r}, *CPL Petitions* I, 72. But two years later, after O'Hiraghty's death, Clement granted Tamlachan to Charles Macheda, the Irish chaplain of the papal nephew Audomer Roger, cardinal of S. Anastasia. The grant to Macheda, who already held a number of Irish benefices, including canonries in Tuam, Annaghdown, Armagh, and Derry, was made on 27 August 1346 on the grounds that Sampford had put off ordination to Holy Orders, and therefore the collation reverted back to the pope. On the same day provision was made to Sampford of an alternative benefice, *Reg. Suppl.* 11, fols. 152^{v}, 164^{r}; *CPL Petitions,* I, 116–17. Though Sampford is consistently described as orator of the archdiocese of Armagh he was not the only proctor employed by O'Hiraghty at the curia: among the petitions presented on his behalf 21 August 1343 was one for an indulgence for his proctors Sampford and Matteo Filippo de Pratis, *Reg. Suppl.* 4, fol. 166^{r}.

[14] *Reg. Vat.* 184, fol. 80^{r}, *CPL* 1342–62, 262.

[15] CPR 1348–50 118, 136.

papal bulls of provision to these benefices, together with those of William Constable and Magister Adam FitzOwen of the Armagh and Meath dioceses respectively, be implemented without interference. FitzOwen was described as FitzRalph's 'official' in a papal document of 8 March 1347 and he stood surety for the payment of the outstanding debts of the archdiocese of Armagh to the papal Camera,[16] while Constable may also have been a member of FitzRalph's episcopal 'family'. Of FitzRalph's three nephews, only one, Richard Radulphi, had a subsequently documented ecclesiastical career. In the original petition which had been granted on 8 May 1344, he was to receive a benefice in the gift of the bishop of Meath, notwithstanding his expectation of one in the diocese of Lichfield. The latter did not materialize and, as subsequent records show, he had still not received a benefice in Meath by 17 June 1351 but was in possession of the rectory of Trim in the same diocese by 15 January 1353.[17] Archbishop FitzRalph preached at this church in Trim on 4 March 1352 and, although the diary contains only a brief note that the sermon had been preached without any reference to the circumstances, it is not improbable that his nephew would have invited his distinguished relative to preach on the occasion of his installation in the new benefice, or shortly afterwards.[18] The reason for Richard FitzRalph junior's inability to make effective a papal provision to this benefice at an earlier date may well have been the presence of an influential local candidate. Letters patent written by the bishop of Meath, William of St.

[16] *Obl. et Sol.* 22, fol. 22^{r}. He was described as bachelor of canon law and received a benefice in the gift of the bishop and clergy of Meath, 27 August 1346, *Reg. Vat.* 174, fols. 124^{v}, 125^{r}, *CPL* 220; *Reg. Suppl.* 11, fol. 151^{v}, *CPL Petitions* i, 116. FitzOwen reappeared 11 August 1361 as supplicant for the archdeaconry of Meath, which had been the subject of a lengthy dispute at the curia involving another former member of FitzRalph's episcopal 'family', William Napton. Napton had been provided to this benefice in response to FitzRalph's petition, but it was disputed. With the archbishop's help Napton received three decisions in his favour but died at Avignon before gaining possession, *Reg. Suppl.* 34, fol. 154^{r-v}, *CPL Petitions* I, 373.

[17] He was granted the reservation of a canonry and prebend in Emly, notwithstanding his expectation of a benefice in the gift of the bishop of Meath, *Reg. Vat.* 206, fol. 88^{v}, *CPL* 420; *Reg. Suppl.* 21, fol. 20^{v}, *CPL Petitions* I, 210.

[18] B, fols. 63^{v}–64^{r}; J, fol. 53^{ra-b}. FitzRalph managed to exert considerable influence in Meath, securing not only the recognition of his visitation rights, but also the right of the church of Armagh to Trim castle. This had been held of the see of Armagh by Roger Mortimer, earl of March, and on his death leaving a minor as heir, it was taken into royal hands. FitzRalph succeeded in collecting the rent, but by 12 December 1363 it was over 2 years in arrears, *Cal. Reg. Sweteman*, 258.

Paul, on 1 December 1348 and referring to an agreement reached by him and his clergy on the one hand and Archbishop FitzRalph and the dean and chapter of Armagh on the other concerning FitzRalph's visitation rights in the diocese of Meath, were witnessed by (among others) Magister Thomas Melton, professor of civil law and rector of the parish church in Trim.[19] Melton does not figure in the papal registers and may have been appointed on the strength of local influence, and FitzRalph junior may have finally secured possession in the event of Melton's promotion or death.

On 12 August 1352 Clement VI granted FitzRalph junior's petition for a further canonry and prebend at Kilmacdonagh in the diocese of Cloyne, but the death of that pope before the papal letters enforcing the grant had been issued made it necessary for the supplicant to petition for its confirmation by Innocent VI on 15 January the following year.[20] The terms both of this latter petition and of a letter which the archbishop addressed to his nephew on 22 February 1354, recounting the episode of the pilgrimage to St. Patrick's Purgatory undertaken by the Hungarian knight George, suggest that Richard junior was actually present in Avignon on both occasions, acting as the agent of FitzRalph. At this point the financial affairs of the archdiocese of Armagh and its outstanding debts to the papal Camera were still under negotiation at Avignon, whereas the archbishop was then deeply involved in the affairs of his province, apart from a brief visit to the English court on business, for which he received a licence from Edward III on 23 April 1353.[21] We know nothing more about the theological studies of Richard junior, but it is at least possible that having graduated at Oxford in the arts faculty (BA by 1344 and MA by 1351) he may have become enrolled as a student of theology at the *studium generale* attached to the papal curia, which during the period of the Avignonese papacy had begun to flourish with more conspicuous success. He was certainly in residence at the curia for most of 1354-7, when he figured frequently in the records of the Apostolic Camera as having made the payments due from Armagh and from several other Irish dioceses which had no regular proctor at the curia.[22]

19 *Cal. Reg. Fleming*, 154-5.

20 *Reg. Vat.* 219, fol. 159^v, *CPL* 1342-62, 476; *Reg. Suppl.* 24, fol. 91^v, *CPL Petitions* I, 233.

21 CCR 1349-54, 537.

22 Hoberg, *Einnahmen*, 210, 255; idem, *Servitienquittungen*, 35-7; and for payments under Clement VI, Mohler, *Einnahmen*, 268, 284.

The placing by FitzRalph of his two remaining nephews, Edmund Radulphi and John Brisbon, respectively in the dioceses of Ossory and Dublin, may also have helped to strengthen his ties with ecclesiastical life in the Anglo-Irish lordship. It also placed a relative in each of the two cathedral chapters whose diocesan ordinaries were then engaged in bitter strife, and at least in the case of Dublin it is a distinct possibility that FitzRalph may have reckoned with the death or eventual deposition of the elderly, now discredited, Archbishop Bicknor. Ossory had been ruled by the Franciscan poet-bishop, the English-born Richard Ledred, since 1317, and he – one of the longest-living of fourteenth-century Irish bishops – would, despite considerable difficulties and periods of absenteeism in England and at the curia, continue to rule his diocese until his death *c.*1360–1. He died around the same time, or very soon after FitzRalph, and was succeeded by the English Dominican provincial, John Tattenhall, who had been the spokesman of the Friars Preachers in the case between FitzRalph and the friars at Avignon.[23] Ledred had probably little personal connection with FitzRalph during the 1340s, when the latter had no particular reason for personal animosity towards a Franciscan bishop and in any case would probably have sympathized with Ledred's case which began to unfold in Avignon shortly before FitzRalph returned to Lichfield in 1344.[24] The origins of this strife lay in the period before 1320 when Ledred had become aware of the existence in his diocese of alleged heretics, and it was to develop into a prolonged and bitter struggle between the bishop and his metropolitan superior, Archbishop Bicknor, over two major issues, the harbouring of heretics in the archdiocese of Dublin and violation of the person and property rights of the bishop of Ossory, the latter with the connivance of Crown officials in the Dublin lordship. Whereas papal records during the 1320s and 1330s displayed a sporadic interest in the long-drawn-out quarrel, when Ledred spent long periods in exile in England working as an auxiliary bishop, it began to assume new dimensions at Avignon in the early 1340s when the bishop of Ossory

[23] *HBC*², 341. Milo Sweteman had been elected by the chapter of Ossory, but the election was quashed by a papal provision in favour of the Dominican, and Sweteman was provided to Armagh, Gwynn, 'Provincial and Diocesan Decrees of the Diocese of Dublin', *Arch. Hib.* 11 (1944), 35.

[24] For Ledred see *DNB* xi. 779–80, and esp. Colledge, *Richard Ledred*, pp. xv–xxxv. The evidence of his poetry suggests that he was well educated, but there is no indication that he studied at any university.

came to the curia in person to make his accusations against Bicknor, whom he alleged had been protecting heretics in his diocese for more than twenty years, including the notorious Robert Couton.[25] Already on 29 June 1343, while FitzRalph was still in Avignon, Clement VI had begun to take an interest in the matter, apparently with a view to sorting out the complexities of the situation,[26] and as soon as he had appointed FitzRalph to the see of Armagh the pope commissioned him and the archbishop of Cashel, the Carmelite Ralph O'Kelly who was also a seasoned curial campaigner, to investigate the entire question and proceed against the archbishop of Dublin as they deemed necessary.[27]

Bicknor, a royal servant who had become archbishop of Dublin in 1317 through papal and royal favour, and subsequently attempted to establish a university at St. Patrick's in Dublin, got into financial and political difficulties during the later years of the reign of Edward II and suffered both royal disgrace and papal excommunication. He continued nominally as archbishop of Dublin until his death on 14 July 1349, but the position of the see was an unhappy one, diocesan administration was neglected, and the personal authority of the archbishop at a low ebb, paradoxically at precisely the time when Bicknor was claiming the title of 'primas Hibernie'.[28] This question of the primacy was, as we shall see, one of the first and most pressing problems which FitzRalph would have to face after his consecration and there is some evidence, which deserves careful consideration, that he was responsible for securing from Innocent VI *c.*1353 a compromise solution of the respective claims of Armagh and Dublin – a solution which, even though it did not put an end to fourteenth-century strife concerning the matter, is still reflected in the nomenclature of the Irish hierarchy, both Catholic and Protestant, to this day.[29]

[25] Neither the identity of Robert Couton, nor the nature of his alleged heresy is known, but he was mentioned by name in the papal documents. He is not identical with the Oxford Franciscan of the same name, *BRUO* I, 507.

[26] *Reg. Vat.* 162, fol. 58^{v}, *CPL* 1342–62, 136.

[27] *Reg. Vat.* 174, fol. 433^{v}, *Reg. Vat.* 176, fols. 212^{r-v}, 216^{r-v}; *CPL* 227, 231–2.

[28] For Bicknor's use of the title see prologue to his constitutions, Gwynn, 'Provincial and Diocesan Decrees', 71.

[29] i.e. 'primas totius Hibernie' for Armagh and 'primas Hibernie' for Dublin, a solution which Archbishop Alen subsequently claimed had been accepted by Innocent VI, *Archbishop Alen's Register*, p. 217. The title 'tocius Hibernie primas' was applied by cameral officials to Bicknor's contemporary in Armagh, Stephen Segrave, *Obl. et Sol.* 8, fols. 69^{v}–70^{v}, when the latter petitioned for redress against two collectors whom he had commissioned to raise a subsidy in order to pay off his debts to

In view of what we have seen of FitzRalph's involvement in the affairs of the see of Armagh and his placing of nephews in benefices both within that archdiocese and in the Anglo-Irish Pale, the possibility of his being chosen for a suitable Irish bishopric cannot have seemed remote. His fellow countryman in Avignon, the procurator-general of the Carmelites since 1327, Ralph O'Kelly – the son of a Drogheda merchant and, as his name suggests, also of mixed race – may have been responsible for introducing FitzRalph to Carmelite circles at the curia, where he preached the widely-circulated sermon on the Immaculate Conception on 8 December 1342.[30] The Carmelite was provided by Clement VI on 7 February 1344 to the see of Leighlin on the mistaken assumption that it had become vacant, and he was consecrated at Avignon two weeks later, before it was realized that the provision could not take effect.[31] He was subsequently appointed on 9 January 1346 to the vacant archbishopric of Cashel, where he remained until his death on 20 November 1361 in an episcopate which coincided almost exactly with that of FitzRalph in Armagh.[32] Like FitzRalph he too began his episcopate with the papal commission to investigate the case of Alexander de Bicknor and the bishop of Ossory.

The death of David O'Hiraghty on 16 May 1346 provided therefore the first suitable opportunity for FitzRalph, since presumably the Carmelite, already consecrated and for many years an influential figure in curial circles, had priority in the case of Cashel. The chapter in Armagh settled on a compromise candidate with remarkable speed: if they had to choose between a candidate of native birth or an Englishman, the result might have been another of the divided, or double elections which

the Camera, but which the collectors refused to hand over. Cited in Boyle, *Vatican Archives*, pp. 171-2, but his date for Segrave's petition as before 21 February 1322 needs correction. Segrave was provided to Armagh on 15 March 1323, following the resignation of Roland Jorz, *Reg. Vat.* 74, fol. 281^v^, *CPL* 1305-42, 229. The text gives the date 21 February 1327, and the case is an excellent illustration of the problems faced by an archbishop of Armagh in 14th-century Ulster.

[30] On O'Kelly see Peter O'Dwyer, 'The Carmelite Order in pre-Reformation Ireland', *Proc. ICHC* (1968), 59, who also drew attention to O'Kelly's clash with Edward III, when the archbishop refused to levy the tax imposed by the parliament of Kilkenny (1346) to meet the cost of the war with France.

[31] *Reg. Vat.* 161, fol. 64^v^; after consecration on 19 February by the cardinal bishop of Porto (Joannes de Convenis, who had also consecrated O'Hiraghty) he was ordered to set out for his see, *Reg. Vat.* 162, fol. 139^v^, *CPL* 1342-62, 125, 139; *Reg. Vat. Aven.* 215, fols. 94^v^-95^r^.

[32] *Reg. Vat.* 169, fol. 33^v^, *CPL* 203.

were a regular feature of capitular life in Irish border areas. But although FitzRalph was of English race and speech, Oxford-educated, and the holder of an important English benefice, he was born in Dundalk and his family was prominent in the commercial and administrative life of the town. Furthermore, although the capitular electors could scarcely have foreseen this, he would try to be scrupulously fair with regard to the rights and prerogatives of both communities within the archdiocese. But it must be stressed that he was far from being an unknown quantity for the electors: he was, or had been, a canon of Armagh and therefore one of their number, and there may have been a certain attraction in electing one who came from their own circles, had already established his reputation as a theologian, was influential and experienced in the ways of the Roman curia, a talented preacher, and an able administrator with genuine pastoral interests. Hence the chapter elected him with a speed which suggests that their decision was unanimous and, apparently unaware of the reservation of the see to the papacy, must have conveyed their choice to Avignon. We can only speculate whether they also notified FitzRalph, then engaged in his normal decanal duties in Lichfield, and whether he accepted or awaited a papal decision. Although Fr. Gwynn assumed that FitzRalph had been notified, possibly by the canon Roger Sampford, and that he conveyed to the chapter his formal acceptance, thereby placing himself as well as the chapter in a false position, the evidence for this view is flimsy and the letter of Clement VI of 31 July 1346 scarcely bears this interpretation.[33] Here the pope simply set aside the election as having been made in ignorance of the papal reservation, which must have taken place at some unspecified date during the episcopate of O'Hiraghty, and went on to appoint FitzRalph by papal provision, having consulted with several cardinals as to the suitability of the choice. This formulation left the matter open, as to whether FitzRalph himself – versed in the ways of the curia – did not upon hearing the news of the capitular election refer the matter to Clement VI for a decision, and by thus appealing to the authority of a pope who would be personally disposed in his favour ensure that the appointment would be allowed to stand, even if the legal reformulation safeguarded papal rights in the matter.

[33] Gwynn, *Studies* (1934), 400–1. The letter is in common form, *Reg. Vat.* 173, fol. 29^{r-v}, *CPL* 217.

The papal reservation may have been an attempt to ensure that the see would be filled without English Crown interference, as Edward III might reasonably be expected to want it for a candidate who would strengthen English influence in the marcher areas beyond the Pale. However, the king, who received the customary notification of the appointment the same day, raised no objection, as he was concerned to secure the now vacant deanery of Lichfield for the keeper of his Privy Seal, John Thoresby.[34] However, the matter was not settled without many more months of negotiations, a situation which helps to explain the delay in setting a date for FitzRalph's consecration and for his final departure to take up his new duties in Ireland more than eighteen months after the papal letter of appointment.

On 5 August 1346 Clement VI issued letters appointing Thoresby at the king's request to the deanery, but the registers of Bishop Roger Northburgh of Coventry and Lichfield show that the office did not change hands so smoothly.[35] For some months to come FitzRalph held on to the office of dean; he had neither done homage for his see nor received back its temporalities. These had been the subject of a royal injunction of 22 June 1346, ordering the justiciar, chancellor, and treasurer in Ireland, together with the barons of the Exchequer in Dublin, to investigate the position with regard to royal rights during previous vacancies in the see of Armagh.[36] In the meantime they were to commit to the dean and chapter of Armagh custody of the temporalities of the see to be held for the duration of the vacancy. The mandate indicated the king's initial good will in the matter, and if FitzRalph was to have difficulty in securing the restoration of the temporalities it was largely because of the effective opposition of royal officials in the Anglo-Irish lordship, who were in a better position to profit from the situation caused by a vacant see, even one with such modest financial assets as Armagh appears to have possessed during these years.[37] Given the well-known problem of conflicting rights and possible dissipation of episcopal property during a vacancy, it was an urgent necessity for FitzRalph to clarify his position as soon as possible, do homage to the king, and secure restoration of the

[34] *Reg. Suppl.* 12, fol. 127^{v}, *CPL Petitions* I, 115. For Thoresby, *DNB* xix. 760–2.

[35] *Reg. Vat.* 173, fol. 285^{r}, *CPL* 218. FitzRalph remained in Lichfield for the rest of 1346, and a dispute arose concerning his continued rights as dean, which were investigated by a commission appointed by the bishop, Reg. Northburgh, ii. fol. 109^{v}.

[36] CCR 1346–49, 31.

[37] Clanchy, 'The Primates and the Church Lands of Armagh', 370–81.

temporalities into his own hands or those of his agents. However, the king's absence on campaign in France posed an added difficulty, and shortly after the battle of Creçy, in a sermon which can be tentatively dated to late September 1346, FitzRalph expressed sentiments which must have been guaranteed to demonstrate his loyalty to the absent king. Discussing the morality of the invasion of France, he defended it against those who objected that it was a war of aggression against another sovereign, who also held his throne and lands by a God-given right. FitzRalph's defence, which sounds like a convenient excuse guaranteed to ensure royal favour, was based on the unsound premiss that Edward's claim to the French throne by hereditary right was universally valid because it was accepted as legal and valid within the realm of England. The sermon was an early indication of the direction in which FitzRalph's thinking was to lead in his subsequent development of the doctrine of dominion by grace. The moral which the preacher wished to communicate concerned the duty of prayer and thanksgiving; one must give thanks for the recent victory and also pray that the king would rule with wisdom and justice, as a king who thus ruled did so because he held his dominion by divine right.[38] Here the argument is circular and not yet clearly worked out, but the possible lines of development are clearly visible.

Meanwhile Bishop Northburgh had appointed a commission to investigate the problem caused by Thoresby's appointment before FitzRalph's departure. Its outcome is unknown, but it probably reached a compromise solution for the intervening period, as FitzRalph continued to exercise his office at least until the end of 1346, and in any case Thoresby was still in France with the king. FitzRalph's last recorded sermon was preached in Lichfield Cathedral on 3 December 1346, the first Sunday of Advent which was a statutory obligation, and in view of the sermon recorded at Burford in Oxfordshire on 6 January 1347 it seems probable that he remained in Lichfield for Christmas, resigning formally as dean around this time and then setting out in the new year for London in order to settle the question of the temporalities. He may have visited Oxford along the way, especially if he felt in need of additional support in his dealings with the king's officials. He did homage to Edward III

[38] B, fol. 19^{r-v}; J, fol. 14vb.

on 15 February 1347, having been obliged formally to renounce the passage in the papal letter of confirmation which was prejudicial to royal claims.[39] Although the bull of consecration issued by Clement VI and the text of the oath which FitzRalph actually took before Bishop Grandisson have survived in the latter's register, and these refer to the candidate's obligation to defend the 'Papatum Romanum ac Regalia Sancti Petri . . . contra omnem hominem,'[40] the papal letter of confirmation referred to in the royal document can only be the bull of appointment issued on 31 July 1346. In it Clement VI expressly reserved all future appointments to the see of Armagh to the papacy, a claim which might well have been the subject of royal concern because potentially damaging to English influence over a part of the Anglo-Irish lordship.[41]

Although no details are known of what passed between FitzRalph and the advisers of Edward III in the spring of 1347, we can assume that there was some hard negotiation. The royal mandates to the justiciar in Ireland, Walter de Bermingham, and to the chancellor of Ireland instructing them to restore the temporalities were not issued for a further two months. Their issue finally on 15 April suggests both that the original consignation of custody to the dean and chapter of Armagh had not been carried out or did not any longer operate, and also that the restoration had not followed automatically once homage to the king had been done. It is possible that the delay was caused by the complicated situation of the war with France, but FitzRalph's subsequent lengthy battle with the Dublin government in order to effect the restitution suggests that the delay was caused by reasons other than negligence and the pressure of other business. On 20 April FitzRalph, now described as 'elect and confirmed' of Armagh, received letters from the king permitting him to nominate his kinsman John Rauf, apparently the head of the family in Dundalk and possessing the necessary authority to represent the archbishop in Ireland, together with William Swayne, as his attorneys in Ireland for one year. This John Rauf figured frequently in the records of the period, as a prominent Dundalk burgess associated with the Dowdalls and

[39] Recorded in the mandate to the Irish justiciar, 15 April 1347, CPR 1345–48, 272.

[40] *Grandisson's Register*, ii. 1023. The passage contained the phrase 'salvo ordine meo', but no reference to a saving clause of the king's rights.

[41] *Reg. Vat.* 173, fol. 29r.

Brisbons, the latter being also related by marriage to the family of FitzRalph, and he had secured a canonry in Dublin for one of their sons.[42]

In this choice of a prominent burgess to represent the new archbishop in Ireland, and presumably to do so primarily against the king's officers concerning the matter of the temporalities, we have another indication that FitzRalph had not allowed his contacts with home and family to lapse completely during his long years abroad. The appointment for one year, and its renewal on 10 July 1347 also with effect for a year, indicates that FitzRalph expected to be detained for some time in England before proceeding to his see, while a further entry in the Close Rolls indicates that these agents were not particularly successful in their dealings with Crown officials in Ireland on the archbishop's behalf. On 10 July 1348 the king had to issue a further mandate to the justiciar Walter de Bermingham, ordering that the temporalities be restored.[43] Although FitzRalph had done homage for the see on 15 February 1347, it had reached the king's ears that some of his ministers in Ireland were unjustly withholding the temporalities and their profits on the grounds that the archbishop had not been consecrated, a situation which Edward III now ordered to be remedied. FitzRalph had in the meantime, in response to his petition, received the bull from Clement VI dated 12 January 1347 permitting him to be consecrated by the prelate of his choice.[44] Having decided to choose his old friend and patron, Grandisson of Exeter, he set out for Devon where his former Oxford colleague, Thomas Buckingham, was chancellor of the diocese, and where the rebuilding of the nave of the cathedral in Decorated (Gothic) style was virtually completed, thus providing a suitable setting for the occasion. We have no reason to assume that contact between the two men had been broken off in the years since FitzRalph had received his first benefices in Exeter through Grandisson's good offices. Grandisson was an exceptionally active prelate, interested in diocesan reform as well as architecture and book-collecting. He visited Avignon occasionally, and was also a regular visitor to Oxford during the

[42] CPR 1345–48, 272; *Dowdall Deeds, ad indicem.* A branch of the Dowdall family established itself *c.*1335 at Termonfechin, where the archbishops of Armagh had a manor and frequently resided, ibid., xvi.

[43] CCR 1346–49, 477. [44] *Reg. Vat.* 174, fol. 355^r, *CPL* 225.

years in which he re-founded and financed the building of the splendid collegiate church of Ottery St. Mary in Devon.[45]

A further problem had however still to be solved before FitzRalph could receive the *pallium* and assume office as archbishop of Armagh, and this concerned the debts which were owed by his four immediate predecessors in the see to the Apostolic Camera. These debts had begun to accumulate because neither Walter nor Roland Jorz ever paid any of the taxes, minute and common services, due upon their being installed in the see. Therefore when Stephen Segrave was appointed on 16 March 1323 he found himself liable for the arrears in tax, and two months later on 11 May he pledged himself to pay in instalments over a period of three years a sum which must have been unrealistic in the light of the actual revenues enjoyed by the incumbent of the see. The common service of the see of Armagh was rated as 1,000 fl., or one-third of the estimated annual revenue of the diocese, but the minute services – calculated on the basis of the number of cardinals actually present at the time of provision and therefore entitled to a share – obviously fluctuated accordingly. The agreement which Segrave made with the officials of the Camera involved a payment of 2,500 fl. to cover his own service and that of his two predecessors, in addition to a further sum equivalent to fifteen minute services, i.e. 166⅔ fl.[46] Neither Segrave nor his successor managed to pay off all of this debt, though O'Hiraghty sent his proctor Roger Sampford on a number of occasions to the curia with (unspecified and presumably small) sums intended as part payment of a debt which, as a result of his own penury, had merely increased by more than a further 1,000 fl. since his provision to the see in 1334. Consequently this outstanding debt, together with the common and service taxes which FitzRalph himself was obliged to pay out of the impoverished resources of the diocese, was the subject of negotiations between Roger Sampford, on behalf of the archbishop-elect, and the Cameral officials in the early months of 1347.[47] One of the

[45] For Grandisson's dealings with the curia concerning the foundation and endowment of Ottery St. Mary and concerning the well-being of clerics from Exeter studying in Oxford, *Reg. Suppl.* 1, fol. 33^r, *Reg. Suppl.* 4, fols. 89^r, 91^r; *CPL Petitions* I, 11, 63–5. Many of these petitions were granted on 6 July 1343 when both Grandisson and FitzRalph were in Avignon.

[46] *Obl. et Sol.* 8, fol. 5^v. See brief discussion of this as example of evidence from cameral registers for Britain and Ireland in Boyle, *Vatican Archives*, pp. 162–3.

[47] On these taxes see William E. Lunt, *Papal Revenues in the Middle Ages*, i (New York, 1934), pp. 81–99.

lengthiest and most detailed entries in the registers of the papal Camera *Obligationes et Solutiones* concerning Ireland in this period records on 8 March 1347 the elaborate arrangements which Sampford had negotiated for the payment of these debts in instalments.[48] All the outstanding debts, those which FitzRalph had inherited from his predecessors and his own in addition, were to be paid in four instalments, each instalment due annually on the feast of St. Gregory (12 March). But this programme of payment was clearly an unrealistic one, far beyond the resources of the archdiocese of Armagh: small sums were paid on FitzRalph's behalf in 1347 and in 1349, and a series of extensions were granted to him after the agreed three years had expired on 12 March 1350.[49]

Once the finances of the see of Armagh had come under scrutiny in the papal Camera, the financial investigators took their search a stage further and brought once more to light the irregularity which has already been noticed: that FitzRalph's predecessors had been lax in their payments of the separate tax for *ad limina* visitations. At this stage FitzRalph was once more in Avignon and in a position to pursue the matter in person. On 5 October 1350 a commission was set up to examine the question, and it duly reported that the papal accountants – in spite of a careful examination of the cameral registers – had failed to find any record of payment of the *ad limina* taxes by an archbishop of Armagh since 1301. Clearly the securities for the outstanding debt which O'Hiraghty had produced in 1343 were no longer regarded as sufficient, and the Camera began to press for payment of the actual sum. Consequently the archbishop was liable for a further series of payments in instalments, and once more partial payments were made by his procurators, further extensions were sought, and although the records of the Camera show that an absolute quittance of all Armagh's debts was acknowledged on 10 May 1356, instalments were still being paid as late as 13 August 1360, occasionally by FitzRalph's nephew, and on the final occasion by his chaplain, Richard Aper.[50]

The register of Bishop Grandisson, a model record of fourteenth-century ecclesiastical administration, provides a

[48] *Obl. et Sol.* 22, fol. 22^{r}.

[49] Partial payments were made in 1347 and 1349, ibid., fol. 52^{r}; ibid., 24, fol. 31^{v}, and for extensions after 1350, ibid., 25, fols. 56^{v}, 78^{v}.

[50] Ibid., 25, fol. 97^{r-v}, 112^{v}, 175^{v}; ibid., 26, fol. 90^{r-v}, 164^{r}, 448^{r-v}.

detailed account of FitzRalph's consecration on 8 July 1347, the Sunday following the feast of the translation of St. Thomas of Canterbury, a prelate whose cult and example was of more than passing interest to both Grandisson and FitzRalph.[51] The consecrating prelate was assisted by three bishops of the south-western dioceses: Ralph of Shrewsbury, bishop of Bath and Wells, Robert Wyvil of Salisbury, and John Trevor of St. Asaph, while those present included the abbots of Buckfast (then Cistercian) and Newenham, also Cistercian, the Premonstratensian abbot of Torre, and the Arroasian abbot of Hartland, the prior of the Augustinian canons at Plympton, as well as numerous clerics, knights, and other laity.[52] Whether representatives of the mendicant communities were present, and simply not included in the account in the register, or whether the friars had already been alienated by Grandisson's extremely cautious policy with regard to licences to hear confessions, cannot be determined.[53] Following the consecration the new archbishop rode in state through the city of Exeter, robed in his pontifical vestments and with his horse arrayed in white trappings 'according to the custom of the Roman curia'. Grandisson himself had been consecrated in Avignon and both he and FitzRalph were familiar with a curial ceremonial more elaborate than that which would be either customary or possible in a remote English diocese.

The account continued with the remark that a few days after his consecration FitzRalph was commissioned by Grandisson to tour the diocese of Exeter confirming children and consecrating churches.[54] However, the commission issued to FitzRalph on 13 July 1347 has also survived in the bishop's register, and it indicates a much wider range of powers conferred upon the new archbishop. In effect it made FitzRalph temporarily the suffragan bishop of Grandisson's diocese and provided the new prelate with an excellent opportunity to gain experience of ordinary diocesan work under an exemplary guide, before setting out for Ireland and his new archdiocese, which he reached at some

[51] *Grandisson's Register*, ii. 1022-4. [52] Ibid., 1022.

[53] Grandisson's restrictive policy with regard to licensing mendicant confessors is reflected in numerous entries in his register, e.g. i. 557, when he quashed existing licences and issued a new list of authorized mendicant confessors subject to his own conditions, and ii. 954, for the conditions he imposed. In the 1350s his register reflected increasing difficulties with the friars at the same time as FitzRalph was developing his opposition to them in Armagh, ibid., ii. 1128, 1143-7, 1186-7, 1208.

[54] Ibid., ii. 1022.

point before Easter 1348. Meanwhile FitzRalph had authorized Roger Sampford to petition the pope for his *pallium*, and on 28 August 1347 when the news of his consecration had obviously not yet penetrated to Avignon, Clement VI issued a mandate to the bishops of Ardagh and Cloyne, respectively Eoghan O'Ferghail and John Brid (the latter the former Cistercian abbot of Combe who had participated in the discussions concerning the beatific vision), to assign the *pallium* to the archbishop-elect, to receive from him the oath of fealty, and to transmit this to the pope. On the same day the pope wrote to FitzRalph, conferring upon him the *pallium* and exhorting him to carry out his duties with humility and justice.[55]

We have already considered the evidence of the sermon diary which provides no indication that FitzRalph's duties as auxiliary bishop in Grandisson's diocese might also have included preaching. Against the suggestion that Grandisson did not encourage a rival episcopal preacher in his diocese, even temporarily, it seems more probable that sermons dating from this period were recorded in some form which did not find its way into the completed sermon diary. The last sermon recorded as having been preached in England by the archbishop while still 'electus', the homily on the Lord's Prayer delivered in London on the occasion of a public procession in Christ Church priory on 11 April 1347, a date which coincided with his presence in London negotiating the restoration of the temporalities of his see, was repeated in Dundalk shortly after Easter 1348 in circumstances which indicated that he had but recently arrived there. It seems therefore probable that he had landed in Ireland, been received by the archdeacon and by that portion of the chapter which resided 'inter Anglos' at or shortly before Easter, and immediately began the intensive preaching tour which brought him to Louth, Ardee, Drogheda, and Mansfieldstown over the next two weeks.

However, all the evidence indicates that he spent but a brief period in Devon with his episcopal mentor. Most of his last months in England appear to have been spent seeking clarification of his own judicial position in Ireland, especially with regard to the disputed primacy and the see of Dublin. The latter was a particularly pressing issue in view of the unusual problem presented by Alexander de Bicknor, and also because a situation was clearly emerging in the course of the year 1347 whereby

[55] *Reg. Vat.* 184, fol. 80^{r}, *CPL* 262.

Clement VI and his curial advisers began to commission Fitz-Ralph to deal with some of the thorniest problems then facing the Irish Church. Understandably perhaps, they were using the Irish ecclesiastic with whom they were most familiar, and in whom they had reason to place confidence as a sort of papal 'trouble-shooter' in Ireland. Such a situation involved his interference in matters which would have lain outside his jurisdiction, unless his position as 'primas Hibernie', affirmed both by Clement VI in his own bull of appointment, and by John XXII for FitzRalph's immediate predecessor, was clarified and also accepted by the English Crown.

Bicknor's tenure of office had begun in auspicious circumstances: he had been the king's treasurer in Ireland and already during the vacancy of the see of Dublin in 1311 before the appointment of John Lech (+ 10 August 1313) he had been the unanimous choice of the cathedral chapters of both Holy Trinity and St. Patrick's.[56] After Lech's death the succession was once more disputed, but Bicknor secured letters from Edward II to Clement V on 18 January 1314, seeking to have his election confirmed.[57] After some delay while Bicknor was engaged on the king's business he went to Avignon to pursue his claim, but Clement's death, followed by the long vacancy until the election of John XXII at Lyon on 7 August 1316, prevented any decision being taken. Bicknor was finally provided to the see on 20 August 1317, consecrated in Avignon five days later, and secured the restoration of the temporalities on 9 September 1317.[58] Much of his subsequent career was to be dogged by financial problems, the first of these being his failure to discharge to the papal curia the debts arising from his provision to the see.[59] Meanwhile having been appointed justiciar in Ireland in 1318 he came to Dublin on Crown business and was duly enthroned in his cathedral. Soon after he set to work to establish a university in Dublin in accordance with the papal authorization.[60] Since the original papal grant had been made, the projected university was hindered by the substantial damage

[56] Hand, 'Rivalry of the Cathedral Chapters', 205.

[57] Rymer's *Foedera*, II. i. 241; CPR 1313–17, 79.

[58] CPR 1317–21, 18.

[59] On 13 March 1333 John XXII described Bicknor to the bishop of Winchester as excommunicate, *Reg. Vat.* 97, fol. 100^{v}, *CPL* 1305–42, 326.

[60] Appointed on 11 August and granted royal protection on 16 August for his journey to Ireland, by 15 March 1319 he had been relieved of his office as justiciar, CPR 1317–21, 196, 199, 317.

done by the Bruce invasion and its aftermath, which underlined the divisions in Irish society and ensured that a university centred on St. Patrick's in Dublin would primarily serve the interests of the Anglo-Irish lordship and not the theological and legal education of the Irish clergy as a whole. Whether or not the university collapsed through lack of provision for students, as claimed by Ware,[61] or whether it was so closely identified with Bicknor – who was certainly the master-mind behind the project – that it flourished or faded with the archbishop's fortunes, cannot be established, but the latter seems the more probable explanation, and Bicknor's fortunes were to be turbulent for the remaining thirty years of his life. Having undertaken several, not particularly successful missions to France on behalf of Edward II, he became involved in a plot to overthrow the Despensers, with the result that on May 1325 the king petitioned the pope to have Bicknor translated elsewhere, giving as his reasons both this bitter enmity towards his minister and his belief that Bicknor was misusing the revenues of the see of Dublin. Bicknor's subsequent allegiance to the party of Queen Isabella and the young prince Edward, as much as the alleged mismanagement of Crown (and ecclesiastical) revenues in Ireland, may have been the real reason for the seizure of the revenues of the see of Dublin into the hands of Edward II's agents, ostensibly in order to ensure the settlement of debts arising out of mismanagement while Bicknor held office in Ireland. However, the fall of Edward II and accession of his son appears to have helped Bicknor at least temporarily, as the young king did not immediately drop his former supporters and even went so far as to support Bicknor in a case of particularly dubious legality against the Franciscan bishop of Ossory.[62] But this return to royal favour did not last long and at the end of a chequered career in the crown service, when Bicknor finally retired as treasurer of Ireland, he was obliged to seek a royal pardon for the various deceptions which he had practised during his tenure of office, when he had clearly made false returns and been guilty of other financial peculations.[63]

The quarrel with Ledred of Ossory was a peculiarly tangled problem, dating back at least to 1320, when on 12 August John

[61] Ware, *De Praesulibus Hiberniae*, p. 112.

[62] Colledge, *Richard Ledred*, pp. xxviii–xxix.

[63] By 14 March 1326 the problem of embezzled funds during his term of office as treasurer in Ireland had come to light, CPR 1324–27, 250.

XXII issued orders to Bicknor that neither Ledred nor the property of his see be molested and to the Irish justiciar, demanding that due reparation be made to the bishop who had been falsely accused, molested by royal officials, deprived of his legitimate income, made the victim of robbery with violence, and thrown into prison with common criminals, while three of his servants were attacked in the town of Kilkenny and severely maltreated.[64] At this stage there is no indication that the matter at issue concerned the heresy trials in the diocese of Ossory, above all that of the celebrated Alice Kyteler, which appears to have reached serious proportions only *c.*1324, and the original dispute may have concerned simply the temporalities of the see of Ossory. By 1324, however, the heresy problem had become acute, and the Kilkenny Franciscan Friar Clyn reported how his confrère and diocesan ordinary had on 2 July of that year heard, judged, and condemned as a heretic Dame Alice Kyteler on account of her soothsaying, witchcraft, offering of sacrifices to demons, and various other malpractices. The trial had taken place in the presence of the Irish justiciar, Thomas Darcy, the chancellor of Ireland and prior of the Knights Hospitallers at Kilmainham, Roger Outlawe, who was a relative of the accused and other members of whose family were involved in the process, while the seneschal of Kilkenny, Arnold le Poer, was also involved.[65] Clyn went on to report that on 2 November 1324 a certain Petronilla of Meath, said to be a follower of Alice's sect and teachings, was condemned on charges of heresy, witchcraft, and sacrificial offerings, and publicly burned – the only such case recorded in medieval Ireland, as Friar Clyn was also able to report.[66] If the bishop's intention had been to make an example of Petronilla he certainly succeeded, as on 20 January 1325 Dame Alice's son William Outlawe formally abrogated his own heresy before the bishop in Kilkenny Cathedral. From an account of the proceedings compiled, it would appear, on the bishop's behalf,[67] we learn that he had made a visitation of his diocese and discovered numerous witches and sorcerers in Kilkenny. Upon further investigation he located the centre of this activity in the wealthy and well-connected Dame Alice,

[64] *Reg. Vat.* 70, fols. 613^{v}–614^{r}, *CPL* 1305–42, 206–7.

[65] Clyn, *Annals of Ireland*, p. 16.

[66] Ibid., pp. 16–17. For a clear account of the proceedings and of Ledred's role see Colledge, *Richard Ledred*, pp. xix–xxiii.

[67] Ed. Thomas Wright, *Proceedings against Dame Alice Kytler for Sorcery in 1324* (Camden Society, 24, London, 1843).

whose four husbands had been disposed of in mysterious circumstances, whereupon the children of these four victims – with the exception of the son by her first husband, also named William Outlawe, who was clearly her ally in her various undertakings – decided to take action against her. The bishop applied to the Irish chancellor for a writ of arrest, but as this was a family matter his application was blocked until Dame Alice was safely out of his jurisdiction. In the meantime the seneschal of Kilkenny had the bishop imprisoned in Kilkenny Castle, but after seventeen days had to release him in default of a charge against him.[68] The bishop's persistent efforts to initiate a heresy-hunt failed, according to the chronicler of these events, for a reason which well illustrates the complexities of the 'two nations' in the Anglo-Irish lordship: Anglo-Norman settler families such as le Poer raised violent protest, in the courts and in the Dublin Parliament, against the ignorance of the 'low-class beggar' from England who dared to accuse of heresy the inhabitants of the island of saints![69]

Although the contemporary narrative indicated that the nest of heresy in Kilkenny was disbanded and its members scattered, either through punishment or exile, and although Edward III would try to take the heat out of the situation by summoning Ledred to England, the matter was far from over and the bishop eventually appealed to the pope and set out for Avignon. During his absence Archbishop Bicknor undertook a visitation of the diocese of Ossory and confiscated the revenues of the see, whereupon Benedict XII sought the intervention of the king on Ledred's behalf, and at the same time exhorted Edward III to have the resources of the secular arm used to aid Bishop Ledred and any other Irish prelates who might be struggling to deal with heretics. At the same time Benedict wrote to the bishops of Ferns and Lismore, ordering them to defend their brother-bishop of Ossory against those prelates and nobles who had seized his property and if necessary to seek the aid of the secular arm,[70] but otherwise no action appears to have been taken until the next pontificate. On 29 June 1343 Clement VI ordered the

[68] Ibid., pp. 8–9. Ledred protested about this treatment to John XXII, who ordered the justiciar in Dublin 12 August 1320 that reparations be made to the bishop for injuries done to him and to members of his household, and arising out of false accusations, as n. 64.

[69] Le Poer addressed him as 'ille vilis rusticus trutannus de Anglia', Wright, *Proceedings*, p. 14.

[70] *Reg. Vat.* 119, fols. 338^{r}, 361^{r}; *CPL* 520, 521–2.

archbishops David O'Hiraghty of Armagh and John O'Grada of Cashel to summon Bicknor to their presence to answer the complaints of Ledred, especially because the Dublin metropolitan was alleged to be harbouring heretics, in particular Robert Couton, and hindering the due process of the ecclesiastical law by obstructing Ledred's appeal to the pope.[71] But these measures also remained ineffective, and Ledred came in person to Avignon. In a series of bulls issued on 9-11 April 1347, Clement made another attempt to settle the matter, presumably on the basis of the more detailed information which the plaintiff provided in person, as these papal documents contain considerable information concerning the course of the strife in Ireland. Bicknor had defended the suspected heretic Robert Couton, forcing Ledred to release him from prison, and then cited the bishop of Ossory to appear before his metropolitan court in Dublin. Ledred, realizing that Dublin was not a safe place for him appealed to the pope, but found that the ports were guarded to prevent his departure by order of the archbishop and the justiciar.[72] He further complained that Bicknor had used the pretext of his metropolitan visitation of the diocese to engage in financial extortion, exacting double procurations to the detriment of the bishop; that for the past twenty years Bicknor had disregarded all ecclesiastical sentences, and for fifteen had been harbouring heretics. Cardinal Bernard d'Alby, the same cardinal who was presiding over the Armenian debates, had been commissioned to conduct an investigation of the entire matter, Bicknor had been summoned to appear before him but had failed to do so.

When this inquiry was initiated is unclear, but it must have been after Cardinal d'Alby entered the curia on 2 August 1339, yet it may be no coincidence that both FitzRalph and the Carmelite Ralph O'Kelly were resident at the curia until respectively the late summer of 1344 and early in 1346, and may have been consulted on an internal Irish affair which was being brought repeatedly to the attention of the curia. Clement VI's group of bulls of 9-11 April 1347 included a provisional absolution from sentence of excommunication for Ledred and a decree

[71] *Reg. Vat.* 162, fol. 58^{v}; *CPL* 1342-62, 136. Roger Sampford was still at the curia and may have been employed to expedite matters such as this concerning the Irish Church. There is no record of a proctor for Ledred before his arrival in person at the curia.

[72] On 18 August 1346 Ledred is described as present in Avignon, *Reg. Suppl.* 11, fol. 139^{V}; *CPL Petitions* I, 115.

annulling whatever had been done by Bicknor to the detriment of the bishop and diocese of Ossory, and placing Ledred together with his city and diocese under the direct authority and protection of the papacy, thereby suspending the metropolitan powers of the archbishop of Dublin over Ossory, its bishop, and inhabitants.[73] The pope also sent on 10 April a mandate to Archbishop Ralph O'Kelly of Cashel and the archbishop-elect of Armagh: they were to investigate the truth of Ledred's complaints, proceed as they saw fit against Bicknor, and, if necessary, to resort to the secular arm.[74]

News of this commission must have reached FitzRalph while he was still in England making arrangements for his episcopal coronation in Exeter, and it is doubtful if he could act on such a delicate matter through his agents in Ireland, both of whom were apparently laymen. But soon after on 4 July 1347 the pope wrote to Edward III, exhorting him to compel the justiciar and government in Dublin to restore the property of the see of Ossory,[75] and the friction between Ledred and Bicknor appears to have died down, or to have been terminated by Bicknor's death, without having required any substantial intervention on FitzRalph's part. Bicknor's successor as archbishop of Dublin was concerned to restore the authority of his see which had been dissipated in this long struggle and, in response to his petition Clement VI issued on 12 July 1351 a mandate to the new archbishop to take over the process which had been initiated by the archbishops of Armagh and Cashel, and to pursue the case to a conclusion, no appeal to the papacy being permitted.[76]

The position of the metropolitan of Dublin after the long years of misrule of Bicknor was a dubious one. A papal commission issued to FitzRalph on 29 September 1347[77] would seem to indicate that the papal deprivation of Bicknor's metropolitan jurisdiction was not limited to that which he might exercise over the suffragan bishopric of Ossory but was also intended to

[73] *Reg. Vat.* 174, fol. 364^{v}, *Reg. Vat.* 176, fol. 216^{r}; *CPL* 226 (9 April), 231 (11 April).

[74] *Reg. Vat.* 174, fol. 433^{v}; *CPL* 227. A similar mandate was issued the following day to the two archbishops, announcing details of the case and the intervention of Cardinal Bernard d'Alby, *Reg. Vat.* 176, fol. 212^{r-v}, *CPL* 231–2.

[75] *Reg. Vat.* 180, fol. 320^{v}; *CPL* 253. This letter was issued 1347 not 1348, Colledge, *Richard Ledred*, p. xxix.

[76] *Reg. Suppl.* 23, fol. 63^{r}; *CPL Petitions* I, 216. Shortly before on 22 June the pope revoked the exemption of Ossory from the jurisdiction of the archbishop of Dublin, *Reg. Vat.* 211, fol. 250^{v}; *CPL* 461.

[77] *Reg. Vat.* 184, fol. 165^{v}; *CPL* 264.

apply to the see of Dublin itself. Otherwise it is difficult to explain why the archbishop of Armagh should be deputed to receive the resignation of Nicholas Allen, abbot of the Augustinian canons of St. Thomas the Martyr in Dublin, when the latter decided to resign in return for an annual pension for life – a resignation which in any case did not take effect.[78] But this commission might also be interpreted as papal recognition that the title 'primas Hibernie' included in FitzRalph's bull of appointment was intended to embrace jurisdiction over all four ecclesiastical provinces in Ireland, even to the extent of interfering within the boundaries of the see of Dublin. It is certain that FitzRalph, before leaving for Ireland, engaged in negotiations with the government in London on the question of the primacy, above all concerning the right of the primate to have his cross carried publicly before him everywhere in Ireland, even within the precincts of Dublin. The attempts of fourteenth-century predecessors to assert this right had resulted in brawls in the streets of Dublin which were scarcely in keeping with the dignity of the primatial office, with the result that they tended to withdraw from public appearances in the area and sought dispensations from personal attendance at Parliament. But FitzRalph was adamant in his insistence on the primatial rights of his see, for which he had clearly documented papal support, and on 5 April 1348 Edward III issued a mandate which amounted to a complete admission of the archbishop's claims: the justiciar and other Crown officials in the Irish lordship were to ensure that the archbishop of Armagh would not be hindered or molested when having his cross carried before him in any part of Ireland, whether he was travelling by horse or on foot, because such was his right by virtue of his primacy and such a privilege had been expressly granted to him by the papacy.[79] But whereas this mandate, and several other royal pronouncements dating from the early stages of FitzRalph's episcopate indicate that he stood at least temporarily in royal

[78] On the same day he was granted the customary faculty to choose a confessor and plenary indulgence at the hour of death, *Reg. Vat.* 184, fol. 310^{r}; *CPL* 272. But he recovered from his illness sufficiently to travel to the curia six years later, where he was provided to the see of Meath on 9 January 1353 and consecrated bishop by Cardinal Pierre Després on 31 January, *Reg. Vat.* 219, fol. 52^{r}, *Reg. Vat.* 222, fol. 305^{v}; *CPL* 475, 488. The consecrating prelate was the papal vice-chancellor in whose presence FitzRalph preached several times. Did he influence this choice of a suffragan in the only diocese within his province in which he was able to exercise full metropolitan jurisdiction?

[79] CPR 1348–50, 105.

favour in this respect, such a situation was partly due to the extremely low ebb of Bicknor's fortunes in the last years of his life, and would not survive unchallenged under the next archbishop.

Within two months of Bicknor's death the situation had changed. The chapter elected the trusted royal agent, John of St. Paul, who the following year would become chancellor of Ireland and among whose impressive collection of benefices was included a canonry of St. Patrick's Cathedral in Dublin; by 4 September 1349 he had secured from Clement VI in a similar procedure to that of FitzRalph's in the case of Armagh the transformation of his election into a papal provision, the see having been reserved to the papacy during the lifetime of Alexander de Bicknor.[80] The new archbishop was a contender for the primacy of a different calibre from Bicknor, and the temporalities were restored to him on 16 December 1349 although his episcopal consecration cannot have taken place until after 8 May 1350[81] while he was still in England. Having discovered that the revenues of his see had suffered considerably from the ravages of Gaelic Irish raiding parties and the high mortality rate in the area, presumably partly as a result of the Black Death as well as the local level of violence, he petitioned the pope and duly received, on 19 March 1352, permission to hold three or more other benefices as should prove necessary to supplement his income and make up for this deficiency.[82] However, it seems indisputable that the first problem to which the new archbishop-elect gave his attention was that of the primacy, or at least the right of the primate to exercise any jurisdiction within the metropolitan province of Dublin. Edward III issued an edict concerning it on 20 November 1349, revoking the letters previously conferred upon FitzRalph permitting him to have his primatial cross carried before him within the territories of Dublin, on the grounds that the king had recently been better informed concerning the basis of the claims of the see of Dublin and was convinced of their justice.[83] Who would

[80] *Reg. Vat.* 192, fol. 41ʳ; *CPL* 312.

[81] On 8 May 1350 Clement VI addressed him as 'archbishop-elect' when reducing his obligations concerning *ad limina* visits, *Reg. Vat.* 194, fol. 416ʳ, and permitting him to retain the fruits of his previous benefices until the Michaelmas following his consecration, ibid., fol. 416ᵛ; *CPL* 335.

[82] *Reg. Vat.* 208, fol. 102ᵛ; *CPL* 432. John of St. Paul clearly undertook a general reorganization: 10 December 1350 Edward III ordered the justiciar and escheator in Ireland to ensure that all alienations of cathedral property made by Bicknor without royal consent were to be revoked, *Archbishop Alen's Register*, pp. 206–7.

[83] CPR 1348–50, 426.

have been in a better position than the new archbishop-elect to influence the king in favour of Dublin's claims? The king's letter went on to suggest that the former decision in favour of the see of Armagh had been secured under false pretences, with the result that the rights of the see of Dublin were grievously impaired, and there was a further danger of armed violence together with other breaches of the peace. Here the king was clearly referring to the efforts of FitzRalph to exert his primatial authority in Dublin during the first year of his active duty in Ireland, which had led to considerable strife and were scarcely in accord with the king's intentions, especially when one considers that the king had on 12 August 1348 envisaged FitzRalph in the role of peacemaker between Edward's loyal subjects in the Anglo-Irish lordship and the native Irish. On that date the king and his Council issued an order, empowering the archbishop of Armagh, together with any available sheriffs, to make peace with those of either race, English or Irish, and throughout the land, who were in opposition to the king and his faithful subjects – a commission which was in effect *plein pouvoir* to negotiate peace settlements in the king's name among the two nations in medieval Ireland.[84]

However, FitzRalph's attempts to defend the Armagh primacy in Dublin during the spring of 1349 may have caused Edward III to have second thoughts about the new archbishop as an instrument of peace and harmony. FitzRalph's visit to Dublin in the period between his last sermon in Drogheda on 25 March 1349 and the death of Bicknor on 14 July, a visit which most probably occurred in April or May, was apparently an attempt to execute the commission which he, together with the archbishop of Cashel, had received almost two years earlier from the pope, namely to investigate the case of the archbishop of Dublin as a harbourer of heretics. This mission on papal authority fell within the terms of the original papal bull guaranteeing the

[84] Ibid., 142. According to Simms, 'The Archbishops of Armagh and the O'Neills', 43–4, the archbishop of Armagh was *ex officio* 'appointed one of the keepers of the peace for County Louth. His mission among the Irish as he saw it was "the exhorting and soliciting them to keep the peace of the king our sovereign lord / towards all his liege people" '. This statement of the primate's functions as seen through English government eyes is taken from 15th-century statutes (*Statutes of Ireland*, 1–12, Edward IV, 367; Henry VI, 207), but there is no reason to assume that either FitzRalph or the 14th-century governors of the English lordship thought differently. FitzRalph's involvement in peace negotiations was not unique. These were a regular feature of the primate's activity, and successive archbishops were present at almost every parley or treaty between English and Irish of the region, Simms, 43.

independence of the see of Dublin from the jurisdiction of Armagh, namely that of Lucius III to John Comyn in 1182 which had contained the saving clause 'nisi per Romanum pontificem vel legatum eius eidem fuerit iniunctum'.[85] FitzRalph was visiting Dublin as legate of the pope, but the account of the events that followed contained in the register of Archbishop Octaviano de Palatio (1478–1513), and which is clearly copied from a document contemporary with the events it described, indicates that he intended to use the occasion to establish the unqualified authority of the archbishop of Armagh as 'primas Hibernie' – as a genuine primacy of jurisdiction and not merely one of honour among the four archbishops.[86] It begins with an account of the royal privilege to FitzRalph as archbishop of Armagh and primate of Ireland concerning his primatial cross, and of Edward III's letters to the magnates of the Irish lordship instructing them to assist FitzRalph in the prosecution of these primatial rights. Whereupon FitzRalph duly visited Dublin, entering the city and processing through it with his cross carried before him until he reached the lodgings in which he resided for three days. During his stay he made a public demonstration of his claims, by having read the privileges of the see of Armagh and the papal bulls guaranteeing its primacy in the presence of the justiciar, Walter de Bermingham, the prior of the Knights Hospitallers at Kilmainham, John FitzRichard, and the Anglo-Irish magnates who happened to be present in Dublin at the time. Against all who opposed the claims of Armagh the archbishop threatened sentence of excommunication, but to no avail. The assembled officials and magnates refused to accept the claims of Armagh and, according to the source copied into the register, allowed themselves to be bribed by Bicknor to obstruct FitzRalph's endeavours, whereupon FitzRalph withdrew to his seat at Drogheda, from which comparative security he proclaimed them all excommunicate. Hence Bicknor had managed to enlist the support of Crown officials in Dublin in defence of his prerogatives in a manner which, if the Armagh source is to be trusted, can only have boded ill for FitzRalph's

[85] Sheehy, *Pontificia Hibernica*, i. 37.

[86] For Octaviano see Gwynn, *The Medieval Province of Armagh*, pp. 7–42. His register (like all other extant Armagh registers formerly in Armagh Public Library, now PRO Belfast) is not an episcopal register in the true sense. It is a large collection of loose documents bound together by Archbishop Ussher in the 17th century, and including items pertaining to the years 1460–1520 regardless of chronological order. There is no modern calendar.

future relations with the Dublin government and also with the king.

The narrative contained in the Armagh document provides a curious sequel to this episode. Within days of FitzRalph's departure from Dublin and excommunication of the opponents of his primacy, the prior of Kilmainham fell ill. The nature of his illness is not described more precisely in the source, but in view of the fact that the Black Death was still raging in the country, it is probable that he fell victim of the plague boils, in which case – given the general medieval respect accorded to the sentence of excommunication combined with the then prevailing state of panic and hysteria caused by the plague – FitzRalph's condemnation of the prior and his associates must have seemed appalling in its implications. A message was dispatched in all haste to the archbishop in Drogheda, assuring him that the prior was repentant and sought absolution, pledging both for himself and for his family that none of them would ever act in a manner detrimental to the interests of the primatial see of Armagh. But it was too late, the prior died of his illness 'through the miracles of St. Patrick', and would have been refused Christian burial had the archbishop not decided that he had shown true repentance and desire to make amends before his death. There is no reason to assume that the narrative in the Armagh register is a complete fiction, though it may have been 'doctored' by supporters of the campaign for FitzRalph's canonization. Hence the psychological implications of the episode, followed shortly after by the death of the archbishop of Dublin, must have been enormous and greatly to FitzRalph's advantage, whereupon the remainder of the prior's supporters, and by implication the supporters of Dublin's claim to the primacy, made their way to Drogheda, humbly sought, and duly received, absolution at the hands of the primate, the archbishop of Armagh.[87]

Although events of the following year were to show that as soon as the see of Dublin was filled by a royal servant more reliable than the wayward Bicknor had been, Armagh's primacy no longer found universal support in governmental circles, and a compromise solution had to be found during the pontificate of Innocent VI, the episode had other implications in the realm

[87] *Octavian's Register*, fol. 279^{r-v}. For Sir John FitzRichard see Charles McNeill (ed.), *Registrum de Kilmainham* (Dublin s.d.), *ad indicem*. The register contains no reference to the manner of his death, but his *Acta* are the last to be included in it. For the use made of the story by Peter Talbot, archbishop of Dublin 1669–80, in a later phase of the primatial dispute, see below, n. 103.

of Irish hagiography. This public assertion of the rights of the see of Armagh and invocation of St. Patrick in support of his claim resulted in a widespread assumption among the faithful of the archdiocese that the saint had miraculously intervened in defence of Armagh's primatial rights, and was further interpreted as a sign that FitzRalph was particularly favoured by the first incumbent of the see. Hence the episode survived in local memory and helped to build up the cult of 'St. Richard of Dundalk' which developed in the area as soon as the remains of the late archbishop were brought back to Dundalk a decade after his death. More practically, the clash in Dublin in the spring or early summer of 1349 indicated that, despite the royal ordinance of 5 April 1348, the entire problem required further clarification. Consequently FitzRalph set out once more for London and Avignon, after about sixteen months in his archdiocese and leaving behind scenes of despair and desolation, above all in the Anglo-Irish Pale where the plague had first appeared, moving from east to west and wiping out particularly large sections of the population in the towns of the eastern seaboard such as Dublin and Drogheda.[88] By now the Black Death had practically spent itself and FitzRalph's departure can scarcely be interpreted as the cowardice of a prelate abandoning his flock, as he had remained in the Dundalk-Drogheda area, based on his two episcopal manors of Dromiskin and Termonfechin, during the worst months of the previous winter, and the account he was to give in the *Proposicio* preached before Clement VI later in the summer of 1349 was based on genuine personal experience of the horrors which befell his flock.[89]

The absence of entries in his sermon diary during the period from May 1348 and September 1351, with a single exception in Ireland preached in the Carmelite church in Drogheda on 25 March 1349 (apart from the Avignon sermons which as we have seen do not form part of the diary proper) was a direct result of the plague conditions when public functions such as sermons were avoided. Hence we are deprived of this guide to his movements for the summer months of 1349 before he appeared in Avignon in August of that year. In view, however, of the fact that on 1 June 1349 Edward III issued a protection to him, as he was travelling to the papal curia with royal permission and

[88] Gwynn, *Studies*, 24 (1935), 25-42; Philip Ziegler, *The Black Death* (London, 1969), pp. 202-5.

[89] B, fols. 246^{v}-251^{v}; J, fols. 177vb-181rb.

on business affecting the state of Ireland, and directed that his church, retainers, and property in Ireland be protected from molestation by the king's officers there, he must have travelled from Ireland to the king's court before heading for Avignon. He got royal permission to be away for one year, as a week later he received letters nominating attorneys to represent him for that period,[90] and around this time he must have also received the royal commission to present Edward III's petition for the extension of the Jubilee indulgence to his kingdoms without the obligation of pilgrimage to Rome, a particularly hazardous undertaking for his subjects in view of the devastated conditions caused by the plague. The 'business' which was the principal cause of FitzRalph's visit to the curia was unquestionably that of the primacy, although he negotiated the state of diocesan finances and the outstanding debts with the papal Camera as well as gaining other concessions while he was there, and it is reasonable to assume that he may have discussed this matter with Edward III or his officials before leaving England some time after the beginning of June. If this hypothesis were true, the result of such a meeting was nevertheless not sufficiently favourable – despite the sign of royal favour indicated by the commission to Clement VI – to prevent the revocation of his primatial rights by the English king in favour of those of Dublin later the same year. By the time this latter edict was issued on 20 November 1349, FitzRalph was in Avignon where, having completed the king's mission with (as it transpired) only partial success[91] and having presented the completed version of his *Summa de Questionibus Armenorum* to the pope, he remained in order to pursue both the question of the primacy and also the most recent cause which he had adopted, that of the secular parochial clergy against the pastoral privileges of the mendicant friars. The primatial issue was doubtless one of the pressing issues to which he referred in the sermon of 6 December 1349 preached in the presence of Clement VI who was, as the evidence of the papal registers indicate, favourably disposed towards the claims of Armagh as the primatial see.[92] Nevertheless, in view

[90] CPR 1348–50, 300, 302.

[91] Ibid. On 18 August 1349, around the time when FitzRalph preached his *Proposicio*, Clement VI issued bulls ordering all metropolitans, including Armagh, Dublin, Cashel, Tuam, Canterbury, York, and the Scottish bishops to publish the Jubilee indulgence in the usual manner, *Reg. Vat.* 192, fol. 1^{v}; *CPL* 311.

[92] In the bull of appointment Clement VI referred to FitzRalph as 'Ibernie primas', but accorded John of St. Paul no such title, *Reg. Vat.* 173, fol. 29^{r}, *Reg. Vat.* 192, fol. 41^{r}.

of his own severe criticism of absentee prelates in the past, FitzRalph felt obliged to justify his own absence from his diocese, and he did so with the argument from conscience discussed above. We may be sure that in his arguments at the curia he employed the claim that his flock regarded the primacy of the ancient see of St. Patrick, to whom they had a particular devotion, as a matter of major priority and that it fully warranted their pastor's personal presence at the papal curia! Furthermore, there is evidence that, as in the case of the other major problems raised by FitzRalph during his stay at Avignon in 1349-51, here also a papal commission was set up to examine the rival claims of Dublin and Armagh with regard to the primacy. Hence the need to await the outcome of its deliberations represented yet another reason for FitzRalph's continued presence at the curia.

He had originally received a royal licence to go to Avignon on 1 June 1349 and, in view of the permission to nominate attorneys to represent him at home for one year, this licence must have foreseen that he would be absent for such a period. However, the situation changed during the winter of 1349-50, most probably because of the new incumbent of the see of Dublin, and Edward III began to press for FitzRalph's return. Three letters issued by the king on 18 February 1350 reflect this new situation. The first was addressed to the cardinal of S. Anastasia and nephew of Clement VI, Audomer Roger, and it described FitzRalph as 'Archiepiscopus tamen Armachaniensis . . . primatem Hibernie se praetendens'.[93] In it the king defended the ancient metropolitan rights of the see of Dublin and drew the cardinal's attention to the fact that the archbishop-elect had sought and obtained a papal examination and confirmation of these metropolitan rights. It had meanwhile reached the king's ears that the cardinal of S. Anastasia had been appointed to examine the privileges of the see of Armagh, and Edward III called upon the cardinal to judge the matter in a manner which would both protect the rights of the archbishop of Dublin and restore peace in a land of violence and rebellion. A similar letter, but without the reference to a commission to examine Armagh's privileges, was sent on the same day to the papal vice-chancellor, Cardinal Pierre Desprès, urging his support for Dublin against possible encroachments by Armagh, while the third letter was addressed to FitzRalph himself. This letter contained an order

[93] Printed in Rymer's *Foedera*, III. i. 190.

to return to his diocese where his flock was suffering from raids and violence of various kinds, and reminded him that he would be better employed in looking after their interests than in the pursuit of privileges which were detrimental to peace and harmony in Ireland.[94]

Hence it would appear that by the time FitzRalph preached before Clement VI on 6 December 1349, or shortly afterwards, the papal nephew had been commissioned to investigate the question of the Irish primacy, especially the documentary evidence and including earlier papal bulls which FitzRalph had laid before the curia in support of the claims of Armagh. The cardinal of S. Anastasia had for a number of years an Irish chaplain, Charles Macheda, for whom he secured several benefices, though Macheda never managed to achieve a bishopric and after the death of his patron he disappeared from the papal registers. His patron appears, however, to have interested himself in the Irish Church and exercised something like the beginnings of a protectorate until his death on 1 December 1352, five days earlier than that of the pope to whom he owed his position.[95] At the same time the English king sought to rally influential curial opinion on the side of Dublin and against FitzRalph. The order to the archbishop to return to his diocese was doubtless motivated less by royal concern for the spiritual well-being of his Irish subjects than for FitzRalph's possible influence at Avignon with regard to the affairs of the 'ecclesia Hibernica'. However, FitzRalph sought and obtained an extension of his licence, and on 7 October 1350 he received permission to remain in Avignon until 2 February 1351, in order to complete the business of his diocese.[96] Meanwhile the king issued on 8 December 1350 letters to the justiciar of Ireland and his officials in Dublin, confirming his edict of 20 November 1349 in favour of the metropolitan rights of the see of Dublin, and ordering them to employ the full rigour of the law against those who persisted in upholding the primatial rights of Armagh within the ecclesiastical province of Dublin,[97] whose archbishop he had in the meantime appointed treasurer of Ireland.

Clement VI's attitude to the rival claims of Armagh and Dublin is made clear by a number of bulls issued to FitzRalph in the early months of 1351. These enabled the archbishop to resolve the conflict between Gaelic and canon law by means of mass

[94] Ibid., 190, 192.
[95] Eubel, *Hierarchia Catholica*, i². 18.
[96] CPR 1348–50, 478.
[97] Ibid., 1350–54, 30.

dispensations for matrimony and ordination to the priesthood, and to promulgate indulgences for those who visited his primatial cathedral on the feast of St. Patrick, as well as for those who contributed over the next ten years to the rebuilding of the cathedral.[98] Clearly FitzRalph had decided to follow the example of the bishops of Exeter and of Coventry and Lichfield, and intended to launch a programme for the restoration of the cathedral fabric in what, by contemporary English standards, must have been a neglected and not particularly imposing edifice. At the same time renewed emphasis on the unique position of his cathedral city, its links with St. Patrick, and the archbishop's own position as 'coarb' of Patrick must have helped impress upon pope and curia that FitzRalph's primatial claims had some justification in the traditions of the Irish Church. Unfortunately, none of the subsequent episcopal registers yield information about the progress of any building programme in Armagh, nor is there much indication that the cathedral was the object of many private benefactions, from either Gaelic or Anglo-Norman members of the archbishop's flock,[99] and it is possible that FitzRalph's attempt to use the cult of St. Patrick and of his see of Armagh in order to boost episcopal authority in the area did not meet with any tangible response among those who were not even prepared to pay their tithes.

In the context of the primatial issue, the most significant aspect of these papal letters was the form of address used. Whereas in the thirteenth century it had been customary to use the archbishop's primatial title, either 'primas Hibernie' or 'primas totius Hibernie', indiscriminately for a variety of letters on matters of secondary importance, under the Avignonese popes the use of the title in papal chancery documents was reserved for the bull of appointment and other solemn occasions.[100] It was rarely used in the normal papal dealings with prelates whose entitlement to such a form of address was unquestioned, but both John XXII and Clement VI made a point

[98] *Reg. Vat.* 201, fols. 135^{v}–136^{r}; *CPL* 387. The letters for Armagh were issued 10 April 1351.

[99] One of the few surviving records of a 14th-century benefaction to the Cathedral of Armagh is the will of Richard Tanner, citizen of Dundalk, 16 September 1335, *Dowdall Deeds*, p. 53. The primatial see did not fare well by comparison with the parish churches, mendicant communities, and hospitals in Drogheda and Dundalk.

[100] For numerous early examples see Sheehy, *Pontificia Hibernica, passim,* but nothing similar is available for the 14th century. These remarks have been worked out on the basis of discussions with Mgr. Hermann Hoberg, Vice-Prefect of the *Archivo Segreto Vaticano*, to whom I am grateful for advice.

of using it when appointing both O'Hiraghty and FitzRalph, and Clement continued to use it with reference to the latter during the primacy dispute, even in this group of bulls, which dealt with routine matters, as though the pope was deliberately emphasizing FitzRalph's primatial status on every occasion. Nevertheless, the eventual resolution of the matter has been the subject of some confusion. FitzRalph had to leave Avignon in the summer of 1351 before any decision was reached in the matter, and it is possible that English intervention prevented such a decision being taken before death removed both Clement VI and the cardinal of S. Anastasia from the scene early in December 1352.

On the basis of an entry in the register of John Alen, archbishop of Dublin from 1529 to 1534, when the problem of the Irish primacy was once more under consideration, it has recently been argued that a solution to the question was reached by Innocent VI, shortly after his election on 18 December 1352.[101] Such a solution apparently involved according to the archbishop of Armagh the title 'primas totius Hibernie' and the archbishop of Dublin that of 'primas Hibernie' – a distinction which survives to this day in the titles of the archbishops of Armagh and Dublin of both major denominations. However, such a decision does not survive in the extant registers of Innocent VI. Archbishop Alen nevertheless recorded that while he was in Rome as proctor of Archbishop William Warham of Canterbury (and his presence at the curia in this capacity can be documented in 1510-13),[102] he consulted the registers of Innocent VI in the pope's private library, concerning some cases which were still pending and in which he was representing the English primate. Here he discovered that Innocent VI, after consultation with some of the cardinals, had issued a decision that the archbishop of Armagh was to be 'primas totius Hibernie' and the archbishop of Dublin 'primas Hibernie' after the manner of the archbishops of Canterbury and York in England.[103] The original of this papal decision has never come to

[101] Watt, *The Church and the Two Nations*, p. 209.

[102] David S. Chambers, *Cardinal Bainbridge in the Court of Rome 1509 to 1514* (Oxford, 1965), p. 79.

[103] *Archbishop Alen's Register*, p. 217. This information was also used by the 17th-century archbishop of Dublin, Peter Talbot, in his *Primatus Dubliniensis, vel Summa rationum quibus innitur Ecclesia Dubliniensis in possessione, ac prosecutione sui Iuris ad Hiberniae Primatum* (Lille, 1674). For English trans. and commentary see W. E. Kenny, *Primatus Dubliniensis* (Dublin, 1947).

light, nor was it recorded in any of the extant registers, though in view of the vicissitudes which the latter have suffered this is in itself not surprising. It may either not have found its way into a register during the pontificate of Innocent VI or it may have been one of the casualties when the registers were transferred from Paris back to Rome at the end of the Napoleonic era.[104] However, a more serious doubt as to this solution having ever been promulgated *as a papal decision* must be considered. If Innocent VI did in fact issue such a compromise decision, it might be expected that such distinctions in titles would be reflected in papal letters issued to these two prelates in subsequent years. But the reverse is in fact true, and whereas Innocent VI continued to refer to FitzRalph occasionally but not consistently as 'primas Hibernie', the archbishop of Dublin was never accorded in papal letters any primatial status, qualified or otherwise.[105] Furthermore, the parties concerned, and in particular FitzRalph's immediate successor in the see of Armagh, Milo Sweteman (1361-80), were not aware that any such decision had been taken, and the latter regarded the matter as still *sub iudice* at the papal curia in a letter which he wrote to Edward III on 27 September 1366.[106]

Archbishop Alen's remarks about the judgement of Innocent VI were made in the form of editorial comment on documents which he had copied into his register, the *Liber Niger Alani*, and his comments on several documents reflect his own interest in the validity of the claim of Dublin to the title Primate of Ireland.[107] His exposition of Innocent VI's alleged views with regard to the analogy of the Irish situation with that of Canterbury and York was appended to a brief injunction from Edward III to the sheriff of Dublin concerning the primacy on 3 October 1366.[108] Here the king stated that as the archbishops of Armagh and Dublin each asserted the right to have his cross carried before him in the other's province, the king had tried to persuade

[104] See Remigius Ritzler, 'Die Verschleppung der päpstlichen Archive nach Paris unter Napoleon I. und deren Rückführung nach Rom in den Jahren 1815 bis 1817', *Römische Historische Mitteilungen*, 6-7 (1962-4), 144-90.

[105] e.g. on 5 April 1354 Innocent VI issued letters conservatory for the archbishop of Armagh to the dean, archdeacon, and chancellor of Kildare. Although the subject matter of the bull had no connection with the primatial dispute FitzRalph was described as 'primas Hibernie', *Reg. Vat.* 226, fol. 149^{r}.

[106] *Cal. Reg. Sweteman*, 224.

[107] *Archbishop Alen's Register*, pp. 248, 272, 274, 286. He claimed (p. 217) that his own bull of appointment from Clement VII contained the title 'primate of Ireland', but there is no such document in his register.

[108] Ibid., p. 216.

them to accept this solution as a compromise. His plea having failed, he summoned them to appear before him in England, but this they also refused to do. The archbishop of Dublin, Thomas Minot (1363–75), who was more accessible to the Dublin government, was therefore to be summoned to answer to the justiciar for his conduct, but Milo Sweteman of Armagh was clearly not as biddable.

The register of Archbishop Sweteman, which frequently provides additional information for the pontificate of his immediate predecessor, has a more detailed account of the episode. Describing himself as chaplain to the king, Sweteman wrote to Edward III on 26 September of the same year. He insisted that, having received the royal injunction, he journeyed to the border of his ecclesiastical province on two separate occasions, 17 and 24 September, in order to negotiate the matter with the archbishop of Dublin. The latter did not turn up on either occasion, but on 24 September his proctors appeared, insisting that the archbishop of Armagh was obliged to obey the king's mandate in all things, and specifically with regard to the mutual recognition of the right to carry the primatial cross.[109] Sweteman's explanation of the reasons why he could not accept this compromise solution was based on the privileged position of the see of Armagh, which had been confirmed by numerous grants from the papacy and from the English Crown, but the most important reason he gave for refusing was that the case which the archbishop of Armagh had brought many years before to the Roman curia concerning the matter was still pending. Sweteman's statement does, however, imply that the question of a possible analogy with the Canterbury-York situation was actually one of the points at issue in the case which had been brought before the papal court, and his reference to the fact that these proceedings had been brought many years before indicates that the case to which he is referring is that initiated by FitzRalph in or soon after 1350. The tenor of this letter therefore confirms the impression that the document which John Alen saw in Rome – and there is no good reason for doubting his testimony – was not a papal decision which had been registered and dispatched. What Alen is more likely to have seen is an entry in a volume of minutes or rescripts pertaining the cases which were still *sub iudice*, or in which no decision was ever reached, which simply tailed off because of

[109] *Cal. Reg. Sweteman*, 224–5.

death or lack of funds of the parties concerned. This happened in FitzRalph's celebrated case against the mendicant orders, and it is not inconceivable that it also happened in his suit against the archbishop of Dublin over the primacy. If this were so, then the document seen by Alen would never have reached the interested parties in Ireland, because it was merely a working instrument in a case which had never been formally brought to a conclusion. But it has more than passing significance as an indication of a shift in papal thinking with regard to a burning question in the Irish Church, and it would be used as a guideline by Counter-Reformation archbishops of Dublin with experience in the ways of the Roman curia. With regard to the primacy, as in other respects, Innocent VI did not share the views of his predecessor.

Meanwhile Edward III took precautions to ensure that the capital of the Irish lordship should no longer be the scene of clashes between FitzRalph and the retainers of the archbishop of Dublin over the primatial question. On 8 December 1350 he sent a mandate to the justiciar, chancellor, and treasurer of Ireland ordering them to prevent the formation of assemblies of armed men to maintain by force the bearing of the primatial cross of the archbishop of Armagh within the city and province of Dublin.[110] A year later, after FitzRalph had returned to Ireland, the king revoked once more his primatial rights within the see of Dublin on practical and legal grounds – they were the cause of disturbances and they violated the bull granted by Innocent III to Archbishop Henry of London (18 May 1216).[111] The following year, on 12 September 1352, the matter came up once more, and the king issued documents to FitzRalph permitting him to be represented through a proctor when summoned to councils and parliaments, as the situation did not permit him to enter the city of Dublin for such purposes with his cross borne before him without risk of molestation.[112] Such a situation had been avoided on account of FitzRalph's absence in Avignon on previous occasions, when the justiciar, Sir Thomas Rokeby, had summoned a great council to Kilkenny in 1350. FitzRalph had just returned to Ireland when a further meeting of the great council took place on 17 October 1351 in Dublin

[110] CPR 1350–54, 30.

[111] On 7 December 1351, *Archbishop Alen's Register*, pp. 207–8. The bull was not issued by Honorius III as the king claimed, see Sheehy, *Pontificia Hibernica*, i. 176–9.

[112] CPR 1350–54, 323, 375.

and on 31 October in Kilkenny, but he would presumably have been expected to attend the Parliament summoned to Dublin in 1353.[113]

Whether he attended this Parliament is not recorded, but he certainly exerted his primatial rights in the Dublin area during the earlier months of 1353, as a royal mandate of 12 May complained that the archbishop of Armagh was still having his cross carried in Dublin, conducting visitations, exercising primatial jurisdiction, and insisting upon bringing the king's faithful subjects for examination in the courts of the church of Armagh, innovations which the king now ordered should cease.[114] From this royal pronouncement it would appear that FitzRalph was indeed assuming unprecedented prerogatives, both by extending his visitations beyond the diocese of Meath – which lay within the Anglo-Norman lordship, but also belonged to his ecclesiastical province of Armagh – into that of Dublin, and also by attempting to extend the juridical competence of the courts of Armagh to cover cases pertaining to other provinces. His attempts to enlarge the number of lawyers and notaries available in his province may be linked with these developments. Collectively these measures illustrate the ambivalent role of the English king in the Irish primacy dispute. Edward III was personally inclined to support the prerogatives of the see of Dublin, possibly both because its incumbent at the time was a loyal servant of the Crown, and also to ensure that the centre of authority in the Irish Church coincided with that of the lordship. Nevertheless, the king was prepared to adopt measures designed to avoid direct confrontation and, while he was not prepared to allow FitzRalph to adopt a provocative stance in Dublin, he did not attempt to forbid the exercise of his primatial rights elsewhere.

ii. The Black Death in Ireland

The great crisis of the mid-fourteenth century, the bubonic plague which spread from the Middle East across Europe in 1348–9, presented – in addition to the social, economic, and demographic problems – a pastoral problem of unprecedented dimensions. It reached the southern ports of England around 24 June 1348, the feast of St. John the Baptist, and having virtually annihilated the densely populated city of Bristol, it

[113] H. G. Richardson and G. O. Sayles, *The Irish Parliament in the Middle Ages* (Philadelphia, 1964²), p. 239.
[114] *Archbishop Alen's Register*, p. 208.

moved westward across the Irish Sea. Although there are some minor variations of opinion concerning which port should be accorded the doubtful honour of having first received the plague in Ireland, most accounts are in general agreement that it – as might be expected – first hit the Anglo-Norman towns of the eastern seaboard, above all, Drogheda and Dublin. It can be tentatively accepted that the first town seriously affected was Drogheda, and that almost simultaneously the plague appeared in Howth and Dalkey, from where it soon overran the capital of the English lordship in Dublin.[1] The sparse account in the Irish annals, which in each case amounts to no more than a brief entry under the year 1349, consists of the single sentence that a great pestilence, which overran Ireland, appeared at Moy Lurg and a large number of people died from it.[2] Its presence in four annals, in virtually the same form with a purely local reference to Moy Lurg in County Roscommon, suggests a common source, and a statement which was originally local in its application appears to have been generalized by its transcription into other annals. However, the sparseness of this description in the Gaelic Irish sources, by comparison with the chroniclers, above all Franciscans, living and working in the towns of the Anglo-Irish lordship who presented a harrowing picture of the disaster,[3] may have a further significance. In the first place it would appear to lend support to the contention of FitzRalph, expressed in his *Proposicio* before Clement VI concerning the extension of the Jubilee indulgence, that the Anglo-Irish colonists were much more severely affected by the plague than were the Gaelic Irish – a claim which in view of the heavy concentration of the Anglo-Norman population in or near the towns, whose standards of hygiene and sanitation encouraged plague-bearing rats to breed, as opposed to the more rural way of life of the Gaelic population, is far from improbable.[4]

[1] Gwynn, *Studies*, 24, 25–9; Otway-Ruthven, *Medieval Ireland*, pp. 267–70.

[2] *Annals of Ulster*, ed. Bartholomew MacCarthy (Dublin, 1893), ii. 491; *Annals of Loch Cé*, ed. William M. Hennessy (RS, London, 1871), ii. 3; *Annals of the Four Masters*, ed. John O'Donovan (Dublin, 1848), iii. 595; *Annals of Clonmacnoise*, ed. Denis Murphy (Dublin, 1896), p. 297.

[3] Clyn, *Annals of Ireland*, pp. 35–8.

[4] There is no modern published study of the Black Death in Ireland, but see Maria O'Kelly, 'The Black Death in Ireland (1348)', unpublished MA thesis, University College, Cork, 1973; also on the 14th-century social and economic history of the Anglo-Norman colony see Kevin Down, in *New History of Ireland*, ii (forthcoming). The population of Ireland before the plague was estimated at *c.*800,000, and the reduction of the population of the colony as a result of the plague at *c.*40–50%.

The most detailed account of the Black Death and its effects in Ireland by a contemporary witness is that of the Kilkenny Franciscan, Friar Clyn, himself apparently a victim in the later stages of the epidemic.[5] He reported that the cities of Drogheda and Dublin were virtually denuded of their population within weeks of the plague's first appearance, adding the detail that in Dublin alone some 14,000 people died between August and Christmas 1348. His account of the nature and symptoms of the plague correspond closely with evidence from other parts of Europe, and he conveyed vividly the atmosphere of fear, revulsion, and despair which prevailed in towns such as Dublin, Drogheda, and his native Kilkenny during the worst months of the pestilence. His description, the solemn testimony included in his account, and the abrupt manner in which his chronicle broke off in the early months of 1349 – most probably because he had fallen victim of the horror which he had described with such compassion – are sufficiently well known not to require further repetition here. However, several passages of his description are of special interest in the context both of the severe pastoral problem which faced the new 'primas Hibernie' and his fellow bishops, and of the bitter opposition to the friars' pastoral work which that primate was to express so soon afterwards.

Friar Clyn reported that fear and horror were so great that few were brave enough to perform works of piety and mercy such as visiting the sick and burying the dead, while the plague was so contagious and swift in its effects that confessor and penitent were often brought to the same grave. He further reported that by Christmas 1348 twenty-five members of the Franciscan community in Drogheda had died, while the same fate befell twenty-three of their confrères in Dublin. Nor was he unduly chauvinistic – he did not ignore Dominican deaths in similar circumstances. When the plague spread inland to Kilkenny, where it raged most severely during Lent of 1349, he recorded that by 6 March eight members of the Dominican community in his native city had also died.[6] Curiously enough he recorded no Franciscan deaths in Kilkenny – perhaps he was himself the first Franciscan victim? Even allowing for the fact that he was more likely to report deaths among his own confrères and fellow-citizens, it is not improbable that the friars may have suffered proportionally heavier losses than other

[5] See concluding section of his account, *Annals of Ireland*, p. 38.
[6] Ibid., pp. 35–7.

groups. The pastorally active mendicants, and above all the Franciscans, were favoured among the laity as confessors, and never more so than when certain death seemed at hand, so that Clyn's account, and even the spectacular losses recorded in the crowded towns of Drogheda and Dublin, do not seem incredible. Although it is impossible to establish figures, or even crude comparisons, for the respective death rates among the friars, with their heavily concentrated urban apostolate, and members of the secular clergy engaged in parochial work – the pages of the papal registers and the capitular decrees of the mendicant orders throughout Europe all tell a similar story of heavy losses and the need for speedy, even if inadequate replacement – the greater probability is nevertheless, that the higher over-all urban death rate combined with the friars' urban apostolate did result in substantially heavier losses on the part of the mendicant orders than among either cathedral clergy, cloistered monastic communities, or even parish curates in rural areas.[7] If this were indeed the case, one might have expected the friars' pastoral contribution to receive some praise rather than the annihilating criticism to which FitzRalph was to subject the friars, and above all the Franciscans, over the next decade.

Nor can FitzRalph have been unaware of what was happening. The plague had first appeared in Drogheda in August 1348, little more than four months after the new archbishop's arrival in the area, and the principal church of that thriving commercial city, the parish church of St. Peter, served as pro-cathedral for the part of the diocese which lay 'inter Anglos'. FitzRalph must have spent the winter months of 1348–9 in the vicinity, hardly in the small manse within the city walls of Drogheda where the primates tended to reside during sessions of a provincial council,[8] but more probably at one of his two episcopal manors, either Termonfechin just outside the city, or Dromiskin some fifteen miles to the north, where he and his household might have been a little better protected. Even there, however, they would have been as vulnerable as FitzRalph's friend Bradwardine was to be when he returned to England as archbishop of Canterbury the following summer.[9] However, we can only speculate on the extent of the losses in FitzRalph's immediate surroundings, though among the clergy of the diocese as a whole

[7] Ziegler, *The Black Death*, pp. 273–4; Knowles, *Religious Orders*, iii. 10–13.

[8] Gwynn, *Medieval Province of Armagh*, pp. 75–6 for this house and the attached property.

[9] *BRUO* I, 245.

they must have been fairly substantial. On his return to Avignon the archbishop petitioned the pope in what was an obvious attempt to increase the availability of priests in the diocese, and on 11 January 1351 he received permission to dispense forty men of illegitimate birth, and twenty sons of priests or married men, in order that they might be ordained and hold benefices.[10]

Such dispensations were a regular feature of Irish ecclesiastical relations with the papal curia in the later medieval period on account of the sharp divergence between the marriage laws of Gaelic Ireland and the canon law of the universal Church,[11] but numbers such as these were exceptional and were clearly intended to cope with a particularly desperate pastoral situation where communities had been deprived of their priest, or often of a succession of priests, during the worst months of the plague. It was a subject upon which FitzRalph was to comment in the course of two separate sermons in 1349 when, in that part of the country with which he was most familiar, the worst phase was over, though as we have seen in the case of the prior of Kilmainham, it continued to claim victims. However, the evidence of these two sermons, preached in very different circumstances and conveying, doubtless by intention, diverging impressions, is somewhat problematic.

The first of these cases marked the resumption of FitzRalph's preaching activity after a break of almost a year, caused no doubt by the avoidance of public gatherings such as medieval sermons tended to be, during the period when the plague was raging most severely. FitzRalph must have arrived in his archdiocese around Easter 1348 and, as has already been noted, engaged immediately in a brief preaching tour of the principal towns in the Anglo-Irish part of his territory. Notes for these sermons have survived in the diary, and we can trace his movements accurately from Dundalk, where he preached on the Thursday after Easter (24 April 1348), to Louth where he delivered a sermon on Low Sunday (27 April), two days later he preached in Ardee (29 April), and from there he proceeded to

[10] *Reg. Suppl.* 22, fol. 222r; *CPL Petitions* I, 207; *Reg. Vat.* 201, fol. 131v; *CPL* 387. For a similar group dispensation, though involving much smaller numbers, issued to Archbishop John O'Grada of Cashel (a member of a Gaelic clerical family which also availed of similar dispensations throughout the 14th century) *Reg. Vat.* 162, fols. 108v–109r; *CPL* 138.

[11] For Gaelic marriage customs and their effect on the enforcement of the canon law see Kenneth Nicholls, *Gaelic and Gaelicised Ireland in the Middle Ages* (Dublin, 1972), pp. 73–6, 91–9.

Drogheda the following Sunday (4 May) and a week later to Mansfieldstown (11 May).[12] With the exception of the first of these sermons, which was a repetition of that preached in London on 11 March 1347 on the topic of the Lord's Prayer, these notes are given in some detail. In the latter case the preacher justified his decision to repeat it with the argument that he had now returned to his own people, by which he presumably meant literally the citizens of Dundalk, and was imitating the example of Christ who taught this as the first prayer to the people of his own blood, the Jews.[13] Hence it seems reasonable to assume that this was indeed the first sermon preached by the new archbishop after his arrival in Ireland. It would be consistent with the suggestion that he had arrived around Easter and almost immediately set out to meet those of his flock who dwelt in the towns of the Pale. Although the notes to the other three sermons are detailed as regards the content, the topics discussed, and the arguments used, the fact of their being notes only, and not complete sermons, makes it difficult to glean from them more than a general impression of how FitzRalph approached his new flock, or how these might have reacted to him. The themes of these sermons are not exactly what one might have expected in the circumstances, being rather more in keeping with a series of Lenten sermons than as an introductory presentation by a new pastor. But it is possible that the archbishop had made up his mind that such topics — with an unwearying concentration on the necessity of baptism for salvation, on prayer, on temptation and the Devil, on sin and penance, reparation and restitution — were what his flock required. He even included, in anticipation of later treatment when he had become more familiar with the situation in his diocese, a general denunciation of usury. In the sermon at Mansfieldstown on 11 May 1348 on the text: 'Tristicia vestra vertetur in gaudium' (Ioh. xvi. 30), he employed the tripartite form which we have seen in some of his Avignon sermons, and dealt with the three elements in the biblical text separately, a pattern which enabled him to express in the section on 'vestra' a prohibition of usury in general terms: 'Dictum fuit quod nemo debet lucrum reportare, cum de alieno mercatur, set de suo unde lucrum iuste reportat.'[14] In sharp contrast to the next sermon preached in Ireland, almost a year later because

[12] B, fols. 42^{v}–45^{v}; J, fols. 34va–37vb.

[13] B, fol. 42^{v}; J, fol. 34^{va-b}.

[14] B, fol. 45^{v}; J, fol. 37ra.

of the plague and delivered in the Carmelite church in Drogheda on 25 March 1349, the notes for these initial sermons contain little that might be regarded as specifically applying to the Irish situation, but appear to have been general moral exhortations to unfamiliar audiences. However, the intervening year, with the horrors of the Black Death, brought the archbishop much closer to the people of the Anglo-Irish lordship, whereupon a totally new awareness of the existence of the 'two nations' and the problems these represented in the realms of social relations, moral theology, and pastoral care becomes evident in the archbishop's public utterances.

The sermon of 25 March 1349 further differed from most of FitzRalph's vernacular sermons in that it dealt with technical theological problems and has survived in the diary in a complete Latin form, as though it also was subsequently revised and included in the diary in order to be used on another occasion. It is also unexpected in its tone, when one considers that it was delivered to an audience consisting presumably of both friars and laity, who must have still been anxious and fearful about the plague which they had managed to escape, but it contains only a single almost perfunctory reference to the 'inundantem pestilenciam'.[15] The general theme of the sermon is, as might be expected in view of the feast-day being celebrated, a Marian one, and the preacher exhorted his hearers to put their trust in the Virgin Mary who would rescue them from their present troubles. By these he meant not only the plague, but a variety of other ills of Anglo-Irish society which he had apparently been studying at close quarters during the previous year, and which he reduced to two basic and related issues: the 'hominum abundantem malivolentiam' or general wickedness of men, and their ignorance, the latter being made particularly acute by the fact that they lived in a land far from any seat of learning which might lead them to wisdom and enlightenment. Such ills were apparently in FitzRalph's eyes no less damaging to the fabric of society than the physical illness of the plague. Both of these themes, ignorance and injustice, together with the need to combat them by means of intensive instruction for both clergy and laity alike, were to become something of a leitmotiv for the primate's work in Ireland over the next few years, and here he developed them for the first time in a manner which was much more stern than the general exhortations on sin, penance, and

[15] Ed. cit., p. 179.

restitution delivered during the previous spring.[16] In its central content this sermon was a development on that preached to the Carmelite community in Avignon more than six years earlier, and it contained a long theological discussion of the wide-ranging privileges granted by God to His Mother, including the Immaculate Conception which is here asserted with even greater conviction than on the earlier occasion, a change of emphasis which might reflect either greater conviction on the archbishop's part than at the beginning of the 1340s or simply the need for more clarity in the formulation of doctrine before a less sophisticated audience.[17]

However, the moral of the sermon was intensely practical and made little concession to the difficult situation in which his flock had found themselves during the previous months, when according to Friar Clyn's account, fear and revulsion had made many neglect their obligations in charity if not in justice.[18] Here FitzRalph discussed the sharp contrast between Christ's mother, who was preserved from all stain of sin, and the audience before him, many of whose faults he attributed to crass ignorance. However, he singled out two faults for special denunciation, and it would appear that he had identified them in the course of a year's close scrutiny of his flock and its *mores* – firstly, the civil war 'inter Anglicos et Hibernicos' and secondly, general theft and dishonesty. In the former case he pointed out to his hearers, most of whom we can presume were 'Anglici', that both rival communities in Ireland were under the impression that it was lawful not merely to rob and plunder those of the opposing community, but also to kill them, and he issued a stern warning that to kill was always gravely sinful except in self-defence.[19] Only an officer of the law, acting in accordance with the prescriptions of that law, had such power. Clearly Fitz-Ralph had begun to concern himself with these conflicts and had heard the excuse that such molestors, presumably in this case molestors of the Gaelic Irish population, were acting as the agents of the Crown and in accordance with the king's law, a

[16] Ibid., p. 183.

[17] Ibid., pp. 184–6. Presumably also for this reason references to theological authorities, a striking feature of the earlier sermon in Avignon, were here restricted to a single allusion to Anselm's *De conceptu virginali*, ch. 18, *MPL* 158, 451. He also referred back to his sermon on the Assumption preached in Lichfield Cathedral 15 August 1345, B, fols. 20^{r}–22^{r}; J, fols. 15va–17va.

[18] *Annals of Ireland*, p. 36.

[19] 25 March 1349, ed. cit., p. 183.

viewpoint which he now explicitly rejected and condemned as erroneous and punishable before God.

In the same vein as his rejection of injury to life and limb by private persons in the name of loyalty to the Crown, he also condemned injury to property on the same pretext: theft, rapine, and plunder were always sinful, according to FitzRalph, and the only adequate form of penitence for such a sin was proper and full restitution. This is a theme which he had frequently mentioned in his Avignon sermons, and he was to return to it again and again, sometimes in exhaustive detail, in the course of his work in Ireland. He was obviously capable of a shrewd appreciation of the manner in which racial dissension could be made the pretext for self-interest and greed, above all in the name of professed loyalty to the king and allegedly justifiable opposition to his unfaithful Irish rebels. These latter could, of course, in the context both of the Gaelic resurgence in the fourteenth century and the increasing independence of the marcher lords beyond the Anglo-Irish Pale, be given a wider definition according as the dictates of self-interest might require, and FitzRalph was careful to give no single group or interest a moral justification for violence and injustice.[20]

He displayed awareness of another and more subtle cause of unrest and dissension among the Irish communities when he turned his attention to the problem of those who could manipulate the law in order to secure for themselves advantages which, while not punishable under the terms of the civil law, were nevertheless morally reprehensible. The example he chose was land, that most sacred commodity in medieval as in modern Ireland, and he made it a vehicle for a discussion which touched upon the problem of dominion. Although he had not yet given expression to his elaborate theory of dominion, whereby all earthly lordship was founded upon God's grace to the individual soul with the inevitable consequence that the sinner was automatically deprived of his right to dominion in the eyes of God even if his rights were still recognized by the secular authority, the germ of its practical application was already visible in this discussion. Clearly FitzRalph had by now established

[20] Ibid. He expressed similar sentiments in Dundalk, 3 April 1356, fulminating against those who destroyed his peace efforts and took the law into their own hands on the grounds that they were acting according to the *lex marchie* of their forefathers, B, fol. 74^{r-v}; J, fol. 61vb.

to his own satisfaction the distinction between the legal rights enforceable in the courts and those which had a moral justification before God. Hence he warned his audience that a cause of grave sin which occurred frequently in their midst (and possibly with even greater frequency in a situation where widows and orphans might be left without legal protection following the plague) was when men seized hold of land or other goods belonging to their neighbour, on a legal pretext which might be valid 'per iudicium legis terrenae', yet a gross violation of the law of conscience and the law of God. These might argue that they had valid possession of this property under earthly law, whereupon FitzRalph raised an argument which he was subsequently to develop in *De Pauperie Salvatoris*, namely that while the civil courts could only judge on the apparent visible realities and therefore, for lack of information which by its very nature remained hidden, make a false judgement, nevertheless, 'falsum iudicium numquam transfert vere dominium'.[21] By doing so, FitzRalph developed a theory of dominion of the just which could never be put into practice, a divinely approved title with no validity before the civil law, a theory which in the final analysis must depend for its implementation on an almost Calvinistic doctrine of the elect and of the sovereignty of the individual conscience. Although FitzRalph was a vigorous exponent of the sovereign right of conscience and the concommitant duty of scrupulous examination which this involved, he was none the less too much a realist and too shrewd in his judgement of Irish problems not to recognize that the practical application of such a doctrine of dominion would reduce a society, which was already given to violence and to manipulation of the law in sectarian interests, to total anarchy.

The stern line taken in FitzRalph's first public sermon since the outbreak of the plague was indicative of the rigorously severe moral theologian, of whom we have already encountered several examples in the Avignon sermons, rather than the compassionate pastor, and as such it was not out of keeping with a widespread approach in fourteenth-century England, pessimistic concerning man's essentially sinful nature and anticipating the sombre, somewhat puritan theology of Wyclif and the Lollards, of whom at least the former looked with respect to FitzRalph as one of the two most formative influences in

[21] Ed. cit., pp. 182-3.

Oxford upon his intellectual and theological development.[22] However, in view of the totally different impression conveyed by FitzRalph in his next sermon, the question must be faced whether he did not strike this grim and stern note with deliberate intent. Behind his words all sorts of suggestions present themselves: did the outbreak of the Black Death and its presence with particularly virulent force among the citizens to whom he was preaching provide an even more effective opportunity for a relatively sophisticated merchant community to engage in plunder and extortion at the expense of the more helpless sections of the population such as widows, orphans, and minors deprived of their guardians? Was there something like a general breakdown of the rule of law even in the Anglo-Irish lordship where the king's writ normally ran with due effect? Was the archbishop addressing in the Carmelite convent not – as some of the sources might lead one to believe – a few desperate survivors of a totally decimated population, but a vigorous and aggressive community whose losses may have merely served to turn them into more militant colonists?[23] In any case his sermon must have made it plain to all that the new archbishop was not an ill-informed and prejudiced English prelate, prepared to accept only one community in his divided diocese while totally rejecting the other. Nor was he prepared to use the institutions of the Church to foster the interests of his fellow colonists at the expense of the Gaelic race. He was already making clear that he intended to impose the same obligations of justice and charity on the colonists in their dealings with the native Irish as vice versa, a policy which was hardly guaranteed to endear him to those whom he regarded as his 'own people' in the area around Drogheda and Dundalk.

However, his sympathy for the position in which his fellow Norman citizens in Ireland found themselves was expressed in a manner which removes any doubt about the archbishop's capacity for compassion. He preached a sermon or *Proposicio* before Clement VI in August 1349 at the behest of Edward III, who wished to have extended to his subjects the benefits of the Jubilee indulgence promulgated for the following year without their being obliged to make the long, arduous, and – in the particular conditions brought about by the Black Death –

[22] Lollard texts referred occasionally to the authority of 'sanctus Ricardus', Hudson, 'A neglected Wycliffite text', *JEH* 29, 263–5.

[23] Gwynn discussed these possibilities, *Studies*, 24, 37.

extremely dangerous journey to Rome and the basilicas of the apostles.[24] This sermon, on the theme: 'Domine salve nos, perimus' (Mt. viii. 25), was an urgent and impassioned plea to Clement VI to give special consideration to those loyal sons and daughters of the Church in the western islands of England and Ireland who, in the present distressing circumstances, were in the most desperate need of the graces to be obtained through the Jubilee indulgence, but were least able to make the necessary journey in order to obtain them. Apart from the petition it contained, entrusted to him by Edward III when he gave him the special licence on 1 June 1349 and which provided at least one formal pretext for this visit to the curia, the sermon deserves consideration for a further reason. It contains the most coherent and detailed statement which we have from FitzRalph's pen of his personal impressions of the Irish situation, the prevailing level of violence, and his interpretation of the social and moral ills caused by the conflicts between the two nations. It must also have provided for his audience a rare opportunity for a first-hand report of conditions in this remote province of Christendom. FitzRalph painted a grim picture of the situation both in England, where the English were constantly at war with the Scots on the northern border, and in Ireland, where English and Irish were opposed to each other with what he called a traditional and inborn hatred.[25] According to his account, robbery and murder were daily occurrences, and it was impossible to make an effective truce between the parties. In spite of such a truce they always resumed their campaign of rapine and murder at the first opportunity. He may already have had reason to examine this situation at first hand, and these remarks suggest that he had attempted to carry out the royal commission issued to him on 12 August 1348, to negotiate for peace where and how he could usefully intervene, acting in the name of the Crown.[26] If this were the case he may already have come to realize the hopelessness of the situation, and the language in which he expressed his disgust at the lack of fraternal charity between the two races is reminiscent not merely of his remarks addressed to the citizens of Drogheda on 25 March of the same year, but also of his comments six years later when he was commissioned to

[24] Nikolaus Paulus, *Geschichte des Ablasses im Mittelalter vom Ursprunge bis zur Mitte des 14. Jahrhunderts*, 2 vols. (Paderborn, 1922–3), ii. 101–23, for a discussion of the Jubilee indulgence.

[25] B, fol. 247^r; J, fol. 177vb–178ra.

[26] CPR 1348–50, 142.

treat for peace with the O'Neill, only to discover that whereas it was possible to negotiate terms with the leaders, these terms would not be observed by supporters on either side. An indication of his despair over the Irish situation was the story he told his audience: the Necromancer of Toledo had asked the Devil which country in the Christian world sent the largest number of souls to hell. The Devil allegedly replied that Ireland had the best claim to this dubious honour, because in that country all men robbed one another, never made restitution, and therefore died without true repentance (this must have become a familiar theme to the curial audiences who had been listening to FitzRalph's sermons over the previous decade), while the constant hatred that burned among the representatives of both nations meant that large numbers died without grace or charity.[27]

FitzRalph's remarks cannot be dismissed as the prejudiced fulminations of a stranger who viewed the problem of violence in Ireland through English eyes, and who automatically assumed that the Gaelic Irish were guilty of rebellion and therefore solely responsible for the disturbances. On the contrary, the sermons which he preached in Ireland, both in 1348–9 and in 1351–6, leave no room for doubt that he was acutely aware of the contribution of his own people, the Anglo-Norman colonists of the Pale, to the uneasy situation which prevailed. All of these sermons were preached before Anglo-Irish audiences, with whom he could communicate in English, and it is a reasonable assumption that in spite of his efforts to restore the cathedral in Armagh and encourage pilgrims to visit it on the feast of St. Patrick,[28] and in spite of his energetic attempts to maintain episcopal authority over the lands of the see of Armagh which lay 'inter Hibernos', he had little personal contact with his Gaelic subjects in the northern part of his diocese apart from the occasional peace-making mission, in which he would have engaged in discussion with their leaders.[29] Nevertheless, in all

[27] B, fol. 247^{r}; J, fol. 178ra. The 'Necromancer of Toledo' is probably to be identified as the English-born Cistercian cardinal Joannes 'de Toledo' (+ 1275). See Villani's description of him: '. . . onde ciò veggendo il Cardinal Bianco, il quale era grante astrolago e maestro di nigromanzia . . .', *Cronaca, lib.* VI. *c.*80 (ed. Milan, 1857), 104; Hermann Grauert, 'Meister Johann von Toledo', *SB München, phil. hist. Klasse* (1901), 111–325; *LTK* v^{2}, 1092. As the Cistercian spent nearly 60 years at the papal curia during the 13th century, and appears not to have returned to England, FitzRalph is most likely to have acquired this information in Avignon.

[28] *Reg. Vat.* 201, fols. 135^{v}–136^{r}; *CPL* 139.

[29] Especially with the O'Neill, see Simms, 'The Archbishops of Armagh and the O'Neills', 45.

of these sermons he never tired of repeating his injunctions about the obligations of justice and charity, of the need for fair business practices on the part of merchants, honesty on the part of lawyers (this latter group seems to have been FitzRalph's particular *bête noire* since his early days at the papal curia), and above all the solemn obligation of restitution, regardless of whether the injured party was English or Irish. If one tried to sum up in a central message the teaching of FitzRalph as expressed in these sermons, it was that the gospel precepts about justice and charity, forbidding fraud, theft, and the infliction of bodily harm, were equally binding upon both races, and that neither the law of God nor that of the English king could be misused in the attempt to secure material advantages or alleged rights over members of the opposing community. Hence his remarks addressed to Clement VI have a ring of truth, as he was describing a situation which he had come to know through personal observation, and the picture he painted can be corroborated from other contemporary sources.[30]

The archbishop continued his sermon in Avignon with a discussion of the reasons why a journey to Rome was so difficult, especially for the subjects of Edward III in England and Ireland, and his remarks, which must have been particularly informative for his audience at the curia, deserve some consideration. He indicated the threefold nature of the danger involved. The first of these resulted from the warlike situation which existed between the English on the one hand, and the Scots and Irish on the other: if the English inhabitants of either island left their homes in large numbers in order to go on pilgrimage, they ran the risk that the opposing nation would immediately avail itself of the opportunity to raid their holdings, steal their cattle, and slaughter their women and children. Here it is significant that he did not include the Gaelic Irish among the subjects of Edward III – recent dealings with the O'Neill in the northern half of his diocese may have made it clear to him that they had no desire to be considered as such. He did not seek the indulgence benefits without the obligation of pilgrimage for them, and he appears to have assumed that they would neither undertake the pilgrimage to Rome themselves nor refrain from attacking the families and property of those who did. His remarks furthermore present an intriguing picture of a wave of English pilgrims which would be exclusively male, whereas all that we

[30] In this case English record material and the Irish annals present a similar story.

know about English pilgrims to Rome in the later Middle Ages indicates that a considerable number of women, both noble and commoner, made the journey as well.[31] The next dangers which faced potential pilgrims from England and from Anglo-Ireland, according to the archbishop, were those of the sea-crossing through waters infested by pirates, and the current war between England and France which meant that the safety of groups of English pilgrims travelling through French territory could not be guaranteed.[32]

A further series of objections which he raised applied specifically to pilgrims from Ireland, whose lower standard of living than that pertaining in England made it extremely unlikely that more than one in every hundred would be able to raise the money to undertake such a journey.[33] Even for those who could, the crossing of the Irish Sea presented an added hazard which those coming from England did not have to face. A seasoned traveller, who had crossed the Irish Sea more than once, FitzRalph may be assumed to have known what he was talking about when he complained about the difficulty of securing a passage. Even at the best of times, he argued, it was often necessary to wait several months at an English port for a favourable crossing, but now under plague conditions the situation was even worse. His argument that the plague affected coastal areas most severely is supported by numerous other sources, resulting in a shortage of sailors and fishermen. Hence there were few left to man the boats, and even the boats, he claimed, had become scarcer becauseof the war between England and France.[34] To add to his gloomy picture, he then raised the pessimistic question whether it would even be possible for the city of Rome to provide adequate supplies of food and other necessities for the stream of pilgrims, or would many of those who had surmounted all other hazards simply starve to death at the tombs of the apostles? FitzRalph's view of the lack of resources in fourteenth-century Rome, while not totally untrue,

[31] See lists of English residents, visitors, and pilgrims in Rome 1333-1514, in 'The English Hospice in Rome', *Venerabile*, 1962, 61-81, 109-44.

[32] B, fol. 247^{r}; J, fol. 177vb. In fact the war was at a low ebb following the fall of Calais to the English, 4 August 1347, and a series of truces helped to maintain an uneasy peace for much of the next decade, McKisack, *The Fourteenth Century*, p. 137.

[33] B, fol. 247^{v}; J, fol. 178ra.

[34] B, fols. 247^{v}-248^{r}; J, fol. 178^{ra-b}. Independent evidence shows that coastal areas were the most severely affected. Apart from the city of Bristol, the coastal regions of Hampshire, Devon, and East Anglia were among the worst affected in England, Ziegler, *The Black Death*, pp. 138-50.

must have been coloured by contemporary opinion at the curia in Avignon.

He also sought to stir up sympathy among his audience for the English subjects of Edward III with the argument that the English population had suffered more severely than either the Irish or the Scots because of the plague.[35] At the time of preaching his contention was probably justified: when he departed from Ireland in the early summer of 1349 the area around the Pale had been the most seriously affected, while the progress westwards into predominantly rural areas occurred during the later months of that year, and in any case did not have the same shattering impact as had been experienced in the close confines of Dublin, Drogheda, and Kilkenny. Similarly on his journey from Ireland to France via the king's court, FitzRalph's route took him through the southern part of England during the summer of 1349, where he could experience at first hand the devastation caused by the earlier phases of the plague, before it moved from south to north. If he sailed from Ireland to Bristol and passed through the south-west he would have encountered particularly acute scenes of desolation. Bristol suffered extremely heavy losses, as did the cathedral city of Exeter, so recently the scene of his own episcopal consecration. One recent historian of the Black Death was inclined to discount the evidence of local Devonshire historians of the eighteenth and nineteenth centuries,[36] one of whom maintained that the plague continued to have a disastrous effect on the area until 1357, while the other included among the consequences of the crisis the fact that it hindered building work on the cathedral nave, paralysed the local woollen trade and all commercial enterprise, and suspended agricultural pursuits.[37] That the latter problem was of long duration, and may even have reached famine proportions, is suggested by an entry on the Patent Rolls for 17 July 1352.[38] FitzRalph received a special royal licence to ship one hundred quarters of wheat as a gift to Bishop Grandisson of Exeter, despite prohibitions of the Irish chancellor against the exportation of corn from Ireland. On the basis of this evidence it would

[35] B, fol. 247^{r-v}; J, fol. 178ra. [36] Ziegler, pp. 139–40.

[37] Respectively Alexander Jenkins, *History of the City of Exeter* (Exeter, 1841), p. 62; George Oliver, *History of the City of Exeter* (Exeter, 1861), p. 74.

[38] CPR 1350–54, 305. Grandisson celebrated the silver jubilee of his episcopal ordination that summer and a gift from his successful protégé was presumably in order, but the choice of gift was unusual and cumbersome, and must have been dictated by the needs of Grandisson and his flock.

seem that the archbishop of Armagh was attempting – despite his own extremely modest resources – to extend a helping hand to his brother bishop in time of crisis.

Hence at the time of preaching in Avignon, FitzRalph had had ample opportunity of experiencing some of the worst effects of the plague, but it was in the nature of things impossible for any observer in August 1349 to present anything like a final report or assessment of the extent of the disaster, or of its relative distribution. An analysis made two years later after the full effects of the pestilence had reached the west of Ireland as well would probably present a different picture. FitzRalph can therefore be regarded as a reliable witness only for the areas within and on the borders of the Anglo-Irish lordship with which he was familiar. The sermon indicates that he had been making some attempt to investigate the extent of the disaster – though the figure he suggested, that two-thirds of the English population died in the epidemic, must now be regarded as improbable. He reported that he had received information to the effect that the 'nacionem Hibernicam aut Scoticam que unius sunt lingue notabiliter attegit sive lesit'.[39] As a result of this remarkable survival of the two enemy nations, the archbishop argued that the king's council would forbid large numbers of English pilgrims to leave their lands and property, or to neglect the defence of the realm, so vulnerable to attacks from either Ireland or Scotland.[40] His argument was therefore based on a contention which – regardless of the figures suggested by modern research – was certainly current opinion among contemporaries in both England and Anglo-Ireland. His feelings of alarm correspond to those of a representative witness from the English midlands, the Augustinian canon in Leicester, Henry Knighton, though in the latter case the proximity and strength of the Scottish threat is the reason for his apprehension. His famous account of the Scottish forces massed on the border, laughing at the sufferings of the English in Cumberland and Durham and deciding that this was their opportunity to invade, only to succumb to the same fate as their enemies, had not yet penetrated to FitzRalph at Avignon.[41] However, it must be pointed out that modern research has tended to support FitzRalph's contention with regard to the lesser impact of the plague in Scotland, even if some recent historians have misinterpreted

[39] B, fol. 247^{r}; J, fol. 178ra.
[40] B, fol. 247^{r-v}; J, fol. 178^{ra-va}.
[41] *Chronicon Henrici Knighton*, ed. Joseph R. Lumby (RS 92, London, 1895).

his account of the situation in Ireland because of their failure to appreciate the distinction which he was making between the English in Ireland and those of Gaelic race.[42]

However instructive FitzRalph's outline of the situation in his remote archdiocese, his vivid portrayal of racial tension, his compassionate account of the suffering and desolation caused by the plague, and of the parallel conditions in Scotland, may have been for his curial audience, his plea met with only partial success. For understandable reasons Clement VI and his curia were interested in promoting active participation in the spiritual exercises connected with the Jubilee indulgence, thereby drawing large crowds of Christians to Rome. Substantial numbers did make the journey, and for many of them their pilgrimage was an act of thanksgiving for having survived the Black Death. Consequently FitzRalph's petition was not granted, possibly on the grounds that it was not in keeping with the spirit of the Jubilee indulgence.[43] The following year however, a change of papal policy was to be observed, doubtless because the situation which FitzRalph had foretold, namely that pilgrims from England and Ireland would be extremely scarce in view of the difficulties involved, proved all too true. The first to benefit from this change of heart were a group of Scottish nobles, including the earls of Ross and Mar, who on 13 June 1350 were granted the privileges of the indulgence without obligation of making the journey to Rome. The reason stated was that Scotland was in a state of war and general destruction, but the plague was not specifically mentioned.[44] On 11 January 1351 the petition of the English royal family, including the king and queen, the prince of Wales, a number of barons, knights, royal counsellors, and higher clergy, was granted subject only to the general condition that they be hindered by reasonable cause from making the journey in person.[45] On the same day FitzRalph also tried to gain a share in the same privilege for his

[42] e.g. Ziegler, pp. 202–3. His difficulty in reconciling the accounts of the course of the plague in Ireland by Clyn and FitzRalph was largely caused by his assumption that when FitzRalph mentioned 'Anglos' he meant the population of England. But he was making a clear distinction between the Anglo-Norman population of Ireland, who lived close to the east coast and who, at the time FitzRalph was preaching, had suffered far heavier losses than the Gaelic population further to the west.

[43] There is no direct evidence for Gwynn's suggestion that Clement VI submitted it to a commission of cardinals, who rejected it as contrary to the purpose of the Holy Year, *Studies*, 24, 42.

[44] *Reg. Suppl.* 22, fol. 52^{v}; *CPL Petitions* I, 200.

[45] *Reg. Suppl.* 22, fol. 41^{r}; *CPL Petitions* I, 207.

flock, including it among a series of petitions which he submitted and which were granted, though with reduced application. Several petitions pertained to his efforts to consolidate the property of the see of Armagh and improve the income of his episcopal *mensa*, and to his attempts to improve the administrative organization of his ecclesiastical province through the appointment of notaries public, while others reflected the need to bring the marriage and family law of Gaelic Ireland into line with the canon law. In addition to these he petitioned for the faculty to dispense from their vows those who had undertaken the obligation to make pilgrimages to Rome, to the shrine of Santiago de Compostella, or to the Holy Land, and in order that his journey to the curia in this Jubilee year might not be totally fruitless, faculties to grant to members of his flock some of the spiritual benefits of the Jubilee indulgence.[46]

The *Proposicio* in which he presented the king's plea was FitzRalph's first curial utterance since his elevation to the see of Armagh. In it he demonstrated that he had in a short period of office at least diagnosed many of the ailments of his Irish flock, even if he could not prescribe effective remedies. He showed a sensitive awareness of the social tensions and practical economic problems which both communities had to face, and in the light of his own family background and of the financial-administrative difficulties of his episcopal see, it is understandable that he interpreted these problems through the eyes of the Anglo-Norman colony. There is no surviving body of evidence for the Church lands of Armagh comparable with the available sources for the estates of the archbishops of Dublin during the fourteenth century, no accounts or evidence for the composition and management of the archbishop's estates, hence FitzRalph's own petitions are a welcome guide to the situation which he found. These petitions, concerning the consolidation of the Church lands of Armagh and the augmentation of his own episcopal income, were the outcome of difficulties which he experienced during his first year in Ireland. Then it must have been forcibly brought home to him that the financial position of an Anglo-Norman prelate in that part of Ireland was a

[46] His petitions were granted enabling men and women of his archdiocese to obtain the Jubilee indulgence at home, permitting him to create additional notaries public, dispense persons related within the forbidden degrees in order that they might marry, and persons of illegitimate birth so that they could be ordained and hold a benefice, but in all cases the numbers for which he had petitioned were substantially reduced, as was curial custom, *Reg. Suppl.* 22, fol. 41^{r}; *CPL Petitions* I, 206.

precarious one. The division of the diocese into an 'English' and an 'Irish' half was territorially an unequal one, the 'English' portion consisting of little more than the tiny county of Louth, but containing the valuable port and trading towns of Drogheda and Dundalk. Much more extensive was the 'Irish' area, covering the modern County Armagh, east Tyrone, and south-east Derry, while the cathedral city itself lay between the lands of the O'Hanlon and the O'Neill. Consequently archbishops of Armagh who were of English or of Anglo-Irish blood found it more comfortable and safer to reside in the vicinity of Drogheda and Dundalk, and leave the care of the cathedral in the hands of the Gaelic dean and canons, most of whom adopted a position of independence in local ecclesiastical affairs. However, the remark that 'no Englishman would dare penetrate (into this area) without the escort of an army',[47] obscures the extent of contact which often did exist between the archbishop and his flock 'inter Hibernos'. Much of this contact was of a financial nature and concerned the administration of the scattered lands of the see of Armagh, of which a substantial portion lay 'inter Hibernos' and were therefore occupied by Gaelic tenants.[48]

FitzRalph's dealings with the papal Camera illustrated the unhealthy financial state of his diocese, but theoretically it could have been the wealthiest in Ireland, richer than Dublin and capable of comparison with some English bishoprics. Generally in the case of an episcopal vacancy in other parts of the country amenable to English jurisdiction, the temporalities were administered by the Crown, whose agents took over the accruing profits. But in the province of Armagh there were a number of sees which never passed out of Gaelic hands – Raphoe, Derry, Clogher, Kilmore, and Dromore – and here the primate enjoyed by custom the right of administration of the vacant diocese in all matters, temporal as well as spiritual. The annual revenue to which the archbishop was in theory entitled accrued from a variety of sources. He was entitled to ecclesiastical dues, such as episcopal thirds and first-fruits, the latter including the first-born of cattle, fatted bullocks when required for his table, and a pig from every herd of swine, together with 4*d.* for every milk cow on his mensal and censual lands.[49] He was also entitled to

[47] Simms, 'The Archbishops of Armagh and the O'Neills', 39.

[48] Glancy, 'The Primates and the Church Lands of Armagh', 382–8. Apart from the two manors in Co. Louth, these lands were mainly located in Armagh and Tyrone, with a concentration of mensal lands around the city of Armagh.

[49] Simms, 39; Glancy, 376.

the first-fruits of crops, and again from his mensal lands the Garbaria, a further share of the crop as corn duty, and to tithes which, it has been argued, could in the diocese of Armagh have consisted only of wool, corn, fish, and flesh.[50] However, this estimate is valid only for the Gaelic part of the diocese, whose economy was exclusively rural and agricultural. But in the trading towns in the English portion the situation was very different, and we know from FitzRalph's sermons that he expected to receive tithes on the sale of various commodities, including wine and timber, while on one occasion a debt due to him from Sir John Plunket, lord of Beaulieu (Bewley), is recorded as consisting of 3 lb. of pepper.[51] Apart from these ecclesiastical dues and the profits from his manors and mensal lands, he was also entitled to annual rents from those who lived on the termon lands within the boundaries of his diocese, whose temporal overlord he was. But a primate residing in County Louth understandably had difficulty in enforcing his right to payment of these dues in the northern part of the diocese, and even in his provisional cathedral city of Drogheda it was not easy to extract that which the primate considered to be his fair dues – hence FitzRalph's constant fulminations against the merchants of Drogheda and their practice of tithe-evasion which ultimately led him to place the city under interdict.

A substantial body of source-material for the middle decades of the fourteenth century testifies to FitzRalph's energetic preoccupation with the administrative problems of his scattered lands, rationalizing them where possible, and attempting to safeguard and increase his episcopal income, not indeed without some success. One of his first recorded acts upon arrival in Ireland as archbishop, when he was able to take stock of the situation in person and doubtless heard reports of the O'Neill raids on the primatial lands,[52] was to safeguard his legal position. On

[50] Ibid., 376. It is virtually impossible to assess the value in actual hard cash of these various revenues to an archbishop residing 'inter Anglos'. Most of our information for diocesan sources of income comes from later references in Sweteman's register. Like FitzRalph, he was an active and successful defender of the material well-being of the see. On his death and during the vacancy before John Colton succeeded, the latter in his capacity as dean of Armagh was entrusted with the administration of the temporalities, and during the 18 months of his administration he delivered to the Exchequer £366. 8*s*. 10*d*. in revenues.

[51] *Cal. Reg. Sweteman*, 222. In his sermon on tithe-evasion preached in Drogheda, 2 December 1352, FitzRalph referred to a wide range of commodities upon the sale of which he expected to receive tithes, B, fols. 62^{v}–63^{v}; J, fol. 52^{ra-vb}.

[52] Simms, 40–1.

6 July 1348 he secured from Edward III a licence, on the grounds that his temporalities were widely scattered, remote from his episcopal seat, and for the most part 'inter Hibernos', enabling him to appoint attorneys to represent him in all pleas, quarrels, and suits for or against him which might come before the courts in Ireland. The following day he named in this capacity his relative John Rauf, and William Swayne, both of whom had already represented him in Ireland the previous year while he was still detained in England.[53] That the archbishop was speaking no less than the truth when he claimed that his lands were scattered, is clearly demonstrated by the two papal documents issued in response to his petitions of 11 January 1351. One of these petitions had been a request that he be permitted to augment the income from his episcopal *mensa*, which amounted to less than £400 sterling annually, by appropriating a number of churches in England and in Ireland, the advowsons of these to be reserved to the archbishop and his successors.[54] Clement VI made the grant, stipulating that FitzRalph should acquire no more than four churches, that these be in Ireland, and that adequate provision should be made for the stipend of a vicar in each case, the four churches to be chosen so that the archbishop's income be increased by a further hundred marks (i.e. £66).[55] On the same day FitzRalph petitioned for the faculty to exchange rents and real property belonging to his *mensa* for others which in the judgement of the chapter of Armagh would be more useful, but as the plea was too vague he was instructed to make it more specific, whereupon it was granted. This specific version is recorded in letters sent by Clement VI to the abbot of the Augustinian canons at Duleek (County Louth), the prior of the Crutched Friars in the Hospital of St. Leonard in Dundalk, and the archdeacon of Armagh. These listed a number of items of property belonging to the episcopal *mensa*, scattered throughout the dioceses of Meath (including the Nober where FitzRalph heard an inquisition in late November 1351),[56] Clogher, Tuam, Elphin, Annadown, and Clonfert, also in the Irish portion of his own diocese, including the early monastic site of Kilmore[57] north of the primatial

[53] CPR 1348–50, 118. [54] As n. 46.

[55] *Reg. Vat.* 203, fol. 194^{r}; *CPL* 298. The archbishop was specifically urged to ensure that 'dicti vicarii possint comode sustentari' (fol. 194^{r}).

[56] *Cal. Reg. Sweteman*, 287.

[57] *Medieval Religious Houses. Ireland*, p. 39. It is not to be confused with the diocesan see of Kilmore farther to the south and west.

city, which had been converted into a parish church and was regarded as one of the principal churches of the diocese 'standing with and dependent upon the cathedral church of Armagh'.[58]

A glance at the monastic map of medieval Ireland[59] is sufficient to show how widely scattered and vulnerable this accumulation of property was, and the necessity of enforcing a policy of consolidation if the archbishop wished, as FitzRalph clearly did, to regain a firm hold over the temporal possessions of his see. But the changes he had in mind could not be carried out overnight; the entire procedure took a number of years to effect, and in the meantime he was concerned to increase the available protection for his property as it stood. On 5 February 1351 Clement VI issued letters to the suffragans of the see of Armagh, bishop William St. Leger of Meath and the bishop of Dromore,[60] and to the abbot of the Augustinian canons at Navan, also in the diocese of Meath, charging them with the protection of the rights, property, and prerogatives of the see of Armagh. FitzRalph had drawn the pope's attention to the difficulty of having personal recourse to the papal court over every local quarrel within his jurisdiction, presumably referring to cases which he could not, or would not settle in the king's courts in Ireland. Consequently the prelates mentioned were deputed to act as judges in all cases in which the archbishop's *mensa* and its property were being threatened by 'occupatores, detentatores, presumptores, molestatores et iniuriatores'.[61]

There was an inherent connection between FitzRalph's two petitions to Clement VI, the one concerning the acquisition of the advowsons of additional churches in order to supplement his mensal income, the other permitting him to dispose of distant property in exchange for more useful items, and both petitions were expressions of a coherent 'estates policy' on the archbishop's part. This connection is made clear by an entry in the register of his successor, Milo Sweteman, referring back to an agreement which FitzRalph had made with Sir Simon Fleming, baron of Slane. Under its terms the primate was to acquire

[58] Glancy, 373. Clement permitted the archbishop to exchange the lands listed for others, not listed, which he and his chapter might consider more useful, *Reg. Vat.* 203, fol. 196^{v}; *CPL* 398–9.

[59] Appended to *Medieval Religious Houses. Ireland.*

[60] *Reg. Vat.* 200, fols. 235^{v}–236^{r}; *CPL* 368. The register includes the name of neither bishop, but this letter is the only evidence for the existence of a bishop of Dromore during FitzRalph's period of office.

[61] *Reg. Vat.* 200, fol. 236^{r}.

advowsons in Slane, Dromconrath, and Killary (both of the latter being situated in the barony of Lower Slane), in exchange for part of the manor of Nober in which the primate had substantial rents.[62] His policy of land-exchanges had not yet been completed when he left Ireland for the last time in the summer of 1356, and upon reaching Westminster he obtained further concessions from Edward III in this respect. An entry on the Patent Rolls for 20 July 1356 added a new dimension to FitzRalph's transactions, as among the advowsons which he wished to acquire were those of the alien priories within the province of Armagh.[63] These were still affiliated to Benedictine houses in Normandy and had been subjected to royal confiscations since the outbreak of the war between England and France. The two alien priories concerned, St. Andrew in Ards (Black Abbey) in County Down and Fore Abbey in Meath, were the subject of protracted financial negotiations which were not completed during FitzRalph's last visit to London. On 26 June(?)[64] 1356 FitzRalph bound himself to pay £200 to the Abbey of St. Mary's at Lonlay in Normandy for the house and lands of St. Andrew in Ards. Provided he was able to gain possession of them in the meantime, he guaranteed to pay over the money at St. Paul's Cathedral in London before 24 June 1360. FitzRalph was in Avignon during the summer of 1360, but the payment was clearly made upon his behalf. When he died, the king took the abbey into royal possession as an alien priory once more, but ultimately restored it to the see of Armagh for a nominal fee when Archbishop John Colton pointed out to Richard II that it had been purchased for the archdiocese by FitzRalph.[65] The latter's transactions over the second priory, that of Fore in Meath which was the property of the Benedictine abbey of St. Taurin at Evreux (Normandy) took place in Avignon, where in 1357 FitzRalph reached an agreement with the abbey's proctor at the curia to purchase the priory for 1,000 fl.[66] But although Sweteman's register contains an entry which implies that FitzRalph had paid 100 fl. on account, the transaction never went through. The reason for this may have been that because of the archbishop's death at the curia the rest of the

[62] *Cal. Reg. Sweteman*, 265. [63] CPR 1354–58, 423.

[64] From Sweteman's register it is not clear whether the date should be 26 June or July, but the entry on the Patent Rolls (as n. 63) makes the former more probable, *Cal. Reg. Sweteman*, 244.

[65] *Medieval Religious Houses. Ireland*, p. 108.

[66] *Cal. Reg. Sweteman*, 264.

money was never paid, and as late as 1418 the priory was still dependent on its mother-house at Evreux.[67]

The tenor of these concessions which FitzRalph received from the king on 20 July 1356 suggests that at that moment he was enjoying exceptional royal favour and had clearly carried out his duties in Ireland to the king's satisfaction. The licence to appropriate the advowsons of the alien priories was granted to him not merely because of the poverty of his see, whose property lay mainly among the king's enemies, but also in recognition of his satisfactory service in Ireland, where he allegedly ruled his lands in the best interests of the Crown and contributed to the preservation of the king's honour. This latter is doubtless a reference to his peace-keeping activities in the marcher area under his control which, despite the king's angry comments six years earlier about the unrest in the area while FitzRalph was in Avignon, had been remarkably peaceful during the subsequent years of his active apostolate in Ireland.[68] In the meantime FitzRalph had exercised his jurisdiction in the area in a manner which, despite his exhortations to fair dealing on the part of both communities, left no room for doubt that he regarded Edward III as 'dominus Hibernie' and legitimate temporal authority in that area.[69] He did occasionally clash with the king, both as dean of Lichfield and as archbishop with primatial ambitions in the province of Dublin, and again in 1357 when he tried to take his case against the friars to the papal court in spite of the Statute of Praemunire.[70] But the differences which FitzRalph as archbishop had with Edward III were not because he was the opponent of an alien English rule, but represented the same type of friction which was part of the normal fabric of Crown-Church relations familiar to every English bishop, but in the Irish context occasionally made more acute.

The difficulties which faced an ecclesiastical administration within the jurisdiction of the Anglo-Irish lordship and caught between the – often competing – rival authorities of Dublin and Westminster are vividly illustrated by the case of the

[67] Ibid., 264, where it is stated that the archbishop paid 100 fl. 'upon union'. See *Medieval Religious Houses. Ireland*, p. 106.

[68] FitzRalph is described on 20 July as having directed the king's business in Ireland and as ruling his lands for the preservation of the king's honour, CPR 1354–58, 423.

[69] On the attitudes of Anglo-Irish primates to the question of who actually held legitimate temporal authority in the archdiocese of Armagh 'inter Hibernos', see Simms, 42.

[70] CCR 1354–60, 399.

collegiate church of Stabannan in County Louth. Edward III presented to it one of his chaplains, John Telyng, on 10 February 1351, only to revoke his grant on 30 March of the same year, having had it brought to his notice that presentation to the church lay in the hands of the chancellor of Ireland, at this point none other than Archbishop John of St. Paul of Dublin.[71] For reasons which are not clear the king enforced his own right of presentation in favour of Telyng again on 1 February and 14 May 1352,[72] thereby rejecting the claims of the Irish chancellor's candidate, John Strode.[73] But the matter did not end there, and the king underwent another change of heart, now lending his support and protection to Strode. On 20 October 1354 he ordered FitzRalph, as ordinary of the diocese in which the church was located, to bring the matter before his court, to weigh up the situation, and find a just solution in accordance with his own episcopal prerogatives and ecclesiastical law, the archbishop's decision to be communicated to the king's court by Easter 1355.[74] The dispute had been caused by the presentation of one candidate under the Great Seal of England and the other under the Irish seal, and significantly the king did not insist on the automatic superiority of a provision made under the former. In view of the important constitutional implications, both for the status of the chancellor in the Irish lordship with regard to his opposite number in England, and for their respective juridical competence in the affairs of the Church within the lordship, it would be of interest to learn how precisely FitzRalph did decide. No record of such a decision has survived, but in view of the fact that John Strode appeared as rector of Stabannan and witnessed peace negotiations between the English colony and the Irish of Oriel and Meath conducted by Archbishop Sweteman nearly twenty years later on 15 July 1373,[75] it seems more probable that he was the successful candidate. The possibility cannot be excluded that Telyng, who disappeared from all records after 1354, may have died, leaving Strode as the only surviving candidate for the rectory. But it

[71] CPR 1350-54, 35, 57, 62. [72] Ibid., 226, 266.

[73] The only person of this name in the papal registers of the period is a John Strode of the diocese of Hereford, who appeared among a list of laymen and clerics of the archdiocese of Dublin, 8 April 1352, *CPL* 455.

[74] CCR 1354-60, 41; CPR 1354-58, 114.

[75] *Cal. Reg. Sweteman,* 223. Strode was still rector of Stabannan 12 October 1375, when he and his chaplains made an agreement with John Douedale of Dundalk concerning property held of the Douedale family, *Dowdall Deeds*, p. 106.

nevertheless seems more probable that the archbishop of Dublin, in his other capacity as an officer of the Crown in Ireland, could ignore the finer points of ecclesiastical legislation or primatial rights and interfere in the presentation to benefices within the archdiocese of Armagh, a situation which can only have helped to make the primatial issue more acute.

iii. The cult of St. Patrick and 'Ritter Georg'

In the fragmentary sermon-note without indication of date or place of preaching with which the surviving form of FitzRalph's diary commenced, the preacher made use of an *exemplum* concerning St. Patrick's Purgatory and the knight who 'solum post Patricii tempus eius purgatorium pro dei amore intravit'.[1] This phrase was to lead to some disagreement between the two previous students of the sermon diary, Hammerich and Fr. Gwynn, and the dating of the sermon in which it occurred has important implications for several aspects of FitzRalph's career. It was delivered on Ash Wednesday, and it contains an attack on mendicant confessors which seems to indicate that it was preached at a time when the archbishop's controversy with the friars had already reached serious dimensions: 'unde dampnant se confessores religiosi, si qui sunt, et alii, qui receptis paucis denariis non inducta restitucione homini de furto aut de usura, aut de iniusto lucro proximi absolucionem inpendunt'.[2] This obligation to restitution was constantly emphasized in FitzRalph's earliest sermons to his Anglo-Irish flock, but the element in this statement which was new was the accusation that those religious who acted as confessors – and it is improbable that he had any others than the friars in mind – were prepared in return for an offering to dispense their penitents from the obligation of restitution of their ill-gotten gains as a necessary precondition for absolution. Although the phrase 'receptis paucis denariis' suggests a contempt which was scarcely in keeping with FitzRalph's last sermon to a mendicant community on 4 October 1349, Hammerich argued that it belonged to a period when the struggle against the mendicants was dawning but not fully ablaze, and he used it to build up his case that the sermon diary provided ample evidence for the genesis and early development of anti-mendicant sentiments in FitzRalph's public utterances before 1350.[3] If one were to accept this hypothesis, the

[1] B, fol. 1^{v}; J, fol. 1va. [2] B, fol. 1^{r}; J, fol. 1^{rb-va}.
[3] *FitzRalph and the Mendicants*, 26–42.

sermon would have to be dated either to FitzRalph's last years in Lichfield or during his first year in Armagh, 1348–9. Although there was a Franciscan convent in Lichfield and FitzRalph could have had an opportunity of studying the friars' confessional practices at close quarters, the sermon is more likely to have been delivered in Ireland for two reasons. Firstly the reference to St. Patrick's Purgatory is more plausible in an Irish context where it had local associations, and secondly the problems that might arise in cases where mendicant confessors erred on the side of leniency in matters of restitution are more consistent with the particular situation prevailing among the 'two nations' in Ireland where ownership and property rights were a constant source of friction, and we have already noticed that FitzRalph had reason to become aware of these problems within a short time of his assuming office as archbishop.

Hammerich built up his argument on the basis of a 'striking inner resemblance' between this fragment and the Epiphany sermon of 1347 preached in Burford.[4] This latter sermon he sought to date to 1348 on the grounds that FitzRalph would have used the English system of dating, and from this he deduced that the now consecrated archbishop of Armagh spent the winter of 1347–8 in Oxford completing the *Summa de Questionibus Armenorum* before setting out for his new diocese, and presumably inadequate library facilities! On the basis of this argument he suggested that the Ash Wednesday sermon also belonged to the year 1348, i.e. 12 March, thereby making it the first recorded sermon preached by FitzRalph upon his arrival in Ireland. If we were to pursue this hypothesis for a moment, it might be further suggested that the archbishop preached this sermon before his own clergy in the 'English' half of the diocese soon after his arrival, and laid down for their information and guidance his own very strict views on the duty of restitution. But this view is based on an unduly distorted interpretation of the evidence. Apart from the problem that the tenor of this criticism of the friar-confessors does not fit a date before 1350 – and most certainly seems out of place during the first weeks after the archbishop's arrival – there is absolutely no reason to assume that the Burford sermon employed a dating any different from the rest of the diary, all of whose entries were standardized – possibly by the unknown English cleric who must have collected FitzRalph's papers after his death in Avignon

[4] Ibid., p. 29.

and been responsible for launching the circulation of the complete sermon diary in England.

However, Hammerich's dating problem stemmed originally from a need to find an adequate explanation for the reference to the knightly pilgrim to St. Patrick's Purgatory also mentioned in the sermon. Fr. Gwynn had assumed that this reference was intended to apply to the most celebrated pilgrim to the Purgatory during FitzRalph's lifetime, the Hungarian knight George Grissaphan, whose much-publicized visit in November-December 1353 resulted in attracting to this remote spot pilgrims from all over Europe during the next century and more, until the intervention of Alexander VI in 1497.[5] There had been previous references to pilgrims to the Purgatory, which was in the care of the community of Augustinian canons close to Lough Derg,[6] including the celebrated knight Owein whose descent into the Purgatory two hundred years earlier in 1153 had been reported by the otherwise unknown Cistercian monk, H. of Sawtry.[7] This tale became enormously influential, circulating in numerous manuscripts, and excerpts from it were frequently incorporated into larger collections, so that it was repeated by Roger of Wendover and Matthew Paris, as well as by Jacopo de Voragine in his *Legenda Aurea*.[8] Hammerich argued that as it was impossible for FitzRalph not to have known

[5] Gwynn, *Studies*, 24, 572. The pope ordered the closure of the cave known as St. Patrick's Purgatory around 17 March 1497, having heard the report of a Dutch friar that both the bishop of Clogher and the community in charge of the Purgatory were demanding a fee from those wishing to enter, a practice which Alexander VI declared simoniacal. Apart from the question of a fee, the Dutchman's account of the requirements for pilgrims are similar to those imposed upon the Hungarian knight George in 1353. The closure in 1497 was the first record of the Purgatory in the *Annals of Ulster*, whereas an unusual feature of the popularity which the Purgatory enjoyed during the later 14th and 15th centuries was that it was totally ignored in Gaelic sources. For the Dutch pilgrim's account and the closure see *Acta Sanctorum*, March ii. 590–1; Gwynn, *Medieval Province of Armagh*, pp. 172–5. The Purgatory was subsequently reopened, presumably by Julius II, and the *Annals* reported (1516) that a French knight visited it and was so well received by the O'Donnell that he sent his host a whole ship with cannon, *Annals of Ulster*, iii. 521; *Annals of Loch Cé*, ii. 225.

[6] *Medieval Religious Houses. Ireland*, p. 193.

[7] See Eduard Mall, 'Zur Geschichte der Legende vom Purgatorium des hl. Patrizius', *Romanische Forschungen*, 6 (1888), 139–97; and for a discussion of other earlier visitors, and alleged visitors, to the Purgatory, Hammerich, 'Eine Pilgerfahrt des XIV. Jahrhunderts nach dem Fegfeuer des hl. Patrizius', *Zeitschrift für deutsche Philologie*, 53 (1928), 25–40.

[8] Roger of Wendover, *Flores Historiarum* (ed. Eng. Hist. Soc., London, 1841), ii. 256; Matthew of Paris, *Chronica Majora* (ed. RS, London, 1874), ii. 192 ff.; Jacopo de Voragine, *Legenda aurea*, ed. Johann G. T. Grässe (Leipzig, 1850), *cap.* 50, pp. 213–16.

about the descent of the knight Owein, his reference in the sermon must have been to this episode, and therefore must have preceded the visit of the Hungarian knight.[9] However, whereas Hammerich's knowledge of the circulation of pious and popular literature in the various vernaculars of later medieval Europe can only be described as encyclopaedic, this argument is not without defects. The Owein-legend circulated in the later Middle Ages, in Latin versions and in numerous translations into French and High German, in a large number of manuscripts, but these were most frequently to be found in convents of nuns, who read collections of this sort in order to incite them to greater penitential efforts. Hence the argument from wide circulation of this kind among a non-scholastic reading public does not necessarily create a watertight argument that a university-trained prelate, living and working in Oxford, Lichfield, and Avignon, might necessarily have been so familiar with the legend that he would have used it as an *exemplum* in the first sermon preached after he had set foot on Irish soil. It is equally possible that he did not accept that the earlier story was based on fact. Furthermore, in view of Hammerich's own arguments that the pilgrimage of the Hungarian knight in 1353, the first which is accurately datable and fully documented,[10] had a profound effect on the subsequent fame of the Purgatory, a place of pilgrimage which was previously little frequented by pilgrims from outside Ireland and apparently virtually unknown within the country itself, it is unlikely that the Anglo-Irish audience to whom FitzRalph would have preached soon after his arrival would have been sufficiently familiar with the place and its connotations, whereas after the visit of the Hungarian knight this would be the case.

Although the circumstances surrounding the pilgrimage of George of Hungary are fairly well known in outline,[11] some further consideration of the episode is necessary here, not merely to correct some misconceptions in the existing picture, but because the events surrounding it are of more than passing significance in the assessment of FitzRalph's years in office as archbishop of Armagh, and especially his readiness to promote the cult of the founder and patron of his archdiocese, thereby

[9] Hammerich, *FitzRalph and the Mendicants*, pp. 28–9.

[10] 'Eine Pilgerfahrt des XIV. Jahrhunderts', 30.

[11] Hammerich (ed.), *Visiones Georgii. Visiones quas in purgatorio sancti Patricii vidit Georgius miles de Ungaria A.D. MCCCLIII* (Copenhagen, 1930); Gwynn, *Studies*, 24, 565–72.

focusing attention on his historical primatial see. Friar Clyn's account of the religious and emotional climate during the worst days of the plague contains a well-known passage in which he described how prelates, priests, and people thronged to a local place of pilgrimage near his native Kilkenny.[12] It is reasonable to assume that even though few could afford to make the journey to Rome and avail themselves of the fruits of the Jubilee indulgence, all such local places of pilgrimage must have been equally frequented during and immediately after the worst phase of the pestilence. It is at least possible that this renewed preoccupation with pilgrimage may also have helped to kindle among the Irish some interest in the places associated with the life of St. Patrick, and this may tentatively be linked with FitzRalph's own efforts to propagate his cult. It has been shown that, whereas throughout the entire Middle Ages St. Patrick's Purgatory was from the Continental point of view the best known of Irish places of pilgrimage, and George of Hungary could justify his decision to go there because of the 'multa mirabilia' of which he heard reports in Compostella, it was completely ignored in Irish sources and, for example, the *Annals* never included any references to it until the late fifteenth and early sixteenth centuries.[13] FitzRalph on the other hand made a deliberate attempt to promote interest in the cult, as can be illustrated by several petitions which he laid before Clement VI. On 10 April 1351 he received permission to grant indulgences to all who visited St. Patrick's Cathedral in Armagh on the saint's feast-day, and also to those who over the next ten years would contribute financially to the restoration of the cathedral,[14] both of which may be regarded as a deliberate attempt to focus attention on the symbolic significance of the ancient see of St. Patrick, even though it lay – as did the Purgatory – 'inter homines minus domitos',[15] and not within the reach of his own personal authority.

He could scarcely have foreseen the course of events, but the episode which more than any other helped to achieve his aim was the decision of George of Hungary to do penance for his

[12] In Timoleague, Co. Carlow, see *Annals of Ireland*, p. 35.

[13] *Annals of Ulster* (1497 and 1516), iii. 417, 521; *Annals of Loch Cé*, ii. 225. *The Annals of the Four Masters* contain no reference to the Purgatory.

[14] *Reg. Vat.* 201, fols. 135^v–136^r; *CPL* 387.

[15] He described it thus in the letter he issued giving general authentication to George's visions, which with several other authenticating documents became the preface of the *Visiones Georgii*, ed. cit., p. 80.

excesses by making the pilgrimage which is so well documented in the *Visiones Georgii* and appended letters of confirmation from ecclesiastical dignitaries in Ireland, including the 'primas Hibernie'.[16] According to his personal testimony, George Grissaphan, son of a Hungarian magnate, left his native land in the service of King Louis of Hungary when the latter campaigned in southern Italy in an attempt to make good his claim to the throne of Naples. Louis of Hungary made two expeditions, in 1347 and in 1350, and it has been suggested in view of the fact that George was only twenty-four years old when he arrived in Ireland in 1353, that he can only have been involved in the second campaign.[17] This view is, however, difficult to reconcile with George's own account of events, and it is more probable that he went to Italy with the first army, was left in charge of the towns and fortresses which the Hungarian king had reduced to obedience, and in particular he captained the garrison of Trani, near Bari. However, his regime was so harsh that he was, as he later confessed, responsible for the murder of more than three hundred and fifty of the local people, as well as numerous acts of robbery and violence, before repenting of his sins and deciding to set out for Avignon to seek absolution at the papal curia.[18] The penance which was imposed upon him in Avignon and the absolution subsequently received in accordance with normal curial procedure in cases of homicide[19] did not, however, satisfy his conscience, and he set out, accompanied by one servant, on foot to the shrine of St. James of Compostella, where he spent a further five months of austerity and penance before deciding that Compostella was overcrowded with pilgrims who disturbed his solitude, and he set out once more on his travels. By now he had heard of the wonders of St. Patrick's Purgatory 'in finibus mundi', in the furthest part of Ireland which he described as the last province in the western world,[20] and again with his servant he set out on foot through Navarre and Gascony, traversed the lengths of France and England, and finally arrived at the church of St. Patrick at Lough Derg which, together with the Purgatory, was in the care of a community of Augustinian canons.[21] Here

[16] The 6 letters are printed ibid., pp. 78–86.

[17] Gwynn, *Studies*, 24, 566. There is no record of a Hungarian knight of that name in service in southern Italy.

[18] *Visiones Georgii*, pp. 87–8. [19] Ibid., p. 89. [20] Ibid., p. 91.

[21] The observance of Arrouaise had been introduced there shortly after 1140, and in the 14th century the community seems to have had a large, if not exclusively, Gaelic element, *Medieval Religious Houses. Ireland*, p. 193.

he was received by the almost centenarian prior Paul, who showed due respect for metropolitan jurisdiction and refused to allow the young man to enter the Purgatory until he had received permission both from the primate and from the ordinary of the diocese of Clogher in which Lough Derg was situated, in the latter case the Gaelic Irish Nicholas MacCathasaigh who had ruled in the diocese since 1320.[22]

From the dates of the documents subsequently issued to George in confirmation of his pilgrimage, a fairly accurate chronology of his movements can be established. He arrived at Lough Derg for the first time no later than the middle or end of October 1353, and he reported that having been thus instructed by the prior, he retraced his steps, taking eight days to reach the presence of FitzRalph, whom we can assume was in the Drogheda-Dundalk area, having returned from the visit to the king's court for which he had received a special licence earlier in the same year.[23] Although he received this strange pilgrim who, 'devotissime et cum lacrimarum effusione' begged to be allowed to enter the Purgatory, and gave him the necessary letters to his suffragan in Clogher and to the prior and canons of Lough Derg, his reactions are not otherwise recorded, but the phrase 'qui locus in diocese Clochorensi inter homines minus domitos situatur' in his subsequent letter of confirmation after George's venture had been completed, may indicate a certain reserve or suspicion concerning a place of pilgrimage over which he had no direct control. In any case George's account made a point of recording that FitzRalph's suffragan, the bishop of Clogher, received him with extreme cordiality, gave him the necessary letters, and sent him back to Lough Derg rejoicing.

Here the preparations for the descent into the Purgatory were made, spanning a further three weeks, in which the knight had to endure both severe fasting and a liturgical programme which must have been daunting to all but the most stalwart souls, before being escorted to the entrance to the cave. At this stage he was accompanied by an entourage which indicates that his pilgrimage had come to be regarded as a local celebrity case – as well it might be in view of the young man's background and bizarre adventures both before and after his decision to repent, which must have made him appear in that remote part of Ireland

[22] Bishop of Clogher 1320-56, *HBC*², 310.

[23] *Visiones Georgii*, p. 92. For FitzRalph's licence to travel to England, CCR 1349-54, 537.

like a being from another world.[24] The entourage included, in addition to the Augustinian prior and canons, the principal local chieftain, presumably the McMahon,[25] and a number of other unnamed nobles, as well as a following of the laity, all of whom were present when the prior performed the final ceremonies, escorted George to the door of the cave, and sealed the door which was to remain closed for the next twenty-four hours. The central part of the *Visiones Georgii* is taken up with the knight's account of the twenty-six visions which, accompanied by the Archangel Michael as his guide, he claimed to have experienced during this period, and the veracity of which was subsequently confirmed by the ecclesiastical authorities most immediately involved. At the end of this period, when he finally emerged, he confessed his experiences[26] and was once more assisted by the canons and by the McMahon who provided him with clothes and other necessities for his subsequent journeys, which initially involved collecting letters of credence from all who had been connected with the episode, and subsequently in delivering the messages which, he claimed and the canons confirmed,[27] had been given to him by the angel – in the best hagiographical tradition. The first of these, which is of immediate interest here, was to FitzRalph himself, while the others were to the pope, the kings of France and England, and the Sultan of Babylon. The core of the messages to the French and English kings, as well as to the pope, concerned the ending of the war between those two kingdoms, while that to the pope contained a further element: a plea to absolve from the sentence of excommunication 'cujusdam principis qui longo elapso tempore iam decessit'.[28] Hammerich was inclined to the view that Ludwig of Bavaria was intended here, but a more likely candidate in a story which had its genesis in a remote part of Gaelic Ireland on the borders of Tir Eoghain and Tir Chonaill, was Edward

[24] The preparations are described in *Visiones Georgii*, pp. 94–5.

[25] '. . . tunc in presencia cuiusdam viri nobilissimi, qui vocatur rex illius patrie, dictus *Magrath*, cum multis alijs nobilibus . . .', ibid., p. 95. Because the McGrath (or Macraith) were hereditary 'coarbs' of the monastery, Hammerich argued that the name of the local king must be also thus identified, 'Eine Pilgerfahrt des XIV. Jahrhunderts', 35, but the variants of all the MSS used in his edition give *Machmathan, Machamahan, Mathamathan, Machani*, and similar versions. Even allowing for Hammerich's description of the text as that of events in Ireland involving an Italo-Hungarian, compiled by a Provençal, and surviving in German MSS (ibid., 37), these are still more plausibly identified as McMahon than as McGrath. The McMahon of the area had raided the monastery in 1207, plundering and reducing it to ashes (*Annals of Munster*, cited in *Medieval Religious Houses. Ireland*, p. 193).

[26] *Visiones Georgii*, pp. 314–15. [27] Ibid., pp. 83–4. [28] Ibid., p. 312.

Bruce who also suffered excommunication at the hands of John XXII and for whom a certain sympathy may have survived in this area.[29] The message to the Sultan of Babylon, which 'continebat magnum et notabile bonum tocius Christianitatis' but was not further elucidated by George in his subsequent accounts, may be deemed to have concerned the predictable objective of the security of the Holy Places.[30]

George's ordeal in the Purgatory must have been completed early in December 1353, as on the 7th of that month the prior of the Augustinians issued a letter proclaiming publicly that the Hungarian knight had carried out his pilgrimage 'iuxta ordinacionem et regulam cenobij nostri'.[31] The prior stressed in his letter the element of confession and guaranteed the truth of all that George would have to tell about his experiences, which seems to suggest that the monks already knew his story and that, instead of bearing a written account of his ordeal and visions (he was unable to read), he would publicize these by word of mouth. From Lough Derg George then proceeded to the bishop of Clogher, with whom he probably spent Christmas, and recounted his experiences, as Nicholas MacCathasaigh duly issued a letter to him on 26 December confirming the veracity of all that George would retail.[32] From Clogher he set out to seek FitzRalph, for whom he had a message to deliver and from whom he also wished to have letters verifying his pilgrimage, but was at first unsuccessful in his attempts to seek an audience with the archbishop. His account does not give any information as to whether FitzRalph was away from the Dundalk-Drogheda area during the month of January or whether he refused to see the bearer of an alleged message for him, but as we shall see from the tenor of a letter which FitzRalph sent to him a month later, it is at least possible that the archbishop was ill during this period. Meanwhile George set out for Dublin where he was received by the prior of the Knights of St. John of Jerusalem at Kilmainham, John Frowick, who also added his confirmation to those of the Augustinian prior at Lough Derg and the bishop of Clogher, though he was careful to specify that he was confirming the validity of their letters and not the veracity of George's

[29] 'Eine Pilgerfahrt des XIV. Jahrhundert', 38. Katharine Simms suggested that the Bruce invasion should be considered as a large-scale episode in the time-honoured custom of importing galloglasses to aid the northern chieftains in their warfare (private communication).

[30] *Visiones Georgii*, p. 313. [31] Ibid., p. 83. [32] Ibid., pp. 84–5.

utterances, which he was clearly not in a position to do.[33] It might reasonably be asked what was the connection of the Hospitaller prior outside Dublin with the episode? The sources provide no clear answer to this question, but in view of FitzRalph's reference in his own subsequent letter of credence to 'literas quorundam militum hospitalis sancti Iohannis Ierosolimitani' which appear to have testified to George's noble Hungarian parentage,[34] it is at least possible that George might have arrived in Ireland with letters of credence from some Hospitallers who were able to testify to his identity, letters which he might have acquired either in southern Italy, or in Avignon, or at a later stage in his wanderings.

The prior of Kilmainham issued his letter on 29 January 1354, but George was still determined to see the archbishop of Armagh before finally leaving Ireland, and headed once more northwards. Through the archdeacon of Armagh, who is unnamed but who invariably was an Anglo-Irish cleric who administered the southern half of the diocese,[35] he sent a message to FitzRalph to the effect that he could not remain much longer in Ireland as he had other messages to deliver but was reluctant to leave the country before delivering the one which the archangel had given him for FitzRalph and which concerned not only the archbishop personally but also the well-being of his diocese. Such tactics had the desired effect, and in a letter which is probably to be dated to Wednesday 19 February 1354, FitzRalph summoned George to him, even offering to send horses for him to avoid unnecessary fatigue.[36] This letter, which was sent from the archbishop's manor at Dromiskin near Dundalk, contained the information that FitzRalph had been at Vespers the previous Monday evening when his archdeacon brought him the letter from George – where the archbishop actually was residing at the time he did not specify – whereupon the archbishop got up at midnight in order to travel to Dundalk the following day, Tuesday, where he arrived after a hard day's journey, more taxing than anything he had undertaken for a long time, and on the Wednesday on which he wrote this letter he was in an exhausted condition at Dromiskin, but nevertheless bade George to come to see him. When one considers the extent to which FitzRalph travelled during his life, and was once more to do in

[33] Ibid., pp. 85–6. [34] Ibid., p. 80.
[35] Gwynn, *Medieval Province of Armagh*, p. 81.
[36] *Visiones Georgii*, pp. 79–80, and translated by Gwynn, *Studies*, 24, 569–70.

1356–7 when he set out once more for Oxford, London, and Avignon, it is difficult to avoid the conclusion that in the early weeks of 1354 he was suffering from some illness, and that this might explain part of the silence of the sermon diary in which no sermons are recorded between the end of 1352 and the spring of 1354. Though as we shall see, another explanation for this lack of preaching activity is also possible.

George's message for FitzRalph concerned the 'absolutionem magne civitatis sui archiepiscopatus, quam dictus primas iniuste interdicebat et excommunicabat, licet non ex malicia, nec ex iniusticia, quamquam videretur, sed quia videbatur sibi civitatem in quibusdam punctis non facere debitum suum nec velle facere'.[37] The suggestion of both Voigt and Hammerich that this was meant to apply to Dublin and that FitzRalph had placed the capital city under interdict because of the refusal there to acknowledge his primacy[38] must be ruled out because the reference is to a city within his own 'archiepiscopatus'. Fr. Gwynn on the other hand linked this message with a sermon which FitzRalph had preached at Drogheda on 2 December 1352 and which contained the most violent attack expressed in the sermon diary on the widespread abuse of the duties and obligations of those who have property or the means of accumulating wealth.[39] Here he fulminated against the fraud practised by local merchants in order to avoid paying their tithes and laid down his own very severe norms as to what actually constituted profit and upon which traders were obliged to yield a tithe to their rector or vicar.[40] In the same sermon the archbishop gave vent to his fury at those who manipulated the law with regard to the sale of property, where they might remain technically within the limits of the law but nevertheless violate obligations in conscience – another example of his oft-repeated recognition that there might be a deep gulf between the stated position of positive law and the claims of divine dominion or lordship which are not enforceable under human law. In the light of this most severe sermon Fr. Gwynn made the extremely plausible suggestion that FitzRalph may have failed to secure redress

[37] *Visiones Georgii*, p. 312.

[38] Hammerich, 'Eine Pilgerfahrt des XIV. Jahrhunderts', 37; Max Voigt, *Beiträge zur Geschichte der Visionenliteratur im Mittelalter* (Leipzig, 1924), p. 181. Hammerich even suggested that the protection of heretics from Ossory might have been a reason for FitzRalph's drastic action against Dublin.

[39] Gwynn, *Studies*, 24, 571; B, fols. 62^{v}–63^{v}; J, fols. 52^{ra-vb}.

[40] B, fol. 63^{r}; J, fol. 52vb.

from the merchants of Drogheda with regard to the payment of tithes – and it is highly unlikely that they would willingly have conformed to his concept of their obligation to pay the tithe on each sale which they made rather than waiting until they could balance their income and expenditure and pay the tithe on their actual profits – and that as a result he placed the city under interdict. Although there are some indications that the text of the sermon diary is defective for much of the period 1353-4, it is also possible that an interdict over the largest city within his area of jurisdiction – together with some indications that FitzRalph may himself not have been in the best of health – may also be responsible for a break in his preaching activity.

The sermon diary subsequently provides occasional indications that the severity of FitzRalph's attitude to moral problems provoked a certain amount of resentment among the trading communities with whom he was dealing, and Fr. Gwynn was led to the further tentative speculation that the archbishop's high-handed ways may have aroused discontent even as far away as the Augustinian convent at Lough Derg. Hence, according to this hypothesis it could be argued that the canons there, who clearly played a decisive part in formulating for George the account of his experiences which he would present to the public, may have suggested to him such an interpretation of his 'message'. On the other hand, if the excommunicated city was in fact Drogheda, it is difficult to understand why a community of canons in a remote part of Gaelic Ireland, in a part of the ecclesiastical province which was clearly under the control of Gaelic clergy and Gaelic chieftains, and where the canons by this late date must have been a largely, if not exclusively Gaelic group, should have been so concerned. Under such circumstances a more probable object of their concern could have been the primatial city of Armagh, which was never susceptible to FitzRalph's jurisdiction and which he may well have had opportunity to place under interdict. In such a case the phrase 'magne civitatis sui archiepiscopatus' would be inappropriate, but the interest of the canons would be explained. In the present state of the evidence, it is unlikely that a satisfactory explanation can be found, and FitzRalph himself in his subsequent letters concerning the episode, even in the letter to his nephew in Avignon, is extremely reticent.

This letter to Richard FitzRalph junior, and another which contained a general proclamation or affirmation of the fact of

George's pilgrimage in terms similar to those used by the Hospitaller prior, were issued by the archbishop from Dromiskin on 22 February 1354, and they make plain that in the meantime George had arrived at FitzRalph's manor and told his story.[41] The letter to FitzRalph junior was the more detailed of the two, and the archbishop provided his nephew with an outline account of the episode, so that he might be able to deal with the matter when George arrived at the curia, but confined himself as regards the 'message' to the remark: 'que vero de nostra persona nobis expressit, ab eo, cum ad vos venerit, fortassis gratis audire aut prudenter poteritis extorquere'.[42] The archbishop's letter to his nephew then concluded with the request to show his letters concerning the affair to the cardinals at the curia. It has been established, on the basis of philological and internal evidence of the text of the *Visiones Georgii* as they have survived, that they were written down in or near Avignon by a Provençal Augustinian friar and presumably on the basis of a verbal report which he received from George himself.[43] These considerations, together with the format of the entire work: a general introduction, followed by the three letters of FitzRalph, respectively to George, the affirmation to all the faithful, and the communication to his nephew, then in strict hierarchical order the letters of the diocesan ordinary, the prior of Lough Derg, the Hospitaller prior of Kilmainham, and finally the account of George's travels, his visions, and messages which he was to deliver, suggest that it was compiled with a specific purpose in mind. Whereas the central core of the story, and of course the letters, all originated in Ireland, the author of the final version included other well-known hagiographical material and above all the earlier account of a knightly pilgrim contained in the Owein legend. Hammerich therefore suggested that, whereas the author, an unnamed Provençal Augustinian, was primarily concerned with the production of a book which the layman might appreciate, combining the traditional with the bizarre and including sufficient moral-theological material for reflection and entertainment, those in Ireland who helped to formulate George's thoughts did intend a propagandistic effect, and in this respect they must be regarded as highly successful.[44]

[41] *Visiones Georgii*, pp. 80-3. [42] Ibid., p. 82.

[43] Hammerich, 'Eine Pilgerfahrt des XIV. Jahrhunderts', 37-40, largely based on Voigt, as n. 38.

[44] Hammerich, as n. 43, 37, and 30-5 for notes on a number of pilgrims – Italian, French, Spanish, and Hungarian – who visited the Purgatory before the closure in

In the light of these considerations, and of the speed with which the Purgatory achieved widespread notoriety and attracted pilgrims from France, Italy, and Hungary, it seems not unreasonable to argue that the written version was composed and began to circulate very soon after George's pilgrimage. By September 1358 the remoteness of Lough Derg had attracted a French pilgrim, Louis d'Auxerre, who reported that as he was coming out of the Purgatory he met Galeotto Malatesta (l'Ungaro) going in, while other sources confirm that this member of the Malatesta clan had made the pilgrimage 'cum familia magna',[45] and on 24 September 1358 Edward III issued letters to both Galeotto Malatesta and to another Italian pilgrim, Niccolò da Beccaio, confirming that both of these had made the descent into the Purgatory.[46] By now the place must have grown rather crowded! Whereas it is conceivable that news of George's exploits had circulated so widely by word of mouth, it is more probable that the written version was by now in circulation, and that it had been prepared in or near Avignon on the basis of George's reports and under the guidance of someone reasonably familiar with the Irish circumstances it reflected. The most likely candidate for this role, and therefore the person who commissioned the Provençal Augustinian to compile the story prefaced with suitable authentication, is none other than the archbishop's nephew, Richard FitzRalph junior. The evidence of his uncle's letter proves that he was in Avignon in the spring of 1354 and in a position to receive George upon his arrival and make the necessary contacts for him to report his story. The records of the papal Camera indicate that the younger FitzRalph was frequently, if not continuously, in residence at the curia over the next three years, and he must have been there when the archbishop of Armagh arrived in 1357 to pursue in person his case against the friars.[47] Consequently he was in an ideal position to secure the services of a local amanuensis, to

1497. There is no critical modern study of the cult, but see Shane Leslie, *St Patrick's Purgatory* (London, 1932); Alice Curtayne, *Loch Derg: St Patrick's Purgatory* (London, 1944).

[45] For sources see Hammerich, art. cit., 32 nn.

[46] Rymer's *Foedera*, iii. 174–5.

[47] He made payments for Armagh and other Irish dioceses 18 July 1353, 5 May and 3 June 1355, 2 April and 10 May 1356, Hoberg, *Einnahmen*, ii. 35, 36, 37; also 28 September 1357, 17 February 1358, ibid., i. 210, 255. He visited Ireland in the meantime and acted as attorney for John Butterly on 21 March 1356, CPR 1354–58, 354.

guide the account which George reported to this Provençal Augustinian, and to provide the accurate background details concerning local conditions which lend conviction to the *Visiones*. At the same time he could render important service to the ecclesiastical province of Armagh and the cult of its patron saint, ensuring the speedy development of the Purgatory to a place of pilgrimage of European renown, and also emphasize the authority of the archbishop of Armagh, the 'coarb' of Patrick and rightful claimant to the title of 'primas Hibernie'. But FitzRalph junior and his uncle could scarcely have anticipated the enthusiastic reception which the German translation of the text received in the south German and Austrian territories, not only in monastic circles but among the aristocracy and educated bourgeoisie.[48] This interest, however, proved a two-edged sword: influential members of the faculty of theology in the University of Vienna condemned George's visions as pure fantasy and subsequently turned their attention to the 'heretical' anti-mendicant views of Archbishop FitzRalph.[49]

iv. Pastoral care and Church reform in a divided society

George Grissaphan's visit to Ireland and St. Patrick's Purgatory occurred roughly in the middle of FitzRalph's longest and most fruitful period of activity as archbishop of Armagh. During the five years between his return from Avignon during the summer months of 1351 and his departure for England early in June 1356, he attempted to devise practical remedies for the flaws he perceived in Irish social and ecclesiastical life. With this purpose in mind he tried to introduce into his province the norms of ecclesiastical government and administration which he had observed in England and on the Continent. Consequently he undertook a programme of ecclesiastical reform, holding synods and visitations, and engaging in preaching tours in order to put into effect reform measures which were directed at those under

[48] See Hans Rupprich, 'Das Wiener Schrifttum des ausgehendes Mittelalters', *SB Wien. Phil. hist. Klasse*, 228, 5 (Vienna, 1954), 157–9.

[49] The best-known critic of the *Visiones* was Heinrich von Langenstein, rector of the University of Vienna 1393–4. See Thomas Hohmann, *Heinrichs von Langenstein 'Unterscheidung der Geister' lateinisch und deutsch. Texte und Untersuchungen zu Übersetzungsliteratur aus der Wiener Schule* (Zurich–Munich, 1977), pp. 44–5, and his criticism was taken up in Felix Faber, *Evagatorium in Terrae sanctae, Arabiae et Egypti Peregrinationem*, ed. Cunradus D. Hassler, 3 vols. (Stuttgart, 1843–9), ii. 482. Criticism of FitzRalph's views on the friars was expressed by the Viennese faculty of theology on 8 March 1413. See Paul Uiblein, *Die Akten der Theologischen Fakultät der Universität Wien (1396–1508)*, 2 vols. (Vienna, 1978), i. 25.

his jurisdiction at all levels – suffragan bishops, parochial clergy, and the laity. As a source of information on these topics his episcopal register would have been particularly valuable, as it would have made possible a more systematic examination of his objectives and achievements than can be gleaned from the sermon diary. The nature of the diary itself prevents it from being other than an uneven and one-sided account, a poor substitute for formal record material, and this defect is made even more acute in the years 1351-6 because of gaps in FitzRalph's preaching and the distinct possibility that several 'quaderni' of the diary are missing.[1] However, the evidence of the diary suggests that much of the reforming activity in these years centred on the two synods which he held in Drogheda, respectively in 1352 and 1355. For neither of these assemblies has a record survived of the legislation enacted, but information can be pieced together from other sources, principally from the diary. In the first case the diary contains a Latin text of the sermon which he preached at the opening of the synod on 7 February 1352; it appears to be virtually complete and provides a vivid picture of the moral abuses against which the archbishop hoped to take action in the course of the synod.[2] The second assembly was also opened with a sermon preached by him, on 5 February 1355, and although the account of this sermon is merely a brief outline of the points raised,[3] a substantial degree of 'follow-up' to the legislation of the synod has survived. Not merely did FitzRalph himself undertake a visitation and preaching tour of the southern half of his own diocese and in the diocese of Meath in the months following the synod, during which he frequently referred back to the provisions enacted, but also the register of Archbishop Swayne (1418–39) contains the statutes of a subsequent provincial council.[4] Five of the decrees of this council are described as having been enacted on the basis of the previous legislation of 'lord Richard', and these pertain for the most part to issues which the sermon diary, including the 1355 visitation sermons, show to have been among FitzRalph's

[1] Gwynn, 'Sermon Diary', 20–1.

[2] Ed. Gwynn, 'Two sermons of Primate Richard FitzRalph', *Arch. Hib.* 14 (1949), 50-65, at 53–63.

[3] Ibid., 63–5.

[4] *Reg. John Swayne*, pp. 8–18. Earlier historians, including Chart, believed that this provincial council had been held under Primate John Colton (1381–1404), but Gwynn argued that they should be dated to Colton's successor, Nicholas Fleming (1404–16), 'Ireland and the English Nation at the Council of Constance', *PRIA* 45 C (1940), 210–12.

principal concerns. Included are statutory measures against those who interfere with the inheritance rights and testamentary dispositions of women, against those who appropriate property belonging to the Church or to individual members of the clergy, guidelines on the obligation of annual confession to one's own parish priest and on the duty of paying tithes and first-fruits.[5] Also included was a series of prohibitions against various forms of entertainment and the maintenance of entertainers: forbidden were mimes, jugglers, poets, drummers, and harpers, and those who extort gifts, presumably in return for their talents and services.[6] Such entertainments were repeatedly forbidden to the clergy in English synodalia, but the tenor of the Armagh statutes seems to imply that FitzRalph's prohibition was absolute and designed to include the laity also.[7] In this case FitzRalph's actions were somewhat unique, and he probably had political and cultural as well as moral-religious objectives in mind. His prohibition may have been directed against the courts and customs of the Gaelic families in the province and against those Anglo-Normans who by the mid-fourteenth century had begun to adopt similar practices. Under such circumstances the enactment of this legislation in 1355, during the years of tension preceding the Statutes of Kilkenny (1366) is not surprising.[8] More difficult to explain is the fact that similar provisions had been enacted by FitzRalph's predecessor, O'Hiraghty, at a provincial council during his episcopate,[9] but we know all too little about this last archbishop of Armagh of Gaelic stock during the later Middle Ages, and an estimate of his attitude to the respective social customs of the two communities is not possible.

Although FitzRalph's opportunities for personal contact with the living conditions and customs of those members of his flock who lived beyond the Anglo-Norman trading colonies in County Louth and in the diocese of Meath are generally assumed to have been minimal, the sermon diary provides evidence of one occasion on which he may have passed through a substantial tract of Gaelic territory, and in view of the fragmentary state of

[5] *Reg. John Swayne*, p. 9. [6] Ibid., p. 11.

[7] Frederick M. Powicke and Christopher R. Cheney (eds.), *Councils and Synods, with other Documents relating to the English Church A.D. 1205–1313*, 2 vols. (Oxford, 1964). See 'joculatores', *ad indicem*.

[8] Geoffrey J. Hand, 'The forgotten Statutes of Kilkenny: a brief survey', *Irish Jurist*, n.s. 1 (1966), 299–312.

[9] *Reg. John Swayne*, p. 11.

the diary for parts of the Irish period there is little reason to assume that he did not make other forays beyond the frontiers of Anglo-Ireland. The one definite occasion was when he preached on 8 September 1351 in Coleraine, a small coastal town far to the north, and inhabited by an isolated English community who were completely cut off from the Anglo-Norman region around County Louth. Gwynn suggested the possibility that FitzRalph returned from Avignon, where he had preached for the last time on 6 March, via England, and from an English port sailed to Ireland in a ship which had reason to call at this isolated outpost.[10] Even if this were the case, it seems probable that he returned from there to the Dundalk area overland, travelling through the territory of the O'Cahan, the Great O'Neill, and O'Hanlon. FitzRalph's decision to visit this region may also have been linked with the censures administered by Edward III to the absentee archbishop while he was still in Avignon: in the king's letters to curial cardinals whose assistance he sought with regard to the conflicting claims to the Irish primacy he drew attention to the state of violence and rebellion which existed in Ireland, and writing to FitzRalph on the same day (18 February 1350) accused the archbishop of being partly responsible for this situation. Here the king reminded FitzRalph that on account of the raids and violence of all kinds which were causing hardship to his flock he ought to return to them and refrain from pursuing personal ambitions. Under these circumstances FitzRalph might have thought it prudent to be seen taking an interest in a community of hard-pressed colonists, though he could not have foreseen that within a generation of his visit the town would succumb before the Gaelic revival.[11] The theme of his sermon, appropriate to the feast of the day, was that of devotion to the Blessed Virgin, and he reminded his audience that she also bore the title of Star of the Sea and had a particular affection for those who lived near the sea, on the islands in a great ocean.[12] Although he made no specific reference to their precarious position, he discussed the link between prudence and moral virtue, and it may not have been coincidence that he made frequent use of the image of the soldier.[13] But apart from this possible allusion, the sermon contained no details which might shed light on the reasons for his visit to

[10] B, fols. 51^v–53^v; J, fols. 42va–44ra; 'Sermon Diary', 28.
[11] Edmund Curtis, *A History of Mediaeval Ireland* (Dublin, 1923^1), p. 263.
[12] B, fol. 51^v; J, fol. 42va.
[13] B, fol. 52^v; J, fol. 43rb.

the area, nor did it indicate particular affinity with the problems of his audience.

By the second half of November he was back in familiar territory, among his own people in Louth and Meath, and he heard an inquisition before twelve jurors at the manor of the Nober in County Meath, where the archbishops of Armagh had extensive property interests.[14] The subject-matter of the inquisition was a purely secular one, concerning internal arrangements in the manor, including the election of officers and regulation of milling obligations, and the archbishop's presence reflected once more his constant concern for the material well-being of his see and its scattered property interests. The season of Advent saw him once more at work in the central area of his diocese around Dundalk and Drogheda, where preparations must have been in hand for the provincial synod to be held early the following year. On 4 December he preached in the parish church of Dromiskin to the local people, but although one of his manors was located there and he was frequently in residence, the sermon – a general instruction on the Last Judgement – gave no indication of particular familiarity with his audience.[15] Two days later he preached in Dundalk, in the church of St. Nicholas on that saint's feast-day. The subsequent decision to transfer his remains from Avignon to this church might suggest that he had a particular veneration for the saint, or at least a special affection for the church. But the brief notes in the diary lend little support for such a theory. On the contrary the archbishop even found time on the feast of a saint primarily venerated as a helper in time of need and bringer of happiness to children, to voice stern warnings about the need for high moral principles and the avoidance of corruption.[16]

But if FitzRalph was aware of the need for severe measures among 'his own people' in Dundalk, and preached to them frequently in less than flattering terms, the brunt of his criticism was reserved for the citizens of Drogheda. His opinion of these was exceedingly low, even by the standards of moral outrage expressed by medieval preachers.[17] He appears to have learned at an early stage that the citizens of this, the largest city in his diocese and a wealthy, economically aggressive merchant

[14] *Cal. Reg. Sweteman*, 287.
[15] B, fols. 53^{v}–55^{v}; J, fols. 44ra–46ra.
[16] B, fol. 56^{r}; J, fol. 46^{ra-b}.
[17] See the numerous examples including some by FitzRalph and Thomas Brinton, bishop of Rochester (1373–89), in Owst, *Literature*², pp. 210–470.

community, were familiar with most of the modern methods of tithe-evasion, of avoiding the accusation of usury while nevertheless profiting from its practice, and – doubtless encouraged by the friars in their midst – were well versed in the means of gaining spiritual benefits after death by means of donations *inter vivos*.[18] Hence FitzRalph had reason to believe that emphatic denunciations of these and other malpractices of an economic nature were more necessary in Drogheda than elsewhere in his diocese, and he returned to these topics here more frequently. A singularly high proportion of the sermons preached in Drogheda returned under one guise or another to tithe-evasion, usury, defrauding the Church and one's business partners, land speculation and rent-evasion, interference with the process of ecclesiastical justice, and with the testamentary rights of minority groups. In the first recorded sermon in Drogheda after his return from Avignon, on 18 December 1351, he discussed the vanity of worldly goods, and the sinfulness of those who cling excessively to such property. In this sermon, which is recorded *in extenso* in the diary and clearly intended for future use, he developed again one of his favourite themes, which he had expounded a decade earlier in Avignon.[19] Previously he had employed it in a manner which implied that he regarded the friars, as the principal beneficiaries of such practices, as equally culpable. He condemned the rich who hoarded their wealth, enjoyed it to the full in life, and intended to bequeath it for the benefit of the poor after death. Here again FitzRalph insisted that such acts were not to be regarded as meritorious; on the contrary they led to eternal damnation. In order to avoid serious sin, he argued, the wealthy must be prepared to detach themselves from worldly pleasures and goods during this life and give alms of their superfluous goods before they find death approaching.[20] But this sermon is still moderate in tone when compared with some of his later outbursts from the pulpit in Drogheda.

The first indication of serious friction between the archbishop and the people of Drogheda was to be found in the sermon preached to them a year later on 2 December 1352, taking the Pauline text 'Induimini dominum Jhesum Christum' (Rom.

[18] Already in *Super Cathedram* (1300) Boniface VIII had recognized that such donations were a major source of the friars' income, and his decision to impose the *portio canonica* to be yielded to the bishop for the secular parochial clergy was an attempt to minimize friction and resentment in this area, see Clem. III. 7. 2, Friedberg, ii. 1161–4.

[19] B, fols. 58^{r}–62^{v}; J, fols. 48ra–52va.

[20] B, fol. 58^{v}; J, fol. 49^{rb-va}.

xiii. 14), and interpreting it in the sense of man's duty to clothe himself with the Christian virtues.[21] The text in the diary is incomplete, breaking off abruptly, but enough of it survives to indicate FitzRalph's opinion of the moral and ethical standards of the citizens. It is mainly devoted to the practical application of the message, contrasting the ideal with the actual situation in the city, where trickery and fraud were common practices, where men had no scruples either in their business dealings with one another or in the fulfilment of their obligations before God. In the case of the latter he returned once more to the obligation of paying tithes, insisting that the clergy's right to tithes was divinely approved and claiming that the flock deliberately deprived the clergy of that right. Frequently the clergy had no option but to accept a compromise solution, or part-payment of the dues to which they were entitled, a situation which FitzRalph condemned as a violent attack on divine lordship.[22] His discussion of the methods employed by traders in order to reduce their tithe liability is an interesting indication of his own concept of the obligation. He complained that they did not pay the tithe at the time of selling their goods or otherwise making a profit, but waited until they could balance their books at the end of the year and then point out that they had little or no profit on the year's trading. FitzRalph on the contrary interpreted the obligation as meaning that they should pay the tithe on each sale – be it of wine, cloth, timber, crops, or livestock – a system which would of course have greatly increased the revenues accruing to the Church.[23] His views clearly did not meet with a very enthusiastic response in the city, but he persisted in the matter and when he still achieved no success, adopted the drastic measure of placing Drogheda under interdict the following year.

These may seem brutal methods, and they certainly reflected the intense concern which FitzRalph displayed for the material, and especially financial aspects of his office. This preoccupation with material affairs could make him a target for the same charges with which he constantly reprimanded his suffragans and clergy, and the excessive care for the goods of this world which he criticized among the laity. On the other hand he found the archdiocese in a desperate financial situation, partly due to the rapacity of English Crown agents during the episcopates of

[21] B, fols. 62^{v}–63^{v}; J, fols. 52^{ra-vb}.

[22] B, fol. 63^{r}; J, fol. 52^{va-b}.

[23] B, fol. 63^{r}; J, fol. 52vb.

his predecessors, and partly because of the weight of papal exactions. The need to restore the situation at home and, no less, the insistence of the papal Camera that an already impoverished diocese should nevertheless have to pay the debts of his predecessors, go a long way to explain his concern for financial problems.

The remainder of the sermon showed that he was similarly concerned that his flock should be honest and just in their dealings with each other, and not solely when the interests of the Church were involved. He was equally severe in his denunciations of usury,[24] and of the methods of those who made false statements about the price of land and other property which was up for sale, though in the latter case it is possible that he had personal experience also in mind. He had recently been engaged in a policy of property exchange, in order to provide the see of Armagh with a more coherent body of temporalities, instead of the widely scattered and therefore uncontrollable lands of his predecessors, and had as a result good reason to become involved in negotiations about the price of property. His emphasis on the duty of serious examination of conscience was reflected in his strictures that even in cases not covered by positive law, where there was no chance of legal redress for the injured parties, the obligation in conscience was still binding. It was not enough to argue, as in the case of the murder of Irishmen or other enemies of the English Crown, that this was done by loyal subjects operating according to the 'lex marchie', or alternatively to argue that an act was not wrong because 'secundum leges regni' there was no specific prohibition of it.[25] Unfortunately the text of the sermon breaks off in all manuscripts at the point at which FitzRalph began to apply his own particular theory of dominion and law, arguing that human law was frequently obliged for social reasons, for the common good, to tolerate hidden wrongs.[26] This was a clear hint in the direction of his theory of dominion, that had eternal validity but was not capable of enforcement under positive law, which at the time of preaching he was already working out in the *De Pauperie*

[24] B, fol. 63^{r-v}; J, fol. 52vb. This had been one of the first topics raised by FitzRalph in Ireland, at Mansfieldstown, 11 May 1348, and it was to remain a burning issue in the diocese. A usury case was brought to trial before his court in Armagh, 31 May 1356 but dismissed as unproven, *Dowdall Deeds*, p. 86. Clearly usury was more easily denounced from the pulpit than proved in court.

[25] B, fol. 63^{v}; J, fol. 52vb. He had already discussed this in Drogheda, 25 March 1349 and would return to it four years later in the light of his experiences as a peace-negotiator between the 'two nations'.

[26] B, fol. 63^{v}; J, fol. 52vb.

Salvatoris. He would soon apply it to the Franciscan controversy over evangelical poverty – here he was using it to resolve the dichotomy caused by the various conflicting systems of law in operation in later medieval Ireland.[27]

The tenor of the sermon to FitzRalph's first provincial synod in 1352 suggests that it was preached to an audience consisting primarily of the higher clergy and including at least some of the suffragan bishops in the province of Armagh. Although the loss of his episcopal register makes it impossible to assess precisely the extent of FitzRalph's contact with his suffragans, the evidence of the registers of his immediate successors suggests no reason to assume that such contact did not exist.[28] Of the ten suffragan bishoprics, Connor was vacant during the early months of 1352 following the death of James O'Kearney the previous year, and nothing is known about Raphoe for this period. Of the others, we have already noted FitzRalph's contact with the diocese of Meath, whose bishop, William St. Leger, is most likely to have been present.[29] Of the dioceses largely in Gaelic hands, the episode concerning George Grissaphan must be taken as an indication that reasonable relations existed between FitzRalph and his suffragan in Clogher, the long-lived Nicholas MacCathasaigh, while the unnamed bishop of Dromore had, on 5 February 1351 – while FitzRalph was still at the curia and was presumably consulted about the appointment, if it did not take place at his prompting – been named as a conservator of the privileges and prerogatives of the see of Armagh.[30] Eoghan O'Ferghail of Ardagh had been elected *c.*1344 and consecrated

[27] Geoffrey J. Hand, *English Law in Ireland 1290–1324* (Cambridge, 1967), pp. 159–218; idem, 'English Law in Ireland, 1172–1351', *Northern Ireland Legal Quarterly*, 23 (1972), 393–422.

[28] The best-documented example is the case of Colton and the bishop of Derry. William E. Reeves (ed.), *Acts of Archbishop Colton in his metropolitan visitation of the diocese of Derry, 1397* (Dublin, 1850).

[29] St. Leger had been archdeacon of Meath under Bishop William of St. Paul O.Carm. (1327–49), *HBC*^{2}, 320. On the latter's death in July 1349, Clement VI provided St. Leger on 5 October, *Reg. Vat.* 195, fol. 48^r; *CPL* 1342–62, 339. On 7 November FitzRalph, then in Avignon, petitioned for the archdeaconry for his 'familiar' William Napton, vicar of St. Nicholas in Dundalk and occasionally FitzRalph's proctor in the papal Camera, *Reg. Suppl.* 21, fol. 82^r; *CPL Petitions* I, 185; *Reg. Vat.* 195, fol. 154^v; *CPL* 341; Mohler, *Einnahmen*, 185, 224. St. Leger died 24 August 1352 and by the time of FitzRalph's second synod the bishop of Meath was Nicholas Allen, formerly abbot of the Augustinian canons of St. Thomas the Martyr in Dublin.

[30] *Reg. Vat.* 200, fols. 235^v–236^r; *CPL* 368. The registered copy of the bull referred to the bishops of Meath and Dromore, and the abbot of Navan (Augustinian canons, see *Medieval Religious Houses. Ireland*, pp. 189–90) simply as NN.

by FitzRalph's predecessor in ignorance of a papal reservation of the see. The fact that he sought and obtained papal confirmation and therefore regularization of his position on 10 February 1352 may have been partly due to the new archbishop's policy of controlling more effectively those under his jurisdiction.[31] Clonmacnoise was ruled by a Dominican friar Henry, while his confrère, the subsequently notorious Bishop Simon, was already installed in Derry, and a Franciscan, Ralph Kilmessan, ruled in Down.[32] Subsequent relations between Archbishop Sweteman and the Dominican bishop of Derry were such that the latter's attendance at the synod need not be taken for granted. But those relations, followed up by Archbishop John Colton's visitation of the diocese in 1397,[33] also indicated the extent to which Derry was regularly subjected to metropolitan jurisdiction. It is also possible that strained relations with the friars may have prevented the attendance of the Franciscan bishop of Down.

How many of these suffragans were actually present is a matter for speculation, but those who did attend heard a sermon which laid down in clear and vigorous language FitzRalph's concept of the duties of a prelate, and an equally vigorous denunciation of the abuses and moral laxity which he professed to observe among some of his fellow prelates. Although he made no specific condemnations, it is possible that he had some of the habits of Bishop Simon of Derry in mind.[34] Taking as his text 'Viri pastores sumus servi tui' (Gen. xlvi. 34), he outlined the work of the bishop as shepherd of his flock, who should be prepared to work in the vineyard of the lord with courage and tenacity, and without seeking material rewards. But so many were, on the contrary, lazy and effeminate, shopkeepers not shepherds, 'ministri diaboli non servi Christi', who would not be

[31] *Reg. Vat.* 211, fol. 177^{r}; *CPL* 458. Eoghan petitioned that, on the death of his predecessor John MacEothaig *c.*1340 (*HBC*^{2}, 309, gives 1343 but without month or day) the diocese was long vacant, whereupon the chapter elected him oblivious of a papal reservation. Eoghan had sought confirmation and consecration from the archbishop of Armagh, presumably O'Hiraghty, as he claimed to have been 8 years in office by 1352. He also claimed to have administered the diocese conscientiously during this period and now, having been made aware of his dubious position (by FitzRalph?), sought and obtained papal confirmation.

[32] *HBC*^{2}, 312, 314, 315.

[33] *Cal. Reg. Sweteman, passim* provides numerous indications of the difficulties caused by the troublesome Dominican. e.g. 14 February 1369 the primate issued a number of orders, among them one exhorting the bishop of Derry to pay the debts he owed to his metropolitan superior, some of which were outstanding since FitzRalph's day, ibid., 284.

[34] Ibid., 223–4, 247–8.

able to answer on the day of judgement as Joseph and his brothers could when interrogated by Pharaoh.[35] The ideal he set before the prelates was threefold, and expressed in simpler, more immediate terms than he had employed when developing his concept of the ideal prelate over a decade earlier in Avignon: sanctity of life, as servant of God; energy in ruling, as men of courage; and wisdom in teaching, as good shepherds. Then he offered them guidelines for a number of problems in moral theology which they would encounter daily, including the degrees of sin involved in the use of the conjugal act for purposes of pleasure and not, as he taught, for procreation. He advised them to exercise prudence in the selection of candidates for ordination, examining carefully both their learning – especially their proficiency in the Bible – and also their personal aptitude for the vocation to the priesthood. But he offered no suggestions to his brother bishops as to how they might ensure that this standard of education be attained, though the provision of adequate facilities for clerical education was clearly the subject of consideration at the later synod.[36] From earlier sermons we know that he was under no illusions about the level of education to be found among the laity, even in a rich and outward-looking city such as Drogheda – he even went so far as to state his belief that ignorance was responsible for many of the ills of Irish society. But it is possible that at the time of convening the first synod in 1352 he had not been confronted to the same extent with the problem of ignorance among his own parochial clergy, whereas by 1355 he had established the dimensions of the problem and drawn some conclusions about its causes and essential remedies. The prelates who neglected to provide for clerical education were probably identical with those who came in for criticism at the first synod on another ground. FitzRalph exhorted his listeners to be courageous in defence of the laws of the Church, reflecting that prelates who neglected to defend them represented a particularly serious problem, and that it was useless to legislate against them as they simply ignored such statutes.[37]

[35] Ed. cit., p. 53; Gen. xlvi, 33–4.

[36] Ibid., pp. 54, 56–7, where he taught a rigorous doctrine concerning 'delectacio in concubito coniugali, que solum fit causa prolis domino serviture . . .', clearly intended as a guideline for the confessional. In the synod of 1355 he drew the assembly's attention to the educational measures devised by Benedict XII for the Cistercians, ed. cit., pp. 64–5.

[37] Ibid., p. 57. FitzRalph clearly welcomed boldness in prelates and here he practised what he preached: any cause he adopted was fought with 'audacia singularis'.

The second half of the sermon was devoted to denunciation, in language so blunt as to border occasionally on the pornographic, of the moral lapses of which some of his fellow bishops were guilty. He accused them of being hirelings and plunderers, thieves, robbers, concerned only with merchandise like shopkeepers, of being fornicators and adulterers, gluttons and drunkards.[38] Some are the cause of great scandal because, not merely are they not the husbands of one wife, but they are the adulterers of many mistresses, instead of which they should take the Church as their bride. Others are equally the cause of scandal because they live each day in such a state of drunkenness, behaving in a filthy and scurrilous manner, that nobody wishes to have the pleasure of their company, and yet at the same time they celebrate the sacraments. Others again are the nepotists, who plunder the movable and immovable goods of the Church in order to provide for their 'nieces and nephews', as they politely call their offspring, and by so doing they impoverish the Church and are unable to show the hospitality which is required of them by their profession. His list of accusations continued with one against those who seized the fruits of their churches, while neglecting to serve them; who were always trying to extract more out of their benefices, while never being there in person to fulfil Christ's command to 'feed my sheep'; who spent their time at the courts of princes, for their own betterment and the ruin of their flocks. He then included a further category, which he called pastors in name and dealers in fact, claiming that they sold to the laity not merely the tithes to which the Church was entitled, but also rewards which should be linked with their spiritual duties, under which category he presumably understood simonists.[39]

How are we to understand this denunciation of the clergy in the Irish Church, or at least in the ecclesiastical province of Armagh? The denunciation included most of the standard abuses, which were the stock-in-trade of medieval preachers and which audiences expected to hear. However, although there was a certain element of convention in such criticism, a distinction should be made between the 'in-group' or internal criticism of the secular clergy, made by a responsible prelate before his

[38] Ed. cit., pp. 58–9, and for Eng. trans. of this passage, Owst, *Literature*², pp. 244–5.

[39] Ed. cit., pp. 60–1. See Becket sermon in the *Audientia causarum* (1341), B, fols. 138^{v}–140^{v}; J, fols. 103ra–105ra.

synodal audience, and the external or 'out-group' attacks on the shortcomings of the secular clergy made by the friars in front of the laity. FitzRalph himself was clearly aware of the need to maintain such a distinction even before becoming a bishop, and explicitly refrained from discussing certain topics in the presence of the laity.[40] In his synodal sermon his references to fornicators and nepotists probably had a more direct application, and were specifically directed at elements either in his audience or under the jurisdiction of those present. A large portion of his province fell within the area of Gaelic Ireland. Despite the reform movement of the twelfth century which had sought to bring Ireland into line with the general practices of western Christendom, the Church had never succeeded in extending its influence beyond the purely religious sphere in Gaelic Ireland, and therefore social customs, family bonds, and the institution of marriage remained a largely secular concern. A practical result of this situation of 'Gaelic secular marriage' was that marriages were easily dissolved and that in the upper classes of later medieval Ireland both men and women frequently had a succession of spouses. Even among the laity many of these marriages were invalid under canon law, as the Gaelic Irish tended to marry their kinsfolk, while their frequent marriages created innumerable ties of affinity. Added to this was the strongly hereditary character of the clerical profession, whereby the clergy entered marriages which were clearly invalid under canon law but valid in Gaelic law, then sought the necessary dispensations from the papacy to hold ecclesiastical benefices, and subsequently also for their sons in spite of their illegitimacy to succeed them in these benefices, or to acquire others.[41] Among his suffragans, and even in communities of monks and canons, FitzRalph must already have encountered this situation, and it is possible that his fulminations were at least partly directed against that substantial group of his clergy, whose Gaelic social customs and family law placed them in a position which was diametrically opposed to the norms of a developed canon law which the archbishop was trying to enforce in the area under his jurisdiction.

[40] Owst, *Literature*², pp. 236-86. See also the strictures of Arundel in his Oxford Constitutions (1408), that preachers should deal with the vices of the clergy in sermons before clerical audiences and attack the sins of the laity when addressing lay listeners, but not vice versa, Wilkins, *Concilia*, iii. 316; FitzRalph's sermon for Palm Sunday 1346 expressed a similar view, B, fol. 27ᵛ; J, fol. 22ʳᵃ.

[41] Nicholls, *Gaelic and Gaelicised Society*, pp. 73-7, 91-102.

FitzRalph concluded with an exhortation to the assembled prelates to work with him during the council for the eradication of some of the ills caused by simony, also to legislate against those who brought ecclesiastical cases before secular courts.[42] Whether his words fell on deaf ears, or whether he succeeded in persuading his brother-bishops to enact a programme of legislation to meet these problems, we do not know. From the first synod no statutes have survived, even indirectly, as the diary contained no sermons or visitation record as was to be the case after the second synod. Nor is it clear that any of the statutes enacted later, almost certainly by Archbishop Fleming and copied into Swayne's register, which were based on FitzRalph's legislation, referred to the first synod. On the contrary most of the topics reflected in this later legislation were those discussed in the synod of 1355.

Whereas FitzRalph's first synodal sermon is preserved in complete form in the diary, in the manner of the Avignon sermons, the second sermon survives only in the form of brief notes or reminders of the points to be raised. This formal difference may have been determined by the audiences to which these were respectively directed. The first was clearly addressed to an audience of higher clergy, presumably including at least some of his suffragan bishops. For most of these, apart from the bishop of Meath, it may have been their first opportunity for a formal meeting with their metropolitan superior. On such an occasion it is not surprising that FitzRalph would have prepared a formal text which survived in full in the diary. On the second occasion there is no indication that bishops were present, and the general tenor of FitzRalph's remarks suggest an audience of clergy at the lower levels of the ecclesiastical hierarchy and concentrated on more local pastoral problems. Under such circumstances the majority of the attendance was probably composed of the Anglo-Irish clergy of Meath and of the English portion of his own diocese – mostly people for whom he must have been a familiar figure. Hence there may have been less need for a formally prepared statement of the problems he wished to bring to their attention.

On the text 'Mundati sunt sacerdos et levite et mundaverunt populum' (Nehemiah xii. 30) he expounded before his audience his concept of the ideal priest. Here there was little trace of that outraged criticism and moral indignation which had characterized

[42] Ed. cit., p. 63.

the earlier sermon, and one is left with the impression that here he was instructing *his own* priests. He laid before them a programme, whose elements are recognizable as a constant feature of his own preaching and practice: the priest is bound to teach his people, and therefore bound to educate himself in sacred subjects; he is to be mediator between God and his flock, and must therefore be exemplary and without blemish himself; he must govern those under his care, and must therefore be capable of giving guidance and justice. Above all he stressed the importance of establishing a relationship between the pastor and his flock, using for the flock's own pastor the term 'proprius' whose interpretation was to be such a bone of contention during the mendicant controversies.[43] From this sermon it emerges that, as far as FitzRalph was concerned, the 'proprius sacerdos' to whom the flock should turn for confession, whose voice they should recognize, whose sermons they should attend, was unquestionably that member of the secular clergy who was their appointed parish priest or curate, and who possessed the privilege of preaching to them and hearing their confessions. Then he went on to consider the foundation of sacred learning which such pastors required for their work as teachers and preachers. This should not be limited to what they have learned by rote from the scripts and notebooks of others – the sort of students' aids with which FitzRalph was familiar since his own days as a student and university teacher. Hence he was in an ideal position to recognize the inadequacy of much of the knowledge thus acquired for the demands of the pastoral situation, in which the priest must himself have a thorough mastery of the message of God which he was supposed to transmit. Such lapses, the archbishop warned, were to be found among the clergy at all levels, among bishops, and among the parochial clergy. Here he set before them the example of his own mentor and patron, Benedict XII, who had included among the reform measures which he had imposed upon his own Cistercian order a number of obligations with regard to higher studies. These included the

[43] Fundamental to the debate about the friars' privilege of hearing confessions of the laity was the question of the meaning of 'proprius sacerdos', and further whether the meaning of that term had remained unchanged since the formulation of the Lateran canon *Omnis utriusque sexus* (1215), V. 38. 12, Friedberg, ii. 887–8. John XXII had attempted to clarify the situation in *Vas electionis* (1321), Extrav. V. 3. 2, ibid., ii. 1291–2, but this statement became one of the most hotly debated elements in the dispute between FitzRalph and the friars. The best general discussion is still Hugolin Lippens, 'Le droit nouveau des mendiants en conflit avec le droit coutumier du clergé séculier du Concile de Vienne à celui de Trente', *AFH* 47 (1954), 241–92.

provision whereby the community had to send suitable candidates to study theology at the common expense and for the common good of the order.[44] Benedict had issued this legislation in July 1335, when FitzRalph was at the curia and in a position to have heard the debates centring on the papal reform measures and the promotion of religious studies in the orders.[45]

FitzRalph had long campaigned for a kind of ecclesiastical meritocracy, for better recognition of the claims of university graduates to benefices, and was apparently trying to establish a direct connection between higher educational attainment and greater suitability for office. But he developed these claims in direct opposition to the existing conditions and on the basis of personal experience. He had suffered personally at the early stages of his career under the system whereby benefices were frequently awarded on the strength of family connections and wealth, while at the same time university masters could barely scrape together enough to survive. There may have been an element of rhetoric in his claims, but he had to face a similar situation as university chancellor, when this issue was one of the *gravamina* laid by the university before the pope.[46] But in an earlier sermon preached in Avignon he had denied wishing to suggest either that pastoral experience was only to be found among doctors of theology or that the simple pastor without a university degree or great pretensions to scholarship might not be a better teacher of his flock.[47] However, he still felt the need for a better standard of theological expertise on the part of those who intended to engage in the pastoral ministry in his province. It is possible that the actual conditions which he encountered in Ireland had made him less idealistic about the pastoral capacities of the simple pastor with little learning or training than he had been a decade earlier in Avignon, when his judgements are more likely to have been based on theory than on personal experience. Furthermore, the need for a well-educated parochial clergy had been brought home to him more forcibly since the beginning of his confrontation with the friars, as the latter regularly employed the argument of their own superior educational attainments and pastoral training, by comparison with the majority of the secular clergy, in defence of their participation in the cure of souls.

[44] Ed. cit., pp. 64–5.
[45] Mahn, pp. 31–75.
[46] See also his sermon before Benedict XII, 25 February 1338, B, fol. 149^{v}; J, fol. 111vb.
[47] In the Becket sermon of 1340, B, fol. 237^{r}; J, fol. 170ra.

The final section of FitzRalph's sermon turned to a consideration, brief in the notes, but presumably expanded in the course of delivery, of the evils to be seen among his own priests, whom he hoped would be salved by the medicine of the present synod. These included the standard abuses and predictable human failings of the clergy with which English synodalia are studded: the clergy enjoyed luxurious living, were lazy and drunken, neglected their duties of hospitality, and were frequently indistinguishable from the laity. Here for the first time in FitzRalph's synodal sermons the friars came in for specific criticism, as usurpers of tithes which were properly due to the Church. It is improbable that FitzRalph meant to imply that the friars were actually laying claim to a share in the tithes. More probable is the suggestion that the friars' lenient attitude in the confessional to the matter of restitution as a necessary precondition for absolution was at issue. The friars were probably inclined to absolve their penitents from the duty of tithe-paying and this was consequently reflected in a loss of diocesan revenue. Equally the friars encouraged the laity to whom they ministered to make legacies and bequests in their favour, and the extent to which the laity made the mendicant orders the objects of their charity also involved a substantial loss of revenue to the secular parochial clergy, and to the diocesan financial system, which was in a far from healthy state despite FitzRalph's own attempts to improve matters. From the friars the preacher moved to the laity, who were also the object of his strictures and against whose failings the council ought to take action. He concluded with a general reference to the categories of offender he had in mind: usurers, perjurers, tithe-evaders, debtors, and those who obstruct the rights of Irishmen and of women to make their wills freely, in defiance of the laws of the king and of God.[48]

That these issues were the subject of synodal legislation is clear from the content of the sermons which the archbishop preached in the course of a visitation in his own diocese and in Meath, which he appears to have undertaken with the specific purpose of ensuring that this legislation be put into operation. Already during his first sojourn in Ireland as archbishop an

[48] Ed. cit., p. 65. Mendicant reluctance to enforce the obligation of tithe-paying on their penitents was common also in England. In 1426 Archbishop Chichele ordered the Franciscan provincial to instruct his friars to stress in their sermons, on pain of ecclesiastical penalties, the necessity of paying personal tithes to parish priests, *The Register of Henry Chichele, Archbishop of Canterbury 1414–1443*, ed. Ernest F. Jacob, iii (Canterbury and York Society, 1945), 156–7.

agreement had been drawn up regulating his visitation rights in the diocese of Meath. The parties to the agreement were respectively the archbishop, dean, and chapter of Armagh on the one hand, and on the other Bishop William of St. Paul of Meath, the archdeacons of Kells and Meath – the latter was then William of St. Leger who succeeded to the bishopric the following year – and the clergy of the diocese. On 1 December 1348 the composition between the two parties was set out in letters patent of the bishop of Meath and his clergy,[49] to the effect that the archbishop and his successors might freely visit the diocese, on the condition that they exacted no more than the sum of £80 in procurations. Half of this sum was to be paid on the day the archbishop entered the diocese, the other half was due within three months following. But payment depended upon a further condition, that three months' notice of the visitation had been given to the bishop of Meath or his representatives, and that the visitation was conducted in accordance with the regulations laid down by Innocent IV in 1254, i.e. every three years.[50] If the archbishop decided to conduct a visitation more frequently, the sums to which he was entitled were accordingly reduced. After two years he was entitled to 80 marks (£53. 6*s.* 8*d.*) and after one year 40 marks (£26. 13*s.* 4*d.*). Any visitation which did not comply with these provisions might be lawfully resisted by the clergy of the diocese, but on the other hand if they resisted the archbishop's legitimate right to visitation, or if they did not pay the agreed procurations, he was entitled to enforce ecclesiastical censures against the offending parties, either in the diocese of Meath or in the portion of the archdiocese of Armagh which lay 'inter Anglos'.[51] At the joint expense of the parties concerned this agreement was to be submitted for papal approval.[52] The bishop of Meath had the necessary documents drawn up by Master William Tadlow, a cleric of the diocese and a public notary, and they were witnessed by

> reverendis et discretis viris magistris Thoma de Meltoun iuris civilis professore rectore ecclesie parochialis de Trym officiali domini episcopi Midensis, Matteo Crompe iuris perito officiali domini archidiaconi Midensis, Michaelo Darcy iuris perito officiali domini archidiaconi de Kenlis, Willielmo de

[49] *Cal. Reg. Fleming*, 154–5.

[50] For the dispute between Bishop Hugh de Tachmon of Meath and Archbishop Reginald of Armagh concerning the latter's visitation rights during the pontificate of Innocent IV see Sheehy, *Pontificia Hibernica*, ii. 218–19 and n.

[51] *Cal. Reg. Fleming*, 154.

[52] Ibid., but the papal registers contain no record of a confirmation.

Monemuta, Ricardo Broun iuris peritis Midensis et Armachane diocesium testibus . . .[53]

This impressive array of legal talent available in the diocese of Meath may have led FitzRalph to reflect on the much less favourable situation in his own archdiocese, and to ensure on his next visit to Avignon that he be permitted to make better provision in the future for the availability of trained notaries in Armagh.

Whether FitzRalph availed himself of these visitation rights assigned to him in this compact before the visitation of 1355 is not clear. His only other recorded sermons in the diocese of Meath were those preached at Trim on 4 March 1352, and at Athboy on 30 November 1354,[54] neither of which give any indication that a visitation was in progress. A visitation would in any case have been unlikely in the later months of 1354, if the second synod of Drogheda and the subsequent visitation were already in the course of preparation. In the former sermon, preached in the parish to which FitzRalph's nephew had been appointed rector, there are no indications of the circumstances of preaching. However, its emphasis on the love of one's neighbour and equality among men, together with references to the fact that the preacher had quoted Augustine's *De Trinitate* and reminded his audience of their Lenten obligations,[55] suggests that the newly installed rector might have invited his distinguished relative to preach an appropriate sermon for the second Sunday in Lent.

After the second synod of Drogheda the situation was very different: during the month following it FitzRalph preached four sermons in the area of Dundalk, Drogheda, and Ardee, and by the end of April had begun his visitation of Meath. The first post-synodal sermon was addressed to the people of his native Dundalk, and it indicated that business practices there were no more to his liking than in Drogheda.[56] His denunciations of the failings of clergy and laity were similar to those of the synodal sermons, and he referred constantly back to the legislation which had recently been enacted to deal with them. The usual complaints about tithe-evasion and usury were repeated, but with an interesting addition concerning usury practices which showed that the Dundalk people must have been familiar with the common procedures in later medieval Europe for avoiding

[53] Ibid., 154-5.
[54] B, fols. 63^{v}-64^{r}, 64^{r}-65^{r}; J, fols. 53^{ra-b}, 53rb-54rb.
[55] B, fol. 63^{v}; J, fol. 53^{ra-b}.
[56] B, fol. 71^{r-v}; J, fol. 59^{ra-va}.

the accusation of usury. FitzRalph accused them of lending sums of money under the pretext of buying rents for a number of years. But this was merely a legal fiction, as the lender paid a price for the rents which was far below their normal market value, and often as low as one third or one quarter. Such purchases, argued the archbishop, were little more than a disguised loan, as the owner of the rents sold his right to these for a certain number of years in return for ready cash. Such a practice, argued FitzRalph, was plainly usury.[57] The synodal legislation against usury and tithe-evasion was stressed again two days later at Ardee, as were the measures enacted against those 'inpedientes iudices ecclesiasticos' who tried to obstruct the work of the ecclesiastical courts and those who interfered with the testamentary rights of minorities already discussed.[58] But the central issue of this sermon was the problem of unsuitable priests who had no genuine vocation to their task, and whom he accused of employing devious methods to secure ordination and promotion to benefices. The situation described by FitzRalph – the buying and selling of titles or rights of admission to the clerical estate, the promise of Masses to be said for the grantors of these titles, and even the solemn promise that those who became priests through these channels would seek no alms or dues from their patrons[59] seems to suggest an interest in becoming members of the clerical estate for reasons other than the promise of financial reward. Was it because of the immunity it offered against being brought to justice in the king's courts, and did FitzRalph mean to imply that members of either or both communities, who may have been guilty of fraud, robbery, or violence, were thereby seeking immunity in a calling for which they were totally unsuited?

On his return to Drogheda early in March FitzRalph preached two sermons for which only fragmentary notes survive in the diary. It is therefore not clear whether he discussed the synodal legislation, though it is quite probable that he did so and saw no reason for further recording it in the diary, which already contained an adequate record of these topics. He returned to the familiar themes which were central to his programme of moral

[57] B, fol. 71^{r}; J, fol. 59rb.

[58] He specifically included those 'inpedientes mulieres libere condere testamentum ac viros hibernicos . . .', B, fol. 65^{v}; J, fol. 54va. The rubric in the diary described the synodal sermon as 'in concilio provinciali', but the notes of subsequent sermons in which FitzRalph referred back to it often used the designation 'concilium generale'.

[59] B, fol. 65^{r-v}; J, fol. 54^{rb-va}.

and spiritual regeneration. Apart from the obligation to pay tithes, which he explained were an acknowledgement of God's right of dominion over man,[60] and usury, he launched another attack on those who held on to their wealth in life and attempted to make up for this by means of large bequests in death. Here he extended the argument, probably to deal with objections raised by members of his flock against his teaching on almsgiving. They appear to have made the excuse that they could not afford to give generously during their lifetime, as the well-being of their own children would suffer, and they claimed that they were not amassing wealth for themselves but for their children. FitzRalph rejected this argument, suggesting that the real reason for this policy of leaving large legacies to the Church was the desire to have one's memory held in respect after death – also a sin of pride.[61] Although these sermons survive in the diary only as fragments, they provide some indication that FitzRalph was not merely indulging in outbursts of moral indignation at the expense of the citizens of Drogheda, but that he had begun to educate them to expect a higher intellectual level in their sermons, citing examples for them from Augustine's *De libero arbitrio* and Aristotle's *Ethics.*[62]

Although no sermons are recorded in the diary for the Easter season of 1355, FitzRalph must have remained in the Dundalk–Drogheda area, possibly making his preparations for the visitation of Meath. The first indication in the diary that the visitation had actually commenced is contained in the note for a sermon preached 'apud Trym in visitatione' on 26 April 1355.[63] It seems reasonable to assume that the visitation did commence in Trim, which was for all practical purposes the centre of the diocese of Meath. The diocese possessed no cathedral, despite attempts in the mid-thirteenth century to commence building, and the church of the Augustinian canons at Newtown by Trim served as a cathedral for Meath until the Dissolution.[64] It is therefore quite possible that FitzRalph initiated his visitation there, and then preached at the parish church in the town. Here

[60] B, fol. 65^{v}; J, fol. 54^{va-b}.

[61] B, fols. 65^{v}–66^{r}; J, fols. 54vb–55rb. Here he spoke 'de cupiditate que adversaria est nostre nacione . . .'

[62] B, fol. 66^{r}; J, fol. 55rb, stressing the obligation in all cases not merely of confession, but also of contrition and satisfaction or restitution.

[63] B, fols. 66^{r}–67^{v}; J, fols. 55rb–56rb. Most of the sermon consisted of a warning to the litigious Palesmen concerning their obligations in justice.

[64] *Medieval Religious Houses. Ireland*, pp. 97–8, 190.

he returned once more to the practical issues which had been preoccupying him since the synod, although the text of the sermon 'Tristicia vestra vertetur in gaudium' (Ioh. xvi. 20) provided the opportunity for a detailed and sensitive explanation of the reasons why divine providence permitted the good to suffer trials and tribulations in this life. His consideration of the prosperity of the wicked gave him the opportunity to put on record once more his views on fair business dealing, and a note in the diary indicates that he had cited numerous examples of fraud and trickery, and the penalties which resulted from them.[65] The only example which he actually recorded, and which may even have been based upon personal experience, concerned the case of a landlord who had lost the original deeds which proved his title in law to certain property. A tenant might take advantage of such a situation and withhold payment of the rent, knowing that he would be protected by the letter of the law, as the title of the real owner cannot be proved under positive law. But FitzRalph tried to make clear to his audience that the tenant's action was nevertheless morally wrong, he was acting in bad faith, had no right to the true ownership of the property, and was bound to make restitution.[66]

Two days after he had preached this sermon FitzRalph received an urgent message from the justiciar, Sir Thomas Rokeby, ordering him to break off the visitation at once in order to attend to more urgent business. The justiciar was at the time at Kildroght in County Kildare, and had received news that Aodh O'Neill was moving on the town of Dundalk with a large army, intending to use the threat of military force as a negotiating instrument.[67] The justiciar was otherwise occupied and could not move northwards with enough troops to defend the area around County Louth, but FitzRalph was instructed to head immediately for Dundalk and negotiate a settlement with the Gaelic leader. Meanwhile the bishop and clergy of Meath were instructed by the justiciar not to regard the visitation as having been interrupted by the archbishop's sudden departure, and were ordered to receive FitzRalph under precisely the same terms upon his return.[68] In view of the fact that FitzRalph

[65] B, fol. 66^{r-v}; J, fols. 55rb–56ra.
[66] B, fol. 67^{r}; J, fol. 56^{ra-b}.
[67] *Rotulorum Patentium et Clausarum Cancellarie Hibernie Calendarium*, ed. Edward Tresham (Irish Record Commission, Dublin, 1828), p. 62.
[68] Ibid. This last clause may refer to the visitation compact made seven years earlier, under whose terms the archbishop could not undertake a new visitation later in the same year, but the continuation of the same one was permissible.

preached in Kells on 14 May, slightly over two weeks later, and was still to be found in the diocese of Meath as late as 21 June, Fr. Gwynn was inclined to doubt whether, in spite of the urgency of the justiciar's order, FitzRalph actually obeyed it and interrupted his visitation. On the evidence of these dates, and because FitzRalph 'was not the man to set aside ecclesiastical business at the bidding of a secular officer',[69] he argued that the archbishop must have succeeded in postponing his commission until the end of the visitation, i.e. until after 21 June at least. Such a decision on his part would have placed 'his own people' in and around Dundalk under considerable strain for a period of some two months. On the other hand we have plenty of evidence for FitzRalph's concern to promote peaceful relations between the Gaelic Irish and Anglo-Norman populations in his archdiocese; we have seen his special concern for his native city of Dundalk, among whose population were still numerous members of his family. The distances from Trim to Dundalk, and from there back to Kells were short enough not to exclude the possibility that FitzRalph did in fact travel northwards as soon as he received the justiciar's message, negotiate some kind of compromise solution with O'Neill, and still be back in Kells in time for the sermon of 14 May. Furthermore, there is no indication of any continuation of the disturbance in the area during the ensuing months, hence the greater probability that the archbishop did actually intervene and achieve some short-term measure of success.[70]

Such a measure of success might tentatively be deduced from the tenor of the subsequent sermons. For the remainder of the visitation – speaking in Kells on the doctrine of the Ascension, and in Greenoge on the border of the archdiocese of Dublin on the obligation of fraternal charity (7 June) – FitzRalph did not return to the problem of violence, though he was to do so the following spring when trouble broke out once more.[71] The only

[69] *Studies*, 25 (1936), 89.

[70] Simms, 'The Archbishops of Armagh and the O'Neills', 45, though her implication that no further disturbances occurred in FitzRalph's lifetime is not borne out by the evidence of his diary.

[71] For the notes of these sermons, B, fols. 67^{v}–70^{r}; J, fols. 56vb–58va. At Kells he exhorted his audience in terms of the Pauline injunction to accept physical punishment (Ad Hebr. xii), but warned against the practices of the 'flagellanti' and the dangers of abuse, B, fol. 68^{r-v}; J, fol. 57ra. In the wave of hysteria which accompanied the Black Death there had been a resurgence of the 'flagellanti' and Clement VI had, on 18 August 1349, issued instructions to a number of bishops, including the archbishops of Armagh, Dublin, Cashel, Tuam, Canterbury, and York, and the

example among the Meath sermons which indicates that it was intended for a trading community, guilty of the familiar failings of usury, perjury, fraud, and tithe-evasion, was the last visitation sermon recorded in the diary, at the rural deanery of Screen on 21 June. It included a somewhat obscure reference to the 'receptores furtorum et furum tanquam collectores tolneti dyaboli', or the Devil's toll-collectors.[72] By now FitzRalph's reservations about the friars' confessional practices, their leniency in the matter of restitution, and the implications of their attitude for the efficient working of the tithe system, had begun to emerge clearly – were the Devil's toll-collectors the friars? And if so, what had prompted the remark in Screen, which had no mendicant community other than one founded fourteen years earlier for Augustinian friars, and these were never FitzRalph's principal *bêtes noires.*[73]

After the Meath visitation, only one more sermon followed in the diary before a gap of nine months, from the end of June until early in April 1356, a period in which it is possible that FitzRalph may have engaged in more protracted negotiations with the O'Neill, in an attempt to restore stable relations between the two communities in the north-east. But the single sermon, that preached in Drogheda on 28 June 1355, has attracted more attention than most of the archbishop's utterances which were not directed against the mendicant friars. Here FitzRalph's target was another form of confraternity whose anti-social practices reflected the manner in which discrimination operated against the Gaelic Irish in commercial and industrial activity, i.e. the trade- and craft-guilds. The guilds, as they existed in Drogheda, were regarded by the archbishop as contrary to the law of charity, because their members bound themselves by oath to exclude from membership those of a certain nation, clearly the native Irish.[74] FitzRalph's sense of

Scottish bishops, to warn their flocks of the dangers of that 'vain religion', *Reg. Vat.* 192, fols. 3^r–4^r; *CPL* 311. Here Clement claimed that some mendicant friars were responsible for encouraging this resurgence of the 'flagellanti', and if this were true it might be a reason for the renewal of criticism of the friars in the pastoral field, as possible fomentors of hysteria. No evidence exists for a connection between these two factors, other than the coincidence that Clement VI shortly afterwards saw fit to have the entire position of the Franciscans (whose extreme wing is more likely to have incited mob hysteria than any other mendicant group) subjected to a thorough examination.

[72] B, fol. 71^v; J, fol. 59vb.

[73] *Medieval Religious Houses. Ireland*, pp. 301–2.

[74] B, fol. 72^v; J, fol. 60va.

fairness had already led him to protest against those who tried to prevent members of the Gaelic race from disposing of their property by testament, and he had constantly stressed that the killing of an Irishman or the seizure of his property by any other than the lawfully appointed officers of the Crown was murder and theft, not 'marcher law'.[75] Now he extended his arguments to embrace the economic discrimination against the Gaelic race which was practised by oath-bound confraternities, who deliberately set out to exclude them from participation in the trade-guilds, and therefore from the benefits involved, such as trading privileges and the apprenticeship of craftsmen. His criticisms of the social and religious customs of the guilds indicate an awareness that they might not always be the innocent and beneficent institutions they claimed to be. He criticized the frequency and splendour of their feasts, the money wasted on wax candles for their processions, and the large donations which they were obliged to make to guild funds, thereby causing them to neglect their obligations in charity towards the real poor.[76] It is possible that the archbishop's strictures against the restrictive practices of the guilds did have a limited success in encouraging some of his flock to accept apprentices from among the native Irish, though with due safeguards. A striking example of this is provided by two indentures dating from the 1350s and providing for the acceptance of two young men as apprentices by Dundalk burgesses. In the first case on 24 July 1351 John Kerseley, a substantial merchant and property-owner in the city, agreed to accept John Ellis, the son of a fellow citizen, to maintain him, and teach him the trade, subject to the usual conditions and obligations.[77] Seven years later on 13 January 1358, another Dundalk merchant, John Rathcoul, took the unusual step of indenturing as an apprentice a young man with a Gaelic name, Nicholas O'Molghallyn (Mulligan), of whom there is no indication in the agreement that he had any sponsor or protector in the town to vouch for his good behaviour. Consequently the terms of his apprenticeship are both more severe and more precisely defined. The young man's obligations, the length of service required of him as an apprentice, and the

[75] Especially at Drogheda, 25 March 1349 and in Dundalk, 3 April 1356.

[76] 'Item ad festum sive convivium eos artant. Item quia cereos supervacue per plateas inaniter et supersticiose consumunt de quorum pecunia possent / multis pauperibus subvenire', B, fols. 72^{v}–73^{r}; J, fol. 60va.

[77] *Dowdall Deeds*, p. 82. Here the apprentice's father was deemed liable should John Ellis waste or lose any of his master's goods.

careful precautions taken to ensure that he neither misappropriated his master's goods nor misbehaved with the womenfolk of his household indicate that Rathcoul was conscious of the possibility that he might be taking a great risk in admitting this unknown quantity.[78] In view of the extreme rarity of such agreements involving members of the Gaelic race, and of the fact that this exceptional case occurred in a merchant community over which FitzRalph might be deemed to have been able to exert influence, it may not be mere coincidence that this agreement was drawn up in Dundalk soon after the archbishop had begun publicly to express his objections to the treatment of the Gaelic Irish by the merchants who formed such an important part of his flock.

In this, as in other concrete cases, FitzRalph was not prepared to accept the existence of racial tensions as an argument in favour of measures which would perpetuate them. While his remarks on this subject must have been as unwelcome to his audiences in Drogheda and Dundalk as his constant denunciations of their greed, rapacity, and fraudulent practices, they must on the other hand have lent a certain conviction to his efforts as peacemaker between the two nations. When his preaching activity resumed once more in the spring of 1356 with a sermon on 3 April in Dundalk on the need for contrition and confession as preconditions for absolution, he returned once more to the racial problem, arguing the uselessness of confession by those who nevertheless continued to rob and kill.[79] He denounced receivers of stolen property, harbourers of thieves and murderers, and in particular those who violated the recently negotiated peace settlement. Here he clearly had those with the O'Neill, who had specifically threatened the town of Dundalk, in mind, when he referred to those 'quo ad facientes guerras pro furtis aut rapinis sive incendiis auctoritate propria sine consensu eorum qui pacem fecerunt, et quo ad excusantes se cum confitentur quod progenitores sui ita fecerunt et quod probi viri et docti eos sic impune facere instruxerunt'.[80] His condemnation of those who fought, stole, burned, and killed on their own initiative and without the consent of the peace-negotiators, clearly reflected his own difficulties. From these remarks it is clear that he had managed in 1355 to reach some form of peaceful settlement with the O'Neills, only to realize

[78] Ibid., pp. 86–7.
[79] B, fols. 73^{r}–75^{v}; J, fols. 60vb–62va.
[80] B, fol. 74^{r}; J, fol. 61va.

that formal cessation of hostilities on the part of the leaders was very different from the elimination of private feuds for petty gain.

He also faced a difficult pastoral situation in which the more militant members of his flock were being encouraged by their confessors to continue these practices. In view of the fact that he was preaching to an almost exclusively Anglo-Norman community in Drogheda, it can be assumed that the atrocities he was condemning were those perpetrated against the native Irish, against which O'Neill had also protested.[81] But who were the 'probi viri et docti' who handed out encouragement and easy absolution for these practices in the confessional, and thereby made his task as peacemaker even more difficult? The archbishop's subsequent condemnation of confession to a stranger, rather than to one's own parish priest to whom had been granted responsibility for the cure of souls, might be taken as an implication that once more he regarded the friars as the culprits. But he was careful to avoid the open suggestion that the four mendicant communities were encouraging a policy of genocide. Furthermore, he had clearly not succeeded in establishing among his own priests a consistent line of action with regard to confessional problems raised by such racial tensions. The problem had received little specific attention in the recent synodal legislation, but the urgency with which FitzRalph discussed the problem now suggests that the O'Neill threat of the previous year had provoked a substantial element among the English of County Louth to take the law into their own hands – understandably if they felt that the justiciar and the Dublin government were unable to provide adequate protection. Hence a situation had developed which FitzRalph felt bound to oppose, whereby rights and obligations in conscience were being ignored and violence justified on the basis of marcher law and the customs of previous generations. In opposition to the archbishop's admonitions about justice and charity these elements adopted the attitude that the law had always condoned such acts of violence in a land where the only security for life and property was physical force and armed resistance. When life and property were at stake many were not prepared to accept FitzRalph's argument of the necessity for anomalies in the law in order to

[81] Under 1354 both the *Annals of Clonmacnoise*, ed. cit., p. 299, and the *Annals of the Four Masters*, ed. cit., iii, 605, recorded that Aodh O'Neill suffered defeat at the hands of an allied force of the O'Neills of Clandeboy and the citizens of Dundalk.

protect the common good, adopting instead the marcher law ('legem marchie sive dyaboli'[82]), condemned by the archbishop. Whether his admonition to them to seek guidance and absolution at the hands of the authorized confessors of his diocese[83] had any effect in such circumstances, must remain an open question, but the evidence from his successor's register suggests that the situation did not improve, and further that the tensions between the 'two nations' were heightened by the strife between rival branches of the O'Neill. When the cathedral city of Armagh was laid under a blockade during the civil war of the late 1360s and the Gaelic Irish dean of Armagh appealed to Archbishop Sweteman, the latter saw no other solution but to call upon the secular arm: excommunication had proved ineffective 'because after absolutions of them by us, and oaths taken to obey the laws of the church . . . they have committed worse deeds than before'.[84] In view of these conditions in the province of Armagh, the complaint made by FitzRalph to Innocent VI on 8 November 1357 that large numbers of his flock were under sentence of excommunication for wilful homicide, robbery, incendiary, and similar crimes, and that the question of their confession and absolution presented a pastoral problem of unprecedented dimensions, was not an exaggeration.

The problem of peace-keeping on the border which ran through his diocese and ecclesiastical province, and the obstacles put in the way of his endeavours by elements among clergy and laity, continued to preoccupy FitzRalph for the remainder of his stay in Ireland, and it was probably one of the items of diocesan business which took him to the king's court in the early summer of that year. The remaining sermons, preached at weekly intervals between 10 and 24 April, reflected his continuing concern. At Termonfechin, preaching to the local people near his manor, he delivered a further explanation of the obligations in charity, expanding on the theme of the Dundalk sermon of the previous week and including examples drawn from his experiences of rough justice while a student in Paris – one of

[82] B, fol. 74^{v}; J, fols. 61vb–62ra.

[83] This warning was the most explicit statement of his objection to confession to a 'stranger', i.e. other than to one's own parish priest, since the *Proposicio* of 5 July 1350, when he had presented a general and systematic statement of his objections to mendicant pastoral activity. Now it was applied to the specific case of his native city, and he argued against the authority of confessors who had not been appointed by the diocesan ordinary, himself, B, fols. 74^{v}–75^{r}; J, fols. 61vb–62ra.

[84] *Cal. Reg. Sweteman*, 276–7; Simms, 46.

the rare occasions on which he ever mentioned having been there.[85] A week later at the Palm Sunday ceremonies in his pro-cathedral in Drogheda, he included only a short homily in deference to the fact that a large congregation of the laity was present and the liturgy was already lengthy,[86] but he still found time for a warning to those who took the law into their own hands, and acted without authority or on the advice of those who were equally bereft of authority. The specific application of his message was couched in terms which can have left his audience in little doubt that his criticism was intended to include the friars, but not necessarily to apply to them exclusively. He warned those who felt tempted to punish private wrongs on their own initiative not to allow themselves to be led astray by their own opinions, or by those of others — be they laymen, secular priests, or regular clerics — who made light of the crimes of murder, theft, or tithe-evasion. But the advice he offered them was clearly directed against the mendicant orders as a valid alternative force in the field of pastoral guidance. He advised his audience that if they had doubt about the application of the rules of justice and charity in individual cases, they ought to seek guidance from their local curate or parish priest, and if necessary to take their problem to a higher authority, to the archdeacon, bishop, or even to the archbishop — a clear indication that he was available to listen to their problems. He had offered similar advice to the people of Dundalk the previous year, and it would appear that the archbishop was prepared to resort to any measures in order to undermine the influence which he saw the friars exerting over his flock. Yet his exhortation to trust their parochial clergy implicitly, because of the latter's obligation to care for their flocks even under threat of death, was an expression of the ideal and not of reality. His synodal sermons showed — even when all allowances are made for rhetorical exaggeration and the conventional denunciations of medieval preachers — that he did not find, or expect to find such devotion to duty among the priests subject to his jurisdiction, whereas the exempt religious whose contribution to pastoral care he wished to eliminate had given proof of their worth in time of crisis. However, a totally dispassionate estimate

[85] B, fols. 75^{v}–77^{v}; J, fols. 62va–64ra.

[86] B, fol. 77^{v}; J, fol. 64ra. Nevertheless, judging by the record in the diary, the sermon was a substantial one, B, fols. 77^{v}–80^{r}; J, fols. 64ra–66ra.

[87] B, fols. 77^{v}–78^{r}; J, fol. 64$^{rb–va}$.

of their relative qualities was scarcely to be expected from the archbishop under the prevailing circumstances, when – rightly or wrongly – he had become convinced that the confessional practices of the exempt religious and the leniency with which they treated grievous offenders, were a major hindrance to his peace-keeping and pastoral policies.

FitzRalph's final sermon in Ireland, on Easter Sunday, 24 April 1356, was of a more private nature. In his own chapel, presumably at the manor of Termonfechin, in view of the fact that he had been in Drogheda a week earlier and had presumably conducted the Holy Week ceremonies there, he addressed his episcopal 'familia', encouraging them to moral renovation and once more emphasizing the role of confession, genuine contrition, and absolution.[88] In such homely and familiar surroundings outspoken denunciation of those who hindered his work for pastoral reform and harmonious relations would have been out of place, and at the time of preaching he clearly did not anticipate a sudden departure from his household in the near future. But the decision to set out for London must have been taken no later than May 1356, as the archbishop had already reached the English midlands and preached in what must have been the familiar surroundings of Coventry parish church on 12 June.[89] In the course of his subsequent involvement in the mendicant controversies he mentioned that he had come to London on diocesan business and had, almost by accident, become involved in the disputes then raging. That his involvement was not totally accidental is indicated both by his own oft-repeated practical objections to the friars' role and by the fact that the completed (or near-completed) manuscript of the seven books of *De Pauperie Salvatoris* accompanied him on his journey and was circulated by the archbishop in Oxford and London. A number of other problems concerning his diocese had occupied much of FitzRalph's attention during the past five years. The primacy issue appears to have lain dormant, but the property transactions which were necessary in order to consolidate the temporalities of the see of Armagh were not yet completed and required royal approval, while the recent trouble on the border with the Gaelic Irish and the tendency of the Anglo-Normans to take the law into their own hands when

[88] B, fols. 80^{r}–81^{r}; J, fol. $66^{ra–vb}$.

[89] B, fols. 81^{r}–82^{r}; J, fols. 66vb–67ra. Here FitzRalph returned to the exposition of the doctrine of the Eucharist delivered in Lichfield Cathedral, 24 March 1345.

threatened or molested was also a matter to be brought before the king. FitzRalph himself could scarcely have foreseen the course which events would take once he involved himself in the mendicant debates in London, and doubtless intended that his visit to the king's court would be as much a routine matter as had been that of 1353. But the publication of *De Pauperie Salvatoris*, the ensuing debates, and FitzRalph's own contribution to those debates, now informed – and inflamed – by his accumulated practical experience of the friars' pastoral work, combined to ensure that the friars and their problems would keep FitzRalph occupied for the rest of his life.

V The Mendicant Controversy

i. Initial stages: the Proposicio *of 1350*

ONE of the most problematic aspects of FitzRalph's career is his apparently sudden change of heart with regard to the four orders of mendicant friars and their role in later medieval society. This change of heart affected FitzRalph's attitude both to the friars' position as academic teachers in the universities and above all to their participation in pastoral work through preaching, hearing confessions, and burying those members of the laity who so wished in their churches – for all of which activities the friars received some financial remuneration – while at the same time continuing to profess allegiance to the mendicant ideal and the obligation in charity of their fellow men to contribute to their support through almsgiving and pious bequests. The question has often been raised as to how it came about that FitzRalph who, initially through his childhood acquaintance with the Franciscans in his native Dundalk, subsequently as student, master, and chancellor of Oxford University, but most especially during his long years of residence at Avignon as supplicant, litigant, and as papal theological adviser on a wide range of topics, was in close and friendly contact with leading members of the mendicant orders, should suddenly become their most bitter opponent and should devote the last years of his life to a systematic attempt to undermine their privileges, their way of life, even their *raison d'être*.[1] FitzRalph had been the colleague of distinguished mendicant theologians as early as the beatific vision controversy, a favoured preacher in the Avignon convents of the Franciscans, Dominicans, and Carmelites, and he made no secret of his admiration for the friars' biblical and oriental studies and for their missionary activities. Furthermore, his subsequent development of the Augustinian doctrine of dominion and grace in *De Pauperie Salvatoris* strongly suggests contact with members of the order of Friars Hermits of St. Augustine, and most probably

[1] For the most thorough examination to date see Hammerich, *FitzRalph and the Mendicants*, pp. 25–47; also Gwynn, *Studies*, 26 (1937), 50–67; idem, *English Austin Friars*, pp. 80–9.

with one of the chief exponents of the doctrine, Guglielmo Amidani da Cremona, prior-general of the order from 1326 to 1342. The latter was appointed bishop of Novara on 17 July 1342, within two months of the accession of his friend and protector to the papal throne as Clement VI, and he did not therefore immediately lose all contact with events and personalities in Avignon. In view of these considerations the attitude which emerged in the course of FitzRalph's first visit to Avignon since his elevation to the see of Armagh requires an explanation.

When he formally launched his attack on the activities and privileges of the friars in the *Proposicio* preached before Clement VI in full consistory on 5 July 1350,[2] he was not propounding a new revolutionary theory. Basing his sermon on the conservative Pauline text: 'Unusquisque in quo vocatus est, fratres, in hoc permaneat apud Deum' (1 Ad Cor. vii. 24), he discussed complaints about the friars which had been common currency during the previous century. At the heart of the matter were two separate but related issues, the first of which was theological, i.e. the doctrine of the poverty of Christ and the apostles that was the basis of the friars', and most particularly of the Franciscans' very existence. The second issue was juridical and concerned the friars' apostolic activity, whereby they engaged in pastoral work outside the parochial structure and exempt from episcopal jurisdiction. Although FitzRalph was subsequently in *De Pauperie Salvatoris* to subject the poverty doctrine, and especially its Franciscan version, to minute analysis, his initial concern, as indicated by this *Proposicio*, was with the second problem, with which he had but recently in the course of his work in Ireland been confronted for the first time at the practical level.

As the issues at stake in the mendicant controversies of the thirteenth and fourteenth centuries have been the subject of a voluminous literature from the pens both of historians and of theologians,[3] it is necessary here only to highlight the aspects which are of particular relevance for FitzRalph's own unique

[2] Ed. cit., pp. 53–73.

[3] For bibliography see Walsh, Hardeby, *AA* 33, 234–5, to which should be added: Amédée Teeaert, 'Deux Questions inédités de Gérard d'Abbéville en faveur du clergé séculier', *Mélanges Auguste Pelzer* (Louvain, 1947), 347–87; Carolly M. Erikson, 'The fourteenth-century Franciscans and their Critics', *FS* 35 (1975), 107–35; 36 (1976), 108–47.

contribution to the controversy. Above all, his work illustrates the fact that the Franciscans must be considered as a case apart, as within a very short time of their foundation the other mendicant orders established a comfortable compromise or *modus vivendi* which enabled them to combine, for the most part without undue tension, the ideal of poverty with the academic and pastoral concerns which soon came to characterize the friars' role in later medieval society. Since their foundation the Franciscans had been divided among themselves on the fundamental issue of poverty, as the original ideals of their founder were no longer realistic once the order began to engage in an active apostolate, when the requirements of preaching and study meant the acquisition of convents, churches, books, and eventually university chairs and the virtual elimination of begging as the friars' principal means of support.

A major problem posed by FitzRalph's analysis of the Franciscan ideal and role in society was determined by his application to the order of a literal interpretation of the original rule of St. Francis. But the latter, although he frequently referred generally to 'evangelical poverty' as that practised by Christ and the apostles, never defined this poverty in material terms. It has been generally accepted however that he intended poverty to mean the renunciation of goods rather than rights, and did not imply that his order should in perpetuity be deprived of all property rights. The question never needed clarification in his lifetime, as the legal questions of property and dominion did not begin to assume a real significance until the later thirteenth century, but by the time FitzRalph was composing his theoretical contribution to the poverty issue in the mid-fourteenth century, the profound implications of theories of dominion were beginning to emerge more clearly. The tangled questions: what was the nature of property and could its use be divorced from ownership? had in the meantime emerged, and largely as the result of Innocent IV's attempt in the bull *Ordinem vestrum* of 14 November 1245 to find a solution to the problem by decreeing that the papacy was the owner of Franciscan property,[4] a solution which would become the most severely contested aspect of the Franciscan poverty

[4] Printed in Eubel, *Bull. Fran. Epitome*, 238-9. The best general survey of the problem is Lambert, *Franciscan Poverty*, and more recently on the social and economic aspects Lester K. Little, *Religious Poverty and the Profit Economy in Medieval Europe* (London, 1978).

controversy until its legal fiction was brought to an end by John XXII in 1323.

Meanwhile papal privileges bestowed on the mendicant orders began the process of exempting them from episcopal control, in some cases placing the bishops in a difficult position by appointing those prelates who were well disposed towards the friars as 'conservatores' of their privileges in order to protect them against the encroachments of their brother-bishops.[5] Such privileges were designed to facilitate the friars in their apostolate and to protect them against molestation by the secular clergy, but they also placed an added strain on the mendicant ideal, especially among the Franciscans who had not found the satisfactory solution which enabled other orders of friars, notably the Dominicans, to own their property and concentrate on their preaching apostolate. FitzRalph denied the fundamental premiss upon which this arrangement was based, arguing that the friar who engaged in pastoral activity and ensured his regular means of subsistence violated his vow of poverty.[6] However, when the friars came under attack in the university sphere, initially in Paris and subsequently at Oxford and Cambridge, the Dominicans were as deeply involved as the Franciscans.[7] The secular masters in Paris, led by Guillaume de S. Amour and Gérard d'Abbéville, adopted a stance which

[5] In *Nimis iniqua* (21 July 1245) Innocent IV had appointed 'conservatores' to protect the friars against episcopal encroachments, *BF* i. 368–9. By now a substantial number of bishops had been drawn from the ranks of the friars, Thomson, *Friars in the Cathedral. The first Franciscan bishops 1226–1261, passim.*

[6] *Proposicio*, 5 July 1350, ed. cit., pp. 70–2.

[7] See Franz X. Seppelt, 'Der Kampf der Bettelorden an der Universität Paris in der Mitte des 13. Jahrhunderts', *Kirchengeschichtliche Abhandlungen*, ed. Max Sdralek, vi (Breslau, 1908), 75–139; Karl Schleyer, *Anfänge des Gallikanismus im 13. Jahrhundert. Der Widerstand des französischen Klerus gegen die Privilegierung der Bettelorden* (Berlin, 1937); Yves Congar, 'Aspects ecclésiologiques de la querelle entre mendiants et séculiers dans la séconde moitié du XIIIe et le début du XIVe, *AHDLMA* 36 (1961), 35–161; M. M. Dufeil, *Guillaume de Saint Amour et la polémique universitaire* (Paris, 1972). In Oxford the Franciscans managed to maintain more peaceful relations with the university than the Dominicans, see Jarrett, *The English Dominicans*, pp. 76–81. Two recent (1975 and 1976) studies of 13th-century university sermons illustrate an interesting contrast between the respective situations in Paris and Oxford. Louis Jacques Bataillon, 'Les Crises de l'université de Paris d'après les sermons universitaires', *Miscellanea Mediaevalia*, 10, 155–69, showed how university preachers, both secular and regular, abused the pulpit as a forum for the propagation of polemic in both Averroist and mendicant controversies. Beryl Smalley, 'Oxford University Sermons, 1290–1292', *Medieval Learning and Literature*, pp. 307–27, noted that whereas the friars 'did make use of their opportunities to put out propaganda for their way of living' (p. 314), both seculars and mendicants tended to mind their manners in the pulpit and refrained from polemic.

FitzRalph was also – though more cautiously expressed – to represent, when they challenged the right of the papacy to grant privileges to the friars exempting them from episcopal jurisdiction and facilitating them in their apostolate. These two further tried to discredit the friars by connecting them with the more suspect implications of Gioachino da Fiore's apocalyptic doctrines,[8] though this aspect of the struggle had few repercussions in the English universities. Nevertheless, a dispute which had begun over university chairs, both in Paris and later in England, soon developed into an attack on the most fundamental principle of the new orders, in short that the mendicant ideal based on the apostolic model was indefensible, even heretical. To the theological struggle was added the juridical one, which in 1350 was central to FitzRalph's criticism, namely whether the friars could preach, hear confessions, and bury the laity in their churches while retaining their privileged position of exemption from ordinary diocesan jurisdiction. The poverty issue has received more attention from historians of these controversies, partly because of the contributions of Aquinas and Bonaventure. But the Franciscan doctor also defended the apostolic activities of his order, insisting that the friars did not intend to usurp the functions of the secular clergy but rather to supplement these where necessary, a task for which their profession of poverty made them eminently suitable.[9] Bonaventure's interpretation of apostolic poverty and the rule of St. Francis became the official doctrine of the order and was incorporated by Nicholas III into the bull of 14 August 1279 *Exiit qui seminat*,[10] a document which was to figure prominently in FitzRalph's own discussions.

[8] Gérard d'Abbéville, 'Contra adversarium perfectionis christianae', ed. Sophronius Clasen, *AFH* 31 (1938), 276–329; 32 (1939), 89–200; Guillaume de Saint Amour, 'De periculis novissimorum temporum', in Brown, *Fasciculus rerum expetendarum*, ii. 9–64. The latter's text was ascribed to FitzRalph in BAV, Vat. Lat. 1037, fol. 1^{r}: 'Liber Almacani contra mendicantes . . .', see Pelzer, *Cod. Vat. Lat.*, II, i. 544–6. For recent work on Gioachino see Marjorie Reeves, *The Influence of Prophecy in the Later Middle Ages* (Oxford, 1969); idem and Beatrice Hirsch-Reich, *The Figurae of Joachim of Fiore* (Oxford, 1971); and the contributions of Herbert Grundmann, recently collected in *Herbert Grundmann, Ausgewählte Aufsätze*, ii, *Joachim von Fiore* (Stuttgart, 1977).

[9] Sophronius Clasen, *Der hl. Bonaventura und das Mendikantentum* (Werl-i-W., 1940). Bonaventure's *questiones* on poverty are edited in *Opera Omnia,* V (Quaracchi, 1891), 117–98. His second *questio* is mistakenly ascribed in CVP 4127, fol. 249rb, to FitzRalph's Franciscan contemporary and critic, Roger Conway, Walsh, 'Hardeby', *AA* 34, 69–71.

[10] Sext. V. 12.3, Friedberg, ii. 1109–21.

At the Council of Lyon (1274) the question of the friars' pastoral privileges was raised once more, and the bishops sought a decision which would protect the position of the parochial clergy. It was claimed that these latter no longer had any defence against the friars' encroachments other than the canon of the Fourth Lateran Council of 1215, *Omnis utriusque sexus*, which obliged all the faithful to confess once a year to their own priest ('proprius sacerdos')[11] – a term which by the time FitzRalph entered the fray had become ambiguous and the subject of controversy. Part of this complexity had already been caused before the end of the thirteenth century, when an assembly of French bishops held in Paris in 1282 interpreted this canon to mean that the faithful were bound to confess in their annual confession to their own priest the sins for which they had already received absolution, thereby questioning implicitly the power of the keys, of binding and loosing which successive popes had devolved upon mendicant confessors.[12] Though John XXII condemned this interpretation in *Vas electionis* (1321),[13] it reappeared in successive phases of the struggle, and particularly in the polemical literature which the legal proceedings between FitzRalph and the friars engendered in 1358 to 1360.[14]

When Cardinal Benedetto Gaetani was papal legate in Paris in 1290 he supported the friars both against the bishops, whose demands with regard to the friars' pastoral privileges he refused, and against the university, to whose delegation of *magistri* he stated the position succinctly if crudely: 'Truly I say unto you (Luc. xxi. 3) before the Roman curia deprives the friars of their privileges, it will destroy the university of Paris'[15] – the Paris theologians might subject the truths of the Bible to scrutiny and debate, but not the privileged position of the friars. However,

[11] V. 38. 12, ibid., ii. 887–8.

[12] Decima L. Douie, 'The Conflict between Seculars and Mendicants at the University of Paris', *Aquinas Papers*, 23 (London, 1954), 26–7.

[13] Extrav. V. 3. 2, Friedberg, ii. 1291–2.

[14] Entitled 'Ordinacio (or Informacio) prelatorum et curatorum regni ffrancie contra abusus privilegiorum et presumpciones fratrum de ordinibus predicatorum et Minorum de consilio Magistrorum in theologia et aliorum Juris peritorum', it was copied in MS Sidney Sussex 64, fol. 5^{r-b}; MS Bodl. 158, fols. 175^{r}–176^{r}; MS Bodl. 865, fols. 24^{v}–26^{v}; MS Lambeth 1208, fol. 96^{r}–98^{r}.

[15] Heinrich Finke, *Aus den Tagen Bonifaz' VIII., Funde und Forschungen* (Münster, 1902), p. vi, quoted in Jürgen Miethke, 'Papst, Ortsbischof und Universität in den Pariser Theologenprozessen des 13. Jahrhunderts', *Miscellanea Mediaevalia*, 10, 94.

the same cardinal, as Boniface VIII, issued the bull *Super Cathedram* (1300), which regulated the relations of the friars with the secular clergy by forbidding the former to hear confessions in any diocese without a licence from the diocesan ordinary. The friars were not to preach at the same time as the bishop ('prelatus'), and they were to pay to the parish church a quarter of all legacies, bequests, and funeral dues which they received from the laity.[16] This latter ruling dealt a severe blow to mendicant poverty, as voluntary offerings were now no longer sufficient and the orders were compelled to seek more stable sources of income, especially in the Franciscan case. But *Super Cathedram* was not simply a negative document: on the one hand it attacked the jurisdictional and financial abuses possible when the hierarchy had no control over the friars' activities, but on the other hand it provided the conditions under which the mendicant orders might exercise a pastoral function with a minimum of friction. Hence modern historians of their respective orders[17] have regarded the bull as a reasonable solution and a foundation for peace between the friars and the secular clergy, but to the early fourteenth-century friars it seemed harsh, and if FitzRalph's criticisms are even partly true it would appear that the secular clergy did not always get a fair deal out of the system either. The substantial support for FitzRalph's attack after the middle of the century indicates that the bull provided no more than an uneasy truce, and that the justification for mendicant privileges was still regarded by many as an open question.

The controversy progressed a stage further during the pontificate of John XXII when the Paris master, Jean de Pouilly, claimed that the powers of the secular clergy were derived

[16] Clem. III. 7. 2, Friedberg, ii. 1161–4. The interpretation of the term 'prelatus' was also discussed in FitzRalph's *Proposicio* of 1350, ed. cit., pp. 56–7.

[17] Lippens, 'Le Droit nouveau des mendiants', 245–6; Uyttenbroeck, 'Le droit pénitentiel', 306–32; Arnold Williams, 'Relations between the mendicant friars and the secular clergy in the later fourteenth century', *Duquesne Studies. Annuale Medievale*, 1 (1960), 22–95. On the practical application of this legislation see Benjamin Z. Kedar, 'Canon Law and Local Practice: the case of mendicant preaching in late medieval England', *Bulletin of Medieval Canon Law*, n.s. 2 (1972), 17–32. He argued that those English bishops who issued licences to friars to hear confessions *and* to preach exceeded their powers under *Super Cathedram*, but that they could find some justification for this restrictive interpretation in early glosses on the bull. With regard to licences to hear confessions, Kedar obscures the distinction between such licences and penitential commissions which were occasionally issued to enable confessors to absolve sins normally reserved for the bishop or his penitentiary – a distinction which is made clear by Williams.

directly from Christ and not indirectly through popes and bishops. Therefore the pope could not free anybody from his obligation to confess a second time to his parish priest as long as the Lateran canon was in force; the papal grant to the friars of the privilege of hearing confessions was based on the recently developed theory that the pope was not only the universal ordinary, but also the 'proprius sacerdos' of every Christian.[18] De Pouilly's attitude was as much a protest against the centralizing tendencies of the papacy as against the friars. He aroused considerable opposition among the latter, but he was in fact upholding the older diocesan system of the earlier middle ages before episcopal authority had been undermined by the growth of centralized papal government, a process in which the friars unquestionably assisted. When attacks on the friars took this form, that they were being used as instruments of papal centralization, John XXII had little alternative but to uphold the mendicant position and condemn De Pouilly's doctrines in *Vas electionis*, and this bull was to play a crucial part in the arguments of the mendicant opposition in the late 1350s.

The same pope also attempted to solve the problem of Franciscan poverty, which had come to a head during a heresy trial at Narbonne in 1321, when one of the Franciscan inquisitors declared that the doctrine of which the Fraticelli were being accused, i.e. that Christ and the apostles had possessed nothing either severally or in common, was not heretical but was a dogma of the Church.[19] Challenged by his Dominican colleague, the Franciscan appealed to John XXII, who duly appointed a commission to examine the question and rescinded temporarily the embargo placed by Nicholas III on free discussion.[20] Although recent studies have done much to modify the picture of this pope as implacably opposed to the Franciscan ideal, theologically insensitive to their problems, and consumed only by a lawyer's passion for definition and clarification,[21] the solution put forward by John XXII in the series of bulls in the early 1320s was essentially a legal one which did little to

[18] See Josef Koch, 'Der Prozess gegen den Magister Johannes de Polliaco und seine Vorgeschichte 1312–21', *Kleine Schriften*, ii. 387–422; Jeffrey G. Sikes, 'John de Pouilly and Peter de la Palu', *EHR* 49 (1934), 219–40.

[19] Decima L. Douie, *The Nature and the Effect of the Heresy of the Fraticelli* (Manchester, 1932), pp. 154–5.

[20] In *Quia nonnumquam*, 26 March 1322, Extrav. Ioann. XXII. 14. 2, Friedberg, ii. 1224; *BF* v. 224. See Tierney, *Origins of Papal Infallibility*, pp. 173–5.

[21] Ibid., pp. 171–204; Lambert, 'The Franciscan Crisis', *FS* 32, 123–43.

solve the doctrinal problem. *Quia nonnumquam* (26 March 1322), which threw the subject open for discussion, became a rallying point for polemical attacks on the Franciscans from all sides,[22] while *Ad conditorem canonum* (8 December 1322) overthrew their position as a possessionless order. By it John XXII renounced for the papacy all dominion over Franciscan goods on the grounds that such dominion was a burden from which only the Franciscans profited – though he subsequently reissued it in a more favourable form, retaining for the papacy ownership of their convents, churches, and libraries.[23] The final blow came the following year with the bull *Cum inter nonnullos* (12 November 1323) which declared heretical the assertion that Christ and the apostles had owned nothing, either severally or in common,[24] thereby paving the way for the new constellation of alliances as the Franciscan general Michele da Cesena, together with Ockham and the canonist Bonagrazia da Bergamo, joined the author of the *Defensor Pacis* at the court of Ludwig the Bavarian in Munich.[25]

There was a close connection between the Franciscan doctrine of poverty and Marsilio's concept of a possessionless clergy dependent for support on the secular power or on donations from private individuals – a view which in some respects anticipated Wyclif on disendowment – and subject to the state in all that did not pertain to the cure of souls.[26] This alliance with the schismatic emperor deprived the Franciscan general of support in his order, whereupon the general chapter succumbed to papal pressure and deposed him, electing in his place the French friar, Guiral Ot, who was subsequently to organize considerable Franciscan support for John XXII's position in the beatific vision controversy. Meanwhile the pope issued *Quia vir reprobus*, specifically directed against the deposed general, but containing a comprehensive summary couched in polemical terms of the papal arguments against Franciscan poverty,[27] and this document also became one of the standard 'authorities'

[22] Above all because it suspended *Exiit qui seminat*, and 'to the Franciscans *Exiit* was almost a second foundation charter, the very Magna Carta of their Order', Tierney, p. 173.

[23] Extrav. Ioann. XXII. 14. 3, Friedberg, ii. 1225–9. The two versions are in *BF* v. 233–46 and nn. See also Tierney, pp. 178–81.

[24] Extrav. Ioann. XXII. 14. 4, Friedberg, ii. 1229–30; *BF* v. 256–9.

[25] Bosl, 'Die "Geistliche Hofakademie" ', 97–129.

[26] For a recent study of Marsilio see Friedrich Prinz, 'Marsilius von Padua', *ZBLG* 39 (1976), 39–77.

[27] 16 November 1329, *BF* v. 408–49.

in the polemic between FitzRalph and the friars. Gradually the issue lost its impetus, especially when the death of John XXII on 4 December 1334 was followed by the demise one after another of the polemists in Munich, and the Franciscan general chapter of 1346 accepted a compromise solution, assisted by some gentle pressure from Clement VI, who was much less rigorous in his attitude towards the mendicant orders than his immediate predecessor Benedict XII had been.[28] But as soon as it seemed the storm had blown over, the first seeds of a new phase of the controversy were sown, and this time FitzRalph emerged, as archbishop of Armagh, as the principal antagonist of the mendicant orders.

In this phase the initiative appears to have been taken by the friars themselves, when their procurators at the curia presented a *Proposicio* before Clement VI and his cardinals, requesting a reconsideration of the bull *Super Cathedram*. They argued that some of its clauses were ambiguous, and petitioned the pope to reinterpret these in favour of the friars; others, which they felt were superfluous, should be revoked; and yet another group of clauses were too harsh and should be mitigated for the benefit of the friars. No copy of this *Proposicio* has survived and we know of its existence only from FitzRalph's references to it at the beginning of his own *Proposicio* of 5 July 1350, which is a direct reply to it,[29] but it is yet another indication of the extent to which the bishops, capitular, and secular clergy of Europe were prepared to rely on *Super Cathedram* as the best available solution to the problem posed by the friars. We do not know what were the immediate circumstances which led to the friars' action at this precise point, but one possibility is an episode which occurred the previous year in Vienna, where the friars complained of secular encroachments on their rights and privileges. The prior of the Augustinian friars in Vienna appealed to the archbishop of Prague, Arnošt von Pardubitz, who was also conservator of the Augustinians' privileges. Meanwhile the papal legate, Cardinal Gui de Boulogne, had arrived in Vienna at Pentecost 1349 and supported the friars' cause.[30] As a

[28] See *Acta*, ed. Ferdinand Délorme, *AFH* 5 (1912), 698–709.

[29] Ed. cit., p. 54, ll. 20–6.

[30] Ludwig Hödl, 'Zum Streit um die Bussprivilegien der Mendikantenorden in Wien im 14. und beginnenden 15. Jahrhundert', *ZKT* 79 (1957), 170–89; Friedrich Rennhofer, *Die Augustiner-Eremiten in Wien* (Würzburg, 1956), p. 72, discussed the arrival of the legate and his grant of permission for the consecration of the new Augustinian church without the approval of the diocesan ordinary (the bishop of

result of his intervention Clement VI issued a decree enforcing *Super Cathedram*, and it is possible that this decision and the problem of implementing it led the friars to take their complaint once more before the pope.[31]

Although FitzRalph in the opening passage of his *Proposicio . . . ex parte prelatorum et omnium curatorum tocius ecclesie*, and on several further occasions in the course of his exposition, explicitly claimed to be speaking on behalf of a number of his fellow prelates, some of whom were actually present at the curia,[32] it is more likely that he would have had the united support of the parochial clergy than that of his brother-bishops. Apart from the consideration that in the mid-fourteenth century a substantial proportion of bishops were still drawn from the ranks of the regular clergy, and especially from the mendicant orders (FitzRalph had several among his own suffragans), many bishops recognized the advantages, in some cases the necessity, of using the friars for pastoral work not merely in remote rural areas and among linguistic minorities, but also in the towns, and every hierarchy had its quota of sympathetic members who acted as conservators of mendicant privileges within their own dioceses or metropolitan jurisdictions.[33] However, one very widespread feature of mendicant communities in the period 1348-50 must have given many, otherwise sympathetic, prelates occasion to reflect: the Black Death had depopulated many convents, at least partly because the friars had taken seriously their pastoral responsibilities in plague-ridden and unsanitary towns, but in order to fill the resulting gaps young and unsuitable persons were admitted, rules were mitigated, and the records of the Dominican and Augustinian as well as Franciscan orders testify to such

Passau) – a decision which reflects the state of relations between the friars and their bishop. Rennhofer does not deal with the problem of confessions. The most recent study of the archbishop of Prague is Jaroslav Polc, 'Ernst von Pardubitz', *Lebensbilder zur Geschichte der Böhmischen Länder*, vol. iii (Munich–Vienna, 1978), pp. 25–43 (with bibliography).

[31] Hödl, art. cit., 185–7, prints the cardinal's letter of 1 August 1349 to the bishop of Passau, and the papal bull of 26 November enforcing *Super Cathedram*.

[32] Ed. cit., pp. 54, 73.

[33] Williams, art. cit., provides numerous examples of the use, even by Grandisson of Exeter who was otherwise sparing in the issue of licences to friars, of mendicants for the Cornish-speaking members of his flock, while bishops in London and the coastal areas employed friars to deal with foreign traders, especially Flemish and German.

circumstances.[34] These conditions may have led many to reflect on the advisability of some general reconsideration of the friars, their function, and their privileges. Although it has been pointed out that FitzRalph was not alone in his criticism, and that the problems which concerned him were to be found not alone in England or Anglo-Ireland but all over western Christendom, it is nevertheless a striking feature – unfortunately given little consideration by historians[35] – that in the period between the mid-fourteenth and mid-fifteenth centuries four of the most notable opponents of the friars in England, and indeed in northern Europe, were Oxford-educated Anglo-Irishmen: FitzRalph, the Cistercian Henry Crumpe, the opponent of Lollardy, John Whitehead, who, however, shared Wyclif's hostility towards the friars,[36] and the dean of St. Patrick's Cathedral in Dublin, Philip Norreys.[37] This concentration of mendicant opposition among the sons of Anglo-Irish colonists was scarcely pure coincidence and the possibility must be considered that elements peculiar to the nature of Anglo-Irish society in the later middle ages made the friction potentially caused by the friars even more acute. That such elements actually existed and helped to highlight this tension in the ecclesiastical province of Armagh during FitzRalph's episcopate will emerge in the discussion below.

The seventeenth-century Irish Franciscan historian, Luke Wadding,[38] who discovered in the course of his work in Rome a

[34] See Hammerich, *FitzRalph and the Mendicants*, p. 46, on the depopulation of Spanish convents, and Knowles, *Religious Orders in England*, ii. 11–12, for similar conditions in England. For the relaxation of standards, both for admission as novices and for election as conventual prior, in the Augustinian order and with special reference to Ireland, see Martin–Meijer, 'Irish Material', 64.

[35] Francis X. Martin, 'An Irish Augustinian disputes at Oxford: Adam Payn, 1402', *Festschrift Adolar Zumkeller*, 298, drew attention to this fact but attempted no explanation. Although the difficulties experienced by FitzRalph in his archdiocese, much of them caused by the peculiarities of the Irish situation, do much to explain his hostility to the intervention of the friars in an already precarious pastoral situation, none of the other three formulated their attacks in direct response to a pastoral problem.

[36] *BRUO* I, 524–5; III, 2037.

[37] *BRUO* II, 1365–6. A native of the Dublin diocese who held several benefices in the English part of the dioceses of Armagh and in Meath, before becoming dean of St. Patrick's in 1457, he began to formulate his attack on the friars as early as *c.*1431 in Oxford. The anti-mendicant question occupied him for much of the 1430s and 1440s, and his views were condemned as heretical after an inquiry conducted by the cardinal protector of the Franciscan order, Domenico Capranica, see *BF* n.s.i. 229–33 (3 and 24 August 1440). On 18 June 1448 Nicholas V excommunicated Norreys, ibid., 621–2.

[38] There is no modern critical monograph on Wadding, but there are some valuable papers in *Father Luke Wadding Commemorative Volume* (Dublin, 1957).

copy of the papal process drawn up while the case for FitzRalph's canonization was under consideration and subsequently conducted an active correspondence on the subject with the bishop of Ossory, David Rothe,[35] included in the *Annales Minorum* his explanation for the origins of the quarrel between the archbishop of Armagh and the Franciscan order.[40] He argued that the archbishop had caused considerable trouble for the Franciscans in both Armagh and Drogheda. From the latter he attempted to seize an ornament which was kept in the Franciscan convent and appropriate it for his own palace. But the mayor of the town, a member of the prominent burgess family Bathe,[41] prevented him from doing so and insisted upon the rights of the friars. Consequently, Wadding continued, FitzRalph was so outraged by this incident that he began his campaign against the privileges of the exempt religious. The source of Wadding's story is somewhat dubious, as it cannot be traced further back than to the *Nitela Franciscanae Religionis* published by an Irish Franciscan, Fr. Dermitius Thadaei, in Lyon in 1627.[42] For this reason Fr. Gwynn was inclined to dismiss the story as founded upon some local tradition, more or less accurate, of the episode as it was remembered by friars from the Drogheda area some three hundred years after the event, and he refused to accept that the incident could have been the main cause of the quarrel between the primate and the friars.[43] It must be conceded that Gwynn was correct at least to this extent: it is improbable that the ownership of an ornament,

[39] Rothe, who corresponded with Wadding under the pseudonym of Nicholas Laffan, was bishop of Ossory from 1618, having previously been vicar-general of of the archdiocese of Armagh. He died in prison, 20 April 1650, Patritium Gauchat, *Hierarchia Catholica*, iv. 267; *HBC*², 405. Apart from his interest in FitzRalph's canonization, he shared the latter's opposition to the friars. On 20 November 1629 Thomas Strange, guardian of the Franciscan convent in Dublin, wrote to Wadding of Rothe '. . . que es un segundo Richardo Armachano, no sólo contra Mendicantes, sino también los regulares no Mendicantes', printed in *Wadding Papers*, p. 320. In an earlier letter, 27 March 1629, the guardian had drawn Wadding's attention to the recent edition in Paris of FitzRalph's anti-mendicant writings, ibid., p. 288 – clearly a reference to the edition (from a Victorine MS which is no longer extant) of the *Defensio Curatorum* and other documents concerning the trial, Paris, 1627. Wadding's letter to Rothe telling of his discovery concerning FitzRalph's possible canonization shows that neither allowed mendicant rivalries to obstruct common scholarly interests, printed in *Wadding Papers*, p. 551.

[40] *Annales Minorum*, viii. 127.

[41] For the Bathe family see *Dowdall Deeds, ad indicem*. The only recorded lord mayor of Drogheda from the family is Edward (1590), ibid., pp. 261–2.

[42] For the Drogheda episode see pp. 206–7. The author has been identified as Anthony Hickey, a member of the Irish Franciscan province.

[43] *Studies*, 25, 82–3.

regardless how precious, in the Franciscan church in Drogheda was the *cause* of the quarrel. But FitzRalph's remarks, made as early as the *Proposicio* of 5 July 1350, should be taken into consideration here. The archbishop reported that he had been approached by the brother of a dead man, whose property had been sequestered by the friars under whose care he had made his will, and with whom he had sought burial. Now the friars were refusing to release to the deceased's brother that property to which he was lawfully entitled, whereupon the latter had appealed to FitzRalph in his capacity as conservator of the friars' privileges. When the archbishop intervened and summoned the friars concerned to his presence, he was insolently and publicly informed that he had been appointed their conservator in order to protect them, not to give judgement against them.[44]

If we place this episode alongside Wadding's account, the picture emerges as something more substantial than a garbled tale dimly remembered over the centuries in a convent which felt itself to be the victim of injustice. The deliberate manner in which FitzRalph included this tale in the first public statement of his objections to mendicant practices,[45] suggests that this episode had been the occasion, if not the actual cause, of his decision to subject the entire question of the privileges and pastoral activity of the exempt religious to more careful scrutiny. The fact that his opposition to the friars' role became even more vigorous in the years after 1350 may be explained by his belief that the reform of ecclesiastical life in the province under his care, which was his major preoccupation during these years, was being hampered by the prevailing conditions. Whether or not the friars 'seriously hampered his work' by their 'deliberate opposition'[46] is not clear from the available evidence, but it is certainly true that his reaction to their activities was to devote the remaining years of his life to a campaign for a general re-think of their role in the life of the late medieval

[44] Ed. cit., pp. 69–70.

[45] Under the terms of *Nimis iniqua* only a bishop could act as a mendicant conservator, hence the episode must have occurred after FitzRalph's return to Ireland as archbishop. On 18 August 1245 Innocent IV appointed the archbishop of Dublin, and the bishops of Ossory and Down, as conservators of Franciscan privileges, and on 17 September the archbishop of Cashel, and the bishops of Cloyne and Cork for the Dominicans, Sheehy, *Pontificia Hibernica*, ii. 113–14, 118. These appointments were not permanent and the office rotated.

[46] Gwynn, *Studies*, 25, 83.

Church, and the reforms he had in mind would have had a detrimental effect on their position. In this context Wadding's attempted explanation deserves to be considered as something more than a fanciful story. It must have rested upon a core of fact which, despite the trials and tribulations of the Irish Franciscan province in the sixteenth century, managed to survive into a more historically conscious age.

Hence the most likely explanation for FitzRalph's sudden and total opposition to the friars is that on acquiring a large diocese to administer he was faced in an acute form with the problem of enforcing episcopal authority. The problem of the exempt religious who exercised a pastoral ministry was made more difficult by the tensions of a racially divided community, and Fitzralph showed an intense awareness of this situation. It can be argued that his previous experience of the mendicant orders had been limited to the atypical situations of the schools at Oxford and the cosmopolitan convents at the papal curia, whereas in the course of his duties as archbishop he encountered the practical problems caused by exempt religious in general, linked with the specific issues which arose when mendicant confessors might abuse the confessional in excessive support for one 'nation' or the other. Close examination of his sermon diary, and especially of several sermons preached in England between his return from Avignon to Lichfield in late 1344 and his departure for Ireland after his episcopal consecration, suggests that he was beginning to be concerned about abuses in the sphere of confession and burial rights but without specifically attributing these abuses to the friars. The general criticism of ecclesiastical failings, of licentious and ignorant clergy, negligent prelates, greedy benefice-hunters, and pluralists which he repeatedly expressed in the Avignon sermons of 1338–44 might be deemed to apply more appropriately to the secular clergy; his constant emphasis on the duty of almsgiving to the involuntary poor in this life rather than testamentary dispositions after death would on the other hand have been more applicable to the friars. As early as 1345, when as dean of Lichfield FitzRalph may have encountered the adverse effects on the parochial clergy (and their revenues) caused by mendicant burial of the laity in or near the churches of their orders, FitzRalph stressed the greater suitability of the parish church as a burial place. Preaching 'in processione facta pro rege et principibus' when the congregation was exhorted to pray for the success of Edward III's ventures in France, probably to be dated 26 June 1345,[47] FitzRalph turned aside to consider the issue briefly, but again without any specific reference to the friars. The following year, preaching at Cannock on 21 May 1346, he was even more explicit in his instructions to those who, acting in ignorance, sought burial in cemetries other than that of their parish church: such action was not merely sinful, but led to eternal damnation.[48] Such a definite statement would appear to have been founded upon knowledge of specific instances which had been brought to the dean's notice while visiting an outlying prebend in the diocese. Whereas there were no mendicant houses in Cannock, both Franciscan and Augustinian friars had churches in nearby Stafford, and it is possible that the preacher had burial in their churches, or in private chapels, in mind.[49] Both of these sermons were delivered in the vernacular and were directed at the laity who might seek burial away from their parish church, not at a mendicant audience whose members might be tempted to encourage such practices.

Another topic which was to be central to the later stages of the mendicant controversies in Avignon, was that of confessional practice, and it drew from FitzRalph critical comment at an early stage. He was particularly concerned with the duty of restitution as a precondition for absolution, and this figured frequently in his sermons, even before he set out for Ireland as archbishop. The first recorded statement of his view 'non est contricio nisi pretereat restitucio' occurred in the vernacular sermon preached in the choir of Lichfield Cathedral on Pentecost Sunday, 15 May 1345,[50] and the topic was further developed in another vernacular sermon preached at Burford on 6 January 1347.[51] A most explicit criticism of the mendicant confessors is to be found in an undated Ash Wednesday sermon copied at the beginning of the diary. Hammerich had argued that this fragment should be dated among the pre-1350 sermons on the grounds of its failure to take into account the several traditions of pilgrims to St. Patrick's Purgatory, and therefore he used it in support of his own contention that FitzRalph's campaign against the mendicant orders was already gathering momentum before he set

[47] Idem, 'Sermon Diary', 49.

[48] B, fol. 32^{v}; J, fol. 26ra.

[49] *Medieval Religious Houses. England and Wales*, pp. 193, 202; *VCH (Stafford)*, iii. 270–1, 273–4.

[50] B, fols. 13^{v}–17^{r}; J, fols. 10vb–13ra.

[51] B, fol. 42^{r-v}; J, fol. 34^{ra-va}.

out for Avignon in 1349.[52] This argument is tendentious and ultimately unsatisfactory, as it is highly improbable that an attack such as '. . . dampnant se confessores religiosi, si qui sunt, et alii, qui receptis paucis denarijs, non inducta satisfaccione, hominem de furto aut de usura aut de iniusto lucro proximi absolucionem inpendunt' should have been launched *before* FitzRalph's sermon in the Franciscan convent in Avignon on 4 October 1349. However, even if we reject Hammerich's argument and leave this sermon aside as not being an indication of FitzRalph's attitude to mendicant confessors before he set out for Avignon in 1349, there are several indications that from 1345 onwards – when he first acquired direct experience in the pastoral sphere -- he was beginning to have reservations about certain kinds of confessional practice, that his criticism was directed both at the confessors who conferred the censured absolution and against the members of the faithful who sought it. But he was still careful to avoid mentioning the friars as specifically responsible for this malaise in confessional practice. It is significant that not even in the *Proposicio* of 5 July 1350, in which his arguments against mendicant confession occupied a central place, did he accuse the friars of the abuse mentioned in the undated Ash Wednesday fragment, that of currying favour among their penitents by 'selling' absolution without imposing the duty of restitution. In any case the Lichfield sermons provide evidence that two of the problems over which he was to clash with the friars, those of confession and burial rights, had a long period of gestation, but it seems that their privilege of preaching and the friction it could cause only came to his attention after he had become archbishop, while even then the implications of the friars' exempt legal position appear only to have impressed themselves upon him gradually.[53]

In the prologue to *De Pauperie Salvatoris* FitzRalph recalled that he and two other doctors of theology had been appointed by Clement VI to investigate certain topics of dissension among the mendicant orders concerning property, dominion, possession, and the right of use, furthermore to examine that apostolic or evangelical poverty professed by the Franciscans.[54] Both Gwynn and Hammerich assumed that FitzRalph received

[52] Hammerich, *FitzRalph and the Mendicants*, pp. 28-9.

[53] But see Kedar, art. cit., for the awareness of FitzRalph's episcopal contemporaries in England, that mendicant preaching required strict control.

[54] Ed. cit., p. 273.

this commission *after* he had preached on 5 July 1350; that the archbishop had launched the campaign on his own initiative, encouraged perhaps by some like-minded prelates who happened to be in Avignon during the Jubilee Year; that Clement VI, who was well disposed towards the friars and embarrassed by the suggestion that he should undertake a wholesale revision and reduction of their privileges, fobbed FitzRalph off with a commission which might never achieve anything in the pious hope that the storm would die down.[55] However, one obstacle to this view is FitzRalph's own statement, also in the prologue to *De Pauperie Salvatoris*, that Clement had issued this commission 'sui regiminis anno octavo', i.e. in the period between 7 May 1349 and 6 May 1350, and before FitzRalph had nailed his own colours to the mast by preaching the *Proposicio* 'Unusquisque'.[56] Although the possibility of an error on the archbishop's part cannot be excluded, the very precision of his statement suggests that he was basing it on a written papal mandate to himself, which he might reasonably be expected to have preserved among the notes from which he composed the dialogue *De Pauperie Salvatoris* and then used as a justification for the text which he was now presenting to Clement's successor, Innocent VI. If we accept this hypothesis, it raises the distinct possibility that when FitzRalph returned to Avignon in 1349 the theoretical issue of mendicant, and especially Franciscan, poverty – as distinct from the legal and practical question of the friars' pastoral privileges, which affected all four orders equally and were the subject of the *Proposicio* of 5 July 1350 – had been re-activated and that the archbishop, a seasoned participant in papal theological discussions since the beatific vision and Armenian episodes and now further experienced in that he had become a conservator of mendicant privileges in Ireland, joined in this new wave of discussions. Hence this situation, combined with the friars' own petition concerning *Super Cathedram*, could have occasioned a general review of the mendicant situation, their pastoral work, privileges, and the theoretical foundation of evangelical poverty, only one fragment of which has come down to us in FitzRalph's consistorial exposition of the pastoral aspect. That this exposition was only part of a larger-scale hearing is indicated by

[55] Gwynn, 'Sermon Diary', 44.
[56] Clement VI was elected 7 May and crowned 19 May 1342, Eubel, *Hierarchia Catholica*, i^2. 18. All extant MSS have the same date for this commission.

FitzRalph's words at the end of the *Proposicio*: 'Cetera, que ad practica pertinent et ad iura, dominus meus Traguriensis hic presens Vestre Sanctitati seriosius, si Vestre Sanctitati placuerit, propalabit'.[57] Here FitzRalph was referring to Bartolomeo, bishop of Traù in Dalmatia, who may possibly have also participated in the Armenian negotiations some years earlier and therefore been an old comrade-in-arms of FitzRalph. Little is known about Bartolomeo other than that he was a canon of Constantinople and resident at the curia in the 1340s; he was appointed bishop of Koter (Kattaro) in Dalmatia on 14 July 1348, consecrated at the curia, and soon exchanged this see for that of Traù on 30 January 1349.[58] His educational qualifications are unknown and, whereas his possible participation in the Armenian negotiations might suggest he possessed a theological training (and therefore a possible identification of one of the two doctors in theology whom Clement VI appointed to examine the poverty question with FitzRalph), the latter specifically introduced him to the commission as a legal expert.[59] Equally puzzling is the implication that a resident of the curia, whether lawyer or theologian with at the most limited experience of the practical problems which mendicant privileges presented at diocesan and parochial level, should be invited to expound on the 'practica' before the consistory. Was this an indication that FitzRalph had in fact few supporters for his standpoint and that the bishop of Traù was the only one present at the curia who was prepared to join him officially in his criticism? Unfortunately the text of Bartolomeo's exposition does not appear to have survived, as it is not to be found in any of the known manuscript collections of material dealing with these mendicant controversies.

When FitzRalph opened this case in 1350 he must have been convinced of his good standing at the curia, having recently presented to Clement VI the *Summa* which was the outcome of his negotiations with the Armenians. In it he had not only done as requested and surveyed the Roman point of view in the dogmatic conflict with the Armenians, but had further upheld the curial position in Western matters of contention, as we have seen in the sections in which he dealt with some of the controverted issues raised in Paris and condemned in Avignon. He also

[57] Ed. cit., p. 73, 11.510–2.

[58] Eubel, *Hierarchia Catholica* i². 177, 490.

[59] He would deal with all that pertained 'per iura', ed. cit., p. 73, 1. 510.

had reason to assume, from the known parallels with Clement VI's own sermons, that his emphasis on the Bible rather than philosophical quibbles would go down well with the present incumbent of the see of Peter with whom, as has already been noted, FitzRalph's friendly, even familiar, relations are suggested by several sermons belonging to this visit to the curia. Nevertheless, he opened his *Proposicio* with a reference to his own personal dilemma caused by the problem which he was about to discuss: on the one hand he felt obliged not to remain silent because of the wishes of prelates at the curia who had chosen him to speak upon their behalf, while on the other he feared to offend his friends the friars ('precaros amicos meos fratres'), a phrase which Hammerich was inclined to dismiss as insincere, maintaining that the sermon of the previous October had been the beginning of the end, the last attempt to obtain a peaceful solution of a long-smouldering conflict before battle commenced – an interpretation which, it is contended in this study, the text of that sermon does not bear.[60] However, developments in the intervening eight months, both the preparation of this *Proposicio* and possibly also the work of Clement VI's commission on the poverty question, must have made FitzRalph aware that the parting of the ways was approaching. It is unreasonable to assume that he would have severed overnight all contact with his former associates among mendicant theologians at the curia, but he must have found himself in a genuine dilemma. Hence the accusation of insincerity here is somewhat beside the point – the archbishop was confronted with a conflict of interests which he sought to resolve in accordance with the needs of his diocese, however questionable his arguments and methods might be judged.

His argument against the friars was above all governed by his view of the role of bishops and secular clergy, as well as the older monastic orders, as belonging within the institutional structure of the Church, whereas the friars were outside it. He commenced with that aspect of *Super Cathedram* which the friars had regarded as obscure and in need of clarification, i.e. their right to preach freely to clergy and people, provided that they did not preach at the time and place where the *prelati* were preaching, unless they had a special licence from the latter

[60] Hammerich, *FitzRalph and the Mendicants*, p. 41.

to do so.[61] Here the question hinged upon the interpretation of the term *prelati*, and if the friars sought clarification it could only be because some bishops and secular clergy were attempting to impose upon it the interpretation which FitzRalph here expounded, namely that *prelati* must be taken to include not only bishops, but all holding office in the Church structure, *curati*, *rectores*, *vicarii*, and *capellani parochiales*; all those having cure of souls, regardless of rank, are *prepositi* and therefore *prelati*! For this opinion FitzRalph offered a threefold proof – from grammar, Scripture, and 'ex racione certa', concluding that the friars were therefore bound to obey even the lowest of these categories, the parish chaplain.[62] Criticizing the impudence of the friars who preached near the parish church when the curate was saying Mass, he pointed out that whereas the curate could only preach to his flock during Mass, the friars had all day to do so, and he concluded – with a sweeping *non sequitur* – that the friars' privilege was anyhow superfluous and ought to be abolished.[63] The second part of the decretal, concerning the friars' right to hear confession and impart absolution to the laity, he regarded as equally superfluous – in this respect also the friars should remain within their original calling. Already in this sermon the confession problem, which was to be crucial to the case of 1357-60, received maximum treatment, and once more the argument was threefold: from the past history of the Church which had managed for twelve hundred years without the friars, from the mendicants' own rule and profession, and because of the divisive and damaging effect they had on Christian society. In the first objection he suggested that if anybody other than the parish clergy were to have this privilege, it should be the members of the older monastic orders 'amplius approbati et amplius incorporati ecclesie . . . qui non solum sunt confirmati, set instituti ab ecclesia'.[64] This argument is tendentious, since the haphazard growth of older monastic congregations, which also acquired privileges of exemption, could scarcely be described as direct 'institution' on the part of the central organs of the Church. However, FitzRalph's use of

[61] Clem. III. 7. 2, Friedberg, ii. 1162; *Proposicio*, ed. cit., pp. 56–7. But see also the restrictions imposed by some English bishops, Kedar, art. cit. On the question of who should be included under the term *locorum prelati* according to the terms of *Super Cathedram*, ibid., 25.

[62] Ed. cit., pp. 56–7, ll. 79–107.

[63] Ibid., p. 57, ll. 110–2.

[64] Ibid., p. 58, ll. 129–31. Almost half of the text, pp. 58–66, was devoted to the problem of confession.

this line of argument against the friars, and in defence of the so-called 'possessionati' who were to be an important element in the anti-mendicant campaign in England and were to draw upon themselves the particular wrath of Wyclif even before he turned against the friars,[65] might have developed in the course of consultations at the curia, especially when one considers the strong preponderance of members of these orders among those members of the college of cardinals who eventually heard his case against the mendicants.

FitzRalph was well aware of the argument that the friars were usually better equipped and educated for pastoral ministry and clearly found it difficult to refute. He therefore circumvented it cautiously, stressing the authority of the bishop with the assertion that if a bishop, on annual visitation, discovered that his curates were unable to provide an adequate ministry, he could select and license suitable friars as confessors, who would then be subject to his authority and virtually act as his curates – a situation which he regarded as infinitely preferable to the friars' independent right to hear confessions at will.[66] Here, however, the archbishop was failing to distinguish between the existing legislation, which provided for a situation that roughly approximated to the suggestion which he was claiming to approve,[67] and abuses of that law which were caused equally by the indiscriminate activity of unlicensed friars and by the laxity of some of his brother-bishops.

His claim that the privilege of hearing confession was diametrically opposed to the friars' own rule and profession reflected a tendency to argue from a literal interpretation of the original rule of St. Francis, regardless of subsequent papal modifications and glosses as well as of the different constitutions of the other mendicant orders. Here he claimed that their vows of poverty and humility were repeatedly violated by the friars' constant attempts to seek the privilege of being confessors,

[65] Robson, *Wyclif and the Oxford Schools*, p. 16, suggested that Wyclif's antagonism towards the endowed religious was first aroused by the circumstances surrounding his disputed wardenship of Canterbury College, from which he was ejected in or soon after the summer of 1370.

[66] Ed. cit., p. 59, ll. 147–57.

[67] He envisaged, as clearly did the author of *Super Cathedram* and the early glossators, that for specific purposes licensed friars might be subject to episcopal jurisdiction, and he implied approval for the view of Joannes Andreae, that the decision on which and how many of the friars suggested by their order should receive a licence rested with the bishop, Joannes Andreae, *Apparatus glossarum in Clementinas* (Venice, 1491), fol. 27^{r}.

as the power to absolve was a great honour which conferred a position of authority and influence when the friars had kings, princes, and nobles as their spiritual sons and daughters – a clear expression of the resentment of the secular clergy at the position of the friars at court throughout western Christendom.[68] FitzRalph concluded that the friars sought such positions out of greed, and in order to secure the temporal advantages connected with the office since, he claimed, they were conspicuously not interested in performing other priestly functions such as administering baptism and the last rites – an accusation which must have caused particular resentment among those who had seen their confrères succumb in large numbers to the recent plague precisely because they had devoted themselves to the latter task. But the preacher extended his oft-repeated teaching on no absolution without restitution to cover his picture of the sinful and covetous friar-confessors: they had obtained this function through the sin of pride and avarice; they exercised it through sin and even if they regretted this sinful acquisition, their regrets could be of no avail until they renounced the office.[69]

The third point made by the archbishop, that it was detrimental to the fabric of Christian society, that it was divisive for those who belonged together (such as husband and wife) to confess to different confessors, that confession lost most of its significance if it were made too easy by confessing to a wandering friar who might appear once a year, rather than to the parish priest who could observe his flock during the entire year, and that it was desirable for a confessor dealing with a penitent at the point of death to know that penitent's past life, had a

[68] Williams, art. cit., provides numerous examples of English bishops who failed to make use of the protection afforded by the canon law. There are no recorded confessional licences in Armagh, not even in the extant registers for FitzRalph's successors so it is not possible to assess whether Irish bishops licensed mendicant confessors, or whether the memory of FitzRalph's difficulties with the friars acted as a deterrent.

[69] Ed. cit., pp. 61–2. FitzRalph was not alone in his claim that the friars made things easier for their aristocratic and wealthy penitents. Piers Plowman painted a vivid picture of the friar, offering Lady Lucre absolution from sexual sins in return for a load of wheat, pointing out that she would fare even better if she were prepared to contribute to a stained-glass window, *Piers Plowman*, B. text, ed. Walter W. Skeet (EETS), iii. 35–63, pp. 33–5. The constant references in contemporary satire to such windows must have been generally understood as meaning the magnificent specimens made for the Franciscan church in London during the first half of the 14th century, and FitzRalph must have also been familiar with this splendid example of mendicant churches, see Erikson, 'The fourteenth-century Franciscans and their Critics', *FS* 35, 121 and n.

certain validity, but his arguments begged at least one major question. He ignored the fact that by the middle of the fourteenth century the friars had achieved a measure of stability and had built up, especially in the towns – where they had their greatest concentration and greatest influence – a regular clientele or flock which, if one can generalize from the pockets of available sources,[70] were also sufficiently stable and permanent to render invalid these objections. FitzRalph's criticisms must, however, have had a greater relevance for rural areas which were occasionally served by itinerant friars and such was a situation with which the archbishop must have been confronted in his first years as archbishop of Armagh. Here there were few urban centres of any consequence outside the towns of Drogheda and Dundalk, which were – especially in the former case – well served by communities of friars with a degree of permanence and stability as indicated above. Vast areas of the diocese, and particularly the Gaelic parts of it, were rural and may have been served by wandering friar-confessors, primarily Franciscans from convents such as that in the cathedral town of Armagh itself, while the friars might easily have been guilty of a further provocation if they extended their wandering ministry into the border area in which they would have clashed with the Anglo-Irish parochial clergy, although the latter were not capable of ministering to any Gaelic-speaking minorities among their flocks.

The argument of fragmentation of families was raised once more by FitzRalph in connection with the mendicants' right of burial of the laity, a privilege which he claimed was detrimental to all parties concerned – the secular clergy who were deprived of their divinely ordained rights, the friars who were drawn into litigation and the acquisition of wealth in direct violation of their profession, and the laity who were deprived of the spiritual benefits which would be theirs if they were buried in the parish church.[71] With regard to the effect on the laity, the least satisfactory aspect of his case, the suitability of the parish church as the only place ordained by God, was assumed rather than argued. His view of the implications for the friars, that it drew them away from their profession of

[70] The question has been examined with regard to Italian mendicant communities and their urban clientele in the 14th and 15th centuries in Walsh, 'The Observant Congregations of the Augustinian Friars in Italy' (MS D.Phil. c. 952, Oxford, 1972).

[71] *Proposicio*, ed. cit., pp. 66–7. He had already hinted at this problem in the Lichfield sermons.

poverty by involving them in litigation and the accumulation of riches in violation of the wishes of their founder, and in the sin of covetousness – he asserted that they were only interested in burying the rich, using the somewhat abusive term 'anclacio', which in this context might best be translated as 'rapacious angling' – was once more based on the application of a literal interpretation of the rule of St. Francis to all mendicant orders. Most plausible was the argument that as the friars were very frequently also the executors of the wills of those laymen and women who sought burial in their churches – a feature which is well documented in the extant wills, as these were frequently drawn up in the convent, witnessed by members of the community, and then deposited in the convent for safe-keeping[72] – the secular clergy often had difficulty in such cases in recovering the canonical portion of the bequests and legacies which was due to them under the terms of *Super Cathedram.*[73] The seculars were often afraid to pursue their rights and bring these cases before their bishops because, FitzRalph adduced, the friars then called on their conservators, and the latter might bring the parish curates into disrepute with a charge of heresy – though here the archbishop was careful to qualify his remarks with 'sicut dicitur'.[74]

Mendicant recourse to the episcopal conservators of their privileges was, as we have seen, a sore point with FitzRalph, and later in the *Proposicio* he aired a further grievance of this kind. Having stated his view of the particular absurdity that, whereas anybody could seek justice against a bishop (and here he tried to have matters both ways by claiming that the bishops were the successors of the apostles in Christ's hierarchy),[75]

[72] For Italian examples of this practice in mendicant communities see Walsh, 'The Observance: Sources for a History of the Observant Reform Movement in the Order of Augustinian Friars', *Rivista di Storia della Chiesa in Italia*, 31 (1977), 40–67.

[73] In the *Defensio Curatorum* FitzRalph complained that if the secular clergy brought an action against the friars for breaches of *Super Cathedram*, they were usually obliged to plead their case before a conservator in some distant place, and were thereby forced to abandon their rights because of the expense. A bishop or wealthy monastery could afford legal proceedings under such circumstances, but the average parish curate could not (ed. Goldast, p. 1397). The litigant who approached FitzRalph to seek justice against the friars, whose conservator the archbishop was, appears not to have experienced this difficulty, above, n. 54.

[74] Ed. cit., p. 67, ll. 348–53.

[75] Ibid., p. 69, ll. 408–9. But FitzRalph had earlier (p. 54, ll. 24–5) taken for granted that the way of life practised (or at least professed) by the friars was the 'via perfeccionis', or apostolic way of life, and this ambiguity was particularly noticeable in the various sections of *DPS*.

nobody could secure justice against the friars, he cited the example of the sequestration of a dead man's property by the friars.[76] In view of the fact that only a bishop could be appointed conservator of mendicant privileges, the episode must have occurred after FitzRalph had become archbishop of Armagh, and is most likely to have occurred in Ireland during 1348–9. His attempted intervention in this case on behalf of the deceased's brother, and the reaction of the friars concerned when he summoned them in order to clarify the matter might go a long way towards explaining why he suddenly decided that the entire system of mendicant privileges and the legal foundations upon which they rested required investigation and revision. Anyhow it must have made clear to him that existing ecclesiastical legislation was of little assistance when dealing with this particular area of friction. It is furthermore tempting to see his concern with possible abuse of property rights by the friars as a chapter in the history of Gaelic and Anglo-Irish tension within his metropolitan jurisdiction, a problem which gradually led him to outspoken statements about the duty of respecting property rights of all one's fellow citizens, even those of opposing communities.

Somewhat as an afterthought he turned in the *Proposicio* to the question of mendicant preaching. Episcopal regulation of such preaching was a haphazard affair in fourteenth-century England, until the anti-Lollard legislation indirectly effected a control of the friars' preaching activity and the content of their sermons.[77] Hence FitzRalph's marginal interest in the question of preaching reflected the views of many of his English episcopal colleagues in the mid-fourteenth century. He used the papal decretals issued for the Franciscans, especially those of Nicholas III and John XXII, to argue that the friars violated their vow of absolute poverty through their privilege of preaching, a privilege which guaranteed them the necessities of life and enabled them to enjoy as by right a secure existence which was denied to the genuine and involuntary poor. He claimed that Nicholas III, expounding on the Franciscan rule in *Exiit*, had exhorted the friars to live by begging, manual labour, and voluntary offerings.[78] These arguments, professedly aimed at all four mendicant orders but in reality determined by Franciscan legislation and profession, lend strength to the view that he had

[76] As n. 44. [77] Kedar, art. cit., 26–30. [78] Ed. cit., pp. 70–2.

already received from Clement VI the commission referred to in the prologue of *De Pauperie Salvatoris*, which involved a specific study of the papal decretals concerning the Franciscans.[79] FitzRalph's attitude to poverty and mendicant privileges was emerging as a literal, almost fundamentalist interpretation of the primitive rule of St. Francis, which had been found by successive popes and by moderate elements in the order over the previous century to be utterly incompatible with a developing and canonically organized order. When FitzRalph did have recourse in his argument to the papal glosses on the rule, he employed them selectively, and he ignored the fact that three of the four mendicant orders owed no allegiance to that rule, that the Dominicans had been expressly constituted as an order of preachers, and that the Augustinians had been called from their hermitages to an active urban apostolate by Alexander IV.[80] Already at this point he seemed to be committing himself to a dangerous position, where the question would soon be asked by his hearers: if the mendicant privileges were a violation of the primitive ideal of the friars, indeed sinful, then what of the popes who concurred with this violation and even encouraged it by granting such privileges? Many of his hearers must have mentally pursued the implications of his argument that not merely did the laity sin by availing themselves of the friars' pastoral services, of confession and burial outside the parish structure, but that the friars sinned even more grievously by performing such functions, in which case the greatest sin of all must lie with those popes who had made the friars' actions possible. FitzRalph may have been aware of these possible implications of papal criticism, and his final argument was an attempt to avoid the impression that he was criticizing Clement VI's predecessors for having granted the friars such extensive rights and privileges: he maintained that those who abused the powers conceded to them deserved to lose them, just as Adam deserved to be deprived of the Garden of Eden and its fruits; therefore the friars deserved to be deprived of their privileges of preaching, hearing confessions, and burial since they had abused them, as all assembled prelates would agree.[81]

Although at this stage he was still couching his arguments

[79] Above, n. 54, and CVP 1430, fol. 1^{ra-b}.

[80] For the bull of union *Licet Ecclesiae Catholicae*, see edition and commentary by Rafael Kuiters, *Augustiniana*, 6 (1956), 9–36.

[81] Ed. cit., p. 72.

against mendicant privileges in terms of his own concern for the friars' moral and spiritual welfare, the solution he envisaged would have amounted to the virtual destruction of the mendicant orders in the form which by the mid-fourteenth century they had achieved. They would have been left with little function or real possibility of gaining a livelihood within the framework of the Church, and their numbers would consequently have been reduced to small bands of incorrigible idealists, such as those who had originally followed St. Francis, and they would only have been able to exercise a marginal influence on Christian society. Older studies of FitzFalph adopted the position that the turning-point in his attitude to the friars and consequently in his entire career occurred *after* he had preached this *Proposicio* in 1350, when he settled down to prepare the detailed study which appeared in *De Pauperie Salvatoris*. It is indisputable that his attacks on the friars became more penetrating and his condemnation more complete after the publication of this dialogue, developing from a plea to have their privileges rescinded towards a position where he appeared to be denying their fundamental assumption that a life of voluntary poverty had a special merit, and consequently denying the justification for their existence. But, as we shall see, what was new in FitzRalph's case following his investigations in the early 1350s was not specifically connected with the pastoral problem, but was rather the way in which he employed as the basis of his argument about poverty the theory of dominion, whereby all lordship, ownership, and jurisdiction was founded on God's grace to the individual soul. In *De Pauperie Salvatoris* FitzRalph was to give the argument against mendicant poverty a philosophical basis and an organic unity, but already by 5 July 1350 he gave proof that he had adopted an extremely critical attitude to the mendicant orders. His fundamental objections to their pastoral function, and consequently to their role in later medieval society, were clearly and forcefully expressed. At this stage they were, however, enhanced by their having been expressed after careful consideration and with a minimum of polemic, before the issues had become confused by conflict and embittered by personalities, as was to be the case in the contributions by both sides during the period 1357–60. Hence FitzRalph never improved on this *Proposicio*, and it remained the most satisfactory statement of his views on the pastoral issue, but it unfortunately received little consideration in the later stages of the conflict.

ii. Dominion and grace: De Pauperie Salvatoris

With the publication in 1356 of the dialogue *De Pauperie Salvatoris* FitzRalph introduced into the smouldering poverty controversy a fresh complicating factor, the theory of dominion founded on grace which was to have such far-reaching implications in the development of both Wyclif's concept of the Church and that of the Czech reformers, Jan Hus and Jerome of Prague.[1] Since R. L. Poole published as an appendix to his edition of Wyclif's *De Dominio Divino*[2] the first four of the seven books of FitzRalph's dialogue in its original version, it has been accepted by modern scholarship that the theory of dominion which Wyclif expounded in the 1370s – initially in *De Dominio Divino* (which was intended to stand as an introduction to his *Summa in Theologia* but whose manuscript circulation appears never to have contained more than the incomplete version surviving in four manuscripts now all in Vienna[3]) and subsequently in *De Civili Dominio*[4] – was borrowed from FitzRalph's elaborate inquiry into the whole theory of lordship, possession, property, and use. Also since the publication of the main corpus of Wyclif's writing around the turn of the century and the attempt to establish a chronology of his works,[5] it has become clear that Wyclif was familiar with the teaching of FitzRalph and cited him frequently in the early philosophical

[1] There is no satisfactory modern study of Wyclif's thought as a whole, but see Workman, *John Wyclif*; Robson, *Wyclif and the Oxford Schools*; on Wyclif's theory of dominion and its place in his system of thought, Michael Wilks, 'Predestination, Property and Power: Wyclif's Theory of Dominion and Grace', *Studies in Church History*, ii (Oxford, 1965), 220-36; Gordon Leff, 'John Wyclif: the Path to Dissent', *PBA* 52 (1966), 143-80; idem, *Heresy in the Later Middle Ages*, ii (Manchester-New York, 1967), pp. 546-9, where he warns against exaggeration of the importance of dominion in Wyclif's thinking: 'Once he had expounded it in the first book of *De Civili Dominio* (i.e. 1376) it had little formative part in his subsequent thinking', ibid., p. 546. Against this view, it must be stressed that Wyclif's contemporaries, and especially his opponents, considered his teaching on dominion sufficiently important to take issue with it and with its source, FitzRalph. See Jeremy I. Catto, 'William Woodford OFM (*c.* 1330-*c.*1397)', (MS D.Phil. d. 4877, Oxford, 1969); Eric Doyle, 'William Woodford's "De dominio civili·clericorum" against John Wyclif', *AFH* 66 (1973), 49-109.

[2] Composed in 1374-5, ed. WS, (London, 1890).

[3] CVP 1339 (upon which Poole based his edition, 1294, 3929, and 3935, all containing other items by Wyclif. CVP 3935 also includes FitzRalph's *Defensio Curatorum*. For the manuscript problem see Poole, ed. cit., pp. vii-xxii.

[4] *De Civili Dominio*, i, ed. Poole; ii-iii (2 parts) ed. Johann Loserth (WS, London, 1885, 1900, 1903-4).

[5] See S. Harrison Thomson, 'The Order of Writing of Wyclif's Philosophical Works', *Českou Minulostí. Essays presented to Václac Novotný* (Prague, 1929), 146-66; idem (with some modification of his own conclusions), 'Unnoticed Manuscripts and Works of Wyclif', *JTS* 38 (1937), 24-36, 139-48.

treatises which, grouped together, form the *Summa de Ente*,[6] and which represent lectures delivered by Wyclif as a master in the arts faculty during the 1360s. Nor were Wyclif's contemporaries and opponents, the Franciscan William Woodford[7] and the Carmelite Thomas Netter of Walden,[8] in any doubt that the immediate source of this questionable teaching was the Anglo-Irish theologian of the previous generation, and Woodford at least was happy to dispose of both Wyclif and FitzRalph in a single argument.[9] Wyclif himself made no secret of the fact that the two Oxford doctors of the previous generation to whom his intellectual formation owed most were Thomas Bradwardine and 'Ardmachanus', and on more than one occasion we find him steering a middle course between the two extremes of thought represented – on some topics but not on all – by these two models.[10] Most obvious of all, a comparison of the texts of *De Dominio Divino* and parts of *De Civili Dominio* with FitzRalph's dialogue indicate the fact all too clearly – not merely did Wyclif take the germ of the idea from his predecessor but often repeated lengthy passages of his arguments.[11]

When *De Pauperie Salvatoris* first circulated in Oxford, no later than the winter of 1356-7, John Wyclif was a fellow of Merton and soon to become a master of arts at Balliol,[12] though he did not begin to publish works which demonstrated his close dependence on FitzRalph until some years later.

[6] Robson, *Wyclif and the Oxford Schools*, esp. pp. 115-217.

[7] *BRUO* III, 2081-2, also Catto and Doyle as n.1.

[8] *BRUO* II, 1343-4. His arguments against FitzRalph, as expounded in his *Doctrinale Antiquatum Fidei*, ii. 187-9; iii. 113-14, esp. concerning the sacramental powers of the simple priest, were taken up by Cardinal Robert Bellarmine, in *De Scriptoribus Ecclesiasticis* (Rome, 1613), p. 237, who warned that FitzRalph's writings, especially the *Summa* and the anti-mendicant works, contained 'multos errores ... de potestate Presbyterorum, de paupertate Christi, et de statu religiosorum'.

[9] Although writing after Wyclif's assault on the friars, Woodford attacked FitzRalph as the source of these theories in his *Defensorum mendicitatis contra Armachanum* (*c*.1394-6), MS Magdalen 75. Woodford deliberately argued that Christ and the apostles held property and civil dominion, accepting the rulings of John XXII for the Franciscans without any gloss or mitigation, Catto, *William Woodford*, p. 192.

[10] e.g. in *De volucione Dei*, ed. Michael H. Dziewicki (WS, London, 1909), pp. 134-79, where Bradwardine and FitzRalph are frequently cited, in each case both critically and with approval, on questions of creation, free will, and divine volition.

[11] Compare texts as contained in *De Dominio Divino*, ed. cit., pp. 1-256, and *De Civili Dominio*, i-iii, *passim*. Occasionally Wyclif disagrees with FitzRalph's arguments, as on the question of whether God can have different lordship over the same thing, *De Dominio Divino*, p. 36.

[12] Robson, *Wyclif and the Oxford Schools*, p. 10; *BRUO* III, 2103-6.

The chronology of Wyclif's earlier, non-theological writings is such a complex problem that it is impossible at this stage to say more than that in *De universalibus* and *De volucione Dei*, both of which must be dated before 1372, Wyclif displayed his familiarity with both the *Summa de Questionibus Armenorum* and *De pauperie Salvatoris*,[13] and it is a reasonable possibility that he read the latter dialogue soon after its publication in Oxford. In the early stages of his academic career Wyclif had no reason for hostility towards the friars in either a university or a pastoral context, and he may not have had any immediate reason to pick up a doctrine which in the debates of 1356–7 was so clearly directed against the mendicant orders. It is certainly true that when he did begin to quote FitzRalph in those treatises from the *Summa de Ente* mentioned above, he tended to go to the Armenian questions for authoritative support on matters of necessity and contingency, and to the later dialogue with regard to philosophical problems, as, for example, creation and annihilation, which FitzRalph had discussed in the early books of *De Pauperie Salvatoris*.[14] Hence not until the 1370s did Wyclif apparently begin to take up the implications of FitzRalph's doctrine of dominion. This, however, led him to develop his concept of ecclesiastical government along lines which the conservative, hierarchically-minded FitzRalph never intended, and this difference of theological outlook eventually led Wyclif to apply the theory of dominion and grace to a purpose which could only be recognized and condemned as heretical, a distinction which FitzRalph's mendicant opponents of a later generation were willing to allow to remain obscure.[15]

Neither of the two main mendicant critics of FitzRalph as

[13] Significantly, Wyclif quoted Books XV–XVII of the *Summa* when dealing with philosophical problems, ed. cit., pp. 184–5, 197, 275–7.

[14] *DPS*, ed. cit., pp. 283–303. It may be significant for the dating of Wyclif's reception of FitzRalph's last dialogue that he cited neither FitzRalph nor Bradwardine in the lengthy passage on annihilation in *De potencia Dei* (*Summa de Ente*, ii, tract 6), ed. cit., pp. 287–315, nor did he take up FitzRalph's arguments about the possible implications of consumption as an act of divine lordship for the conversion of the elements in the Eucharist, *DPS*, p. 303.

[15] Esp. Woodford, whose attacks on Wyclif's view of dominion are the earliest known, Doyle, art. cit., 50. Lollard sanctification of FitzRalph did nothing to improve his orthodox image in the eyes of mendicant critics at Oxford towards the end of the 14th century. See also Wilks, art. cit., 235, who regarded Wyclif's doctrine of dominion as 'the reverse of revolutionary', but interpreted it as a 'smoke-screen of predestinarian speculation', enabling Wyclif to reconstruct the old lay ideal of a theocratic monarchy and a proprietary church – dimensions which FitzRalph never considered.

the inspiration of Wyclif named any other theologian who might have been the common source for the doctrine, and whereas Wyclif openly acknowledged his debt to FitzRalph, the latter did not at any stage name his source – he tended to cite only those sources he was opposing, but rarely the authority for an opinion which he was defending. Hence the question has to be faced: how and when did FitzRalph come to be convinced of the truth of his views about the essential relationship between lordship and grace, a conviction which is the foundation of his dialogue. When did he first express interest in these problems? As we have already seen in his lectures on the Sentences, the only extant work whose composition antedated his visits to Avignon and exposure to current influences there, there was no allusion in the entire text to problems of lordship and jurisdiction. The Avignon sermons of the years 1335 and 1338–44 are equally devoid of evidence of a personal interest in these questions, but there are several brief allusions in the Armenian questions which indicate that during the later stages of his longest stay at Avignon his attention had at least been drawn to the issue. In Book X, Chapter 4, where he discussed the general question of hereditary rights and the possibility of hereditary claims to ecclesiastical jurisdiction, he inserted a short digression which is significant as the first clear indication of his future line of development:

> So far as I can judge [argued Ricardus] no man in the state of mortal sin has true lordship over other creatures in God's sight. He ought rather to be called a tyrant, a thief or a robber, though he may keep the name of king or prince or lord, by reason of possession or hereditary succession, or the approval of the people who are subject to him, or by some other human law. But he has no true lordship until he repents, and until the grace of penance has restored him to a state that is acceptable to God.[16]

Here the implications of the statement were not worked out in detail, an indication perhaps that FitzRalph was himself not yet aware of the direction in which such a theory would lead him, though he had been exposed to its formulation.

The dialogue *De Pauperie Salvatoris* contains very few direct references to sources apart from the Bible and the Decretals, Aristotle, Augustine, and the Lombard,[17] and Fr. Gwynn was

[16] S, fol. 75va; Vat. Lat. 1033, fol. 76^{r}; Vat. Lat. 1035, fol. 105^{va-b}.

[17] Occasionally also the Pseudo-Dionysius (a text in the schools), Clement of Alexandria, and Anselm's *Cur Deus homo*, which he cited regularly in the sermons and the *Summa*. Understandably the decretals, and especially the pronouncements

the first to question further the evolution of the theories underlying the dialogue. He traced them back to several of the most important representatives of the Augustinian theological school, all members of the order of Friars Hermits of St. Augustine, and principally to Aegidius Romanus, the official doctor of the order.[18] Aegidius's doctrine was formulated in the treatise *De ecclesiastica potestate*, composed in 1302 at the height of the conflict between Boniface VIII and Philip the Fair and representing an extreme interpretation of the principles of *De Civitate Dei* in sharp contrast to the author's earlier Thomist-Aristotelian treatise *De Regimine Principum* (*c.* 1285).[19] In the later treatise Aegidius set out the theory of spiritual and temporal power in its most uncompromisingly ecclesiastical form and it is an intriguing paradox in the development of medieval ecclesiology and political thought that a doctrine which was first put forward as a defence of hierocratic claims of papal monarchy should, within the space of three generations, become the basis from which Wyclif would develop a most formidable attack on papal jurisdiction. The latter, drawing also from Marsilio's vision of a possessionless Church dependent entirely upon the state, would totally upset Aegidius's argument that all lordship can only exist with justice under and through the Church. It has universal lordship over all things temporal and only its faithful members have just and righteous lordship. Such a theory was based on the general principle that lordship, as a gift from God, must be founded on divine justice, and that such justice is lacking in all who, either through sin or lack of baptismal regeneration, are without grace. From this it followed that original and mortal sin deprived both the infidel and the sinner of all rights to lordship, jurisdiction, and property.

Subsequently the doctrine was traced further by Ullmann, who was able to identify its application in the hierocratic defence of papal jurisdiction against secularist claims by Alanus, the English (or more probably Welsh) canonist who taught at Bologna in the early thirteenth century,[20] and showed its further development though Hostiensis and Cardinal Petrus

of Nicholas III and John XXII concerning the Franciscans, are most frequently cited in the later books not printed by Poole, where FitzRalph moved from the theoretical and general to a particular discussion of the Franciscan case.

[18] *English Austin Friars*, pp. 35–73.

[19] *De ecclesiastica potestate*, ed. Richard Scholz (Weimar, 1929).

[20] Walter Ulmann, *Medieval Papalism* (Cambridge, 1949), pp. 133–7. For Alanus see also *LTK* i^2. 265.

Bernardi to the pontificate of John XXII. These curialist lawyers had been seeking a principle which would enable them to argue that temporal authority had no validity without the sanction of the spiritual power. They needed a theoretical justification for the confiscation of the property of condemned heretics, and through this theory of dominion they could define heresy as a just cause for the withdrawal of ownership. Here it is worth noting that the canonists – unlike FitzRalph and Wyclif, and indeed unlike the papal publicists of the early fourteenth century who used the theory in ecclesiastico-political terms – regarded dominion as commensurate with ownership as sanctioned by civil as well as divine law and, being consequently concerned only with the implication of the theory in so far as it was enforceable under positive law they avoided much of the paradox which diminished the force of later developments of the argument.

Subsequent exponents of the doctrine within the Augustinian order attempted to modify the rigour of Aegidius' teaching. The first to consider the problem, Giacomo da Viterbo, attempted to reconcile the more extreme views of his former Paris master with accepted Aristotelian principles.[21] In turn his own pupil Alessandro da S. Elpidio, while staunchly defending papal claims against the schismatic emperor Ludwig the Bavarian, modified Aegidius' doctrine suffiently to permit the legality of natural society and forms of government under infidels, while Agostino Trionfo, in the *Summa de Potestate Ecclesiastica* dedicated to John XXII (1320) which is otherwise a statement of the most extreme curialist doctrines of the age, distanced himself cautiously but perceptibly from this particular tenet of his order's official doctor.[22] At this stage it might have appeared that the leading theologians of the Augustinian order had become aware of the doctrine's potential implications and quietly allowed it to disappear from the scene, were it not for the fact that it emerged again in the mid-1320s from the pen of

[21] As Capocci, Giacomo in Perini, *Bibl. Aug.* i. 191–6; Gwynn, *English Austin Friars*, pp. 61–2. His contribution to the problem was edited by H.-X. Arquillière, *Le Plus ancien traité de l'église. Jacques de Viterbo, De Regimine Christiano (1301–2)* (Paris, 1926).

[22] Gwynn, pp. 62–4. Alone among this group of publicists, Agostino Trionfo has received a detailed modern study: Michael Wilks, *The Problem of Sovereignty in the Later Middle Ages. The Papal Monarchy with Augustinus Triumphus and the Publicists* (Cambridge, 1964), though the question of dominion founded on grace receives only marginal treatment.

one who must be regarded as no less representative of the order's theological tradition than any of the three mentioned above. Also a master of theology and elected prior-general of the order at the general chapter of Florence (1326) in succession to Alessandro da S. Elpidio, who had died a few months earlier,[23] Guglielmo Amidani da Cremona had already come out in defence of the papal position against the recently published *Defensor Pacis* (1324). As one of the theologians commissioned by John XXII to examine the *Defensor Pacis*, the Augustinian composed his *Refutatio Errorum*, in which the arguments of Aegidius Romanus are used, often verbatim, to prove the 'potestas directa' of the spiritual power, and to deny the view that all things temporal should be subject to the secular power.[24]

The general significance of this *Refutatio* lies in the fact that a prominent theologian at the curia thought it prudent to defend the most extreme conclusions of Aegidius Romanus without any modification of papal claims in favour of those of the temporal power, indicating not only that this doctrine had left a deeper impression on the tradition of the Augustinian order than might otherwise appear, but also that such an anti-Thomist (-Aristotelian) doctrine might expect a favourable reception at the papal court within a short time of the canonization of Aquinas in 1323. Guglielmo da Cremona ruled his order as prior-general for sixteen years at a time when the conflict between pope and emperor was at its height, during the last years of John XXII and the entire pontificate of Benedict XII – when reform of the religious orders (including the Augustinians) was a burning issue. Accurate details concerning his movements during this period are few, but he must have been based at Avignon for most of the time, apart from visitations and general chapters held in outlying provinces of the order. The extant decrees of six general chapters over which he presided indicate a constant concern for promotion of higher studies in the order; he had been consulted by John XXII on at least one occasion; he co-operated with Benedict XII over the Augustinian reform decrees, and his appointment to the see of Novara on 17 July 1342, soon after Clement's accession, might

[23] The decrees of this chapter are printed in *AA* 4 (1912).

[24] Gwynn, *English Austin Friars*, pp. 64-5; Daragh MacFhionnbhairr (ed.), *Guillelmi de Villana Cremonensis tractatus cuius titulus reprobatio errorum* (Corpus Scriptorum Augustinianorum 2, Rome, 1977).

be taken as an indication of his good standing with the new pope, with whom he had long shared common ground in their joint opposition to the *Defensor Pacis.*[25] Consequently it seems reasonable, in default of evidence to the contrary, to accept Gwynn's hypothesis that the Augustinian prior-general worked in roughly similar circles to those with which FitzRalph was connected in Avignon during the same period, and that FitzRalph thereby came in contact with him and with his doctrine of dominion and grace, which found tentative expression in the work of the 'Armachanus' before culminating in *De Pauperie Salvatoris.*[26]

We have already encountered, in the *Proposicio* of 5 July 1350, a statement of FitzRalph's belief in God's grace as a foundation for valid lordship and exercise of authority and jurisdiction, with the corollary that those who abused such rights and privileges deserved to be deprived of them.[27] At this stage his treatment was brief, but possible lines of development may have been clear to members of his audience who could remember the arguments of the publicists in defence of papal prerogatives during the struggles of the previous three decades. Whereas FitzRalph's first explicit reference to the question came in Book X of his *Summa*, he had already in several sermons given serious consideration to the duties of prelates and other Church dignitaries, and their suitability for such positions – a theme which he later developed more fully, but with the friars rather than his fellow bishops as the target for his criticism. With regard to the passage in the *Summa de Questionibus Armenorum*, Michael Wilks has warned against the danger of lifting it out of context: he maintained that FitzRalph had in mind here the problem of a kingdom seized by conquest and was therefore arguing that in such a case there could be no natural right of government,[28] an interpretation which the passage concerned does not really bear and which, at the immediately practical and political level is substantially at variance with the arguments for the English conquest of France which FitzRalph preached at the procession of 26 June 1345.[29] However, Wilks very aptly pointed out that in connection with

[25] Eubel, *Hierarchia Catholica*, i². 372.
[26] Gwynn, *English Austin Friars*, pp. 66–7.
[27] *Proposicio*, ed. cit., p. 72.
[28] Wilks, art. cit., 230 n.
[29] In that sermon he had argued exclusively on the basis of hereditary right, regardless of any claim to dominion founded upon grace, B, fol. 19ᵛ; J, fol. 15ᵛᵃ⁻ᵇ.

the development of FitzRalph's doctrine of dominion, we are so accustomed to considering him 'as a sort of prototype of Wyclif that we sometimes tend to forget that he was a publicist in the Roman curia at Avignon, elaborating a concept which had been developed earlier in the century by such men as Aegidius Romanus and Augustinus Triumphus'.[30] He might have further added that such publicist activity was guaranteed to be well received in the circles around Clement VI, that most hierocratically-minded of Avignonese popes.[31] It would certainly be a grave mistake to see FitzRalph either as an architect of social revolution, the development of whose doctrine of dominion was 'merely an attempt to find a new basis for authority and wealth in a rapidly changing society',[32] or as a forerunner of disendowment and the Calvinist ethic. To interpret him in terms of what Wyclif, the Lollards, or the Reformers in Prague subsequently made of his thesis, is to ignore the manner in which an orthodox, ambitious, and essentially conservative and hierarchically-minded prelate made his own a doctrine which had been hierocratic in its conception.

The precise significance to be attached to Wyclif's doctrine of dominion, both in terms of his own concept of the Church and of Christian society, and also in the context of the religious revolution of the later middle ages, has been the subject of some recent studies, though their results present nothing like an agreed picture.[33] All who have considered the topic have also discussed *en passant* the dialogue which was its immediate source, but direct and detailed consideration of FitzRalph's own thought on the subject in its own terms and with specific

[30] Wilks, art. cit., 229.

[31] Clement VI's political theory has been studied by Diana Wood, 'The Political Theory of Pope Clement VI', 2 vols. (Unpublished Ph.D. Thesis, University of London, 1976).

[32] For this interpretation see Reginald R. Betts, 'Richard fitzRalph, Archbishop of Armagh, and the Doctrine of Dominion', *Essays in Czech History* (London, 1969), pp. 160–75, at 161. When this, essentially Marxist, interpretation of FitzRalph's doctrine of dominion first appeared (1949) it was critically reviewed by Aubrey Gwynn, *IHS* 6 (1950–1), 131–3. In 1938 Hammerich had already suggested that FitzRalph's doctrine of dominion, as taken over by Wyclif, 'became a decisive factor – with several peripathies – in the fundamental principles of the conception of society in the rich capitalistic and Calvinist countries, viz. in England, Scotland, Holland, Switzerland, the older parts of the U.S.A.', *FitzRalph and the Mendicants*, p. 84.

[33] Especially the works of Betts, Leff, and Wilks. William Farr, *John Wyclif as Legal Reformer* (Leiden, 1974), gave some consideration to Wyclif's concept of the Church, but not to his theory of dominion.

reference to the poverty and mendicant controversies which brought it into being has unfortunately remained buried in two unpublished doctoral theses.[34] Hence it will be necessary here to consider the particular form which FitzRalph gave to the doctrine, also the circumstances which gave rise to and substantially coloured his interpretation of this extreme Augustinian teaching.

Although, as we have seen, his earlier works contained several indications of the possible direction which his thinking might take, FitzRalph did not work out the implications of the doctrine in any public exposition before the dialogue *De Pauperie Salvatoris*. As he revealed in his preface, the subject had been under discussion at Avignon at least since the year 1349–50,[35] and from what we know of the continuity of the doctrine among the pro-papal publicists since the turn of the century (apart from its essentially practical application by the canonists) we can assume that it never completely lost currency in curial circles. However, it had towards the end of the 1340s acquired a new dimension, when the possibility of its application to the Franciscan poverty question was dimly perceived. When the commission consisting of FitzRalph and two other theologians had failed to reach any satisfactory conclusion, several cardinals who had followed the discussions with interest, including Etienne Aubert, the future Pope Innocent VI, suggested that FitzRalph undertake a closer investigation of the entire question.[36] Hence, at their personal request, or so he claimed, FitzRalph began to plan the theological investigation which ultimately resulted in the *De Pauperie Salvatoris*, adopting as previously in the *Summa de Questionibus Armenorum* the dialogue form, in order to facilitate free discussion of the various options. In this formal respect he differed from Wyclif, whose treatment of the subject is generally accepted as having originated in a series of university lectures, circumstances which account not only for the lack of order and endless repetitions,

[34] Helen Hughes, '"De Pauperie Salvatoris" of Richard FitzRalph of Armagh' (Manchester, 1927); Richard O. Brock, 'An Edition of Richard FitzRalph's "De Pauperie Salvatoris", Books V, VI and VII' (University of Colorado, 1954).

[35] FitzRalph's description of the papal commission which occasioned *DPS* suggests that the matter was then of more than academic interest, ed. cit., p. 273.

[36] Ibid., pp. 273–4. Aubert had been a cardinal since 20 September 1342, Eubel, *Hierarchia Catholica*, i². 18, and had been present at the curia during the debates about reform of the religious orders. His own attitude to the mendicant problem as pope was ambivalent.

but also for the numerous disclaimers and qualifications of the latter's argument, intended no doubt to protect him against a possible charge of heresy.[37] However, as will emerge from this brief investigation of FitzRalph's work on the subject, he too was unable to avoid in his treatment of the issues involved a certain element of confusion, which was probably unavoidable given both the intellectual parentage of the doctrine and the archbishop's double concept of law.

Work on the dialogue was interrupted by FitzRalph's enforced departure from the congenial atmosphere of Avignon in the early summer of 1351, when the royal licence and Edward III's patience with the archbishop's primatial aspirations had finally come to an end. Over the next five years FitzRalph was primarily occupied with the administration of his archdiocese and ecclesiastical province, with one recorded visit to England, and possibly a period of illness before or during the visit to Ireland of George of Hungary. However, he did manage to finish his dialogue 'inter fluctus pastoralis officii sine intermissione in partibus Hibernie inundantes, cum fuissent paululum mitigati intervalla temporum quasi furtive (novit Omnipotens) michi surripui'.[38] This was not mere rhetoric and, as we have seen, there can have been few quiet moments during these years in Ireland. But he did manage to put the work into circulation by 1356, as he was able to report on 18 December 1356 in the first of the series of anti-mendicant sermons preached in London during the winter of 1356-7 that he had already sent the dialogue to the pope and cardinals for their comments and approval, at the same time making known its contents among his friends and colleagues in Oxford.[39] However, this haphazard genesis did not fail to leave its mark on the completed work which – even allowing for the dialogue technique which permitted the author to raise a number of extraneous issues – is extremely diffuse in conception and organization, and does not appear to have been based upon a preconceived and coherent plan. It has been argued that the reason for this lack of clarity both in organization and in line of argument was due to the fact that FitzRalph was himself not absolutely clear about his attitude to the issues involved or the solutions to be adopted,[40]

[37] Wilks, art. cit., 228. [38] *DPS*, ed. cit., p. 273.

[39] As Sudoris' printing of these London sermons is virtually useless, they will be cited from the MSS of the sermon diary. B, fol. 94^{v}; J, fol. 75rb.

[40] Gwynn, *English Austin Friars*, p. 68. Hughes, pp. 165-200, discussed the

and it is certainly indisputable that this dialogue is considerably less dogmatic in its utterances than the anti-mendicant sermons which followed soon after. Hence it is possible that FitzRalph used the dialogue both as a means of clarifying his own thoughts and of provoking further discussion. To this suggestion may be added a further probability, namely that the final section of the dialogue – especially Book VII which is most specifically connected with the practical application of his views to the mendicant problem – was composed in Ireland. It is even more disorganized, and certainly more subjective, than the preceding sections and it was the portion of the text upon which FitzRalph's mendicant critics concentrated, thereby compelling him at a later stage in the proceedings at Avignon to write an eighth book in order to clarify his position.[41]

For the unwary reader, relying on the printed edition, Poole's decision to publish only Books I–IV might lead to the assumption that these books alone dealt with the theoretical problem of dominion, property, possession, and use. However Book V continued in the same vein, discussing the lordship of angels and that enjoyed by Adam and Eve before their fall, together with the origins of civil society after Adam's sin,[42] before making the transition in the final four chapters to the concrete problems of the foundation of the friars' case and justification for their existence, i.e. the alleged possessionless status of Christ and the apostles.[43] These five books were planned and executed with more care than the rest, Book VI (the longest of the seven) begins to show signs of deterioration, while Book VII marks a definite decline in the coherence of FitzRalph's conception of

anomalies and contradictions to be found in the various parts of the dialogue, attributing them to a double line of thought, an imperfect fusion of Augustinian and Aristotelian theories of the origins of earthly law and authority. Similar ambiguities clouded the arguments of FitzRalph's Oxford opponent, see Walsh, 'Hardeby', *AA* 33, 253–4; 34, 8–9.

[41] For the limited MS circulation of Book VIII see Appendix, p. 472, 474–5.

[42] CVP 1430, fols. 64ra–76rb. The remark that 'there is no hint in any of these (i.e. the first 5) books of the real issue which FitzRalph has set himself to face', *English Austin Friars*, p. 68, scarcely seems justified. Already in Book IV, ed. cit., pp. 436–40, there is a detailed discussion of the papal interpretation of 'dominium' and 'proprietas' in *Exiit qui seminat.* Similarly Mathes' statement in 'The Poverty Movement and the Augustinian Hermits', *AA* 32, 16, that the first 5 books 'seem to have no connection at all with the question at issue', does little justice to the originality of what FitzRalph was trying to do, i.e. to use the discussion about theories of dominion as a basis for a more ecclesiologically orientated consideration of the poverty question.

[43] CVP 1430, fols. 74rb–76rb.

his subject. Hence it seems most probable that these first five books, and possibly also part of Book VI, were composed at Avignon during 1350–1. Although the papal registers indicate that he was busy securing the creation of additional offices and the necessary dispensations for the proper functioning of his archdiocese, in addition to pursuing his primatial claims and sorting out the finances of the Church of Armagh in relation to the papal Camera, FitzRalph must have had more time for serious study and reflection during these last months in Avignon than could have been possible over the next five years in Ireland.[44] These earlier books also contained the most detailed consideration of the theoretical aspects of the problem, again supporting the present writer's contention that FitzRalph set to work on the subject in the firm belief that he was continuing in the tradition of the papal publicists, whereas the later sections reflect his concern with the immediate and practical problems posed by the Franciscan profession, status, and activities, and with the relevant papal legislation which a prelate in his position might feel bound to consider. Hence while the thirty-seven chapters of Book VI are devoted to an exhaustive dicussion of the case for evangelical poverty, Book VII examines the discrepancies, real and apparent, between the legislation issued by Nicholas III for the Franciscans and the various utterances of John XXII in his decretals, and in the polemical *Libellus*, 'Quia vir reprobus', which he issued as a bull against Michele da Cesena.

Whereas both of these sections betray the marks of hasty composition, Book VII alone appears to have been added as an afterthought in the earliest datable manuscript — it has been argued elsewhere that this manuscript most probably originated at Oxford in the period *c.*1356 to 1357.[45] The practical orientation of these later books not merely strengthens the impression that they were composed in response to the immediate Irish situation of the early 1350s when the archbishop had less reason to concern himself with the philosophical basis for his theory, but it also ensured that these were the principal target of the mendicant counter-attacks during the later stages of the controversy in London and Avignon. FitzRalph was himself at least partly responsible for this development as in the course of

[44] Book VI is contained in CVP 1430, fols. 76rb–97rb, and Book VII at fols. 103ra–118vb. Fols. 97^{v}–102^{v} are blank.

[45] Walsh, 'Manuscripts of FitzRalph in Vienna', 67–71, and Appendix, p. 475.

the London sermons of the winter of 1356–7 he largely summarized the arguments contained in the dialogue and concentrated heavily on the issues discussed in these sections – doubtless because they had been composed most recently and with specific reference to a controversial situation similar to that which he encountered upon his arrival in London in the summer of 1356. That the – albeit scrappy – seventh book was part of the original plan, whereas Book VIII was not, is made plain both by the reference in the prologue to 'seven books' and by FitzRalph's further comment in the course of the sermon preached in the *aula* of Bishop Michael Northburgh of London on 18 December 1356 to the effect that he had already completed a work in seven books on the burning topic which was the subject of this sermon, and had circulated it in Avignon and Oxford.[46] Furthermore, the extremely limited manuscript circulation of the eighth book of the dialogue, usually to be found separately from the main body of the text, indicates that it attracted little interest outside Avignon and outside the circles most immediately connected with the legal proceedings which came to an end on the archbishop's death. The single exception in this manuscript circulation is the copy which was made for Adam Easton and which contains the entire eight books written as a single work. In view of Easton's known extensive stay at the curia from 1369 onwards,[47] it must have been copied from a complete text put into circulation in Avignon towards the end of FitzRalph's life.

The central problem which the archbishop set himself to solve, and which was raised by his discussion partner Iohannes at the outset of the dialogue, concerned the nature of the apostolic way of life upon which the mendicant orders based their existence. Iohannes questioned how it could be possible for several holy men, including SS. Basil, Augustine, Benedict, Dominic, and Francis, to inaugurate separate orders with differing rules, and still maintain that they all conformed to the apostolic way of life. He further pointed out that even for the Franciscan order there seemed to be a considerable discrepancy

[46] He told his audience: 'scripsi de ille materia septem libellos, quos domino nostro pape et quibusdam dominis meis cardinalibus approbandos seu discuciendos atque corrigendos, si oporteret, direxi, et Oxonie eciam ad eos legendum volentibus communicandos iam tradidi . . .', B, fol. 94^{v}; J, fol. 75rb. It would be interesting to know if FitzRalph had any particular cardinals in mind, whose views he would have welcomed, and if these were eventually appointed to hear the case, but on this point all sources are silent.

[47] *BRUO* I, 620–1 for his movements.

between the meaning of 'paupertas' as contained in the rule of St. Francis and as explained in the bull of Nicholas III *Exiit qui seminat* on the one hand, and in the decretals and *libellus* of John XXII on the other.[48] In reply Ricardus carefully drew attention to the suspension by John XXII of the ban which Nicholas III has imposed in *Exiit* on all further discussion or glossing of his interpretation of the Franciscan rule, and then went on to point out that the problem was caused by conflicting meanings attached by the various parties to the terms 'lordship', 'property', 'possession', 'right of use', and the voluntary renunciation of those rights. With the aim of clearing up this confusion he now intended to conduct a thorough examination of the true senses and meanings of these words, commencing with a discussion of the nature of dominion as pertaining to God and his creatures. He distinguished clearly between 'proprietas' and 'dominium': all 'dominium' belonging to the individual is not necessarily 'proprietas'. Similarly 'dominium' must always be distinguished from 'ius utendi': whereas the former always and truly included the latter, the reverse was not necessarily the case. Equally he argued that 'dominium' was to be distinguished from 'possessio', which he saw as an extension of 'dominium' and a middle point between it and the 'ius utendi'.[49] Here he argued that nobody having dominion could make use of that dominion unless he also possessed the property to which that dominion pertained, a statement which indicates that in the initial stages of his deliberations FitzRalph did not envisage the possibility of a dominion which could have no validity in this life, because it was unenforceable under positive law. At this stage, doubtless under curial influence, he still shared a view of dominion similar to that employed by the canonists.[50]

However, FitzRalph was to shift his position in the course of composition of the dialogue, on this and on other topics in the light of his direct experience with the friars, so that by the time he came to consider the practical aspects of the problem in Books VI and VII the difficulties caused by the double line of argument emerged more clearly. This intellectual confusion

[48] These fundamental questions were raised by Iohannes at the beginning of Book I, ed. cit., p. 277. [49] Ibid., pp. 278–81.

[50] He distinguished between legal possession and dominion: 'quoniam nemo habens dominium potest uti suo dominio nisi prius rem dominatam possideat, et possessio rei de iusticia dominio debetur; unde constat quod ipsa possessio a dominio suo distinguatur', ed. cit., 281.

appears to have been caused both by the long gestation of the work and the shift of purpose during the intervening years in accordance with change circumstances – a shift from theoretical to practical being most clearly identifiable in the caesura between Books V and VI – and by the complex nature of FitzRalph's own arguments. The first five books provided an exhaustive discussion of the abstract problems of dominion, possession, use, and property in relation to the divine gifts of creation and grace, thereby laying the foundation for a discussion of the mendicant ideal of poverty, the degree of possession and renunciation of property rights it implied, its justification in Scripture, also of the privileges which had already been showered on the friars and whose abolition the archbishop had already argued was in the interests of the over-all fabric and healthy pastoral life of the later medieval Church.

FitzRalph began to lay this foundation by explaining to Iohannes the nature of God's lordship from the moment of creation, as creation was the necessary precondition for lordship. Subsequently, he argued, God assumed government and maintenance of his creatures, acts which FitzRalph saw as corresponding to possession and use, rather than to lordship.[51] He also distinguished between God's lordship and that enjoyed by his creatures, providing an exhaustive discussion of the use of material things enjoyed by man under divine lordship.[52] Books II and III were devoted to a consideration of the natural or original lordship enjoyed by man before Adam's fall, a lordship subject to the qualification that it concerns only that which is lent by God to man and is therefore not true lordship. It is, however, the 'ius sive auctoritas originalis possidendi naturaliter res sibi natura subiectas conformiter racioni, et eis plene utendi sive eas tractandi'.[53] Such original lordship is then distinguished from the lordship which can be acquired under positive law by the fact that it cannot be refused when granted, nor can it be abdicated except through sin. Once more it is emphasized that positive laws were made necessary because of sin; they became imperative in order to repress evil and ensure that the good live in peace and order. Hence it follows that the civil lordship exercised through kings and princes would have been superfluous before the fall.[54] But then

[51] Ibid., pp. 283–7.
[52] Ibid., pp. 297–316.
[53] Ibid., p. 335.
[54] Ibid., pp. 370–1.

Fitzralph introduced a qualification, indicating that he was not totally prepared to abandon Aristotelian views of the State. He admitted that all might not deserve equal use of lordship, even before the fall some would have been pre-eminent over others, and that even then some laws would have been necessary for the regulation of the social order.[55]

In Book III the discussion centred on the relationship between original lordship and actual possession and use, and on the objects thus affected. Possession, he argued, is not a right itself, but merely a title to just and righteous lordship, but FitzRalph still had difficulty in establishing whether private property would have existed had it not been for the fall of Adam.[56] Here the problem of reconciling the titles granted by original lordship with those enforceable under positive law emerges once more, and it becomes clear that FitzRalph is no closer to answering his own practical questions, because the two levels upon which he understood lordship — original and civil — prevented rather than proposed a solution of the actual problems of wealth and poverty. Again in Book IV, dealing with specific problems of property and civil dominion, possession and the various types of 'ius utendi' which might exist without necessarily involving lordship or ownership, the same difficulty emerges. Central to this discussion was the bull of Nicholas III, *Exiit qui seminat*, and the interpretation it contained of the controversial terms: 'dominium, proprietas, ius utendi', and FitzRalph criticized that pope for not having appreciated the distinction between 'dominium', which is common to all just persons and cannot therefore be abdicated, and 'proprietas' whereby property is limited to a single person. In the light of this distinction, he argued, the papal ruling that the followers of St. Francis should conform to the terms of the original rule by abdicating the 'dominium vel proprietatem' of their goods, and retaining only a simple right of use, was labouring under a false impression.[57] At this stage the argument seems to have changed direction, and it is difficult to avoid the impression that here at the beginning of Book IV, with the restatement of Nicholas III's problematic ruling and the introduction of a further refinement of FitzRalph's theory of dominion, there may have been a break in composition. Now there emerges a further qualification of civil lordship, that of divine sanction:

[55] Ibid., pp. 371–3. [56] Ibid., pp. 394–9. [57] Ibid., pp. 436–7.

ideally civil lordship is that original lordship which is justified by grace, practically it is that which has the sanction of positive law.

Much of the argument in Book IV is devoted to proving that a man in the state of mortal sin lost his lordship over temporal goods, but unlike the canonists who applied this argument to heretics and their property he never suggested that either the Church or the secular arm should deprive such sinners of their actual civil proprietorship of such goods. An extension of this thesis, which Wyclif pursued and formulated clearly, but which FitzRalph was careful to avoid, was a denial of the power of the sinful priest to carry out validly the functions of his office, and especially to administer the sacraments. However, FitzRalph's most vocal opponent among his younger Oxford contemporaries, the Augustinian friar Geoffrey Hardeby – incidentally the only opponent of FitzRalph who took issue specifically with *De Pauperie Salvatoris* and not with the anti-mendicant sermons and tracts – virtually put words into FitzRalph's mouth.[58] He rejected FitzRalph on this point with the argument that lordship was not dependent on the state of grace, as the priest in mortal sin could validly administer the sacraments; even if degraded by his bishop he still had the power of transubstantiation, and even when excommunicate he nevertheless maintained his sacerdotal powers.[59] Here the Augustinian is closer to Wyclif's view as interpreted by Wilks: 'however much the prelate himself was damned, the divine power still flowed through his office . . . with the officer, so to speak, a sleeping partner in the business.'[60] Nevertheless, in view of the peculiar genesis of Hardeby's *Liber de vita evangelica* as a compendium of Oxford disputations,[61] one is led to speculate whether this, unquestionably heretical, extension of FitzRalph's doctrine to include ecclesiastical office did not arise in the discussions at Oxford motivated by the circulation there of *De Pauperie Salvatoris* in 1356–7.

Book V was largely devoted to a theoretical discussion of the

[58] *Liber de vita evangelica*, Ch. vi, Bodl. MS Digby 113, fol. 20^{v}–21^{r}. Wilks argued that the traditional interpretation of Wyclif's statements on this point (in *De potestate papae*, ed. Loserth (WS, London, 1907), pp. 34–5, 131, 203–5) did little justice to Wyclif's 'intellectual shrewdness and perspicacity', 'Wyclif's Theory of Dominion', 223–4.

[59] MS Digby 133, fols. 20^{v}–21^{r}.

[60] Wilks, art. cit., 226.

[61] For the arguments in favour of this interpretation see Walsh, 'Hardeby', *AA* 33, 184–93.

lordship enjoyed by Adam in the state of innocence, the extent to which he held possession, and the lordship enjoyed by angels, in an attempt to reinforce FitzRalph's own view of common original dominion before the fall.[62] At the root of this argument was the contention that before the fall all temporal possessions had been common to all men, and that private property was introduced to the world only as a result of sin. Consequently the just, being in the state of grace, shared equal dominion over all things. But this argument ignored the possibility of various distinctions between proprietorship and temporal lordship in practice, and also the fact that no just man could have the complete use of his original dominion in a manner useful to him. Such dominion would be constantly impeded in its exercise by the proprietorship and lordship of temporal things and the use of property by others, all of which had the divine approval according to the Aristotelian–Thomist school, and against such property and lordship there could be no natural right. In sermons, especially those preached in Ireland in the early 1350s, FitzRalph showed his awareness of the limitations imposed on original lordship by legally sanctioned private property, but he was clearly arguing for a double legality – that sanctioned by God and that recognized by man, in a manner similar to that suggested by Wyclif.

In Book VI FitzRalph moved to immediate practical issues, including scriptural justification for the mendicant poverty practised by the Franciscans in analogy, as they claimed, to the life of Christ and the apostles. Here the evangelical counsels to poverty and renunciation were examined, together with the question of Christ's kingship of the Jews and his civil dominion under human law, the dominion enjoyed by the apostles, their renunciation of property, the degree of poverty they practised, and above all their mendicancy. Opening with a discussion of the various grades of poverty, FitzRalph argued for a flexible definition of that poverty to which one might bind oneself by a vow and followed the directive of Nicholas III that no profession of poverty should be so extreme as to exclude the necessary means of life.[63] Hence the degree of poverty to be observed by a vow must vary, not only with the conscience of the person

[62] Esp. Bk. V, Ch. 13, on the nature of Adam's dominion, CVP 1430, fols. 70va–71ra.

[63] Bk. VI, Ch. 3, CVP 1430, fols. 78vb–79vb. The directive of Nicholas III is *Exiit qui seminat*, Sext. V. 12. 3, Friedberg, ii. 1109–21.

involved, but also with the circumstances of place and time, with his status and office, and with other human imponderabilia – an argument which could be used to justify the wealth and status of prelates like himself who were precluded by their obligations from living a life of extreme poverty.[64] At this stage FitzRalph's attitude was still ambivalent: he was not yet prepared to deny that such a life of mendicancy, based on a voluntary vow of perpetual poverty, could be meritorious in spiritual terms, but he was not convinced that the justification for such a life lay in the fact that Christ and the apostles had observed extreme poverty in that sense.[65]

His main argument here is from Scripture, using the New Testament to demonstrate that this could not have been the apostolic way of life, as Christ and the apostles had material objects beyond bare necessity, preserving them for future use. As a result those who observe such a degree of poverty by renouncing all things were not truly imitating the apostolic model which neither taught nor practised such poverty.[66] In this category FitzRalph included all the friars implicitly, though his remarks were directed specifically against the Franciscans, and indeed by the mid-fourteenth century only the extreme Franciscan Spirituals actually observed such a degree of poverty. But here FitzRalph also displayed a greater sensitivity to the spirit of the Gospel, rather than slavish adherence to the literal meaning, when he pointed out that the numerous exhortations of Christ to renounce earthly goods for the sake of greater perfection were intended, not as a command to renounce all lordship and right of possession of such things, but an exhortation to renounce them as a means to a higher end, i.e. a means of avoiding that excessive care and solicitude for worldly goods which drew men away from the Christian example. Hence he regarded the gospel precepts not as an absolute condemnation of property – as a prelate and staunch upholder of the hierarchical establishment he could scarcely do otherwise – but as a guideline for those who chose to adopt

[64] Bk. VI, Ch. 19, CVP 1430, fol. 87^{rb-va}. This was essentially an extension of the earlier argument that one might renounce the desire for temporal possessions without abdicating dominion, Bk. VI, Ch. 5, CVP 1430, fol. 79rb.

[65] He argued that Christ and the apostles were able to provide for the future, Bk. VI, Ch. 4, CVP 1430, fol. 79va.

[66] But on the other hand he was prepared to concede the possibility that certain followers of Christ might adopt such a way of life by a vow, Bk. VI, Ch. 8, CVP 1430, fol. 81va.

this path to salvation unencumbered by wordly cares. He was prepared to concede the merit of those who wished to live a monastic form of life and take a vow of strict poverty, but the argument raised by Iohannes that Nicholas III had described Franciscan poverty as 'evangelica atque perfecta',[67] led FitzRalph into an elaborate discussion of the circumstances in which such a vow of extreme poverty was permissible. Here he showed a genuine concern that the poverty ideal could and frequently did lead to contempt of the ecclesiastical hierarchy, who were obliged to make provision for the future and could not afford the irresponsible luxury of living from day to day. Consequently he was prepared to accept the validity of such vows only when accompanied by adequate safeguards for the ecclesiastical authority, and in particular for that of the bishops.[68]

Having disposed of that argument – though without directly answering Iohannes' query – the archbishop moved on to a discussion of the 'principium formale' of absolute poverty, dividing such poverty into five degrees. The strictest of these, he argued, consisted in the abdication of all secondary rights of use, of all civil lordship, and involved the retention of that original lordship which was common to all in the state of grace. Under such circumstances possessions were held only by the common natural right of use, a form of possession which, he argued, corresponded roughly with the teaching and practice of the apostles.[69] But his analogy between the manner in which Christ and the apostles might make use of a dwelling place without actually owning it either severally or in common, and members of a monastic community, was a false one. It failed to take account of the fact that the exponents of the monastic life, whom he was prepared to support, had titles to their properties under civil law, while the apostles, according to his own arguments, had no civil right of use.[70] The next stage of his argument was equally unrealistic. Here he claimed that the common temporal goods of all men were only divided after Adam's fall, when each individual claimed his own private property. A restoration of the original situation was achieved,

[67] Bk. VI, Ch. 9, CVP 1430, fol. 81vb.

[68] Bk. VI, Ch. 10, CVP 1430, fol. 82ra.

[69] Bk. VI, ch. 17–18, CVP 1430, fols. 85va–86va.

[70] The apostles resembled Adam's state before the fall '. . . in statu sue innocentis originis . . .', Bk. VI, Ch. 18, CVP 1430, fol. 86va.

when Christ abolished all such distinctions of property and re-created with his apostles the community of all things.[71] This argument had equally little validity in the practical circumstances of the society with which FitzRalph was familiar. It was enforceable neither under civil nor canon law, as even the latter had made elaborate provision for ownership of ecclesiastical property in a manner which did not permit the common ownership of all the just.

Papal willingness to condone, and even actively encourage, the mendicant position with regard to the ownership, possession, and use of property was an embarrassing problem for FitzRalph. Despite their personal links, respectively to the Cistercians and to the Benedictines, neither Benedict XII nor Clement VI – the popes to whom FitzRalph was personally most indebted – showed any inclination to hostile measures against the practice of mendicant poverty. FitzRalph had therefore to exercise caution in his discussion of the justification for papal exercise of civil lordship over the goods of the Franciscans. The papal action itself he defended on the grounds that it was motivated not by personal greed nor even by the desire for profit for the Church, but simply by paternal affection for the order concerned.[72] By analogy he considered the position of prelates in the Church, who had possessions without being personally wealthy, as they held these goods in their capacity as ministers of the Church for the benefit of the poor. Consequently these goods were intended only as a means of fulfilling their obligations in charity.[73] Again his remarks reflected a theoretical situation, the position as it ought to be, not as it actually was. When one recalls his own sermons preached at Avignon before he joined the ranks of the bishops, one must seriously doubt his conviction that the office-, benefice-, and pension-hunters who haunted the halls of the papal palace would regard the wealth and possessions which they hoped to acquire in this light.

Despite the volume of FitzRalph's anti-mendicant writings, only rarely did he consider the separateness of the Franciscan

[71] For this reason Ricardus rejected Iohannes' claim that Christ had civil dominion because he was the natural heir to the kingdom of the Jews, Bk. VI, Ch. 18, fol. 86^{va-b}.
[72] Bk. VI, Ch. 31, CVP 1430, fol. 93va.

[73] Ibid., for an elaborate defence of clerical property, which did not involve additional civil lordship, because such property required only original dominion in order to be used lawfully.

case from that of the other mendicant orders, and in doing so confine his condemnation exclusively to the followers of St. Francis. One such occasion occurred in Book VII of the dialogue, in which he sought to determine the nature and quality of that Franciscan poverty which they claimed was an imitation of the apostolic example.[74] On the basis of FitzRalph's definition of apostolic poverty, the Franciscans must therefore claim to practise a form of poverty which involved holding temporal possessions under original lordship, and sharing their use with all the just. On this assumption the Franciscans took pride in observing a stricter form of poverty than that of the other mendicant orders – unjustly according to FitzRalph. He maintained that their claim was false and fictitious, and stood in stark contrast with their actions. They violated this vow of extreme poverty in countless ways, most blatantly by transferring the civil lordship of their property to the pope, thereby gaining for their possessions greater security, instead of making them available for the common use of the just. They had therefore acted contrary to their profession, had sinned by procuring such a reservation in violation of their profession, and continued to sin by passively tolerating the continuance of such a situation.[75] Once more FitzRalph was in difficulty over the extent of papal responsibility, guilt, and therefore sinfulness in the matter. At least to the extent that successive popes permitted the friars to accept a ruling and live according to a law which restricted the community of the natural law in others, thereby giving the friars occasion to commit sin, are the popes declared to have been guilty.[76]

Having thus argued the case that the friars violated their profession, FitzRalph moved on to what appears to have become, at least in the later stages of composition of the dialogue, his central principal purpose. He had already given advance warning of this in the *Proposicio* of 1350, but here the sinfulness of all mendicant privileges was to be clearly articulated. At this point the carefully drawn distinction between the

[74] Bk. VII, Ch. 10, CVP 1430, fols. 111rb–112va. Iohannes raised the problem that, whereas the Dominicans profess complete poverty, they have possessions in common in a manner which conflicts with the ruling of Nicholas III for the Franciscans. In reply Ricardus cited the various rulings of Gregory IX, Innocent IV, and Alexander IV to show that the papal interpretation of Dominican poverty was that they should have 'pauca propria', fol. 111^{rb-va}.

[75] Bk. VII, Ch. 5, fols. 104vb–106va.

[76] Esp. Nicholas III, '. . . non potest . . . a peccato totaliter excusari', fol. 106ra.

Franciscans on the one hand and the remaining mendicant orders on the other became a superfluous encumbrance, and a case built upon the evidence of the Franciscan order is made to serve all four orders equally with regard to their unsuitability for the pastoral scene. Here he emphasized, even more firmly than in 1350, the juridical problem caused by the friars' exempt status: they neither possessed juridical competence themselves, nor were they subject to that of their bishop. He also returned to the issue that the privilege of hearing confessions was a violation of the friars' professed obligation of humility, primarily because they had managed to become confessors to the higher levels of society, with corresponding access to honours, powers, and riches.[77] The archbishop's attitude was understandable in that it reflected the true situation, whereby the ruling classes of western Christendom did to a remarkable extent choose their confessors and closest spiritual advisers from the ranks of the mendicant orders. The reasons for this are another matter, and FitzRalph maintained that easier absolution, flattery in return for favours, and material rewards, were the reasons for the friars' popularity in the confessional. But where his argument fell down was in its failure to consider the extent to which the friars had also made themselves the poor man's friend. By the mid-fourteenth century, and especially in urban areas, an adequately functioning, humane, and charitable, yet theologically informed pastoral care would have been impossible without the friars' co-operation. Unfortunately we know all too little about the pastoral situation in Anglo-Irish towns such as Drogheda and Dundalk, but the substantial presence of the friars especially in the former, and the heavy losses which they suffered during the Black Death, suggest pastoral participation on their part. Regardless, however, of whether FitzRalph had personal experience of the positive aspects of mendicant participation in pastoral activity, or whether he chose to ignore it as not relevant to his present purpose, these were unquestionably borne out by the harmonious relations which existed between mendicant communities and municipal authorities throughout Europe in this period.

[77] Bk. VII, Ch. 6, fols. 106va–108ra. This chapter, and Chs. 7, 16, and 18, were omitted from the original text in this MS. Whereas most of Bk. VII was written in a different hand from the preceding 6 books, these additions were made, both in the table of contents and in the text itself, by the first hand. These corrections are consistent with the suggestion that this was a working copy dating from *c.*1356–7.

Once more FitzRalph returned to the contested issue of burial of the laity in mendicant churches, claiming that this practice defrauded prelates and secular clergy of their rights and therefore violated the great commandment of charity towards one's neighbour, by stealing not merely his temporal but also his spiritual goods.[78] But this was clearly a marginal issue in his eyes, and the crucial question from which all other ills associated with the friars' pastoral activity were seen to derive, was that of the confessional. The latter, he correctly assumed, was the key to the friars' enormous influence over the mass of the laity, to a greater degree than was possible through their preaching activities, and the influence gained in the confessional was in turn responsible for the decision of so many laymen and women either to seek mendicant burial or to make substantial donations or legacies to the churches of the friars, and in many cases to do both. Consequently the first indications of FitzRalph's criticism of the friars in his sermons preceding the *Proposicio* of 1350, and in this *Proposicio* itself, stemmed from his concern over confessional practice; and through the legal proceedings in Avignon from 1357 to 1360 it became even clearer that this was the central and crucial issue, while all other questions of mendicant poverty, preaching, and public activities were relegated to the role of supporting arguments.

FitzRalph therefore condemned the friars both for engaging in pastoral activity and for having sought permission to do so. They did not accept these pastoral functions because they were freely offered by successive popes, but they had been wrung from the latter in response to the petitions of the friars and of their influential protectors. This was a contradiction of their profession, and the friars were therefore a divisive canker and a source of danger to the hierarchical structure of the Church. In the archbishop's condemnation of the diversity of religious orders one can almost foresee Wyclif nodding approvingly in the wings.[79] FitzRalph's recommendation to Innocent VI amounted almost, but not quite, to a similar condemnation of 'private religions', as he exhorted the pope to take drastic action

[78] Bk. VII, Ch. 6, 'Nunquid vere quis diligit proximum suum, a quo non solum bona temporalia, set eciam spiritualia, sine eius culpa gestit aufferre? Non video fieri ita posse', fol. 107ra.

[79] It anticipates his denunciation of 'private religions', first expressed in *De apostasia* (1381) and becoming more violent in the later years of his life.

and abolish all privileges of exemption for religious orders, mendicant and others. By doing so he would put an end to the individual peculiarities in the practice of poverty and mendicancy and incorporate all religious into the hierarchy once more as one flock under one shepherd, all living harmoniously under that evangelical form of poverty which accorded with the natural law, as FitzRalph understood and expounded it.[80]

The implications of these sentiments were more radical than any other criticism of the friars by FitzRalph or any other prelate previously. On the one hand he expressed a recognition that the friars' rule and profession of poverty as the apostolic way of life represented an implicit challenge to the outward forms of papal monarchy and the institutional Church, and of the hierarchy whose members claimed that their lives were modelled on the same apostles. But on the other hand the archbishop, perhaps unwittingly, twisted the original curial doctrine in such a manner as to provide ammunition for later critics. These would carry the inferences logically deducible from his teaching much farther than his immediate purposes had required, into areas which he had not foreseen. Above all, they would extend his strictures not merely to the friars and other religious orders, but to the hierarchical order which FitzRalph had explicitly striven to protect.[81]

When one sifts through the mass of contradictions expressed in the various parts of *De Pauperie Salvatoris*, it is possible to identify in FitzRalph's argument that his theory of dominion by grace disqualified the friars from the position they enjoyed, two basic aspects. The first arose from his belief that those who abused a possession or privilege deserved to be deprived of them. The friars sinned grievously in a number of ways: they violated their self-professed vow of extreme poverty in countless ways, the most blatant being the fiction whereby the civil lordship of their property could be transferred to the pope, while they enjoyed its use and did so in a security which could not be enjoyed by the involuntary poor. Although this was no longer the canonical position, having been abolished by John XXII, FitzRalph still regarded it as an indication of the friars' inherent sinfulness. Furthermore, the friars' pastoral privileges

[80] Bk. VII, Ch. 6, CVP 1430, fol. 108ra. This plea is specifically directed at the pope 'sanctitatis domini nostri presentis', who is the dedicatee of the diaglogue.

[81] Especially Wyclif in *De ecclesia*. On his doctrine of the Church see Leff, *Heresy in the Later Middle Ages*, ii. 516–45.

were a violation of their vow of humility. They usurped a position in pastoral care to which they had no entitlement, claiming its material rewards and therefore effectively 'stealing' from the secular clergy. Hence when measured against the standards of their own professed vows and mendicant rule, they stood convicted of grievous sinfulness and were thereby deprived of their dominion and pastoral privileges. The second aspect, which concerned the absolute validity of their vows and mendicant rule, was more problematic, and FitzRalph's treatment correspondingly more tentative. It involved a rejection of the grounds upon which the friars based their claims to dominion, i.e. the alleged similarity between their way of life and that of Christ and the apostles. It led FitzRalph to deny that the friars might have the use of goods over which they did not have civil dominion, as such a situation had no foundation in the Gospels, and it also led him to deny the merit of a vow of poverty which involved mendicancy. He was careful to exclude from his strictures the vow of personal poverty taken by a monk whose community held corporate property, and clearly did not foresee his doctrine as an instrument of disendowment of the 'possessionati'.

In effect the message of *De Pauperie Salvatoris* was that FitzRalph's earlier solutions to the mendicant problem were incapable of success because they did not go far enough. He had previously suggested the abolition of mendicant privileges for practical reasons, because they interfered with the duties of bishops and parochial clergy, because they did harm both to the friars themselves and to their flocks, and because they were a source of scandal. Such an abolition would have radically altered the structure and function of the mendicant orders, but it would have permitted them to survive. But in this dialogue FitzRalph provided a battery of arguments – theological, philosophical, and ecclesiological – for the dissolution of the mendicant orders entirely, the basis of his case being that his thorough examination of the concepts of dominion and possession, and the right of use in relation to the divine gifts of creation and grace, had demonstrated the errors of the friars' ways and consequently the worthlessness of their profession.

However, in spite of his exhaustive discussion of terms in the first five books of the dialogue, the whole question of lordship, ownership, property, and grace was constantly bedevilled by ambiguities and conflicting usage of terms. At the outset

FitzRalph had pointed out that a major problem in the interpretation of the decretals was caused by Nicholas III, having considered 'dominium' and 'proprietas' as synonomous terms, and there had undoubtedly been a considerable refinement of terminology in the course of the two generations between *Exiit qui seminat* (1279) and John XXII's series of pronouncements on the subject of Franciscan poverty – a refinement which was due in no small measure to the work of the Augustinian publicists on behalf of papal dominion. But the major problem was rooted in the theoretical, idealistic basis of FitzRalph's argument. Like Aegidius Romanus he never attempted a practical application of the theory in this life, where the common dominion of the just would necessarily be restricted in its use by the civil power. Consequently when an opponent of FitzRalph's theory, such as the Oxford Augustinian, Geoffrey Hardeby, tried to counter his arguments by reducing them to practical terms, he occasionally misinterpreted and distorted the archbishop's frame of reference. John XXII has also recognized that the distinction between lordship over and 'ius utendi' of consumable goods, though large in the mind of FitzRalph and of the Franciscan rigorists,[82] had little relevance in practice.

But on the basis of examination FitzRalph could argue that grace alone entitled a person to the exercise of lordship over temporal things and conferred upon all the just an equal right to their use. Hence the only kind of poverty worthy of the designation 'evangelical poverty' was that which consisted in the abdication of civil lordship, relying only on the original lordship appropriate to man in his natural state of creation and grace. The friars could not claim to practise such poverty, as once they agreed to the papal reservation of the lordship over their temporal goods and therefore the restriction of the original dominion of all others, they deviated from this evangelical ideal. Furthermore, their other privileges, which gave them an extraordinary status within the Church and disturbed the foreordained relations of the heavenly and ecclesiastical hierarchies, were illegal, hence their religious life lost its value and all members were in a state of sin. This state of sin had further obvious consequences, according to FitzRalph's scheme of things: since dominion and all other acts of jurisdiction were dependent on grace, the friars – like Adam and Eve – lost their

[82] Walsh, 'Hardeby', *AA* 34, 8, 14.

original lordship and with it their spiritual jurisdiction in the pastoral sphere, thereby rendering null and void their work in the confessional and pulpit: their absolution was meaningless and their preaching illegal.

One logical consequence of such teaching was summed up by the Marxist historian of the Hussite movement, R. R. Betts, in the implication that the title to exercise office and authority, as well as the enjoyment of property, was to be a subjective one, namely being in a state of grace. It implied that no man, be he prelate, king, judge, or merchant, might have any right to exercise functions implicit in his office or profession by virtue of election, appointment, or consecration, or by virtue of inheritance, purchase, licence, or charter. 'It was a doctrine which was able to unmake popes, to trample episcopacy underfoot, to mutilate monasticism.'[83] Rights of sons to the inheritance of their fathers, of labourers to their daily wage, could all be subjected to the same criteria. A further conclusion, which FitzRalph was careful to avoid, but which was deduced from his dialogue by a mendicant opponent and subsequently propounded by Wyclif and the Lollards, concerned the effectiveness of the sacraments when administered by a sinful priest. Such a doctrine undermined belief in the efficacy of the sacraments: 'no man could be sure that he was not in original sin for want of effective baptism, no woman could be sure that she was lawfully married; there would be no assurance of legitimacy, none that the sacrament of the altar was effectively performed; orders would be in doubt – absolution a conjecture, and supreme unction a gamble.'[84] Pope, cardinals, and hierarchy might be among the 'foreknown'; where then did that leave the hierarchical structure of the visible Church?

However, it took Wyclif, Hus, and Jerome of Prague, as well as the commission appointed by the council fathers at Constance who examined their views, to reach such a precise formulation of the dangerous implications contained in FitzRalph's doctrines. A storm of protext and criticism greeted the original circulation of the text in 1356, at Oxford, where it soon became the subject of academic controversy (and where Wyclif as regent master in the arts faculty may have encountered it at an early date), in London, where FitzRalph summarized its most important conclusions in a series of public sermons,

[83] Betts, 'FitzRalph and Dominion', 160–1.

[84] Ibid., 164–5.

and at Avignon, where he had sent it for papal approval and where the procurators-general of the four mendicant orders soon took action against it. But all this criticism concerned the immediate and obvious issue, and did not consider the possibility that the preacher of social justice in the border areas of the Anglo-Irish Pale might become the prophet of egalitarianism, challenging thereby the institutions of Church and State. These critics were concerned with the implications of the doctrine for the mendicant way of life, not merely with the friars' practice of poverty, but with the entire range of academic and pastoral privileges upon which they had built their position of authority and influence. The extent to which FitzRalph's mendicant critics limited their attention to these practical issues, rather than considering possible long-term ecclesiological implications which might be drawn from FitzRalph's teaching, is illustrated by one striking and apparently paradoxical factor: the general lack of interest on the part of these critics in *De Pauperie Salvatoris* as compared with the attention they devoted to the refutation of the anti-mendicant sermons, initially in London during the winter and spring of 1356–7, and then at Avignon, where a series of *Proposiciones*, *Libelli*, and counter-accusations reflected the cut-and-thrust of the debate during the legal proceedings of 1357–60.

iii. FitzRalph v. the Friars at the papal court

When FitzRalph left Ireland in the early summer of 1356, he apparently intended nothing more than a routine visit to London and the king's court, such as that for which he had received permission three years earlier (though there is no independent evidence that he actually travelled on that occasion). If the account he laid before Innocent VI and the assembled cardinals on 8 November 1357 is to be believed, he only became involved in this phase of the mendicant controversies by accident: he recalled how he had come to London on business concerning the Church of Armagh, and in the English capital found a dispute raging between mendicant doctors of theology and secular clergy concerning the degree of poverty practised by Christ and the apostles. His opinion on the matter was sought, and he was invited to preach a series of sermons from the most influential pulpit in London, St. Paul's Cross.[1] In

[1] *Defensio Curatorum*, ed. Goldast, ii. 1392.

view of the subsequent involvement of the dean of St. Paul's, Richard Kilwington, in the proceedings at Avignon, and of his long-standing acquaintance with FitzRalph since they had disputed and lectured together at Oxford, such an invitation does not seem improbable. Furthermore, other factors indicate that friction between regular and secular clergy over the involvement – and popularity – of the friars in pastoral activity had become acute. Successive popes were repeatedly obliged to respond to hostile situations throughout Europe by re-issuing *Super Cathedram*, ordering bishops and secular clergy to observe its provisions.[2] Benedict XII re-issued it in 1335 and 1337, Clement VI in 1343, 1344, 1347, 1349–51, while Innocent VI, Urban V, and Gregory XI issued it at least once during each year of their pontificates, thereby showing a strong concentration in the years after 1349. All of these numerous re-issues were at the request of bishops, capitular, and secular clergy, scattered all over Europe and all apparently prepared to accept the solution offered by *Super Cathedram*. The bull appears to have become the standard recipe, and when FitzRalph's case provided no new solution each pope simply confirmed it each year wherever requested and regardless of whether it worked or not. However, at the same time English episcopal registers of the early 1350s show that even bishops who had previously been prepared to grant extensive concessions to the friars working in their dioceses were becoming more cautious in their attitude to all friars, and positively hostile towards the Franciscans.[3] Both sides in the dispute felt that they had legitimate grievances. The friars saw the secular clergy as jealous of mendicant educational qualifications and pastoral success, and of the concomitant financial rewards. The secular clergy, in their turn, had a case which was well stated in a bill of complaints drawn up by the clergy of the province of Canterbury and submitted to a provincial council held in London on 16 May 1356.[4] The bill repeated the frequent claim that the friars abused their privilege of mendicancy and failed to observe their profession of poverty. They rode about the country on fine horses and

[2] Hammerich, *FitzRalph and the Mendicants*, p. 11. For the re-issues in the mid-14th century see *BF* vi. *passim*.

[3] *Grandisson's Register*, ii. 1128, 1143, 1144–7, 1186–7, 1208; *Trillek's Register*, ii. 20, 61, 232.

[4] PRO, D.L. 42/8, fols. 79^{v}–80^{r}, discovered by the late William A. Pantin. For a similar series of complaints by the London clergy in the time of Archbishop Pecham (1287) see Wilkins, *Concilia*, ii. 168.

lived in ornate and luxurious quarters, more fitted to major prelates of the realm. They ignored the laws and customs of the province of Canterbury, slandered the clergy, and flattered the nobility. Under the guise of religion they meddled in the private and public affairs of the rich and powerful, in order to increase their own wealth and influence, thereby damaging the fabric of the English Church. The document continued with the complaint that much of this influence was obtained through the friars' laxity in the confessional: they absolved their penitents too easily and dispensed from the obligation of restitution. More than forty years ago, when this document came to light, Gwynn pointed out the similarity between these *gravamina* and the almost contemporary satire directed against the friars by the author of *Piers Plowman*,[5] and much recent research has underlined the persistence of this type of criticism in political and Lollard poetry.[6] More significantly in this context, the complaints bear a striking resemblance to the abuses which FitzRalph had been attributing to the mendicant confessors in his diocese over the previous five years.

Hence, as Gwynn noted, 'FitzRalph was thus coming to a city where criticism of the friars was rife',[7] but the evidence already reviewed suggests that this criticism was mainly concerned with practical objections to the friars, and in particular with their active and influential role in the pastoral area. Yet FitzRalph's remarks to Innocent VI conveyed a slightly different impression, namely that the theoretical dispute about the poverty of Christ and consequent validity of the mendicant ideal was uppermost in the London controversies of 1356. If this were indeed the case and, as FitzRalph announced in public a few months later, he had recently 'published' the completed dialogue *De Pauperie Salvatoris* in Oxford and Avignon – a publication which would scarcely have passed unnoticed in London where active theological teaching was largely in mendicant hands – the invitation to participate in the dispute becomes even more comprehensible. It also raises a further question. Bradwardine's views on predestination had become common currency in interested circles long before their formal publication *c.*1344. Even though FitzRalph had spent most of

[5] *Studies*, 26 (1937), pp. 51–2.

[6] See Erikson, 'The fourteenth-century Franciscans and their Critics', for a discussion of recent literature on the subject.

[7] *Studies*, pp. 26, 52.

the previous five years in Ireland, and not in the Oxford-London area, it is possible that knowledge of the commission set up by Clement VI and of FitzRalph's recently developed views on dominion and poverty was beginning to circulate before the formal publication of the dialogue, and may have been partly responsible for a renewed interest in the poverty question in London during the mid-1350s.

The first indications that poverty was under discussion came from FitzRalph himself. He travelled from Ireland to London via Coventry, where he preached in the parish church on Pentecost Sunday, 12 June. The notes in his diary for this sermon are brief, alluding to the fact that he had drawn on an earlier Pentecostal sermon, and also that he used material subsequently incorporated into the sermon preached a fortnight later.[8] Clearly FitzRalph did not enter the Coventry sermon in his diary until after he had reached his destination in London. At Coventry he discussed a number of problems relating to confessional practice, including doubts over the distinction between venial and mortal sin, and with conflicts of jurisdiction arising from abuses of confessional procedure. He developed a conservative line of argument, stressing the authority of Church councils and of bishops, and also the greater value of confession made to one's own parish priest or his vicar or curate.[9] Therefore it seems that, regardless of any poverty dispute which he might find in progress upon arrival in London, he had already launched his own campaign against mendicant confession before reaching the capital. His first recorded sermon in London was preached to a community of nuns in the East End, 'in ecclesia monalium Londoniensis ad partem orientalem', possibly the Augustinian canonesses of Clerkenwell or Shoreditch.[10] In this sermon for the feast of Corpus Christi (23 June) the preacher confined himself to an exposition of the doctrine of the Eucharist. Presumably anti-mendicant polemic was not considered an appropriate topic for nuns' ears.

Three days later he preached at St. Paul's Cross, a formal sermon on the love of God and of one's neighbour. Here he displayed a range of learning unusual in his popular vernacular sermons and it was probably tailored for his first major public appearance in the city. The burning questions of mendicant

[8] B, fols. 81^{r}, 82^{r}–86^{r}; J, fols. 66vb–67ra, 67va–70rb.
[9] B, fol. 81^{r}; J, fol. 67ra.
[10] *Medieval Religious Houses. England and Wales*, p. 229.

poverty and confession were raised only indirectly, as a violation of the command to love one's neighbour by depriving the secular clergy of their divinely appointed role, and with more than a hint that the friars' activities had no justification in Scripture.[11] But the approach was restrained and, although the notes in the diary for this sermon are detailed, they contain no reference to an incident which he subsequently recalled. On 18 December 1356, preaching in the *aula* of the bishop of London, he recalled that in the course of a sermon preached at St. Paul's Cross the previous summer he had denied the scriptural justification for Christ's mendicancy, and in the heat of the moment went so far as to wager his Bible that no friar could find a text anywhere in the Bible which would prove the mendicants' claim in this respect.[12] It would appear that the archbishop had a habit of making wagers! According to his account a friar preached at St. Paul's Cross in reply. His identity is unknown, but it may have been the Franciscan theologian, Roger Conway, then in residence at the London Greyfriars.[13] He took up the challenge but, FitzRalph maintained, avoided the issue by appealing not to the text of Scripture itself, but to the gloss – and Conway frequently resorted to the authority of the glossators in his own identifiable contributions to the controversy.[14] The sermon of 26 June was, according to FitzRalph's diary, the only one preached at St. Paul's Cross that summer, but another statement which he made in Avignon the following year leaves open the possibility that he preached more antimendicant sermons during this period in London, which did

[11] B, fol. 85^{v}; J, fols. 69vb–70ra.

[12] B, fol. 94^{v}; J, fol. 75rb.

[13] For Conway see *BRUO* I, 459, also the papal bull of 10 February 1355 permitting him to become a member of the London Franciscan convent, 'at which the nobles of the realm are wont to meet', *Reg. Vat.* 229, fol. 192^{r}, *CPL* 1342–62, 563. In this bull he was described as guardian of the Worcester convent, a description which led Glanmor Williams, *The Welsh Church from Conquest to Reformation* (Cardiff, 1976^{2}), p. 83, to suggest that he was Welsh-born (in the garrison borough of Conway) though not necessarily of Welsh parentage. There is no adequate printed study of Conway, but see the unpublished thesis by Paulinus Lavery (*Antonianum*, Rome, 1930).

[14] His *Defensio Mendicantium* was printed in Goldast, ed. cit., ii. 1410–44, following FitzRalph's *Defensio Curatorum*. Goldast was clearly under the impression that Conway's *Defensio* was a reply to that of FitzRalph, but see Lavery, pp. 51–2; Walsh, 'Hardeby', *AA*, 34, 64–71. Conway developed a more moderate, less extreme 'Franciscan' attitude towards poverty when he replied to FitzRalph at Avignon, and thus anticipated his Oxford confrère, William Woodford. Conway's contribution to the poverty, as opposed to the pastoral controversy, is contained in Bodl. MS Rawl. G. 40, fols. 42^{r}–48^{r}.

not find their way into the diary. The one containing the original wager of his Bible may have been one of these.[15]

In any case evidence for the events of the summer of 1356 is sparse, and it is not clear whether the disputing parties in London had become aware of the contents of *De Pauperie Salvatoris*. Certainly the surviving notes for his London sermons during the summer months indicate that he, at least, did not make the contents public in any formal sense, nor did he base the summer sermons on the doctrine of dominion as worked out in his dialogue. Was he awaiting reactions from a preliminary private circulation in Oxford, or was he still preparing it for publication? It is equally uncertain whether there had been any poverty controversy in progress before his arrival, or whether he was its instigator. Hence these opening skirmishes may have preceded the formal publication of his work in England. He could already have forwarded it to Avignon, but the evidence of the diary suggests that he spent much of the autumn in the Oxford area, made known there the text of the dialogue, and possibly engaged in disputations on its contents. His presence in the area is confirmed by three sermons preached at Deddington, a village north of Oxford, on 16 and 18 October and on 1 November 1356.[16] In the first of these he returned to a topic already raised in St. Paul's Cathedral on 17 July, when he had accused mendicant confessors of not imposing an adequate penance in the case of grave sin.[17] He ruled that grave sins be taken to the ordinary of the diocese for absolution and, in case his hearers were still in doubt as to what such sins constituted, he spelt them out – murder, theft, sacrilege, and incest.[18] The first Deddington sermon touched briefly on questions of mendicancy and dominion, while the second continued the subtle build-up of the case against the friars as violators of the first basic commandment to love their

[15] FitzRalph's remark at the beginning of the *Defensio Curatorum* that he had preached 'septem aut octo sermones' on the subject in London implies that in addition to the 6 known anti-mendicant sermons of 1356–7, there may have been others which did not survive in the diary, ed. cit., p. 1392. It is of course possible that FitzRalph did not note the remark concerning the wager in the diary at the time of preaching, but the general tenor of the controversy suggests that this episode occurred later than the summer, possibly in the course of the sermon preached on 1 November 1356 by an unnamed Franciscan on the 4 grades of poverty, 'ut mihi fuerat reportatum', ibid., p. 1402, and that FitzRalph had preached an intermediate sermon between that date and 18 December which does not survive in the diary.

[16] B, fols. 87^{r}–92^{v}; J, fols. 71ra–75ra.

[17] B, fols. 86^{r}–87^{r}; J, fols. 70rb–71ra.

[18] B, fol. 88^{r-v}; J, fols. 71vb–72ra.

neighbours – meaning of course the secular parochial clergy.[19] In the third, on the feast of All Saints, FitzRalph instructed his audience in the correct veneration of the saints, probably a more appropriate topic in a small quiet village than fulminations against the friars. But he coupled his exhortations to venerate the saints with a series of warnings, reminding his audience of the dangers of confusing veneration of a saint's image and memory with idolatry and superstition, and he particularly warned against the kind of abuses which might surround the cult of the Marian shrines of Lincoln, Walsingham, and Newark – a type of pastoral abuse for which the friars could not in this case be blamed.[20] These remarks were subsequently taken from context by Wyclif, who ignored the archbishop's earlier exhortation to venerate those singled out by the Church as worthy of example, and used the warning as an authoritative support for his own rejection of the cult and veneration of the saints.[21]

By the date of preaching of this sermon John Wyclif was a rising young philosopher at Merton, making a name for himself in the arts faculty, where he appears to have taught for an unusually long time, while also engaged in the study of theology.[22] Although he was subsequently to take over the underlying doctrine of dominion and grace formulated by FitzRalph, and to develop that doctrine far beyond its original purpose as a tool of anti-mendicant criticism, spelling out implications which a conservative prelate like FitzRalph would have scarcely conceded, there is no evidence for any initial impression left by the publication of the dialogue on the young bachelor of arts after 1365.[23] Nor is there much evidence for debate and discussion of FitzRalph's theory in the schools in the late 1350s, although the subsequent development of Wyclif's thinking ensured that his acknowledged source also came under scrutiny in the years of the papal condemnations, and one can

[19] B, fols. 88^{v}–91^{r}; J, fols. 72rb–74ra.

[20] B, fol. 92^{r}; J, fol. 74va.

[21] Benrath, *Wyclifs Bibelkommentar*, pp. 34–5, cites Wyclif's version of FitzRalph's remarks. According to Wyclif (MS St. John's 171, fol. 263^{r}), the passage was taken 'de sermone 60 de omnibus sanctibus', although this sermon is not number 60 in any extant MS. Wyclif gives however a very accurate rendering of FitzRalph, according to B, fol. 92^{r} (where the sermon is number 64), with only two minor changes of wording, neither of which alter the sense.

[22] For Wyclif's career in the arts faculty see *BRUO* III, 2103–4.

[23] Robson, *Wyclif and the Oxford Schools*, is silent on the matter.

see in the work of William Woodford something like an official university reaction against a deceased but none the less authoritative teacher.[24] Apart from Wyclif's own philosophical teaching as formulated in his *Summa de Ente*, and of the Durham Benedictine, Uthred of Boldon and his circle – none of whom showed much interest in problems of dominion until the Wycliffite application was spelt out in the 1370s – Oxford thought in these years is a largely unwritten page in the intellectual history of the university, and few names of distinction stand out.[25]

Among the exceptions was the Augustinian regent master, Geoffrey Hardeby, the only mendicant doctor of the day recorded as having taken seriously the challenge presented by this novel attack on the whole concept of mendicant poverty. Whereas many subsequent friar-critics, notably Roger Conway, provided competent refutations of FitzRalph's view on mendicant poverty and pastoral privileges as these were developed in the *Defensio Curatorum* and other contributions to the hearing at Avignon, or even – as in the case of William Woodford almost a generation later – replied to the eighth book of *De Pauperie Salvatoris*, which had been composed in Avignon to combat the friars' counter-charges after 1357, Hardeby was the only one who addressed himself specifically to the problem as expressed in the seven books of the dialogue put into circulation in Oxford before 18 December 1356, which were the subject of Chapters V–XI of his *Liber de vita evangelica.*[26] Whereas Hardeby revised some of his work at a later date in order to publish a compendium of his Oxford disputations, he never rethought his views on poverty in the light of developments in the controversy beyond 1356–7. Similarly his refutation of FitzRalph on the canonical-pastoral problem was based almost exclusively on the *Defensio Curatorum*, the *Proposicio* preached on 8 November 1357, whose manuscript circulation and early printings reveal it to have been the most influential piece of anti-mendicant polemic published during the later middle ages. Hence a large section of the *De vita evangelica* stands as a unique surviving contribution to the controversy from the mendicant side, unique in that it alone was a response

[24] Esp. throughout the *Defensorium mendicitatis,* MS Magdalen 75.

[25] One exception is the unpublished thesis, S.L. Forte, 'A Study of Some Oxford Schoolmen of the middle of the fourteenth century' (MS B.Litt., Oxford 1949).

[26] Bod., MS Digby 113, fols. 14^{v}–48^{r}.

to the application of FitzRalph's theory of dominion to the problem of mendicant poverty, unclouded by subsequent debate over the pastoral issue and by the polemical note introduced in the later stages at Avignon.

Similarly Chapters XIV–XVII of Hardeby's work, devoted to a defence of the friars' role in the pastoral sphere,[27] were based on the *Defensio Curatorum*, whose contents must – in view of the strong presence of English friars at the curia pursuing the case against FitzRalph – have become known in Oxford without delay.[28] The format of both groups of chapters of *De vita evangelica* indicate that they must have originated in a series of *questiones ordinarie* or *questiones disputate*. Hardeby, in accordance with accepted procedures did not name any of his fellow disputants, but external evidence suggests that he must have engaged in a series of disputations with supporters of the archbishop's point of view. The first of these disputations must have taken place after the publication of *De Pauperie Salvatoris*. This section of Hardeby's work shows few indications of subsequent revision, other than the very occasional inclusion of an opinion subsequently encountered, but he was able to cite book and chapter of FitzRalph's dialogue, implying that the disputation took place after the entire text was circulating in Oxford, and that the disputants were not dependent on reported versions of FitzRalph's views. Similarly the disputations upon which Chapters XIV–XVII were based indicate that the participants already knew the *Defensio Curatorum* in its entirety. In the light of Courtenay's discoveries about the course of academic debate among bachelors disputing with each other under the guidance of a regent master, and their readiness to incorporate into their discussions the content of current controversies, such disputations on the content of these two works by FitzRalph might easily have taken place under the regency of a mendicant master.[29]

On the basis of his magisterial sermon, preached in St. Mary the Virgin on 27 November 1356, it would appear that Hardeby incepted as doctor of theology and commenced regency around the same time as FitzRalph's text became known in the university. We may assume a two-year regency, which was common among secular masters and among regulars whose orders did not have a long queue of candidates waiting to incept, and which

[27] Bodl., MS Digby 113, fols. 58^v–96^v.
[28] Below n. 95.
[29] Courtenay, *Adam Wodeham*, pp. 75–112.

would have run from late 1356 until the summer of 1358. If *De Pauperie Salvatoris* had become the subject of debate among the bachelors, secular and mendicant, disputing under his regency, it is also possible that the regent master himself devoted to their arguments a series of *questiones* during the same academic year. Hardeby's arguments suggest that a wider range of implications inherent in this doctrine of dominion than FitzRalph had been prepared to spell out, were raised in the course of the disputations. FitzRalph had been careful to avoid the implication that a state of sin and consequent loss of dominion might have any effect on the valid exercise of priestly or episcopal powers. He never considered the question of whether the sinful priest might validly celebrate the Eucharist or administer the sacraments. But Hardeby's reply did not avoid these issues, and he rejected any suggestion of a diminution of the priestly powers of the sinner, virtually putting words into the archbishop's mouth and certainly raising the possibility that those who debated the *De Pauperie Salvatoris* had considered this aspect of the problem also.[30] Whatever the merits of modern speculation whether FitzRalph actually went 'all the way' in his anticipation of Wyclif's teaching on dominion, the meagre information to be inferred from these *questiones* suggests that some of his contemporaries thought he did.

The next stage of the controversy is well known. FitzRalph had returned from Oxford to London by 18 December, when he preached in the *aula* of Bishop Michael Northburgh of London on the text: 'Dirigite viam domini' (Ioh. i. 23). Like all of the other London sermons it was preached in the vernacular and preserved in the diary in a substantially expanded Latin version.[31] Even so, it cannot have made easy listening for his audience, being primarily devoted to abstract questions of Christ's poverty and his capacity for dominion and ownership, and it summarized the conclusions contained in the early books of *De Pauperie Salvatoris*. There is no evidence for an immediate reaction to the sermon, and after a gap of five weeks it was followed up on 22 January 1357 with a further sermon, this time at St. Paul's Cross. Here, on the text: 'Quodcumque dixerit vobis facite' (Ioh. ii. 5) he moved on to deal with the practical problem which had formed the subject of the later parts of *De Pauperie Salvatoris*, rejecting the concept of

[30] MS Digby 113, fol. 20^{r-v}.

[31] B, fols. 92^{v}–98^{v}; J, fols. 75ra–79ra.

mendicant poverty as without scriptural foundation and in no sense to be equated with the life-style of Christ and the apostles.[32] These two sermons represented the essence of his case against the theory and practice of mendicancy, powerfully argued by a master of the exegetical approach which this problem required.

After a further gap of five weeks the next instalment came, this time directed against the separate problem of the friars' pastoral activity and especially the question of confession, which was to dominate much of the proceedings at Avignon. From the same pulpit on 26 February the exposition of the text: 'Dic ut lapides isti panes fiant' (Matth. iv. 3)[33] was made the vehicle for the most explicit attack yet on those pastoral abuses which FitzRalph had consistently denounced among the Anglo-Irish of County Louth. Beginning with an attack on those who violated their obligation to pay tithes, a practice in which the London merchants were scarcely less talented than their counterparts in Drogheda and Dundalk, he accused these merchants of neglecting to pay tithes to the secular clergy and at the same time seeking absolution from this sin at the hands of the friars. FitzRalph argued that such absolution was invalid and merely the cause of graver sin, and went on to attack the position of the friars as confessors throughout the city. In this sermon he showed for the first time an awareness of the need to combat the accusation that he was repeating the errors of Jean de Pouilly, by insisting that in spite of confession to a duly licensed and authorized friar, the faithful were still bound to confess all their sins to their own parish priest before receiving the Eucharist at Easter, in accordance with the Lateran canon *Omnis utriusque sexus*. This accusation was to be made the basis of heresy charges brought against him and his supporters at Avignon in 1358, and it is not unlikely that the friars had raised it during the London controversy.

In any case they seized upon the canonically unsound elements in FitzRalph's case against the pastoral activity of their members, and on 7 March representatives of the four mendicant orders met in the chapter-house of the London Greyfriars. The choice of the Franciscan headquarters may reflect their specially vulnerable position as the principal target of the

[32] B, fols. 98^{v}–106^{r}; J, fols. 79ra–84ra, essentially summarizing parts of Book VII of the dialogue.

[33] B, fols. 106^{r}–112^{r}; J, fols. 84ra–87vb.

archbishop's attacks, though it may also suggest that the instigator of the protest was Roger Conway, soon to emerge as one of FitzRalph's most formidable opponents. The assembled friars, priors, and representatives of the London convents, under the presidency of Thomas Soude, a Franciscan and possibly guardian of Greyfriars, drew up a list of twenty-one alleged errors which they found in the archbishop's public utterances, dealing with the poverty of Christ, the mendicancy professed and practised by the friars, the papal legislation guaranteeing the friars' role in the pastoral sphere, and their own particular performance in that area. They made no direct reference to the implications of the theoretical problem of dominion, but in the preamble they defended their confessional practice, maintaining that they only heard the confessions of those who came freely to them in accordance with the papal mandate, and stressing that they always imposed 'penitencias salutares pro modo culparum'.[34] These twenty-one clauses, of which the first five dealt with Christ's life on earth, mendicant state, and teaching on the subject of mendicancy, the next six with the friars' practice of mendicant poverty, and the remaining ten with the pastoral issues of preaching and hearing confessions, were incorporated into an *Appellacio* drawn up by a public notary, Richard Upton of the diocese of Lichfield, in the name of the prior of the London Augustinians, John of Arderne, who acted as proctor for the four orders of friars. He duly set out on 10 March for FitzRalph's London lodgings, bearing the membrane scroll which contained the *Appellacio*. On being received by members of the archbishop's household, the friar proclaimed to them its contents and presented them with a copy.[35]

The friars did not have to wait long for a reply. Two days later FitzRalph preached once more at St. Paul's Cross. Taking as his text the words of St. Paul: 'Nemo vos seducat inanibus verbis' (Eph. v. 6), he dealt with each of the twenty-one articles in turn.[36] The vernacular sermon, as delivered, must have been a lengthy and powerful piece of oratory, but even at that he was obliged to summarize his arguments in the aural text and reserve his more detailed exposition for the written Latin version.

[34] The circumstances of the meeting are described in detail in the preamble to the text of the *Appellacio*, which survives in a single manuscript, MS Sidney Sussex 64, fol. 4^{r-v}. On the contents of this MS see Walsh, 'FitzRalph and the Friars', 224–5.

[35] MS Sidney Sussex, fol. 4^{v}.

[36] B, fols. 112^{v}–127^{r}; J, fols. 88ra–96va.

Gwynn rightly remarked that this sermon, in manuscript form, deserves to be regarded as a pamphlet, and it has survived as a vigorous piece of anti-mendicant polemic with a circulation independent of the sermon diary and even, in isolated cases, independently of the other London sermons.[37]. In it FitzRalph considered the poverty and pastoral problems jointly. With regard to poverty he went to the root of a problem which had troubled all mendicants, and especially the followers of St. Francis: the patent dichotomy between the rule of poverty which they professed to observe and the wealth and splendour to which, through their popularity with the faithful, they had become accustomed. He questioned the ambition and lust for power which led them to accept office as confessors of kings and princes. He questioned the sincerity of a vow of poverty which permitted them to live in splendour – their churches were larger and more magnificent than cathedrals, their living quarters luxurious, their cellars full of good wine. They had fine belfries and cloisters, the latter spacious enough for armed knights to hold tournaments there. They had valuable collections of books, ornaments more precious than most prelates, with the possible exception of the pope.[38] Nor were his accusations simply shafts in the dark. His audience must have been familiar with the mendicant churches in the city, especially the lofty Greyfriars, upon which two generations of craftsmen had worked and which, by the time FitzRalph came to London, must have been virtually completed and its magnificent set of thirty-six stained-glass windows in place.[39] The church and convent, which had an average community of eighty or ninety friars, were probably more spectacular, but the communities of Austin, Black, and Carmelite friars were not much worse off.[40] Many members of the audience must have been able to contrast this splendour, of which they were being so evocatively reminded, with the genuine poverty of so many of the secular

[37] e.g. Cambridge, MS Peterhouse 223, fols. 35^{v}–43^{v}, where it circulated with the *Defensio Curatorum* and other documents pertaining to the Avignon phase of the controversy; Rome, Bibl. Casanatensis 948 (B. III. 15), fols. 104vb–116rb, together with a random selection of 16 of FitzRalph's sermons, including some preached in Ireland, some at the curia, and some anti-mendicant sermons. It is also to be found in CVP 3935, 3937, and 4244.

[38] B, fol. 117^{r}; J. fol. 90^{v}. He also accused them of seeking the honour of being confessors to kings and princes, rather than to the poor and humble, B, fol. 119^{r}.

[39] Charles L. Kingsford, *The Grey Friars of London* (Aberdeen, 1915), pp. 38–9.

[40] See the entries, with guide to sources, in *Medieval Religious Houses. England and Wales,* pp. 186, 197, 201.

clergy. The preacher heightened the effect still further by quoting the rule of St. Francis clause by clause, contrasting its provisions with the friars' way of life so familiar to himself and his audience.[41] Few would have stopped to consider that not merely was this rule no longer capable of a literal interpretation once the group of original Franciscans had become an international order, but also that three of the four orders being thus indicted owed no allegiance to that rule.

Equally subjective was FitzRalph's approach to the pastoral issue. From the days of his earliest Avignon sermons he had shown an awareness of the pastoral problem presented by 'ignorantia sacerdotium', and here he returned to the question once more. He argued the desirability of confession to one's own priest rather than to a licensed friar, unless there were grave reasons for not doing so. Reluctantly he conceded the truth of the argument that the friars were usually better equipped for pastoral work, that they had a higher standard of theological learning and better training for preaching and pastoral care. Then, somewhat inconsistently, he claimed that the friars appointed their less learned members to pastoral work and especially to hear confessions – a claim whose falsity is most convincingly demonstrated by the registers of his brother-bishops in England, which list numerous licences issued to friar-doctors.[42] He also grudgingly allowed that an acceptable 'grave reason' for the choice of a mendicant confessor in favour of one's own priest might be the latter's defective education, but at the same time insisted that the parish priest was more suitable than a friar with four times his learning because the former knew his penitent, whereas the latter was an outsider.[43] In this sermon one can see emerging FitzRalph's attitude to the problem of confession to a licensed friar, the validity of absolution granted by such a friar, and the need to avoid falling into the errors of Jean de Pouilly concerning the obligation of a second confession. FitzRalph was beginning to formulate his arguments for the desirability of a second confession to one's own priest, not because of any inherent defect in the friar's powers of binding and loosing and therefore in the absolution administered, but on legal and social grounds: the canons, and especially *Omnis utriusque sexus* still required it, and the

[41] B, fols. 120^{v}-121^{r}; J, fols. 92vb-93ra.
[42] See the evidence presented in Williams, art. cit., *BRUO* and *BRUC*, *passim*.
[43] B, fols. 121^{v}-122^{r}; J, fol. 93^{rb-vb}.

authority of the parish priest would be undermined if he had no means of checking up on a parishioner who declared that he had confessed to a licensed friar and came to receive the Eucharist in his parish church at Easter.[44] But the sermon also provided the first indications, and the subsequent proceedings in Avignon would confirm this impression, that whereas FitzRalph could argue powerfully and convincingly on the poverty issue when his scriptural expertise came to his aid, he was out of his depth in the canonical problem posed by the conflicting interpretations of *Omnis*, *Super Cathedram*, and *Vas electionis*.

This sermon was also seen as an indictment of the mendicant orders, a declaration of war made in one of the most public places in London. Already in the course of the sermon he told his audience that the friars were taking steps to have him silenced, seeking an injunction from the king – not without the prospect of success, as Edward III and his queen were usually prepared to befriend the friars. A royal order had already been secured preventing Dean Richard Kilwington from preaching against the friars' privileges, and it was intended to secure a similar one against FitzRalph.[45] An indication of the friars' success in their objective is the fact that FitzRalph preached no further sermon from St. Paul's Cross. His only further recorded sermon in London, on 25 March, was from a much less prestigious pulpit, that of St. Mary's Newchurch, and here he strayed from the theme of the day to launch another bitter attack on the friars' confessional practices.[46] Yet another, even more convincing indication of royal intervention against the archbishop's cause was the mandate issued by Edward III on 31 March. The king stated that it had been brought to his attention that FitzRalph was about the leave the country on a mission which was not further specified in the royal mandate, but which could only have been an attempt to take his case to the papal curia in defiance of the Statute of Praemunire.[47] The king forbade FitzRalph to leave the country, and on 7 April issued further orders to the sheriff of London and the keepers of the ports on the south-eastern coast, instructing them to ensure that no religious, or any other person, in particular no Augustinian

[44] B, fols. 124^{v}–125^{r}; J, fols. 94va–95rb. [45] B, fol. 113^{r}; J, fol. 88va.

[46] B, fols. 56^{v}–58^{r}; J, fols. 46va–48ra. This sermon is out of order in all extant MSS of the diary.

[47] Rymer's *Foedera*, III. i. 353.

friar, might leave the country without royal licence.[48] These measures were clearly designed to prevent the principal participants from taking their case to Avignon, but in van. FitzRalph arrived during the summer of 1357 and the Augustinian John of Arderne was there in time for the formal opening of the proceedings the following November. Meanwhile Innocent VI attempted to reduce tension by issuing *Frequentes hactenus* on 8 September, ordering the enforcement of the provisions of *Super Cathedram* in London.[49]

Ware suggested that the guardian of the Franciscan convent in Armagh was one of those who cited FitzRalph to the papal curia after the London sermons of 1356–7,[50] and his view is lent some support by the fact that the archbishop, chapter, priests, and people of the city and diocese of Armagh petitioned Innocent VI for a reaffirmation of *Super Cathedram* in their interests. The pope complied with this request in a letter of 25 August 1357 to the abbots of Mellifont and St. Mary's, Navan, ordering them to ensure that *Super Cathedram* be enforced in the diocese.[51] Shortly after this, the bull was re-issued in London, and throughout northern and central Germany, and in northern Italy. This mass re-issue preceded a wave of subsequent reaffirmations of the bull during the years 1358–60 – including Sweden, Hungary, Constance, Basel, and Strassburg, the ecclesiastical province of Mainz, in Bohemia and the lands of the 'Wenzelskrone', as well as in York and Durham – while FitzRalph's case was at its height.[52] The issue for Armagh may well be an indication that by August 1357 FitzRalph had arrived in person at the curia, delivered the petition from the clergy and people of his diocese in support of his case against the friars, and received as an interim solution the re-issue of the bull in question, though the problem must be left open whether the archbishop's flock was as united in its desire to secure a settlement detrimental to the friars as the terms of the petition seem to imply.

When the case finally opened in Avignon its tenor suggests that the first move in these curial proceedings was made by the

[48] CCR 1354–60, 399.

[49] *Reg. Vat.* 232, fol. 345^r, *CPL* 1342–62, 583, and copied in MS Sidney Sussex 64, fols. 127^r–128^r. For FitzRalph's arrival in Avignon in summer 1357 see *Mon. Fran.* i. 358.

[50] James Ware, *A Commentary on the Prelates of Ireland* (Dublin, 1704), p. 14.

[51] *BF* vi. 305, n. 724.

[52] *BF* vi. *passim.*

friars, but then FitzRalph took over the initiative. He retaliated both by replying to their charges, in the *Proposicio* of 8 November, and by initiating counter-proceedings of his own, petitioning for a commission of cardinals to hear his case against them. The *Proposicio* was delivered before pope and cardinals in full consistory, and FitzRalph apparently received papal permission to present his plea in person and not through a consistorial advocate. The reasons for this decision are unclear – it may have been determined by the need to save his meagre resources for the pursuit of the case if further aid was not forthcoming from his fellow bishops, or by his own undoubted talent for presenting a persuasive case, backed up by his own personal influence at the curia. He brought his case, not before the court of the Apostolic Palace, but before the cardinals' tribunal, which might be expected to work more quickly.[53] The petition, which is undated in the surviving copies, but which referred back to the *Proposicio*, reviewed the situation briefly, stating the charges made in the *Appellacio* of 10 March 1357, which had become the basis of the friars' case and of the archbishop's own reply.[54] However, the actual statement of FitzRalph's position, in sufficient detail to inform curial audiences, was contained in the *Proposicio*.

He opened this *Proposicio* with a review of the situation as it had developed since his arrival in London, where – as he claimed – the poverty controversy was already in progress when he reached the capital. On invitation he delivered some seven or eight sermons – he appeared not too definite about the precise number, but his declaration suggests that he either included among these the essentially moderate sermons preached during the summer of 1356, or else that there had been others which never found their way into the diary. From these sermons nine conclusions were deduced by the friars, on the basis of which they delated him to the papal curia:

[53] On consistorial procedures see Guillaume Mollat, *The Popes at Avignon* (trans. from 9th edn., London, 1963), pp. 294–6.

[54] The petition survives in seven MS collections of material pertaining to these proceedings, including MS Sidney Sussex 64, fols. 110^r–111^r. To the list in Walsh, 'FitzRalph and the Friars', 233–4, n. 37, should be added CLM 11882, fols. 206^r–209^r, and the single printing, in a rare edition of the *Defensio Curatorum* (Paris 'apud Petrum Billaine', 1633), pp. 140–7. This printing, which also included two of FitzRalph's contributions to the Avignon phase of the controversy: *Quoniam (quia) in proposicione nuper facta* (pp. 95–140), and the *Libellus* 'Coram vobis' (pp. 148–67), was based on a Victorine manuscript no longer extant in any Paris collection.

I Christ was always poor during his life on earth, but not because he wanted or loved poverty for its own sake

II He never begged voluntarily

III He never taught voluntary mendicancy

IV He actually taught that nobody should beg voluntarily

V Nobody can prudently assume a vow of mendicant poverty for perpetual observance

VI The Franciscan rule does not impose the obligation of mendicant poverty

VII The bull of Alexander IV condemning the *Libellus* of Guillaume de Saint Amour did not contradict any of the preceding conclusions[55]

VIII The parish church is a more suitable place for the confessions of the parishioners than the churches of the friars

IX Equally the bishop's church is more suitable for confessions than mendicant churches.

These conclusions, which differ slightly in grouping and emphasis from the twenty-one clauses of the *Appellacio*, but were a reasonable deduction from the final sermon at St. Paul's Cross which followed it, became the basis of FitzRalph's case at Avignon. He did not attempt to deny that he taught along these lines in sermons and published statements, but presented a lengthy justification of his stand. Although seven of the nine conclusions dealt with mendicancy, the main issue in the *Proposicio* and in the subsequent proceedings was the friars' pastoral role, above all, confession to the friars, which represented only two of the disputed conclusions. Despite the stated order of the nine points, FitzRalph began his argument with the pastoral question, devoting most of the *Proposicio* to its various implications. He insisted on the parish church as the proper place for parishioners' confessions, ordained by God and confirmed by law. Equally the position of the parish priest was laid down by divine law, and his greater suitability as confessor was justified by his personal knowledge of his flock. The friars were outsiders, and their churches had only been approved for these purposes in response to their incessant demands and petitions to the papacy. While being careful to avoid open criticism of the successive popes who made the friars' pastoral position possible, FitzRalph came dangerously

[55] *Defensio Curatorum*, ed. cit., p. 1392. For Alexander IV's condemnation of the *Tractatus brevis de periculis novissimorum temporum* (1255) in the bull of 5 October 1256, see *BF* ii, 160–2.

close to suggesting that the power to bind and loose, and therefore to absolve, was greater in a secular priest than in a friar authorized by the papacy. His arguments, frequently little more than his own opinion stated as fact, implied that the friars were engaged in a large-scale deception at the expense of their pastoral charges, that they took advantage of the laity's defective understanding of the canonical position and enticed them to be buried in mendicant churches. He also returned to the claim that the friars fraudently deprived the secular clergy of their legitimate tithes by failing to instruct their penitents in the obligation to pay them, and by granting easy absolution to those who failed to fulfil these obligations.[56]

At this point he launched the oft-quoted philippic against confessional practices in his archdiocese: he claimed to have some two thousand members of his flock, who were involved annually in sentences of excommunication for crimes of homicide, robbery, and arson, many of them doubtless reflections of the racial tensions in the border areas under his jurisdiction. Of these, he argued, only about forty came to him or his penitentiaries to seek absolution from these 'reserved' sins, yet all of them received the Eucharist, claiming to have been absolved from their sins. Such absolution, he claimed, could only have been obtained from the friars operating within his diocese.[57] His remarks indicate a serious pastoral problem, though his figure of two thousand need not be taken very seriously. Like all medieval orators his attitude to numbers was casual, and he made equally inaccurate estimates of student numbers at Oxford, whose decline in the mid-fourteenth century he attributed to unscrupulous methods of recruitment of young boys into the mendicant communities there.[58]

These methods of recruitment were already a cause for concern among the university authorities, and it is possible that FitzRalph came to Avignon intending to add this element to his list of *gravamina* against the friars. His case was strengthened by the evocative picture which he painted for pope and cardinals

[56] *Defensio Curatorum*, pp. 1393–4.

[57] Ibid., p. 1394. Not merely in Ireland were the friars accused of regarding human life as cheap and absolution for murder a triviality. Anonymous poems of the later 14th century in England claimed that if a man killed his entire family and confessed to a friar, he might receive absolution for less than the price of a pair of shoes, and that he might be absolved from murder and fornication for less than six pence, Wright, *Political Poems*, i. 266, ii. 270, and cited in Erikson, *FS* 35, 120–1.

[58] *Defensio Curatorum*, p. 1398.

of a despairing English parent whom the archbishop had encountered the same day as he set out from his lodgings for the papal palace. The Englishman had told him that he had travelled to Avignon in order to seek papal assistance in his plight. Shortly before Easter 1357 his young son, not yet thirteen and a student in Oxford, had been enticed by the friars – he did not specify which order – to join their community. The boy's parents were not permitted to talk to him except under the surveillance of a friar, and although the parents believed that the boy was being kept against his will they were powerless to intervene in the situation.[59] Such cases were, according to FitzRalph, common in England, and were a reason for the startling decline in student numbers at Oxford from an alleged 30,000 while he was a student there to a mere 6,000 by 1357. Apart from the fact that neither figure can be accepted as a realistic one for the student population of medieval Oxford, any impression of declining numbers in the 1350s can reasonably be explained in terms of the Black Death.[60] However, there is independent evidence to show that this was not simply a case of FitzRalph clutching at any charge which he might use against the friars. During these years mendicant policies of recruitment, especially among younger students, were giving cause for concern and the university authorities became obliged to take steps to deal with the matter.

On the grounds that the nobility were afraid to send their sons to Oxford, the university passed in 1358 a series of statutes forbidding the friars to admit into their orders any member of the university under the age of eighteen, or to send such youths to other convents of their order to be admitted. The penalties for breach of this statute were severe: all friars of the order concerned would be debarred from all university acts, from hearing and giving lectures, in Oxford and elsewhere for a year following the prohibited admission of such a novice. These statutes also attacked the 'wax' doctors, 'doctores

[59] Ibid., p. 1397.

[60] The figures given in Salter, *Medieval Oxford* (OHS 1936), p. 100, of *c*.1,500 students for the early 14th century, and *c*.1,000 a century later, have been queried recently by Trevor H. Aston, 'Oxford's Medieval Alumni', *Past and Present*, 74 (1977), 3–40, who estimated an average for the 14th and 15th centuries of *c*.1,100–1,300, with *c*.250 friars, ibid., 6–7. *CPL* contains numerous cases for the 20-year period following the Black Death in which religious petitioned the pope for a reduction of the age of ordination, in order to help them restore their depleted numbers, and the universities must have experienced a similar situation.

cereorum', who had obtained their degrees not on their own merits but through the influence of the rich and powerful. Their letters were sealed with wax, which would stand up to fire no more than the learning of such doctors would stand up to examination. These doctors are to be identified as the young men induced into the mendicant orders, whose education has been neglected but who have been taught to curry favour with the great, and win their degrees by this method rather than through normal channels. As a result they preach and teach what they do not understand and thereby cause great harm to the Church.[61] This legislation, which in any case was equally a reflection on the weakness of university authorities which could admit to such a situation, did not survive unchallenged. The friars appealed to the papal court and on 1 June 1365, Urban V ordered the archbishop of Canterbury, and the bishops of London and Lincoln to ensure that the chancellor and regent masters of the university revoked these statutes.[62] Nor did the problem pass unnoticed in contemporary literature, and the accusation that the friars, especially Franciscans, stole young students – many of them little more than children – while at university, recurred frequently and was subsequently taken up by Wyclif.[63]

Nor was this FitzRalph's only grievance relating to the friars' academic activity: he complained that he sent several parish curates from his diocese to study – presumably at Oxford – but they had to return home in disgust because they were unable to purchase any theological textbooks, nor even a Bible, because the friars, who could afford to buy books on all subjects, arts, theology, canon and civil law, and medicine, grabbed everything that came on the market. Clearly he had attempted to put into practice the educational ideals which he had expounded at the second synod in Drogheda and sent some of his parochial clergy to acquire more theological expertise than was possible at home. It is not difficult to sympathize with his claim that if these would-be students were faced with such a situation, they would become so demoralized that no cleric would remain in the Church apart from the friars with, as FitzRalph argued, disastrous results for the Church as a whole.[64]

The notarial instrument or 'acta causae' of 14 November

[61] Printed in *Mun. Acad.* i. 207–8.
[62] *Reg. Vat.* 254, fol. 127^{r-v}, *CPL* 1362–1404, 52.
[63] Erikson, *FS* 35, 112–5.
[64] *Defensio Curatorum*, pp. 1398–99.

recorded the content of FitzRalph's case against the accusation of John of Arderne and introduced a new set of participants on the opposing side, the procurators-general of the four mendicant orders at the curia: Guillaume de Militiis O.P., Giacomo da Montepulciano O.F.M., Bernardo de Catalonia O.E.S.A., and Arnold of Teng O.Carm.[65] Although FitzRalph continued to regard John of Arderne as the nominal adversary, this London Augustinian appears to have ceded place to the official procurator of his order and took no formal part in the hearing.

The function of the cardinals' tribunal was a limited one. It did not deliver a final judgement, but instituted summary legal proceedings and then referred the case to the pope for judgement. An investigation of the composition of the tribunal appointed in this case provokes the speculation whether Innocent VI might not have been prepared to reverse the policy of his predecessor and may have chosen cardinals sympathetic to FitzRalph's cause. Guillaume Court, cardinal-bishop of Tusculum, was a Cistercian, like his uncle Benedict XII, to whom he owed his elevation to the College of Cardinals. He had been his uncle's closest colleague and by the 1350s was the only survivor of that reforming circle which gathered around the Cistercian pope in the later 1330s. He held a number of English benefices by papal provision, including the archdeaconry of Wells, he had presided over heresy trials in which Castilian and Provençal Franciscan Spirituals were condemned,[66] and he also shared FitzRalph's interest in the problems of the Christian East.[67] Pierre du Cros, bishop of Auxerre and cardinal of S. Martino al Monte, had formerly employed as his chaplain Richard Kilwington, who was provided to the deanery of St. Paul's at the cardinal's request,[68] and both of these cardinals would the following year become involved once more in the affairs of the Catalan Grand Company.[69] Elias de Saint Yrieux, bishop of Uzès and cardinal of S. Stefano in Celiomonte, was a

[65] The instrument or 'Recordacio commisionis facte' is copied in the same MSS as the petition, above, no. 54.

[66] For Court see Eubel, *Hierarchia Catholica,* i^2. 17, 81; Baluze, *Vitae Pap. Avin.* i. 206, 212–3, ii. 320–4, 412; Schimmelpfennig, 'Benedikt XII. als Reformpapst', 40–1. For his condemnation of the Franciscan Giovanni da Castiglione (d'Orcia) see Alexander Patschovsky, 'Strassburger Beginenverfolgungen im 14. Jahrhundert', *Deutsches Archiv,* 30 (1974), 110.

[67] Setton, *The Papacy and the Levant*, i. 183.

[68] Eubel, *Hierarchia Catholica*, i^2. 19; Baluze, i. 256, 286, ii. 411–2.

[69] Setton, *The Papacy and the Levant*, i. 465 n.

Benedictine.[70] Hence all three cardinals were French, two were members of the older endowed monastic orders, the 'possessionati', who might be expected to show little sympathy for the mendicant ideal – a factor which did not escape FitzRalph as he aimed a little flattery in their direction in the course of the *Proposicio*.[71] Furthermore, two of the three, one regular and the secular member, drew revenues from English benefices. If FitzRalph had the weight of influence of the *ecclesia Anglicana* behind his appeal, the members of the tribunal might have been sympathetic.

A fourth cardinal had originally been nominated, Francesco degli Atti, bishop of Florence and cardinal of S. Marco, but illness forced his withdrawal before proceedings could commence. Of all these cardinals he was best qualified to judge the case. A canonist, he had several years earlier as bishop of Chiusi (1348–53) composed a *Tractatus de canonica portione et de quarta*, which became a widely consulted manual on the problem.[72] The friars must have had mixed feelings about his participation. Unlike FitzRalph he would have conceded their right to pastoral involvement in principle, but in his treatise he defended the bishops' rights to the *portio canonica* on a wide range of offerings and not simply on burial dues, and would probably have sympathized with many of FitzRalph's objections. Whereas canonist opinion generally supported the friars' position on confession against that of Jean de Pouilly, and was divided on the necessity of licences for mendicant preaching, on the question of the canonical portion under the terms of *Super Cathedram* the canonists tended to uphold the rights of the bishops and secular clergy.[73] There was, however, at least one member of the College of Cardinals who was prepared to support FitzRalph's position on confession, which was dangerously close to that of De Pouilly and condemned in *Vas electionis*. This was Nicholas de Bessia, bishop of Limoges and created cardinal deacon of S. Maria in Via Lata by Clement VI, who submitted a *Libellus* in favour of FitzRalph's position during the proceedings.[74]

[70] Eubel, *Hierarchia Catholica*, i². 19, 120; Baluze, i. 318, ii. 412, 447–8.

[71] *Defensio Curatorum*, p. 1399.

[72] See *Dizionario biografico degli Italiani*, iv. 545–6; Richard C. Trexler, 'The Bishop's Portion: generic pious legacies in the late middle ages in Italy', *Traditio*, 28 (1972), 432–4, 449–50.

[73] Canonist opinion is discussed in Haren, *A Study of the 'Memoriale Presbyterorum'*, i. 402–9.

[74] Mentioned by the author of the *Replicaciones* on behalf of FitzRalph against

Most of our information concerning these proceedings is drawn from the *Processus summarius*, a day by day account of the sittings of the tribunal.[75] It shows that the cardinals were meticulous in the hearing of evidence from both sides, but clearly reluctant to take a decision. During the winter and spring of 1357–8 they often adjourned the case for several weeks at a time, possibly in order to attend to other curial business. Less openly partial to FitzRalph than one might have expected, they deliberated, hesitated, and finally sought papal approval before deciding on 14 November that the archbishop's case be even admitted to the curial court.[76] The next meeting of judges, parties, and procurators on 21 November accomplished nothing beyond distributing copies of the procurators' statements and fixed a further date for 2 December to discuss these. Another delay followed while objections were raised on FitzRalph's behalf, because of some alleged but unspecified defects in the depositions. The tribunal considered these objections, but judged them beyond their competence.[77] After further consultations with the pope, these procedural difficulties were resolved and it was agreed that the tribunal should meet again on 19 December to hear the parties expound the *Libelli, articuli et capitula* upon which they based their respective cases.

On that date FitzRalph's procurator introduced his *Libellus: Coram vobis . . .* which contained the main elements of his case against the friars' pastoral privileges. He based his argument on the obligation of confession to one's own priest imposed in 1215 by *Omnis utriusque sexus*, which further decreed that anybody wishing to confess to another must first obtain a licence from his 'proprius sacerdos'.[78] Although *Super Cathedram* (1300) had been an attempt to legislate for the new pastoral

Roger Conway, Paris, Lat. 3222, fol. 160rb. For Nicholas de Bessia see Eubel, *Hierarchia Catholica*, i². 18, 301; Baluze, i. 381–4; ii. 247, 281, 290. After FitzRalph's death he changed his attitude sufficiently to accept in 1366 the office of cardinal protector of the Franciscans, Wadding, *Annales Minorum*, viii. 201. Or was his support 'bought' with the Franciscan largesse of which FitzRalph's supporters complained?

[75] The only surviving copy is in MS Sidney Sussex 64, fols. 111^{v}–113^{v}.

[76] Ibid., fol. 111^{v}. On the limited competence of a tribunal of cardinals, who had to receive for each case they examined a specific delegation of authority stating their powers, Mollat, *The Popes at Avignon*, p. 298.

[77] MS Sidney Sussex 64, fols. 111^{v}–112^{r}.

[78] Ibid., fols. 115^{r}–118^{v}. To the list of surviving MSS in Walsh, 'FitzRalph and the Friars', 236 n. 45, should be added CLM 11882, fols. 198^{r}–206^{r}, and the printed edn. of 1633, above, n. 54. For the decree *Omnis*, V. 38. 12, Friedberg, ii. 887–8.

situation created by the friars, its failure to clarify the continued validity of previous legislation encouraged the friars to adopt the attitude that the prescriptions contained in *Omnis* were no longer to be enforced. The attitude of Jean de Pouilly that confession to a friar, even if properly licensed under the terms of *Super Cathedram*, did not fulfil the obligation imposed by the Lateran canon, and that those who confessed to a friar were therefore bound to confess the same sins again to their parish priest before receiving the Eucharist at Easter, had been condemned in *Vas electionis* by John XXII. But even that experienced canonist had failed to clarify whether the relevant sections of the Lateran canon were still binding. The root of the problem lay therefore in the fact that *Super Cathedram* was ambiguous, both legally and theologically. Not merely did it fail to clarify the position with regard to previous legislation, it also failed to define the nature of absolution imparted by a licensed friar. The canonists, who were in doubt about the extent of episcopal powers with regard to preaching as well as confessional licences,[79], were equally uncertain about the *nature* of the friars' confessional powers, and opinion was sharply divided. The view of Bernard of Parma that a friar validly licensed by his bishop still required the permission of the 'proprius sacerdos' remained a minority view,[80] but William of Monte Lauduno adopted a standpoint which was reflected in much of the subsequent debates. He argued that, whereas annual confession to the 'proprius sacerdos' was not required by law if the parishioner had confessed to a licensed friar, there was none the less a practical pastoral problem involved if the parish priest had to administer the Eucharist to a parishioner whom he did not know to be contrite and to have confessed his sins. Hence the desirability of repeating the confession 'ex quadam aequitate et congruentia'.[81]

The majority of contemporary canonist opinion shared William's basic premiss; it supported *Vas electionis* and rejected the legal obligation for a second confession. The weight of this opinion might have been a reason for FitzRalph's striking neglect of the opinions of fourteenth-century glossators – they could be of no assistance to him. On the other hand none of his

[79] Kedar, art. cit.

[80] Haren, *A Study of the 'Memoriale Presbyterorum'*, i. 404–8.

[81] A Benedictine, he expressed this view in the 'Apparatus super Clementinas', *Repetitiones Iuris Canonici*, iv (Cologne, 1618), 320.

previous literary output had given reason to assume that he was familiar with canonist sources. Throughout the *Defensio Curatorum* and his subsequent contributions to the proceedings his sources of authority were the Bible and the relevant decretals, but without any consideration of the substantial body of commentary which these decretals had evoked in the early decades of the fourteenth century. In this respect he differed from mendicant opponents, such as Hardeby, who was well versed in the work of the canonists of his own and the previous generation. However, although FitzRalph gave no direct indication of familiarity with the work of William of Monte Lauduno, he may have been aware of the general drift of canonist opinion, and at one point in the *Defensio Curatorum*, in which he was striving to avoid the impression that he shared the errors of Jean de Pouilly, he developed a point to which he had already alluded in the sermon of 26 February 1357. This was the suggestion that De Pouilly had erred by questioning the quality or degree of powers conferred on a licensed friar, by suggesting that the friar's authority to bind and loose was less than that of the parish curate, whereas FitzRalph now argued that the distinction was really a formal and legalistic one determined by the nature of the existing legislation, whose ambiguities he tacitly admitted. The penitent was obliged to re-confess the same sins simply because of the existence of the Lateran canon of 1215.[82]

However, FitzRalph never pursued the implications of this argument and continued to work for the total abolition of the mendicant privilege of confession. His proposed solution was one which could comment itself neither to the pope nor to the friars. He wanted all modifications contained in *Vas electionis* to be eliminated and the bull reduced to conformity with the decree of 1215 which antedated the advent of the friars on the pastoral scene. His argument implied rejection of the curial theory whereby the pope was both the universal ordinary and the 'proprius sacerdos' of every Christian, and of the papal policy which employed the friars as instruments of centralization and closer control. At no time did he use the argument of the superior authority of the first decree, issued by a general council, over the later ones, which were papal pronouncements, but his discussion of these bulls left no room for doubt that,

[82] *Defensio Curatorum*, p. 1395.

whether for reasons of principle or pragmatism, he accorded more weight to the Lateran canon.

The archbishop's demand, if implemented, would have had profound implications for the later medieval Church and for the development of its social role, it would have reversed the trend of papal policy over the previous one and a half centuries, deprived the orders of their influence and appeal in the communities they served and from whom they sought their livelihood, and it would have forced the bishops back into total dependence on the secular clergy to fulfil all the pastoral commitments of their dioceses. This demand put the cardinals in a quandary, and they seized upon the opportunity for a Christmas recess and adjourned until 15 January 1358. Then the friars' *Libellus* was introduced, and in further sessions of 29 January, 15 February, and 22 March the tribunal heard the *Excepciones* of each party in reply to the *Libellus* of the other, while Jacques de Seve, a curial advocate in FitzRalph's employ, argued a series of *Allegaciones* against the mendicant case, and a second curial advocate, Pietro da Perugia, replied for the friars.[83]

In the *Excepciones* the case assumed an even more polemical tone, and the friars' procurators sezied the opportunity for a personal attack on FitzRalph, which ultimately developed into a formal accusation of heresy. They denied his authority to prosecute the case (not, as we shall see, without good reason), accused him of doctrinal errors, and argued that as his actions deserved the sentence of excommunication, he ought to be treated as an excommunicate and excluded from the papal courts.[84] They petitioned for his other writings, especially the London sermons, to be introduced before the tribunal as evidence against him, and claimed that he was conspiring with bishops, parish priests, and other benefice-holders in England and elsewhere to ensure the destruction of the mendicant orders. The *Excepciones* then concluded with a sweeping condemnation of FitzRalph's *Libellus* as vague and obscure, capricious and calumnious, and a plea that in order to avoid prejudice to their own case, his should not be admitted for

[83] MS Sidney Sussex 64, fols. 112^{r}–113^{r}. The principal reply to the friars' *Libellus* was not contained in FitzRalph's *Excepciones* to it, but in the *Allegaciones* of Jacques de Seve, ibid., fols. 121^{r-v}, 123^{r}–125^{r}. Those of Pietro da Perugia appear not to have survived and we know of his participation only from the *Processus summarius*.

[84] Ibid., fol. 120^{r}.

consideration until after judgement had been awarded on the basis of their own submissions.[85] This latter plea illustrates the ambiguous nature of the proceedings. The exact nature of the case which the cardinals were appointed to hear was never defined precisely. The first formal charge had come from the friars and FitzRalph had both replied to that charge and petitioned for a commission to hear his own counter-charge. The tribunal thus constituted heard evidence from both sides indiscriminately and without distinguishing two separate cases. But when FitzRalph's *Excepciones* were presented, it was argued on his behalf that the cardinals' mandate only gave them jurisdiction to hear the case as presented in FitzRalph's supplication and not any case which the friars might present.[86] The friars naturally adopted the opposite view, and the tribunal, without making any formal ruling on its own competence, continued to hear both sides simultaneously as though it were an open inquiry.

The friars' *Libellus* resembled much of their polemical contributions in defence of their own position, in that it made no attempt to discuss the canonical or pastoral merits of their activities, but concentrated entirely on FitzRalph's propaganda campaign designed to bring them into disrepute. It made no attempt to justify the friars on the grounds of superior educational qualifications, but listed the works which illustrated FitzRalph's erroneous teaching on the doctrine of mendicant poverty – the London sermons, *De Pauperie Salvatoris*, and the supplement to it in the form of forty-five articles which circulated as the eighth book of the dialogue.[87] With an ironic twist the friars turned FitzRalph's own doctrine, that those who committed grave sin (i.e. by slandering the friars) were deprived of their ecclesiastical and temporal dominion, back on the archbishop himself. Throughout the *Libellus*, but not in the subsequent *Excepciones*, they described him as 'Ricardus se asserens

[85] Ibid., fol. 120^{v}.
[86] Ibid., fol. 112^{v}.
[87] Ibid., fol. 119^{r-v}. The friars' procurators referred to 54 articles by FitzRalph on *DPS*, and presumably meant Book VIII of the dialogue in the form of 45 articles, which he added at Avignon. These had a limited circulation compared with the rest of the dialogue and survive in Paris, Lat. 3222, fols. 1ra–77vb; Berlin (East, GDR) Deutsche Staatsbibliothek, MS Magdeburg 47, fols. 252vb–309ra; Cambridge, MS Corpus Christi 180, fols. 90ra–128vb (a MS of the entire 8 books compiled for Adam Easton OSB, before 1381); MS Lambeth 121, fols. 138^{r}–179^{r}. Of these Lat. 3222 is undoubtedly the earliest text, and the MS may have been compiled at Avignon during or soon after the proceedings concerned.

archiepiscopus et primatus prefatus'. The subsequent manuscript dissemination of his anti-mendicant writings lends weight to their accusation that FitzRalph conducted a widespread propaganda campaign and had his statement of the case distributed and preached by the secular clergy throughout the Western Church, and not merely in England and at the curia. The remedy demanded by the friars' procurators was an extreme one, that the entire corpus of FitzRalph's writings against the friars be condemned and that he be debarred from all public comment on the subject in future.

Such harsh treatment from the tribunal was unlikely, but the cardinals were aware that indiscriminate propaganda could inflame the situation further. According to the author of the *Processus summarius*, whose sympathy for FitzRalph occasionally seeps through the façade of factual narrative, the friars were denouncing him in their sermons as a scandalmonger, heretic, heresiarch, even Antichrist or the Devil incarnate.[88] One would like to know the identity of such preachers, as neither the mendicant procurators-general nor English friars of such meticulous orthodoxy as Roger Conway, or the Dominican William Jordan, both of whom had arrived in Avignon by the spring of 1358, seem likely candidates for the role. At first glance the obvious culprits for such sentiments might appear to be the Spiritual Franciscans, already to be found in large groups in the Provençal towns and countryside, where they regularly fell foul of the Inquisition. But against this view, there was a paradoxical yet undeniable similarity between some of FitzRalph's criticism of current mendicant practices, especially with regard to the possession of property and practice of poverty, and that of the Franciscan extremists. In the London sermons and in his Avignon statements FitzRalph's argument invariably lacked the subtlety, even ambiguity, of *De Pauperie Salvatoris*, and in this cruder form he, like the Spiritual Franciscans, pleaded for a literal interpretation of the rule of St. Francis without mitigation by glosses or papal privileges. Both objected, though for different reasons, to the privileged position of the friars in pastoral and academic fields, and FitzRalph's gibe that the manner in which the friars were spending money in pursuit of their case against him indicated that they were neither as poor nor as dependent on the proceeds of mendicancy as they

[88] MS Sidney Sussex 64, fol. 112^{v}.

pretended, must have met with agreement in circles which would otherwise have little in common with a conservative pillar of the hierarchical establishment. FitzRalph must have had reason to envy the collective resources of the mendicant orders, which enabled them to mount a comprehensive campaign against him, especially as the testimony of Richard Kilwington showed that he received neither financial nor moral support from his fellow bishops and the members of his cathedral chapter, and implied that FitzRalph suffered such a crushing defeat at the friars' hands that he had no hope of recouping his expenses. An indication of the lengths to which the friars were prepared to go in order to finance their campaign against FitzRalph is provided by two letters of the Augustinian prior-general, Matteo d'Ascoli, of 16 November 1358. In the first, addressed to the provincial of the province of Cologne and presumably but one of a number of similar letters to all provincials of the order, the recipient was ordered to ensure that a levy of ten florins be paid from each province to help meet the crippling expenses of the defence against the archbishop of Armagh. The second letter indicated the general's readiness to resort to even more desperate measures: he permitted the procurator-general of the order, who was in dire financial straits because of the court case, to divert money from the fund collected to forward the process of canonization of their confrère, Nicolò da Tolentino, and use it in the present emergency.[89] Without comparable backing from the English hierarchy FitzRalph could scarcely compete with the friars on equal terms.

This lack of authoritative support from English bishops for FitzRalph's cause may have been determined by their reluctance to force a crisis, as a result of which they might be obliged to do without the useful and often necessary services of the friars in their own dioceses. It may also have been a case of instincts of self-preservation prevailing among those who could foresee some of the implications of FitzRalph's case. As early as 1350 he had seemed to be committing himself to a dangerous course when, by arguing that the friars' privileges were a violation of the ideals of their founders and even sinful, he was indirectly attacking the popes who approved such violations. But whether they realized that the gap between FitzRalph's

[89] For Kilwington's remarks see Lat. 3222, fol. 113va. For the text of the general's letters see Martin-de Meijer, 'Irish Material', 66–7.

standpoint and that of the Fraticelli and Spiritual Franciscans was not an unbridgeable one, is another question.

These questions do not permit a clear answer, but there is independent evidence that the polemic at Avignon continued. On 23 January 1358 the tribunal issued an injunction preventing both parties from preaching in public or disputing in the schools on matters pertaining to the case while it was still *sub iudice.*[90] At Oxford discussion arising from the subject was ranging even farther afield, and a letter from the chancellor, John de Hothum, and regent masters of the university, addressed to FitzRalph, indicated their anxiety over at least one aspect which was emerging from the controversy.[91] Obviously the line of argument pursued by Hardeby in his *questiones* was neither unique nor the most radical: a member of the university was advocating that, because of the sinfulness of the clergy, Church property should be confiscated and divided among scholars and soldiers, and that both tithes to the secular clergy and offerings to the friars should be abolished. Further details were to be supplied to FitzRalph by the bearer of the letter, but one significant detail was committed to paper. The offender, whose identity is unknown, had powerful protectors. Although his punishment was to be exclusion from all university acts until he should recant in public, he refused to do so because he was confident of the support of certain English magnates. It is tempting to think of Wyclif as a possible identification of this unknown disputant, but this is improbable in view of his continued silence on the question of dominion for more than a decade after FitzRalph's death. The letter was dated 26 March, but without any year, and it must have been sent to FitzRalph at Avignon – possibly in 1358 – as it requested him to bring the matter to the attention of the pope.

It is probable that this case should be linked with the text of a public recantation to be imposed upon a certain 'frater Johannes', a doctor of theology and presumably still actively teaching in Oxford. The recantation was to be sworn in the prsence of the superior of his order, and of the chancellor, John de Hothum, and the regent masters, in the church of St. Mary the Virgin after the university sermon on the Sunday following the feast of St. Frideswide, i.e. 19 October 1358. As an

[90] MS Sidney Sussex 64, fol. 111^{r}.

[91] Ibid., fol. 126^{v}. For Hothum, provost of the Queen's College and chancellor 1357–9, see *BRUO* II, 969–70.

additional punishment the friar was fined 100 shillings, payable to the university, and could never again lecture in theology without the special permission of the chancellor and regent masters. He was being punished for having declared in the schools that tithes belonged more rightly to the friars than to the parish clergy, that the king had the right to deprive ecclesiastics of their temporalities, and that the university was a school of heresy.[92] It is not clear from the surviving text of the document, which was a formula for the forthcoming recantation, nor from the chancellor's register,[93] whether the friar in question ever actually swore to the provisions it contained, but it seems probable that he was involved in the same university controversy as the subject of the chancellor's letter to FitzRalph, and at least possible that the two men were identical.

There is little evidence for the friars' claim, recorded in the *Processus summarius*, that a number of English prelates were conspiring with FitzRalph for the elimination of the mendicant orders.[94] But it is clear that the secular clergy continued to express their opposition to the friars' activities and privileges, with at least the tacit support of their bishops while the case was being heard. The proceedings were adjourned from 22 March until 26 June, a delay which FitzRalph felt to be in the friars' interests, and he secured papal approval for the return to the tribunal of Francesco degli Atti, who might have been expected to share some of FitzRalph's views on the canonical issue, in place of Elias de Saint Yrieux who had fallen ill. Meanwhile a delegation of English friars appeared before the pope, headed by Roger Conway and John Tatenhall, the Franciscan and Dominican provincials, and including John de Waldeby O.E.S.A., John Couton O.Carm., Richard of Soleville O.F.M., and William Jordan O.P.[95] They petitioned the pope to compel the English bishops to punish all who led the faithful astray by slandering the friars and attacking papal powers of dispensation, and they expressed concern that this

[92] Printed in *Mun. Acad.* i. 208–11.

[93] In the so-called *Registrum A*, which is discussed by Graham Pollard, 'The oldest Statute Book of the University', *The Bodleian Library Record*, 9 (1968), 69–81.

[94] MS Sidney Sussex 64, fol. 111^{v}.

[95] Ibid., fol. 113^{r-v}, and for the text of their petition, fol. 125^{v}. For Conway above, nn. 13–14; John Tatenhall, *BRUO* III, 2221; John de Waldeby, ibid., III, 1957–8; William Jordan, ibid., II, 1022. The MS gives W. Couton, but the Carmelite in question must be John Couton, English provincial 1359–62, *BRUO* I, 507. The Franciscan Richard of Soleville cannot be identified.

defamatory preaching would deprive them of the loyalty and financial support of their flocks. As a practical remedy to the situation however, all they could suggest was that the pope reaffirm the provisions of *Super Cathedram* and *Vas electionis* in their favour.

Some indication of the papal attitude is provided by the account of the next stage of the proceedings in the *Processus summarius*. Innocent VI was reluctant to issue any document which conceded the friars' point in principle, i.e. which was a formal recognition and condemnation of these alleged defamatory activities, lest it might prejudice the case which was *sub iudice*. But on the recommendation of the tribunal he ordered the vice-chancellor to issue a letter to the English prelates, which would cover the immediate situation but without conceding a principle. Through the vice-chancellor the friars obtained a *minuta*, or draft document drawn up in accordance with the terms of their petition. FitzRalph, 'super hoc munitus', appealed against this *minuta*, had it quashed, and the vice-chancellor prevented under pain of excommunication from bringing it before the tribunal.[96] To seasoned curial campaigners this altercation must have appeared as a falling-out of old allies and an indication that the once-influential group of protégés of John XXII could no longer carry that weight which it had done in the past. FitzRalph had on several occasions been invited to preach in the chapel of Cardinal Pierre Després, a fellow countryman of John XXII from Cahors and a cardinal since 1320, who held the office of vice-chancellor from 1348 until his death on 30 September 1361.[97] On 27 June the tribunal considered the *minuta* and the proposed alternative document before adjourning for a further week. Here the *Processus summarius* ends, though there is independent evidence that the hearing continued for some time longer, probably until FitzRalph's death, without reaching a conclusion.

The *minuta* under discussion was clearly the forerunner of *Gravem dilectorum*, but with one important difference. The *minuta* was precisely what the friars' procurators had asked for – an unequivocal statement of the friars' value in the pastoral

[96] MS Sidney Sussex 64, fol. 113ᵛ.

[97] Eubel, *Hierarchia Catholica*, i². 15; Paul M. Baumgarten, *Von der apostolischen Kanzlei. Untersuchungen über die päpstlichen Tabellionen und die Vizekanzler der Heiligen Römischen Kirche im XIII., XIV. und XV. Jahrhundert* (Cologne, 1908), 104–7.

field, and a condemnation of all interference and molestation by the secular clergy. It did not include the saving clause 'lite pendente', which appeared in the final form of the bull issued on 1 October 1358, and which stipulated that the case was still before the papal courts but left the bishops free to take interim action as necessary.[98] The debate before the tribunal had obviously continued and this compromise solution adopted. Furthermore, the 'lite pendente' clause indicated that the cardinals had not yet reached a verdict but still intended to do so.

The events and documents alluded to in the *Processus summarius* represented but one aspect of the debate in progress, the formal legal proceedings before the tribunal and as presented by the participants and their procurators. But the unofficial contributions to the case, some of them in direct defiance of the papal prohibition of 23 January 1358, were at least equally revealing. FitzRalph is recorded as having preached only two more sermons in Avignon between the *Proposicio* of 8 November 1357 in which he launched his case, and his death exactly three years later. On All Saints Day, 1 November 1358, a month after the issue of *Gravem dilectorum* which, even in its final compromise form, must have represented a defeat for the archbishop's case, he was invited to preach once more in the vice-chancellor's chapel. It was expected that Innocent VI would attend, but he was prevented by illness. FitzRalph nevertheless made use of the opportunity for another attack on the friars, in particular their practice of mendicancy.[99] The views on almsgiving which he expressed added further fuel to the flames and met with a fiercely critical response from his mendicant opponents. An indication of FitzRalph's continued influence at the curia is provided by the fact that he soon received another invitation to preach before the pope, which he used in an attempt to clarify the situation. This sermon, preached in Innocent VI's private chapel on the feast of Epiphany 1359,[100] contained the most extreme statement of FitzRalph's views on a problem which had preoccupied him for much of the past twenty years. Now he promised eternal

[98] The bull is printed in *BF* vi. 316–17; Augustus Theiner, *Vetera Monumenta Hibernorum et Scotorum* . . . (Rome, 1864), p. 313; Luigi Torelli, *Secoli Agostiniani* (Bologna, 1659–86), vi. 27–8. The minute is copied in MS Sidney Sussex 64, fol. 126^{r}.

[99] B, fols. 127^{r}–134^{v}; J, fols. 96va–100vb.

[100] B, fols. 241^{r}–246^{v}; J, fols. 173va–177vb. This sermon was included by the compiler of the diary with the anti-mendicant *proposiciones* at the end of the collection.

damnation to all who continued to enjoy their worldly goods in life and hoped to remedy the defect by generous benefactions after death – a practice from which the friars benefited more than any other section of the community, and which they themselves warmly encouraged. The pope's reaction to this line of argument is unknown, but the sermon was itself an indication that the friars had not succeeded in totally discrediting FitzRalph or in depriving him of all his influence at the curia. It can only have increased the embarrassment of the tribunal and made them even more reluctant to reach a decision against him.

During these months at Avignon FitzRalph's pen was busy. He completed the eighth book of *De Pauperie Salvatoris*, in which he set out to clarify his position and counter some of the objections raised against his views, especially on mendicancy. Hence most of the book was devoted to an analysis of the bull *Exiit qui seminat* and its provisions concerning the profession of poverty and the circumstances in which begging was permitted.[101] On the pastoral issue he repeated many of his old arguments, but he can hardly have enhanced his popularity in curial circles when he argued that not merely when the friars acquired property and impugned their profession of poverty did they commit mortal sin and incur sentence of excommunciation, but also when they took salaried appointments as penitentiaries. The superiors who permitted them to do so (and by inference the authority which conferred the appointment) were equally guilty.[102] The argument of his debating partner Iohannes that they were doing all this with papal dispensation and therefore quite legitimately, is rejected, and FitzRalph countered that the papal privilege to preach and hear confession might mitigate the friars' sin but did not eliminate it, as such privileges merely encouraged the friars not to conform to the rule and testament of St. Francis. Even the argument that St. Francis' testament, a subject of controversy in the Franciscan order since the founder's death, was not considered binding by a large body within the order, failed to meet with FitzRalph's approval.[103] On confession he continued to hold to the argument formulated in *Defensio Curatorum* about the nature of De Pouilly's error and about the binding force of the Lateran

[101] Esp. in the second half of the text, Chs. XXI ff., Lat. 3222, fols. 40va–78ra.
[102] Ibid., fol. 21^{ra-vb}.
[103] Ibid., fols. 28ra–29vb.

canon in spite of all subsequent papal legislation, and no new arguments were added to those already to be found in his formal contributions before the tribunal.

During the same period he also published a series of objections and replies, *Quia in proposicione nuper facta*, and the articles on *Vas electionis* which circulated under the title *De audientia confessionum.*[104] It has been demonstrated that this latter work, and not the *Defensio Curatorum*, provoked Conway's *Defensio Mendicantium*, which was composed in 1359.[105] By now interest was concentrated almost exclusively on the interpretation of *Vas electionis* and the disputed doctrine of De Pouilly, and one result of Conway's contribution, which effectively shifted the issues away from poverty and mendicancy and back to the pastoral question, was the re-issue of *Vas electionis* in a bull addressed to Conway on 14 July 1359.[106] In effect this bull was a judgement against FitzRalph, as the central element in his case as outlined in the *Libellus* was the need to replace *Vas electionis* with a new ruling which would eliminate the anomalies of the existing legislation and reaffirm the exclusive rights of the secular clergy to hear confessions in fulfilment of the annual obligation. Furthermore the course of the proceedings demonstrate that this *Libellus*, which concentrated primarily on the pastoral issue, and not the *Defensio Curatorum*, was FitzRalph's official statement of his case before the tribunal.

This concentration on De Pouilly's errors had a further result, in that it enabled FitzRalph's opponents to charge with heresy anybody heard repeating the views of De Pouilly as condemned in *Vas electionis*, and the contributions to the controversy introduced by FitzRalph and in particular by Richard Kilwington indicate that the heresy charge was being taken seriously. Apart from Jacques de Seve and the other unnamed curial advocates employed by FitzRalph, few supporters are recorded as having taken part in his case. The author of the *Scriptum cuiusdam iuvenis*, which survives as part of the collection in

[104] MS Sidney Sussex 64, fols. 89^r–105^v. Both texts had a wide MS circulation.

[105] Lavery, op. cit., pp. 50–1, 60. One of the MSS of Conway's text, Wolfenbüttel, MS Helmst. 311 (formerly in the possession of Flaccius Illyricus) contains, fol. 82rb, an 'explicit' stating that it was preached in consistory in 1359, and the same MS dated to 1360 the reply to FitzRalph by the Dominican, Barthelmy of Bolsenheim, fol. 88ra. This dating, if correct, strengthens the impression that the case continued after the issue of *Gravem dilectorum*, and was only concluded by FitzRalph's death.

[106] MS Sidney Sussex 64, fol. 108^r.

Lat. 3222,[107] was a weak reed upon which to build a defence. His argument that in the state of innocence all goods were held in common and all men were equally rich, was little more than a string of quotations from the Old Testament in favour of wealth and possessions as a mark of divine favour. He repeated the views of Augustine on manual labour for monks and concluded with a brief discussion of the 'sophisticatio mendicantium et detecṣtio ypocrisie eorum'.[108] Cardinal Nicholas de Bessia composed a *Libellus* on *Vas electionis* in support of FitzRalph's position, of which no copy appears to have survived. Its existence is known only from a single reference in eight articles directed against Conway's *Defensio Mendicantium.*[109] Although the rubric in the single surviving text of these articles described them as 'Replicaciones Ricardi archiepiscopi Armachani . . . contra opusculum ffratris Rogeri Conewey',[110] the author of the text occasionally referred to 'meus Armachanus', and it is in fact a compilation of arguments drawn from FitzRalph's works but put together by another hand, who supported the views expressed. In the circumstances the most likely author is Kilwington. The writer explained his involvement as a result of a promise made to FitzRalph in London, and referred to his own treatise on *Vas electionis*, which he had presented to the tribunal.[111] Kilwington used the term 'meus Armachanus' on at least one other occasion, and he has been tentatively identified as the first anti-mendicant spokesman to reply to Conway after the latter had transferred from Worcester to London in the spring of 1355.[112] But at this stage, which must have been towards the end of the proceedings, it is difficult to avoid the impression that the argument had exhausted itself, and Kilwington – if indeed he was the author – limited himself to picking at technicalities and correcting minor points of detail in the friars' argument. It is also possible that he was never as deeply committed to the cause as FitzRalph, and

[107] Lat. 3222, fols. 103va–111rb.
[108] Ibid., fol. 108vb.
[109] Ibid., fol. 160^{rb-va}.
[110] Ibid., fols. 159ra–194va.
[111] Ibid., fols. 159rb, 160rb. The only plausible explanation for the composition of this text is that Kilwington put FitzRalph's arguments against Conway together, frequently citing the archbishop's own words in the first person. A similar composite text, made up of FitzRalph's anti-mendicant arguments and subsequently ascribed to him, is contained in MS Bodl. 784, fols. 86va–108ra.
[112] *DNB* xi. 353; Wood, *History and Antiquities of the University of Oxford*, ed. Gutch, i. 475.

simply continued to provide support because he had promised to do so.[113]

Wood cited three works by Kilwington in support of FitzRalph's cause, and Kingsford assumed that none of them survived. However, two of them can be identified among the collection in Lat. 3222,[114] and the third – described by Wood as *Contra mendicitatem otiosam*[115] – is unlikely to be identical with the treatise on *Vas electionis*. Neither of these last-named works has been identified in any collection of anti-mendicant material. The second work mentioned by Wood as *Contra Rogerum Conway* is identical with 'In causa domini Ardmacani Allegaciones magistri Ricardi (i.e. Kilwington) devoti vestri contra fratres'.[116] These were a capable defence of FitzRalph's fitness to prosecute the case and were concerned primarily with procedural technicalities rather than with the actual subject-matter of the case.[117] He argued that FitzRalph was a fit person to conduct the case, and that the pope had formally heard his proposition in consistory and admitted his petition. Furthermore, FitzRalph was acting only in the public interest, to prevent abuses and therefore to save souls. The nature of his 'actio' was that of a 'popularis actio', not an attempt to secure a personal favour.[118] Then Kilwington explained FitzRalph's action in terms of the Good Samaritan. FitzRalph had fallen among thieves, who deprived him of his rightful tithes and offerings, slandered him, and left him half dead. The thieves were of course the friars, and the Good Samaritan or agent of consolation should be the assembled cardinals in consistory who had power to provide a just remedy for the situation.[119] Kilwington made no attempt to deny the friars' charge that FitzRalph had taken the matter to Avignon on his own authority, without the support of his brother-bishops. Nor had he consulted his own cathedral chapter in Armagh, a chapter

[113] He stated as much in one of his contributions to the case: 'Sic puto quod ego fidelis inveniar in eo quod sibi promisi Londoniis . . .', Lat. 3222, fol. 159rb.

[114] Kingsford in *DNB* xi. 353.

[115] Wood, ed. cit., i. 475.

[116] Lat. 3222, fols. 111va–116rb.

[117] He prefaced his remarks with the statement that the *Allegaciones* already contributed to the main topic of the case, fol. 111va. His main concern was to show 'quod dominus Archiepiscopus Armachanus sit persona habilis et sufficiens ad prosequendum causam contra fratres deductam in libello suo super statu universalis ecclesie sine consensu capituli sui et absque scientia seu auctoritate aliorum prelatorum seu inferiorum suaditur per raciones subscriptas', ibid.

[118] Ibid., fols. 111vb–112ra.

[119] Ibid., fol. 113^{ra-va}.

which he seems to have treated in an even more cavalier fashion than that of Lichfield some twenty years earlier. Kilwington further implied that FitzRalph's case was faring very badly, with no possibility of recouping the heavy expenditure involved.

From this contribution it is also clear that the friars considered FitzRalph a heretic and excommunicate, 'ex tamquam talis repellendus ab agendo'. Kilwington rejected the argument that FitzRalph was therefore barred from conducting his case: he was not a heretic in the canonical sense, having constantly protested his willingness to submit all his views to the correction of the Holy See.[120] But the heresy charge was obviously taken seriously, as FitzRalph's ally felt compelled to cite canonist opinion, including that of Hostiensis, to show why the archbishop was not canonically a heretic, and also to distinguish various kinds of heresy and prove that a heretic need not necessarily be excommunicate. When dealing with this and other objections, concerning the formal aspects of FitzRalph's *Libellus*, Kilwington showed himself the better canonist of the two, citing a range of glossators in defence of FitzRalph's statement, before going on to demonstrate a number of technical defects in the *Libellus* of the friars and to raise procedural objections regarding their conduct of the case.[121] Kilwington's case must have been further strengthened by developing differences among the friars' procurators. Whereas the Franciscans and Dominicans held together, the Carmelites developed one variation and the Augustinians yet another. Their rhetoric got out of hand and the representatives of the four orders ceased to present a united front – at least from Kilwington's point of view – and he seized upon these inconsistencies as reasons for rejecting their charge that FitzRalph was a heretic.

But independent evidence shows that the heresy charge was taken seriously. Another, unnamed adherent must have been a dubious asset to the archbishop's cause. He was allegedly the propagator of some bizarre views, and charges of heresy brought against him by Roger Conway were heard in the summer of 1358. An instrument of 23 July 1358 (specifically) indemnified FitzRalph against legal action in connection with this heresy

[120] Lat. 3222, fols. 113vb–114rb. He pointed out, reasonably enough, that everything that FitzRalph had to say about the friars had been said in the presence of the pope, who had raised no objection to his continuing with the case.

[121] Ibid., fols. 114va–115va.

trial, and if the curious piece of doggerel appended to the instrument in the Sidney Sussex manuscript was supposed to represent the substance of these heretical propositions, their absurdity makes it impossible that they should be associated with a theologian of FitzRalph's calibre.[122]

Although FitzRalph was protected from charges of heresy, all the evidence indicates that he was losing ground at the curia and that he had little reason to expect further episcopal support, from England or elsewhere. The contest between the friars and the secular clergy was widespread, but the reluctance of powerful interests to commit themselves to FitzRalph's extreme position of total condemnation of the mendicant orders lent the dispute a local and personal character when it finally reached the papal court. Many prelates affected by the dispute over the friars' activities took steps within their own dioceses and in accordance with the available canonical machinery to regulate those activities, thus enabling them to continue to profit from participation in the pastoral field by religious whose level of education and commitment was usually higher than that of the average parish curate.

Surviving manuscripts of the literature generated by the controversy indicate more interest in the German lands than in Latin countries, but no German, Austrian, or Bohemian allies are known to have come forward in support of FitzRalph. The only evidence for contemporary preoccupation with the mendicant controversies in the Bohemian lands points in a different direction. FitzRalph's heated and insulting letter from Avignon to the Franciscan bishop of Bisignano, Giovanni Marignola, while the latter was in attendance at the court of Charles IV in Prague, revealed that the Franciscans had sought him out as a suitable champion in their case against the archbishop of Armagh.[123] Bishop Giovanni had declared his intention to come

[122] MS Sidney Sussex 64, fol. 108^{v}; MS Lambeth 1208, fols. 100^{v}–101^{v}. Only the former contains these 'theses': 'Tenor autem dictorum Armachanorum talis est videlicet; Verbum divinum non aliter est in natura assumpta quam in lapido, Deus non est aliter in sacramento altaris quam in buffone, Qualiter tamquam pater non divinus distinguitur a filio distinguitur a divina essencia, Non aliter distinguitur pater in divinis a filio quam essencia distinguitur ab utroque'. Although this ditty implied several adherents, only one faced charges and his identity remains a puzzle. The author of the *Scriptum cuiusdam iuvenis*, Lat. 3222, fols. 103va–111rb, seems an unlikely candidate, as this treatise reveals his views as fairly conventional argument against the friars.

[123] Ed. Dobner, *Monumenta Hist. Bohemia*, ii. 73–4.

to his confrères' defence, to visit Avignon in person, and take up the matter with the enemy of his order. Having heard of his intentions, doubtless from Franciscan circles at the curia who would scarcely have concealed the proposed intervention of an episcopal supporter on their side, FitzRalph wrote to Bishop Giovanni in Prague, warning him that it would be unwise for the Franciscan, now an old man, to enter the field against a more distinguished adversary, himself. He indulged in a display of bravura by reminding the Franciscan that thirty years earlier he had dealt successfully with more distinguished minds, such as Ockham and Burely. Marignola might have been able to pose at the imperial court as the apostle of the orient, who had visited India and China, but FitzRalph maintained that such claims to fame would be of no use to him in the present circumstances.[124] The letter must have been written *c.* 1358, but there is no indication that Marignola had taken any active part in the controversy before his own death, which took place shortly after, as on 22 March 1359 Innocent VI appointed a successor to the see of Bisignano in place of the recently deceased prelate.[125]

Equally little assistance was forthcoming for FitzRalph from England, and the statements of John of Reading and Thomas Walsingham, both members of the 'possessionati' and no friends of the friars, that FitzRalph lost his case through lack of funds, are at least partly substantiated by Richard Kilwington.[126] Although Henry Knighton maintained that FitzRalph did have a 'subsidium de clero', that he had travelled to Avignon with a number of clerical supporters, and that the abbot of St. Alban's acted as his procurator,[127] there is no other evidence for this, and the presence of such a powerful supporter would scarcely have escaped the notice of the compiler of the *Processus summarius*, and of Kilwington, much less the notice of Walsingham, himself a monk of St. Alban's. There are also indications that Edward III may have supported the friars against the obstreperous archbishop of Armagh. On 26 March 1358 royal protection

[124] Ed. Dobner, *Monumenta Hist. Bohemia*, ii. 73–4.

[125] Eubel, *Hierarchia Catholica*, i^2. 136.

[126] John of Reading, *Cronica*, ed. Tait, p. 131; Thomas Walsingham, *Historia Anglicana*, ed. Riley, i. 285. According to the latter, FitzRalph was able to sustain his opinions at the curia in the initial stages, but then the promised subsidy from the English clergy did not come while the friars spent vast sums in order to preserve their privileges.

[127] *Chronicon Henrici Knighton*, ed. Lumby, ii. 93–4.

was extended to William Jordan, then Dominican prior of York, travelling abroad in the king's service, while on 3 October that protection was extended until summer 1359 as Jordan remained abroad on the same business.[128] Jordan had arrived in Avignon as part of the delegation of English friars within weeks of the first royal letter and it is possible that he was sent to the curia because of royal interest in the friars' case, and that he was ordered to remain at his post until the case was concluded.

However, the net result of the inquiry was a reaffirmation of the status quo. It can be inferred that the proceedings continued until FitzRalph's death in November 1360, as the Alsatian Dominican, Barthelmy of Bolsenheim, preached his refutation of the archbishop's case in full consistory earlier in the same year.[129] and as there is no evidence for a further papal decision beyond the interim solution contained in *Gravem dilectorum* on 1 October 1358. But FitzRalph was fighting a hopeless case, and the standpoint from which he chose to fight it was ill conceived. Even apart from the fact that it required an expertise in canon law which he did not possess, most canonist opinion was in favour of *Super Cathedram* and *Vas electionis*, and of the manner in which these had operated during the first half of the fourteenth century. Therefore, with the canonical position essentially in favour of the friars, these could be faulted – as could many of the bishops[130] – for violations of the canonical procedures which governed their activities, but FitzRalph was on dangerous ground when he advocated the reversal of a considerable body of papal legislation in order to have the friars' privileges eliminated entirely. The tribunal attempted to be fair to both sides and, while it was reluctant to see a prelate of FitzRalph's standing totally discredited, his uncompromising attitude must have been the cause of embarrassment.

There is no evidence that Innocent VI was ill disposed towards FitzRalph. On the contrary there is reason to believe that he attempted to find a peaceful solution to the Irish primatial dispute at the beginning of his pontificate, and FitzRalph was clearly permitted to use the primatial title in all the documents submitted to the tribunal.[131] Innocent VI had

[128] CPR 1358-61, 27, 101. [129] Above, n. 105.

[130] See Williams, art. cit., for the negligence of many English bishops, who failed to make use of the available legislation for the control of mendicant pastoral activity.

[131] See esp. the documents transcribed in MS Sidney Sussex 64, fols. 108-128,

furthermore been willing to provide FitzRalph with a prestigious platform as late as 6 January 1359. He also granted a number of the archbishop's petitions for additional benefices for members of his household, whose composition had clearly changed since his departure from Ireland in the summer of 1356. During his first ten years as archbishop of Armagh he had surrounded himself with Anglo-Irish clerics, members of families resident within the dioceses of Armagh and Meath, some of them linked to him by ties of blood and kinship. While the legal battle was at its height in the early autumn of 1358 he secured on 14 August a benefice in the diocese of York for Peter Stapleton of the diocese of Durham, and on 5 September another in the diocese of St. Andrews for John Kenan Meri, both of whom are described in the papal registers as his clerks.[132] Is the changed complexion of his episcopal family to be explained in terms of their allegiance to his anti-mendicant campaign? Were Kenan Meri and Stapleton to be numbered among the 'pluribus aliis clericis' who, according to Knighton, went to his assistance?

The other members of his following who figure in the last references to him in the papal registers are less surprising. On 5 September 1359 John Galtrim, a medical doctor and a cleric of the Meath diocese, was to receive a canonry in St. Patrick's, Dublin, despite the fact that he already held benefices in Meath and Ferns,[133] while in the final reference to FitzRalph as still living he secured on 10 September 1360 for his kinsman Walter Douedall the right of succession to the canonry and prebend vacated by the recently deceased John Galtrim.[134] On this occasion FitzRalph's petition included an additional piece of information. Douedall was actually present with him in Avignon in September 1360. Was this an indication that FitzRalph's health was already failing, and that he had summoned his relative to help him wind up his affairs, at the same time gaining for him the financial security of an additional benefice while there was still time? No evidence of a university degree or other

where FitzRalph's primatial title is included even in the text of documents which were of an official nature, and whose originals must have passed the scrutiny of curial officials.

[132] *Reg. Suppl.* 31, fols. 241^{r}, 266^{r}, *CPL Petitions*, 334, 332 (fol. 241^{r} is bound out of order in the register).

[133] *Reg. Suppl.* 32, fol. 175^{r}, *CPL Petitions*, 347.

[134] *Reg. Suppl.* 33, fol. 252^{v}, *CPL Petitions*, 359.

theological training is adduced in support of the petition for Douedall's benefice, and there is no reason to believe that he would have taken an active part in the mendicant controversy. Nor, apparently, did he attempt to have the archbishop's remains brought back to Ireland immediately after his death, and it is possible that the eventual decision to do so was based upon FitzRalph's posthumous reputation among his former flock in the Anglo-Irish Pale.

A notable feature of this final group of petitions which FitzRalph submitted in the papal curia was the lack of any relating to the affairs of his diocese — in marked contrast to his previous lengthy visit to Avignon after becoming archbishop. Apart from the negotiations involving the alien priories within his province, the papal records feature nothing of interest for the diocese since the petition of 31 May 1355, when FitzRalph sought and secured four additional notaries to carry out the legal and administrative work of his diocese.[135] Was this perhaps an indication of lack of interest in Irish diocesan affairs during the final years of his life, when the campaign against the friars seems to have become his all-consuming passion, or a realization that he was never likely to return, that his work as archbishop of Armagh was at an end, even if not completed? The attitude of Innocent VI towards his personal petitions and towards his case would not suggest that papal opposition was the reason for the virtual eclipse of his diocese and its affairs from the records.

However, no signs of papal favour could obliterate the fact that FitzRalph's cause represented an implied challenge to papal powers of dispensation, and in such circumstances a pope had no option but to uphold the status quo. Despite FitzRalph's disclaimer that they had no divinely ordained place in the hierarchical order, the mendicant friars had become a powerful element in the ecclesiastical establishment. FitzRalph might with some justice argue that such a position of influence was — at least for the Franciscans — a departure from their original ideal, and therefore a vindication of his own viewpoint. But without a solid body of episcopal support behind him, which was conspicuously lacking, his chances of success were minimal, and his case — but not the controversy — died with him. A striking feature of the end of FitzRalph's life is that we know

[135] *Reg. Suppl.* 28, fol. 96^{v}, *CPL Petitions*, 287.

virtually nothing about the manner or the circumstances of his death – in sharp contrast to the wealth of documentation concerning his lengthy and colourful career. Even the date has been the subject of some uncertainty, as those sources which record the death of the Irish primate are all slightly later in date than the actual event, and none of these are of an official nature. Similarly, we know nothing about the obsequies, which presumably took place in the papal curia, as the translation of his remains to Ireland did not take place for at least another ten years, but information about where he found a temporary grave in Avignon, or who might have officiated at his obsequies, whether they took place under a cloud of papal or curial disfavour, is simply not available.

His death in November 1360, followed within a year by that of Roger Conway, Richard Kilwington, and two members of the tribunal, meant that the case was deprived of its principal participants and the issue was temporarily allowed to subside, though it continued to trouble the universities of Paris (during the 1360s) and Oxford (a decade later under Wyclif). Both Conway and Kilwington are recorded as having been buried in London,[136] and this would indicate that their presence in Avignon was no longer required after the death of FitzRalph. Few were prepared to share his obsession with the problem of the mendicant orders. His pursuit of the friars evolved from his interpretation of what constituted the Church's best interests, but finally became an end in itself. Taking the long view, his total obsession during the last four years of his life with the friars, and with the related problems of dominion, poverty, and pastoral privileges, has led historians to distort the perspective, to view this episode as the guiding principle of his life and its exponent as the precursor of John Wyclif. The proliferation of his anti-mendicant writings, whose propagandist purposes ensured them a wider circulation than his pastoral sermons, and in circles such as secular cathedral chapters and monastic communities of the 'possessionati' – all of whose libraries had a rate of survival far above the average for medieval books – further encouraged undue emphasis on this aspect of his career. At the same time the fight against the friars was easier to document than the work of a prelate in a remote area of fourteenth-century Europe whose episcopal register has not survived. In

[136] Respectively *BRUO* I, 459, and II, 1051.

the short term his image was distorted by the legacy, real and imagined, which he left to Wyclif and the Lollards, especially in the development of Wyclif's doctrine of dominion and in the exegetical approach of the Lollard Bible, and by the wave of mendicant polemic which could now point to the 'Armachanus' as the fountain-head from which all Wycliffite heresy flowed.

Epilogue

Lollard saint and the cult of 'St. Richard of Dundalk'

After FitzRalph's death in Avignon Innocent VI did not make any attempt to fill the see again as speedily as had been the case following the death of O'Hiraghty, when Clement VI had immediately provided the capitular nominee. FitzRalph had died at the curia, and from the papal point of view there could be no doubt about the legal position of his see. It was reserved to the pope, and such property as the archbishop possessed personally, which after the crippling expenditure of three years of legal action cannot have amounted to much apart from books, papers, and diocesan records, would automatically revert to the papal treasury.[1] As there is no contemporary evidence for Raphael of Volterra's claim that FitzRalph had been created cardinal, the question of papal permission to make a will for the disposal of his property did not arise.[2] Hence it is possible that, with the approval of family interests as represented in Avignon by Walter Douedall, the care of his unpublished papers was entrusted to a literary executor, and in view of the exclusively English circulation of the complete sermon diary, Richard Kilwington is the most likely candidate for this office. The disappearance of FitzRalph's episcopal register, which he is most likely to have had in his possession in London and Avignon during the last years of his life, can also be easily explained by the lack of interest of an English executor, such as Kilwington, in the diocesan affairs of Armagh.

Eventually on 29 October 1361 Innocent provided the former dean of Ossory, Milo Sweteman, who had been elected by the chapter of that see upon the death of the controversial Franciscan bishop, Richard Ledred, but had seen the election quashed by the pope in favour of the English Dominican and participant

[1] For the papal right to the 'spoils' of such prelates, esp. the regulations of John XXII and Benedict XII, see Hans E. Feine, *Kirchliche Rechtsgeschichte: die katholische Kirche* (Cologne-Graz[5], 1972), p. 349.

[2] *Commentariorum Urbanorum Raphaelis Volaterrani*, Bks. 3 and 21 (Basel, 1544). Ware, *De Praesulibus Hiberniae*, p. 21 also knew of this claim and rejected it.

in the case against FitzRalph, John Tatenhall.[3] Meanwhile during the interregnum the see of Armagh was administered by the legal expert and Gaelic canon of the chapter, Isaac O'Culean, who acted as commissary on behalf of the dean and chapter and who had presumably administered the diocese, or at least the Gaelic portions of it, while FitzRalph was out of the country from 1356 to 1360. We know of his activities in this capacity only from an entry in Sweteman's register, the record of a series of *Acta* dating from April 1361 when O'Culean conducted an inquiry into the rights of the prior of the Hospitallers in Ireland to present Sir Thomas Waleys, a cleric of the diocese of Armagh, to the vicarage of Carlingford.[4] A further link with the past and pointer towards the future, was provided by an entry in the papal registers of petitions for 27 August 1361. John Colton, who would eventually succeed Sweteman in the Irish primacy and who had been master of Gonville Hall in Cambridge from its initial endowment until 1360,[5] successfully petitioned for the treasurership of the diocese of Dublin.[6] In the petition he described himself as chamberlain of the late archbishop of Armagh, a designation which may either suggest that he held the position as an absentee benefice – but which seems unlikely from the general tenor of the petition – or that the recently deceased archbishop had more connection with Cambridge than might otherwise have been expected.

After FitzRalph's death interest in him continued, initially under two forms: the collection of his sermons and some of his anti-mendicant writings with a view to wider circulation, in England and elsewhere, and the propagation of his cult in his own native area of Counties Louth and Meath. Before long, as we shall see, a further dimension with more significant implications developed, as the archbishop came to be regarded as the father of Wyclifism and the godparent of Lollardy. With regard to the first of these aspects, the circulation of FitzRalph's literary output, it is possible that both of his relatives, Walter Douedall and Richard FitzRalph junior, were present at the curia when the archbishop died, but the most likely person actually to have undertaken the task of preparing the sermons for 'publication' was unquestionably Kilwington. He had been associated with

[3] *HBC*², p. 308. For Sweteman and Tatenhall see *BRUO* III, 2220, 2221 respectively.
[4] *Cal. Reg. Sweteman*, 219–20. [5] *BRUC*, 150–1.
[6] *Reg. Suppl.* 35, fol. 181ᵛ; *CPL Petitions*, 375.

FitzRalph for many years, he possessed the necessary intellectual qualifications for such a task, his sense of personal loyalty and commitment to the archbishop's cause had been amply demonstrated by the events of the previous three years, and he is known to have returned to England, where he died and was buried in his cathedral of St. Paul's by March 1362.[7] On the other hand, although it has been suggested that FitzRalph's nephew may have been responsible for propagating the cult of St. Patrick's Purgatory, and possibly also FitzRalph's primatial claims, while in Avignon as procurator for Armagh and other Irish dioceses, there is no evidence that he took any active part in his uncle's legal battle at the curia, or even that he was still alive in 1360. Similarly in the case of Douedall there is nothing to indicate that he might have been actively involved in the endeavour to preserve his kinsman's sermons for posterity, nor even that he had any academic or university training – the petition for his benefice did not claim him as a student or graduate of any kind. But it is possible that he may have supported and encouraged such a project, especially as it must have been known – to him, to Kilwington, and to others – that FitzRalph was in the process of revising his sermons with a view to publishing at least the formal ones preached in Avignon, about the informal entries for English and Irish sermons contained in the diary.

Nevertheless, it appears to have been more than coincidence that FitzRalph and his relatives had close connections with the Church in the diocese of Meath, that a bishop of Meath eventually gave the necessary impetus to launch the cult of 'St. Richard of Dundalk', and that its greatest area of impact outside FitzRalph's native town of Dundalk was the diocese of Meath. Ten days before the archbishop's death in Avignon, Innocent provided on 6 November 1360 the dean of Limerick, Stephen Wall (de Valle), to be bishop of that see in succession to Stephen Lawless (+ 28 December 1359).[8] Wall, an alumnus of Oxford University and of sufficient standing in the Anglo-Irish lordship to be entrusted with the office of treasurer of Ireland for a brief period March to June 1368, was translated to Meath on 19 February 1369.[9] As bishop of Meath, Wall is recorded as having been responsible for the return of FitzRalph's remains to Dundalk, where he was re-interred in the church of St. Nicholas and where his tomb survived into the mid-seventeenth

[7] *BRUO* II, 1051. [8] *HBC*^{2}, p. 330. [9] *BRUO* III, 1966.

century.[10] The chronicler of St. Mary's Abbey, who is the earliest source for the return of the remains and of Wall's involvement, gave no date for the event, but it must have been between his translation to Meath and his death in Oxford on 10 November 1379.[11] Ware repeated the same version without citing a source, and dated the return to 'about the year 1370', and it is possible that Wall visited Avignon on the occasion of his translation from Limerick to Meath and brought back the deceased primate's remains in or soon after 1370.[12]

The English Benedictine chronicler, Thomas Walsingham, whose sympathy for FitzRalph in the struggles against the friars has already been noted, provided the earliest indications that FitzRalph's new tomb was becoming a place of devotion and pilgrimage. The first signs of the cult of 'St. Richard of Dundalk', which was to survive in the 'English' part of his diocese and in Meath until the Reformation, were beginning to emerge. Under the year 1360 Walsingham recorded FitzRalph's death, but dated to the feast of St. Edmund the Confessor (20 November), and reported the transfer soon after of the remains to his birthplace, Dundalk, 'in which place countless miracles are wrought to God's praise'. The second entry, for 1377, added: 'About this time God, declaring the justice which Master FitzRaffe had shown on earth whilst he lived . . . works daily many miracles through the merits of the said Richard of Dundalk: whereby, as it is said, the friars are ill pleased.'[13] Walsingham doubtless had a double purpose when he inserted this entry into his chronicle. He could embarrass the friars as well as record the posthumous glory of the archbishop who had devoted the last years of his life to opposing them. His sentiments resemble very closely those of contemporary political satirists, who frequently made the friars their target and sought protection against them through 'the Armachan, whom the Lord hath crowned in heaven'.[14]

The date of the second entry suggests that the alleged miracles at the tomb of 'St. Richard' began soon after the translation of his remains. This date fits well with the evidence that Urban VI, soon after his accession to the papal throne in April 1378, set up a commission to inquire into the life and miracles, fame, and

[10] *Chartularies of St Mary's Abbey Dublin*, i. 393.

[11] *HBC*², p. 320.

[12] Ware, *De Praesulibus Hiberniae*, pp. 20–1; idem, *De Scriptoribus Hiberniae* (Dublin, 1639), i, 69–72.

[13] Walsingham, *Chronicon Angliae* (ed. RS), pp. 48,400; also *DNB* vii. 197.

[14] Wright, *Political Poems*, i. 259; cited in Erikson, *FS* 36, 118.

reputation of FitzRalph. Clearly the first moves had been made in an attempt to secure his canonization, and the pope's action was a response to petitions, which in their turn were presumably based upon the archbishop's reputation for sanctity in his native area and on the numerous miracles alleged to be a result of his intercession. One member of this commission was Cardinal Perrino Tomacelli,[15] who on 9 November 1389 was elected pope as Boniface IX. He had been one of the more enthusiastic proponents of FitzRalph's cause and two days after his accession he ordered Archbishop John Colton, together with the bishops of Meath and Limerick, Alexander Petit de Balscot and Peter Curragh,[16] to conduct another inquiry 'super vitae sanctitate et miraculis bonae memoriae Ricardi archiepiscopi Armachani'.[17] The sees of Limerick and Meath had been connected with Stephen Wall during his lifetime, and the choice of these bishops may have been connected in some way with the efforts made twenty years earlier by Bishop Wall to promote the archbishop's cult. One can only speculate on the reasons for papal interest in the cause of a man whose reputation was being seriously challenged, not only by the friars because of his attitude towards themselves, but also as the intellectual parent of some of Wyclif's more questionable tenets, at a time when these had been brought to the attention of curial theologians by Adam Easton.[18]

On the other hand FitzRalph had by the late 1370s become a venerable figure in the Anglo-Irish Church, and in the uncertain months and years following the outbreak of the schism in the papacy, when Irish allegiance to Rome in deference to English political wishes could not be taken for granted, it might have been considered prudent to heed the wishes of Anglo-Irish Church leaders. However such a solution explains only Urban's initial action. By the accession of Boniface IX the situation, not merely in the Church within the Anglo-Irish lordship but in

[15] See Arnold Esch, in *Dizionario biografico degli Italiani*, 12 (Rome, 1970), 170–83. He had been created cardinal in 1381, at the same consistory as the English Benedictine, Adam Easton, who was engaged in the campaign against Wyclif at the curia, Eubel, *Hierarchia Catholica*, i^2. 24.

[16] Alexander Petit was bishop of Meath 1386–1400, while Curragh succeeded Wall in Limerick in 1369 and held the see for thirty years, *HBC*^{2}, pp. 320, 330.

[17] The only record of this inquiry is ASV, Indice 320, fol. 42^r.

[18] For Adam Easton see Knowles, *Religious Orders*, ii. 56–8; *BRUO* I, 620–1; William A. Pantin, 'The *Defensorium* of Adam Easton', *EHR* 51 (1936), 675–80; Leslie J. McFarlane, 'The Life and Writings of Adam Easton, O.S.B.', 2 vols. (unpublished Ph.D. thesis, University of London, 1955).

most of Gaelic Ireland as well, had become clear and a concession of this nature would be superfluous. Even more so was the case ten years later, when on 28 January 1399 Boniface IX – who, it may be recalled, had a copy of the *Summa de Questionibus Armenorum* made for him at Perugia in 1393 – responded to a further initiative from Armagh. Primate Colton and his fellow investigators had completed their inquiry, and they petitioned that a similar examination of the case be undertaken in England, because of FitzRalph's long associations with London, Lichfield, and Oxford. As a result, a further commission was issued to Colton, to the bishop-elect of Bangor, and the abbot of Oseney, to examine reports of miracles which were alleged to have taken place in England.[19] There was a certain irony in such an investigation being ordered at a time when the candidate in question was being claimed as a Lollard saint,[20] but there is no indication that the papal inquiry concealed any ulterior motives. It was a routine procedure in response to reports from Ireland which were apparently made in good faith. At this point however the trail of evidence in the process of canonization stops, probably because of unfavourable replies from England. Richard Young, who had been archdeacon of Meath before his elevation to the see of Bangor, was an Oxford man and a frequent visitor to the curia during the 1390s.[21] He was well placed to know that by now the wealth of evidence against FitzRalph was regarded by his old university as overwhelming. Oxford theologians, and in particular the mendicant masters whose numerical strength in the faculty of theology was still undiminished, were not slow to point to the connection between Wyclif's teaching and that of the 'Armachanus', and at the same time Lollard sources continued to emphasize their debt to 'sanctus Ricardus'. Most strikingly the author of the Lollard prologue to the second recension of the English Bible, tentatively identified by modern scholars as John Purvey, appealed to the authority of 'Armachanus' in

[19] *Reg. Lat.* 69, fols. 181^v–183^r; *CPL* 1396–1404, 245.

[20] From *c.* 1376 Wyclif frequently referred to FitzRalph as 'sanctus Richardus', or 'sanctus Armachanus', see *De Civili Dominio*, iii, ed. cit., *passim, De blasphemia*, ed. cit., p. 232. Nicholas of Hereford also referred to him as 'sanctus Ricardus' in his Ascension Day sermon, 1382, MS Bodl. 240, fol. 848^v, and cited in Hudson, 'A neglected Wycliffite text', 263 n. The Wycliffite author of the *Opus arduum*, a commentary on the Apocalypse, also did so, Hudson, 265, as did the satirical poets cited by Erikson, *FS* 35–6, *passim.*

[21] *BRUO* III, 2137–8. He acted as papal chaplain and auditor of causes in the papal palace, 1397–9.

support of his understanding of Scripture,[22] and a recent study has shown the extent of Lollard dependence, not merely on the exegetical methods of Nicholas of Lyra, but also on the views of FitzRalph as expounded in his dialogue with Iohannes in the early books of the *Summa de Questionibus Armenorum.*[23] We have already seen that FitzRalph's dependence on Scripture went beyond the immediate need to find common ground with his Armenian debating partners, and that he stressed the literal sense of Scripture as a powerful method of right reasoning – an aspect of his thinking which might have attracted Wyclif's attention to him in the first place.

Under these circumstances, it would have been virtually impossible for the archbishop's canonization cause to have prospered. Unfortunately no record of the proceedings has survived, though it was still extant in the early seventeenth century when it was discovered in the Vatican by Luke Wadding and was the subject of correspondence between himself, Archbishop Ussher, and Bishop David Rothe of Ossory, all of whom were interested in FitzRalph but for different reasons. The silent demise of the canonization process was therefore due to a combination of factors. The mendicant orders would have put the entire weight of their influence into the attempt to block such a move, which would have conferred the official recognition of sanctity upon the most dangerous adversary they had encountered for over a century. The extent to which anti-mendicant polemic was identified with the name of FitzRalph in the years immediately after his death is illustrated by the testimony of the Czech scholar, Adalbert Rankonis de Ericinio.[24] As master of arts and former rector of the University of Paris he had come to Oxford, where he must have made contact with FitzRalph personally during the academic year 1356-7, as he became the possessor of the earliest extant manuscript of the original seven books of *De Pauperie Salvatoris*, a manuscript whose extensive annotations and corrections suggest that these may even have been the work of FitzRalph himself.[25] As might be expected from one who

[22] Josiah Forshall and Frederick Madden (eds.), *The Holy Bible: made from the Latin vulgate by John Wycliffe and his followers* (Oxford, 1850), p. 48.

[23] Minnis, ' "Authorial intention" and "literal sense" in the exegetical theories of Richard FitzRalph and John Wyclif', 1-30.

[24] Vojtěch Raňkuv von Ježov, *BRUO* III, 1547; Jaroslav Kadlec, *Leben und Schriften des Prager Magisters Adalbert Rankonis de Ericinio* (Münster, 1971).

[25] For this MS, now CVP 1430, see Walsh, 'The Manuscripts of Archbishop Richard FitzRalph', 67-71.

took a copy of FitzRalph's dialogue with him to his native Bohemia, Adalbert Rankonis was no friend of the friars, and at the University of Paris in the early 1360s when he returned to the study of theology and lectured on the Sentences, his opposition to the friars in the university was well known. The possibility that his support for FitzRalph's views might have been the subject of disputations is suggested by a letter which he wrote to the Augustinian canon, Konrad Waldhauser, on 10 December 1365, shortly before Adalbert's return to Prague. He spoke of his reputation in the university 'quod Parisius publice dicitur et quasi super certa per mendicantes predicatur, quod ego sum secundus Armachanus'.[26] His tone implied that the friars studying and teaching in Paris could have paid the Bohemian 'baccalarius sententiarius' no finer compliment. Furthermore, the debates in the Caroline University in Prague during the years following 1369–70, and especially the doubtful propositions put forward by Heinrich Totting von Oyta while still a student of theology, concerning the powers of the sinful priest,[27] suggest that pre-Hussite reforming circles in the Bohemian capital did not have to wait for Wyclif. The generally accepted chronology of the reception of Wyclif's theological and philosophical works in Prague and the identification of the channels through which they were received may need some modification,[28] but long before such a transmission was possible FitzRalph's dialogue was known in Prague and its implications and the arguments of others who thought along similar lines were open to discussion.

Wyclif's debt to FitzRalph was never in doubt. He acknowledged the authority of 'Armachanus' on a variety of topics, citing him with approval on grace, sin, lordship, and property, on poverty and the religious life, on the rights and duties of prelates with regard to the property of the poor, though he frequently criticized him in arguments concerning free will, divine volition, and God's foreknowledge. His Lollard sympathizers and mendicant opponents were agreed on this debt, and historians since R. L. Poole have accepted that Wyclif's doctrine of

[26] Ed. in Kadlec, p. 337. [27] Ibid., pp. 14–19.

[28] i.e. that whereas Wyclif's philosophical writings became known in Prague by the 1390s when the presence of a Bohemian princess in England as consort of Richard II increased intellectual as well as diplomatic contact between the two countries, the theological works only became known there during the first decade of the 15th century, and largely thanks to the labour of two Czech scholars who came to work in England, Mikuláš Faulfiš and Jiří Kněhnic, respectively *BRUO* II, 670–1, 1059.

dominion was essentially that of FitzRalph, though the latter applied it more cautiously and in the context of his own, not Wyclif's vision of the Church. Historians have differed as regards the ultimate importance in Wyclif's system, and above all in his concept of the Church, of the teaching he took over from FitzRalph, but not as regards its origin.

Even more complex are the varying interpretations of the strands of continuity which may be deemed to lead from Wyclif through Hus and the Bohemian reformers to the doctrine of the elect expounded by John Calvin some two centuries later, strands which were substantial enough to attract the disapproving attention of a staunch supporter of the Tridentine settlement such as Cardinal Robert Bellarmine.[29] In spite of the unfavourable attention which resulted from Lollard enthusiasm, FitzRalph's work continued to attract interest, and the unusually wide manuscript circulation throughout Europe is a clear indication that he was remembered not simply for his opposition to the friars, nor only in circles which might welcome ready-made arguments against the mendicant orders, powerfully and convincingly formulated. The friars themselves continued to interest themselves in FitzRalph's other work, and a fair proportion of the extant manuscripts of his *Commentary on the Sentences* and of the *Summa de Questionibus Armenorum* originated in mendicant houses. The limited circulation of the *Commentary on the Sentences* may have been a genuine reflection of its lack of originality and appeal, but the remarkably large number of surviving manuscripts of the *Summa*, especially those dating from the first half of the fifteenth century when the question of reunion with the eastern Churches was still a burning issue, told a different tale. The cumulative evidence of this manuscript tradition, comprising abstract and academic theological speculation in treatises and sermons, moral exhortation, and social comment in vernacular sermons in England and Ireland, concern for the wider implications of the Church in east and west, as well as the more colourful anti-mendicant polemic, represented a literary presence in and an impact upon the learned and ecclesiastico-political life of Continental Europe matched by no Irishman in medieval times.

There is ample evidence that, in spite of the failure of the canonization process, his cult survived in Ireland in the diocese of Meath and in the 'English' half of the diocese of Armagh, and

[29] *De Scriptoribus Ecclesiasticis*, p. 237.

that it did so with the blessing of successive primates. Although Richard FitzRalph junior disappeared from the records even before his uncle's death, and individual members of the Dowdall family wielded little ecclesiastical influence in the area until the elevation of George Dowdall to the primacy on 17 March 1543 on the eve of major changes in the province,[30] family connections may have helped to keep FitzRalph's memory alive in the area. An episode which figured in the fifteenth-century primates' registers, and which may be tentatively dated to 1437, indicates that this memory was a lively one. A chaplain of Athboy in the deanery of Trim, who had confessed to a charge of incontinence, was charged in the primate's court to pay the sum of six shillings and six pence towards the repair of the windows in the Franciscan church in Drogheda, and to visit barefoot the relic of the True Cross in Christ Church Cathedral in Dublin and the shrine of 'St. Richard of Dundalk': failure to comply with this sentence would result in excommunication.[31] Both Trim and Athboy were in the diocese of Meath, and the inclusion in this penance of a pilgrimage to St. Richard's shrine may be taken as evidence that the cult was still strong in the dioceses of Meath and Armagh.

Fifty years later there is a further indication of the survival of the cult, and once again it is associated with Trim. In 1485 a parliament was held at Trim, roughly coinciding with the death of Richard III and the accession of Henry VII. The statute roll of this parliament is now lost, but Sir James Ware cited an extract from it, recording that 'a chantry was confirmed in the church of St Nicholas at Dundalk in honour of God, the Blessed Virgin, St Nicholas and St Richard of Dundalk'.[32] This chantry was distinct from the tomb of FitzRalph in the same church of St. Nicholas, which was still the centre of the local cult. On 20 June 1545 Archbishop Dowdall held a synod at St. Peter's Drogheda, at which it was ordained that henceforth the feast of St. Richard of Armagh would be celebrated annually in the

[30] *HBC*², p. 383 and n.; Gwynn, *Medieval Province of Armagh, ad indicem.*

[31] Cited in FitzMaurice-Little, p. 188. FitzMaurice had assumed that this entry was taken from the register of Nicholas Fleming (1404–16), whereas Little suggested that of John Swayne (1418–39), which would be more in keeping with the date of 1437. However, neither register contains such an entry, nor has it been possible to locate it in any of the subsequent (for the most part uncalendared) 15th-century registers. Gwynn, *Medieval Province of Armagh*, p. 271 n., suggested that FitzMaurice may have copied it from some older secondary source.

[32] Ware, *The Whole Works,* ed. Harris, p. 508.

diocese on the day after the feast of SS. John and Paul (27 June), and the form of celebration was to include nine lessons.[33] But the extant Antiphonary of Armagh had already included the feast of St. Richard on 14 March, but without the nine lessons, and Dowdall's action was consequently not the inauguration of a feast-day for his distinguished kinsman, but the provision of a new date and a more elaborate liturgy for a feast which had already been in existence. Hence it would appear that Dowdall was doing his best to ensure that due liturgical honour would be paid to his predecessor nearly two hundred years after FitzRalph's death. Not even the opposition of the friars, which was still to be detected in the resentful utterances of Wadding and others as late as the early seventeenth century (when the role of the friars as the pastoral agents of the Counter-Reformation was a contentious issue), had been able to prevent the cult from surviving into the reign of Henry VIII.

The latest piece of evidence for the survival of FitzRalph's tomb is a description by Sir Thomas Ryves, contained in a work published in London in 1624 in reply to Bishop David Rothe, and defending James I against charges of tyranny and oppression of the Irish Church.[34] Ryves had come to Ireland with Sir John Davies in 1612 and assumed various offices, including the chancellorship of the Primate's Prerogative Court which he managed to hold at least until 1640. However, the opposition of the Church of Ireland caused him to return to England *c.* 1622–3, and after *c.* 1625 he took little further part in Irish affairs. However, he reported that while in Ireland he had seen FitzRalph's tomb, defaced and mutilated, but still standing at that late date. By now the devotional cult must have become no more than a memory, but the archbishop's personality and work once more became the object of attention, both polemical and scholarly. In 1613 Bellarmine saw fit to warn against FitzRalph's errors concerning priestly powers, evangelical poverty, and the status of the mendicant friars, citing the authority of Thomas Netter of Walden and linking FitzRalph with the pernicious teaching of John Wyclif.[35] Almost simultaneously Melchior Goldast von

[33] Gwynn, *Medieval Province of Armagh,* pp. 269–71.

[34] *Regiminis Anglicani in Hibernia Defensio Adversus Analecten.* (i.e. the bishop of Ossory), (London, 1624), iii. 40. For Ryves (Rives), a Wykhamist and sometime Fellow of New College, Oxford, see *DNB* xvii. 561–2 and R. Buick Knox, *James Ussher, Archbishop of Armagh* (Cardiff, 1967), pp. 42–4. Ryves aroused the opposition of the Irish bishops, including Ussher, because of the extent of his control over the affairs of the Church of Ireland.

[35] Above, n. 29.

Haiminsfeld (1578–1635), lawyer, historian, and chancellor of the University of Giessen, included the *Defensio Curatorum* and Conway's *Defensio Mendicantium* with the political works of Ockham in his collection of sources for the legal history of the Holy Roman Empire.[36] During the succeeding decades an awareness becomes visible of the need for a general re-think of the role of the friars in the new pastoral situation created by the Counter-Reformation, leading to a new wave of interest in FitzRalph's anti-mendicant writings, and several printings of the *Defensio Curatorum* and other relevant documents followed. From the letter of an Irish Franciscan in Louvain, Francis Matthews, to Wadding dated 29 August 1631 it is clear that at least one of these printings in Paris was instigated by Paul Harries. This bitterly anti-mendicant English priest resident in Dublin has already been identified as the 'Paulus Veridicus' who used MS Lansdowne 393, and compiled the *Tabula sermonum* in this copy of the diary.[37] Rothe combined an interest in FitzRalph's life and work with an intense dislike of mendicant involvement in pastoral work, and seventeenth-century Franciscans accorded the bishop of Ossory the title 'secundus Armachanus', of which Adalbert of Rankonis had been so proud.[38] These altercations, together with the work of Ussher, Wadding, and Anthony Hickey, combined to ensure that the memory of FitzRalph was kept alive in the first half of the seventeenth century.[39]

[36] *Monarchia*, ii (Frankfurt, 1612). Two centuries earlier Laurentius Aretinus had already linked FitzRalph with Franciscan political thinkers, esp. Ockham, in his *Liber de ecclesiastica potestate*, cited in Karla Eckermann, *Studien zur Geschichte des monarchischen Denkens im 15. Jahrhundert* (Abhandlungen zur Mittleren und Neueren Geschichte 75, Berlin, 1933), p. 163.

[37] *Wadding Papers*, p. 568. From Matthew's letter it emerged that Harries was also responsible for an English translation of *Defensio Curatorum*, the first such translation recorded since that of John of Trevisa in the late 14th century. Two years earlier Thomas Strange, Franciscan guardian in Dublin, had written to Wadding, 27 March 1629, informing him of a recent printing of FitzRalph 'contra Mendicantes' in Paris, ibid., p. 288.

[38] Strange to Wadding, 20 November 1629, and again from London 26 May 1630, ibid., pp. 319–20, 368.

[39] Ussher's interest in FitzRalph is documented in MS Lansdowne 393, where the sermon diary was annotated by Ussher and by Ware. Both made extracts from it, now BL, MSS Add. 4792–4793; Bodl. MS Rawl. C. 850, see Gwynn, 'Sermon Diary', 5–6, 12. There is no evidence for Boyle's suggestion that the copy of the process of canonization found in the 17th century and mentioned in the Wadding correspondence had been found in Ussher's library and then offered to Wadding, *Bibliotheca Sanctorum*, xi (Rome, 1968), 174–5. From Rothe's letter to Wadding it is clear that the latter had found the document in the Vatican and, although Rothe was in regular correspondence with Ussher, he did not indicate that another copy had turned up in Armagh, *Wadding Papers*, pp. 548–55.

The years of Cromwellian rule changed all this, and though Protestant archbishops of Armagh continued to take a scholarly, antiquarian interest in their famous predecessor, nothing remained of the tomb or cult of 'St. Richard'. The Protestant primate, John Bramhall (1660-3) became interested in FitzRalph's tomb, possibly through his friendship with Sir James Ware, who returned to Dublin after the Restoration. According to Ware, shortly before Bramhall's death on 25 June 1663, the Primate visited his diocese with the intention, among other things, of repairing the cathedral. While in Dundalk he inquired where FitzRalph had been buried and resolved to erect a monument to his memory.[40] The fact that he had to make inquiries in 1663 suggests that nothing was left of the tomb which Ryves had seen prior to 1622-3, and doubtless it – but apparently not the memory of the cult – had been wiped out in the Cromwellian era. As late as 8 July 1726 a deed drawn up in Dundalk could refer to lands and tenements 'joyning Saint Richard's Abby'.[41] Unfortunately it is not possible to identify the site of these tenements, nor is there any record of such an abbey in Dundalk. It is indeed improbable that such an abbey could have existed, even if one accepts that Irish usage of the designation 'abbey' is notoriously imprecise. The church implied in the document cannot have been the parish church of St. Nicholas where FitzRalph was buried, and the only other religious houses in Dundalk before the Dissolution had been the Franciscan friars and the priory of St. Leonard, a hospital of the Crutched Friars,[42] though nothing remains today of either building. More probably local tradition, which knew of the original shrine and maintained the memory of 'St. Richard of Dundalk', simply associated with that memory the ruin of an ecclesiastical building which had no connection with him. Ironically, it is possible that popular tradition had given his name to the ruins of the Franciscan convent and church, with which he had family and childhood connections, but against whose community he subsequently fought so bitterly.

In the final analysis he was remembered primarily as the enemy of the friars, the bitter opponent of mendicant partici-

[40] Ware, p. 124.

[41] Joseph Martin, 'Old Title Deeds of Co. Louth. Some Dundalk Deeds, 1707 to 1843', *County Louth Archaeological Journal*, 10 (1941–4), 146.

[42] *Medieval Religious Houses. Ireland*, pp. 212–13, 249.

pation in the life of the medieval (and Counter-Reformation) Church. But his life-work as theologian and diocesan reformer attracted few, apart from the scholar-prelates of the early seventeenth-century Irish Church who approved, and at the other extreme curially-minded theologians such as Bellarmine, who saw him as the heresiarch who begat Wyclif. The legacy of Wyclif, and especially his doctrine of dominion, has bedevilled the historical picture of FitzRalph almost as much as the anti-mendicant issue has done. Whereas a critical investigation of Wyclif's debt, real and imagined, to his Oxford predecessor would require another, and very different study from the present one, it may be suggested that the availability of printed texts of the Wycliffite corpus – in itself most welcome – has helped to propagate this distortion. It has been made all too easy to count the large number of times when FitzRalph was quoted by Wyclif and to ignore the factors that, not merely did later medieval schoolmen quote one another frequently, but that FitzRalph, together with Ockham and Wodeham (who were of little use to Wyclif) and Bradwardine, whom Wyclif used at least as frequently as the 'Armachanus', were the most quoted English schoolmen of the two preceding generations. It would have given more occasion for comment had Wyclif *not* expressed interest in the views of FitzRalph.

But FitzRalph did not appear suddenly from nowhere in the 1350s to provide the conservative opponents of the friars with a powerful case for a return to the pre-1200 situation, nor to furnish the architects of social and ecclesiastical revolution in the late fourteenth and early fifteenth centuries with their intellectual foundations – though the tendency of posterity to link him with these phenomena helped to promote the wide circulation and preservation of his work, including those writings which were linked with neither controversial issue. This situation, taken in conjunction with his exceptionally well-documented ecclesiastico-political career, helped to make FitzRalph the most significant personality linking Ireland with the intellectual world of continental Europe during the millenium between Columbanus and Luke Wadding. From his unusually large and wide-ranging *œuvre* it is possible to build up a picture of a versatile and capable, if turbulent individual, equally at home in the cut-and-thrust of academic debate in Oxford, in the cosmopolitan world of Avignon where he could experience at first hand the cultural and religious links between East and West, and between the Latin-Mediterranean world and his Anglo-Irish homeland, as well as in the racially divided border diocese of Armagh.

His work in the schools reveals him as a vigorous and active teacher, though one who cannot be claimed as one of the most original or stimulating minds in Oxford at a time when competition was keen. But a combination of ability and patronage helped him on the road to success, and not even the Stamford Schism, which may have been provoked by his own belligerent handling of a difficult university situation, could damage his reputation seriously. At Avignon, helped by the coincidence of the beatific vision controversy, he secured recognition and opportunities to broaden his own intellectual horizons to include Byzantium and Armenia, at least a nodding acquaintance with Hebrew and Islamic scholarship, and contact with the missionary-minded friars who made this oriental lore possible. The combination of Avignon experiences and pastoral needs led him to a new, and much-disputed concentration on the Bible. He began to express interest in biblical exegesis, though it is questionable whether one can speak of his own approach in terms of scholarly discipline. It was more a common-sense method of interpreting Scripture to meet immediate situations – with the Armenians in Avignon, for his flock from the pulpit, and against the friars everywhere. Apart from the interest in 'orientalia' which it reveals, the *Summa* showed FitzRalph as coming to identify himself with the papal drive for more concentration on scriptural studies, and with curial orthodoxy against the wilder speculations of the 'moderni' in the schools. He tended generally to emphasize the value of sacred rather than secular scholarship and, despite his years of experience of curial litigation he extended his suspicion of secular scholarship to include the law, leaving himself at a disadvantage when the struggle with the friars required an expertise in the canon law. However, his much-disputed move from scholasticism to Scripture was a natural result of the course of his career. The active pastor and preacher did not need scholastic arguments – they would scarcely have been effective against the merchants of Drogheda and Dundalk who refused to pay tithes and operated a closed shop against apprentices of Gaelic Irish birth!

At Lichfield FitzRalph had been able to develop a talent for diocesan administration, and he could experience in the work of Northburgh and Grandisson the interest of English bishops in new styles of building – an interest which the resources of the see of Armagh did not permit him to pursue as he would have wished. Lichfield also brought him into conflict with the English Crown, a foretaste of the reaction of Edward III when the archbishop of Armagh began to make unprecedented claims regarding the Irish primacy and tried to take the mendicant issue to the papal court. Such clashes with the Crown were a regular feature of the Church in Ireland, and the practice of 'Rome-running' was an inevitable consequence. FitzRalph never lost contact with the Irish Church during his years abroad, and already in Lichfield before his elevation to the see of Armagh he adopted the Irish custom – when in doubt appeal to Rome. From his earliest Avignon sermons he can be seen developing the concept of the ideal pastor – prelate and parish priest – with more than a hint that he took Becket as his model. He shared with Grandisson a lifelong interest in and admiration for the murdered archbishop of Canterbury and, although he initially professed to admire Becket for not engaging in litigation (unlike Archbishop Stratford against FitzRalph), it is possible that he also saw Becket as his model when he took up the cudgels towards the end of his life for a cause which he believed to be vital to the best interests of the universal Church.

Arising from his preoccupation with the ideal pastor, the seeds of FitzRalph's anti-mendicant attitude began to form. He became concerned about confessional practice, the duty of restitution, the problem of testamentary bequests and eventually, in Ireland, the confusion between morality and politics which appeared to condone murder and theft across the racial divide. His episcopal career represented an important chapter in the history of the see of Armagh, its cult of St. Patrick, and primatial claims, its internal organization and relations with the papal curia. FitzRalph worked, not merely for the pursuit of his own primatial claims, but for the consolidation of the temporal possessions of the see of Armagh, for diocesan and moral reform, and for the education of his clergy. He was a preacher of undoubted eloquence, sensitive to the moods and needs of his various audiences, possessed of an impressive scriptural learning and Latin style, capable of fearlessness, clarity, and stubbornness – and towards the end of his life showing a talent for insulting polemic. If he directed this against the friars, it was less for the motive of personal jealousy which lay behind many anti-mendicant attacks, than because of his own knowledge of the common experience of his priests, of the pastoral situation, and of what he regarded as a particularly disruptive element in circumstances which were already difficult. In Ireland he devoted his own pastoral and preaching talents to a campaign against social conflict, economic discrimination, and especially against the justification of murder and theft on racial grounds. He attempted to cope from the pulpit with a problem which, six hundred years later, still has not found a solution.

Appendix

*Notes on the circulation of FitzRalph's writings and on some of the principal manuscripts**

During the fourteenth and fifteenth centuries FitzRalph's sermons, theological, and polemical writings had an exceptionally wide circulation, partly – but not exclusively – because his campaign against the friars helped to make him one of the most prominent and frequently quoted prelates of the later Middle Ages. In the attempt to establish a definitive corpus of FitzRalph manuscripts, 182 codices have so far been located in European libraries, whereas none have been discovered in non-European collections.[1] A substantial proportion of these manuscripts contains a single large-scale work by FitzRalph, either the *lectura* on the Sentences, *Summa de Questionibus Armenorum*, or *De Pauperie Salvatoris*, frequently with the addition of occasional sermons or anti-mendicant treatises. A smaller number contains collections of sermons, either the entire sermon diary or portions of its latter section, which is composed of the more formal sermons. However, the vast majority of the 182 manuscripts are 'Sammelhandschriften', miscellaneous collections which contain, among other authors, individual pieces by FitzRalph, occasionally sermons of a pastoral–theological interest, but above all, his anti-mendicant sermons and treatises, including 84 copies of his philippic preached against the friars on 8 November 1357 at Avignon, the *Defensio Curatorum.* This most famous piece of anti-mendicant polemic was also translated into Middle English by that prolific translator, John of Trevisa (1326–1402).[2] It received several printings in the late fifteenth century (being the only work by an Irishman to survive in an incunabulum), and many more in the sixteenth and seventeenth centuries.

Apart from the *Defensio Curatorum*, no single work by FitzRalph had a

*A complete catalogue of the extant corpus of FitzRalph MSS, containing an extensive introduction on the MS tradition is being prepared by the present author, and no attempt is made here to duplicate its findings. In the notes on individual MSS which follow, reference will be made to printed descriptions, where such an adequate description exists. Furthermore no attempt is made to consider doubtful MSS attributed to FitzRalph, such as the putative 'Distinctiones' in Cambridge, Peterhouse College, MS 223, or the various rearrangements of his anti-mendicant arguments, which will be discussed in detail in the catalogue.

[1] For a preliminary list see Richard Hayes, *Manuscript Sources for the History of Irish Civilisation* (Boston, Mass., 1965), ii. 150–2. At the time of publication his list, compiled with the assistance of Ludwig Bieler and Aubrey Gwynn, stood at 83, of which two were not actually MSS of his works: one was directed against him, and the other was a later anti-mendicant text based on his arguments.

[2] For his work as a translator see H. S. Bennett, *Chaucer and the Fifteenth Century* (Oxford History of English Literature, II. ii, Oxford, 1947), p. 299 and *passim.* His translation of FitzRalph survives in BL, MS Harl. 1900; Cambridge, St. John's College, MS 204.

wider circulation than the *Summa de Questionibus Armenorum*, of which no fewer than 37 complete, or substantially complete, texts and eight fragments have been identified, while it also received a printing in the early sixteenth century. It circulated initially from two principal centres, the papal court and the schools of Paris, but made a minor impact on English and Irish audiences. Only two full texts and four fragments survive in English collections, while Trinity College Dublin possesses two complete texts of English provenance which were formerly in the library of Archbishop James Ussher.[3] In Paris the *Summa* was unquestionably FitzRalph's most popular work, and one of the conclusions to be drawn from the surviving manuscript evidence is that Parisian theologians displayed little interest in FitzRalph's anti-mendicant contributions. Nor did they display much more interest in his pastoral-theological sermons, which are sparsely represented in French collections by comparison with the monastic and cathedral centres of the 'Germania Sacra'. With regard to his *lectura* on the Sentences, we have already seen that theological circles around the Sorbonne and the Franciscan *studium* in Paris showed interest in it as long as the topics it discussed were 'en vogue' in the schools, whereas the character and subject-matter of the *Summa* ensured its wider appeal. Oriental lore, in whatever form presented, was always popular, and the *Summa* must have been almost a standard work in the major Parisian libraries of the later fourteenth and fifteenth centuries. Of the extant number of complete texts, roughly one-quarter are either now located in Paris (and known to have emanated from Parisian collections – the Sorbonne, S. Germain-des-Près, Grand-Carmes, Collège Louis le Grand, S. Victor), or are known to have been made and acquired originally in Paris.[4]

The second major centre for the dissemination of the *Summa* was the papal court, both before and after its return to Italy, though the fate of the Avignonese collections under Benedict XIII (Pedro de Luña) inevitably ensured a higher survival rate of the 'Italian' curially-based manuscripts.[5] Apart from a general humanist interest in all things Greek or oriental, a further factor contributed to the relative popularity of the *Summa* in the Italian peninsula during the fifteenth century. In the light of attempts to re-establish union between the eastern and western Churches at the Councils of Basel and of Ferrara–Florence there was a revival of interest in Greek views of purgatory, satisfaction, and indulgences, and of the beatific vision – an interest reflected in, among others, surviving texts belonging to Cardinals Juan de Torquemada and Nicholas Cusanus (the latter only a

[3] London, Lambeth Palace, MS 158, and Oxford, New College, MS 90, contain complete texts. Cambridge, Corpus Christi College, MS 156; Pembroke College, MS 5 (the first 10 books); London, BL, MS Harl. 106 (a fragment similar to that of MS Corpus Christi 156 – extracts from Book XIII concerning indulgences); Oxford, Lincoln College, MS 18 (the letter of dedication to the two Armenian prelates and most of Book I). Trinity College Dublin, MSS 189 and 190 contain complete texts.

[4] See BAV, Vat. Lat. 1035 (bought in Paris by the later cardinal, Juan de Torquemada, while a student of theology); Kraków, MS 1599 (above, p. 130); Paris, Bibliothèque universitaire (Sorbonne), MS 225; Bibliothèque mazarine, MS 895 (440) and MS 896 (1174); Bibliothèque nationale, Lat. 12438, Lat. 14578, Lat. 15974.

[5] BAV, Vat. Lat. 1033, and Vat. Lat. 1034.

fragment), and a copy made for the lord of Cesena, Domenico Malatesta Novello (1418–65).[6]

The widespread interest in FitzRalph's work generated in Central Europe by the storm over dominion and grace, and by his attacks on the friars, ensured that the *Summa* also circulated there, and seven manuscripts have been located – two each in Vienna, Prague, and Cracow, and that made for Johannes Scharpe, a priest of the diocese of Münster who became a fellow and eventually provost of Queen's College, Oxford, wrote against Wyclif, and subsequently returned to Germany as a canon of Lübeck.[7] His text is unique in that it is not a direct copy of the *Summa*, but a rearrangement which omitted the dialogue form. Scharpe clearly had this manuscript made for himself: he left untouched the basic structure of the nineteen books, but revised the text, varying the form for his own purposes and drawing conclusions and interpretations from the interplay between Ricardus and Iohannes – a factor which lends the manuscript an independent significance in the transmission and reception of FitzRalph's arguments.

The principal factor in the strong representation of FitzRalph manuscripts in Central European collections was the image of his role as 'teacher' and precursor of Wyclif, both in terms of the controverted doctrine of dominion which assumed unprecedented dimensions in the Hussite controversies up to and including the Council of Constance, and in terms of the condemnation of religious orders, especially mendicant orders. After the original impetus given by Adalbert of Rankonis, who made FitzRalph's work known in pre-Hussite Prague, and in addition to the resentment which his attacks aroused among the strong mendicant representation in the theological faculties of Prague and Vienna, the 'Armachanus' was clearly seen in both of these centres as a major component in the corpus of Wycliffite ideas, in both their intellectual and popular dimensions, and in this context he was copied, circulated, and – depending on standpoint – received with enthusiasm or suspicion.

A further category of manuscript tradition, which was previously deemed to have been negligible, but which now must be recognized as substantial, is that of the individual non-mendicant sermons, mainly of a pastoral–theological nature. A number of manuscripts, including Innsbruck, Universitätsbibliothek MS 234, CLM 16058 and 23474, as well as the Klosterneuburg and Göttweig manuscripts, testify to a substantial circulation of FitzRalph's Avignon sermons. Many of these circulated already while their author was still dean of Lichfield, and therefore their relative popularity owed more to their quality as sermon literature, to a growing recognition of the value and interest of sermons emanating from curial circles in Avignon, and little or nothing to FitzRalph's subsequent notoriety as a result of his campaign against the friars, or to the natural interest among secular and cathedral clergy, and among the older monastic orders, in 'friar-baiting'.

[6] Vat. Lat. 1035; Hospital zu Kues, MS 64; Cesena, Biblioteca Malatestiana, Pluteo Dest. XIX. 1. Malatesta Novello was responsible for the building of this library (1447–52) close to the Franciscan convent and *studium*.

[7] Originally Magdeburg, Domgymnasium, MS 47, now (under the same shelf-mark) in Deutsche Stasstsbibliothek, Berlin (East, GDR). For Scharpe see *BRUO* III, 1680.

Cambridge. Corpus Christi College, MS 180.
For a description of this manuscript, now in the collection acquired by the Elizabethan archbishop of Canterbury, Matthew Parker (1504–75), see Montague R. James, *A descriptive Catalogue of the Manuscripts in the Library of Corpus Christi College Cambridge*, 2 vols. (Cambridge, 1909–12) i. 420–1.

Together with Lambeth Palace MS 121, it is one of the only two manuscripts in existence which contain the entire eight books of *De Pauperie Salvatoris*. It was made for Adam Easton, a Benedictine of the priory of Norwich, before his elevation to the College of Cardinals on 21 December 1381, and contains at the end of Book VII (top of folio 88rb) the inscription: LIBER D(OMI)NI / ADE ESTONE / MONACHI NOR / WICENSIS. Folios 88^{v}–89^{r} are blank, and folio 89^{v} contains the following: 'Incipit liber domini Armachani archiepiscopi de mendicitate fratrum et eorum privilegiis', which is the eighth book, in the form of 45 chapters, of the dialogue and was composed by FitzRalph at Avignon in 1358 to 1359. The same title is given in the two manuscripts which contain the eighth book alone: Paris, Bibl. nat., lat. 3222, and Deutsche Staatsbibliothek, Berlin (East GDR), MS Magdeburg, Domgymnasium 47, and by the Franciscan William Woodford in his reply, contained in Oxford, Magdalen College MS 75. Although Book VIII was added after Easton's note of ownership, it was written in the same hand as the rest of the manuscript, which is, however, not that of Easton himself, who is known to have annotated Corpus Christi College MS 74. Presumably Easton had access to the entire text, including Book VIII, during his lengthy sojourn at Avignon, where he resided intermittently from 1368 onwards, as secretary to the Benedictine Cardinal Simon Langham, and later as proctor of the English Benedictines at the curia. He subsequently transferred with the court of Gregory XI to Rome and composed a most valuable account of the election of Urban VI. A student of theology at Oxford from before 1355, he incepted as doctor in 1363–4 and acted as prior of Gloucester College in 1366. He was in residence in Oxford continuously apart from a brief period when he was recalled to Norwich to organize preaching by the monks in the cathedral and to lead the opposition against the friars. Pantin[8] dated this recall to some point between 1357 and 1363, most probably before 1360, and he linked the eagerness of the Norwich community to have a worthy champion against the friars with the financial support which the English Benedictines were providing for FitzRalph's cause in Avignon – though we now know that this support cannot have been very substantial. In any case Easton must have been present in Oxford during 1356–7, when FitzRalph launched there the first seven books of *De Pauperie Salvatoris* and they became the basis of debate on the entire mendicant question in the schools for a brief period. Hence it is possible that Easton acquired his manuscript of the first seven books there at some stage before his departure from Oxford for Avignon, and from all that is known of Easton's meticulousness in ensuring that the defective portion of any incomplete manuscript acquired by him be copied and

[8] Pantin, *The English Church in the Fourteenth Century*, pp. 175–7.

included,[9] it is understandable that, upon discovering that there was an eighth book, he had that copied also.

The entire manuscript is the work of an English scribe, possibly Easton's secretary, and there is no indication of whether it was written down in Avignon or in England. This is also true of the illumination on folio 1ra (see *frontispiece*), which is clearly the work of someone who, like Easton, was familiar with the archbishop's controversy with the friars and sympathetic with his point of view. Whereas in his *Defensorium*, Easton opposed its interpretation by Wyclif, he appears to have accepted in principle the theory of dominion by grace,[10] and Easton's miniaturist obviously took FitzRalph's part: in the initial the 'Armachanus' is writing 'Sanctissimo' in a book, while a dove flies towards him. Above him and to the right are a Dominican and a Franciscan, with a devil standing on the latter's shoulders and a devil beneath them. Below are an Augustinian and a Carmelite, each standing upon a devil.

Cambridge. Sidney Sussex College, MS 64.
See Montague R. James, *A descriptive Catalogue of the Manuscripts in the Library of Sidney Sussex College Cambridge* (Cambridge, 1895), pp. 46–7; and in greater detail Walsh, 'Hardeby', *AA* 33 (1970), 216–220. The contents of this manuscript, and in particular the documents relating to the hearing of FitzRalph's case in Avignon, are discussed extensively in Walsh, 'FitzRalph and the Friars'.

Città del Vaticano. Vat. Lat. 1033, 1034, 1035, 1036.
Four texts of the *Summa de Questionibus Armenorum*, dating between 1380 and the mid-fifteenth century. For a reliable description, including notes on possessors, see Pelzer, *Codices Vaticani Latini*, II. i, 541–44.

Kraków (Cracow). Bibliotheca Jagellónica, MS 1599 (DD. VI. 1).
This manuscript, which was copied in Paris in 1375 and contains no other work apart from the *Summa*, is yet another illustration of the extent to which Paris was a major centre for the dissemination of this work. It also indicates both that the Polish clergy found FitzRalph's work useful in their dealings with the Ruthenians, who shared many of the views of the Armenians, and that suspicion of FitzRalph's orthodoxy during the pontificate of Boniface IX had penetrated to Poland, see flyleaf: 'Iste liber est datus per magistrum Laurencium de Ratibor,[11] professorem, pro libraria magistrorum in quo continetur Armachanus (Anglicus) De questionibus Armenorum, scriptus ac finitus per manus Gherardi Busonis, Parisiis studentis, a.d. 1375 in vigilia Petri et Pauli apostolorum, a.m.d.g. Amen' (fol. 184vb). Underneath another hand, which added 'Anglicus' in the preceding inscription, wrote: 'Et in certis punctis et locis est hereticatus et condempnatus et post mortem incineratus per ecclesiam romanam tempore Bonifacii noni.' It would be interesting to know more about the

[9] Ibid., p. 181. [10] Ibid., p. 130.

[11] See also his 'Determinacio' on behalf of the University of Cracow delivered at the Council of Basel in Kraków, Bibliotheca Jagellónica, MS 1217 (AA. II. 15). See also Werner Marschall, 'Schlesier auf dem Konzil von Basel', *AHC* 8 (1976), 294–325.

source of this information, and its implication that suspicion of some elements in FitzRalph's writings had reached such a point during the pontificate of Boniface IX that a work, or at least portions of it, were declared heretical and burned – especially in the light of proceedings for FitzRalph's canonization which were in progress during that pontificate, and the fact that Boniface IX had a copy of the *Summa* made for his personal use at Perugia in 1393 – was he, after all, suspicious?

London. British Library, MS Lansdowne 393.
The best published description is contained in Gwynn, 'Sermon Diary', 5-7. For further information on the identity of the seventeenth-century possessor and compiler of the *Tabula Sermonum*, 'Paulus Veridicus', alias Paul Harri(e)s, above, p. 182, and for his various controversies on the one hand with Archbishop Ussher, and on the other with the mendicant orders see *DNB* ix. 21. For individual sermons this manuscript occasionally gives better readings than B or J, but Gwynn's remark, 'Sermon Diary', 6, that it is unique among texts of the entire sermon diary in that it contains a copy of the articles on *Vas electionis*: 'Quia in proposicione nuper facta' is misleading – this text is added to manuscripts of the diary in both B and J, and in the original hands of these manuscripts.

Oxford. Bodleian Library, MS Bodl. 144.
See Gwynn's description in 'Sermon Diary', 2-4. This manuscript was the principal basis for his discussion of the format of the sermon diary, drawing attention to the essentially different character of both parts. However, his remark that the sermons up to and including the third Sunday in Lent 1357 (12 March) 'have all the appearance of being entries in a regular sermon diary' (ibid., 3), needs qualification. The London sermons of 1356-7 were clearly revised and polished in Latin after aural delivery, and the version contained in the diary is most definitely not that which was spoken from the pulpit.

Oxford. St. John's College, MS 65.
See Gwynn, 'Sermon Diary', 4-5; Neil Ker, *Medieval Libraries of Great Britain. A list of surviving books* (London, 1964^2), p. 313, for the note of possession by the Benedictine Johannes Savell (1479), before it passed by a curious combination of purchase and begging ('emit et mendicavit') to an unnamed deacon then studying in Oxford. It subsequently passed to the Dominican convent at Warwick, where it was in the possession of the prior provincial, Nicholas Stremer, in 1501.

Paris. Bibliothèque nationale, cod. lat. 3222.
See the description in *Catalogue général des manuscrits latins*, iv, 371-3, which dates the manuscript to the late fourteenth century. On internal grounds it should be dated somewhat earlier, and may even have been contemporary with the proceedings FitzRalph v. the friars, for which it provides so much information, especially concerning the work of Richard Kilwington and the otherwise unknown supporters of the 'Armachanus'. Folios 1ra–77vb contain a beautifully written text of Book VIII of *De Pauperie Salvatoris*, which is the earliest known surviving copy of this

work and may have been made for one of the participants in the proceedings. Although the subsequent transfers of possession of this manuscript in the sixteenth and seventeenth centuries are well known (see *Catalogue*, 373), there is no indication of its fourteenth-century provenance and/or possessors.

Paris. Bibliothèque nationale, cod. lat. 15853.*
There is no adequate printed description of this manuscript, but see Leff, *FitzRalph Commentator*, pp. 177–81, and above, p. 39–40. A mid-fourteenth-century vellum manuscript, consisting of i + 193 folios, in two columns, and the property of the Sorbonne master Johannes Gorre, it circulated under the misleading ascription 'Thomas Hibernicus'.

Wien (Vienna). Österreichische Nationalbibliothek, CVP 1430.
For this manuscript, Adalbert of Rankonis's text of *De Pauperie Salvatoris*, see Walsh, 'The Manuscripts of Archbishop Richard FitzRalph', 67–71. It has been suggested that the hand which wrote the extensive marginal annotations and interpolations, which were incorporated into the body of the text in all subsequent manuscripts, was that of FitzRalph himself. It was unquestionably the hand of someone close enough to him to have been involved in the final stages of composition of the work, possibly a secretary or another scribe, but equally likely to have been the archbishop himself. Leff, *FitzRalph Commentator*, p. 179, suggested that the marginal notes in Paris, lat. 15853, were the work of FitzRalph. This is a different hand from the distinctive angular hand which annotated CVP 1430. In the case of the Paris manuscript the notes are genuine marginalia and not part of the substance of the text, and it is more probable that this annotator was an interested scholar in Paris, possibly even the original owner, Johannes Gorre. However, at this stage of study of the manuscripts of the FitzRalph corpus, the question must remain open, and unless another text annotated in a contemporary hand or one which is clearly an autograph is discovered for purposes of comparison, there can be no definitive answer. In this case the more probable identification for FitzRalph's hand must remain that of the annotator of CVP 1430, because of the nature of the interpolations.

*CLM 8943 also contains 2 *articuli* from FitzRalph's *lectura*, Bk. II q. 1, in the same form as they are preserved in Florence, Bibl. naz. A.III.508, fols. 81va–83rb, 87rb–89va.

Bibliography

MANUSCRIPT MATERIAL: UNPRINTED SOURCES

(*a*) *Archival Material*

ARMAGH
Registers of the Archbishops of Armagh, 1361 ff. (several volumes contain pre-1361 material). Deposited in BELFAST, Public Record Office, transcripts in the Library of Trinity College, Dublin
CITTÀ DEL VATICANO, Archivio Segreto Vaticano
Indices
Obligationes et Solutiones (Fondo Camerale 1295 ff.)
Registra Avenionensia (1316 ff.)
Registra Lateranensia (Dataria Apostolica 1389 ff.)
Registra Supplicationum (Dataria Apostolica 1342 ff.)
Registra Vaticana (1073 ff.)
LICHFIELD, Cathedral Archives
Register of Roger Northburgh, Bishop of Coventry and Lichfield 1322–58
LINCOLN, Cathedral Archives
Register of William Burghersh, Bishop of Lincoln 1320–40
LONDON, Public Record Office
D.L. 42/8

(*b*) *Codices**

BERLIN (East, GDR), Deutsche Staatsbibliothek
MS Magdeburg 47 (formerly Magdeburg, Domgymnasium MS 47)
BRUXELLES (BRUSSELS), Bibliothèque nationale (royale)
MS 506
MS 2583
CAMBRIDGE
Corpus Christi College MS 74
Corpus Christi College MS 156
Corpus Christi College MS 180
Pembroke College MS 5
Peterhouse College MS 223
St. John's College MS 204
Sidney Sussex College MS 64

*This list includes only those codices directly cited in this study, and makes no claim to be a complete list of all manuscripts containing works by FitzRalph, let alone all those either pertaining to the controversies discussed or those containing texts based upon his arguments.

CESENA, Biblioteca Malatestiana
  Pluteo Dest.XIX.1
CITTÀ DEL VATICANO, Biblioteca Apostolica Vaticana
  Ottobon.Lat. 179
  Ottobon.Lat. 869
  Vat.Lat. 955
  Vat.Lat. 1033
  Vat.Lat. 1034
  Vat.Lat. 1035
  Vat.Lat. 1036
  Vat.Lat. 1037
  Vat.Lat. 1110
  Vat.Lat. 4006
  Vat.Lat. 4353
  Vat.Lat. 11517
DUBLIN, Trinity College
  MS 189
  MS 190
FIRENZE (FLORENCE), Biblioteca nazionale
  MS Conventi soppressi A.III.508
  MS Conventi soppressi A.VI.611
GÖTTWEIG (Niederösterreich), Stiftsbibliothek
  MS 124
  MS 151
  MS 157
  MS 329
HAMBURG, Staatsbibliothek
  MS St Petri-Kirche 30 b.
INNSBRUCK, Universitätsbibliothek
  MS 234
KLOSTERNEUBURG (Niederösterreich), Stiftsbibliothek
  MS 204
  MS 789
KRAKÓW (CRACOW)
  MS 1217 (AA.II.15)
  MS 1599 (DD.VI.1)
KUES, Hospital zu
  MS 64
LICHFIELD, Cathedral Library
  MS 89
LONDON
  British Library
    Additional MSS 4792–4793
    MS Harl. 106
    MS Harl. 1900
    MS Royal 6.E.vii
    MS Royal 17.A.xxvi
  Lambeth Palace Library
    MS 121
    MS 158

MS 1208
Westminster Abbey Library
MS 1
MAINZ, Stadtbibliothek
MS 217
MÜNCHEN (MUNICH), Bayerische Staatsbibliothek
CLM 8943
CLM 11882
CLM 14190
CLM 16058
CLM 23474
NEW YORK, Columbia University Library
MS Plimpton 156 (formerly MS Phillipps 4633)
OXFORD
Bodleian Library
MS Ashmole 794
MS Bodl. 144
MS Bodl. 158
MS Bodl. 240
MS Bodl. 493
MS Bodl. 784
MS Bodl. 865
MS Digby 113
MS Hebr. 1466
MS Rawl. G.40
MS Rawl. C.850
MS Tanner IV
Lincoln College MS Lat. 18
Magdalen College MS 75
Merton College MS H.3.12 (340)
Merton College MS H.3.13
New College MS 90
Oriel College MS 15
St. John's College MS 65
St. John's College MS 171
PARIS
Bibliothèque mazarine
MS 895 (440)
MS 896 (1174)
Bibliothèque nationale
Lat. 3222
Lat. 12438
Lat. 14538
Lat. 15853
Lat. 15974
Bibliothèque universitaire (Sorbonne)
MS 193
MS 225
PISA, Seminario arcivescovile
MS 159

ROMA (ROME), Biblioteca Casanatense
MS 948 (B.III.15)
SALZBURG, Erzabtei Sankt-Peter
MS b.X.18
ST. PAUL IM LAVANTTAL (Kärnten), Stiftsbibliothek
MS 23
TROYES, Bibliothèque municipale
MS 505
WIEN (VIENNA), Österreichische Nationalbibliothek
CVP 1294
CVP 1339
CVP 1430
CVP 3929
CVP 3935
CVP 3937
CVP 4244
CVP 5076
WOLFENBÜTTEL, Herzogliche Bibliothek
MS Helmst. 311
WORCESTER, Cathedral Library
MS Q 71

MANUSCRIPT MATERIAL: UNPUBLISHED THESES

Brock, Richard O., 'An Edition of Richard FitzRalph's "De Pauperie Salvatoris", Books V, VI and VII' (Ph.D., University of Colorado, Boulder, 1954).

Catto, Jeremy I., 'William Woodford OFM (c.1330–c.1397)', (D.Phil., University of Oxford, MS D.Phil. d.4877, 1969).

Forte, Stephen L., 'A Study of some Oxford Schoolmen of the middle of the fourteenth century' (B.Litt., University of Oxford, MS B.Litt., c.10–11, 1949).

Haren, Michael J., 'A Study of the "Memoriale Presbyterorum", a fourteenth-century confessional manual for parish priests', 2 vols. (D.Phil., University of Oxford, MS D.Phil. d.6097–8, 1975).

Hughes, Helen, ' "De Pauperie Salvatoris" of Richard FitzRalph of Armagh' (Ph.D., University of Manchester, 1927).

Jenkins, Hester T., 'Lichfield Cathedral in the Fourteenth Century', 2 vols. (B.Litt., University of Oxford, MS B.Litt. d.538–9, 1956).

Lavery, Paulinus, 'De Fr. Rogerii Conway O.F.M. vita et operibus deque eiusdem controversiis cum Richardo Radulpho, Archiepiscopo Armachano' (L.Hist.Eccl., Antonianum, Rome, 1930).

Macfarlane, Leslie J., 'The Life and Writings of Adam Easton OSB', 2 vols. (Ph.D., University of London, 1955).

O'Kelly, Maria, 'The Black Death in Ireland (1348)', (M.A., University College Cork, 1973).

Simms, Katharine, 'Gaelic Lordships in Ulster in the Later Middle Ages' (Ph.D., University of Dublin, 1976).

Walsh, Katherine, 'The Observant Congregations of the Augustinian Friars in Italy' (D.Phil., University of Oxford, MS D.Phil., c.952, 1972).

Weisheipl, James A., 'Early Fourteenth Century Physics of the Merton "School" ' (D.Phil., University of Oxford, MS D.Phil. d.1776, 1956).

Wood, Diana, 'The Political Theory of Pope Clement VI', 2 vols. (Ph.D., University of London, 1976).

PUBLISHED MATERIAL

(Items already included in the list of Abbreviations are not repeated here, except in the case of first printings of articles subsequently published in collected form)

Acta Sanctorum, ed. Johannes Bollandus *et al.* (Antwerp–Brussels, 1643 ff.).

Aegidius Romanus, *De ecclesiastica potestate*, ed. Richard Scholz (Weimar, 1929).

Alexander, Jonathan J. G., and Gibson, Margaret T., *Medieval Learning and Literature. Essays presented to Richard William Hunt* (Oxford, 1976).

D'Alverny, Marie-Thérèse, 'Deux Traductions latines du Coran au moyen âge', *AHDLMA* 22–23 (1947–8), 69–131.

Anawati, George C., 'Nicolas de Cues et le problème de l'Islam', *Nicolò Cusano agli inizi del mondo moderno. Atti del congresso internazionale in occasione del V centenario della morte di Nicolò Cusano, Bressanone, 6–10 settembre 1964* (Facoltà di Magistero del l'università di Padova 12, Florence, 1970), 141–73.

Andreae, Johannes, *Apparatus glossarum in Clementinas* (Venice, 1491).

Annals of Clonmacnoise, ed. Denis Murphy (Dublin, 1896).

Annals of the Four Masters, ed. John O'Donovan, 7 vols. (Dublin, 1848–51).

Annals of Loch Cé, ed. William M. Hennessy, 2 vols. (RS, London, 1871).

Annals of Ulster, ed. William M. Hennessy and Bartholomew MacCarthy, 4 vols. (Dublin, 1897–1901).

Arquillière, H.-X. (ed.), *Le Plus ancient traité de l'église, Jacques de Viterbo, De regimine christiano (1301–2). Étude des sources et édition critique* (Paris, 1926).

Aston, Trevor H., 'Oxford's Medieval Alumni', *Past and Present*, 74 (1977), 3–40.

Bale, Johannes, *Scriptorum Illustrium Maioris Britanniae Catalogus*, 2 vols. (1st edn., Ispwich and Wesel, 1548, 2nd edn., Basel, 1557–9).

— *Index Britanniae Scriptorum*, ed. Reginald L. Poole and Mary Bateson (Oxford, 1902).

Balić, Carol, 'Henricus de Harclay et Ioannes Duns Scotus', *Mélanges offerts à Étienne Gilson* (Toronto–Paris, 1959), 93–121.

Baluzius, Stephanus, *Vitae Paparum Avenionensium*, ed. Guillaume Mollat, 4 vols. (Paris, 1916–22).

Bataillon, Louis Jacques, 'Les Crises de l'université de Paris d'après les sermons universitaires', *Die Auseinandersetzungen an der Pariser Universität im XIII. Jahrhundert* (Miscellanea Mediaevalia, 10, Berlin–New York, 1975), 155–69.

Baudry, Léon, *Guillaume d'Occam: sa vie, ses œuvres, ses idées sociales et politiques* (Paris, 1949).

Baumgarten, Paul M., *Von der apostolischen Kanzlei. Untersuchungen über die päpstlichen Tabellionen und die Vizekanzler der Heiligen Römischen Kirche im XIII., XIV. und XV. Jahrhundert* (Cologne, 1908).

Bellarmino, Robertus, *De Scriptoribus Ecclesiasticis* (Rome, 1613).

Benedikz, B. S., *A Catalogue of the Lichfield Cathedral Library Manuscripts*, revised version (Birmingham, 1978).

Bennett, H. S., *Chaucer and the Fifteenth Century* (Oxford History of English Literature, II.ii, Oxford, 1947).

Benrath, Gustav A., *Wyclifs Bibelkommentar* (Berlin, 1966).

Betts, Reginald R., 'Richard FitzRalph, Archbishop of Armagh, and the Doctrine of Dominion', *Essays in Czech History* (London, 1969), 160–75. First printed in *Essays in British and Irish History in Honour of James Eadie Todd*, ed. M. A. Cronne, T. W. Moody, and D. B. Quinn (London, 1949), 46–60.

Bibliotheca Cluniacensis, ed. Martin Marrier and André Duchesne (Paris, 1613).

Bolton, Brenda, 'The Council of London of 1342', *Councils and Assemblies* (Studies in Church History, 7, Cambridge, 1971), 147–60.

Borenius, Tancred, *St Thomas in Art* (London, 1932).

Bosch, Ursulà, *Andronikos III Palaiologos* (Amsterdam, 1965).

Bosl, Karl, 'Die "geistliche Hofakademie" Ludwigs des Bayern', *Der Mönch im Wappen* (Munich, 1961), 97–129.

Bottin, Francesco, 'Un testo fondamentale nell'ambito della "nuova fisica" di Oxford', *Antiqui et Moderni. Traditionsbewusstsein und Fortschrittsbewusstsein im späten Mittelalter* (Miscellanea Mediaevalia, 9, Berlin–New York, 1974), 201–5.

Bradwardine, Thomas, *De causa Dei contra Pelagium*, ed. Henry Savile (London, 1618).

Brady, Ignatius, 'The Development of the Doctrine of the Immaculate Conception in the fourteenth century after Aureoli', *FS* 15 (1955), 175–202.

Brincken, Anna Dorothee von den, *Die 'Nationes Christianorum Orientalium' im Verständnis der lateinischen Historiographie* (Kölner historische Abhandlungen, 22, Cologne–Vienna, 1973).

— 'Die universalhistorischen Vorstellungen des Johann von Marignola OFM. Der einzige mittelalterliche Weltchronist mit Fernostkenntnis', *Archiv für Kulturgeschichte*, 49 (1967), 297–339.

Brown, Edward (ed.), *Fasciculus rerum expetendarum et fugiendarum*, 2 vols. (London, 1690).

Brown, Stephen F., 'Walter Burleigh's Treatise "De suppositionibus" and its influence on William of Ockham', *FS* 32 (1972), 15–64.

— 'Walter Burley's "Quaestiones in librum Perihermeneias" ', *FS* 34 (1974), 200–95.

Buytaert, Eligius M., 'The Immaculate Conception in the Writings of Ockham', *FS* 10 (1950), 149–63.

Callus, Daniel A. (ed.), *Robert Grosseteste, Scholar and Bishop. Essays in Commemoration of the Seventh Centenary of his Death* (Oxford, 1955).

— 'Robert Grosseteste as Scholar', ibid., 1–69.

Chambers, David, S., *Cardinal Bainbridge in the Court of Rome 1509 to 1514* (Oxford, 1965).

Chambre, William de, *Continuatio Historiae Dunelmensis,* in Henry Wharton, *Anglia Sacra,* i (London, 1691), 765-84.

Charland, Thomas M., *Les Artes Praedicandi. Contribution à l'histoire de la rhétorique du moyen âge* (Paris-Ottawa, 1938).

Chronicon Henrici Knighton, ed. Joseph R. Lumby, 2 vols. (RS, London, 1889-95).

Clasen, Sophronius, *Der hl. Bonaventura und das Mendikantentum* (Werl i. W., 1940).

Clucas, Lowell M., 'Eschatalogical Theory in Byzantine Hesychasm: a parallel to Joachim da Fiore?', *Byzantinische Zeitschrift,* 70 (1977), 324-46.

Collectanea, ed. Charles R. L. Fletcher, Montague Burrows, *et al.,* 4 vols. (OHS 1885-1905).

Congar, Yves, 'Aspects ecclésiologiques de la querelle entre mendiants et séculiers dans la séconde moitié du XIIIe et le début du XIVe siècle', *AHDLMA* 36 (1961), 35-161.

Constable, Giles, *The Letters of Peter the Venerable,* 2 vols. (Cambridge, Mass., 1967).

Courtenay, William J., 'John of Mirecourt and Gregory of Rimini on whether God can undo the past', *Recherches de théologie ancienne et médiévale,* 39 (1972), 224-56; 40 (1973), 147-74.

— 'Ockhamism among the Augustinians: the case of Adam Wodeham', *Scientia Augustiniana. Studien über Augustinus, den Augustinismus und den Augustinerorden. Festschrift P. Dr.theol. Dr.phil. Adolar Zumkeller OSA* (Cassiciacum 30, Würzburg, 1975), 267-75.

— 'The Sentences-Commentary of Stukle: a new source for Oxford theology in the fourteenth century', *Traditio,* 34 (1978), 435-8.

— 'Augustinianism at Oxford in the Fourteenth Century', *Augustiniana,* 30 (1980), 58-70.

— 'The Effect of the Black Death on English Higher Education', *Speculum,* 55 (1980), 696-714.

Crombie, Alistair C., 'Grosseteste's Position in the History of Science', *Robert Grosseteste, Scholar and Bishop,* ed. Callus, 98-120.

Curtayne, Alice, *Loch Derg: St Patrick's Purgatory* (London, 1932).

Curtis, Edmund, *A History of Mediaeval Ireland,* (1st edn., Dublin, 1923, 2nd edn., London, 1938).

— and McDowell, Robert B., *Irish Historical Documents 1172-1922* (London, 1943).

Dalton, John M., *The Collegiate Church of Ottery St Mary* (Cambridge, 1917).

Daniel, Norman, *Islam and the West. The making of an image.* (Edinburgh, 1960).

Dean, Ruth J., 'The earliest known Commentary on Livy', *Mediaevalia et Humanistica,* 3 (1945), 86-98; 4 (1946), 110 (Corrigenda).

— 'Cultural Relations in the middle ages: Nicholas Trevet and Nicholas of Prato', *Studies in Philology,* 45 (1968), 541-64.

— 'Nicholas Trevet, Historian', *Medieval Learning and Literature,* ed. Alexander-Gibson, 328-52.

Denholm-Young, Noël, 'Richard de Bury (1287-1345)', *TRHS* 4th ser. 20 (1937), 135-68.

Denifle, Heinrich, *Die Entstehung der Universitäten des Mittelalters* (Berlin, 1885).
Denton, Jeffrey H., *English Royal Free Chapels 1100-1300. A constitutional study* (Manchester, 1970).
Dizionario Biografico degli Italiani (Rome, 1960 ff.).
Dobner, Gelasius, *Monumenta Historica Bohemiae nusquam antehac edita*, 6 vols. (Prague, 1764-85).
Dondaine, Antoine, ' "Contra Grecos". Premiers écrits polémiques des dominicains d'Orient', *AFP* 21 (1951), 320-446.
Douie, Decima L., *The Nature and the Effect of the Heresy of the Fraticelli* (Manchester, 1932).
— 'The Conflict between Seculars and Mendicants at the University of Paris', *Aquinas Papers*, 23 (London, 1954).
Doyle, Eric, 'William Woodford's "De dominio civili clericorum" against John Wyclif', *AFH* 66 (1973), 49-109.
— 'A Bibliographical List by William Woodford, OFM', *FS* 35 (1975), 93-106.
— 'William Woodford on Scripture and Tradition', *Studia Historico-Ecclesiastica. Festgabe für Professor Luchesius G. Spätling OFM*, ed. Isaac Vázquez (Bibliotheca Pontificii Athenaei Antoniani, 19, Rome, 1977), 481-504.
Dugdale, William (and Dodsworth, Roger), *Monasticon Anglicanum*, 3 vols. (London, 1655-73).
Dunbabin, Jean, 'Aristotle in the Schools', *Trends in Medieval Political Thought*, ed. Beryl Smalley (Oxford, 1965), 65-85.
Dykmans, Marc, *Robert d'Anjou: la vision bienheureuse. Traité envoyé au pape Jean XXII* (Miscellanea Historiae Pontificiae, 30, Rome, 1970).
— *Les Sermons de Jean XXII sur la vision béatifique* (ibid., 34, Rome, 1973).
— *Pour et contre Jean XXII en 1333. Deux Traités avignonnais sur la vision béatifique* (Studi e Testi, 274, Città del Vaticano, 1975).
— 'Le Cardinal Annibal de Ceccano et la vision béatifique', *Gregorianum*, 50 (1969), 343-82.
— 'À propos de Jean XXII et de Benoît XII. La libération de Thomas Waleys', *AHP* 7 (1969), 115-30.
— 'Le Dernier sermon de Guillaume d'Alnwick', *AFH* 63 (1970), 259-79.
— 'Les Frères Mineurs d'Avignon au début de 1333 et le sermon de Gautier de Chatton sur la vision béatifique', *AHDLMA* 46 (1971), 105-48.
— 'Le Cardinal Annibal de Ceccano (vers 1282-1350), étude biographique suivi du testament du 17 juin 1348', *Bulletin de l'institut historique belge*, 43 (1973), 134-344.
— 'De Jean XXII au concile de Florence ou les avatars d'une hérésie gréco-latine', *RHE* 68 (1973), 29-66.
Eckermann, Karla, *Studien zur Geschichte des monarchischen Denkens im 15. Jahrhundert* (Abhandlungen zur Mittleren und Neueren Geschichte, 75, Berlin, 1933).
Edwards, Kathleen, *The English Secular Cathedrals in the Middle Ages. A constitutional study with special reference to the fourteenth century* (Manchester-New York, 1967).

Ehrle, Franz, *Historia bibliothecae Romanorum pontificum tum Bonifatianae tum Avenionensis* (Rome, 1890).

Emden, Alfred B., 'Northerners and Southerners in the Organization of the University to 1509', *Oxford Studies presented to Daniel Callus* (OHS, n.s. 16, 1964), 1–30.

Enchiridion Symbolorum, ed. Heinrich Denzinger–Adolf Schönmetzer (Barcelona–Freiburg–Rome–New York, 1963).

The English Hospice in Rome, *The Venerabile*, Sexcentenary Issue, 21 (Rome, 1962).

Erikson, Carolly M., 'The fourteenth-century Franciscans and their Critics', *FS* 35 (1975), 107–35; 36 (1976), 108–47.

Etzweiler, James P., 'John Baconthorpe: "Prince of the Averroists"', *FS* 36 (1976), 148–76.

— 'Baconthorpe and Latin Averroism', *Carmelus*, 18 (1971), 235–92.

Eubel, Conrad, *Bullarii Franciscani Epitome* (Ad Claras Aquas, 1908).

Farr, William, *John Wyclif as Legal Reformer* (Studies in the History of Christian Thought, 10, Leiden, 1974).

Feine, Hans E., *Kirchliche Rechtsgeschichte: die katholische Kirche* (5th edn., Cologne–Graz, 1972).

Feret, Pierre, *La Faculté de théologie de Paris et ses docteurs les plus célèbres, moyen âge*, 4 vols. (Paris, 1894–7).

Finke, Heinrich, *Aus den Tagen Bonifaz' VIII. Funde und Forschungen* (Münster, 1902).

— (ed.), *Acta Aragonensia*, 3 vols. (Berlin–Leipzig, 1908–22).

Fitzmaurice, Edward B., and Little, Andrew G., *Materials for the History of the Franciscan Province of Ireland, A.D. 1230–1450* (Manchester, 1920).

FitzRalph (see Radulphi, Ricardus).

Fletcher, Charles R. L., 'The University and Cardinal Gailard de Mota (1325–1345)', *Collectanea*, i.16–26.

Fordun, John, *Scotichronicon*, ed. Thomas Hearne, 5 vols. (Oxford, 1722).

Forshall, Josiah, and Madden, Frederick (eds.), *The Holy Bible: made from the Latin vulgate by John Wycliffe and his followers* (Oxford, 1850).

Frame, Robin, 'Power and Society in the Lordship of Ireland, 1272–1377', *Past and Present*, 76 (1977), 3–33.

Garrod, Heathcote W. (ed.), *Merton College Injunctions of Archbishop Kilwardby 1276* (Oxford, 1929).

Gay, Jules, *Le Pape Clément VI et les affaires d'orient (1342–52)*, (Paris, 1904).

Gérard d'Abbéville, *Contra adversarium perfectionis christianiae*, ed. Sophronius Clasen, *AFH* 31 (1938), 276–329; 32 (1939), 89–200.

Giese, Wolfgang, 'Asienkunde für den kreuzfahrenden Westen. Die "Flos historiarum terre orientis" des Hayto von Gorhigos (O.Praem.) aus dem Jahre 1307', *Secundum Regulam Vivere. Festschrift für P. Norbert Backmund O.Praem.*, ed. Gert Melville (Windberg, 1978), 245–64.

Gilbert, John T. (ed.) *Chartularies of St Mary's Abbey, Dublin: with the Register of its House at Dunbrody, and Annals of Ireland*, 2 vols. (RS, London, 1884).

Gill, John, 'Pope Urban V (1362-70) and the Greeks of Crete', *OCP* 39 (1973), 461-8.
Gilson, Etienne, *La Philosophie au moyen âge. Des origines patristiques à la fin du XIVe siècle* (2nd edn., Paris, 1952).
Glancy, Michael, 'The Primates and the Church Lands of Armagh', *Seanchas Árdmhacha*, 5 (1970), 370-96.
Glorieux, Palémon, *Répertoire des maîtres en théologie de Paris au XIIIe siècle* (Paris, 1933).
— *La Faculté des arts et ses maîtres au XIIIe siècle* (Paris, 1971).
Golubovich, Girolamo, *Bibliotheca bio-bibliographica della terra santa e dell'oriente francescano*, iv (Quaracchi, 1923).
Grauert, Hermann, 'Meister Johann von Toledo', *SB München, phil.hist. Klasse* (Munich, 1901), 111-325.
Gregoras, Nikephoros, *Historia*, ed. L. Schopen and I. Bekker (Bonn, 1829-55).
— *Rhomäische Geschichte: Historia Rhomaike*, German trans. and notes by Jan Louis van Dieten (Stuttgart, 1973).
Gregorii de Arimino O.S.A. Registrum Generalatus 1357-1358, ed. Albericus de Meijer (Fontes Historiae Ordinis S. Augustini. Prima Series: Registra Priorum Generalium 1, Rome, 1976).
Grundmann, Herbert, *Ausgewählte Aufsätze. Teil 1, Religiöse Bewegungen; Teil 2, Joachim von Fiore; Teil 3, Bildung und Sprache* (Schriften der Monumenta Germaniae Historica, 25, 1-3, Stuttgart, 1976-8).
Guidi, Pietro, *Inventari di libri nelle serie dell'Archivio Vaticano (1287-1459)*, (= Studi e Testi, 135, Città del Vaticano, 1948).
Guillaume de St Amour, *De periculis novissimorum temporum*, printed in Brown, *Fasciculus rerum expetendarum*, ii.9-64.
Guillemain, Bernard, *La Court pontificale d'Avignon 1309-1376. Étude d'une societé* (Bibliothèque des Écoles françaises d'Athenes et de Rome, 201, Paris, 1966).
Gwynn, Aubrey, 'The Medieval University of St Patrick's, Dublin', *Studies*, 27 (1938), 199-212, 437-54.
— 'The Sermon Diary of Richard FitzRalph, Archbishop of Armagh', *PRIA* 44 C (1937), 1-57.
— 'Ireland and the English Nation at the Council of Constance', ibid., 45 C (1940), 183-233.
— 'Provincial and Diocesan Decrees of the Diocese of Dublin during the Anglo-Norman period', *Arch.Hib.* 11 (1944), 31-177.
— 'Two Sermons of Primate Richard FitzRalph', ibid., 14 (1949), 50-65.
Hammerich, Louis L., 'Eine Pilgerfahrt des XIV. Jahrhunderts nach dem Fegfeuer des hl. Patrizius', *Zeitschrift für deutsche Philologie*, 53 (1928), 25-40.
— (ed.), Visiones Georgii. Visiones quas in purgatorio sancti Patricii vidit Georgius miles de Ungeria A.D. MCCCLIII, *Det Kgl. Danske Videnskabernes Selskab. Historisk-filologiske Meddelelser*, 18,2 (Copenhagen, 1930).
Hand, Geoffrey J., 'The Rivalry of the Cathedral Chapters in Medieval Dublin', *JRSAI* 92 (1962), 193-206.
— 'The Medieval Chapter of St Patrick's Cathedral, Dublin: the early period (c.1219-c.1279)', *Repertorium Novum*, 3 (1964), 229-48.

Hand, Geoffrey J., 'The forgotten Statutes of Kilkenny: a brief survey', *Irish Jurist*, n.s.1 (1966), 299-312.
— *English Law in Ireland 1290-1324* (Cambridge, 1967).
— 'English Law in Ireland, 1172-1351', *Northern Ireland Legal Quarterly*, 23 (1972), 393-422.
Harvey, John, *English Medieval Architects* (London, 1954).
Harvey, Margaret, 'Two "quaestiones" on the Great Schism by Nicholas Fakenham, OFM', *AFH* 70 (1977), 97-127.
Hayes, Richard J., *Manuscript Sources for the History of Irish Civilization*, 11 vols. (Boston, Mass., 1965).
Hechisch, Barnabas, *De immaculata conceptione beatae M.V. secundum Thomam de Sutton OP et Robertum de Cowton OFM* (Rome, 1958).
Historical MSS Commission Reports (London, 1870 ff.).
Hödl, Ludwig, 'Zum Streit um die Bussprivilegien der Mendikantenorden in Wien im 14. und beginnenden 15. Jahrhundert', *ZKT* 79 (1957), 170-89.
Hoffmann, Fritz, *Die Schriften des Oxforder Kanzlers Iohannes Lutterell. Texte zur Theologie des vierzehnten Jahrhunderts* (Leipzig, 1959).
Hohmann, Thomas, *Heinrichs von Langenstein 'Unterscheidung der Geister' lateinisch und deutsch. Texte und Untersuchungen zu Übersetzungsliteratur aus der Wiener Schule* (Münchener Texte und Untersuchungen zur deutschen Literatur des Mittelalters, 43. Zürich-Munich, 1977).
Holinshed, Raphael, *Chronicles of England, Scotland and Ireland*, ed. J. Johnson *et al.*, 6 vols. (London, 1807).
Hudson, Anne, 'A neglected Wycliffite text', *JEH* 29 (1978), 257-79.
Jacob, Ernest F., 'Petitions for Benefices from English Universities during the Great Schism', *TRHS* 4th ser. 27 (1945), 41-59.
— *The Register of Henry Chichele, 1414-43*, 4 vols. (Canterbury and York Society, Oxford, 1938-47).
Jacopo de Voragine, *Legenda aurea*, ed. Johann G. T. Grässe (Leipzig, 1850).
James, Montague R., *The Ancient Libraries of Canterbury and Dover. The catalogues of the libraries of Christ Church Priory and St Augustine's Abbey at Canterbury and St Martin's Priory at Dover* (Cambridge, 1903).
— *A descriptive Catalogue of the Manuscripts of the Library of Sidney Sussex College Cambridge* (Cambridge, 1895).
— *A descriptive Catalogue of the Manuscripts of the Library of Corpus Christi College Cambridge*, 2 vols. (Cambridge, 1909-12).
Jarrett, Bede, *The English Dominicans* (London, 1921).
Jenkins, Alexander, *History of the City of Exeter* (Exeter, 1841).
John of Reading, *Chronica*, ed. James Tait (Manchester, 1914).
Jones, W. R., 'The Armenian Church and the Papacy in the Fourteenth Century: Richard FitzRalph's Critique of Armenian Christianity', *The Armenian Review*, 25 (1972), pt. I, 3-9.
Juárez, Agustin Una, 'Aristóteles y Averroes en el siglo XIV. Las Autoridadas "Mayores" para Walter Burley', *Antonianum*, 52 (1977), 326-58, 680-94.
Jugie, Martin, 'Barlaam', *DHGE* 6 (Paris, 1932), 817-34.

Jugie, Martin, 'Barlaam est il né Catholique?', *Échos d'Orient,* 39 (1940), 100–23.

Jusserand, Jean J., *English Wayfaring Life in the Middle Ages,* 4th edn. (London, 1950).

Kadlec, Jaroslav, *Leben und Schriften des Prager Magisters Adalbert Rankonis de Ericinio, aus dem Nachlass von Rudolf Holinka und Jan Vilikovský* (Beiträge zur Geschichte der Philosophie und Theologie des Mittelalters, neue Folge 4, Münster, 1971).

Kaeppeli, Thomas, *Le Procès contre Thomas Waleys OP. Études et documents* (Dissertationes Historicae, 6, Rome, 1936).

— 'Note sugli scrittori domenicani di nome Giovanni di Napoli', *AFP* 10 (1940), 48–76.

Kedar, Benjamin Z., 'Canon Law and Local Practice: the case of mendicant preaching in late medieval England', *Bulletin of Medieval Canon Law,* n.s. 2 (1972), 17–32.

Ker, Neil R., *Medieval Libraries of Great Britain. A list of surviving books* (2nd edn., Royal Historical Society, London, 1964).

Kingsford, Charles L., *The Grey Friars of London* (Aberdeen, 1915).

Kitchel, Mary Jean, 'Walter Burley's Doctrine of the Soul: another view', *MS* 39 (1977), 387–401.

— 'The "De Potentiis Animae" of Walter Burley', *MS* 33 (1971), 85–113.

Knowles, M. David, *The Religious Orders in England,* 3 vols. (Cambridge, 1948–59).

Knox, R. Buick, *James Ussher, Archbishop of Armagh* (Cardiff, 1967).

Koch, Josef, *Durandus de S. Porciano* (Beiträge zur Geschichte der Philosophie und Theologie des Mittelalters, 26, Münster, 1927).

— *Kleine Schriften,* 2 vols. (Storia e Letteratura, 127–8, Rome, 1973).

— 'Die Magister-Jahre des Durandus de S. Porciano OP und der Konflikt mit seinem Orden', *Miscellanea Francesco Ehrle,* i (Studi e Testi, 37, 1924), 265–306. Reprinted in *Kleine Schriften,* ii, 7–118.

— 'Der Prozess gegen den Magister Johannes de Polliaco und seine Vorgeschichte (1312–1321)', *Recherches de théologie ancienne et médiévale,* 5 (1933), 391–422. Reprinted in *Kleine Schriften,* ii, 387–422.

— 'Neue Aktenstücke zu dem gegen Wilhelm Ockham in Avignon geführten Prozess', ibid., 7 (1935), 353–80; 6 (1936), 79–93, 168–97. Reprinted in *Kleine Schriften,* ii, 275–365.

— 'Der Kardinal Jacques Fournier (Benedikt XII.) als Gutachter in theologischen Prozessen', *Die Kirche und ihre Ämte und Stände. Festgabe für Joseph Kardinal Frings,* ed. W. Corsten, A. Frotz, P. Linden (Cologne, 1960), 441–52. Reprinted in *Kleine Schriften,* ii, 367–86.

Kölmel, Wilhelm, *Regimen Christianum. Weg und Ergebnisse des Gewaltenverhältnisses und des Gewaltenverständnisses (8. bis 14. Jahrhundert),* (Berlin, 1970).

— 'Apologia Pauperum. Die Armutslehre Bonaventuras da Bagneoregio als soziale Theorie', *Historisches Jahrbuch,* 94 (1974), 46–68.

Kohler, Charles, 'Lettres pontificales concernant l'histoire de la Petite Arménie au XIVe siècle', *Florilegium Melchior de Vogüé* (Paris, 1909), 308–23.

Konrad von Megenberg, *Werke. Ökonomik I—II,* ed. Sabine Krüger (Monumenta Germaniae Historica 500-1500, Staatsschriften des späteren Mittelalters. III.Band. Die Werke des Konrad von Megenberg, 5.Stück: Yconomia, Stuttgart, 1973-7).

Krajcar, J., 'The Ruthenian Patriarchate', *OCP* 30 (1964), 65-84.

Kretzmann, Norman, 'Richard Kilwington and the Logic of Instantaneous Speed', *Studi sul XIV secolo in memoria di Anneliese Maier*, a cura di Alfonso Maierù e Agostino Paravicini Bagliani (Storia e Letteratura 151, Rome, 1981, forthcoming).

Kritzeck, James, *Peter the Venerable and Islam* (Princeton, 1964).

Kuiters, Rafael (ed.), 'Licet Ecclesiae Catholicae', *Augustiniana,* 6 (1956), 9-36.

Laiou, Angeliki, 'Marino Sanudo Torsello, Byzantium and the Turks', *Speculum,* 45 (1970), 374-92.

Lambert, Malcolm D., *Franciscan Poverty, the doctrine of the absolute poverty of Christ and the apostles in the Franciscan Order 1210-1323* (London, 1961).

— 'The Franciscan Crisis under John XXII', *FS* 32 (1972), 123-43.

Lang, Albert, *Die Entfaltung des apologetischen Problems in der Scholastik des Mittelalters* (Freiburg i. Br., 1962).

Leff, Gordon, *Bradwardine and the Pelagians* (Cambridge Studies in Medieval Life and Thought, 2nd ser. 5, Cambridge, 1957).

— *Gregory of Rimini. Tradition and Innovation in Fourteenth-Century Thought* (Manchester, 1961).

— 'The Changing Patterns of Thought in the earlier fourteenth century', *Bull. J. Rylands Library,* 43 (1961), 343-72.

— 'John Wyclif: the Path to Dissent', *PBA* 52 (1966), 143-80.

— *Heresy in the Later Middle Ages. The relation of heterodoxy to dissent c.1250-c.1450,* 2 vols. (Manchester-New York, 1967).

— *William of Ockham. The Metamorphosis of Scholastic Discourse* (Manchester, 1975).

Leire Guimaraens, Francisco da, 'La Doctrine des théologiens sur l'Immaculée Conception de 1250 à 1350', *Études Franciscaines* n.s. 3 (1952), 181-203; 4 (1953), 23-51, 167-87.

Leland, John, *Commentarii de Scriptoribus Britannicis ex autographo Lelandino edidit Ant. Hall* (Oxford, 1709).

Lerner, Robert E., 'A Note on the University Career of Jacques Fournier, O.Cist., later Pope Benedict XII', *ASOC* 30 (1974), 66-9.

Leslie, Shane, *St Patrick's Purgatory* (London, 1932).

Lippens, Hugolin, 'Le Droit nouveau des mendiants en conflit avec le droit coutumier du clergé séculier du concile de Vienne à celui de Trente', *AFH* 47 (1954), 241-92.

Little, Andrew G., *The Grey Friars in Oxford* (OHS 1892).

Little, Lester K., *Religious Poverty and the Profit Economy in Medieval Europe* (London, 1978).

Loenertz, Raymond-Joseph, *La Societé des frères pérégrinants. Étude sur l'orient dominicain* (Dissertationes Historicae, 7, Rome, 1937).

— 'Ambassadeurs grecs auprès du pape Clément VI (1348)', *OCP* 19 (1953), 178-96. Reprinted in *Byzantina et Franco-Graeca,* ed. Peter Schreiner, i (Rome, 1970), 285-302.

Lotharii Cardinalis (Innocentii III) de miseria humane conditionis, ed. Michele Maccarrone (Lucca, 1955).

Lunt, William E., *Papal Revenues in the Middle Ages*, 2 vols. (New York, 1934).

Lydon, James F., *Ireland in the Later Middle Ages* (The Gill History of Ireland, 6, Dublin, 1973).

— 'The Bruce Invasion of Ireland', *Historical Studies*, 4 (1963), 111–25.

MacFhionnbhairr, Daragh (ed.), *Guillelmi de Villana Cremonensis tractatus cuius titulus reprobatio errorum* (Corpus Scriptorum Augustinianorum, 2, Rome, 1977).

McGrade, Arthur S., *The Political Thought of William of Ockham* (Cambridge Studies in Medieval Life and Thought, 3rd ser. 7, Cambridge, 1974).

McGrath, Fergal, *Education in Ancient and Medieval Ireland* (Dublin, 1979).

McKisack, May, *The Fourteenth Century 1307-1399* (The Oxford History of England, 5, Oxford, 1959).

McNeill, Charles (ed.), *Registrum de Kilmainham* (Irish Manuscripts Commission, Dublin 1932).

MacNiocaill, Gearóid, *Na Búirgéisí*, 2 vols. (Dublin, 1964).

Mahn, Jean-Berthold, *Le Pape Benoît XII et les cisterciens* (Paris, 1949).

Maier, Anneliese, *Ausgehendes Mittelalter. Gesammelte Aufsätze zur Geistesgeschichte des 14. Jahrhunderts*, 3 vols. (Storia e Letteratura, 97, 105, 138, Rome, 1964–77), with *Addenda* in iii.609–13.

— *Die Vorläufer Galileis im 14. Jahrhundert* (Storia e Letteratura, 22, Rome, 1949, revised edn., 1966).

— *An der Grenze von Scholastik und Naturwissenschaft. Studien zur Naturphilosophie des 14. Jahrhunderts* (Essen, 1943, 2nd edn., Storia e Letteratura, 41, Rome, 1952).

— *Zwischen Philosophie und Mechanik* (Storia e Letteratura, 69, Rome, 1958).

— 'Diskussionen über das aktuell Unendliche in der ersten Hälfte des 14. Jahrhunderts', *Divus Thomas*, 25 (1947), 147–66, 317–37. Reprinted in *Ausgehendes Mittelalter*, i, 41–85.

— 'Annotazioni autografe di Giovanni XXII in codici vaticani', *Rivista di storia della chiesa in Italia*, 6 (1952), 317–22. Reprinted in *Ausgehendes Mittelalter*, ii,81–96.

— 'Zu einigen Problemen der Ockhamforschung', *AFH* 46 (1953), 161–94. Reprinted in *Ausgehendes Mittelalter*, i,175–208.

— 'Ein unbeachteter "Averroist" des 14. Jahrhunderts: Walter Burley', *Medioevo e Rinascimento. Studi in onore di Bruno Nardi*, ii (Florence, 1955), 477–99. Reprinted in *Ausgehendes Mittelalter*, i,101–21.

— 'Verschollene Aristoteleskommentare des 14. Jahrhunderts', *Autour d'Aristote. Recueil d'études de philosphie ancienne et médiévale offert à Monsigneur A. Mansion* (Louvain, 1955), 515–41. Reprinted in *Ausgehendes Mittelalter*, i,237–64.

— 'Zu einigen Sentenzenkommentaren des 14. Jahrhunderts', *AFH* 51 (1958), 369–409. Reprinted in *Ausgehendes Mittelalter*, i,265–305.

— 'Das Problem der Evidenz in der Philosophie des 14. Jahrhunderts', *Scholastik*, 38 (1963), 183–225. Reprinted in *Ausgehendes Mittelalter*, ii,367–418.

Maier, Anneliese, 'Der Katalog der päpstlichen Bibliothek in Avignon vom Jahr 1411', *AHP* 1 (1963), 97-177. Reprinted in *Ausgehendes Mittelalter*, iii,77-157.

— 'Zu einigen Handschriften der päpstlichen Bibliothek von Avignon. Nachtrag zur Edition des Katalogs von 1411', *AHP* 2 (1964), 323, 38. Reprinted in *Ausgehendes Mittelalter*, iii,159-66.

— 'Die "Bibliotheca Minor" Benedikts XIII. (Petrus de Luna)', *AHP* 3 (1965), 131-91. Reprinted in *Ausgehendes Mittelalter*, iii,1-53.

— 'Zwei unbekannte Streitschriften gegen Johann XXII. aus dem Kreis der Münchener Minoriten', *AHP* 5 (1967), 41-78. Reprinted in *Ausgehendes Mittelalter*, iii,373-414.

— 'Zu einigen Disputationen aus dem Visio-Streit unter Johann XXII', *AFP* 39 (1969), 97-126. Reprinted in *Ausgehendes Mittelalter*, iii, 415-45.

— 'Zwei Prooemien Benedikts XII.', *AHP* 7 (1969), 131-61. Reprinted in *Ausgehendes Mittelalter*, iii,447-79.

— 'Eine unbeachtete Quaestio aus dem Visio-Streit unter Johann XXII', *AFH* 63 (1970), 280-318. Reprinted in *Ausgehendes Mittelalter*, iii, 505-42.

— 'Schriften, Daten und Personen aus dem Visio-Streit unter Johann XXII', *AHP* 9 (1971), 143-86. Reprinted in *Ausgehendes Mittelalter*, iii,543-90.

Mall, Eduard, 'Zur Geschichte der Legende vom Purgatorium des hl. Patrizius', *Romanische Forschungen*, 6 (1888), 139-97.

Mandalari, Giannantonio, *Fra Barlaamo Calabrese maestro del Petrarca* (Rome, 1888).

Mariani, Ugo, *Chiesa e Stato nei teologi agostiniani del secolo XIV* (Rome, 1957).

Marschall, Werner, 'Schlesier auf dem Konzil von Basel', *AHC* 8 (1976), 294-325.

Martin, Francis X., 'The Irish Augustinian Reform Movement in the fifteenth century', *Medieval Studies presented to Aubrey Gwynn S.J.*, 230-64.

— 'An Irish Augustinian disputes at Oxford: Adam Payn 1402', *Festschrift Adolar Zumkeller*, 289-322 (see Courtenay).

— and Meijer, Alberic de, 'Irish Material in the Augustinian Archives, Rome, 1354–c.1620', *Arch.Hib.* 19 (1956), 61-134.

Martin, Joseph, 'Old Title Deeds of Co. Louth. Some Dundalk Deeds, 1707 to 1843', *County Louth Archaeological Journal*, 10 (1941–4), 138-48.

Mathes, Fulgence A., 'The Poverty Movement and the Augustinian Hermits', *AA* 31 (1968), 5-154; 32 (1969), 5-116.

Matthew of Paris, *Chronica Majora*, 7 vols. (RS, London, 1872-83).

Mercati, Giovanni, *Se la versione dall'ebraico del codice Veneto Greco VII sia di Simone Atumano arcivescovo di Tebe* (Studi e Testi, 30, Città del Vaticano, 1916).

Meyendorff, John, 'Un mauvais théologien de l'unité au XIVᵉ siècle: Barlaam le calabrais', *1054-1954. L'Église et les églises. Études et travaux offerts à Dom Lambert Beauduin*, ii (Chevotoque, 1955), 47-64.

— *Introduction à l'étude de Grégoire Palamas* (Paris, 1959), English trans. *A Study of Gregory Palamas* (London, 1964).
— *Byzantine Hesychasm: Historical, Theological and Social Problems* (Variorum Reprints, London, 1974).
Miethke, Jürgen, 'Papst, Ortsbischof und Universität in den Pariser Theologenprozessen des 13. Jahrhunderts', *Miscellanea Mediaevalia*, 10 (Berlin–New York, 1975), 52–94.
Minnis, Alistair J., ' "Authorial intention" and "literal sense" in the exegetical theories of Richard FitzRalph and John Wyclif: an essay in the medieval history of biblical hermeneutics', *PRIA* 75 C (1975), 1–30.
Modana, Leonello, *Catalogo dei codici ebraici . . . di Bologna* (Florence, 1889).
Mohan, G. E., 'The "Quaestio de Relatione" attributed to Ockham', *FS* 11 (1951), 273–303.
Mollat, Guillaume, *Les Papes d'Avignon* (10th edn., Paris, 1965).
— *The Popes at Avignon* (trans. from 9th French edn., London, 1963).
— 'Contribution à l'histoire du Sacré Collège de Clément V à Eugène IV', *RHE* 46 (1951), 22–122, 566–94.
Monck Mason, W. H., *History and Antiquities of the Collegiate and Cathedral Church of St. Patrick, near Dublin* (Dublin, 1820).
Moody, Theodore W., Martin, Francis X., and Byrne, Francis J. (eds.), *A New History of Ireland* (Oxford, 1976 ff.).
Moorman, John, *A History of the Franciscan Order* (Oxford, 1968).
Mortier, Daniel A., *Histoire des Maîtres généraux de l'ordre des frères prêcheurs*, 7 vols. (Paris, 1903–13).
Muldoon, James, 'The Avignon Papacy and the Frontiers of Christendom: the Evidence of Vatican Register 62', *AHP* 17 (1969), 125–95.
Munimenta Academica, ed. Henry Anstey, 2 vols. (RS, London, 1868).
Murdoch, John E., 'Mathesis in Philosophiam Scholasticam Introducta: the rise and development of the application of mathematics in fourteenth-century philosophy and theology', *Arts libéraux et philosophie au moyen âge* (Paris, 1969), 215–54.
Netter, Thomas (Waldensis), *Doctrinale Antiquatum Fidei ecclesiae catholicae advers. Wiclefitas et Hussitas*, 3 vols. (Venice, 1571).
Nicholls, Kenneth, *Gaelic and Gaelicised Ireland in the Middle Ages* (The Gill History of Ireland, 4, Dublin, 1972).
Nicol, Donald, 'Byzantine Requests for an Oecumenical Council in the fourteenth century', *AHC* 1 (1969), 69–85. Reprinted in *Byzantium: its Ecclesiastical History and Relations with the Western World* (Variorum Reprints, London, 1972).
— 'The Byzantine Church and Hellenistic Learning in the fourteenth century', *Studies in Church History*, 5 (1969), 23–57. Reprinted in *Byzantium . . .*, as above.
Oberman, Heiko A., *Archbishop Thomas Bradwardine, a fourteenth-century Augustinian. A study of his theology in its historical context* (2nd edn., Utrecht, 1958).
— *Werden und Wertung der Reformation. Vom Wegestreit zum Glaubenskampf* (Spätscholastik und Reformation, 2, Tübingen, 1977).
— and Weisheipl, James A., 'The Sermo Epicinius ascribed to Thomas Bradwardine', *AHDLMA* 33 (1958), 295–329.

Guillelmi de Ockham opera politica, ed. Jeffrey G. Sikes *et al.*, 3 vols. (Manchester, 1940–56).

O'Dwyer, Peter, 'The Carmelite Order in pre-Reformation Ireland', *Proc. ICHC* (Dublin, 1968), 49–62.

Oliver, George, *History of the City of Exeter* (Exeter, 1861).

—— *Lives of the Bishops of Exeter and a History of the Cathedral* (Exeter, 1861).

Orme, Nicholas, *English Schools in the Middle Ages* (London, 1973).

Otway-Ruthven, Annette J., *A History of Medieval Ireland* (London, 1968).

Oudenrijn, M. A. van den, *Das Offizium des hl. Dominikus des Bekenners im Brevier der "Fratres Unitores" von Ostarmenien. Ein Beitrag zur Missions- und Liturgiegeschichte des vierzehnten Jahrhunderts* (Dissertationes Historicae, 5, Rome, 1935).

Pantin, William A., *The English Church in the Fourteenth Century* (Cambridge, 1955).

—— 'The "Defensorium" of Adam Easton', *EHR* 51 (1936), 675–80.

Paravicini Bagliani, Agostino, 'Un matematico nella corte pontificia del secolo XIII: Campano da Novara (+ 1296)', *Rivista di storia della chiesa in Italia*, 27 (1973), 98–129.

Parry, J. H. (ed.), *Register of John Trillek, 1344–1361*, 2 vols. (Cantilupe Society [Hereford] – Canterbury and York Society, 1910–12).

Patschovsky, Alexander, 'Strassburger Beginenverfolgungen im 14. Jahrhundert', *Deutsches Archiv*, 30 (1974), 56–198.

Paulus, Nikolaus, *Geschichte des Ablasses im Mittelalter vom Ursprunge bis in die Mitte des 14. Jahrhunderts*, 2 vols. (Paderborn, 1922–3).

Peck, Francis, *Academia Tertia Anglia, or the Antiquarian Annals of Stamford* (Stamford, 1727).

Pelzer, Auguste (Augustus), *Codices Vaticani Latini* Tom.II, pars i (Città del Vaticano, 1931).

—— 'Les 51 articles de Guillaume Occam censurés en Avignon en 1326', *RHE* 18 (1922), 240–70.

Perini, David, *Bibliographia Augustiniana*, 4 vols. (Florence, 1929).

Petrarca, Francesco, *Epistolae Familiares*, ed. Vittorio Rossi (Edizione nazionale, Florence, 1931).

Petrowicz, Gregorio, 'I Fratres Unitores nella Chiesa Armena', *Euntes Docente*, 22 (Festschrift Cardinal Agaganian, 1969), 309–47.

Piana, Celestino, 'Un sermone inedito su l'assunzione della Vergine di Riccardo FitzRalph, Primate d'Irlanda (+ 1360)', *Studi Francescani*, 3. ser., 20 (1948), 115–25.

Podskalsky, Gerhard, *Theologie und Philosophie in Byzanz. Der Streit um die theologische Methodik in der spätbyzantinischen Geistesgeschichte (14./15. Jh.), seine systematischen Grundlagen und seine historische Entwicklung* (Byzantinisches Archiv, 15, Munich, 1977).

Polc, Jaroslav, 'Ernst von Pardubitz', *Lebensbilder zur Geschichte der Böhmischen Länder 3, Karl IV. und sein Kreis* (Munich–Vienna, 1978), 25–43.

Pollard, Graham, 'The oldest Statute Book of the University', *The Bodleian Library Record*, 8 (1968), 69–92.

Powicke, Frederick M., *The Medieval Books of Merton College* (Oxford, 1931).

— and Cheney, Christopher R. (eds.), *Councils and Synods*, 2 vols. (Oxford, 1964).
Prince, John, *Damnonii Orientales Illustres: or The Worthies of Devon* (Exeter, 1701).
Prinz, Friedrich, 'Marsilius von Padua', *ZBLG* 39 (1976), 39–77.
Puschel, Brita, *Thomas à Becket in der Literatur* (Beiträge zur englischen Philologie, 45, Bochum, 1963).
Radulphi, Ricardus, *Summa de Questionibus Armenorum*, ed. Johannis Sudoris (Paris, 1511).
— *Proposicio 'Unusquisque'* (see Hammerich).
— 'Sermons' (see Gwynn, Piana, Zimmermann).
— *Defensio Curatorum* (printed Louvain, 1475, Paris, 1485, Rouen, 1485, Lyon, 1496, Paris, 1627, Paris, 1633; in Goldast, *Monarchia s. Romani imperii*, ii.1393–1410; Brown, *Fasciculus rerum expetendarum*, ii.466–86.
— *De Pauperie Salvatoris*, Books I–IV, ed. Reginald L. Poole, in John Wyclif, *De dominio divino* (WS, London, 1890), 257–476.
Reeves, Marjorie, *The Influence of Prophecy in the Later Middle Ages. A Study in Joachimism* (Oxford, 1969).
— and Hirsch-Reich, Beatrice, *The Figurae of Joachim of Fiore* (Oxford Warburg Studies, 8, Oxford, 1972).
Reeves, William E. (ed.), *Acts of Archbishop Colton in his Metropolitan Visitation of the Diocese of Derry*, 1397 (Dublin, 1850).
Reichert, Benedictus M., *Acta Capitulorum Generalium Ordinis Praedicatorum*, 3 vols. (Monumenta Ordinis Praedicatorum Historica, Rome, 1898).
Rennhofer, Friedrich, *Die Augustiner-Eremiten in Wien. Ein Beitrag zur Kulturgeschichte Wiens* (Cassiciacum, 13, Würzburg, 1956).
Richard, Jean, *La Papauté et les missions d'orient au moyen âge (XIIIe–XVe siècles)*, (Collections de l'École Française de Rome, 33, Rome, 1977).
Richard de Bury (d'Aungerville), *Philobiblon*, ed. and trans. E. C. Thomas (London, 1888).
Richardson, H. G., and Sayles, G. O., *The Irish Parliament in the Middle Ages* (Philadelphia, 1952).
Ritzler, Remigius, 'Die Verschleppung der Päpstlichen Archive nach Paris unter Napoleon I. und deren Rückführung nach Rom in den Jahren 1815 bis 1817', *Römische Historische Mitteilungen*, 6–7 (1962–4), 144–90.
Robert of Gloucester, *The Life and Martyrdom of Thomas Becket Archbishop of Canterbury*, ed. W. H. Black (Percy Society, 19, London, 1845).
Robson, John A., *Wyclif and the Oxford Schools. The Relation of the 'Summa de Ente' to the Scholastic Debates at Oxford in the later fourteenth century* (Cambridge Studies in Medieval Life and Thought, n.s.8, 2nd edn., Cambridge 1966).
Roger of Wendover, *Flores Historiarum* (ed. Eng. Hist. Soc., London, 1841).
Rose-Troup, F., *Bishop Grandisson, Student and Booklover* (Plymouth, 1929).

Roth, Cecil, *The Jews of Medieval Oxford* (OHS, 1951).
Rotolorum Patentium et Clausarum Cancellarie Hibernie, ed. Edward Tresham (Irish Record Commission, Dublin, 1828).
Roure, M. L., 'Insolubilia Walteri Burlei', *AHDLMA* 37 (1970), 262–84.
Runciman, Steven, *The Last Byzantine Renaissance* (Cambridge, 1970).
Rupprich, Hans, 'Das Wiener Schrifttum des ausgehende Mittelalters', *SB Wien, phil.hist.Klasse*, 228, 5 (Vienna, 1954).
Russell, Frederick H., *The Just War in the Middle Ages* (Cambridge Studies in Medieval Life and Thought, 3rd ser. 8, Cambridge, 1975).
Ruysschaert, José, *Codices Vaticani Latini 11414–11709* (Città del Vaticano, 1959).
Ryves, Thomas, *Regiminis Anglicani in Hibernia Defensio Adversus Analacten.* (London, 1642).
Salter, Herbert E., *The Oxford Deeds of Balliol College* (OHS, 1913).
— *The Medieval Archives of the University of Oxford*, 2 vols. (OHS, 1917–19).
— 'The Stamford Schism', *EHR* 37 (1922), 249–53.
— *Registrum Cancellarii Oxoniensis*, 2 vols. (OHS, 1932).
— *Medieval Oxford* (OHS, 1936).
Savage, Henry E., *The Fourteenth Century Builders* (Lichfield, 1916).
— *The Great Register of Lichfield* (Lichfield, 1923).
— *Richard FitzRalph, sometime Dean* (Lichfield, 1928).
Scaduto, Mario, *Il monachismo basiliano nella Sicilia medioevale* (Rome, 1947).
Schepers, Heinrich, 'Holcot contra dicta Crathorn', *Philosophisches Jahrbuch*, 77 (1970), 320–54; 79 (1972), 106–36.
Schimmelpfennig, Bernhard, 'Zisterzienserideal und Kirchenreform. Benedikt XII. (1334–42) als Reformpapst', *Zisterzienser-Studien*, iii (Berlin, 1976), 11–43.
Schirò, Giuseppi, 'I rapporti di Barlaam Calabro con le due Chiese di Roma e di Bisanzio', *Archivio storico per la Calabria e la Lucania*, 1 (1931), 325–57; 2 (1932), 71–89, 426–37; 5 (1935), 59–77; 6 (1936), 80–99, 302–25; 8 (1938), 47–71.
Schleyer, Karl, *Anfänge des Gallikanismus im 13. Jahrhundert. Der Widerstand des französischen Klerus gegen die Privilegierung der Bettelorden* (Berlin, 1937).
Schmaus, Michael, 'Zur Diskussion über das Problem der Univozität im Umkreis des Johannes Duns Scotus', *SB München, phil.hist. Klasse*, 4 (München, 1957).
Schmidt, Wieland, 'Richard de Bury – ein anti-höfischer Höfling', *Philobiblon*, 19 (1975), 156–88.
Schmitt, Clémens, *Un Pape réformateur et un défenseur de l'unité de l'Église. Benoît XII et l'ordre des frères mineurs* (Quaracchi–Florence, 1959).
Schmitz, Philibert, 'Les Sermons et discours de Clément VI, OSB', *RB* 41 (1929), 15–34.
Schneyer, Johann Baptist, *Repertorium der lateinischen Sermones des Mittelalters für die Zeit von 1150–1350* (Beiträge zur Geschichte der Philosophie und Theologie des Mittelalters, 43, Münster, 1969 ff.).
Scholz, Richard, *Unbekannte kirchenpolitische Streitschriften aus der*

Zeit Ludwigs des Bayern (1327-1354), 2 vols. (Bibliothek des Deutschen Historischen Instituts in Rom, 9-10, Rome, 1911-14).

Seppelt, Franz X., 'Der Kampf der Bettelorden an der Universität Paris in der Mitte des 13. Jahrhunderts', *Kirchengeschichtliche Abhandlungen*, ed. Max Sdralek, 6 (Breslau, 1908), 75-139.

Setton, Kenneth M., *The Papacy and the Levant (1204-1571)*, vols. 1-2 (The American Philosophical Society, Philadelphia, 1976-8).

— 'The Byzantine Background to the Italian Renaissance', *Proc. Am. Phil. Soc.* 100 (1956), 1-76.

Shapiro, Herman, 'A note on Walter Burley's Exaggerated Realism', *FS* 20 (1960), 205-14.

— 'More on the "Exaggeration" of Burley's Realism', *Manuscripta*, 6 (1962), 94-8.

Sheehy, Maurice P. (ed.), *Pontificia Hibernica: Medieval Papal Chancery Documents concerning Ireland*, 2 vols. (Dublin, 1962-5).

Sikes, Jeffrey G., 'John de Pouilly and Peter de la Palu', *EHR* 49 (1934), 219-40.

Simms, Katharine, 'The Archbishops of Armagh and the O'Neills 1347-1471', *IHS* 19 (1974), 38-55.

— 'The Concordat between Primate John Mey and Henry O'Neill (1455)', *Arch.Hib.* 34 (1976-77), 71-82.

Skeat, Walter W. (ed.), *Piers Plowman*, by William Langland, B text, EETS original ser. 28, 38, 54, 67, 81 (London, 1867-85).

Smalley, Beryl, *The Study of the Bible in the Middle Ages*, 2nd edn. (Oxford, 1952).

— (ed.), *Trends in Medieval Political Thought* (Oxford, 1965).

— 'John Baconthorpe's Postill on St. Matthew', *Medieval and Renaissance Studies*, 4 (1958), 91-145.

— 'Oxford University Sermons, 1290-1293', *Medieval Learning and Literature*, ed. Alexander-Gibson (Oxford, 1976), 307-27.

Statutes and Ordinances and Acts of the Parliament of Ireland, King John to Henry V, ed. H. F. Berry (Dublin, 1907).

Talbot, Peter, *Primatus Dubliniensis, or the Primacy of the See of Dublin by Peter Talbot, D.D., Titular Archbishop of Dublin* (Lille, 1674), trans. W. E. Kenny (Dublin, 1947).

Tanner, Thomas, *Bibliotheca Britannico-Hibernia, sive de scriptoribus qui in Anglia, Scotia et Hibernia ad saeculum XVII initium floruerunt* (London, 1748).

Teeaert, Amédée, 'Deux Questions inédités de Gérard d'Abbeville en faveur du clergé séculier', *Mélanges Auguste Pelzer* (Louvain, 1947), 347-87.

Thadei, Dermitius (= Hickey, Anthony), *Nitela Franciscanae Religionis* (Lyon, 1627).

Theiner, Augustus, *Vetera Monumenta Hibernorum et Scotorum historiam illustrantia* . . . (Rome, 1864).

Thomson, S. Harrison, 'The Order of Writing of Wyclif's Philosophical Works', *Českou Minulostí. Essays presented to Václav Novotný* (Prague, 1929), 146-66.

— 'Unnoticed Manuscripts and Works of Wyclif', *JTS* 38 (1937), 24-34, 139-48.

Thomson, Williell R., *Friars in the Cathedral. The first Franciscan Bishops 1226-1261* (Pontifical Institute of Mediaeval Studies, Studies and Texts, 33, Toronto, 1975).

Tierney, Brian, *Origins of Papal Infallibility 1150-1350. A Study on the Concepts of Infallibility, Sovereignty and Tradition in the Middle Ages* (Studies in the History of Christian Thought, 6, Leiden, 1972).

Tournebize, Henri-François, *Histoire politique et religieuse de l'Arménie depuis les origins des Arméniens jusqu'à la mort de leur dernier roi (l'an 1393)* (Paris, 1900).

— 'Arménie', *DHGE* iv. 290-1.

Trapp, A. Damasus, 'Augustinian Theology of the Fourteenth Century', *Augustiniana,* 6 (1956), 146-274.

— *et al.* (eds.), *Gregorii Ariminensis OESA Lectura super Primum et Secundum Sententiarum.* Tomus IV super Secundum (*Dist.*1-5); Tomus V super Secundum (*Dist.* 6-18). (Spätmittelalter und Reformation. Texte und Untersuchungen, ed. Heiko A. Oberman, Berlin-New York, 1979).

— 'Notes on the Tübingen Edition of Gregory of Rimini', *Augustiniana,* 29 (1979), 239-41; 30 (1980), 46-57.

Trevisa, John (of), Dialogus inter Militem et Clericum, Richard FitzRalph's Sermon: 'Defensio Curatorum', and Methodius: 'þe Bygynnyng of þe World and þe Ende of Worldes', ed. Aaron J. Perry (Early English Text Society, Oxford, 1925).

Trexler, Richard C., 'The Bishop's Portion. Generic Pious Legacies in the late middle ages in Italy', *Traditio,* 28 (1972), 397-450.

Tsirpanlis, Constantine N., 'The Career and Political Views of Marc Eugenicus', *Byzantion,* 44 (1974), 449-66.

Turley, Thomas, 'Guido Terreni and the Decretum', *Bulletin of Medieval Canon Law,* n.s.8 (1978), 29-34.

Tylenda, Joseph N., 'Calvin and the Avignon sermons of John XXII', *ITQ* 41 (1974), 37-52.

Uiblein, Paul, *Die Akten der Theologischen Fakultät der Universität Wien (1396-1508),* 2 vols. (Verband der wissenschaftlichen Gesellschaften Österreichs, Vienna, 1978).

Ulmann, Walter, *Medieval Papalism* (Cambridge, 1949).

— 'John Baconthorpe as a Canonist', *Church and Government in the Middle Ages. Essays presented to C. R. Cheney on his 70th Birthday* (Cambridge, 1976), 223-46. Reprinted in *Scholarship and Politics in the Middle Ages* (Variorum Reprints, London, 1978).

— 'Boniface VIII and his Contemporary Scholarship', *JTS*, n.s.27 (1976), 58-87. Reprinted in *Scholarship and Politics in the Middle Ages.*

Uyttenbroeck, C., 'Le droit pénitentiel des religieux de Boniface VIII à Sixte IV', *Études Franciscaines,* 47 (1935), 171-89, 306-32.

Vidal, J.-M., *Benoît XII (1334-1342). Lettres communes et curiales analysées d'après les registres dits d'Avignon et du Vatican,* 3 vols. (Paris, 1903-11).

Volaterranus, Raphael, *Commentariorum Urbanorum Raphaelis Volaterrani . . .* (Basel, 1544).

Voigt, Max, *Beiträge zur Geschichte der Visionenliteratur im Mittelalter* (Leipzig, 1924).

Vries, Wilhelm de, *Rom und die Patriarchate des Ostens* (Munich, 1963).
— 'Die Päpste in Avignon und der christliche Osten', *OCP* 30 (1964), 85-128.
Wadding, Luke, *Annales Minorum*, 31 vols. (Quaracchi, 1931 ff.).
Father Luke Wadding Commemorative Volume (Dublin, 1957).
Wadding Papers, ed. Brendan Jennings (Irish Manuscripts Commission, Dublin, 1953).
Wallis, John E., *Lichfield Cathedral* (London, 1975).
Walsh, Katherine, 'The Manuscripts of Archbishop Richard FitzRalph of Armagh in the Österreichische Nationalbibliothek, Vienna', *Römische Historische Mitteilungen*, 18 (1976), 67-75.
— 'The Observance: Sources for a History of the Observant Reform Movement in the Order of Augustinian Friars', *Rivista di storia della chiesa in Italia*, 31 (1977), 40-67.
— 'An Irish Preacher at Avignon: Richard FitzRalph's Sermons to the Dominican Friars', *Xenia medii aevi historiam illustrantia, oblata Thomae Kaeppeli*, 2 vols. (Storia e Letteratura, 142, Rome, 1978), i, 401-15.
— 'The Later Medieval Schoolman in Theory and Practice', *Innsbrucker Historische Studien*, 2 (1979), 171-6.
— ' "Böhmens Vater – des Reiches Erzstiefvater"? Gedanken zu einem neuen Bild Kaiser Karls IV', *Innsbrucker Historische Studien*, 3 (1980), 189-210.
— 'Klemens VI. und Stift Stams. Predigttätigkeit in Avignon und Frühhumanismus in Tirol am Beispiel von MS 234 der Universität Innsbruck', *Studien und Mitteilungen zur Geschichte des Benediktiner-Ordens und seiner Zweige*, 92 (1981), forthcoming.
Walsingham, Thomas, *Historia Anglicana* 1272-1422, ed. Henry E. Riley, 2 vols. (RS, London, 1863-4).
Ware (Waraeus), James, *De Praesulibus Hiberniae Commentarius* (Dublin, 1665).
— *A Commentary on the Prelates of Ireland* (Dublin, 1704).
— *De Scriptoribus Hiberniae* (Dublin, 1639).
— *The Whole Works of Sir James Ware concerning Ireland, revised and improved in three volumes*, ed. Walter Harris (Dublin, 1739-45).
Warner, George, *Queen Mary's Psalter. Miniatures and Drawings by an English Artist of the 14th Century, reproduced from Royal MS 2 B VII in the British Museum* (London, 1912).
Watt, John A., *The Church and the Two Nations in Medieval Ireland* (Cambridge Studies in Medieval Life and Thought, 3rd ser.3, Cambridge, 1970).
— *The Church in Medieval Ireland* (The Gill History of Ireland, 5, Dublin, 1972).
— 'Negotiations between Edward II and John XXII concerning Ireland', *IHS* 10 (1956), 1-16.
— Morrall, John B., and Martin, Francis X. (eds.), *Medieval Studies presented to Aubrey Gwynn S.J.* (Dublin, 1961).
Weakland, J. E., 'Pope John XXII and the Beatific Vision', *Annuale Medievale*, 19 (1968), 76-84.
Webb, J. J., *Municipal Government in Ireland* (Dublin, 1918).

Weisheipl, James A., 'The Curriculum of the Faculty of Arts at Oxford in the Early Fourteenth Century', *MS* 26 (1964), 143-85.

— 'Developments in the Arts Curriculum at Oxford in the Early Fourteenth Century', *MS* 28 (1966), 151-75.

— 'Repertorium Mertonense', *MS* 31 (1969), 174-224.

Weiss, Günther, *Joannes Kantakuzenos – Aristokrat, Staatsmann, Kaiser und Mönch – in der Gesellschaftsentwicklung von Byzanz im 14. Jahrhundert* (Wiesbaden, 1969).

Weiss, Roberto, 'The Greek Culture of South Italy in the later middle ages', *PBA* 37 (1953), 23-50. Reprinted in *Medieval and Humanist Greek. Collected Essays by Roberto Weiss* (Medioevo e Umanesimo, 8, Padua, 1977), 13-43.

— 'England and the Decree of the Council of Vienne on the Teaching of Greek, Arabic, Hebrew and Syriac', *Bibliothèque d'Humanisme et Renaissance*, 14 (1952), 1-9. Reprinted in *Medieval and Humanist Greek*, 68-79.

— 'The Study of Greek in England during the fourteenth century', *Rinascimento*, 2 (1951), 209-39. Reprinted in *Medieval and Humanist Greek*, 80-107.

— 'The Translators from the Greek at the Angevin Court of Naples', *Rinascimento* 1 (1950), 195-226. Reprinted in *Medieval and Humanist Greek*, 108-33.

— 'Petrarco e il mondo greco', *Atti e Memorie dell'Accademia Petrarca di Lettere, Arti e Scienze di Arezzo*, n.s. 36 (1952-3), 65-96. Reprinted in *Medieval and Humanist Greek*, 166-92.

Wharton, Henry (ed.), *Anglia Sacra*, 2 vols. (London, 1691).

Wilkins, David, *Concilia Magnae Britanniae et Hiberniae, A.D. 446-1718*, 4 vols. (London, 1737).

Wilks, Michael, *The Problem of Sovereignty in the later middle ages. The papal monarchy with Augustinus Triumphus and the publicists* (Cambridge Studies in Medieval Life and Thought, n.s.9, Cambridge, 1964).

— 'Predestination, Property and Power: Wyclif's theory of dominion and grace', *Studies in Church History*, 2 (Oxford, 1965), 220-36.

Williams, Arnold, 'Relations between the mendicant friars and the secular clergy in the later fourteenth century', *Duquesne Studies. Annuale Medievale*, 1 (1960), 22-95.

Williams, H. F. Fulford, 'The Vestments of Bishop Grandisson now in the Azores', *Report and Transactions of the Devonshire Association*, 94 (1962), 613-22.

Williams, Glanmor, *The Welsh Church from the Conquest to the Reformation* 2nd edn. (Cardiff, 1976).

Wood, Anthony à, *The History and Antiquities of the University of Oxford*, ed. John Gutch (Oxford, 1792).

Wood, Diana, 'Maximus sermocinator verbi Dei: the sermon literature of pope Clement VI', *The Materials, Sources and Methods of Ecclesiastical History* (Studies in Church History, 11, Oxford, 1975), 163-72.

Workman, Herbert B., *John Wyclif*, 2 vols. (Oxford, 1926).

Wright, Thomas (ed.), *Proceedings against Dame Alice Kyteler for Sorcery in 1324* (Camden Society, 24, London, 1843).

— *Political Poems and Songs relating to English History, from the*

accession of Edward III to that of Richard II, 2 vols. (RS, London, 1859–61).
Wrigley, John E., 'Clement VI before his Pontificate: the early life of Pierre Roger, 1290/91-1342', *The Catholic Historical Review*, 56 (1970), 433-73.
Wyclif, John, *De apostasia*, ed. Michael H. Dziewicki (WS, London, 1889).
— *De civili dominio*, i, ed. Reginald L. Poole; ii–iii, ed. Josef Loserth (WS, London, 1885–1904).
— *De dominio divino*, ed. Reginald L. Poole (WS, London, 1890).
— *De blasphemia*, ed. Michael H. Dziewicki (WS, London, 1893).
— *De ecclesia*, ed. Josef Loserth (WS, London, 1886).
— *De ente: librorum duorum excerpta*, ed. Michael H. Dziewicki (WS, London, 1909).
— *De potestate papae*, ed. Josef Loserth (WS, London, 1907).
Xiberta, Bartolomeu M., *Guiu Terrena, carmelita de Perpignà* (Barcelona, 1932).
— 'De elementis doctrinalibus in controversia de immaculata B.V. Mariae conceptione', *Carmelus*, 1 (1954), 199–235.
Zacour, Norman P., 'Talleyrand: the Cardinal of Périgord (1301–64)', *Tr.Am.Phil.Soc.*, n.s. 50, pt.7 (1960), 1–83.
Zenner, Joseph R., 'Armachanus über Widersprüche und Irrthümer in der heiligen Schrift', *ZKT* 15 (1891), 348-61.
Ziegler, Philip, *The Black Death* (London, 1969).
Zimmermann, Benedict M., 'Ricardi Archiepiscopi Armacani Bini Sermones de Conceptione B.V. Mariae . . . annis 1342 et 1349', *Analecta Ord. Carm. Discalc.*, 3 (1931), 158–89.
Zumkeller, Adolar, 'Die Augustinerschule des Mittelalters: Vertreter und philosophisch-theologische Lehre', *AA* 27 (1964) 167–262.

Index of Manuscripts Cited

General Index

Not included in this index are names of modern authors cited in the bibliography, references to England, Ireland, Anglo-Irish etc., nor references to FitzRalph's career. References to individual writings by him are included.

The following abbreviations are used:

ab. = archbishop
b. = bishop
c. = count
card. = cardinal
d. = diocese
emp. = emperor
kg. = king
O.Carm. = Carmelite
O.Cist. = Cistercian
OESA = Augustinian friar
OFM = Franciscan
OP = Dominican
O.Praem. = Premonstratensian
OSA = Augustinian canons regular
OSB = Benedictine
q. = queen